The Bedford Companion
to Shakespeare

An Introduction with Documents

>—<

The Bedford Companion to Shakespeare

An Introduction with Documents

>‹

SECOND EDITION

RUSS McDONALD

University of North Carolina at Greensboro

Bedford/St. Martin's

BOSTON ◆ NEW YORK

For Bedford/St. Martin's

Developmental Editor: Karen S. Henry
Production Editor: Arthur Johnson
Production Supervisor: Catherine Hetmansky
Marketing Manager: Richard Cadman
Editorial Assistants: Katherine Gilbert, Caroline Thompson
Copyeditor: Cynthia Benn
Text Design: Claire Seng-Niemoeller
Cover Design: Zenobia Rivetna
Cover Art: Detail of *A Fête at Bermondsey,* c. 1570 by Joris Hoefnagel. Courtesy of the Marquess of Salisbury.
Composition: Stratford Publishing Services
Printing and Binding: Haddon Craftsmen, Inc., an RR Donnelley & Sons Company

President: Charles H. Christensen
Editorial Director: Joan E. Feinberg
Editor in Chief: Karen S. Henry
Director of Marketing: Karen Melton
Director of Editing, Design, and Production: Marcia Cohen
Managing Editor: Elizabeth M. Schaaf

Library of Congress Control Number: 00–106455

Manufactured in the United States of America.

6 5 4 3 2 1
f e d c b a

For information, write: Bedford/St. Martin's, 75 Arlington Street, Boston, MA 02116
(617-399-4000)

ISBN: 0–312–24880–6

Published and distributed outside North America by
PALGRAVE, Houndmills, Basingstoke, Hampshire RG21 2SX and London.
Companies and representatives throughout the world.
PALGRAVE is the new global academic imprint of St. Martin's Press LLC
Scholarly and Reference Division and Palgrave Publishers Ltd. (formerly
Macmillan Press Ltd.).

ISBN: 0–333–94711–8

A catalogue record for this book is available from the British Library.

Acknowledgments

Acknowledgments and copyrights appear at the back of the book on pages 427–29, which constitute an extension of the copyright page. It is a violation of the law to reproduce these selections by any means whatsoever without the written permission of the copyright holder.

This book is dedicated to five great teachers

Avis Hartley

George Walton Williams

Robert Y. Turner

Cyrus Hoy

Stephen Booth

Preface

>‹

Teachers of Shakespeare face an acute version of a problem that vexes most English professors: how to do justice both to the literary works on the syllabus and to the culture that helped to generate them. *Hamlet,* to take a familiar example, begs to be studied in light of Elizabethan anxiety about the health of the queen, the problem of royal succession, and early modern ideas about subjection and power. However, *Hamlet* itself is such a rich and complex work of art that class time spent talking about Elizabeth, Essex, and James or about sixteenth-century political theory can be seen as class time stolen from such major topics as Hamlet's language, the parallel structures of action, the emotional power of tragedy, and the play's metadramatic brilliance. The increased historical awareness characteristic of recent scholarship has sharpened our sense that an understanding of a play depends on familiarity with multiple contexts, and yet such a conviction does not cancel our obligation to teach principles of literary analysis that reveal the pleasures of the text. For Shakespeareans, this dilemma is compounded by modern students' difficulties with the early modern idiom. It's all very well to talk loftily about Renaissance politics, but if readers can't comprehend the words in the first two scenes of *Hamlet,* the result is frustration and disappointment both for instructor and class members. Then there is the further problem that Hamlet exists in three different texts, two of them "good" and one of them "bad." Instructors and students need help with the multitude of textual and extratextual matters that the study of William Shakespeare entails.

    The Bedford Companion represents an attempt to put the Shakespearean text into cultural perspective without causing it to disappear. The book is designed as a vehicle for efficiently conveying facts and ideas that will inform class discussion and enhance students' comprehension of Shakespearean drama. First, the chapters themselves contain an abundance of introductory information on which instructors can build. The treatment of Elizabethan performance in Chapter 4, for example, should generate questions about the staging of crucial episodes not specifically examined in the chapter, such as the tomb scene of *Romeo and Juliet*. Further, coming to terms with the spareness of the original staging leads easily to an appreciation of the opulent poetry in the same scene. Second, the documents that follow each chapter lend themselves to correlation with a wide range of plays. The excerpts from *Patriarcha*, Sir Robert Filmer's defense of royal authority, and from King James's 1610 speech to Parliament should stimulate students to hear the rhetoric of Richard II, Claudius, King Lear, and Prospero in terms of contemporary political writing. Or certain chapters might be profitably considered in relation to particular plays, such as the chapter on the family in connection with *As You Like It*. The combination of introduction and primary materials offers students something unavailable elsewhere. Shakespeare criticism abounds, but students need critical readings much less than they need contextual data about early modern society, religion, literary theory, economics, politics, printing, language, and theater.

The feature that distinguishes this volume is its collection of documents and illustrations. These comprise a broad range of primary materials: maps of London and Stratford, selections from Holinshed's *Chronicles*, facsimiles of pages from Shakespearean quartos, royal proclamations, portraits of Elizabeth and James, excerpts from contemporary literary criticism, passages from handbooks on courtship, political treatises, and an acerbic commentary on urban fashion. Such examples constitute a partial introduction to early modern English culture, and students and instructors who find themselves fascinated with a passage can seek out supplementary material as well as additional or contradictory examples in modern texts, facsimiles, or microfilm versions of the originals. For a discussion of editorial policy — a glance through the book will reveal that some excerpts are modernized and some not — see the Introduction. (Several other notes are included in the section titled "To the Reader," which follows this preface.)

Although my professional bias leads me to favor the poetic over the historical, this book is not a receptacle for extraliterary, contextual information that students need to know but that I don't want to talk about. On the contrary, to exploit the metaphor contained in the title, this book is a genuine companion, one that goes along with a volume of Shakespeare and carries on a dialogue with it. I employ it in my own classes as a means of allowing students to consider questions that require explanation and reflection: the instability of the Shakespearean text, the problematic definition of a literary "source," early modern dogma about the family (and challenges to it), the religious controversies of the late sixteenth century, changing critical notions of literary modes, and so on. Happily, other instructors have used the book as well, and their experiences and commentary have prompted me to make a number of alterations and what I hope are improvements for this second edition.

To begin with, the sequence of chapters has been changed to reflect student need and demand. In questionnaire responses about the first edition, the book's users emphatically urged that the language chapter be assigned early; thus, it now follows the biography chapter. The most obvious addition is a new chapter on Shakespeare in performance from the Restoration to the end of the twentieth century, on stage and in film. Naturally, the choice of documents and illustrations for this chapter is personal, idiosyncratic, and by definition unsatisfactory, representing only a fraction of the available material. In selecting them I have tried to walk a middle way between overly familiar favorites and arcane pieces that deserve their obscurity. The scope of the theatrical history narrated in this chapter is also limited, confined (with one or two exceptions) to British and American productions.

The material changes in many of the existing chapters are also substantial. The most significant additions consist of generous excerpts from women's writing: Isabella Whitney's poem bidding farewell to London, Elizabeth Cary's *Tragedy of Mariam,* sonnets by Lady Mary Wroth, the powerful conclusion to the Countess of Pembroke's translation of Robert Garnier's *Tragedy of Antonie,* Aemilia Lanyer's defense of Eve from *Salve Deus Rex Judaeorum,* and Lady Anne Southwell's "Letter on Poetry." The chapter on language (now Chapter 2) contains several new pieces, including Erasmus's call for translating the New Testament into English, a section of Lever's *The Art of Reason,* and excerpts from Montaigne's "On the Vanity of Words" with a corresponding passage on eloquence from Daniel's *Musophilus.* Also, the chapter on Shakespeare's reading has been broadened somewhat; in the representation of daily life, more attention is given to women's work with the addition of selections from a popular cookbook and from Elizabeth Clinton's *Countess of Lincoln's Nursery;* the topic of sports makes an appearance in a passage on games from Mulcaster's *Positions;* and the chapter on politics and religion now includes more material about religion, notably a vivid excerpt from Hooker's *Laws* and parts of *The Catholics' Supplication* and Muriel's *Answer to the Catholics' Supplication.* Revisions have been made to reflect recent scholarship, as in the case of the Peacham drawing of *Titus Andronicus.* Very little has been omitted, although some lengthy selections (the homilies, for example) have been abbreviated slightly. The bibliography has been updated, and a list of the most useful and popular Shakespearean Web sites has been appended. Once again, author and publisher welcome responses and suggestions for further improvement. Likewise, we would appreciate being informed of errors that, despite the efforts of many, I have allowed to creep into the finished volume.

By a rough estimate, about half the living Shakespeareans in the United States and England have helped with this book, and I wish to express my profound gratitude for the assistance received.

Staff members at several libraries have responded helpfully to requests: Jackson Library at the University of North Carolina at Greensboro, especially

Nancy Fogarty and Mark Schumacher; the Folger Shakespeare Library, particularly Elizabeth Walsh and Lori Johnson; Perkins Library at Duke University; the Huntington Library; and the British Library. The English Department at Greensboro has generously provided me with course relief and research assistance, for which I thank James Evans and my colleagues.

I gladly acknowledge my undergraduate and graduate students at Greensboro and the University of Rochester for helping to shape the contents and the form of *The Bedford Companion*. In effect, they are its collective parents.

At the beginning of the project, almost two hundred members of the Shakespeare Association of America answered a questionnaire about their teaching habits and preferences, and that detailed information has been enormously useful. My thanks to all who took the time to reply.

Albert Braunmuller, James Longenbach, Catherine Loomis, Gail McDonald, and Michael Warren read the entire manuscript, correcting factual errors, adjusting faulty emphases, making valuable suggestions about coverage, and improving my prose style. Others performed similar service in reading one or more chapters: Thomas Berger, Stephen Booth, William Carroll, Maurice Charney, Miriam Gilbert, Christopher Hodgkins, Arthur Kinney, Carole Levin, Margaret Maurer, Robert Miola, Gail Kern Paster, Russell Peck, Bruce Smith, Susan Snyder, Valerie Traub, Paul Werstine, and George Walton Williams. I deeply appreciate the efforts of all these kind and careful readers.

For guidance in choosing the documents and illustrations, I am grateful to many of those listed above, as well as to Roslyn Knutson and Debora Shuger. Both generously supplied me with copies of primary materials and helped me to locate difficult items. Gratitude for advice, illuminating conversation, and scholarly favors goes to Peter Blayney, Susan Cerasano, Alan Dessen, Frances Dolan, Andrew Gurr, Frank Melton, Hugh Parker, Mary Tonkinson, Gina Wilkins, and Perez Zagorin.

Since this book is designed chiefly for the classroom, I take pleasure in thanking Peggy O'Brien and Jeanne Addison Roberts for involving me in the NEH-sponsored Teaching Shakespeare Institute at the Folger Library. For ten years the Institute served me as a Shakespearean pedagogical laboratory: many sections of this book were first devised for its participants, and its workshops and small groups permitted the testing of various practices in the teaching of Shakespeare. I learned not only from the hundreds of high-school teachers, but also from the master teachers and resident and visiting scholars associated with the program.

In preparing the second edition, I have again amassed a pile of debts. It is a pleasure to express my gratitude first to those listed above who also assisted with the revision. As general editor of the Bedford Shakespeare Series, Jean Howard took a clear-headed approach and made balanced and valuable recommendations. The new chapter on Shakespeare in performance would have been impossible without the herculean labor of Barbara Hodgdon and Russell Jackson, who neglected their own work to give me thorough, meticulous, and prompt readings. (They also preserved me from a number of gaffes.)

Since the appearance of the first edition Catherine Loomis has been collecting and sending me relevant items from her wide reading in the English Short Title Catalogue, and her generosity has made the quest for new documents much easier. Suzanne Gossett, Elizabeth Hageman, Elaine V. Beilin, Theodora Jankowski, David Bevington, Martha Rozett, Wendy Wall, Carol Rutter, and Georgianna Ziegler also thoughtfully suggested new material; my inability to incorporate all of their recommendations should not be held against them. Stephen Orgel and Britton Harwood kindly corrected some errors and ambiguous statements in the first edition. For responses to and conversation about that edition, scholarly favors, and other sorts of help, I thank Gail McDonald, Julie Solomon, Coppélia Kahn, Ruth Morse, Maureen Quilligan, Linda Gregerson, David Bergeron, Geraldo de Sousa, Valerie Wayne, Stephen Buhler, Grace Ioppolo, Stanley Wells, Tim Barkley, and Jack McDonald. Sylvia Morris at the Shakespeare Centre Library in Stratford was efficient and generous in aiding my search for photographs; Betsy Walsh at the Folger surpasses her own high standard of expertise and helpfulness each time she is called upon, which is often.

The following instructors were generous in their responses to a question naire about the first edition, and I am grateful: Thomas H. Blackburn, Swarthmore College; Kathleen Blumreich, Grand Valley State University; Barbara Bono, State University of New York at Buffalo; Stephen Buhler, University of Nebraska at Lincoln; Suzanne Gossett, Loyola University; Claudius W. (Bill) Griffin, Virginia Commonwealth University; Jennifer Glosh Herbert, University of Akron; Christopher Highley, Ohio State University; Theodora A. Jankowski, Washington State University; Gordon Lell, Concordia College; Kate Levin, City College, City University of New York; Robert McHenry, University of Hawaii; Caroline McManus, California State University at Los Angeles; Robert T. Mundhenk, Northampton Community College; Lori Newcomb, University of Illinois, Urbana; Marianne Novy, University of Pittsburgh; Peter G. Platt, Barnard College; Rachel E. Poulsen, Loyola University; Karen Raber, University of Mississippi; Nicholas Ranson, University of Akron; Lisa Schnell, University of Vermont; Barbara Sebek, Colorado State University; Lolly Smith, Everett Community College; Alison Taufer, California State University at Los Angeles; Frances Teague, University of Georgia; and Kathleen Thornton, University of Albany.

Karen Henry of Bedford/St. Martin's deserves to have her name on the front of this volume. For three years, after we first met on a bus at a meeting of the Shakespeare Association of America, she labored tirelessly and cheerfully on the first edition, helping me get a confused heap of materials into print. She has been as thoroughly involved in the preparation of the second edition. What makes her an extraordinary editor is her pedagogical sensitivity. A teacher without a classroom, she knows instinctively what students need and is able to help an author fulfill those needs. Thanks also to many others at Bedford/St. Martin's, especially Charles Christensen, Joan Feinberg, and Lori Chong Roncka. Arthur Johnson's meticulous attention to the manuscript has improved it substantially, and his efficiency and good humor have made light work of what might have been a tedious job. I also gratefully acknowledge the assistance of Jacob Molyneux in proofreading the first edition and Maggie DiVito in proofreading the second.

The length of these lists notwithstanding, there are a few people I have forgotten to thank. To them, apologies and thanks.

Once again, I can only gesture at the depths of my gratitude to my wife and son for their forbearance, good will, and senses of humor.

To the Reader

—>‹—

A few notes having to do with early modern conventions may be helpful.

In Shakespeare's England, the new year officially began not on January 1 but on March 25 (the feast of the Annunciation, or "Lady Day"). Apparent inconsistencies in dates sometimes arise from this feature of the early modern calendar; diaries and legal documents can be particularly confusing. For example, King James's payment to the King's Men recorded in February 1603 was actually made in the year we call 1604. When a document printed here contains such a date, the inconsistency is signified with a slash mark — in the example above, 1603/04. When a document does not contain the date itself, as with King James's speech to Parliament (March 21, 1609), the year has been silently modernized (here, to 1610).

Several of the facsimiles and unmodernized documents presented here contain "yᵉ"or "yᵗ." These signs are simply abbreviations for the words *the* and *that*. The *y* derives from the Old English letter **Þ** and served the printer as an economy, since the *t* and *h* which it replaced were common letters often needed elsewhere. *Y* is pronounced "th" (never "ye," as in the modern "Ye olde gifte shoppe").

Some financial records contain the monetary abbreviations £ (or *l*), *s*, and *d*. £ stands for pound (from the Latin *libra*), *s* for shilling (from the Latin *solidus*), and *d* for pence (from the Latin *denarius*). Other abbreviations and peculiarities can lead to confusion. In monetary sums recorded in Henslowe's *Diary*, for example, the last *i* is printed as *j*, as in the figure "iiij s" (four shillings). Elizabethan spelling made no distinction between *i* and *j*, although they were pronounced differently.

In reproducing selections from sixteenth- and seventeenth-century printed texts, I have mostly used original editions (or microfilm copies of them) as copy text. All quotations from Shakespeare, unless otherwise noted, are taken from *The Riverside Shakespeare* (1974), edited by G. Blakemore Evans.

Contents

><

PREFACE   VII

TO THE READER   XIII

→ *Introduction*   *I*

Shakespeare in Our Time   1
The Uses of a Companion   3
The Illustrations and Documents   4
Three Troublesome Topics: Terminology, Modernization, and Money   7
A Final Word   8

→ CHAPTER I
*Shakespeare, "Shakespeare," and the Problem
of Authorship*   *II*

Early Life   12
London: The First Decade   15

London: Maturity   19
Retirement   22
The Anti-Stratfordians   24
What Is an Author?   26

ILLUSTRATIONS AND DOCUMENTS

The House Known as Shakespeare's Birthplace   29
Record of Shakespeare's Baptism   29
Map of Stratford-upon-Avon   31
Francis Meres, From *Palladis Tamia: Wit's Treasury*   32
The Royal License for Shakespeare's Company   33
A Plague Bill   33
John Ward, Vicar of Stratford, From His *Diary*   34
Detail from the "Agas" Map of London (With Shakespeare's Lodging
   Indicated)   34

→ CHAPTER 2
"To What End Are All These Words?":
Shakespeare's Dramatic Language

36

Early Modern English   38
Rhetoric   42
Wordplay   44
The Forms of Dramatic Language   47
Language as Theme   55

ILLUSTRATIONS AND DOCUMENTS

Desiderius Erasmus, From the Foreword to the Third Edition of the
   Latin New Testament   59
Thomas Wilson, From *The Art of Rhetoric* (Of Composition)   60
Samuel Daniel, From *Musophilus*   62
Michel de Montaigne, From "Of the Vanity of Words"   63
Roger Ascham, From *The Schoolmaster*   64
Ralph Lever, From *The Art of Reason, Rightly Termed Witcraft*   66
George Puttenham, From *The Art of English Poesy*   68
Baldassare Castiglione, From *The Book of the Courtier*   73
Chart of the Relative Proportions of Poetry and Prose
   in Shakespeare's Plays   77

→ CHAPTER 3
Theater à la Mode: Shakespeare and the Kinds of Drama 79

Comedy 81
Tragedy 85
History 90
Romance 94
Mixed Modes 97

ILLUSTRATIONS AND DOCUMENTS

Sir Philip Sidney, From *The Defense of Poesy* 99
Elizabeth Cary, From *The Tragedy of Mariam, Fair Queen of Jewry* 100
Aristotle, From *Poetics* 101
Title Page of *Richard III* (First Quarto) 105
William Lambarde, From His Notes of a Conversation with Queen Elizabeth I about *Richard II* 107
John Fletcher, From His Preface to *The Faithful Shepherdess* 107
Thomas Rymer, From *A Short View of Tragedy* 108

→ CHAPTER 4
Performances, Playhouses, and Players 109

Going to a Play, Circa 1595 109
The Playhouses 114
The Companies 120
The Theater and the Authorities 123

ILLUSTRATIONS AND DOCUMENTS

Map Showing the Playhouses in Shakespeare's Time 128
Henry Peacham, Sketch Accompanying Lines from *Titus Andronicus* 128
Inventory of Theatrical Costumes (From Henslowe's Papers) 129
Remains of the Rose Playhouse 132
Two Plans of the Rose Playhouse 133
C. Walter Hodges, Illustration of the Second Globe 134
Copy of De Witt's Sketch of the Swan Playhouse 135
Wenceslas Hollar, Detail from *Long View of London* 137

Philip Henslowe, Log of Plays from His *Diary*   137
Testimony about a Performance of *Richard II*   140
Record of King James's Payment to the King's Men   140
Thomas Heywood, From *An Apology for Actors*   141
Edward Alleyn, Letter to His Wife   143

→ CHAPTER 5
"I Loved My Books": Shakespeare's Reading   *145*

Shakespeare and the Classics   147
Major Influences   149
Indirect Sources   154
Shakespeare's Favorites   158

ILLUSTRATIONS AND DOCUMENTS

Edward Hall, From *The Union of the Two Noble and Illustre Families
   of Lancaster and York*   163
From the Geneva Bible   164
Giovanni Battista Giraldi Cinthio, From *Gli Hecatommithi*
   (The Principal Source for *Othello*)   169
From *The Book of Common Prayer* (The Order for the Burial
   of the Dead)   171
John Foxe, From *Acts and Monuments*   174
A Moralized Ballad   178
Sir William Strachey, From *A True Reportory of the Wreck and Redemption
   of Sir Thomas Gates* (A Source for *The Tempest*)   180
Christopher Marlowe, From *Tamburlaine the Great*   182
Sir Philip Sidney, Two Sonnets from *Astrophil and Stella*   183
Lady Mary Wroth, Two Sonnets from *Pamphilia to Amphilanthus*   184
Raphael Holinshed, From *The Chronicles of England, Scotland, and Ireland*
   (Second Edition)   185
Plutarch, From *Lives of the Noble Grecians and Romans* (Translated by Sir
   Thomas North)   186
Mary Sidney Herbert, Countess of Pembroke, From Her Translation of
   The Tragedy of Antonie by Robert Garnier   187
Ovid, From *Metamorphoses* (Translated by Arthur Golding)   190

→ CHAPTER 6
"What Is Your Text?" *194*

What Is a Shakespearean Text? 195
From Pen to Press: The Printing of Renaissance Plays 198
   Illustration of the Folding and Printing Process 200
Shakespeare's Plays in Print 201
Some Examples of Textual Instability 206
Shakespeare's Texts and the General Reader 210

ILLUSTRATIONS AND DOCUMENTS

Title Page of *Titus Andronicus* (First Quarto) 211
Title Page and Catalogue of the First Folio 212
Illustration of a Seventeenth-Century Print Shop (Frontispiece to
   Edmund Rive's *Twelve Rules Introducing to the Art of Latin*) 214
Facsimile of the Last Page of *King Lear* (First Quarto) 215
Facsimile of "To be or not to be" from *Hamlet, Prince of Denmark*
   (First Quarto) 216
Facsimile of "To be or not to be" from *Hamlet, Prince of Denmark*
   (1623 Folio) 217
A Comparison of the Work of Compositors A and B on the 1623 Folio 218

→ CHAPTER 7
Town and Country: Life in Shakespeare's England *219*

London 221
The Suburbs 224
The Countryside 225
Rural Life 228
The Daily Routine 231
Clothing 231
Getting and Spending 233

ILLUSTRATIONS AND DOCUMENTS

William Harrison, From *The Description of England* (The Conditions
   of English Inns and Overnight Travel) 237
John Stow, From *Survey of London* (The Location of Tradesmen
   in London) 238

Isabella Whitney, From "The Manner of Her Will, and What She Left to London" 239

Thomas Platter, From *Travels in England* (The Thames River) 241

Lupold von Wedel, From *Journey through England and Scotland* (A Visit to the Bearbaiting Arena) 241

Thomas Nashe, From *Christ's Tears over Jerusalem* (The Brothels of Suburban London) 242

Gervase Markham, From *The English Husbandman* (Rural Domestic Architecture and Interior Design) 243

John Moore, From *A Target for Tillage* 245

Sir Anthony Fitzherbert, From *The Book of Husbandry* (What Works a Wife Should Do) 246

William Harrison, From *The Description of England* (Dining Customs) 248

Richard Mulcaster, From *Positions . . . for the Training Up of Children* (Chapter 27, "Of the Ball") 248

William Harrison, From *The Description of England* (Fashion) 250

John Murrell, From *A Delightful Daily Exercise for Ladies and Gentlewomen* 252

→ CHAPTER 8
Men and Women: Gender, Family, Society   *253*

The Situation of Women 253

Patriarchy 259

Primogeniture 263

Marriage and Money 265

Family Life 269

The Social Structure 273

Conclusion: The Body Politic 277

ILLUSTRATIONS AND DOCUMENTS

Aristotle, From *Historia Animalium* 278

William Vaughan, From *Natural and Artificial Directions for Health* 279

Lady Anne Southwell, Letter on Poetry 279

Aemilia Lanyer, From *Salve Deus Rex Judaeorum* 281

Sir Robert Filmer, From *Patriarcha, or The Natural Power of Kings* 283

From *An Homily of the State of Matrimony* 285

William Gouge, From *Of Domestical Duties: Eight Treatises* 290

Sir Thomas Smith, From *De Republica Anglorum: The Manner of Government or Policy of the Realm of England* (Of Children)   292

George Whetstone, From *An Heptameron of Civil Discourses* (Household Laws to Keep the Married in Love, Peace, and Amity)   292

Elizabeth Clinton, From *The Countess of Lincoln's Nursery*   293

Ben Jonson, On My First Son   295

Excerpts from Conduct Books   295

Sir Edward Coke, From *The Third Part of the Institutes of the Laws of England* (Of Buggery or Sodomy)   296

Richard Barnfield, From *The Tears of an Affectionate Shepherd Sick for Love, or The Complaint of Daphnis for the Love of Ganymede*   298

Queen Elizabeth I, List of Royal Proclamations   299

Queen Elizabeth I, Royal Proclamation against Vagabonds and Unlawful Assemblies   301

Queen Elizabeth I, Edict Arranging for the Expulsion from England of Negroes and Blackamoors   302

→ CHAPTER 9
Politics and Religion: Early Modern Ideologies   303

An Absolute Monarchy?   304

Councillors   306

The Monarchs   308
   The "Ermine Portrait" of Elizabeth I   309
   Portrait of James I, by Paul van Somer   310

The Church   315

The Ideology of Order   318

Shakespeare's Theater and the Problem of Authority   322

The Stage and Its Opponents   324

ILLUSTRATIONS AND DOCUMENTS

Sir Thomas Smith, From *De Republica Anglorum: The Manner of Government or Policy of the Realm of England* (Of Parliament and the Monarchy)   326

Queen Elizabeth I, The Tilbury Speech   328

King James I, From *A Speech to the Lords and Commons of the Parliament at Whitehall*   328

King James I, Secret Letter to Sir Robert Cecil   331

King James I, Letter to George Villiers, Duke of Buckingham   332

Sir John Harington, Letter Describing the Revels at King James's Court   333

Niccolò Machiavelli, From *The Prince*   334

King James I, From *Basilikon Doron*   336

Simon Forman, From His *Diary* (On a Dream about an Encounter with Queen Elizabeth)   339

John Field and Thomas Wilcox(?), From *An Admonition to the Parliament*   340

From *The Catholics' Supplication* and *An Answer to the Catholics' Supplication*   343

From *An Homily against Disobedience and Willful Rebellion*   345

Richard Hooker, From *Of the Laws of Ecclesiastical Polity*   349

Philip Stubbes, From *The Anatomy of Abuses*   351

→ CHAPTER 10

From Bracegirdle to Branagh: Shakespeare in Performance from 1660 to the Present   353

Innovations, Technical and Theatrical   354

Actors and Their Roles   357

American Shakespeare   363

Twentieth-Century Stages, Modern and Postmodern   366

Shakespeare Screened   376

ILLUSTRATIONS AND DOCUMENTS

David Garrick as King Lear (After a Painting by Benjamin Wilson)   383

Nahum Tate, From *The History of King Lear*   383

Three Lady Macbeths (Sarah Siddons, Ellen Terry, Judi Dench)   386

Ira Aldridge as Othello   388

Playbill Advertising a Gala Performance of *Julius Caesar* (Featuring the Three Booth Brothers)   389

Norman Wilkinson's Set Design for *Twelfth Night*   390

Robert Edmond Jones's Set Design for John Barrymore's *Hamlet* (New York and London)   391

John Barrymore's Script for *Hamlet* (Directed by Arthur Hopkins)   392

William Hazlitt, Review of *A Midsummer Night's Dream* (From *The Examiner*, January 21, 1816)   393

Two Productions of *A Midsummer Night's Dream* (Charles Kean, London; Peter Brook, Stratford-upon-Avon)   395

Robert Speaight, Review of Peter Brook's *A Midsummer Night's Dream*
  (From *Shakespeare Quarterly*)   398
Laurence Olivier as Henry V   400
Kenneth Tynan, From *He That Plays the King*   401
Titus (Directed by Julie Taymor)   405

BIBLIOGRAPHY   406

APPENDIX: Shakespeare Resources on the Web   422

INDEX   430

Introduction

✦

From the time Shakespeare's plays first began to appear, they have not only attracted people to the theater but also led many to want to read the texts. Many of the plays were printed during the dramatist's lifetime, some more than once, and seven years after Shakespeare's death his theatrical colleagues published a nearly complete collection of his plays in one volume, the book we know as the First Folio of 1623. For the better part of the next three centuries, people continued to attend performances or read Shakespeare for pleasure (privately and in groups), and many literate households owned editions of his works. But Shakespeare became a subject of academic study in Britain and America only at the end of the nineteenth century, when English literature was established as a discipline and British and American poetry, fiction, and drama began to displace classical literature written in Greek and Latin. The works of William Shakespeare were quickly and properly installed at the center of the canon of literature written in English, and they still occupy this prominent position, whatever additions and modifications the canon may have undergone. More people are studying William Shakespeare today than at any other point in the last four hundred years.

Shakespeare in Our Time

The rapid expansion of the Anglo-American college and university system after the Second World War introduced millions of new students to Shakespeare's plays, but methods of study have undergone important changes in the past fifty years, and these developments help to account for the publication of the book you are now reading. In the 1950s and 1960s, Shakespeare study was dominated by a style of literary analysis called new criticism, which focused on the verbal details of poetry, drama, and prose fiction. Close reading of the Shakespearean passage has by no means been abandoned, but the past two decades have seen an adjustment in the relative importance of literary text and historical context. According to recent thinking, the cultural forces to which any Renaissance writer was inevitably subject demand greater notice: civic, court, and international politics; religious controversy; economic prosperity or depression; scientific discoveries; fashions in clothing, architecture, furniture, gardening, and music; tensions among social and economic classes; developments in legal practice; changes in literary taste; and the effects of plague and weather, to name some of the most powerful determinants. This broader concept of literary study is sometimes referred to as new historicism, or cultural poetics. But whether we accept such labels or not, critics today are reluctant to think of the play or poem as a verbal icon and thus to regard the culture from which it emerged merely as background, a niche in which to display the literary object. Although Shakespeare the author has scarcely disappeared, he now looks less like a free agent.

The complex process of artistic production and response also entails the conditions of another culture, however — that of the respondent. What we call "Shakespeare" is an artistic phenomenon resulting from an interaction between an early modern playwright's words and the environment in which they are heard or read. The performance of *Hamlet* that Shakespeare's original audience witnessed, with Richard Burbage playing the Prince of Denmark on the open stage of the Globe in the suburbs of Elizabethan London, is a very different phenomenon from the spectacular production enjoyed by those Victorians who filled the vast spaces of the Lyceum Theatre to watch Henry Irving play the same part, or the film version seen by the young Americans who lined up at their local cineplex to see Ethan Hawke's modern Prince. The branch of study known as performance criticism has recently begun to explore the assumptions and decisions that inform every production of a Shakespeare play. Yet another proof of the dynamic relation between the literary object and those who receive it appears in the unprecedented growth of feminist criticism. Thirty years ago such a critical school scarcely existed, and certainly not by that name. Now it is without question one of the most influential modes of Shakespeare study. In the words of Jeanne Addison Roberts, "One of the most beneficial effects of feminism is that it has given us a new Shakespeare." But what does this mean, to possess a "new" Shakespeare? What happened to the old one? And how many are there?

Recognition that who we are determines what Shakespeare is need not imply critical chaos nor generate undue anxiety in the student who comes to study him for the first time. We have the texts, problematic though they may be, of thirty-four plays that Shakespeare seems to have written alone, of three or four others on which he probably collaborated, and of 154 sonnets, two narrative poems, and a handful of lyrics. These furnish a practically inexhaustible source of study, discovery, and pleasure. But how are they to be approached?

As literary artifacts? theatrical scripts? dramatic poems? documents in English political history? records of a power struggle among social classes? depictions of ongoing gender conflicts? archival evidence in the history of ideas? The answer to all these questions is yes. Every critic, every instructor, every student will address the texts differently, and that is as it should be. But the most successful encounter with Shakespeare's works occurs when the person confronting them is well informed about the texts, their creator, and the culture from which they arose.

The Uses of a Companion

This book is designed to supply information, ideas, and contextual material that will promote such a productive encounter. Its ten chapters enact, roughly speaking, a progression from the biographical to the cultural. The first three chapters introduce the writer and his tools, presenting the facts of his life and career, considering the state of the English language and the way he employed it, and examining the dramatic modes that he embraced, enriched, and altered. These are followed by chapters devoted to the conditions of the professional theater at the turn of the seventeenth century (Chapter 4), the kinds of books that Shakespeare read and that shaped his choice of dramatic stories (Chapter 5), and the complex process by which his plays made their way into print (Chapter 6). Chapters 7 through 9 expand the scope, offering a broadly sketched picture of the cultural milieu of which Shakespeare was a product and which he helped to produce. These chapters supply details of daily life in early modern England; information about marriage customs, the family unit, and larger social communities; and, finally, a glance at the political players and ideological issues that concerned the subjects of Queen Elizabeth and King James. Chapter 10, the last chapter and new to this edition, surveys the production of the plays since the Restoration, exploring the very different Shakespeares that emerge from the major periods of the British and American stage and cinema.

Each of these chapters is inevitably incomplete. The topics treated in each of the early ones have been the subject of a number of excellent books. For the later chapters, on early modern social and political life, the issues are so vast and complex that they have inspired shelves of books. Readers are encouraged to seek additional information and opinions, and the supplementary bibliography at the end of the book is designed to promote further investigation. On the subject of Shakespeare's biography, for example, Samuel Schoenbaum's excellent *William Shakespeare: A Documentary Life* can supply further details and fill in gaps that result from the spatial limitations of this book. Also inevitably, each chapter is partial in its presentation of the topic, reflecting my personal sense of those facts and ideas most relevant to Shakespeare study at the beginning of the twenty-first century. My own bias is toward Shakespeare as artist, a predisposition that prizes language and its arrangement into patterns, but I attempt to keep it from eclipsing other topics and approaches.

Occasionally, as with the authorship controversy, contrary views are deliberately included within the chapter discussions. And the primary documents at the end of each chapter make available a wealth of material on a broad range of issues.

The Illustrations and Documents

This book is distinguished chiefly by its presentation of illustrations and documents, so a word is in order about what they are, how they were selected, and how they might best be used. Simply speaking, the documentary materials are meant to illustrate or clarify the topics discussed within each chapter. To take an example from the first chapter: in a paragraph on the fortunes of the house in which William Shakespeare was born, the reader is parenthetically directed to page 29, where the first illustration is an eighteenth-century drawing of that structure. For a different kind of example, Chapter 7 contains a brief discussion of Elizabethan clothing (pp. 231–33) that sends the reader to the next-to-last document in the chapter, an excerpt from William Harrison's *Description of England* of 1587, in which the Elizabethan commentator surveys what Londoners are wearing and remarks acidly on the follies of fashion.

Most chapters offer several types of documentary material, from illustrations and maps to facsimiles of pages from early modern texts to excerpts from pertinent books and records. The nature of the accompanying material depends to a great extent on the subject of the chapter. Chapter 6, for instance, outlines the transmission of the text from Shakespeare's manuscript to a stage version to a printed copy to a modern edition and also includes several photographs of pages from quarto versions and from the 1623 Folio. As the subject of inquiry widens to social and political issues, the primary materials become more discursive. Chapter 9, "Politics and Religion: Early Modern Ideologies," presents a passage from the early modern political theorist Sir Thomas Smith, a generous excerpt from *An Homily against Disobedience and Willful Rebellion*, a letter and parts of a speech and treatise by King James I, a section of an inflammatory Puritan pamphlet addressed to Parliament, and other such polemical writing.

Most of this material is well known to the specialist, and some of it familiar even to the beginning student of Shakespeare. A few illustrations, such as the copy of Johannes de Witt's drawing of the Swan Playhouse or the title page of the 1623 Folio, are reproduced everywhere. The frequency with which such items reappear in studies of Shakespeare attests to their explanatory value, and it would have been perverse not to provide them. Certain selections are relatively new, such as the photograph of the foundations of the Rose Playhouse, unearthed in 1989. Many of the documents exist in modern editions but are not immediately accessible to the student. Examples of this type include the excerpts from Edward Hall and Raphael Holinshed, on which Shakespeare based his history plays, and the passage from a translation of the Scriptures that Shakespeare would have known, the Geneva Bible of 1560. A few of the documents, such as William Gouge's *Of Domestical Duties: Eight Treatises,* a Jacobean marriage manual with a decidedly Christian, patriarchal slant, have rarely been reprinted since the seventeenth century.

It is difficult to articulate a single criterion for the selection of primary materials. In considering what to include, I sought, and usually took, advice from specialists in each of the ten major areas treated here, although in no case was it possible to print all the materials recommended. In general my goal has been to negotiate a middle way between the obvious and the arcane. Certain documents — such as the list of theatrical costumes from Henslowe's papers — have been chosen to illuminate topics treated in the chapter; others — such as John Foxe's compelling report of the execution of two Protestant martyrs — are included because the interest of the narrative far outweighs the document's relevance to the specific concerns of the chapter. The doubts and complaints about the documentary materials that will arise in some readers' minds are probably just: it may be objected that the excerpts and illustrations are idiosyncratically chosen, that there are too few of them, and that the few selected are too brief. In response, I would plead the limitations of space and reply that the book contains over a hundred items offering an imaginative thoroughfare into Shakespeare's world. It is doubtful that any two experts could agree on an ideal list. Instead, this is one scholar-teacher's idea of what would be helpful.

That said, however, this selector would still urge the student confronting these chunks of early modern thought and experience to be cautious. In the first place, the materials reproduced in this book offer a selective and minuscule sampling, the tip of the tip of the iceberg. We have inherited a partial and perhaps unrepresentative view of life in sixteenth- and seventeenth-century England, a view shaped and colored by what has come down to us in written form. Moreover, the surviving legacy was originally determined by what was printed and sold during the period, or by what was deemed worthy of preservation. For example, royal documents are more likely to have survived than a tailor's daily account books. And far more women wrote poetry than published it.

Second, much of the material available to us, notably political writing and handbooks on conduct, must be approached warily because of its prescriptive character. In other words, the claims of these various writers must not be taken as gospel. Many of the documents are presented not as proof of how things were in the period, but as expressions of how certain people thought things ought to be. One of the clearest instances of this difference would be James I's speech to Parliament in 1610 on the role of the monarchy. In that oration the king proclaims the divine basis of royal authority, but the modern reader must not therefore assume that such a position was universally accepted. Quite the opposite. That the speech was given at all implies considerable resistance to the monarch's argument, and independent sources confirm the strength of such tensions between James and Parliament in just those years. In other words, every document must be examined with a question about its context and its conditionality. Even the maps and illustrations, which would seem to be safe enough, are potentially misleading: the copy of the de Witt drawing of the Swan may have been the worst of ten such sketches from the period, but because this is the one that has survived, we have latched onto it.

With these provisos in mind, the reader may elect to use the chapter discussions and documents in several ways. As indicated, the chapters have been arranged in a pattern moving from the specific to the general, from Shakespeare's life through his working habits to the culture he inhabited. They need not be studied in this order, of course. In fact, the first nine chapters might with equal profit be approached in reverse, so that acquaintance with early modern ideology and society precedes and prepares the reader for study of Shakespeare's place in that milieu. Since most of the documents and illustrations have been chosen to accompany information or clarify concepts discussed in the chapters, readers will find their understanding enhanced if they refer, as directed in the text, to the appropriate item at the end of the chapter.

Some of the primary materials can be employed independently of the chapters to which they are attached. To mention the most obvious of possibilities, many of the excerpts from Shakespeare's sources — Hall, Holinshed, Cinthio, and Strachey, for example — might serve as the basis for class discussion or as the starting point for an essay about the particular plays deriving from the sources. But more general uses present themselves as well: *An Homily of the State of Matrimony*, for instance, or the advice on prudence and passion given in Whetstone's *Heptameron of Civil Discourses* might be studied in conjunction with the representation of marriage in many of the comedies (most obviously *The Taming of the Shrew*) and some of the tragedies as well. The excerpt from Filmer's *Patriarcha* may be employed to illuminate the conflicts in *As You Like It, King Lear,* and other plays. Or the selections in Chapters 7 through 9 might be read on their own as a kind of crash course in early modern English history.

Examining these documents alongside Shakespeare's plays, students may begin to wonder about the nature of influence. Throughout the nineteenth century and well into the twentieth, scholars spent considerable energy identifying and scrutinizing texts that Shakespeare must have read and relied on in the creation of his dramas and poems. Chapter 5 makes use of much of this labor, and the documents in that chapter afford a glimpse of some of the major sources. Recently, however, scholarship has come to adopt a more relaxed understanding of influence, first recognizing that an author need not have read a particular text to be familiar with its ideas, and, second, that the existence of such a book means that the author's audience would have been aware, either directly or indirectly, of its contents. Gouge's marriage pamphlet, for example, was published after Shakespeare's retirement, but its treatment of the theory, history, and practice of matrimony records what a substantial portion of Shakespeare's contemporaries thought about such issues. Thus it furnishes us with a set of opinions (and, implicitly, contrary ideas) that were circulating in Shakespeare's culture and that audiences would have brought with them to performances of such marriage plays as *Much Ado about Nothing* and *Othello.*

Three Troublesome Topics:
Terminology, Modernization, and Money

A comment about terminology. The period under scrutiny, the end of the sixteenth and beginning of the seventeenth century, goes by at least two names, the traditional *Renaissance* and the more recent *early modern*. Those who prefer the second name believe that *Renaissance* privileges the period unfairly by endorsing the notion of "awakening" and thus implying an unwarranted superiority to the preceding "dark ages." Partisans of the term *Renaissance* sometimes claim that to speak of early modern England is to appropriate for our own purposes a period of history distinct and in significant ways alien from our own. It is probably fair to say that *Renaissance* looks to the past, since it acknowledges the rebirth of classical learning in sixteenth-century England, whereas *early modern* looks forward, locating there the origins of capitalism and other forms of modernity. To my way of thinking, each term has its virtues and its limitations, and so this book uses both (as well as the more specific *Tudor, Elizabethan, Jacobean,* and *Stuart*). I have tried to employ each as context would seem to dictate: hence, *Renaissance* tends to dominate at the beginning of the book, where literary matters are central, while *early modern* becomes more frequent as attention shifts to social and political institutions.

I have also avoided a slavish consistency in modernizing the form of primary materials. Most of the texts are presented here using modern American spelling and punctuation. Chief among the many reasons for this choice is that, since comprehension of an argument or narrative is of paramount importance for most of the documents, modernized spelling makes the passage easier to read, understand, and remember. Not to modernize would be to estrange the reader from the text unnecessarily, and in the wrong ways. One wants to preserve the historical strangeness of the *ideas* being presented, and retention of old spelling would make the distinctiveness of those ideas harder to see, not easier. Moreover, original spelling interposes a screen between the modern reader and the historical text that Shakespeare's contemporaries would not have had to look through. The sixteenth-century reader's eye processed the original spelling as automatically as a modern eye does modern spelling. Looked at in this way, the decision to modernize constitutes a paradoxical form of historicism. Another determinant is that virtually everyone today reads Shakespeare's plays in modern-spelling editions. Thus, not to modernize collateral documents would be to make Shakespeare seem more accessible and familiar than his contemporaries, more like us than like them, and that would be a falsification. In a very few cases, with short passages or documents of a particular kind — the list of costumes belonging to the Lord Admiral's Men, for example — the original spelling has been preserved to expose the reader to the conventions of early modern spelling and punctuation, especially their fluidity and inconsistency. Glosses of potentially unfamiliar words appear in brackets in the text; footnotes, it was felt, would be disruptive (although a few footnotes are included for definitions that extend beyond a word or two).

A final vexing question concerns money and how to think about it. Readers of the following chapters will occasionally come across a monetary figure and wonder what it means. They should probably not seek to translate the amount into modern terms, since the number of variables involved makes it virtually impossible to provide equivalents for what things cost in Shakespeare's day. Even though records of prices survive, they are misleading. In the first place, most people didn't purchase many of the same commodities we buy, such as fruits and vegetables, which came from people's gardens. Second, technology has altered the cost of making and distributing other necessities, and thus has changed their value in relation to other articles: suits of clothing, those not made at home, were exceedingly expensive to purchase because they were not available off the rack but tailored individually. Third, the cash economy was much more thoroughly developed in London than in villages or the countryside, where shops were scarce and a system of barter and exchange was widespread. Finally, the changes in value brought on by inflation, which was especially fierce toward the end of the sixteenth century, practically defeat any effort to contextualize prices and wages in any given year. Instead of seeking modern equivalents, we will do better to compare the price of a given item with the cost of other commodities and services at roughly the same time. This topic is treated at greater length in Chapter 7, where some such equivalents can be found.

A Final Word

Shakespeare has continued to sell — in bookstores, theaters, and schools. His appeal seems in no danger of diminishing, but as the world changes, readers need more help comprehending certain features of his work and his culture. This book was conceived as a tool for reuniting text and context, for bringing the work of art into closer proximity with its formative conditions. *The Bedford Companion* will have served its purpose if the reader is able to connect the words, characters, actions, and ideas of Shakespeare's texts with the political institutions, social practices, theatrical milieu, discursive habits, literary scene, and printing process that contributed to their creation. It reflects some of the changes in recent thought described at the beginning of this introduction, specifically the return of historical criticism, because its assemblage of documents permits the reader to situate the text culturally. But it also seeks, even while admitting the inescapable connection between scholarship and the era that produced it, to avoid a single critical dogma or agenda. This book does not survey the major schools of critical thought; such guides are available elsewhere. Most of the time, and insofar as possible, I leave the task of literary interpretation to the reader.

Having argued that people study Shakespeare in multiple ways and for a variety of reasons at different times, I would qualify that claim by suggesting the presence of a constant factor in human responses to the plays: the pleasure his works afford. To be sure, the conditions of reception determine the kinds of satisfaction — aural, intellectual, theatrical, social, economic. But usually people study Shakespeare because they like to. The main purpose of this book is to amplify those pleasures. When I first went to England as a student, I spent a weekend in Oxford and then hitched a ride to Stratford-upon-Avon for the day. After attending a performance at the Royal Shakespeare Theatre, I found myself unwilling to leave the town, and so I stayed for a week, going to every play in the repertory, and to some more than once. They were the most beautiful things I had ever seen. This book is one product of a lifelong effort to remain in Shakespeare's world and to entice others into it.

CHAPTER I

Shakespeare, "Shakespeare," and the Problem of Authorship

✕

The playwright William Shakespeare was born in Stratford-upon-Avon, a market town about a hundred miles northwest of London, in April 1564. A Tudor building that stands today in Henley Street is shown to millions of visitors as the house in which the playwright was born, and that building (illustrated on p. 29) may serve as an emblem for the problems of Shakespearean biography. In structure and appearance it seems to be Elizabethan, and parts of it may even be original, but the house is substantially different from the way it was in the middle of the sixteenth century. Originally there were two buildings, an eastern and a western structure, that John Shakespeare, the playwright's father, purchased at different times and that have since been joined to make the present one. In 1552 there was a midden heap outside the house, an illegal garbage dump for which the authorities levied a fine. Part of the ground floor housed the leather business in which John Shakespeare was engaged. The playwright inherited the buildings upon the death of his father and may have rented the eastern structure as a coaching inn. In the eighteenth century, as Shakespeare's reputation grew, a birth room was identified and efforts were made to save and memorialize the building. Now the house is a primary exhibit in the tourist industry that has come to dominate life in Stratford. In Shakespeare's day there was no gift shop. Even mildly skeptical visitors will find themselves wondering about the authenticity of "the birthplace" and about how faithfully modern appearances are able to convey historical truth.

So it is with the story of William Shakespeare's life. The narrative that most of us know bears some resemblance to the facts, but myths and distortions have accumulated over the centuries, and the uneasy mixture of truth and legend has prompted contradictory reactions to the problem of Shakespearean biography. On the one hand, many people still relish and repeat the colorful, sentimental tales that originated in the hundred years or so following Shakespeare's death — that he delivered rousing speeches while helping his father butcher animals; that he left Stratford a fugitive after being caught poaching deer at Charlecote, the nearby estate of Sir Thomas Lucy; that he got his start in the London theaters taking care of the horses of gentlemen who arrived for performances — in other words, he served as a kind of parking attendant — and then joined the company and became its principal playwright. On the other hand, the spuriousness of many of these tales has led some people to dismiss not only the myths but also the facts that scholars have carefully and certainly established about Shakespeare's life in London and Stratford. A further product of this skepticism has been the urge to propose more suitable candidates for authorship of the works traditionally assigned to Shakespeare.

Both of these extreme positions, sentimental credulity and radical disbelief, are mistaken. We do not know as much as we would like about William Shakespeare the man, but we do know much, and what we know makes a convincing case for a glover's son from a small town in Warwickshire going to London in his young manhood, finding his way into the theatrical world by acting and writing, and producing the plays and poems that have captured the imagination of the world. This chapter will offer a brief survey of Shakespeare's life, seeking to separate fact from fiction and, insofar as possible, to give a human face to the celebrated figure from the distant past and a different culture. This much might have been done fifty years ago. Two recent developments demand further consideration, however. In the past few years the proponents of the earl of Oxford as the author of Shakespeare's plays have been pressing their claims with unusual volume, and thus the legitimacy of that case needs to be examined. Second, recent literary theory has begun to reshape our sense of authorship: we have been reminded that works of art are the products not merely of an individual writer's genius but also of the culture that produced that writer. This principle is especially pertinent to that author of authors who made his name in the Elizabethan theater, where more than in most artistic arenas the final product was the result of a collaborative process involving writers, copyists, actors, censors, audiences, and printers. We need to do as much as possible to learn the facts about William Shakespeare's life, but finally the life is less important than the work.

Early Life

William Shakespeare was born to Mary and John Shakespeare in April 1564, their third child and first son. The infant was baptized on April 26, and since by ecclesiastical order the sacrament had to be performed within a few days of birth, his birthday has traditionally been assigned to April 23. Already we have entered the realm of myth and sentiment: April 23 is St. George's Day, the date given over to celebration of England's patron saint and therefore appropriate for the birth of England's greatest poet; April 23 is also the date of Shakespeare's death fifty-two years later, and so it offers tempting symmetry. That the precise hour and day of Shakespeare's birth are unknown is insignificant compared with the relative abundance of detail that survives about his family, thanks to town records and the parish register of Holy Trinity Church: we know that he was probably born in late April 1564 because he was baptized on Wednesday the 26th, as indicated in the church record reproduced on page 30; that his parents were John and Mary Shakespeare of Stratford; that he grew up with four younger siblings, brothers named Gilbert, Edmund, and Richard, and a sister named Joan; that three other sisters, two older and one younger than he, died in infancy or youth;[1] and that the family lived in the house in Henley Street throughout Shakespeare's boyhood. The historical records of the town itself are relatively full as well. Stratford had been a center of trade since the twelfth century, when Richard I licensed its Thursday market, and the basic street plan, depicted in the eighteenth-century map on page 31, was laid out in medieval times and has not changed much.

John Shakespeare, having moved to Stratford from a nearby village and found a wife, Mary Arden, in another neighboring village, became a prominent citizen of the town. Turning his back on the agricultural pursuits of his own family, he became a glover, or *whittawer,* one who treated the hides of animals and made and sold soft leather goods such as gloves, belts, and purses. He quickly became involved in town government, serving in several responsible positions, ranging from ale-taster (an officer who ascertained that loaves of bread weighed what they were supposed to and that ale was up to standard) to constable to burgess to alderman and finally to bailiff, the small-town equivalent of mayor. When William was about twelve years old, John Shakespeare's fortunes began to decline: he failed to attend town council meetings, began to sell property apparently to raise cash, was fined for failing to make a court appearance, was replaced as alderman in 1586 for shirking his responsibility, and in 1592 was reprimanded "for not comminge monethlie to the churche . . . [i]t is sayd . . . for feare of processe for debtte" (qtd. in Halliday 442). Some scholars attribute these absences to recusancy, a religiously motivated unwillingness to conform to the practices of the Church of England. It is possible that John Shakespeare and his family may have held Catholic sympathies, as did many English people less than half a century after Henry VIII's break with Rome. Financially and socially, things improved at the very end of his life, perhaps as a result of his son's professional success in London. In 1596 the playwright petitioned for and was granted a family coat of arms, apparently on behalf of his father, whose application had been denied some years earlier, and in 1601, the year of his death, John Shakespeare again occupied a place on the town council. The story of Shakespeare's parents is representative of many small-town tradesmen in the sixteenth century — success in business, modest

---

[1] The Shakespeares' first child, Joan, died sometime between her birth in 1558 and the christening of her sister, also named Joan, in 1569; the second, Margaret, died in infancy in 1562; and the last, Anne, died at age seven in 1579.

social prominence, and public service. In this case the fruits of hard work were imperiled by adversity, but in the end balance was restored. Their eldest son would achieve even greater financial success and social prominence, but the means to those ends lay in London, where he ventured probably in his mid-twenties.

Shakespeare's youth in Stratford requires a good deal of speculation, since much biographical information from the period is based on legal records in which children were not mentioned. But it is fairly safe speculation, given what we know of his family. As the son of a prominent citizen, he probably attended the Stratford grammar school, an institution established for the male offspring of just such people; sons of burgesses attended free. There he would have learned Latin and begun a rigorous course of reading in the great Roman authors.[2] We may assume that he attended church. Even if the Shakespeare family were secretly loyal to Rome, they apparently adhered to the law and conformed to Anglican practice (perhaps excepting John Shakespeare's 1592 lapse mentioned earlier). We may also conclude that, at least in some small way, Shakespeare helped his father in his business and developed an acquaintance with the agricultural and mercantile practices of the region in which he spent his first twenty years.

As Shakespeare comes of age, the record becomes more ample. In November 1582 the young man married the not-so-young Anne Hathaway, eight years older than her eighteen-year-old groom and three months pregnant at the wedding. In May of the next year, their daughter Susanna was christened, followed in 1585 by twins named Hamnet and Judith. Most biographers thus assume that Shakespeare resided in Stratford through his twenty-second year. Concerning the next seven years, until Shakespeare surfaced in London in 1592, the record is virtually silent; this is the period known to biographers as "the Lost Years." Theories abound as to what the young man might have been doing during this phase. The tale that he fled town to escape punishment for poaching was first mentioned nearly a century after his death. It is possible that he joined a troupe of players touring the provinces and thus made his way into the margins of the theatrical world centered in London. One of the earliest biographers, John Aubrey, reports that Shakespeare "had been in his younger years a schoolmaster in the country." Recent scholars have revisited that possibility by connecting it with the Shakespeares' alleged Catholic sympathies. Specifically, some believe that the teenaged William Shakespeare was employed, perhaps even before his marriage, as a tutor by an important Catholic family in Lancashire, the Hoghtons. They have sought to document that connection by studying the movement of certain schoolmasters between Stratford-upon-Avon and Hoghton Tower, a known center of recusant activity and a kind of safe house for fugitive priests and Continental agents of the Counter-Reformation. Further research may confirm these suggestions, but at present the claim is still open to dispute. Wherever he went upon leaving

[2]See Chapter 2 for more on Shakespeare's education.

Stratford, he must have arrived in London toward the end of the 1580s, just as the public theaters were beginning to flourish.

London: The First Decade

That Shakespeare is mentioned in 1592 as a presence to be reckoned with on the London theatrical scene indicates that he had been active there for some time. This first reference — a dig at a relative newcomer — seems to derive from professional jealousy. Robert Greene was a university-educated rake, pamphleteer, and playwright who obliquely attacked Shakespeare in a piece written just before Greene's death:

> [F]or there is an upstart Crow, beautified with our feathers, that with his *Tygers hart wrapt in a Players hyde*, supposes he is as well able to bombast out a blanke verse as the best of you: and beeing an absolute *Iohannes fac totum*, is in his owne conceit the onely Shake-scene in a countrey.

Scholars have made much of the images and allusions herein, some of their surmises probably justified, some of them probably not. That the "upstart Crow" implies a novice or parvenu seems obvious, but it may also refer to Shakespeare's lack of a university education; Greene was proud of his. The second phrase, "beautified with our feathers," has been taken to mean that Shakespeare the young actor depended on playwrights like Greene for his lines; it could also depict Shakespeare as the adapter or thief of others' plays and dramatic ideas. The charge of vicious hypocrisy is cloaked in a phrase twisted from Shakespeare's own *Henry VI, Part 3*, where York assails Queen Margaret as a "tiger's heart wrapp'd in a woman's hide." And Greene concludes with another jab at pretension, attacking a young theatrical jack-of-all-trades (*Iohannes fac totum*) who presumes to think himself an artist.

If Shakespeare had provoked envy by the early 1590s, he had also attracted favorable attention. In the same year as Greene's attack, another London writer, Thomas Nashe, referred to the uncommon success of the *Henry VI* plays, noting that tens of thousands of spectators had thrilled to the heroics of one of its characters. But success arrived in another guise as well. In 1593 Shakespeare first appeared in print with the narrative erotic poem *Venus and Adonis* dedicated to Henry Wriothesley, the third earl of Southampton. The nature of the relationship between poet and dedicatee is unclear: was it personal, or a conventional case of patronage? Whichever it was, the connection seems to have been durable and important, for a year later Southampton found himself the recipient of Shakespeare's second narrative poem, *The Rape of Lucrece*. The two poems may owe their existence to the outbreak of plague in 1593: the sixteenth-century London historian John Stow reports that almost 11,000 people died in London between December 1592 and December 1593 — this in a city of 200,000 residents — and the proportions of the epidemic led to the closing of the theaters. Thus Shakespeare may have used the idle days away from the playhouse to seek more remunerative literary work.

Eighteenth-century legend has it that Southampton gave Shakespeare a thousand pounds in recompense for the poems. Further, Southampton is sometimes identified with the comely young man of the sonnets, which Shakespeare may have begun to compose during this period of theatrical inactivity. Whatever the terms of the Southampton connection, it adds color and detail to our understanding of Shakespeare's extraordinary literary and social success.

The sequence of 154 sonnets divides into two groups, 1–126 and 127–54, and contains characters and implied narratives. In the first series, an older poet affectionately praises a beautiful young man, sometimes longingly, and urges him to marry. In the later group, the speaker confesses passion for and anguish at a mistress, a faithless "Dark Lady." If the earl of Southampton was not the young man of the first group of sonnets, who was? Who is the Dark Lady? Does the adjective *dark* refer to her hair color, her complexion, or her shady character? Who is the rival poet who makes an occasional entrance? When were the sonnets written? These primary questions are usually accompanied by others about the ordering of the poems, the circumstances of their publication, the sexual proclivities of the poet, and (above all) whether the implied narrative in the sequence represents poetically the lived experiences of actual persons. To some extent, of course, the sonnets must be a record of their creator's emotional biography, as is the case with every work of art by every artist; but when the amorous and sexual energies are as various and complex as those exhibited here, and when the poet is as celebrated as Shakespeare, the temptation to speculate, and even to assume a direct relationship between the work and the life, becomes nearly irresistible. However, scholarship (both historical and interpretive) has been notoriously unsuccessful in its attempts to solve the mysteries of the sonnets, and thus it seems prudent, given the limited space available here, to confine commentary to the place of these poems in Shakespeare's artistic output.

Arguments about the dating of the poems are almost as numerous and contradictory as those about who is dating whom *in* the poems. Although the entire sequence was not published until the Quarto of 1609, some of the sonnets were written in the 1590s, as part of the Elizabethan vogue for sonneteering. English poets had been writing sonnets for decades, many of them in the style of the Italian poet Petrarch, but the publication of Sir Philip Sidney's sonnet sequence *Astrophil and Stella* in 1591 generated a rush of similar verse. (It might be added that the obvious historical identities of the characters in that collection have helped to encourage the inspection of Shakespeare's sonnets for similar evidence.) Shakespeare was to some extent following literary fashion, and presumably the closing of the theaters in the period 1592–94 gave him leisure for lyric as well as narrative verse. Whether or not the poems were written for publication, initially they circulated in manuscript: Francis Meres, a literary commentator writing in 1598, refers in his *Palladis Tamia* (see p. 32) to Shakespeare's "sugared sonnets among his private friends." Versions of two of the sonnets were printed in a poetry anthology of 1599; in 1609 the 154 that exist were published together, along with Shakespeare's short poem "A Lover's

Complaint." The most recent editor of the sonnets, Katherine Duncan-Jones, has contested the orthodoxy that the sonnets are mainly products of the 1590s. Believing that Shakespeare himself authorized the publication of the 1609 collection, and finding in some of the poems allusions to public events between 1604 and 1608, she argues that, while some of the sonnets were unquestionably Elizabethan, many were composed after 1603–04. Whether the poet authorized or oversaw the publication of the volume, we do not know. Whether he or someone else is responsible for the arrangement of the poems, we do not know. Whether the poet's sexual biography is relevant to the narrative in the sequence, we do not know. These questions are tantalizing, and it is vain to discourage speculation. But as compelling as the story of the sonnets seems to be, and as beautiful as the sonnets are as poems, Shakespeare was by trade a playwright. Following his occasional flirtations with narrative and lyric verse, he always returned to the playhouse.

The reopening of the theaters coincided with, and perhaps to some degree produced, a shuffling of personnel and leadership in the London acting companies. Scholars have been unable to ascertain which theatrical company (or companies) first employed Shakespeare as actor and playwright — the Queen's Men, Pembroke's Men, and Lord Strange's Men are frequently mentioned possibilities — but in 1594 he joined Richard Burbage and six other players to form a new company under the sponsorship of Henry Carey, Lord Hunsdon, who at that time served as lord chamberlain. The formation of this theatrical troupe occurred at the point when Shakespeare the playwright was attaining artistic maturity, and so 1594 ushered in a period of relative stability: with Burbage taking the leading roles and Shakespeare providing scripts such as *Richard II* (the first installment of what would become the great second cycle of English history plays), *A Midsummer Night's Dream*, and *Romeo and Juliet* in 1595–96, the company began playing regularly at the Theatre just north of the city walls, and within a few years became the most successful theatrical troupe in England. They began to appear at court, playing at Greenwich Palace (presumably for Queen Elizabeth herself) during the Christmas season of 1594 and eventually giving more royal performances than any other contemporary theatrical company.

"Stability," however, was as evanescent in the theater then as it is now. Two years later, in 1596, the actors experienced troubles with their lease when the owner of the land on which the Theatre stood got sticky about his terms, and the company was forced to find another playing space. This crisis ended happily, leading ultimately to the construction of the Globe and, after a series of complicated transactions, the acquisition of a second theater, the indoor Blackfriars. By the time James I came to the throne in 1603, Shakespeare's was unquestionably the premier English theatrical company, and the new king, hoping to associate his name with success, chose to patronize it, as the royal license (p. 33) indicates. Renamed the King's Men, the troupe continued to perform for almost four decades, surviving Shakespeare's death in 1616 and Burbage's in 1619; they succumbed finally, as did all such enterprises, to Parliament's closing the theaters in the 1640s. It is fair to say that Shakespeare's contribution as author helped to secure the prominence and endurance of the company.

The year 1594 also saw the first publication of a Shakespeare play, *Titus Andronicus,* although his name was not listed on the title page. Such neglect of the writer by the publisher was not uncommon unless the author was sufficiently well known to increase sales, which at this point Shakespeare apparently was not. Famous or no, playwrights rarely had much say in the publication of their plays, since the script legally belonged to the theatrical company that produced it.[3] What did sell books, apparently, was the record of performances: the title page of *Titus Andronicus* (reproduced on p. 211) advertises that "it was Plaide by the Right Honourable the Earle of Darbie, Earle of Pembrooke, and Earle of Sussex their Seruants." Similarly, five more of Shakespeare's plays were published over the next four years (*Romeo and Juliet* in two versions) without his name attached, although the names of the companies that performed them do appear. In 1598, with the quarto publication of *Love's Labor's Lost,* the title page attributes the work to Shakespeare, as is the case for most of the plays published subsequently (including some that he apparently did not write). By the end of the 1590s Shakespeare had written most of his history plays and many of his most popular comedies. Francis Meres, the critic who mentions the private circulation of the sonnets, compares him in the same passage to the Roman masters of comedy and tragedy, Plautus and Seneca, naming several of Shakespeare's comedies and histories, the two tragedies written so far, and the narrative poems. (See the excerpt from Meres's *Palladis Tamia* on p. 32.) By the turn of the seventeenth century Shakespeare had become the most successful playwright in London.

He had not broken his ties with his hometown, however, as various financial and other documents attest. His wife and children apparently remained in Stratford while he lived in London, and it seems likely that he made regular trips back and forth during the twenty years or so that he worked in the capital. The journey would have taken four days on foot, perhaps two on horseback. Shakespeare's only son, the twin Hamnet, died in August 1596. In that same year the College of Heralds granted the Shakespeares the coat of arms that had been denied John Shakespeare almost thirty years before. In May 1597 William Shakespeare purchased New Place, the second-largest house in Stratford; the spread also included two barns, two gardens, and two orchards. In London during the mid-1590s, he lived near Bishopsgate, fairly near the Theatre, where his company played; in 1600 he is known to have lived on the South Bank of the Thames River, probably as a result of the company's having built the Globe there in 1599; in 1604 he lodged with a French family, the Mountjoys, in Silver Street near St. Olave's Church. The map of London on page 35 indicates the exact location of the Mountjoy house.

Although his growing fame as a playwright made him a valuable asset to the company and he maintained his normal rate of production, writing an average of two plays each year, he also continued to perform, acting in Ben

[3]Some of the complexities of the publication process will be clarified in Chapter 6, "What Is Your Text?"

Jonson's *Every Man in his Humour* in 1598 and again in Jonson's *Sejanus* in 1603. He may have acted in other plays as well, although these are the only two in which surviving records indicate that he took a role. Given the familiar conception of Shakespeare the natural genius transcending the vicissitudes of the material world — as in Milton's description of "sweetest Shakespeare, fancy's child, / Warbl[ing] his native woodnotes-wild" — it is worth emphasizing the hands-on quality of his professional activity. He was actively engaged, as actor, shareholder, and supplier of scripts, in the financial affairs of the company. It is true that the nature of the documents that survive — court records, details of lawsuits, transfers of property — tends to highlight the commercial side of the man's life at the expense of the artistic. But in our rush to celebrate the art we have tended to slight the revelatory value of these mundane financial details: Shakespeare was a businessman as well as an artist.

London: Maturity

Shakespeare's growing prosperity is attributable not so much to his writing as to his status as a shareholder in the Lord Chamberlain's Men. When the Globe was erected from the timbers of the original Theatre in 1599, Shakespeare was listed as one of the ten "housekeepers," or shareowners. He is also recorded as one of the seven housekeepers of the indoor playhouse at Blackfriars in 1608, when the company obtained the right to use the building as a theater. (James Burbage, Richard's father, had acquired Blackfriars in 1596, perhaps out of concern for the difficulties with the landlord of the Theatre, but neighborhood protest prevented its theatrical use at that time.) If the investments in property that Shakespeare continued to make in Stratford are a reliable guide, his profit from these enterprises was handsome. He bought 127 acres of land in Old Stratford (a suburb of the town) for £320 in May 1602 and then a cottage opposite New Place later that same year; in 1605 he invested £440 in "a lease of tithes" — something like stock in an agricultural enterprise — for property in and around Stratford. Interestingly enough, although most biographers think he had by this time retired to Stratford, he purchased a house in London in 1612, near the theater in the Blackfriars district. Perhaps he was following the example of his colleague Richard Burbage, who had made similar investments, or it may be that he did not deem his theatrical career finished. Shakespeare kept a close eye on his account books, and during the last twenty years of his life, beginning with the purchase of New Place, there was a lot to count. To note these financial transactions or to acknowledge Shakespeare's keen business sense is not to discount his imaginative gifts and literary achievement. Rather, it is to modify the portrait of the otherworldly artist and to admit that art and commerce are often productive partners.

Around 1600, after a decade of writing mostly comedies and histories, Shakespeare changed artistic direction. Thus began the great tragic phase, starting with *Julius Caesar* in 1599 and *Hamlet* shortly thereafter and continuing through *Macbeth* in 1606 and *Antony and Cleopatra* and *Coriolanus* about 1607 or 1608. Although he continued to write comedies, the comic spirit informing the plays is noticeably altered. *All's Well That Ends Well* (c. 1603) and *Measure for Measure* (1604), although their endings are technically "happy," deal with problematic subjects: in the first case a young woman insists on marrying an immature, unworthy man who doesn't want her, and in the second a novice must defend herself against the sexual harassment of a corrupt civic official as she seeks to save her brother from being executed for fornication. These plays exhibit tonal ironies so bitter and representations of human activity so unflattering that at times it is difficult to remember that they are comedies. Another problematic play from these years, *Troilus and Cressida*, is even more difficult to classify. In its dark assessment of human experience and achievement it more nearly resembles *Othello* or *King Lear* than *Much Ado about Nothing* or *As You Like It*. And yet it is not clearly a tragedy either.

The impetus for this shift of direction remains one of the great mysteries of Shakespeare's career, for which various explanations have been offered. Psychological: Shakespeare the man experienced some kind of personal crisis brought on perhaps by the death of his son and his father or by some unrecorded emotional event. Practical: perhaps performances of tragedies drew audiences in greater numbers. Formal: Shakespeare had tired of writing the kinds of plays to which he had devoted the previous ten years and sought to experiment with the theatrical possibilities of tragedy. Literary: tragedy had long been considered the more important mode, superior to comedy in its themes and range. Cultural: Shakespeare's darkening vision reflects the increasing pessimism of his society about politics, economics, and the social structure. We are not likely to learn the actual reason for this artistic reversal, if there was only one, and even if we did, we would need a corresponding explanation for yet another change, the shift that occurs around 1608 and leads to the creation of the late romances. The Jacobean Shakespeare differs from the Elizabethan Shakespeare, but to seek the man in the work is to court frustration and uncertainty.

Shakespeare's second decade in the theater differed from the first in a number of meaningful ways. First, he enjoyed professional security, remaining with the company he had helped to found until his retirement from the theater and return to Stratford. Second, he became, practically speaking, an unofficial court dramatist. As principal playwright for the King's Men, Shakespeare saw much of his contemporary work performed for King James and the royal family — notably *Measure for Measure, Othello,* and *King Lear* — and many of the earlier plays that they would have missed before their arrival in London in 1603 were revived for court performance. *Macbeth* must have been written with James's experience and taste in mind: the Scottish king took pride in his legendary descent from the family of Banquo, had narrowly escaped assassination in the Gunpowder Plot of 1605 (when a group of radical Catholics planted explosives that would detonate at James's opening of Parliament), had published a treatise on witchcraft, and was known to like short plays, which *Macbeth* conspicuously is. Third, with the company's acquisition of a second theater in 1608, Shakespeare found himself writing not only for the usual spectators at the Globe but also for a more exclusive audience. The indoor house at Blackfriars, although frequently referred to as a "private theater" from the days when children's companies had performed there, was in fact as public as the Bankside amphitheaters. But it was smaller, the absence of natural light meant that performances could be held at night and lit by candles, and the admission price was higher. Thus Blackfriars is thought to have attracted a more aristocratic, fashionable crowd. Finally, Shakespeare's rate of productivity slowed down slightly, to about one play each year, perhaps an understandable consequence of his success and increasing age but probably also of reduced opportunities for playing. The plague had returned to London with a vengeance: between 1603 and 1610 the public theaters were closed almost as much as they were open. The authorities prohibited public gatherings when the number of deaths per week in London and its suburbs reached a certain level, usually forty but sometimes thirty or fifty. (See the plague bill from 1609 on p. 33.) The reduction in business caused by the plague was perhaps counterbalanced by the increased receipts from two theaters instead of one, and certainly the payments for royal performances must also have helped offset losses. In any case, Shakespeare and his colleagues dominated the English theatrical scene, and by the end of his career in London he was rich and famous.

Exactly when the end of his London career came and why he elected to end it are difficult to determine. The turn to romance that occurred around 1608 needs to be assessed with the same restraint appropriate to the shift into tragedy. Despite the wishful claims of nineteenth-century Shakespeare worship, or bardolatry, Shakespeare's theatrical career does not conclude with a glorious, autobiographical farewell disguised as a play (*The Tempest*). He was experimenting up to the end, sometimes successfully, sometimes not. *Cymbeline*, for example, written about 1609-10, a year or two before *The Tempest* and probably before *The Winter's Tale*, is a fascinating, beautiful, and at times bizarre piece of work, for the dramatist was stretching himself in ways that critics and audiences have sometimes found baffling. And even if we could see the last plays as a progression of affirmative steps leading to the triumph of *The Tempest*, we would still have three texts to deal with, *Henry VIII*, *The Two Noble Kinsmen*, and *Cardenio* (this last one now lost). These unusual plays were written with John Fletcher, who was to be Shakespeare's successor as chief dramatist of the King's Men. Some believe that Shakespeare had retired to Stratford by about 1611 and composed his portions of these plays while living in retirement, and it could be that *The Tempest* or even earlier plays were written under such conditions. But we have few historical details to flesh out the bare skeleton of his final years as an artist.

Shakespeare's last years in the theater should probably be considered representative of his career as a whole. He did what a good professional might have been expected to do, what he had always done, inventing or at least developing new dramatic forms to suit his tastes and please audiences. This was an especially useful gift to a company needing to attract spectators to two theaters, and Shakespeare at the last, as at the first, was sensitive to the opportunities of theatrical space: the magical tone and effects of the late plays bespeak a deliberate effort to exploit the resources of the new indoor theater. Even on the verge of retirement he was still helping the company by collaborating with Fletcher. Whether this was a relationship of mentor to pupil or merely a practical arrangement is uncertain: Fletcher was hardly a beginner, having had several successes with Francis Beaumont. Presumably Shakespeare's name on a play helped to bring in customers, although it may be that the younger Fletcher, developer of the new and fashionable tragicomedy, was by 1612 the greater draw. Businessman that he was, Shakespeare would have remained interested, in every sense, in the company's financial health.

Retirement

The available information about Shakespeare's last few years is mostly financial or legal. Presumably he lived at New Place with his wife and in proximity to his two daughters, one of them now married, and the other surviving members of his family. His mother died in 1608, seven years after his father; in 1612 and 1613 his brothers Gilbert and Richard were buried; his sister Joan lived in the western half of the Henley Street property. Although an enormous fire ravaged much of Stratford in July 1614, Shakespeare seems to have suffered no direct loss. A heated controversy over property occurred in that same summer, however, when two powerful landowners in town attempted to enclose a large meadow at Welcombe, just outside Stratford, a common area in which many citizens, Shakespeare among them, had a financial interest. Since the enclosure would apparently have converted farmland to pasture for grazing sheep, thus reducing employment, diminishing the tithe-profits of investors, and possibly increasing claims on civic charity, fierce resistance arose in the town council, with Thomas Greene, a kinsman of Shakespeare, leading the effort to block the project. The enclosers actually began to dig up the earth with the intent of planting hedges, but men, women, and children from the town came into the meadow with spades and set about to fill the ditches. Although Shakespeare's name is listed in several of the surviving documents, no one has been able to determine satisfactorily where he stood on the issue. Perhaps his sympathies were divided, or perhaps he was attempting to placate both parties by refusing to take a firm position. As often happens in such matters, the case lasted longer than some of the litigants. The Welcombe controversy made its way slowly through the legal system until it reached the king's chief justice, Sir Edward Coke, who denied the attempt to enclose; that was in April 1616, the same month and year that Shakespeare died.

The lack of solid information about Shakespeare's last years has left a gap that legend has been eager to fill. For example, the cause of Shakespeare's death is unknown, but John Ward, the vicar of Stratford in the mid–seventeenth century, supplies a tantalizing story of a party in which Shakespeare, drinking with his literary friends Ben Jonson and Michael Drayton, contracted a fever that led to his death. (In his play *Bingo*, the modern English playwright Edward Bond depicts an imagined version of this occasion, along with an unflattering view of Shakespeare's participation in the Welcombe enclosure dispute.) This anecdote, recorded in Ward's diary entry given on page 34, is typical of the ambiguous nature of biographical evidence: it occupies one sentence in a series of entries in a notebook; it is cryptic and medically questionable; and it is possibly true nonetheless. Although Ward was not born until twelve years after Shakespeare's death, he was well connected in Stratford, knew the playwright's daughter personally, and presumably was familiar with local gossip. We may wish to believe some version of this nearly contemporary story, but where do we draw the line between legend and fact?

In March 1616 Shakespeare seems to have known that his life was nearing its close because he sent for his attorney to alter his will, probably in reaction to his daughter Judith's recent marriage. (Shakespeare ensures that Judith's new husband, Thomas Quiney, does not take advantage of her for her portion. A man of dubious reputation, Quiney pleaded guilty to impregnating another woman not long before his marriage to Judith; a month after the wedding, the woman and infant died in childbirth.) The will has occasioned much debate: eighteenth-century admirers of its author found the testament cold and un-poetic, and many have been disturbed by the one ambiguous reference to his wife, Anne. (He bequeaths her his "second best bed" and its linens.) In *Shakespeare: A Biographical Handbook,* Gerald Eades Bentley persuasively contends that the will is typical of a comfortable landowner at the beginning of the seventeenth century (Bentley 61). The dying Shakespeare left remembrances and gifts to various relations, friends, and colleagues — his fellow actors were to receive money to buy memorial rings — but most of the estate devolved to his daughter Susanna and her husband, the local physician John Hall. His books would have gone to them and thus remained at New Place. Of Shakespeare's theatrical manuscripts there is no mention, but this is as it should be, since the plays belonged technically to the company that had produced them. In the eyes of the law, the handwritten manuscripts would have had no value.

We cannot be sure why Shakespeare did not provide specifically for his wife, and too little is known about local practice to be certain whether, as in some parts of England, she would have automatically inherited one-third of her husband's estate, the "widow's portion." The most plausible suggestion is that Anne Shakespeare, who in 1616 was about sixty years old, would naturally have remained a resident of New Place and would have been provided for by her inheriting daughter. But what about the "second best bed"? In this case, as Samuel Schoenbaum says pointedly, we have a "choice between cynicism and sentiment" (*William Shakespeare: A Compact Documentary Life* 304). Other contemporary wills refer to pieces of furniture in their order of value, specifically to second-best beds, and it may be that the second-best bed would have been the one shared by husband and wife, the best being reserved for guests. Yet the phrase does not seem entirely innocent. Across the gap of time, the legacy appears to have been either a kind of mordant joke hinting at marital difficulty or an affectionate sexual souvenir.

Shakespeare was buried where he was baptized, in Holy Trinity Church in Stratford, beneath a stone slab carved with the following verse:

Good Frend for Jesus Sake Forbeare,
To Digg the Dust Enclosed Heare:
Bleste Be Yᵉ Man Yᵗ Spares Thes Stones,
And Curst Be He Yᵗ Moves My Bones.

The dead man's wishes have been respected: the tomb remains undisturbed in the chancel of the church, although the number of pilgrims walking across the grave led to such deterioration by the eighteenth century that the authorities had to replace the stone and inscription. Early in the seventeenth century a monument was erected, a painted bust of the poet done in the conventional funerary style, that has lasted to this day.

Seven years after his death, the book we know as the First Folio — its actual title is *Mr. William Shakespeares Comedies, Histories, & Tragedies* — was published in London. John Heminges and Henry Condell, two of the fellow actors remembered in the will with rings, assembled manuscripts and earlier published versions of Shakespeare's plays and arranged for them to be collected into a single printed volume containing thirty-six plays, half of them published for the first time. Although the book did not appear until 1623, the idea for such a volume must have arisen several years before, and the actual printing took more than a year. Heminges and Condell may have been inspired by the example of Ben Jonson, who in 1616 had published a folio volume consisting of his plays, masques, and poems, called *Workes*. As the compilers seem to have been aware, and as the prefatory verse contributed by Jonson himself enunciates, this book is Shakespeare's everlasting monument.

The Anti-Stratfordians

A question frequently asked by the general public is whether the works attributed to Shakespeare were in fact written by the man from Stratford. Such skepticism is fueled from time to time by those who cannot bring themselves to accept that a glover's son from a small provincial town could have written the plays, and who have spent a great deal of energy attempting to convince the world that the real author of the Shakespeare canon is someone else. Although a slew of nominees have been proposed over the last two centuries, from Christopher Marlowe to Queen Elizabeth, the favorites are Francis Bacon and Edward de Vere, earl of Oxford. What these two men have in common is their aristocratic status, and it is on this ground that the Baconians and Oxfordians usually stake their claim. (It is probably worth mentioning that, while both Bacon and de Vere were titled, de Vere's status was much higher than Bacon's. Bacon was knighted in 1603 and much later became an earl, whereas de Vere, the descendant of an old and distinguished family, inherited the title of seventeenth earl of Oxford.) The doubters do not question the existence of William Shakespeare of Stratford, and some even acknowledge his participation in the London theatrical scene; but he is reckoned to be a front man for an aristocratic writer who would not permit his name to be linked to the popular theater.

The anti-Stratfordian argument is based in two areas: education and class, with the first being a less inflammatory version of the second. No one, it is said, could have attained the learning and sophistication required to write Shakespeare's comedies, histories, and tragedies without the benefit of a university education. In order to strengthen this contention, its proponents some-times characterize William Shakespeare not only as lacking a university education but as actually illiterate. Since most Englishmen who attended universities in the sixteenth century were members of the nobility, the argument about education is in fact an argument about class. To some, it is intolerable to suppose that a person from the lower middle class — and from the country, at that — produced the works that are considered the pinnacle of Western literary achievement. Thus it is necessary to propose an aristocratic substitute as the author.

In the nineteenth century, Francis Bacon was the choice of the anti-Stratfordians as the true author of "Shakespeare's" plays. Far outstripping other pretenders, he even inspired the production of a journal, *Baconiana*, in which the plays were meticulously scrutinized for secret clues to Bacon's authorship. But recently Bacon's fortunes have waned while those of another candidate have waxed. Edward de Vere lived from 1550 to 1604, spent much of his time at the court of Elizabeth, wrote some poetry, associated with most of the major figures in politics and the arts, and in midcareer retired to the country with an annual pension from the Crown. His candidacy has benefited lately from the advocacy of one of his descendants, who has assumed direction of the Shakespeare-Oxford Society and devoted a great deal of energy to polemics about the authorship question. Given this degree of attention, Oxford's candidacy can serve to represent the claims of all the pretenders and the conspiracy theories attached to them.

In brief, the Oxfordians propose that the plays exhibit such a detailed knowledge of court politics and of social practices at the highest echelons that their creator must have had firsthand knowledge of such a milieu. According to this view, a tradesman's son from the provinces could not have had access to such people and customs, and thus the plays' author must have been a courtier-poet such as de Vere. The accompanying postulate is that, given the rigid power structures of the Tudor court and the hypersensitivity of an aging monarch, the regime would never have permitted such an insider to take credit for dramas such as *Richard III*, *Richard II*, and *Love's Labor's Lost*. Whether or not they were deemed to comment on recognizable persons and events, the plays concern themselves with such sensitive issues as the abuse of royal power, political hypocrisy, courtly vanity, monarchical madness, and regicide. And since Elizabeth's watchful councillors would not have tolerated potentially negative representations of royal concerns, two stratagems were employed. First, all traces of aristocratic origins and connections were expunged from the plays and poems so as to maintain the fiction of humble authorship, a task accomplished by the supreme authority of Elizabeth's chief ministers, the Cecil family. Second, a decoy, a beard, was required to play the role of playwright: enter William Shakespeare of Stratford.

This is hardly the place for a lengthy refutation of the Oxfordian or Baconian position, but some instances of stretched logic and special pleading ought to be noticed. To begin with, the doubts about Shakespeare's education are hardly decisive. Although the Stratford archives do not supply us with William

Shakespeare's report card, we may be reasonably sure that, as the son of a town burgess, he attended the local school and earned over some ten years a thorough grounding in Latin grammar and literature. He received the kind of classical education, in short, that would have given him a taste for fiction, history, and poetry, and would have stimulated and enabled him to continue his education on his own. Moreover, literary history is replete with examples of young people from modest beginnings who had no university training but who made distinguished contributions to literature. In fact, Shakespeare's contemporary Ben Jonson did not attend a university but, diligently building on his excellent grammar school education, became one of the most learned and creative figures of his age.

Oxford's death in 1604 creates chronological bars to his candidacy. The historical record indicates that *Macbeth* and *The Tempest* were written circa 1606 and 1611, respectively, and more important, they depend explicitly on events that occurred after Oxford's death, notably the Gunpowder Plot of 1605 and the circulation in 1610 of pamphlets about the New World. Many other obstacles present themselves, such as books that Oxford could not have known before his death but that indisputably served as sources for the plays. And the poems that de Vere is known to have written under his own name do little to recommend him as the author of *A Midsummer Night's Dream* or *Hamlet*.

Perhaps the most damning refutation of the various pretenders' claims is the ingenuity needed to demonstrate that the real author has secretly encoded his name in various Shakespearean works and that such signals can be revealed only through complicated cryptographic schemes. As recently as 1987 an attorney named Penn Leary published a book called *The Cryptographic Shakespeare: A Monograph Wherein the Poems and Plays Attributed to William Shakespeare Are Proven to Contain the Enciphered Name of the Concealed Author, Francis Bacon.* The earl of Oxford's supporters are hardly less fanciful, finding "E-d-w-a-r-d d-e V-e-r-e" peppered among the sonnets, the poems, and even the prefatory "To the Reader" that begins the First Folio.

The strongest case against Oxford or Bacon or Marlowe or anyone, however, arises not from a barrage of negative arguments but rather from the positive evidence placing William Shakespeare of Stratford in London between 1592 and 1612, connecting him to the theatrical scene there (specifically his membership in the King's Men), and identifying him with the published texts that derived from public performances and that bear his name.

What Is an Author?

The authorship question has taken a new turn in the past three decades owing to changes in theory and criticism that have affected the study of literature. Scholars and critics have challenged the romantic image of the artist as an individual and transcendent genius and supplanted it with a broader, culturally based model of authorship. Much attention is given to the writer's social and institutional affiliations, a primary goal being to identify as specifically as possible the conditions and details of the writer's participation in a discursive community. In poststructuralist criticism, the earlier notion of authorial autonomy has yielded to awareness of the embeddedness of dramatic texts in social, economic, and political structures. To some extent, the artist is a subject, inescapably responsive ("subjected") to the local forces of history, politics, and literature.

The work of Stephen Greenblatt and Louis Adrian Montrose, both writing under the influence of the French theorist Michel Foucault, has been especially influential in prompting revision of our comfortable notion of the imaginative master working in splendid isolation. As Greenblatt puts it, "There may be a moment in which a solitary individual puts words on a page, but it is by no means clear that this moment is the heart of the mystery and that everything else is to be stripped away and discarded. Moreover, the moment of inscription, on closer analysis, is itself a social moment" (*Shakespearean Negotiations* 4–5). In other words, the literary productions of a writer such as Shakespeare are conditioned and determined by historical and social forces that vastly complicate simple notions of authorship and artistic responsibility. Whereas earlier scholars sought to identify books that a writer might have known or to describe scientific debates or economic practices incorporated into a work, recent critics have relaxed the definition of artistic influence. Now major political figures or particular social practices are seen as contributing to the creation of the literary text whether any direct relation to that text can be demonstrated or not. Thus an author becomes something of a channel for a flood of cultural forces, and authorial control over the process of creation — the creator's *authority* — tends to be spread into the culture at large.

Montrose, for example, sees *A Midsummer Night's Dream,* a play celebrating within its fiction the royal marriage of Theseus and Hippolyta and perhaps performed as part of the celebration of an aristocratic wedding, as shaped to a large degree by the cultural presence of Elizabeth I.

> Whether or not Queen Elizabeth was present at the first performance of *A Midsummer Night's Dream,* her pervasive *cultural presence* was a condition of the play's imaginative possibility. This is not to imply that *A Midsummer Night's Dream* is merely an inert "product" of Elizabethan culture. The play is rather a new *production* in Elizabethan culture enlarging the dimensions of the cultural field and altering the lines of force within it. Thus, in the sense that the royal presence was itself represented within the play, it may be said that the play henceforth conditioned the imaginative possibility of the Queen. ("'Shaping Fantasies'" 62)

This reciprocity between the cultural field and the literary artifact is one of the primary tenets of what has come to be called new historicist analysis of early modern literature. Although the passage illustrates the new historicist concern with how dramatic texts work to change the culture that produced them, what is especially important for our purposes is Montrose's insistence on the dispersal of responsibility for the creation of the play. Thus, Queen Elizabeth, in one sense, participates in the authorship of *A Midsummer Night's Dream*. In the postmodern critical climate, the writer of Shakespeare's plays is perceived to have a slightly lesser role in the process of literary creation than would have been true fifty years ago.

The diminution of individual agency in recent theory coincides with a fundamental truth about the stage, one that has always been recognized but that has assumed greater importance in recent years — the collaborative nature of the theatrical enterprise. In some ways the theater is the most socially embedded of all the arts, depending as it does upon a direct process of exchange between performer and spectator and thus subordinating the contribution of the writer. Moreover, Shakespeare's plays are the products of a complex process of creation, realization, and transmission. Even if we hold to the notion of the solitary artist scribbling in a garret, we must recognize that the script of *King Lear* as it was delivered to the company on the first day of rehearsals in the 1605–06 season may well be very different from the version that we confront when we sit down to read it in a modern edition. The text of the play probably underwent changes at several junctures: in the hands of the scribe who copied out the parts for the actors, in the company's progress from first rehearsal to public presentation, between the opening and subsequent performances or even revivals, in the making of a copy to send to the printer, and in the compositorial labor that finally produced the printed text. *King Lear* is a particularly telling example of the complex stages of production because there are two versions, one that appears in the Quarto of 1608 and another in the Folio of 1623, and the discrepancies between them have led scholars to detect an act of revision that further complicates the notion of an "authorized" text.

These theoretical and critical developments help to put the mysteries of biography in perspective. Finally it matters less who wrote the plays than that they were written and that we continue to admire and enjoy them. This is not to say, however, that our curiosity about literary creativity is illegitimate and the identity of the playwright irrelevant. We know that life informs art, and we continue to learn how that transaction occurs. In her fascinating psychological study *Shakespeare the Actor and the Purposes of Playing*, Meredith Skura proposes that William Shakespeare's experience as a performer — the familiar narcissism of the actor — forcefully influenced the forms and ideas of his dramas, particularly in the creation of such figures as Richard III and Iago. Finally, it is important to remember that the case is never entirely closed. Shakespearean biography has been painstakingly constructed from the most detailed and mundane forms of evidence, and while we should not expect astounding revelations — a signed note in Shakespeare's hand, turned up in a Warwickshire barn, claiming authorship of plays from *The Comedy of Errors* to *Cardenio* — it is possible that new discoveries will help to answer some of the questions that continue to tease us.

✦ The House Known as Shakespeare's Birthplace   *c. 1762*

This drawing, from a watercolor by Richard Greene, depicts the house in Henley Street, Stratford-upon-Avon, in which Shakespeare's parents lived at the time of his birth. Despite alterations over the past four centuries, the house is still standing.

✦ Record of Shakespeare's Baptism   *1564* ➤

This page from the baptismal record of Holy Trinity Church, Stratford-upon-Avon, shows the original notation of Shakespeare's baptism on April 26, 1564. The relevant phrase is in Latin: *Gulielmus filius Johannes Shakspere* (William son of John Shakspere). The "xxx" was added later to designate the famous name.

October 26	Hamnissa filia Johannis Exemworth de adoxmiteston nolga
28	Elizabeth filia T Royers
November 5	Agnes filia Stephani Burman
11	Thomas filius Gulielmi Smyth
11	Agnes filia Thomæ Hirres
17	Johanna filia Richardi Roberts
27	Richardus filius Rogeri Banister
December 1	Richardus filius Johannis Hemming
5	Gulielmus filius Gulielmi Hearing
7	Henricus filius Henrici Ffeild
14	Rodolphus filius Richardi Castell
15	Antonius filius Gulielmi Brasford
22	Johannes filius Thomæ Bayliss
24	Aliria Rogeri Paxepoynte
Januari 5	Robertus filius Richardi Martyn
5	Richardus filius Humfredy ff Index
9	Francisca filia Johannis Hauley
9	Nicholaus filius Richardi Barbar de drayton
13	Helena filia Nicholai Cope
14	Johanna filia Roberti Arthar
23	Elizabeth filia Thomæ Hunt
28	Richardus filius Johannis ff prey
30	Aliria filia davidis Gately
30	Anna filia Henrici Wagstaffe
February 2	Aliria filia Gulielmi Brace
14	Gulielmus filius Rogeri Bett
23	Aliria filia Rodolphi Cawdrey
23	Catarina filia Brandi Prewe
27	Aliria filia Richardi Greenway
26	Agnes filia Thomæ Horne de Bushopton
28	W filius Richardi Herbarte

1564

April 3	Edwardus filius Thomæ Sheffeld
6	Benedicta filia Thomæ Fflemming
22	Johannes filius william Brooks
26	Gulielmus filius Johannes Shakspere XXX
may 3	Humfredus filius william furse
4	Aliria filia Johannis Rogers de bushopton
12	Johannes filius Johannis Golford
21	Richardus filius Gulielmi Ball de Bushopton
	Per Richard minter

→ Map of Stratford-upon-Avon

c. 1768

This plan of Shakespeare's hometown was made by Samuel Winter around 1768. Despite the late date of the map, the layout of the town was essentially the same in the eighteenth century as it was in Shakespeare's day, and as it is now. Note particularly the location of the birthplace (#18) in Henley Street and New Place (#16) at the corner of Church Street and Chapel Lane.

→ FRANCIS MERES

From *Palladis Tamia: Wit's Treasury* 1598

Meres's book, a compendium of philosophical and literary observations, evaluates England's literary scene at the end of the sixteenth century by comparing modern writers with their ancient counterparts. Shakespeare appears as the master of several genres and dramatic modes, and his repeated mention is one of the first and strongest indicators of his prominence at the end of the 1590s. The principal Roman writers invoked are Ovid, the poet whose stories of mythological transformation appear in his *Metamorphoses;* Plautus, the dramatist whose comedies Shakespeare adapted directly in *The Comedy of Errors;* and Seneca, the touchstone for classical tragedy.

A comparative discourse of our English Poets,
with the *Greek, Latin, and Italian Poets.*

. . . [T]he English tongue is mightily enriched, and gorgeously invested in rare ornaments and resplendent habiliments by Sir *Philip Sidney, Spenser, Daniel, Drayton, Warner, Shakespeare, Marlowe,* and *Chapman.* . . .

As the soul of *Euphorbus* was thought to live in *Pythagoras:* so the sweet witty soul of *Ovid* lives in mellifluous & honey-tongued *Shakespeare,* witness his *Venus* and *Adonis,* his *Lucrece,* his sugared Sonnets among his private friends, &c.

As *Plautus* and *Seneca* are accounted the best for Comedy and Tragedy among the Latins: so *Shakespeare* among the English is the most excellent in both kinds for the stage; for Comedy, witness his *Gentlemen of Verona,* his *Errors,* his *Love's Labor's Lost,* his *Love's Labor's Won,*[1] his *Midsummer Night's Dream,* & his *Merchant of Venice:* for Tragedy his *Richard II, Richard III, Henry IV, King John, Titus Andronicus* and his *Romeo and Juliet.*

As *Epius Stolo* said, that the Muses would speak with *Plautus'* tongue, if they would speak Latin: so I say that the Muses would speak with *Shakespeare's* fine filed phrase, if they would speak English. . . .

As *Pindarus, Anacreon,* and *Callimachus* among the Greeks; and *Horace* and *Catullus* among the Latins are the best Lyric Poets: so in this faculty the best among our Poets are *Spenser* (who excelleth in all kinds) *Daniel, Drayton, Shakespeare, Bretton.* . . .

[T]hese are our best for Tragedy, the Lord *Buckhurst,* Doctor *Leg* of Cambridge, Doctor *Edes* of Oxford, master *Edward Ferris,* the Author of the *Mirror for Magistrates, Marlowe, Peele, Watson, Kyd, Shakespeare, Drayton, Chapman, Dekker,* and *Benjamin Jonson.* . . .

[T]he best for Comedy among us be *Edward* earl of Oxford, Doctor *Gager* of Oxford, Master *Rowley* once a rare Scholar of learned Pembroke Hall in Cambridge, Master *Edwards* one of her Majesty's Chapel, eloquent and witty *John Lyly, Lodge, Gascoigne, Greene, Shakespeare, Thomas Nashe, Thomas Heywood, Anthony Munday* our best plotter, *Chapman, Porter, Wilson, Hathway,* and *Henry Chettle.* . . .

---

[1]*Love's Labor's Won* is the puzzling title that scholars have not been able to trace. It may be either the title of a lost play or an alternate title for an existing comedy such as *The Taming of the Shrew.*

[T]hese are the most passionate among us to bewail and bemoan the perplexities of Love: *Henry Howard* Earl of Surrey, Sir *Thomas Wyatt* the elder, Sir *Francis Brian*, Sir *Philip Sydney*, Sir *Walter Raleigh*, Sir *Edward Dyer, Spenser, Daniel, Drayton, Shakespeare, Whetstone, Gascoigne, Samuel Page* sometimes fellow of *Corpus Christi* College in Oxford, *Churchyard, Bretton*.

↬ The Royal License for Shakespeare's Company   *1603*

From its formation in 1594 until 1603, Shakespeare's company was known as the Lord Chamberlain's Men. King James assumed patronage of the troupe in a document dated May 19, 1603, from which this passage is taken. The new title, the King's Men, was retained until the closing of the theaters in 1642.

We . . . do license and authorize these our Servants Lawrence Fletcher, William Shakespeare, Richard Burbage, Augustine Phillips, John Heminges, Henry Condell, William Sly, Robert Armin, Richard Cowley, and the rest of their associates freely to use and exercise the art and faculty of playing comedies, tragedies, histories, interludes, morals, pastorals, stageplays, and such others like as they have already studied or hereafter shall use or study as well for the recreation of our loving subjects as for our solace and pleasure when we shall think good to see them during our pleasure.

↬ A Plague Bill   *1609*

Reproduced below is a plague bill, a civic document specifying the number of deaths in London. It records that 364 people died in the environs of London, 177 of the plague, between August (Augusto) 24 and 31. The last printed line indicates that seventy-three parishes are clear of the plague, while forty-eight are infected.

→ JOHN WARD, VICAR OF STRATFORD

From His *Diary* 1662–63

These remembrances are taken from the diary of John Ward, vicar of Stratford (1662–81). Although Ward was born after Shakespeare's death, his diary offers reported details about Shakespeare's life and death, as well as references to his descendants.

Shakespeare had but two daughters, one whereof Mr. Hall, the physician, married, and by her had one daughter, to wit, the Lady Bernard of Abingdon. . . .

I have heard that Mr. Shakespeare was a natural wit, without any art at all; he frequented the plays all his younger time, but in his elder days lived at Stratford, and supplied the stage with two plays every year, and for that had an allowance so large, that he spent at the rate of £1,000 a year, as I have heard.

Remember to peruse Shakespeare's plays, and be versed in them, that I may not be ignorant in that matter. . . .

Shakespeare, Drayton, and Ben Jonson had a merry meeting, and it seems drank too hard, for Shakespeare died of a fever there contracted. . . .

→ ## Detail from the "Agas" Map of London ➤

With Shakespeare's Lodging Indicated

This detail from the "Agas" map of London (drawn in the late sixteenth century) shows the house where Shakespeare lived around the time he wrote *Othello* and *Measure for Measure*. According to testimony in a 1612 trial, Shakespeare apparently rented a room ("one Mr Shakespeare that lay in the house") from Christopher Mountjoy and his family. The house, indicated by a circle, stands near the northern wall of the city, on the northeastern corner of Silver ("Sylver") and Monkswell ("Muggle") Streets.

CHAPTER 2

"To What End Are All These Words?":
Shakespeare's Dramatic Language

><

One major assumption informs this chapter: that Shakespeare's language is a primary source of our pleasure in his plays, not an obstacle to appreciation, not something we must overcome in order to understand the stories. In other words, there is no such thing as in other words. Shakespeare in other words is not Shakespeare. There is no denying the appeal of the tales he dramatized, but as Chapter 5 will indicate, Shakespeare rarely invented them, preferring instead to appropriate stories that he read or biographies of historical figures or plots of plays he had seen and turn them into theatrical vehicles for his company. His characters have captured and held the imaginations of audiences over three centuries, but these persons are what they are because of what they say. The unparalleled success of Shakespeare's stories and characters depends on the communicative power of Shakespeare's language, and this chapter will suggest some ways of making his language more available to the twentieth-century reader. Once we become alert to the potential power of Shakespeare's words, especially to the sensuousness of their sounds and patterns, then we have access to pleasures and meanings that take us to the heart of his dramatic enterprise.

This chapter, then, constitutes an effort to alleviate a modern reader's difficulties with the language of a Renaissance playwright, but such an attempt at clarification cannot account for the distinctive brilliance of Shakespeare's poetry and prose. An introduction to such problems as pronoun usage, fluid syntax, wordplay, and verse forms in the sixteenth and seventeenth centuries leaves a number of essential topics unexplored. The most important of these is probably figurative language. Modern readers are immediately struck by the density and richness of Shakespeare's dramatic verse, and a primary source of that impression is the abundance and power of the images and metaphors in which characters express their thoughts. The properties we value in expository prose — simplicity, brevity, "naturalness" — are irrelevant to Shakespeare. We read and listen to his verse precisely because of its artificiality, its poetic appeals to the ear and to the mind's eye. Figurative language delights the senses and the intelligence by expressing one idea in terms of another, and in the hands of the greatest poets, the imagery employed for such expression is richly connotative, creating a network of pictures and ideas that resonates with other images, ideas, and themes throughout the poem or play.

Near the beginning of *Macbeth,* just before the murder of King Duncan, Banquo remarks to his son on the late hour, the dark night, and the fatigue that overwhelms him.

> There's husbandry in heaven,
> Their candles are all out. Take thee that too. [*Gives him his belt and dagger.*]
> A heavy summons lies like lead upon me,
> And yet I would not sleep.   (2.1.4–7)

The sky (heaven) is described as an economical household in which all sources of light (the stars and moon) have been extinguished. Some powerful force (like lead) calls the speaker to sleep (a heavy summons), and yet he resists. The ideas could have been expressed much more plainly, but the power of the lines rests in their resonance. The nouns — "husbandry," "candles," "summons," "lead" — are evocative in themselves, but in the context of the action they become even more charged with meaning. "Husbandry" connotes household management or government, which Macbeth is about to disrupt, and we have just heard Lady Macbeth ridicule her "husband" for cowardice or unmanliness. In handing the dagger to his son, Banquo foreshadows the hallucinated dagger that Macbeth imagines in his soliloquy a few lines later, as well as the actual dagger that he carries away from the murder. At the end of this scene, a ringing bell "invites" or summons Macbeth to perform the murder; in act 3 Banquo faces the even heavier summons of death, brought by the murderers Macbeth has engaged. The heaviness of lead evokes a burden of foreboding that marks all these early scenes. In her subsequent madness, Lady Macbeth, fearing the dark, carries a candle, and darkness in the moral sense — evil — is a principal subject of the play.

This brief sketch barely suggests the imaginative associations of a typical passage of figurative language. It represents what this chapter will not do, and it is included to indicate the kind of analysis that readers must learn to do for themselves. An increased sensitivity to poetic resonance should be the goal of anyone approaching Shakespeare's plays, but no matter how adept we become, still greater sensitivity is always possible. Subsequent readings always generate new imaginative connections. Shakespeare's verbal power is an inexhaustible subject; finally it is a mystery. The magic of his language, its irresistible attraction, is a result of an artistic imagination speaking to the imagination of the audience, and figurative language is the medium for that communication. As we learn from *A Midsummer Night's Dream*, images, imagination, and magic are all of a piece.

Early Modern English

The modern reader unacquainted with sixteenth- and seventeenth-century English will encounter certain technical difficulties with Shakespeare's language, quite apart from the writer's distinctive poetic and rhetorical effects. One such obstacle is provided by verbs with inflected endings, such as "hath" for the modern "has," "doth" for "does," "goeth" for "goes," and similar early modern forms that can immediately brand the text as old-fashioned and alien. It may be some comfort to discover that a few of these forms were beginning to sound old-fashioned at the time that Shakespeare was employing them, and they were gradually being displaced by more modern usage. We should keep in mind, moreover, that he frequently mixes the older endings with the modern "has," "does," and "goes," relying at times on the archaic style to achieve formality or intensity or a particular rhythmic goal but avoiding any consistent pattern.

The most familiar point of confusion among the older forms is what might be called the pronoun problem, or the frequent appearance of "thou," "thee," "thy," "thine," and "ye," words that serve for many to typify the strangeness of early modern speech. Here patterns of usage can be discerned, because certain of these pronouns, more so than the verbs, carry traces of meaning that Shakespeare frequently exploits. We cannot hope to recover the Renaissance listener's ear for such differences, a trained sensitivity that had become second nature, but awareness of the broad categories of usage can help us recognize the potential significance of a shift from one form to another. Sometimes, of course, these changes are not meaningful. For certain speakers or groups of speakers, pronoun usage was a matter of personal taste.

Where we employ "you" for all references to the second person, the Renaissance speaker had a choice between "you" and "thou." (It simplifies matters to know that "ye" and "thee" are merely the objective cases of "you" and "thou" — the equivalent of "me" in relation to the nominative "I" — and thus the same rules apply as for "you" and "thou.") "You" is the standard second-person pronoun in English, but other languages retain a distinction between different uses of "you," such as *tu* and *vous* in French, or *tu* and *usted* in Spanish, and familiarity with the different functions of these words can help with Renaissance usage. To speak very broadly, "you" was normally used in the plural; in certain circumstances it was used in the singular, for example, in speaking to a social superior or a parent, thus connoting respect or formality. "Thou," on the other hand, implied familiarity and was used for speaking to social inferiors, children, or loved ones.

Although Shakespeare does not usually employ these pronouns in any consistent pattern, he sometimes exploits their connotations for dramatic effect.

For example, a deliberate shift from "you" to "thou" functions as a signal. In the first meeting between Petruchio and Katherina in *The Taming of the Shrew,* Petruchio passes back and forth between "you" and "thou" as he shifts between the polite and the personal. Katherina, however, resisting his overtures throughout the contest, attempts to keep him at a distance by consistently addressing him as "you" (2.1). The only exception occurs at the end of the scene when Katherina, on hearing Petruchio announce to her father that "upon Sunday is [their] wedding-day," responds with "I'll see thee hang'd on Sunday first." As this exchange suggests, the superiority implied by the speaker who employs "thou" makes it especially useful for insults. Old Queen Margaret in *Richard III* repeatedly uses the more familiar "thou" to lash out at her enemies, as in her curse on Richard: "Thou elvish-mark'd, abortive, rooting hog! / . . . / Thou slander of thy heavy mother's womb! / Thou loathed issue of thy father's loins!" (1.3.227–31).

Familiarity need not connote disrespect, however; it can also imply intimacy, as when lovers address each other as "thou." When Romeo and Juliet first meet at the Capulet party, for example, she properly addresses the attractive stranger as "you," whereas the more impetuous Romeo quickly shifts into the more familiar form: "Thus from my lips, by thine, my sin is purg'd [*Kissing her.*]" (1.5.107). Before their next meeting, as Juliet stands at her window meditating on her feelings, she has already adopted the more personal mode: "O Romeo, Romeo, wherefore art thou Romeo?" (2.2.33).

The other circumstance in which "thou" is always appropriate is the direct address to God or to divine powers generally, as when Henry V utters a prayer of thanks on learning of the small number of English dead at the battle of Agincourt: ". . . O God, thy arm was here; / And not to us, but to thy arm alone, / Ascribe we all!" (4.8.106–08). Or, similarly, Edmund's devotion to his own private deity in the second scene of *King Lear:* "Thou, Nature, art my goddess, to thy law / My services are bound" (1.2.1–2). As I have indicated, the numerous subtleties of such uses are no longer understood by most modern English speakers, but a feeling for the major distinctions will immeasurably enrich our responses to the social and personal dynamics of Shakespeare's characters and their dialogue.

All of these examples indicate that the English language available to Shakespeare was undergoing a period of transition from older, medieval forms to the patterns and diction more like those we use today. In fact, this was a period of rapid linguistic expansion, the result of numerous historical events and pressures. The most notable was the widespread use of the printing press — invented on the Continent in the first half of the fifteenth century and first used in England by William Caxton in 1474 — which made written language much more widely available in the sixteenth century than it had been in the fifteenth. Along with, and in great part due to, this mechanical aid came a corresponding increase in the number of readers, as education became more common among young men, particularly those residing in cities and towns. That literacy was increasing is indicated by the characters Shakespeare creates: those who cannot read, such as Capulet's servant in the second scene of *Romeo and Juliet,* are treated as comic butts. One stimulus to the increase in literacy was the desire to read the Bible, and the new possibility of doing so. For centuries the Scriptures had been available only in Latin, Greek, and Hebrew, but as the English language became more respectable and as the forces of the Reformation gained support, humanist scholars began to translate the Bible into the vernacular so that the common people could read the word of God for themselves. This practice became a topic of great controversy in the first half of the sixteenth century, although English Protestants were not the only advocates for a vernacular Bible, as is suggested by the excerpt from Erasmus, one of the great Catholic humanists (see p. 59). In short, more books and more people to read them help to account for the extraordinary number of changes in the English language in the years between 1500 and 1600. And in this dynamic period the language moved from a state that Chaucer would hardly have found strange to one that in many ways resembles our own.

Shakespeare's vocabulary can be a stumbling block, especially for readers. In the theater the speaking actor frequently relies on tone, semantic drive, narrative context, and body language to communicate the sense of utterly unfamiliar terms and phrases, but on the page such words become more noticeable and confusing. Among some scholars at the time, English was thought to be lacking in the expressive possibilities of a rich language such as Latin, and so writers at the end of the sixteenth century regularly invented, borrowed, or altered words to suit their narrative and expository needs. This practice of borrowing and inventing new words became so widespread that it provoked a reaction against "inkhorn terms," or fancy words just created. Many pedagogues, notably Thomas Wilson, urged writers to maintain a balance between the Latinate and the Anglo-Saxon, but some patriotic defenders of English wanted to purge the language of all foreign influence. (See the excerpt from Lever's *Art of Reason* on p. 66.) As knowledge increased in both the arts and sciences, so did the apparatus required to communicate that knowledge. The Saxon-Germanic foundations of English vocabulary were supplemented by an immense number of borrowings from Latin, some of them direct appropriations and others indirect derivations through French, a legacy of the Norman invasion led by William the Conqueror in 1066.

Shakespeare's own vocabulary seems to have been exceptionally large — about 29,000 words, nearly twice that of the average American college student — which attests to his acquaintance with a far wider range of specific topics and terms than the modern reader usually commands. Even more troublesome than those terms that we could know if our experience were broad enough are the many words that we probably could not, such as those that have dropped from common use, like "bisson" (blind), or those that the playwright seems to have created from Latin roots (or to have taken up shortly after their invention) but that did not catch on, such as "conspectuities" (eyesight or vision) or "unplausive" (doubtful or disapproving). Especially confusing are those words that have shifted meaning over the intervening centuries, such as "proper" (handsome), "nice" (squeamish or delicate), "silly" (innocent), or "cousin" (kinsman, that is, not necessarily the child of an aunt or uncle). In confronting these changes resulting from the vagaries of linguistic fashion, however, we should also remember that many Shakespearean words familiar to us would have been strange to Shakespeare's audience because they were the products of his invention or unique usage: "assassination," "bump" (in the sense of swelling or protuberance), and "dwindle."

Words and their meanings present fewer difficulties, however, than do the many sentences in which the words seem to be set down in an unfamiliar order. This is because the most significant difference between early modern English and our own is that over the past four centuries we have tended to standardize the positions into which the words are placed. Nowadays, as a rule the subject appears first, then the verb, and then the direct object or complement, with various modifiers and other subordinate elements distributed where they won't get in the way and won't disrupt what is felt to be the logical order. Even in the middle of the sixteenth century, grammarians attacked the convolutions of Latin syntax and called for "natural" phrasing in the composition of English prose (see p. 60). From Thomas Wilson and Francis Bacon in the sixteenth century to George Orwell and E. B. White in the twentieth, prominent advocates for simplicity and clarity have shaped our concept of normal English syntax. Bacon believed that to devote too much attention to style was to neglect the actual object of expression and instead "fall in love with a picture."

But Shakespeare, as an artist, was in the business of creating stage pictures out of poetry and therefore was influenced by considerations more numerous and varied than mere simplicity: iambic pentameter, particular rhythmic effects, a need for emphasis, principles of characterization (young women speak differently from old men, servants from kings), and larger aural questions of pace and variety. Fluidity is the rule in the Shakespearean sentence, and so we encounter an immense number of syntactic possibilities. Direct objects may open the sentence when we would normally expect a subject, as in Hamlet's complaint to his mother: ". . . Sense sure you have, / Else could you not have motion" (3.4.71–72). Prepositional phrases or modifying clauses sometimes intrude in positions that strike us as abnormal or may even violate what we have come to know as rules. At a crucial moment in *Hamlet,* for example, the Ghost speaks a sentence that may reflect Shakespeare's training in Latin but that sounds to our ears like a stunning dangling modifier:

> Sleeping within my orchard,
> My custom always of the afternoon,
> Upon my secure hour thy uncle stole,
> With juice of cursed hebona in a vial,
> And in the porches of my ears did pour
> The leprous distillment.   (1.5.59–64)

In this crucial sentence three introductory phrases delay the arrival of the subject, which (grammatically) should be "I" but is in fact "thy uncle." This error embodies the initial problem of the play: Claudius replaces Old Hamlet. Moreover, in a small but effective way the suspensions that begin the sentence heighten suspense about the identity of the criminal and the means of death.

Virtually every scene is enriched by such manipulations of syntax, and as Shakespeare becomes more mature and playful, the variety of his syntactic arrangements increases remarkably. In the early plays, lines tend to be end-stopped, that is, the length of phrases and clauses is governed by, or at least corresponds to, the length of the poetic line.

> Now out of doubt Antipholus is mad,
> Else would he never so demean himself.
> A ring he hath of mine worth forty ducats,
> And for the same he promis'd me a chain:
> Both one and other he denies me now.   (*The Comedy of Errors* 4.3.81–85)

By the end of Shakespeare's career, enjambment is the rule: the tyranny of the poetic line has been vanquished by the claims of the sentence.

> Give me my robe, put on my crown, I have
> Immortal longings in me. Now no more
> The juice of Egypt's grape shall moist this lip.
> Yare, yare, good Iras; quick. Methinks I hear
> Antony call; I see him rouse himself
> To praise my noble act.   (*Antony and Cleopatra* 5.2.280–85)

But we have now moved beyond the conditions of Renaissance discursive models into the realm of style or, as Shakespeare's contemporaries would have known it, rhetoric.

Rhetoric

Apart from such technical problems, Shakespeare's language is puzzling to the modern reader because, generally speaking, the twentieth century takes a very different attitude toward verbal expression than did the sixteenth. Modes of dramatic or poetic speech that appealed to the Renaissance taste for abundance and decoration may strike us as inflated, elaborate, or excessively ornamented. Characters in modern plays seem to speak more "naturally" than their Shakespearean counterparts, but modern forms of theatrical language are no more real than those spoken by the characters in *Hamlet*. Both styles of speech are arranged and artificial; the differences arise from their authors' dependence on different conventions. The practices of sixteenth-century dramatic language were developed and refined by playwrights who were committed to the value of eloquence and thoroughly grounded in the study of rhetoric.

In the 1570s Shakespeare probably attended the King's New School, the local grammar school in Stratford-upon-Avon, where the system of primary education was devoted to the study of Latin. English literature as a separate discipline for study and appreciation did not become a feature of British education until the end of the nineteenth century. In fact, well into the second half of the sixteenth century, many poets and scholars considered the English language an unworthy medium for the production of literature and hardly an appropriate subject for study. Chaucer was acknowledged as the brilliant exception, but Latin was still the preferred language for artistic or philosophical expression. The monarch and court were often entertained with dramatic performances in Latin; as indicated earlier, many churchmen and scholars objected to the translation of the Bible into the vernacular; the principal models for poetry or drama or even philosophical or historical writing — for any kind of serious discourse, that is — were Roman or Greek, or occasionally their Italian or French derivatives.

Shakespeare and his schoolmates were immersed in Latin grammar and literature, as the grammar school curriculum described in Chapter 5 will attest. Each student would have been required to translate, memorize, recite, and — most relevant for our understanding of Shakespeare's creativity — imitate the works he read. In learning to compose verses and speeches, that is, in the equivalent of present-day composition courses, the young scholars would have written in Latin. The method of double translation designed to increase their proficiency is described in the numerous handbooks for teachers published in the Renaissance by such scholar-teachers as Roger Ascham and John Brinsley. These pedagogues instruct the master to begin by reading aloud from a poetic passage that the students have never heard before, preferably some verses of Ovid. The pupil translates the passage read aloud from Latin into English, and then reverses the process, rendering the English version back into Latin as near to the original as possible (see Ascham's instructions, p. 64).

By means of such drills, students not only became familiar with the conventional patterns into which words were arranged but also became sensitive to the effects of those arrangements. The Romans themselves had begun the process of analyzing and organizing the stylistic methods of their great writers. In elaborate treatises devoted to the principles of composition, writers such as Cicero and Quintilian identified, explained, and illustrated numerous verbal patterns such as metaphor, apostrophe, paradox, and a multitude of others. Known as figures of speech, schemes, or tropes (verbal "turns"), these forms of expression were associated specifically with particular narrative situations, emotional states, or literary effects. These classical theorists and cataloguers inspired their Renaissance counterparts to produce rhetorical handbooks for those who wished to write in English. George Puttenham's *The Art of English Poesy* (see p. 68) and John Hoskyns's *Directions for Speech and Style,* among many other such guides, converted classical examples into their English equivalents and supplied an abundance of native examples. The educational system that inculcated these forms of rhetoric was not limited to slavish translation, however. As students advanced, they were eventually given poetic or dramatic situations taken from the classical authors and asked to amplify the episode or invent language appropriate to the scene. And in some cases, notably those of Shakespeare and other brilliant Elizabethans such as Sir Philip Sidney, Edmund Spenser, John Donne, and Ben Jonson, imitation led to creation, reproduction to original artistic production.

The systematized forms of rhetoric inculcated in the classroom and outlined in these handbooks were so familiar to the educated Elizabethan that it was easy for a playwright to get a laugh by simply referring to them. Grumio in *The Taming of the Shrew* predicts that Petruchio will dazzle Katherina with his verbal skills, or "rope-tricks," Grumio's own blunder for rhetorics, or "rhet-tricks": "She may perhaps call him half a score knaves or so. Why, that's nothing; and he begin once, he'll rail in his rope-tricks. I'll tell you what, sir, and she stand him but a little, he will throw a figure in her face, and so disfigure her with it, that she shall have no more eyes to see withal than a cat" (1.2.110–15). The apparently uneducated Grumio may not know "rope-tricks" from "rhet-tricks" or rhetorics, but even he employs a classically sanctioned figure of speech in playing on the words "figure" and "disfigure." Polonius, the old counselor in *Hamlet,* is exceedingly vain about his rhetorical skills, which leads the Queen to complain "More matter with less art." *Love's Labor's Lost,* one of Shakespeare's earliest comedies, vigorously mocks the pedantic rigidity associated with Tudor systems of rhetoric. Many of its jokes escape most of us because the educational system that fostered them no longer exists. (Readers five hundred years from now will probably be similarly puzzled by references in our literature to "grinds," "the thesis paragraph," "physics for poets," and other staples of the American high-school or college experience.) It is vital that we try to appreciate the delight in ornament and pleasure in pattern that characterize Renaissance literature. As C. S. Lewis puts it,

> Rhetoric is the greatest barrier between us and our ancestors. . . . Nearly all our older poetry was written and read by men to whom the distinction between poetry and rhetoric, in its modern form, would have been meaningless. The "beauties" which they chiefly regarded in every composition were those which we either dislike or simply do not notice. This change of taste makes an invisible wall between us and them.   (61)

In order to break down this wall, we will do well to think of rhetoric as a species of verbal play. As such, it was an indispensable tool for a Renaissance playwright whose first aim was to amuse his audience.

Wordplay

We cannot hope to recover the automatic acquaintance with most forms of rhetoric that a sixteenth-century playgoer of average education would have had; the names and functions of the many tropes and figures have become the province of specialists. But we must be aware of how meaningful such patterns were to the age that produced Shakespeare, and more important, we must use our knowledge of the existence of those systems to understand the Renaissance delight in language, its taste for copiousness or elaboration, and its pleasure in verbal games. The touchstone for such matters is Shakespeare's — and his culture's — fondness for wordplay.

In act 2, scene 3, of *Much Ado about Nothing,* Beatrice enters seeking Benedick, who has just been tricked into believing that she is in love with him.

When she delivers her message, "Against my will I am sent to bid you come in to dinner," and leaves the stage after a moment of additional backchat, Benedick turns to the audience to offer a reading of the invitation: "'Against my will I am sent to bid you come in to dinner' — there's a double meaning in that." In this case Benedick is mistaken: Beatrice means what she says and no more. But in a larger sense he is right, if we consider that Beatrice has yet to acknowledge her attraction to Benedick and that she has been sent to provoke Benedick by the very pranksters who fooled him. Benedick's triumphant discovery of a double meaning is especially ironic because in almost any other case he would have been correct. Double meanings, the kind found most obviously in puns and other forms of wordplay, pervade Shakespeare's work; and one source of their abundance is that Shakespeare is an eloquent spokesman for his age's perception of the ambivalence of all human experience.

Samuel Johnson reflected an eighteenth-century bias toward the rational and the solemn when he criticized Shakespeare's fondness for the pun, complaining that "a quibble [a pun], poor and barren as it is, gave him such delight, that he was content to purchase it, by the sacrifice of reason, propriety and truth. A quibble was to him the fatal Cleopatra for which he lost the world, and was content to lose it" (qtd. in *The Works of Samuel Johnson* 7:74). But for most writers of the Renaissance, especially Shakespeare, wordplay carried no such moral charge. Preachers as well as playwrights eagerly embraced its temptations, taking advantage of double meanings in order to amuse their audiences and cultivate an awareness of the delights and the dangers of human speech. The prominence of the pun demonstrates that words, like the human actions they describe, are subject to multiple interpretations.

The most obvious form of wordplay is the homonym, in which a single sound calls forth more than one meaning. Pistol, the cowardly soldier in *Henry V*, resolves to quit the French campaign and return home to a life of crime: "To England will I steal, and there I'll steal" (5.1.87). A similar case is Hamlet's retort to Claudius's complaint that his "son" appears sullen, that "the clouds still hang on" him. The Prince replies, "Not so my lord, I am too much in the sun" (1.2.67). Hamlet is suffering under the light of public scrutiny, unnaturally made to be the son of two fathers, and oppressed by his role as the son of a murdered father. But human speech abounds with many looser forms of the pun, to which the classical rhetoricians gave a variety of names: *paronomasia, agnominatio, antanaclasis, syllepsis*. The anonymous Roman author of the *Rhetorica ad Herennium* defines *paronomasia* as "a figure in which, by means of a modification of sound or change of letters, a close resemblance to a given verb or noun is produced, so that similar words express dissimilar things." A Shakespearean instance of this variation is Falstaff's line to Prince Hal, "were it not here apparent that thou art heir apparent." Modern terms for the pun are more familiar but no less various: a quibble, a *double entendre,* an equivocation, a play on words. A useful way to describe its operation is as an exercise in substitution, a figure in which one meaning displaces another. Alternatively, it may be seen as a competition for dominance among two or more legitimate meanings. In all these cases, the principle in which wordplay is grounded is that the pun exposes differences among similar phenomena, or, conversely, reveals likeness in difference.

Shakespeare's plays exhibit many different kinds of puns — characters employ them consciously and unconsciously, for example — and they serve multiple functions. Wordplay often provides humor when a secondary meaning is released unexpectedly. It may reveal character, as in *Richard III*, when Richard of Gloucester employs double meanings to promote his double-dealings in quest of the English crown. Richard is a witty punster, but his quibbles are often sinister rather than comic. In fact, the automatic association of laughter with the pun is a modern phenomenon, one of the barriers that C. S. Lewis notes between the sensibilities of the sixteenth century and those of the twentieth. For Shakespeare and his contemporaries, wordplay could be a tool for seriously exploring the discrepancy between surface and substance.

The noncomic pun (as well as the humorous one) performs at least two important general functions. First, it supplies the audience with a kind of intellectual pleasure, allowing it to move nimbly back and forth among various meanings of a single term. Baldassare Castiglione comments on the way that such puns "inspire wonder" or admiration rather than humor, as the listener admires the speaker's "ingenuity" and appreciates the "richness" of the speaker's verbal ability (see the excerpt from *The Book of the Courtier* on p. 73). Many of Shakespeare's speakers evoke just this kind of intellectual admiration. In *Romeo and Juliet*, for example, a tragedy loaded with double meanings, comic and serious, a particularly complicated series of puns breaks forth when the Nurse enters with bad news (Tybalt's death) and Juliet fears for Romeo:

Hath Romeo slain himself? Say thou but *ay,*
And that bare vowel *I* shall poison more
Than the death-darting *eye* of cockatrice [mythical monster].
I am not *I,* if there be such an *ay,*
Or those *eyes* shut, that makes thee answer *ay.*
If he be slain, say *ay,* or if not, no.
Brief sounds determine my weal or woe.   (3.2.45–51)

The wordplay here serves numerous functions, some already mentioned: it suggests passionate confusion, of course, and thus reveals character. The passage is also "one of Shakespeare's first attempts to reveal a profound disturbance of mind by the use of quibbles" (Mahood 70). But more than this it exercises the listener's intelligence, creating new senses out of a single syllable and leading the listener repeatedly to adjust and reinterpret the aural world. This pleasure is analogous to the larger intellectual and emotional exercise that the play as a whole promotes, as it pushes the audience back and forth between the interpretive poles of hope and judgment, sympathy and despair.

The other primary function of the pun is to open a window onto the main ideas of a play, capturing in individual words the conflicts and complex meanings of its characters' experience. In *Henry IV, Part 1,* for example, Falstaff's incessant punning establishes a contest among more and less legitimate meanings of the same sound, just as the play itself dramatizes a contest for the crown, a struggle that arises from Bullingbrook's doubtful legitimacy. At the battle of Shrewsbury that ends the play, the disguised kings sent onto the battlefield to confuse the enemy function as visual puns: they look alike, indeed they all look like King Henry, but they don't mean the same thing. So it is with double meanings in those comedies based on the confusion of twins, *The Comedy of Errors* and *Twelfth Night.* In Viola and Sebastian, an identical outward appearance conceals two very different persons, just as a homonym permits two distinct meanings. By exploiting such confusing resemblances, Shakespeare stimulates his audience's sense of the richness of the world and reveals the perils of drawing premature and certain conclusions about almost anything.

The impact of the serious pun is especially apparent in *Macbeth.* It is not merely that the text is rife with wordplay, although it is: gild/guilt, surcease/success, success (as in *victory/that which follows*), peerless (as in *unparalleled/alone*), consequence (as in *what follows/importance*), done (as in *performed/finished*), and done/Duncan (done-kin)/Dunsinane/Donalbain/ "dunnest smoke of hell." Equally significant is that the action of the play depends on the trickiness of words. Having placed his faith in the witches' prophecies, Macbeth finds that he has erroneously believed "th' equivocation of the fiend / That lies like truth" (5.5.42–43). He is vanquished, finally, by a pun. "None of woman born / Shall harm Macbeth," say the witches, and so he thinks himself immune. But Macduff, his conqueror, was "untimely ripped" from his mother's womb, delivered in Caesarean fashion. Ambiguity can be deadly: "Double, double, toil and trouble."

The Forms of Dramatic Language

If the intervening centuries have altered our attitude toward wordplay, they have also changed the conventions of dramatic speech: characters in modern plays rarely speak in verse. Thus a brief survey of Shakespearean forms of speech will yield a common set of terms so that we may proceed to notice how the forms of language function. These patterns divide, to begin with, into two: prose and poetry. Further subdivisions may be made, particularly in Shakespeare's poetry, but the dominant form is unrhymed iambic pentameter, or blank verse. I shall give considerable attention to the kinds of Shake-spearean poetry, including blank verse, but for the sake of convenience I begin with prose.

The easiest definition of prose is that it is everything that isn't poetry — the newspaper, political orations, psychology textbooks, this chapter you are reading now. The problem with such a definition is that it requires you to know what poetry is so that prose can be distinguished from it. At this point the easiest maneuver is to examine the physical appearance of the lines as they are printed in the book: in so doing we can usually tell the difference between poetry and prose because prose goes all the way to the end of the page, whereas poetry doesn't. This distinction works a little better, although there are still gray areas where it can be hard to differentiate. English prose, our ordinary language, often arranges itself into rhythmic patterns, and sometimes these can become so regular that the sounds of the prose resemble the rhythms of poetry. Some public speakers, the occasional Southern senator or preachers in some African American churches, can develop their prose utterances into an elaborately patterned and highly musical performance. Although the concentration and intensity of poetic language give it an affective power not found in most prose, a good speaker can make prose utterances as potent as poetry. One of the most memorable passages in *Hamlet* is the Prince's eloquent "What a piece of work is a man" (2.2.303–08). Unlike the play's verse soliloquies, this speech depends not on the poetic alternation of syllables but instead draws its rhythmic power from patterns of verbal repetition. Some of Shakespeare's prose is extremely poetic, and some of his poetry is decidedly prosaic. Even experts disagree on whether to print certain passages as poetry or prose. But usually we can distinguish between the two, and as will become clear, it matters that we do so.

In *A Midsummer Night's Dream* a group of workers — "rude mechanicals," as they are called by one of the fairies — prepares a play to be performed at the wedding celebration of Duke Theseus and his bride, Hippolyta. These amateur actors, as they cast and begin to rehearse their play — which is itself written in an old-fashioned, singsong style of poetry — speak in prose, as when Bottom the weaver proposes a solution to the problem of frightening the ladies in the audience with a lion on stage: "Nay; you must name his name, and half his face must be seen through the lion's neck, and he himself must speak through, saying thus, or to the same defect: 'Ladies,' or 'Fair ladies, I would wish you,' or 'I would request you,' or 'I would entreat you, not to fear, not to tremble'" (3.1.36–41).

It used to be said, with some regularity, that Shakespeare used prose mainly to establish social class. This is undeniably one of its functions in the opening scene of *Julius Caesar,* where the laborers have taken to the streets of Rome on a holiday, and in the mechanicals' scenes of *A Midsummer Night's Dream.* Bottom and company speak in prose, the least formal and least "elevated" kind of dramatic speech available, not only because they are the lowest members of society depicted in the play, but also because they function as "clowns." In other words, the identification of prose with the lower social and economic classes inadequately represents the variety of Shakespeare's practice. Among the aristocracy prose may also indicate informality, as when Theseus and the young lovers comment to one another, in prose, on the progress of the mechanicals' performance. High-born characters often speak in prose: over half of *As You Like It* is written in prose, and Rosalind, the banished Duke's daughter, is one of its most gifted speakers. Prose is especially arresting when it marks a departure from the usual form of blank verse. In the first encounter between Olivia and the disguised Viola in *Twelfth Night* (1.5), for example, Shakespeare signifies Olivia's growing infatuation with Viola/Cesario by causing her to shift from the casual prose she has been using to the verse that the attractive young page speaks. Thus one of the most important characteristics of prose is that it is not poetry.

In the tragedies particularly, prose can measure a collapse of some kind, as when a character who has spoken grand and controlled verse is reduced to disordered prose. In the fourth act of *Othello*, the hero exhibits just such a change of register when he falls under the spell of Iago's insinuations about his wife's faithlessness.

OTHELLO: What hath he said?
IAGO: Faith, that he did — I know not what he did.
OTHELLO: What? what?
IAGO: Lie —
OTHELLO: With her?
IAGO: With her? On her; what you will.
OTHELLO: Lie with her? lie on her? We say lie on her, when they belie her. Lie with her! 'Zounds, that's fulsome! Handkerchief — confessions — handkerchief! To confess, and be hang'd for his labor — first to be hang'd, and then to confess. I tremble at it.   (4.1.31–39)

Even such a short passage as this one displays not only the sudden shift from verse to prose — the three utterances preceding Othello's long speech make up one complete line of iambic pentameter — but also the disintegration of logical structure within a prose passage, as Othello moves toward incomprehensibility. Such a strategic deployment of prose attests to Shakespeare's acute ear for dramatic variety. Early in his career he recognizes and takes advantage of the tonal effects produced by an alternation between two forms of speech. Even though an audience may not immediately or consciously register the distinction between a speech in prose and a speech in poetry, it is subconsciously affected by their relative degrees of structure, and such aural differences help to establish and maintain a mood or tone that supports the dramatist's larger purpose.

Early in his career Shakespeare rarely wrote in prose. *Richard III*, for example, an early play of some thirty-five hundred lines, contains only about fifty lines of prose, or less than 2 percent. *Hamlet*, on the other hand, a play of slightly greater length and of similar gravity, but written in the middle of his career, contains about nine hundred lines of prose, or almost 30 percent. (See the chart on p. 77.) This difference indicates that as he developed artistically and increased his command of his dramatic tools, Shakespeare became considerably more flexible. About five years after *Richard III*, in *Henry IV, Part 1*, Shakespeare exploited with great subtlety the different effects obtainable from poetry and prose. Prose is the language of the everyday, the standard form of speech in the tavern at Eastcheap. The most gifted speaker of prose in this play is Sir John Falstaff, whose influence over the young prince — a dubious influence in the opinion of the court — is signaled most obviously in the way Prince Hal mimics the old rascal's linguistic forms. Throughout the first half of the play, except for the one verse soliloquy declaring his intention to surrender the pleasures of Eastcheap, spoken at the end of act 1, scene 2 ("I know you all"), the Prince speaks only prose in the tavern or in the company of Falstaff and his drinking companions; at the end of act 3, however, in Eastcheap and in the presence of the ne'er-do-wells he has hitherto addressed only in prose, the Prince shifts into verse. (It is worth noting that at this point Falstaff also adopts verse, parodying the Prince's new style.) Hal's commitment to the more formal voice audibly establishes his assumption of royal responsibility; when he "throw[s] off" the "loose behavior" of the first three acts, he also throws off the loose and informal patterns of prose. And members of an oral culture like Shakespeare's would probably have been more sensitive than we are to such a change.

The patterns of poetry on which Shakespeare depends vary from the rigorously structured to the flexibly organized, but the single feature that they all have in common, the quality that distinguishes poetry from prose, is music. One source of this poetic music is rhyme — and I speak here primarily of end rhyme, the repetition of sounds, a combination of vowels and consonants, at the end of two verse lines. Shakespeare does not employ an abundance of rhymed verse, although he does so from time to time, especially at the beginning of his career. As he matures poetically, he relies on rhyme to create certain specific effects: perhaps to heighten the emotional effect of a passage, occasionally to poke fun at the speaker, and most often to close off a scene, to indicate with a rhymed couplet that the episode is over. Helena, Lysander, and Hermia speak rhymed verse in the first act of *A Midsummer Night's Dream;* the following is an excerpt from Helena's first soliloquy:

> How happy some o'er other some can be!
> Through Athens I am thought as fair as she.
> But what of that? Demetrius thinks not so;
> He will not know what all but he do know;
> And as he errs, doting on Hermia's eyes,
> So I, admiring of his qualities.
> Things base and vile, holding no quantity,
> Love can transpose to form and dignity.   (1.1.226–33)

Rhyme enhances the music already created by the rhythm of the passage, but its singsong effect also introduces a delicately critical comment on the baffled Helena's perception of her misery. This excerpt exposes a feature of Renaissance language often puzzling to modern ears, that pronunciation was apparently as unfixed as syntax: here "eyes" rhymes with "qualities," although we cannot be sure whether "eyes" is pronounced *ees,* whether "qualities" concludes with a long *i* sound, or whether the sound might have been something in between. The resort to rhyme often pays ironic benefits, even in the tragedies: the tidy closure of Hamlet's second soliloquy, ". . . the play's the thing, / Wherein I'll catch the conscience of the King," seems so self-assured and definitive as to undercut and cast doubt on the prince's sudden confidence.

In the soliloquy just quoted, Helena speaks rhymed iambic pentameter, but other kinds of rhymed poetry often arrest the ear. Consider Oberon's chant as he applies a magic lotion to Titania's eyes:

What thou seest when thou dost wake,
Do it for thy true-love take;
Love and languish for his sake.
Be it ounce [lynx], or cat, or bear,
Pard [leopard], or boar with bristled hair,
In thy eye that shall appear
When thou wak'st, it is thy dear:
Wake when some vile thing is near.   (2.2.27–34)

This is tetrameter, lines with four beats, and the effect of combining such short lines and end rhymes sounds simple but is in fact complex. The combination creates something like an incantation (Oberon is, after all, casting a spell on Titania) and thus implies a magical mood; but violating as it does the five-beat pattern established in Oberon's normal pentameters, these short verse lines can be heard as jaunty or even humorous music for what is arguably one of the cruelest actions in the play.

The use of rhymed poetry decreases as Shakespeare matures artistically. *A Midsummer Night's Dream* is exceptional in that 45 percent of its lines are written in rhymed verse, a higher percentage than for any other play in the canon. We may attribute this to at least two probable causes: first, to the unreal, artificial, dreamlike quality for which Shakespeare is striving, and second, to the fact that one of the main subjects of *A Midsummer Night's Dream* is poetry itself — verse as a product of the imagination. Therefore, Shakespeare fits his method to his meaning.

The primary means by which Shakespeare creates musical effects is not rhyme but rhythm, the ordered repetition of syllables in verse lines. And by far the most significant poetic structure he employs is poetry that does not rhyme, more specifically, unrhymed iambic pentameter, or blank verse. The blank verse line is decasyllabic, composed of ten syllables; put another way, there are five iambic units per line. An iamb is simply a unit of sound with two beats, the first unstressed and the second stressed: da-DA. Multiply that by five and you have a line of iambic pentameter, or *penta*-meter. But what is the value of devoting time to identifying kinds of verse and differentiating iambic pentameter from trochaic trimeter? Actors do not deliver the lines in this exaggerated fashion; if they did, the result would be ludicrous and the audience would be heading for the exits. So how does it help to know about this kind of verse? And when we do know about it, what have we got? In the first place, the naming of parts is an instructive exercise. To know the components of a machine is to come closer to an understanding of how it works. Next, not to be too mystical about it, the rhythms of the verse affect us even though we may not be conscious of their effect. The five units of iambic pentameter give the line a basic structure, much like the time signature of a piece of music. We may not know that *Stars and Stripes Forever* is in four/four time, but if it were not played that way we would certainly hear the difference.

According to Sir Philip Sidney in *The Defense of Poesy* — and linguists have confirmed the perception — blank verse is particularly well suited to the natural rhythms of English speech, and so it serves as a useful medium for

Shakespeare's drama. It was relatively new when Shakespeare took it up. Although the rhymed ten-syllable line had been the primary English poetic form since Chaucer's time, the earl of Surrey created blank verse when he gave up rhyme for his translations from Virgil's *Aeneid* (c. 1540), and indeed Shakespeare's appropriation of it accounts in large part for the dominance of blank verse during the last three hundred and fifty years of English poetry. Most of Shakespeare's most memorable poetic creations — "To be or not to be," "Tomorrow and tomorrow and tomorrow," "The quality of mercy is not strained," "Now is the winter of our discontent" — draw their power from the poet's skillful manipulation of the pentameter line.

Here is Titania, speaking in blank verse, when she refuses to surrender the Indian boy to Oberon:

> The fairy land buys not the child of me.
> His mother was a vot'ress of my order,
> And in the spiced Indian air, by night,
> Full often hath she gossip'd by my side,
> And sat with me on Neptune's yellow sands,
> Marking th'embarked traders on the flood;
> When we have laugh'd to see the sails conceive
> And grow big-bellied with the wanton wind;
> Which she, with pretty and with swimming gait,
> Following (her womb then rich with my young squire)
> Would imitate, and sail upon the land
> To fetch me trifles, and return again,
> As from a voyage, rich with merchandise.
> But she, being mortal, of that boy did die,
> And for her sake do I rear up her boy;
> And for her sake I will not part with him.   (2.1.122–37)

Although the listener does not hear "The FAIR-y LAND buys NOT the CHILD of ME," the five-beat structure works on the ear nonetheless. The smooth musicality of the meter, the regular repetition of unstressed and stressed sounds, combines with other forms of repetition (words, phrases, consonants, and vowels) to create a mood of intense emotion, even awe. The lyrical regularity of the iambic pattern entrances the listener into sympathy with the speaker, and as the speech draws to its close, Shakespeare intensifies that sense of enchantment by an even subtler manipulation of the rhythm. The multisyllabic words that have been integrated into the poetic line ("imitate," "merchandise") are abandoned in the last two lines in favor of monosyllables that reinforce the incantatory tone. Everywhere in the canon such subtle variations help to shape the mood and meaning of a speaker's words.

Such bending or breaking of the iambic pattern is a crucial Shakespearean poetic strategy. Depending on the requirements of the speech or character or situation, iambic pentameter may be fiercely regular or it may be scarcely regular at all. And irregularity can make a huge dramatic difference. Consider this single line from *Julius Caesar,* one of the most famous lines in all of Shakespeare: "Friends, Romans, countrymen, lend me your ears!" If the line were entirely regular, we would hear it as

Friĕnds, Rómăns, cóuntrўmén, lĕnd mĕ yŏur eárs!

But it is irregular. Antony begins with a stressed syllable, overturning the established iambic pattern just at the moment that he takes control of the political events in the play. But he does not merely reverse the stress of the normal iamb. Instead, he follows that initial stress ("Friends") with another stress ("Ro-") that then restores the regular pattern of unstressed-stressed (da-DA). The reestablished pattern is quickly broken again by the force of the imperative "lend," part of an inversion ("lend me") inserted into the middle of the line. In scanning it, therefore, we hear it as follows:

Friĕnds, Rómăns, cóuntrўmén, leńd mĕ yŏur eárs!

Other patterns are audible as well. For example, the line accelerates: it begins with a monosyllable and then stops, continues with a word of two syllables and then stops, proceeds with a noun of three syllables (all of these nouns being similar to one another in meaning) and then stops, and finally provides the listener with the momentary release of "lend me your ears," a phrase of four words to complete the pattern of increasing syllables. The iambic pattern is retained, but only barely, and with competing patterns grafted onto it. A struggle between the rhythmic form of the verse and the semantic claims of the sentence creates an aural tension within the line, and this is a struggle for authority not unlike the competition for power occurring at this moment between Brutus and Antony. Such variation of the blank verse pattern to make meaning is heard everywhere in Shakespeare — in Hamlet's self-lacerations ("O, what a rogue and peasant slave am I!"); in Richard III's furious confrontation with a realm he seeks to master ("And I — like one lost in a thorny wood, / That rents the thorns, and is rent with the thorns"); in Cleopatra's suicide speech ("Give me my robe, put on my crown"). The more alert we are to such aural effects, the better we understand Shakespeare's talent.

A Midsummer Night's Dream offers an excellent opportunity for judging the variety and sophistication of Shakespeare's dramatic poetry because the playwright has built into the dramatic structure a foiling device, an example of bad poetry. The play-within-the-play, the Pyramus and Thisbe episode, sets off and calls attention to the excellence and beauty of his own creation; this is one of the early and simple instances in which Shakespeare attempts such a contrast. Moreover, this bad poetry is funny. The play-within-the-play mocks the style of drama that Shakespeare must have seen in his youth and that was still popular with certain audiences even during the years when *Twelfth Night* and *Hamlet* were being written. Most especially it mocks the bald and primitive style of verse that some of Shakespeare's predecessors composed. This is Pyramus's discovery of Thisbe's bloody mantle:

But stay! O spite!
But mark, poor knight,

What dreadful dole is here!
 Eyes, do you see?
 How can it be?
O dainty duck! O dear!
 Thy mantle good,
 What! stain'd with blood?
Approach, ye Furies fell!
 O Fates, come, come,
 Cut thread and thrum,
Quail, crush, conclude, and quell! (5.1.276–87)

This doggerel is not too far removed from the following passage from Thomas Preston's *Cambyses,* written in the form known as *fourteeners* (referring to the number of syllables per line) about twenty-five years before *A Midsummer Night's Dream.* This is the king's death speech:

Who but I in such a wise his deaths wound could have got?
As I on horse back up did leap, my sword from scabbard shot,
And ran me thus into the side, as you right well may see —
A marvels chance unfortunate that in this wise should be!
I feel myself a dying now, of life bereft am I,
And Death hath caught me with his dart, for want of blood I spy.
Thus gasping heer on ground I lye; for nothing I doe care;
A just reward for my misdeeds my death doth plaine declare.

This comparison is pertinent because Shakespeare seems to have had *Cambyses* in mind as he composed his comedy. Preston's play is titled *A Lamentable Tragedy, Mixed Full of Pleasant Mirth, Containing the Life of Cambyses, King of Persia,* which may be a source of the description of the Pyramus and Thisbe play as "tragical mirth."

A still more instructive poetic comparison emerges when we juxtapose the verse Bottom speaks as the dying Pyramus with a passage that Oberon delivers to Puck in act 2:

     Thou rememb'rest
Since once I sat upon a promontory,
And heard a mermaid on a dolphin's back
Uttering such dulcet and harmonious breath
That the rude sea grew civil at her song,
And certain stars shot madly from their spheres,
To hear the sea-maid's music? (2.1.148–54)

Some of the most prominent features of Bottom's doggerel are present, especially internal rhyme and insistent alliteration, but their effect here is very different. Bottom's short lines make the rhyme come so rapidly that its effect is comic rather than magical or tragic; Oberon's unrhymed pentameters are spacious and majestic. The figurative language in Oberon's remembrance is specific and palpable; in Bottom's lament it is trite. Most listeners will immediately recognize that Oberon's verse is fresh and powerful, whereas Bottom's is ludicrous. Having sensed the differences, we should make it our business to learn how to articulate them.

Language as Theme

These several verbal forms and patterns serve as tools, affective instruments designed to move the audience, to give pleasure, to engage, to amuse, to excite. Having established what these tools are, we must forget them, temporarily at least, and begin to consider how they work. Shakespeare's early plays give us an unusually candid look at how he causes these instruments to function. Around 1592 or 1593, Shakespeare seems to have experienced an epiphany, discovering more or less suddenly the almost limitless power of language. Our knowledge of dates is sketchy here, but we can still make a reasonable guess about which plays came at this time, and in works such as *Love's Labor's Lost* and *Richard III* particularly, we observe a sudden explosion of rhetorical ability, a sense of exuberance, of power at what words can do. The astonishing language of these plays has something of *The Sorcerer's Apprentice* about it, as if a young magician had suddenly come upon the secret of his magical powers and had begun to see how far he could push them. Moreover, it is at this same time that Shakespeare begins to explore the implications of the word *play*. He begins to think seriously about the dramatic text as a representation of reality: as he explores the relationship between life and the stage, between the world and the word, the idea of the theater becomes a major theme in his work. Shakespeare the dramatist begins playfully to examine the implications of his play, and Shakespeare the poet asks the same questions of language. Probably the most fruitful text for studying this topic is *Richard III*.

Usurper, hunchback, infanticidal psychopath — Richard is also a master of language. We are both repelled and attracted by him, complementary responses that he provokes chiefly on the basis of what he says. In his case at least, words speak louder than actions. At no point in the text is he shown killing anyone; others carry out his mischief for him, and they do so because Richard tells them or asks them or promises them something to do it. Richard gets what he wants with words, and his gift for language is almost unparalleled, as the very first lines of the play attest. Shakespeare's introduction of his heroic villain is characteristically original. The playwright is faithful to the demands of Tudor politics: because Richard was ultimately defeated at Bosworth by the earl of Richmond, who became Henry VII and grandfather of Shakespeare's queen, Elizabeth I, the Tudor dynasty had an investment in demonizing Richard. Shakespeare does not attempt to mitigate or to disguise Richard's wickedness. But, predictably, he does the unpredictable: he makes his villain a wit, a jokester, an actor. And Richard is such a memorable villain because his words are unforgettable.

Here is Richard III's notorious opening soliloquy:

Now is the winter of our discontent
Made glorious summer by this son of York;
And all the clouds that low'r'd upon our house
In the deep bosom of the ocean buried.
Now are our brows bound with victorious wreaths,
Our bruised arms hung up for monuments,
Our stern alarums chang'd to merry meetings,
Our dreadful marches to delightful measures.
Grim-visag'd War hath smooth'd his wrinkled front,
And now, in stead of mounting barbed steeds
To fright the souls of fearful adversaries,
He capers nimbly in a lady's chamber
To the lascivious pleasing of a lute.
But I, that am not shap'd for sportive tricks,
Nor made to court an amorous looking-glass;
I, that am rudely stamp'd, and want love's majesty
To strut before a wanton ambling nymph;
I, that am curtail'd of this fair proportion,
Cheated of feature by dissembling nature,
Deform'd, unfinish'd, sent before my time
Into this breathing world, scarce half made up,
And that so lamely and unfashionable
That dogs bark at me as I halt by them —
Why, I, in this weak piping time of peace,
Have no delight to pass away the time,
Unless to see my shadow in the sun
And descant on mine own deformity.
And therefore, since I cannot prove a lover
To entertain these fair well-spoken days,
I am determined to prove a villain
And hate the idle pleasures of these days.   (1.1.1–31)

The rhetorical fireworks in this passage are calculated to win the audience over to Richard, to exhibit his self-conscious wit, his pleasure in patterns, and his taste for performance. The speech begins with sweeping contrasts: war becomes peace, clouds are swept away by sunshine, chaos is converted into order, Lancaster yields to York, winter becomes summer. Each of the first two pairs of lines expresses one of these antitheses, and then Shakespeare begins to compress, shifting back and forth between war and peace within the same line. But all these oppositions merely serve as prologue to the larger contrast that informs the speech (and indeed the play as a whole), the conflict between Richard and everyone else. The soliloquy is typical of Richard's language because it illustrates the audacity and pride with which he aims his eloquence at his adversaries. He shows off his verbal ingenuity to the audience in the first scene; in the second scene he tells Lady Anne that he has killed her husband and her father-in-law, and then he woos her in marriage anyway; when the young prince of York asks for Richard's dagger the villainous uncle replies "with all my heart"; and Richard informs Queen Elizabeth that he intends to marry her daughter (his niece) and make her his queen. Most of the principal conflicts in *Richard III* are dramatized in rhetorical terms. And, forced to take sides, we choose Richard, at least at first. He talks us into it.

One way he does so is with beguiling sounds and images. His first line contains a metaphor ("winter of our discontent"), his second a pun ("son of York"), his third a quadruple internal rhyme ("clouds . . . low'r'd . . . our house"), and so we might proceed throughout the speech, noting particularly Richard's enthusiasm for seductive sounds. We hear the insistent repetition of consonants, "Unless to see my shadow in the sun" (alliteration, with assonance); the repetition of vowels, "Now are our brows bound" (assonance, with alliteration); the repetition of a word at the beginning of successive lines (anaphora); rhythmically and semantically balanced phrases, "dreadful marches to delightful measures" (isocolon); and other showy aural effects. This passion for patterns, for elaborate rhetorical arrangements, is shared with Richard by other characters in the play, notably his three main female adversaries, Lady Anne, old Queen Margaret, and Queen Elizabeth, and makes itself felt in virtually every scene. The point, of course, is that the great enthusiast for rhetoric is Shakespeare. The young playwright, like each of his characters, seeks to hold audiences by the skillful manipulation of words.

In suggesting that Richard is a kind of actor, we should remember that the Greek word for actor is *hypokrites*, our "hypocrite," one who pretends to be what one is not. We might also say that Richard is a kind of playwright, an artist, with a plot to gain the Crown, a script written to put himself on the throne, and a sensibility that causes him to think in theatrical terms: "Plots have I laid, inductions dangerous" (1.1.33). We might even see Richard as something of a critic, offering rave reviews of his own performance, as when he turns to the audience immediately after Lady Anne has yielded to him: "Was ever woman in this humor woo'd? / Was ever woman in this humor won?" (1.2.27–28).

The point of these metaphors, of course, is that Shakespeare depicts Richard as a creature of prodigious — if perverted — imagination, and in this respect Richard's most important descendant is Iago in *Othello*. In seeking, for whatever complicated set of reasons, to destroy his friend and superior officer, Iago imagines a scenario in which Othello will play the role of the wronged husband and brutally punish his faithful wife. It is Iago's talent for language and fiction — or lies — that permits him to realize those imagined circumstances. Iago takes the same attitude toward words that he takes toward other people: they are merely instruments, vehicles that he uses on the road to vengeance. An audience's moral revulsion at Iago's plot is overpowered, at least occasionally, by its admiration for his wicked creativity and his skillful use of words. And yet for all the linguistic verve and imaginative talent of a Richard or an Iago, these gifted speakers are finally guilty of betraying the word, of using language dishonestly. In Shakespeare's book this is a very serious offense. Words are the medium of the imagination, and the imagination is Shakespeare's means of livelihood. The perils of imagination as registered by the perversion of language is one of Shakespeare's abiding themes.

But the complement is also true. Creatively arranged words repeatedly bear witness to the positive uses of the imagination. In *Much Ado about Nothing*, the witty lies that Don Pedro and friends invent for tricking Beatrice and Benedick into falling in love with each other exhibit the benefits of imaginative invention. Similarly, in many of the other comedies, the disguises adopted by the heroines — Rosalind in *As You Like It*, Viola in *Twelfth Night* — serve as visual emblems of a verbal performance that leads to marriage and harmony. The great tragedies also are often said to be studies in the duality of language. Macbeth, as I have indicated, is finally betrayed by a kind of pun when he mistakenly interprets the witches' prophecies about his being vulnerable only to one "not born of woman." And yet the same play insists that if words can destroy, they can also enrich. Macbeth delivers some of the most stirring and memorable speeches in all of literature. Iago's lies and plots are illusions that demonstrate the deadly power of words; and yet those lies and illusions make up the dramatic fiction of *Othello* that — as a theatrical creation — demonstrates the opposite, the positive and living power of language. Language — its beauties, its power, its inadequacies, its dangers, its pleasures — is never far from the center of Shakespeare's thinking. Paradoxically for modern readers, as soon as we become comfortable enough with the technical properties of Shakespeare's language to forget them, to concentrate on what the playwright is talking about, we find that much of the time he is talking about language itself, and we are never allowed to forget it.

➜ DESIDERIUS ERASMUS

From the Foreword to the Third Edition
of the Latin New Testament

1522

Translated by Robert P. Adams

Erasmus of Rotterdam (1466–1536), one of the most erudite scholars of his time and one of the promoters of the Renaissance in England, here takes up the question of whether the Bible should be made available to the common people in the language they speak. The status of the vernacular was a source of fierce controversy between the religious reformers (mostly Protestant) and the establishment (mostly Catholic) in the early sixteenth century, and even though Erasmus remained faithful to Rome, he characteristically took an independent position. Such translations indicate the new esteem that the English language was gaining among the learned.

Some think it a fault, though venial, if the holy books are translated into French or English. But the evangelists had no hesitation about writing in Greek what Christ spoke in Syriac. Nor did the Latin fathers fear to turn the speeches of the apostles into Latin, thereby spreading the Word across the world in the form of the Vulgate [the Latin Bible]. No law prevented Jerome from translating the Holy Writ into his native Yugoslav. I myself would like to see it turned into all the languages there are. Christ wants his gospel to be spread as widely as possible. He died for all; he wants to be known by all. It would serve that end if his books were turned into all the languages of all the nations; or else if, by decree of the princes, those three languages [Latin, Greek, and Hebrew] to which the divine philosophy has been entrusted were taught to all the peoples. If the power of the Roman emperors could bring about within a few years that Frenchmen, Germans, Spaniards, Africans, Egyptians, Asians, Cilicians, and Palestinians all spoke Latin and Greek, even on everyday occasions — and for no better reason than to facilitate the commerce of an empire not destined to survive long in any case — how much more should we be concerned that the rule of Christ, which is to last forever, should be spread through all the regions of the earth? At present, Christianity is narrowly contracted, for what reasons I cannot guess, unless, as I suspect, there are men who would rather maintain their secular power under the pretext of Christianity in their own little corner of the world than see Christ himself ruling over the entire globe. But on this topic there will be more to say on another occasion, when it can be said more forcefully. Now let me hasten on with my task, and ask why it should seem improper that anyone should recite the Gospel in that language to which he was born, and which he understands — a Frenchman in French, a Briton in English, a German in German, an Indian in Indian? To me it seems much more improper, not to say ridiculous, that a layman or a woman should mumble their psalms or recite their prayers like trained parrots in a language where they don't understand what they are saying. I agree with Saint Jerome that the glory of the Cross would be more advanced and its triumphs made more splendid if it were celebrated by all the races of mankind, each one speaking its own language — if the farmer driving his plough could chant a passage in his native tongue from the mystic psalms, if the weaver sitting before his loom could lighten his labor with a chapter from the gospel, if the sailor standing by his tiller could chant some favorite selection, if the matron sitting at her spinning-wheel could hear some scriptural story recited by her maid or niece.

→ THOMAS WILSON

From *The Art of Rhetoric* 1553

Of Composition

Thomas Wilson (1525?–1581) was one of the many humanist educators who sought to apply the rhetorical principles of classical oratory to the writing of English. In this section of *The Art of Rhetoric*, he considers the appropriate ways of "composing," or putting words together in proper order (from the Latin *com*, "with," and *pos*, "put"). Note particularly Wilson's simile designed to suggest that, in the sentence as in society, man should naturally come before woman.

When we have learned usual and accustomable words to set forth our meaning, we ought to join them together in apt order, that the ear may delight in hearing the harmony. I know some Englishmen that in this point have such a gift in the English as few in Latin have the like, and therefore delight the wise and learned so much with their pleasant composition, that many rejoice when they may hear such, and think much learning is got when they may talk with them. Composition, therefore, is an apt joining together of words in such order that neither the ear shall espy [observe] any jar, nor yet any man shall be dulled with overlong drawing out of a sentence, nor yet much confounded with mingling of clauses, such as are needless, being heaped together without reason and used without number. For by such means the hearers will be forced to forget full oft what was said first, before the sentence be half ended, or else be blinded with confounding of many things together.

Some again will be so short, and in such wise curtail their sentences, that they had need to make a commentary immediately of their meaning, or else the most that hear them shall be forced to keep counsel.

Some will speak oracles that a man cannot tell which way to take them; some will be so fine and so poetical withal, that to their seeming there shall not stand one hair amiss, and yet everybody else shall think them meeter [more appropriate] for a lady's chamber than for an earnest matter in any open assembly.

Some will rove so much, and babble so far without order, that a man would think they had a great love to hear themselves speak.

Some repeat one word so often that if such words could be eaten and chopped in so oft as they are uttered out, they would choke the widest throat in all England. As thus: "If a man knew what a man's life were, no man for any man's sake would kill any man, but one man would rather help another man, considering man is born for man to help man and not to hate man." What man would not be choked, if he chopped all these men at once into his mouth and never drunk after it? Some use overmuch repetition of some one letter, as "Pitiful poverty prayeth for a penny, but puffed presumption passeth not a point, pampering his paunch with pestilent pleasure, procuring his passport to post it to hell-pit, there to be punished with pains perpetual." Some will so set their words that they must be fain to gape after every word spoken, ending one word with a vowel and beginning the next with another, which undoubtedly maketh the talk to some most unpleasant. As thus: "Equity assuredly every injury avoideth."

Some will set the cart before the horse, as thus: "My mother and my father are both at home," even as though the goodman of the house did wear no breeches, or that the gray mare were the better horse. And what though it often so happeneth (God wot [knows] the more pity), yet in speaking at the least let us keep a natural order and set the man before the woman for manners' sake. Another coming home in haste after a long journey saith to his man: "Come hither, sir knave, help me off with my boots and my spurs." I pray you, sir, give him leave first to pluck off your spurs ere he meddle with your boots, or else your man is like to have a mad plucking. Who is so foolish as to say the "council and the king," but rather the "king and his council," the "father and the son," and not contrary. And so likewise in all others, as they are in degree first, evermore to set them foremost. The wise, therefore, talking of divers [several] worthy men together, will first name the worthiest and keep a decent order in reporting of their tale.

Some end their sentences all alike, making their talk rather to appear rhymed meter than to seem plain speech, the which as it much delighteth being measurably used, so it much offendeth when no mean is regarded. I heard a preacher delighting much in this kind of composition, who used so often to end his sentence with words like unto that which went before, that in my judgment there was not a dozen sentences in his whole sermon but they ended all in rhyme for the most part. Some not best disposed wished the preacher a lute, that with his rhymed sermon he might use some pleasant melody, and so the people might take pleasure divers ways and dance if they list [like]. Certes [Surely] there is a mean, and no reason to use any one thing at all times, seeing nothing delighteth — be it never so good — that is always used.

Quintilian [Roman rhetorician] likeneth the colors of rhetoric to a man's eyesight. "And now," quoth he, "I would not have all the body to be full of eyes, or nothing but eyes, for then the other parts should want their due place and proportion." Some overthwartly [perversely] set their words, placing some one a mile from his fellows, not contented with a plain and easy composition, but seek to set words they cannot tell how; and therefore one not liking to be called, and by print published, "Doctor of Physic," would needs be named of "Physic Doctor," wherein appeared a wonderful composition (as he thought), strange undoubtedly, but whether wise or no, let the learned sit in judgment upon that matter. Another. "As I rose in the morning," quoth one, "I met a cart full of stones empty." Belike the man was fasting when the cart was full, and yet we see that through strange composition this sentence appeareth dark.

Some will tell one thing twenty times, now in, now out, and when a man would think they had almost ended, they are ready to begin again as fresh as ever they were. Such vain repetitions declare both want of wit and lack of learning. Some are so homely in all their doings, and so gross for their invention, that they use altogether one manner of trade and seek no variety to eschew tediousness.

Some burden their talk with needless copy [*copia,* too many words] and will seem plentiful when they should be short. Another is so curious and so fine of his tongue that he cannot tell in all the world what to speak. Every sentence seemeth common, and every word generally used is thought to be foolish in his wise judgment. Some use so many interpositions both in their talk and in their writing, that they make their sayings as dark as hell.

Thus when faults be known, they may be avoided, and virtue the sooner may take place, when vice is foreseen and eschewed as evil.

→ SAMUEL DANIEL

From *Musophilus* 1599

Cast in the form of a dialogue, Daniel's poem is one of the great affirmations of Renaissance humanism. This excerpt, taken from the soaring conclusion, asserts the civilizing power of eloquence, declaring the capacity of words to do no less than change the world. It also posits the connection between language and empire, looking back to Rome (lines 951–56) and forward to British colonial expansion (lines 957–62).

Pow'r above pow'rs, O heavenly *Eloquence,*
 That with the strong rein of commanding words,   940
 Dost manage, guide, and master th'eminence
 Of men's affections, more than all their swords:
 Shall we not offer to thy excellence
 The richest treasure that our wit affords?
Thou that canst do much more with one poor pen   945
 Than all the pow'rs of princes can effect:
 And draw, divert, dispose, and fashion men
 Better than force or rigor can direct:
 Should we this ornament of glory then
 As th'unmaterial fruits of shades, neglect?   950

Or should we careless come behind the rest
   In pow'r of words, that go before in worth,
   When as our accents equal to the best
   Is able greater wonders to bring forth:
   When all that ever hotter spirits expressed   955
   Comes bettered by the patience of the North?
And who in time knows whither we may vent
   The treasure of our tongue, to what strange shores
   This gain of our best glory shall be sent,
   T'enrich unknowing Nations with our stores?   960
   What worlds in th'yet unformed Occident
   May come refined with th'accents that are ours?
Or who can tell for what great work in hand
   The greatness of our style is now ordained?
   What pow'rs it shall bring in, what spirits command,   965
   What thoughts let out, what humors keep restrained,
   What mischief it may pow'rfully withstand,
   And what fair ends may thereby be attained.

→ MICHEL DE MONTAIGNE

From "Of the Vanity of Words"

1580

Translated by John Florio, 1603

The great French essayist Michel de Montaigne, whose work Shakespeare read, probably in Florio's translation, presents a skeptical counterargument to the humanist enthusiasm for language and rhetoric. Whereas Daniel's *Musophilus* celebrates the power of words, Montaigne's essay explores the empty, deceptive, and pretentious qualities of language.

A rhetorician of ancient times said that his trade was to make small things appear and seem great. It is a shoemaker that can make great shoes for a little foot. Had he lived in Sparta, he had doubtless been well whipped for professing a false, a cozening, and deceitful art. And I think Archidamus King of that city did not without astonishment listen unto the answer of Thucydides, of whom he demanded whether he or Pericles was the strongest and nimblest wrestler; whose answer was this, *Your question Sir, is very hard to be decided; for if in wrestling with him I give him a fall, with his fair words he persuadeth those that saw him on the ground that he never fell, and so gets the victory.* Those that mask and paint women commit not so foul a fault; for it is no great loss, though a man see them not as they were naturally born and unpainted. Whereas these profess to deceive and beguile, not our eyes but our judgment, and to bastardize and corrupt the essence of things. Those commonwealths that have maintained themselves in a regular, formal, and well governed estate, as that of

Crete and Lacedemon, did never make any great esteem of orators. Ariston did wisely define rhetoric to be a science to persuade the vulgar people, Socrates and Plato to be an art to deceive and flatter. And those which deny it in the general description do everywhere in their precepts verify the same. The Mahometans, by reason of its inutility, forbid the teaching of it to their children. And the Athenians, perceiving how pernicious the profession and use thereof was, and of what credit in their city ordained that their principal part [the main purpose of rhetorical strategies], which is to move affections, should be dismissed and taken away, together with all *exordiums* and *perorations*. It is an instrument devised to busy, manage, and to agitate a vulgar and disordered multitude; and is an implement employed but about distempered and sick minds, as physic is about crazed bodies. . . .

I know not whether [words] work that in others, which they do in me. But when I hear our architects mouth-out those big and rattling words of *pilasters, architraves, cornices, frontispieces, Corinthian,* and *Doric* works, and such like fustian-terms [tough words] of theirs, I cannot let [prevent] my wandering imagination from a sudden apprehension of Apollidonius his palace, and I find by effect that they are the seely [simple] and decayed pieces of my kitchen door. Do but hear one pronounce *Metonymia, Metaphor, Allegory, Etymology,* and other such trash-names of grammar, would you not think they meant some form of a rare and strange language? They are titles and words that concern your chambermaid's tittle-tattle.

→ ROGER ASCHAM

From *The Schoolmaster* 1570

Scholar of Latin and Greek and tutor to Queen Elizabeth, Roger Ascham (1515–1568) was one of the most learned men of his day. His posthumously published *Schoolmaster* is designed to instruct the teacher in educating students effectively. The excerpt printed here offers advice on the proper means of teaching Latin, particularly the system of double translation from Latin into English and then back into Latin.

After the child hath learned perfectly the eight parts of speech, let him then learn the right joining together of substantives [words or phrases serving as nouns] with adjectives, the noun with the verb, the relative with the antecedent. And in learning further his syntaxes, by mine advice, he shall not use the common order in common schools, for making of Latins: whereby, the child commonly learneth, first, an evil choice of words (and right choice of words, saith Caesar, is the foundation of eloquence); then, a wrong placing of words; and lastly, an ill framing of the sentence, with a perverse judgment, both of words and sentences. These faults, taking once root in youth, be never or hardly plucked away in age. Moreover, there is no one thing that hath more either dulled the wits, or taken away the will of children from learning, than the care they have to satisfy their masters, in making of Latins.

For the scholar is commonly beat for the making, when the master were more worthy to be beat for the mending, or rather marring of the same, the master many times being as ignorant as the child, what to say properly and fitly to the matter. . . .

There is a way, touched in the first book of Cicero, *De Oratore,* which, wisely brought into schools, truly taught, and constantly used, would not only take wholly away this butcherly [brutal] fear in making of Latins, but would also, with ease and pleasure, and in short time, as I know by good experience, work a true choice and placing of words, a right ordering of sentences, an easy understanding of the tongue, a readiness to speak, a faculty to write, a true judgment, both of his own and other men's doings, what tongue so ever he doth use.

The way is this. After the three Concordances learned, as I touched before, let the master read unto him the *Epistles* of Cicero, gathered together and chosen out by Sturmius [German scholar (1507–1589), editor of Cicero], for the capacity of children.

First, let him teach the child, cheerfully and plainly, the cause and matter of the letter; then, let him construe it into English, so often as the child may easily carry away the understanding of it; lastly, parse it over perfectly. This done thus, let the child by and by both construe and parse it over again, so that it may appear that the child doubteth in [is uncertain in] nothing that his master taught him before. After this, the child must take a paper book, and sitting in some place where no man shall prompt him, by himself, let him translate into English his former lesson. Then showing it to his master, let the master take from him his Latin book, and pausing an hour, at the least, then let the child translate his own English into Latin again, in another paper book. When the child bringeth it, turned into Latin, the master must compare it with Tully's [Cicero's] book, and lay them both together: and where the child doth well, either in choosing, or true placing of Tully's words, let the master praise him, and say, "Here you do well." For I assure you, there is no such whetstone, to sharpen a good wit and encourage a will to learning, as is praise.

But if the child miss, either in forgetting a word, or in changing a good with a worse, or misordering the sentence, I would not have the master either frown or chide with him, if the child have done his diligence, and used no truantship therein. For I know by good experience that a child shall take more profit of two faults, gently warned of, than of four things, rightly hit. For then, the master shall have good occasion to say unto him: "Tully would have used such a word, not this; Tully would have placed this word here, not there; would have used this case, this number, this person, this degree, this gender; he would have used this mood, this tense, this simple, rather than this compound; this adverb here, not there; he would have ended the sentence with this verb, not with that noun or participle, etc."

In these few lines, I have wrapped up the most tedious part of grammar, and also the ground of almost all the rules, that are so busily taught by the master, and so hardly learned by the scholar, in all common schools: which after this sort, the master shall teach without all error, and the scholar shall learn without great pain, the master being led by so sure a guide, and the scholar being brought into so plain and easy a way. And therefore, we do not contemn [scorn] rules, but we gladly teach rules, and teach them, more plainly, sensibly, and orderly than they be commonly taught in common schools. For when the master shall compare Tully's book with his scholar's translation, let the master, at the first, lead and teach his scholar to join the rules of his grammar book with the examples of his present lesson, until the scholar by himself be able to fetch out of his grammar every rule, for every example, so as the grammar book be ever in the scholar's hand and also used of him as a dictionary, for every present use. This is a lively and perfect way of teaching of rules: where the common way, used in common schools, to read the grammar alone by itself, is tedious for the master, hard for the scholar, cold and uncomfortable for them both.

Let your scholar be never afraid to ask you any doubt, but use discreetly the best allurements you can, to encourage him to the same, lest his overmuch hearing of you drive him to seek some misorderly shift: as, to seek to be helped by some other book, or to be prompted by some other scholar, and so go about to beguile you much, and himself more.

With this way, of good understanding the matter, plain construing, diligent parsing, daily translating, cheerful admonishing, and heedful amending of faults, never leaving behind just praise for well doing, I would have the scholar brought up withal, till he had read and translated over the first book of *Epistles* chosen out by Sturmius, with a good piece of a comedy of Terence also.

→ RALPH LEVER

From *The Art of Reason, Rightly Termed Witcraft*   1573

The Art of Reason is Lever's entry in the sixteenth-century controversy over the expansion and uses of the English language. His project is to accommodate the demand for new words, a result of the expansion of knowledge, by combining English words rather than borrowing from French or Latin. The first excerpt is from "The Forespeech," Lever's justification of his system. Following that, from "The Second Book," is his presentation of the *saywhat,* his recommended term for what might otherwise be called a kind of "definition."

To prove that the art of reasoning may be taught in English, I reason thus. First, we Englishmen have wits, as well as men of other nations have, whereby we conceive what standeth with reason, and is well done, and what seemeth to be so, and is not. We have also framed unto ourselves a language, whereby we do express by voice or writing all devices [ideas] that we conceive in our mind, and do by this means let men look into our hearts, and see what we think. Then, as Englishmen can compass this art by wit, so can they also declare and set it forth by speech. Now whereas a number of men do suppose that our language hath no words fit to express the rules of this art, and whereas some men do argue that it must needs be so because they that speak or write thereof at large use terms and words that no mere Englishman can understand, it is plain that neither their supposition is true nor yet their reason good. For as time doth invent a new form of building, a strange fashion of apparel, and a new kind of artillery and munitions, so do men by consent of speech frame and devise new names fit to make known their strange devices. As for strange and inkhorn terms (used of many without cause), they argue a misuse to be in the speaker, but they prove not directly that there is any lack in our language, no more than the rudeness of lawyers' Latin proveth that there is a want of good words in the Latin tongue. I see and confess that there be *Plura rerum, quam verborum genera* (that is, more things than there are words to express things by) and do know withal that Aristotle found that want [deficiency] in the Greek tongue, which for fineness of speech and store of words far excelleth all other languages. Yet is there this help in speech, that we oft use many words to express one thing: yea and sometimes one word is used to signify sundry matters. Moreover, one language borroweth of another, and where there is want, men sometimes devise new names and compounded terms. So that after a man hath conveyed any new device in his head, and is desirous to have the same published [publicized] and made common to many, he findeth ever some shift by one mean or other to make the same known. And because there is not so good a way to do it by as speech, man maketh that his chief mean. Thus ye may see the original groundwork and beginning of arts. Man first doth conceive trim [well-made] devices in his head, and then (as the Poets do feign of Jupiter) is pained as a woman in travail [labor], till he have uttered and published them to be seen and commended of others. So that whenas arts are begun at the first by one, and after labored by many, they grow by continuance of time to perfections, as well in the utterance of the speech, as in the device of the mind. As for devising of new terms and compounding of words, our tongue hath a special grace, wherein it excelleth many other, and is comparable with the best. The cause is for that the most part of English words are short, and stand on one syllable apiece. So that two or three of them are oft times joined in one.

Of these kind of words, I have devised many and am now to give a reason of my doing. But first I desire thee (gentle Reader) not to scoff at them afore thou know what they mean; or that thou has found out thyself or learned of others more apt and fit terms than they are. . . .

We therefore that devise understandable terms compounded of true and ancient English words do rather maintain and continue the antiquity of our mother tongue than they that with inkhorn terms do change and corrupt the same, making a mingle-mangle of their native speech and not observing the property [integrity] thereof. They that will have no new words devised where there is want seem not well to consider how speech groweth, or wherefore it was devised by man. For names are not given unto things afore the things themselves be invented. Therefore old names will not serve to make new devices known.

OF A SAYWHAT, AND OF THINGS THAT ARE HANDLED AND INTREATED OF IN LIKE MANNER THAT IT IS. CHAP. 4.

A saywhat is a saying showing what a thing is, as man is a wight [being], indued [endowed] with sense and reason. . . .

GENERAL RULES APPERTAINING TO A SAYWHAT

Five points are to be observed in a perfect saywhat.

1

First, that the saywhat show what the kinred [family, category] is.

2

Secondly, that it contain neither more nor less matter than it should.

3

Thirdly, that it stands of [is distinguishable from] the next kind, having most proper differences put thereto.

4

Fourthly, that it be plain.

5

Fifthly, that it be brief.

→ GEORGE PUTTENHAM

From *The Art of English Poesy* 1589

One of the most thorough of sixteenth-century guidebooks, George Puttenham's *The Art of English Poesy* (published anonymously) is a treasury not only of rhetorical instruction but also of information about Elizabethan education and society in general. It is divided into three books, the first on the importance and the proper kinds of poetry, the second on metrical models, and the third on the definition and function of rhetorical tropes. Included here are Puttenham's introductory remarks on the value of poetic ornament found at the beginning of Book 3 and two sections from Book 3,

Chapter 19: the first contains a discussion and illustration of some rhetorical figures; the second is his explanation of "the rebound," a central figure in sixteenth-century wordplay.

BOOK 3, CHAPTER 1

Of Ornament Poetical

As no doubt the good proportion of any thing doth greatly adorn and commend it, and right [just] so our late remembered proportions do to our vulgar poesy: so is there yet requisite to the perfection of this art another manner of exornation [ornamentation], which resteth in the fashioning of our maker's language and style to such purpose as it may delight and allure as well the mind as the ear of the hearers with a certain novelty and strange manner of conveyance, disguising it no little from the ordinary and accustomed; nevertheless making it nothing the more unseemly or misbecoming, but rather decenter and more agreeable to any civil ear and understanding. And as we see in these great Madames of honor, be they for personage or otherwise never so comely and beautiful, yet if they want their courtly habiliments or at leastwise such other apparel as custom and civility have ordained to cover their naked bodies, would be half ashamed or greatly out of countenance to be seen in that sort, and perchance do then think themselves more amiable in every man's eye, when they be in their richest attire, suppose of silks or tissues and costly embroideries, than when they go in cloth or in any other plain and simple apparel. Even so cannot our vulgar poesy show itself either gallant or gorgeous if any limb be left naked and bare and not clad in his kindly clothes and colors, such as may convey them somewhat out of sight, that is, from the common course of ordinary speech and capacity of the vulgar judgment, and yet being artificially handled must needs yield it much more beauty and commendation. This ornament we speak of is given to it by figures and figurative speeches, which be the flowers, as it were, and colors that a poet setteth upon his language of art, as the embroiderer doth his stone and pearl, or passements of gold upon the stuff of a princely garment, or as the excellent painter bestoweth the rich Orient colors upon his table of portrait: so nevertheless as if the same colors in our art of poesy (as well as in those other mechanical arts) be not well tempered, or not well laid, or be used in excess, or never so little disordered or misplaced, they not only give it no manner of grace at all but rather do disfigure the stuff and spill [spoil] the whole workmanship, taking away all beauty and good liking from it, no less than if the crimson taint, which should be laid upon a lady's lips, or right in the center of her cheeks, should by some oversight or mishap be applied to her forehead or chin, it would make (you would say) but a very ridiculous beauty, wherefore the chief praise and cunning of our poet is in the discreet using of his figures, as the skillful painter's is in the good conveyance of his colors and shadowing traits of his pencil, with a delectable variety, by all measure and just proportion, and in places most aptly to be bestowed.

BOOK 3, CHAPTER 19

Of Figures Sententious, Otherwise Called Rhetorical

Now if our presuppoal be true, that the poet is of all other the most ancient orator, as he that by good and pleasant persuasions first reduced the wild and beastly people into public societies and civility of life, insinuating unto them, under fictions with sweet and colored speeches, many wholesome lessons and doctrines, then no doubt there is nothing so fit for him, as to be furnished with all the figures that be rhetorical, and such as do most beautify language with eloquence and sententiousness. Therefore, since we have already allowed to our maker his auricular figures, and also his sensible, by which all the words and clauses of his meters are made as well tunable to the ear, as stirring to the mind, we are now by order to bestow upon him those other figures which may execute both offices, and all at once to beautify and give sense and sententiousness to the whole language at large. So as if we should entreat our maker to play also the orator, and whether it be to plead, or to praise, or to advise, that in all three cases he may utter, and also persuade both copiously and vehemently.

And your figures rhetorical, besides their remembered ordinary virtues, that is, sententiousness, and copious amplification, or enlargement of language, do also contain a certain sweet and melodious manner of speech, in which respect they may, after a sort, be said auricular: because the ear is no less ravished with their current tune, than the mind is with their sententiousness. For the ear is properly but an instrument of conveyance for the mind, to apprehend the sense by the sound. And our speech is made melodious or harmonical, not only by strained tunes, as those of music, but also by choice of smooth words: and thus, or thus, marshaling them in their comeliest construction and order, and as well by sometimes sparing, sometimes spending them more or less liberally, and carrying or transporting of them farther off or nearer, setting them with sundry relations, and variable forms, in the ministry and use of words, do breed no little alteration in man. For to say truly, what else is man but his mind? which, whosoever have skill to compass, and make yielding and flexible, what may not he command the body to perform? He therefore that hath vanquished the mind of man hath made the greatest and most glorious conquest. But the mind is not assailable unless it be by sensible [of the senses] approaches, whereof the audible is of greatest force for instruction or discipline: the visible, for apprehension of exterior knowledges, as the philosopher saith. Therefore the well tuning of your words and clauses to the delight of the ear, maketh your information no less plausible to the mind than to the ear: no, though you filled them with never so much sense and sententiousness. Then also must the whole tale (if it tend to persuasion) bear his just and reasonable measure, being rather with the largest than with the scarcest. For like as one or two drops of water pierce not the flint stone, but many and often droppings do, so cannot a few words (be they never so pithy or sententious) in all cases and to all manner of minds, make so deep an impression, as a more multitude of words to the purpose discreetly and without superfluity uttered: the mind being no less vanquished with large load of speech, than the limbs are with heavy burden. Sweetness of speech, sentence, and amplification are therefore necessary to an excellent orator and poet; he may in no wise be spared from any of them.

And first of all others your figure that worketh by iteration or repetition of one word or clause doth much alter and affect the ear and also the mind of the hearer, and therefore is counted a very brave figure both with the poets and rhetoricians, and this repetition may be in seven sorts.

ANAPHORA, or the Figure of Report.   Repetition in the first degree we call the figure of *report,* according to the Greek original, and is when we make one word begin and, as they are wont to say, lead the dance to many verses in suit [in sequence], as thus:

> *To think on death it is a misery,*
> *To think on life it is a vanity:*
> *To think on the world, verily it is*
> *To think that here man hath no perfect bliss.*

And this written by Sir Walter Raleigh of his greatest mistress in most excellent verses:

> *In vain, mine eyes, in vain you waste your tears,*
> *In vain, my sighs, the smokes of my despairs,*
> *In vain you search th' earth and heavens above,*
> *In vain you seek, for fortune keeps my love.*

Or as the buffoon in our interlude called *Lusty London* said very knavishly and like himself:

> *Many a fair lass in London town,*
> *Many a bawdy basket borne up and down,*
> *Many a broker in a threadbare gown,*
> *Many a bankrupt scarce worth a crown,*
> *   In London. . . .*

ANADIPLOSIS, or the Redouble.   You have another sort of repetition, when with the word by which you finish your verse, you begin the next verse with the same, as thus:

> *Comfort it is for man to have a wife,*
> *Wife, chaste, and wise, and lowly all her life.*

Or thus:

> *Your beauty was the cause of my first love,*
> *Love while I live, that I may sore repent.*

The Greeks call this figure *anadiplosis,* I call him the *redouble* as the original bears.

EPANALEPSIS, or the Echo Sound, Otherwise the Slow Return. You have another sort of repetition, when you make one word both begin and end your verse, which therefore I call the *slow return*, otherwise the *echo sound*, as thus:

> *Much must he be beloved, that loveth much,*
> *Fear many must he needs, whom many fear.*

Unless I called him the *echo sound*, I could not tell what name to give him, unless it were the *slow return*.

EPIZEUXIS, the Underlay, or Cuckoo Spell. You have another sort of repetition, when in one verse or clause of a verse, you iterate one word without any intermission, as thus:

> *It was Maryne, Maryne that wrought mine woe.*

And this bemoaning the departure of a dear friend.

> *The chiefest staff of mine assured stay,*
> *With no small grief, is gone, is gone away.*

And that of Sir Walter Raleigh's very sweet:

> *With wisdom's eyes had but blind fortune seen,*
> *Then had my love, my love for ever been.*

The Greeks call him *epizeuxis*, the Latins *subjunctio*, we may call him the *underlay;* me thinks if we regard his manner of iteration, and would depart from the original, we might very properly, in our vulgar and for pleasure call him the cuckoo spell, for right as the cuckoo repeats his lay, which is but one manner of note, and doth not insert any other tune betwixt, and sometimes for haste stammers out two or three of them one immediately after another, as *cuck, cuck, cuckoo,* so doth the figure *epizeuxis* in the former verses, *Maryne, Maryne,* without any intermission at all.

PLOCHE, or the Doubler. Yet have you one sort of repetition, which we call the *doubler,* and is as the next before, a speedy iteration of one word, but with some little intermission by inserting one or two words between, as in a most excellent ditty written by Sir Walter Raleigh these two closing verses:

> *Yet when I saw my self to you was true,*
> *I loved my self, because my self loved you.*

And this spoken in common proverb.

> *An ape will be an ape, by kind as they say,*
> *Though that you clad him all in purple array.*

Or as we once sported upon a fellow's name who was called *Woodcock,* and for an ill part he had played entreated favor by his friend.

> *I pray you entreat no more for the man,*
> *Woodcock will be a woodcock [fool] do what you can.*

Now also be there many other sorts of repetition if a man would use them, but are nothing commendable, and therefore are not observed in good poesy, as a vulgar rhymer who doubled one word in the end of every verse, thus:

adieu, adieu,
my face, my face.

And another that did the like in the beginning of his verse, thus:

To love him and love him, as sinners should do.

These repetitions be not figurative but fantastical, for a figure is ever used to a purpose, either of beauty or of efficacy: and these last recited be to no purpose, for neither can you say that it urges affection, nor that it beautifieth or enforceth the sense, nor hath any other subtlety in it, and therefore is a very foolish impertinency of speech and not a figure. . . .

ANTANACLASIS, or the Rebound. You have another figure which by his nature we may call the *rebound,* alluding to the tennis ball which being smitten with the racket rebounds back again, and where the last figure before played with two words somewhat like, this playeth with one word written all alike but carrying divers senses, as thus:

The maid that soon married is, soon marred is.

Or thus better because *married* and *marred* be different in one letter:

To pray for you ever I cannot refuse,
To pray [prey] upon you I should you much abuse.

Or as we once sported upon a country fellow who came to run for the best game, and was by his occupation a dyer and had very big swelling legs:

He is but course [coarse] to run a course,
Whose shanks are bigger than his thigh:
Yet is his luck a little worse,
That often dyes before he dye.

Where you see this word *course* and *dye,* used in divers senses, one giving the *rebound* upon the other.

→ BALDASSARE CASTIGLIONE

From *The Book of the Courtier* *1528*

The Book of the Courtier, written in Italian at the beginning of the sixteenth century and translated into English by Sir Thomas Hoby (pub. 1560), became one of the most influential books in early modern Europe. Purporting to record the conversations of a group of aristocrats, it promotes the humanist values of learning, civility, gracefulness, wit, and the dignity of man. This passage (in a modern translation) explores the pleasures of wordplay and, by implication, the power relations associated with the skillful use of puns.

The discussion continuing, Bernardo said:

"You have now heard all I have to say about those jokes which rely on a continuous narration; so now we should talk of those which consist in a single remark, and whose sharp wit is concentrated in a brief sentence or word. And just as with the first kind of amusing anecdote one must, when telling the story or indulging in mimicry, avoid resembling clowns and parasites and those who make others laugh by their own foolishness, so in these terse comments the courtier should guard against appearing malicious or spiteful, or repeating witticisms and quips merely to tease and wound. Because such men often have their whole body deservedly chastised for the sins of their tongue.

"Now, of the spontaneous jokes that consist in a brief remark, those which arise from some ambiguity are the most effective, although they do not always arouse mirth, since they are more usually praised for their ingenuity than for their humor. For example, a few days ago our Annibale Paleotto was talking to someone who was recommending him a tutor to teach his sons grammar and who, after commending the teacher for his learning, when he came to the question of his salary said that as well as money he wanted to have a room furnished for living and sleeping, because he lacked a bed. Annibale immediately retorted: 'Then how can he be learned, if he hasn't read?'[1] You see how well he exploited the ambiguous meaning of *non aver letto*. But since these puns are very subtle, in that someone employs words in a sense quite different from what is given them by everyone else, it appears that, as I have said, they inspire wonder more often than laughter, except when they are accompanied by something more. The kind of witticism that customarily arouses laughter occurs when we expect to hear one thing and the one who is talking says something different, and this is called the 'unexpected retort'; and if there is also some double meaning, then the witticism becomes extremely rich, as happened the other day when there was a discussion about making a fine brick floor for the Duchess's room, and after a lot had been said you, Gian Cristoforo, remarked: 'If we could get the Bishop of Potenza and lay him flat it would suit the purpose well, since he is the biggest born fool I ever saw.' Everyone laughed out loud, for you made a pun by splitting the word *mattonato* into two; and then in addition your saying that a bishop should be laid flat and used for the floor of a room was a totally unexpected notion, and so the joke was very pointed and very funny.[2]

"However, there are many different kinds of pun; and so one must be cautious in their use, hunting carefully for the right words, and avoiding those that cause the joke to fall flat and seem too labored, or, as we have said, that are too wounding. For example, once when several companions met at the house

[1]The pun is on *letto*, which means either "bed" or "read."
[2]*Matto nato* means a "born fool" and *mattonato* a "brick floor."

of one of their friends, who happened to be blind, after the host had asked them to stay for dinner, they all left except one, who remarked: 'Well, I'll stay, since I see you've got an empty place.' And he pointed his finger at the man's empty socket. This of course is too cruel and discourteous, for it wounded the blind man's feelings to no purpose and without provocation; moreover, the jibe could have been at the expense of all those who are blind, and sweeping insults of this kind give no pleasure, because they appear to be premeditated. Of this sort was the remark made to a man who had lost his nose, namely: 'Where, then, do you rest your spectacles?' or 'How do you smell the roses every year?'

"Among other witticisms, however, those are very elegant which depend on turning someone's own sarcastic remarks against him, using the very same words as he does, and hoisting him with his own petard. For example, there was the litigant who, in the presence of the judge, was asked by his adversary: 'What are you barking for?' And he retorted: 'Because I see a thief.' The same kind of joke was when Galeotto Marzi was on his way through Siena and stopped in the street to ask the way to the inn; and when a Sienese noticed how corpulent he was, he laughed and said: 'Others bring their baggage along behind but this fellow carries his in front.' And Galeotto retorted: 'That's what you have to do in a land of robbers.'

"There is another kind still, which we call playing on words, and this relies on changing a word by adding or taking away a letter or a syllable, as when someone said: 'You must be more experienced in the literature of the *latrines* [Latins] than of the Greeks.' And to you, madam [Emilia Pia], a letter was addressed: 'To signora Emilia impia' [unholy, cruel].

"It is also amusing to quote a verse or two, putting it to a use other than what the author intended, or some other common saying, perhaps to the same purpose, but with a word altered. Thus a gentleman who had an ugly and shrewish wife, being asked how he was, replied: 'Just you imagine, seeing that *Furiarum maxima iuxta me cubat.*'[3]

"And Girolamo Donato, when in company with many other gentlemen he was making the Stations in Rome [the seven churches of Rome] during Lent, encountered a group of beautiful Roman ladies; and when one of the gentlemen said: '*Quot colum stellas, tot habet tua Roma puellas,*' he immediately added: '*Pascua quotque haedos, tot habet tua Roma cinaedos,*'[4] pointing out a group of young men who were coming from the other direction.

"Then there is the way in which Marc'Antonio dalla Torre spoke to the Bishop of Padua. For there was a nunnery in Padua in charge of a cleric who was thought to be extremely devout and learned, and who used to go the familiar rounds of the convent, often hearing the nuns' confessions. And then five of the mothers, and there were no more than as many again, became pregnant, and the father was seized by the Bishop after he had tried unsuccessfully to run away. He immediately confessed that because of the temptation of the

---

[3]This is a play on Virgil's "*Furiarum maxima iuxta accubat*" (*Aeneid* VI, 605–06), meaning "Lying nearby the greatest of the Furies. . . ," to give the sense "The greatest of the Furies sleeps with me."
[4]The line from Ovid's *Ars Amatoria* (*Art of Love*) running "Your Rome has as many girls as the sky has stars" is answered by: "Your Rome has as many homosexuals as the meadows have kids."

devil he had got those five nuns pregnant, and consequently my Lord Bishop was resolved to chastise him very severely. However, the culprit was a very learned man and so he had very many friends, all of whom made efforts to help him; and along with the others Marc'Antonio also went to the Bishop to plead with him to be lenient. After they had been very insistent, recommending the culprit and pleading in extenuation the easy opportunities he had been given, the frailty of human nature, and various other factors, the Bishop said at length: 'I will do nothing for him, because I have to render my account to God.' They still insisted, however; and then the Bishop added: 'What shall I answer when on the Day of Judgment the Almighty says to me: *"Redde rationem villicationis tuae?"*' To which Marc'Antonio swiftly replied: 'My Lord, in the words of the Evangelist: *Domine, quinque talenta tradidisti mihi; ecce alia quinque superlucratus sum.*'[5] At this the Bishop could not stop from laughing and he greatly mitigated both his anger and the punishment he had designed for the wrongdoer."

[5]Namely, God will say: "Give an account of your stewardship" (Luke 16.2), and the bishop should answer: "Lord, you delivered five talents [coins] to me: see, I have gained over and above them five more" (Matthew 25.20).

Chart of the Relative Proportions of Poetry and Prose in Shakespeare's Plays

This table, reprinted from *The Complete Pelican Shakespeare*, edited by Alfred Harbage, indicates the relative amounts of poetry and prose in each play, and other information.

	Total Lines	% Blank	% Rhyme	% Prose	Scenes	Casts Men	Women	Songs	Longest roles (with count for those over 500 lines)
COMEDIES									
Errors	1756	65.8	21.5	12.7	11	11	5		Antipholus S., Adriana, Dromio S.
Shrew	2584	72.5	5.8	21.7	12	19	4	2	Petruchio (549), Tranio, Katherina
T.G.V.	2199	68.7	5.8	25.5	19	13	3	1	Proteus, Valentine, Julia
Dream	2106	35.4	45.5	19.1	7	15	6	2	Theseus, Helena, Bottom
L.L.L.	2667	21.8	43.1	35.1	9	13	5	2	Berowne (591), Navarre, Princess
Merchant	2564	73.5	5.5	21.0	19	16	3	1	Portia (565), Shylock, Bassanio
A.Y.L.	2636	35.2	10.3	54.5	22	17	4	5	Rosalind (668), Orlando, Touchstone
Much Ado	2549	25.3	3.0	71.7	17	14	4	2	Benedick, Leonato, Don Pedro
Twelfth Night	2423	31.4	7.3	61.3	18	11	3	4	Toby, Viola, Feste
Merry Wives	2598	9.6	3.8	86.6	21	16	4	1	Falstaff, Mrs. Page, Mr. Ford
All's Well	2760	43.6	10.3	46.1	23	8	6		Helena, Parolles, King
Measure	2671	59.0	3.4	37.6	15	17	5	1	Vincentio (820), Isabella, Lucio
HISTORIES									
1 Henry VI	2676	88.0	11.9	0.1	19	39	3		Talbot, Joan, York
2 Henry VI	3062	82.1	3.2	14.7	18	43	4		York, Margaret, Henry
3 Henry VI	2902	95.5	4.4	0.1	22	40	3		Warwick, Edward, Richard

(continued)

	Total Lines	% Blank	% Rhyme	% Prose	Scenes	Casts		Songs	Longest roles (with count for those over 500 lines)
						Men	Women		
Richard III	3602	93.8	4.4	1.8	23	40	5		Richard (1124), Buckingham, Elizabeth
John	2560	94.9	5.1	0.0	15	18	4		Faulconbridge (520), John, Constance
Richard II	2755	80.9	19.1	0.0	18	26	5		Richard (753), Bullingbrook, York
1 Henry IV	2954	54.3	2.7	43.0	17	32	3		Falstaff (585), Hotspur (545), Hal (535)
2 Henry IV	3182	48.7	2.6	48.7	17	39	5	1	Falstaff (593), Hal, Henry
Henry V	3176	57.2	3.2	39.6	20	39	4		Henry (1025), Fluellen, Canterbury
Henry VIII	2804	95.1	2.6	2.3	16	36	4	1	Henry, Wolsey, Katherine
TRAGEDIES									
Titus	2521	93.2	5.2	1.6	13	21	3		Titus (687), Aaron, Marcus
Romeo	2964	71.0	16.6	12.4	21	21	4	1	Romeo (591), Juliet (509), Laurence
Caesar	2453	92.5	1.3	6.2	13	36	2		Brutus (701), Cassius, Antony
Hamlet	3776	66.3	5.7	28.0	20	25	2	3	Hamlet (1422), Claudius (540), Polonius
Troilus	3326	63.0	6.1	30.9	18	24	4	1	Troilus, Ulysses, Pandarus
Othello	3228	78.4	3.1	18.5	15	14	3	3	Iago (1097), Othello (860), Desdemona
Lear	3195	69.9	5.3	24.8	22	22	3	4	Lear (697), Edgar, Kent
Macbeth	2113	80.3	12.1	7.6	26	25	7		Macbeth (681), Lady Macbeth, Malcolm
Timon	2281	66.4	7.0	26.6	17	27	2		Timon (795), Apemantus, Flavius
Antony	3019	90.5	1.3	8.2	36	30	4	1	Antony (766), Cleopatra (622), Caesar
Coriolanus	3294	77.4	0.8	21.8	27	29	4		Coriolanus (809), Menenius, Volumnia
ROMANCES									
Pericles	2322	59.7	22.4	17.9	22	22	7		Pericles (592), Marina, Simonides
Cymbeline	3266	79.9	6.3	13.8	23	24	3	2	Imogen (522), Posthumus, Iachimo
Winter's Tale	2946	71.5	3.1	25.4	14	15	6	6	Leontes (648), Paulina, Autolycus
Tempest	2026	71.4	7.5	21.1	9	15	4	7	Prospero (603), Ariel, Caliban

CHAPTER 3

Theater à la Mode:
Shakespeare and the Kinds of Drama

><-

According to the English novelist Somerset Maugham, "There are three rules for writing the novel. Unfortunately, no one knows what they are." The joke exposes the ambivalence felt by writers and critics about the wish for a formula for fiction, whether narrative or dramatic. Although it would be comforting to have a set of rules for writing a successful play, this notion contradicts what writers know instinctively — that plays can't be written according to formula. Ever since Aristotle's attempt to describe the principles of tragedy sometime in the fourth century B.C., people have wanted to codify the rules for literary forms, disseminate those rules, and discourage deviation from them. Yet in practice dramatic modes are irregular and ever-changing. Literary history records an expansion of formal classifications, and even if such categories are not as complicated and various as Polonius thought ("tragical-comical-historical-pastoral"), they still tend to combine and overlap.

Practicing playwrights have usually been less concerned with the "laws" of form than some eighteenth-century critics and modern educators have, but it is nevertheless useful to know something about these literary kinds, especially their historical appeal and their affective powers. For clarity and convenience, I will refer to drama as a *genre,* like other forms of literature such as novels or lyric poetry, and to the various subgenres of drama as *modes.* The range of theatrical modes in the English Renaissance was enormous, from morality plays performed in innyards to satiric comedies played by children's troupes, from the bloody spectacle of Thomas Kyd's *Spanish Tragedy* in the public theater to the historical dignity of Elizabeth Cary's unperformed *Tragedy of Mariam,* the first drama by a woman published in England (see p. 100). While a modern reader may find it helpful to be aware of what English spectators at the turn of the seventeenth century expected when they went to see a comedy or a tragedy, a prerequisite for such awareness is the recognition that the boundaries between the several dramatic forms were not clearly fixed.

In terms of his attraction to different modes, Shakespeare's career divides conveniently into two phases. In general, we may see the first ten-year period, from about 1590 to 1600, as devoted to comedies and histories, and the second decade, from about 1601 to 1611, as focused on tragedies and romances. The division is rough, however, for each decade contains major examples of the other modes. Early in his career Shakespeare wrote at least two tragedies, *Titus Andronicus* and *Romeo and Juliet,* and many of the history plays composed during this period take the form of tragedy. But for the most part Shakespeare spent his first ten years producing histories, or chronicle plays, and experimenting with various kinds of comedy, from the farcical and classically influenced *Comedy of Errors* to the fantastic *Midsummer Night's Dream* to romantic comedies such as *Much Ado about Nothing* and *As You Like It.*

The second decade is similarly varied. From about 1601 to 1607 Shakespeare wrote mainly the major tragedies, including *Hamlet, Othello, King Lear,* and *Macbeth;* then in the last four or five years of his career he turned to romance, or tragicomedy, creating magical plays such as *The Winter's Tale* and *The Tempest.* But this half exhibits major exceptions as well. In the midst of this tragic phase he also produced *All's Well That Ends Well* and *Measure for Measure,* two plays variously described as *dark comedies, tragicomedies,* and *problem plays,* but which are recognizably comic in shape and effect. And the play that no one seems to know how to categorize, *Troilus and Cressida,* was also composed about this time, perhaps in 1601 or 1602; some complete editions of Shakespeare place it among the tragedies, some with the comedies. To make matters even more complicated, there is the matter of collaboration: at the very end of his writing career, perhaps after he had left London for Stratford, Shakespeare and his younger colleague John Fletcher worked together on three plays, *Henry VIII, The Two Noble Kinsmen,* and the lost *Cardenio.* And recently some scholars have begun to think that Shakespeare may also have collaborated with other playwrights, most notably with Thomas Middleton on *Timon of Athens* (Wells and Taylor 501–02).

Shakespeare's dramatic structures faithfully represent the variety and complexity of the theatrical culture he inhabited: comedy and tragedy constitute the major kinds of drama, but there is considerable permutation in each, the boundaries between modes are not clear, and virtually all the subgenres interpenetrate and modify one another. All this is true about practice; it is not true about early modern theory. Twentieth-century ideas about dramatic form are considerably more subtle than those expressed in the sixteenth and seventeenth centuries. The First Folio divides Shakespeare's plays into three kinds — comedies, tragedies, and histories — and as the documents that follow this chapter indicate, contemporary theorizing about dramatic forms was for the most part rudimentary. The categories I have mentioned and will analyze below represent comparatively recent attempts at critical description: for example, *romance* did not exist as a dramatic classification in the Renaissance, although its characteristics and appeal were generally acknowledged. It is important to keep in mind that practice usually precedes theory; that is, certain forms of comedy and tragedy are associated with particular emotional and ideological effects, but they generate these effects because Shakespeare's own formal experiments created such possibilities.

Comedy

Comedy refers to a literary structure, be it drama or novel or film, that moves toward a happy ending and implies a positive understanding of human experience. Comedy is usually funny, although this is not a prerequisite. Dante's great poem depicting the movement of the human soul toward a final union with God is called *The Divine Comedy*. Although there are moments of grim humor in the sections devoted to the punishment of sinners — the flatterers must live in excrement, for example, condemned to swim in what they used to sling — *The Divine Comedy* is not known for its jokes. But it is comic in form and in outlook. In most comedy the happy ending involves a marriage or at least some kind of union or reunion that resolves the conflict and brings the characters into a state of harmony. In *The Divine Comedy*, the marriage is between the human soul and God; in less elevated works, the final union is more carnal. Comedy moves from confusion to order, from ignorance to understanding, from law to liberty, from unhappiness to satisfaction, from separation to union, from barrenness to fertility, from singleness to marriage, from two to one.

This progression is easily discerned by comparing the opening and closing of *A Midsummer Night's Dream*. At the beginning, Duke Theseus is impatient at having to cool his passion and to wait for the day of his wedding to Hippolyta; Hermia is in love with Lysander but is ordered by her father and the Duke to marry Demetrius, who professes love for her; Helena loves Demetrius, who used to love her but now scorns her; Oberon and Titania, king and queen of the fairies, are engaged in a marital brawl that is disturbing the mortal world. In contrast, the end of the play celebrates three marriages and one remarriage. Although the promised joy may be mitigated somewhat, things are better at the end than they were at the beginning. After the festivities of the last act, it is vital that we recognize where the characters go as they leave the stage, and it is the same destination in all of Shakespeare's comedies.

They go off to bed. There may be a dinner first, or a dance of some kind, but these are more polite and social images of the kind of union that will ultimately take place when the hero and heroine are alone together. Love first, then marriage, then sexual union, then, implicitly, birth. At the end of Henry Fielding's *Tom Jones*, when the proper Squire Allworthy remarks that Tom will use his "best endeavours" to deserve Sophia, the vulgar Squire Western responds: " 'His best endeavours!' cries Western; 'that he will, I warrant un. —— Harkee, Allworthy, I'll bet thee five pounds to a crown we have a boy tomorrow nine months.' " Embedded within the proper congratulations is a joke about the wedding night and youthful virility and fertility. Sexual union is seen as the happy conclusion that will perpetuate the species. In *Much Ado about Nothing*, the confirmed bachelor Benedick justifies his unexpected attraction to Beatrice with the words, "the world must be peopled." The characters act on their intuition that the world is good, that life is worth living, that conflict will ultimately find a positive resolution.

Well, yes, one might say, but what about the jokes? The word *comedy* is more likely to conjure up a favorite sitcom or the Marx Brothers than Dante or Fielding, and such a response is entirely legitimate, since one of comedy's main attractions is the laughter that derives from wordplay, intricate plotting, and pies in the face. But the mirth we associate with comedy depends on our acquaintance with the conventions of the form, especially its customary ending. In other words, we laugh because we know that the characters are protected from serious harm, because we have the distance to enjoy the jokes, because nobody is going to be seriously injured on that banana peel. Modes of literature offer us images of life filtered through a certain kind of lens, and the closure of the comic fiction directs us to conclude that there is good reason to laugh at the world, that life leads finally to satisfaction and away from despair, that problems can be solved, that happiness is possible. It promotes the value of wit, especially in the service of genuine feeling; it sides with youth and passion over age and money; its principal effects are ironic pleasure and confirmation of the social order.

The complementary values just mentioned, wit and desire, provide a spectrum along which we may arrange the major examples of dramatic comedy. So different in emphasis are the various types that it might be more appropriate to talk about *comedies* than *comedy*. To name only the most obvious examples, there is farce, satire, slapstick, intrigue comedy, romantic comedy, tragicomedy, religious comedy, and comedy of manners. However earthy the plot and language, virtually all comedy has a religious dimension. The words we use to talk about the endings indicate as much, words such as *grace, faith, pardon, union*, and *love*. At the same time, however elevated and romantic, virtually all comedy has a ridiculous dimension. Sixteenth-century critics tended to emphasize the ridiculousness, as the passage from Sir Philip Sidney's *Defense of Poesy* (see p. 99) suggests. Characters behave foolishly, get themselves into embarrassing scrapes, and find themselves turned into asses — literally in *A Midsummer Night's Dream*, and figuratively in a multitude of other works.

Herein lies the paradox on which theatrical comedy, and especially Shakespearean comedy, depends. Critics may expatiate on harmony, joy, and perpetuation of the species, but people go to see these kinds of plays because they want to be made to laugh. In other words, although the comic ending affirms that men and women can find happiness and that the world is a comprehensible and benevolent place, this clarification occurs only in the last five minutes. For some two hours, the audience is asked to concentrate on and take pleasure in misunderstanding, confusion, envy, and foolishness. The emphasis of comedy is positive, but the human being is shown to be a small and silly creature. The comic dramatist, depending on the point of view that motivates and shapes the work, may elect to emphasize the reconciliation over the comic conflict. In an early play like *The Comedy of Errors* (1592–94), based directly on two plays by the Roman dramatist Plautus, Shakespeare spends most of his energy magnifying and exploiting the confusion generated by two sets of twins. Several years later, in another twin comedy, *Twelfth Night* (1601–02), the misunderstandings still evoke laughter and derision, but here the playwright complicates the tone by exploring the pleasures of romantic love and offering large doses of melancholy and music. No comedy is purely farcical or purely romantic, and Shakespeare is the master of the combined response. All his comedies are hybrids, complicated mixtures of farce and romance, sunshine and shadow, absurdity and profundity.

Nature seems to endorse amorous or procreative desires, conspiring to assist the characters in their fulfillment. In *A Midsummer Night's Dream*, for example, the fairies Oberon and Puck represent natural forces, or supernatural forces that control natural forces, and Oberon's natural impulse is to give the characters what they want, to arrange that Demetrius fall back in love with Helena. In this respect Oberon acts as a stand-in for the playwright, who guarantees that conflicts are resolved and desires gratified — usually, that is. Several Shakespearean comedies have problematic endings, in which the promised marriage is delayed or in some way compromised. In *Love's Labor's Lost*, for instance, a messenger enters amid the jollity of the final scene to announce the death of the Princess's father. Consequently, her wedding, along with several others that have seemed inevitable for most of the play, is postponed for a year, and Berowne, the main male character, is sent for that year to exercise his wit among the sick. This unconventional ending is uncharacteristic for such an early comedy. As Shakespeare continues to explore the tonal possibilities of comedy, the romantic unions come to seem less joyous and more inflected with irony and potential failure. Such irony tinges even the title of one of the problem comedies, *All's Well That Ends Well*, for the happy ending to which it refers amounts to a forced marriage between a persistent young woman and a personally unappealing young man who has declared repeatedly that he doesn't want her. In performances of *A Midsummer Night's Dream*, Demetrius's affectionate return to Helena is usually convincing; in stagings of *All's Well That Ends Well*, Bertram's final acceptance of *his* Helena is usually not.

The conventions of comedy, like those of all literary modes, are consistent with the customs of the society in which a comedy is produced; the society of early modern England was patriarchal and authoritarian, inhospitable to disruption or disorder. Shakespeare's comedies, then, can be seen as instruments of social stability in their representation of the unshakable power of husbands, aristocrats, and other dominant cultural voices. It is true that in *A Midsummer Night's Dream* Shakespeare sides with Hermia in her desire to marry Lysander and thus rejects her father's proprietary claim that she should marry Demetrius, the man he chooses. Egeus's insistence on his right to dispose of his daughter as he wishes indicates, particularly in his use of pronouns, the conventional expectations surrounding arranged marriages:

Scornful Lysander, true, he [Demetrius] hath my love;
And what is mine, my love shall render him.
And she is mine, and all my right of her
I do estate unto Demetrius.   (1.1.95–98)

In *Romeo and Juliet*, the parallel tragedy written at about the same time, Juliet's father at first mouths enlightened sentiments about needing his daughter's consent before he agrees to her marriage to Paris; but by the fourth act he echoes Egeus in his intemperate assertion of his fatherly right. Although both plays reject such paternal claims, endorsing the daughters' desires for companionate marriage (a wedding of two kindred souls), they reflect the cultural anxiety pervading early modern England, when notions of romantic love were beginning to challenge the norms of patriarchal authority in the matter of marriage.

Even though he sides with his young women, however, Shakespeare finally marries them to husbands whose superior power is assumed: the last scene of *A Midsummer Night's Dream* presents the exchange of one male authority figure for another. Although the other women, particularly Titania and Hippolyta, seek to assert their independence from their husbands, the play ends with their submission. In the wood near Athens where the main events take place, Oberon magically overrules his wife's desire that she be allowed to keep a little Indian boy as her page, and he takes revenge on her by mating her temporarily with the monstrously transformed Bottom. At the end of this episode Titania yields to Oberon and returns to the role of submissive wife. Likewise, Hippolyta seems to understand much better than Theseus what has happened to the lovers in the forest, "the story of the night," but after hesitating, she keeps quiet and lets her husband think what he likes. Viewed from a feminist perspective, *A Midsummer Night's Dream* becomes a story of female independence thwarted by male power, a depiction of a society in which women either fail to fulfill their desires or, if they do, are able to look no further for that satisfaction than another man.

This problem is especially acute in *The Taming of the Shrew*. For many years critics and audiences regarded Katherina as a miserable, unsocialized creature whose refusal of suitors and defiance of her father are signs of a maladjusted personality and an uncontrolled ego. Thus Petruchio's scheme of marrying her in a wild ceremony and depriving her of food and sleep until she learns to behave — "he kills her in her own humor," as one of the servants puts it — becomes an exercise in comic justice issuing in marriage and quiet life: ". . . amid this hurly I intend / That all is done in reverend care of her" (4.1.203–04). In a play full of disguises, role-playing, and transformations carried out in the name of love, Petruchio apparently transforms Kate from miserable shrew to gratified partner. But the same plot can be staged as an insensitive, even cruel exertion of male power, a sexist suppression of female desire in the interests of financial advantage and patriarchal norms. According to this more recent view, Kate's long, final speech about the need for wives to submit to their husbands is nothing more than "a ventriloquization of male superiority" (Boose 193) and the play less a boisterous comedy than an unpalatable document in the history of misogyny.

Which is it? And might this reading not pertain to other comic texts as well? *As You Like It* may be seen as a play in which the unparalleled wit of a Rosalind is squandered on the unworthy Orlando, or *The Merchant of Venice* as a kind of male fantasy in which Portia's dead father controls her choice of a husband by arranging the riddle of the caskets of gold, silver, and lead. What about *Measure for Measure*, in which the young novice Isabella spends much of the play defending her chastity against the sexually rapacious Angelo but finds herself in the last act claimed in marriage by the very Duke who has conspired to protect her? All these opposing interpretations constitute legitimate reactions to the conflicts of value and ideology out of which the plays are constructed. Each reading, positive or negative, festive or critical, depends on the reader's or the theatrical director's decision to emphasize certain actions and ideas at the expense of others. The ambiguity is inherent in the clashes of gender and generation that all literature represents. It is Shakespeare's extraordinary sensitivity to both sides of these questions that makes his plays almost infinitely amenable to such different responses.

Tragedy

A glance at the title page of a complete volume of Shakespeare reveals that comedies are usually given general titles: *The Comedy of Errors, Much Ado about Nothing, All's Well That Ends Well*. One explanation for this phenomenon, put forward by Northrop Frye in his *Anatomy of Criticism,* is that comedy tends to focus on the group or community. In *As You Like It,* for example, an audience takes satisfaction not only in the happiness of Rosalind and Orlando but also in the wedding of Celia and Oliver and in the restored authority of Duke Senior. The titles of the tragedies, on the other hand, indicate a more limited emphasis: *Hamlet, Prince of Denmark; Romeo and Juliet; Richard II; Othello, the Moor of Venice; Antony and Cleopatra.* In these dramas the audience is invited to witness the misfortunes of charismatic and powerful individuals. *Tragedy* refers to a literary structure that moves toward an unhappy ending and thus implies an unfavorable assessment of human experience. Death is the tragic counterpart to the marriage that concludes comedy. Not only does the hero or heroine die, but others do also, often at the hands of the tragic figure. Tragedy ends in annihilation, misery, separation, loss. It is a pedagogical cliché that order is invariably restored at the end of Shakespearean tragedy, but this gesture hardly compensates for the death of a Hamlet or the unspeakable suffering of a King Lear. The emphasis is on failure, waste, disappointment, and self-destruction. The form of tragedy that Shakespeare helped to shape was developed from a variety of sources: from ancient tragedy, primarily Roman rather than Greek, and from medieval and early Tudor English tragedy, which stressed the moral benefit to be derived from watching the horrifying experiences of fallen princes. Sidney's description (see p. 99) reflects contemporary thinking about the affective power of tragedy. In Shakespeare's particular treatment of the mode, the poignancy of the action derives from the dramatic irony: it is the tragic figure's talent that leads to destruction.

The tragic pattern is clearly visible in *Macbeth*. A heroic and patriotic nobleman, rewarded for extraordinary courage and service to his king, is made Thane of Cawdor and granted the favor of a royal visit. By the end of the play this noble figure has become a lonely and fearful monster, guilty not only of murdering the king his kinsman but even of infanticide and the pollution of his kingdom. The audience last sees Macbeth as a head on a pole when Malcolm is crowned King of Scotland. Tragedy promotes the impression that hope is futile, that the heroic figure, no matter how magnificent, can never escape the traps that await anyone who inhabits our imperfect and even vicious world. Nature seems to conspire against humans rather than cooperate with them — the benevolent sprites of *A Midsummer Night's Dream* or the unnamed providential forces that assist the characters in *The Comedy of Errors* or *Much Ado about Nothing* become the witches who tempt Macbeth or the distant and inscrutable gods of *King Lear*.

Like comedy, Shakespearean tragedy depends on a paradox. Although the curve of the action is negative and completes itself with the death of the hero — the occasion, Aristotle says, for pity and fear (see p. 101) — an undeniable effect of this action is to create admiration for the tragic protagonist. It would be irresponsible of us to conclude that the tragic figure is merely a victim of unfair circumstances or a vicious environment: the hero bears responsibility for the misery that ensues. Macbeth, demonic prophecies notwithstanding, is a murderer. But it is a curious paradox that audiences admire him anyway. Tragedy is sometimes defined as a great person suffering greatly, and the heroic reaction of the tragic figure to extreme suffering commands immense respect and sympathy. Ironically, that heroism also serves to console the spectator: the world may be a wicked place, the deck may be stacked against us, but the tragic action demonstrates that the human creature is capable of extraordinary heroism and endurance.

Our admiration for an Antigone or a King Lear is a function not only of their courage, but also of their own consciousness of the cause of their suffering. Lear's mad confession to the blind Gloucester discloses that awareness — his sense of his tragic error — and makes for one of the most poignant moments in the play:

> . . . They flatter'd me like a dog, and told me I had the white hairs in my beard ere the black ones were there. To say "ay" and "no" to every thing that I said! "Ay," and "no" too, was no good divinity. When the rain came to wet me once, and the wind to make me chatter, when the thunder would not peace at my bidding, there I found 'em, there I smelt 'em out. Go to, they are not men o' their words: they told me I was every thing. 'Tis a lie, I am not ague-proof.   (4.6.96–105)

The old king admits to a blind man his own blindness and mortality. Having inhabited the untrustworthy realm of the court and believed the flattery of his wicked daughters, King Lear had regarded himself as different from ordinary men, immune to the infections of the world. Now he has come to recognize that he is only a man as other men are, that his saying something does not make it so, that the rain falls on him as it does on the beggar and the thief, that he is vulnerable, finally, to the fevers ("agues") that afflict us all. The experience of tragedy is the discovery of mortality, and this understanding deepens the tragic paradox visible in the experience of the hero: the ability to recognize one's weakness constitutes an enormous strength.

So the tragic playwright, like the writer of comedy, may encourage in the audience a range of possible responses. The emphasis may fall on the horrors of the human situation, or on the hero's inspiring reaction to those horrors. Just as comic characters may be simultaneously foolish and delightful, tragic figures may be both monstrous and admirable. And just as comedy is both ridiculous and reassuring, tragedy is dispiriting and uplifting at the same time.

Attention to the tragic protagonist should not lead us to neglect the political implications of tragedy. Recent critics particularly urge that we redirect our attention to the local and ideological resonances that plays such as *Hamlet* and *Macbeth* must have had in England at the turn of the seventeenth century. For contemporary audiences, tragedy was inevitably political, a representation of the actions of monarchs and a study — however guarded — of the problem of good government. Many of the crucial issues of Shakespeare's day were represented in the stories he elected to dramatize in his tragic phase between 1599 and 1608: succession and regicide (*Hamlet* and *Macbeth*), political division and monarchical irresponsibility (*King Lear*), pride and absolutism (*Julius Caesar* and *Coriolanus*), financial folly (*Timon of Athens*), political conspiracy (*Julius Caesar* and *Macbeth*), the conflict of personal desire and political responsibility (*Antony and Cleopatra*). Such topically relevant issues have frequently been acknowledged, with critics arguing variously that the tragedies represented either barely veiled critiques of contemporary political practices (*Coriolanus*) or endorsements of contemporary orthodoxy (*Macbeth*).

Responses to *Macbeth* pointedly illustrate the course of recent political criticism. The play has long been regarded as a fictional defense of Jacobean ideology, especially given the notoriety of the Gunpowder Plot, an attempt to assassinate the king on a royal visit to open Parliament in November of 1605. At that time, the King's Men were performing frequently at court, James's preference for short plays was well known, and the Stuarts' legendary lineal connection to Banquo was a familiar tenet of royal mythology. But such an interpretation assumes authorial intention, and many poststructuralist critics have shifted from a focus on a playwright and his hero to a culturally founded understanding of dramatic writing. Materialist critics contend that the term *tragedy,* in the traditional sense, is an "honorific" means of mystifying Shakespeare's plays and promoting an old-fashioned conception of moral action and human freedom that ignores the ideological implications of all texts. Instead, these critics assert, plays like *Macbeth* should be read "dissidently," "against the grain," as exposures — whether intentional or not is incidental — of the apparatus of power in the Jacobean state. One of the best-known exponents of the critical school known as cultural materialism, Alan Sinfield, offers a passionate statement of this view:

> It is often said that *Macbeth* is about "evil," but we might draw a more careful distinction: between the violence the state considers legitimate and that which it does not. Macbeth, we may agree, is a dreadful murderer when he kills Duncan. But when he kills Macdonwald — "a rebel" (1.2.10) — he has Duncan's approval. . . .
>
> Violence is good, in this view, when it is in the service of the prevailing dispositions of power; when it disrupts them, it is evil. A claim to a monopoly of legitimate violence is fundamental in the development of the modern state; when that claim is successful, most citizens learn to regard state violence as qualitatively different from other violence, and perhaps they don't think of state violence as violence at all (consider the actions of police, army, and judiciary as opposed to those of pickets, protesters, criminals, and terrorists). *Macbeth* focuses major strategies by which the state asserted its claim at one conjuncture.   (95)

The focus of political criticism has also been redirected. Sinfield and other critics, particularly feminist writers such as Janet Adelman and Lynda Boose, read the tragedies as exposures of misogynist and racist ideology. *Macbeth* and *Coriolanus* may be seen as critiques of the savagery and repression that constituted early modern constructions of masculinity, *Othello* and *Antony and Cleopatra* as documents of the tendency of Western societies to distance and finally to destroy what they perceive as threats from blacks, women, and other such manifestations of the "other."

However we read the tragedies, as the stories of great individuals or critiques of social practice, two matters need clearing up — or at least bringing up, since they've proved resistant to repeated efforts to clarify and put them in perspective. The first is the doctrine of the *tragic flaw*, the second the effect known as *catharsis*, and both are part of the critical tradition descending from Aristotle's discussion of tragedy in the *Poetics*. As numerous scholars have pointed out, the notion of a flaw actually represents a mistranslation of the Greek *hamartia*, a term more properly understood as an error in action rather than as a fatal weakness of character. To think of the tragic hero as afflicted with a "fatal flaw" is to simplify and misunderstand the complex problem of the tragic protagonist and the society with which he or she is in conflict. (In fact, the very simplicity of the idea helps to account for its popularity.) To say that all tragic figures are flawed to a greater or lesser extent is not to make much progress in distinguishing them from other dramatic characters in tragedy and comedy, or in life for that matter. Defining the tragic figure mainly in terms of a flaw makes it too easy for us to pigeonhole the experience of a complicated character and thus insulates us from complicity in that character's responsibility or guilt. Once again, the appropriate word is *paradox*, a radical form of irony. Tragic drama presents its audience with a spectacle in which heroic men and women are destroyed by their own capable hands, victims of the very traits that set them apart from the rest of us.

Hamlet is frequently described as flawed by an inability to make up his mind, but the term *procrastination* does not do justice to the experience that *Hamlet* represents. The Prince of Denmark is a seeker of truth, a subtle thinker who wants to know the facts and then to act rightly on the basis of what he knows. The play represents the collision between the hero's admirable aim and the traps and obstacles that the world places in his way. Hamlet's hesitation may derive from a laudable moral repugnance at undertaking the role of the avenging son, and in any case it seems right that he should proceed cautiously. But his idealism carries a tragically high price — the death of Polonius, the suffering and suicide of Ophelia, and the entrapment of the hero in the very world he has set out to oppose. Nor does the term *ambition* capture the complexity of tragic experience explored in *Macbeth*, although the relative simplicity and emotional directness of the Scottish play have led thousands of students to approach it in that way. Ambition is only one facet of Macbeth's persona, and it becomes comprehensible only when seen in relation to his other dominant characteristics, particularly his superhuman courage and his irrepressible moral sensitivity. That Shakespeare is not concerned chiefly with ambition is indicated by the placement of Duncan's murder: it occurs very early, at the beginning of the second act. The audience is invited to concentrate instead on the *consequences* of killing the king, on those horrible feelings and events that result from, or, as the etymology of *con-sequences* suggests, "follow with," the act of murder.

The tragic flaw is a problem because it is misleading; the trouble with catharsis is that it is nebulous. According to Aristotle, tragedy "effects through pity and fear the purgation of these emotions." Things seem clear enough until we come to that last phrase, "the purgation of these emotions." Most audiences have no trouble feeling pity for the experience of a character like King Lear, and the spectacle of tragic waste and misery is a fearsome thing. But commentators on the *Poetics* have debated at length the question of purgation. A modern authority on the treatise, Stephen Halliwell, believes that Aristotle proposed the idea of catharsis as a defense of the theater, a counterargument to the Platonic distrust of poetry and drama. Plato feared that the theatrical experience threatened the audience, and implicitly society at large, by stimulating and releasing in the spectator dangerous feelings that ought to be kept under control. Aristotle, on the other hand, saw tragedy as a channel for containing such emotions.

According to Halliwell, catharsis should be understood "as a powerful emotional experience which not only gives our natural feelings of pity and fear full play, but does so in a way which conduces to their rightful functioning as part of our understanding of, and response to, events in the human world" (90). Such an emotional experience entails the spectator's recognition that no one is exempt from the suffering represented in tragedy. In the Aristotelian view, "the heart of tragedy" resides "in the poetic demonstration of ways in which suffering is entangled in even the finest strivings of human action" (Halliwell 91–92), and the normal response to such a demonstration is pity and fear. This conception of catharsis returns us, then, to the tragic paradox, in which the hero's gifts are also the cause of his or her fall. Both the idea of *hamartia* and the problem of catharsis are still much discussed in analysis of tragedy, probably too much so. It is worth pointing out that a philosopher's reflections on the emotional effect of Greek tragedy may be of limited relevance to a sixteenth-century English audience's experience of Shakespeare's efforts in that form, and also to our own.

The inevitable tendency to invoke Aristotelian theory probably reflects our desire to comprehend and define as precisely as possible the effect of tragedy, and probably we should resist that impulse. Such definitions are rarely satisfactory. Elizabethan literary critics conceived of tragedy in didactic terms, seeing it as a warning against the dangers of tyranny, usurpation, and political unrest. But Shakespeare, following the lead of his immediate predecessor Christopher Marlowe, extended the possibilities of the form far beyond those narrow limits. Most significantly, he complicated the psychological dimension of the central character and the audience's sense of relation to that character. Shakespeare encourages a simultaneous engagement and detachment that make every tragedy different from every other, every performance of *Hamlet* or *Macbeth* different from every other, and every spectator's response different from every other. Each performance impresses each spectator with varying degrees of sympathy, judgment, identification, distance, pity, and fear. Rather than seeking to make Shakespeare's practice conform to an ancient theory, we should devote our energies to clarifying and articulating our own mixed reactions.

History

Shakespeare's history plays probably offer the greatest challenge to the modern reader and spectator because they are less familiar than comedy and tragedy. It may help us to know that the chronicle play or history was also less familiar to Shakespeare and his audiences than comedy and tragedy because it was being invented at the very moment that Shakespeare began working in the form. The great classical tragedies with which the Renaissance was familiar tended to focus on the experience of a heroic figure, not a series of historical events. The more influential model for Shakespeare's histories was the English political-morality play, in which the subject was tyranny or insurrection and the emphasis given to the health of the body politic; such plays included John Bale's *King Johan* (c. 1530) and Thomas Sackville and Thomas Norton's *Gorboduc* (c. 1562). Thus Shakespeare's history plays were to some extent dramatic experiments, narrative plays whose dramatic kind and emotional impact, positive or negative, depended somewhat on the historical episode being staged. And even when the requisite moral response was unambiguous, the play itself was almost always a hybrid, a combination of comic and tragic effects. To a great extent, Shakespeare was making it up as he went along.

Richard III is a good indicator of this formal indeterminacy. Technically, the play is a tragedy: it is so advertised on the title page of the First Quarto and in the Folio (see p. 105). And it is tragic, particularly in the medieval sense, portraying as it does a fall from a high position brought about by the tragic figure's own errors or crimes. To many members of a Tudor audience, however, the ending of *Richard III* would have been an occasion for rejoicing: the deformed tyrant is defeated at the battle of Bosworth Field by the earl of Richmond, the future Henry VII and grandfather of Queen Elizabeth. As the conqueror puts it, "The day is ours, the bloody dog is dead" (5.5.2). The play's effect is further complicated by the fact that Richard's murderous schemes for attaining the crown are drawn from the bag of tricks usually associated with comedy, and Shakespeare's clever dramatic structure seduces the audience into sharing Richard's confidences and participating in his plots. At the same time, the deeds that constitute the plot are appalling: for all the verve and glee with which he carries out his schemes, Richard is a criminal. The play's final effect is mixed. Morally and intellectually, spectators are led to applaud the victory of Richmond and the punishment of Richard; theatrically, they lament the death of Richard, against whose histrionic talent Richmond hasn't a chance.

This mixture of comic and tragic stories and of perceptions about those stories also characterizes the group of plays known as the Great (or Second) Tetralogy, which includes *Richard II; Henry IV, Part 1; Henry IV, Part 2;* and *Henry V.* Modern critics see these plays as a group, and some refer to them as "The Henriad." While no one can prove that Shakespeare initially conceived of them as a cycle, it seems clear that by the time he started writing *Henry IV, Part 2,* he had begun to perceive the shape of an epic story beginning with Bullingbrook's usurpation of the throne in *Richard II* and ending with his son's victory at the battle of Agincourt. This cycle comprises several potentially tragic and comic actions. The fate of Richard II is tragic in the loose sense of a fall from a high place, but it qualifies in a more sophisticated sense of the term as well, in that Richard's faith in his divinely sanctioned privilege is what leads him to undo himself. Moreover, the epiphany he experiences in the prison cell just before his assassination adds a heroic dimension to a character who may until this point have seemed a fool. Similarly, the difficulty of distinguishing naiveté from heroism appears with particular force in the portrayal of Harry Percy — Hotspur — the rival of the Prince of Wales in *Henry IV, Part 1.* Hotspur's absolute commitment to honor leads him to act recklessly in challenging the king but also to misread the significance of his diminished forces. Like the tragic figures of whom he is an early version, the young rebel enacts a story of wasted talent.

The clearest case of squandered ability is that of Sir John Falstaff, whose experience strikes audiences as alternately comic and tragic. In *Henry IV, Part 1,* Falstaff seems to be the irresistible comic figure who can't be kept down or shaken off. Descended from the Roman stock character known as the *miles gloriosus* (the braggart soldier), Falstaff is the play's clown, the childish drunkard blessed with divine immunity. At the end of the battle of Shrewsbury, Prince Hal stands over the inert and apparently deceased figures of Hotspur and Falstaff, but as soon as Hal exits, Falstaff rises to declare his unreadiness to die. In *Henry IV, Part 2*, Falstaff exhibits many of the same conventionally comic traits, but his ending is prototragic. Although Shakespeare postpones his death until *Henry V*, where the Hostess describes it in a memorable passage, Falstaff truly is finished at the end of *Part 2* when the Prince banishes him. The old fool is vanquished largely by excessive faith in his own wit, charm, and verbal skill.

The entire tetralogy may be regarded as an enormous comedy weighted with intense tragic insights. Looked at from one perspective, the cycle presents the success story of the Prince of Wales, who expiates his father's crime, leads his country to victory at Agincourt, and, in the archetypal comic conclusion, marries the princess of France. But this positive interpretation requires that a great deal be suppressed — the human cost of Bullingbrook's usurpation, particularly the death of Richard and the ensuing civil war; Prince John's lying to the rebels at Gaultree Forest, one of many instances of verbal deception; Hal's apparently heartless rejection of Falstaff; the self-serving motives with which the church promotes and justifies Henry's invasion of France; and the slaughter of the French prisoners. After the joyous spectacle that concludes *Henry V*, the audience hears an epilogue in which these harmonies are contradicted by a glimpse into the near future. Speaking of Henry as the "star of England," the Chorus summarizes and prophesies:

> Fortune made his sword;
> By which the world's best garden he achieved,
> And of it left his son imperial lord.
> Henry the Sixt, in infant bands crown'd King
> Of France and England, did this king succeed;
> Whose state so many had the managing,
> That they lost France, and made his England bleed.   (Epilogue 6–12)

This tension between achievement and failure, promise and disappointment, although it influences our responses to all four plays, is especially keen in *Henry V*, where interpretive incompatibility is built into our experience of the play. Norman Rabkin, in a brilliant essay called "Rabbits, Ducks, and *Henry V*," argues that the play is like an inkblot: we can see either a rabbit or a duck, but never both at the same time (33–62). At one moment Henry V appears to be the model of a Christian king whose victory and marriage are grounds for celebration and approval. At the same time he seems the model of a Machiavellian self-server who banishes his former friends, unjustifiably invades France, breaks his word to his own men, and ignominiously slaughters the French prisoners. History is difficult to read.

One of the most beguiling scenes in *Henry IV, Part 2*, is the meeting of Falstaff and Justice Shallow in the latter's orchard in Gloucestershire, where the two old men reflect on their younger days and lament the passing of time and the loss of many of their old chums. If spectators are touched by the ancient Justice Shallow's memories of his hell-raising days as a law student, they may be shocked when, as the old man leaves the stage, Falstaff confides in them:

I do see the bottom of Justice Shallow. Lord, Lord, how subject we old men are to this vice of lying! This same starv'd justice hath done nothing but prate to me of the wildness of his youth, and the feats he hath done about Turnbull Street, and every third word a lie. . . . And now is this Vice's dagger become a squire, and talks as familiarly of John a' Gaunt as if he had been sworn brother to him, and I'll be sworn 'a ne'er saw him but once in the Tilt-yard, and then he burst his head for crowding among the marshal's men. I saw it, and told John a' Gaunt he beat his own name, for you might have thrust him and all his apparel into an eelskin.

(3.2.302–07; 319–26)

Shakespeare uses the reminiscence and the commentary on it to introduce doubts about the truth of memory and thus about the reliability of history, the very form in which he himself is working and that the audience is watching. All that has amused and touched us, according to Falstaff, has been a fiction, but that qualifier, "according to Falstaff," is a crucial part of the problem. For after ridiculing Justice Shallow for name-dropping about John of Gaunt, Falstaff drops the name of John of Gaunt. Whose version is accurate? And, implicitly, whose version of the story of the House of Lancaster is reliable?

It depends, of course, on who is telling the story. The Great Tetralogy, compared to the First, exhibits an increased consciousness of the mediated and conditional nature of all historical writing, and this axiom has exerted a strong influence on recent critics. The parallel phrases now used to describe this perception are "the textuality of history" and "the historicity of texts." The "textuality of history" suggests that history can be represented only in texts, that we know what happened in the fourteenth and fifteenth centuries only by means of written records, and that such verbal documents are subject to the limitations and complexity of language. Likewise, the "historicity of texts" asserts that all written language (whether plays or letters or textbooks) is inextricably rooted in its own time and culture, and that comprehension of any historical writing requires an awareness of the milieu that produced it. The emergence of these ideas has significantly affected critical response to Shakespeare's history plays. In the first half of the twentieth century, the prevailing view, expressed most emphatically by E. M. W. Tillyard in his *Shakespeare's History Plays*, was that the history plays reflected an ordered conception of the universe to which virtually everyone in the culture subscribed. Shakespeare was an orthodox writer, and that was as it should be. Recent critics, among them Stephen Greenblatt and other subscribers to the school of criticism known as new historicism, or cultural poetics, have dissented, arguing that Shakespeare's plays did not merely reflect the hierarchical and oppressive views of his place and time, but that they actually helped to produce and sustain the dominant political theory. In other words, these critics see the plays not merely as effects of ideology but as creators of it.

There are modern and postmodern variations on all of these cultural readings. Some believe that the histories, like the later tragedies, were intentionally subversive of Tudor orthodoxy; others, that they were unconsciously so. Greenblatt and other new historicists hold that the histories served the Crown as an outlet for subversive doctrine, as a container of rebellious impulses that might have erupted in the streets had they not been released and defused within the confines of the public theaters. It is indisputable that the Tudor and Stuart regimes were aware of — and wary of — the power of historical theater to influence political feeling. In February 1601 the Lord Chamberlain's Men were paid by supporters of the earl of Essex to stage a performance of Shakespeare's *Richard II*, the play in which a strong and popular leader deposes an increasingly unpopular and ineffectual monarch. The rebellion failed, a member of the company was summoned to explain its presentation of the play (see excerpt on p. 140), and Elizabeth herself was apparently conscious of the performance and its significance, as her comments to William Lambarde indicate (see p. 107). What all this suggests is that history plays are no less complex than comedies and tragedies. The theater has political power, but Shakespeare's histories reveal the difficulty of attempting to determine and control the nature of that power.

Romance

At the end of his career Shakespeare experimented with a new dramatic mode that we call romance. His efforts in this form include *Pericles, Cymbeline, The Winter's Tale,* and *The Tempest,* as well as the two collaborations written at the very end of his career with John Fletcher, *The Two Noble Kinsmen* and probably *Cardenio.* Never one to be bound by the Roman models to which some of his contemporaries were faithful, Shakespeare was by this time uncommonly adventurous in combining kinds and adapting into drama the various tales and narratives that appealed to him. Many of his contemporaries were adventurous too, for by about 1608 the London stages offered audiences a range of choice: historical tragedy, domestic tragedy, imitations of classical tragedy, romantic comedy, city comedy, satire, prodigal-son plays, apprentice-makes-good stories, chronicle plays, and tragicomedy. Francis Beaumont and John Fletcher, writing under the influence of Continental models, were gaining attention for their development of English tragicomedy in plays such as *Philaster* and *A King and No King.* Shakespeare's last plays most resemble this kind of tragicomedy, which, as Fletcher's description makes clear (see p. 107), threatens its audience with disaster or death and abruptly changes gears so that the action comes to a happy ending.

The romance form is difficult to define, particularly because it has appeared and reappeared repeatedly in the history of literature. I do not wish to suggest that romance — or any of the modes I have discussed — is a transhistorical category that works the same across all cultures and all periods. But there is something familiar about romance, as Howard Felperin points out: "To the extent that all literary experience involves a journey into another world inherently removed from present time and place, all literature is fundamentally romantic" (*Shakespearean Romance* 7). Romance seems to exhibit many of the same properties in its various manifestations, whether in the mode of Greek romance, from which much Renaissance literature derives; or in medieval quest romance, such as Sir Thomas Malory's *Morte d'Arthur;* in Edmund Spenser's epic poem *The Faerie Queene;* in its later appearance among the nineteenth-century poets we know as the Romantics; and in modern cinematic versions, such as the Western or the space epic. A touchstone for the formal and tonal properties we are concerned with is George Lucas's *Star Wars,* with its otherworldly locations, youthful hero, displaced princess, battles between the agents of good and evil, and supernatural Force. The most productive approach to Shakespearean romance is to offer a series of descriptions, none comprehensive but each contributing a partial explanation of the effect or shape of the form.

As a distinctive kind of comedy, romance arrives at a happy ending by an unusually perilous route. As our sense of the term implies, the action usually involves amorous desire and fulfillment, but the essential characteristic of fictional romance is an adventure story. Etymologically the word derives from the same root that gives us both the French and German words for "novel," *roman.* The main characters must endure a series of hazards and trials that lead ultimately to success and reward. The form is given to extremes, for the ending is not only happy but joyous, even revelatory, and the progression to that ending is much more arduous than in traditional comedy. In other words, the fundamentally comic shape of the action is darkly colored by tragic concerns and perceptions: the marriage or reunion that ends the play is preceded in the middle by some form of catastrophe, either death or some similarly grave loss.

These tonal oppositions of inexpressible despair and joy are matched by other extremes. *Pericles,* for example, opens with a riddle that the hero must solve for King Antiochus; the answer reveals the king's incest with his daughter. A wide geographical range is employed as well. Pericles travels throughout the Mediterranean; *Cymbeline* takes place in ancient Britain, ancient Rome, and the wilds of Wales; and *The Tempest* is set on a magical island. Often temporal limits are ignored: *The Winter's Tale* covers a period of sixteen years. At the conclusion of the hero's trials, magic or the supernatural contributes to the ending, often creating a sense of miracle. The vaguely providential force that, in the earlier comedies, seems to safeguard the characters and bring about a happy resolution is here specifically identified with divine protection, and in several of the plays this immortal force is theatrically incarnated, as in Jupiter's appearance in a dream at the end of *Cymbeline* or Diana's in *Pericles.* Such instances of theophany, or the appearance of a god or goddess, attest to the religious affinities of Shakespearean romance.

The cardinal feature of the form, the key to its emotional power, is the gap between the desperate middle and the joyful ending. Characters in these plays are able to recover what seemed irretrievably lost, what they themselves have foolishly attempted to destroy: penitent husbands find themselves reunited with wives they wished dead; lost children are restored to their parents; impossible wishes are granted. It has often been pointed out that the *Odyssey* is the first romance, an adventure story that is also a love story, and one that delays the pleasure of Ulysses' homecoming for twenty years by taking him all over the known world (not to mention a visit to the underworld). And it is this wandering that makes the poem; that's what it's about. So with Shakespeare's romances. Although we look forward to the endings, the playwright spends most of his time not ending the play and then, when he finally does so, surprising us. So crucial is this incongruity that we might say that Shakespeare makes his romances *about* endings, playing self-consciously on the audience's desire for a happy outcome. These are fantasy plays that stimulate, frustrate, and fulfill our fantasies of resolution, but above all they force us to examine and evaluate our need for satisfactory closure. At the end of *Cymbeline*, the sleeping hero dreams that Jupiter descends from above and explains to his family why their son has had to endure such misery: "Whom best I love, I cross; to make my gift, / The more delay'd, delighted" (5.4.101–02). The god insists that waiting for fulfillment intensifies the emotion, that the more difficult the trial, the more satisfying the victory.

But Jupiter appears in a character's dream, distanced from the audience and even from the reality of the play-world. In other words, the deity's appearance is a form of illusion occurring within a play that is itself an illusion. This dramatic tactic confirms the principle that the choice of a mode implies particular meanings about the world and the human experience of it. By turning at the end of his career to stories of fantasy and magic, Shakespeare has committed himself not only to the power of the imaginary, but also to the value of fiction in general. This turn to romance is especially revealing because the tragedies seem obsessed with the perils and deceits of illusion. The apparitions of the deceptive witches in *Macbeth*, the fatal trickery of Iago's performance in *Othello*, or the lies of the elder daughters in *King Lear* — all these betray Shakespeare's mistrust of theatricality and perhaps even doubt about his own profession. As Anne Righter puts it in discussing the "Tomorrow and tomorrow and tomorrow" speech, "The final attitude of Macbeth, the passionate reduction of all human endeavour to the meaningless posturing of a player on a darkening stage, is scarcely flattering to the theatre. Such an image expresses not only the hollowness of life, but also the degradation and stupidity of the actor's profession" (169). Shakespeare's late interest in romance suggests a reversal in his thinking; his professional doubts, if not dismissed, appear to have been at least allayed.

Thus in the last plays the instances of spectacle tend to be affirmative rather than threatening, a point best demonstrated in the powerful last scene of *The Winter's Tale*. Hermione, dead, or apparently dead, for sixteen years, has been memorialized in a statue, and as her penitent husband, the one responsible for her death, stands before it, the statue comes to life. This spectacular moment could be terrifying: as Paulina puts it, ". . . you'll think / (Which I protest against) I am assisted / By wicked powers" (5.3.89–91). But instead of a demonic show, Paulina presents her audiences, both onstage and in the theater, with what amounts to a miracle. The appropriate response is spiritual wonder at an act of grace. As Paulina also says, "It is requir'd / You do awake your faith" (5.3.94–95). A statue, a work of art, an imitation of life, suddenly becomes "real," a miracle that occurs in a play that is itself an imitation of life, a fiction in which imaginary persons come to life for the pleasure of a credulous audience. Shakespeare prizes the indistinguishability of the illusory and the actual. The artificiality of all experience, with Providence as the artist, the divine play-wright, is the great theme of Shakespeare's last phase. Here it would be fitting to cite Prospero's famous "Revels" speech from the fourth act of *The Tempest* about the unreality of the whole world; instead, I shall quote a much more contemporary instance of the same perception, from Cormac McCarthy's novel *The Crossing* (1994): "For this world also which seems to us to sing of stone and flower and blood is not a thing at all but is a tale. And all in it is a tale and each tale the sum of all lesser tales and yet these also are the selfsame tale and contain as well all else within them" (143).

Mixed Modes

A great many of Shakespeare's plays transgress the formal boundaries described in this chapter and are therefore difficult to classify. In certain come-dies, particularly those written after his initial efforts at farcical and romantic comedy, the ironies can become so bitter and the obstacles to joyful closure so formidable that the work may seem nearer to tragedy than to its comic sib-lings. *The Merchant of Venice* is probably the most illustrative example of the high cost of comic resolution. The lovers' gathering at Belmont in act 5, musi-cal and joyous though it may be, is overshadowed by their intolerable treat-ment of Shylock in the trial scene (4.1). The movement toward assimilation that normally unites the cast in the last moments is not strong enough to include Shylock, who is stripped of his wealth, his daughter, and his religion and who leaves the stage for the last time in act 4. Although the merchant Antonio is present for the festivities in the last act, he has no partner and must go home alone. *Twelfth Night* closes with a similar if less extreme case of rejec-tion, when Malvolio refuses the Countess's offer of reconciliation and storms off the stage vowing revenge. A few moments later, another Antonio, clearly infatuated with his friend Sebastian, is left alone as the pairs of lovers exit together. Virtually all comedy rejects or neglects someone — a father who won't agree to a marriage, or a malcontent family member like Don John in *Much Ado about Nothing* — but most of the time the audience sanctions this exclusion of the uncooperative individual in the interests of community. Such characters do appear in the early plays, but as his comedies become more tonally complicated, Shakespeare contrives to give such people a greater claim on our emotions, to make the rejection more disturbing, and even to endanger the expected comic festivity.

Likewise in tragedy the audience's need to sympathize with the protagonist is often thwarted or made more difficult by an emphasis on the character's weaknesses. Historically, the critical reception of *Othello*, for example, reveals that some readers find the protagonist so hasty and foolish in his suspicions of Desdemona's fidelity that they feel only contempt, a response expressed in one of the early critiques of the play, Thomas Rymer's *A Short View of Tragedy* (see p. 108). When such foolishness is heightened by a director or the actor playing Othello, sympathetic engagement or tragic pity and fear may be pushed aside by scornful laughter. Similarly, in *Antony and Cleopatra,* the Queen of Egypt can be played as a dishonest and manipulative opportunist. Just as comic joy is subject to being compromised or diminished, the potential for antiheroic mockery always lurks beneath the surface of the tragedies. Shakespeare encourages such doubts more readily in some plays than in others, and no matter how subtle the ironic suggestions may be, directors can take those cues and adjust the emotional tone, thus promoting a dramatic experience that Shakespeare himself might not have recognized. Such is the ambiguous nature of human behavior and the vehicles created to depict it.

It should be clear by now that each of Shakespeare's modes is plastic, subject to reshaping by the playwright and reconsideration by critical history, and that almost none of the plays fits neatly into a box that we can label comedy or tragedy. *Twelfth Night,* a play in which almost everyone wants to get married, ends with a song that does not ignore the miseries of marriage: "But when I came, alas, to wive, / With hey ho, the wind and the rain." And the King's Men apparently finished their performances of tragedy with a rousing jig, as was the custom in the early modern playhouses. It may be difficult for us to comprehend a theatrical experience in which *Hamlet* is followed by a jolly dance performed by some of the players who have just expired in the final scene. But Elizabethan audiences were evidently used to such contrarieties, and Shakespeare exploited rather than suppressed them. His own subtle and even contradictory understanding of human experience prompted him to reconstruct and complicate the dramatic forms he inherited, to push the formal boundaries. This remaking of his medium to suit his meaning is probably the most powerful evidence of Shakespeare's artistic originality.

In fact, great playwrights have regularly strained against conventional limits, reconceiving forms in accord with their expressive needs and exploiting the interrelation of dramatic modes. Anton Chekhov wrote *The Cherry Orchard* as a comedy, but Konstantin Stanislavsky, the original director, produced it as a tragedy. Both labels seem apt. Our contemporary playwright Tom Stoppard was alert to the fragility of dramatic modes when he produced an adaptation called *Dogg's Hamlet* that includes almost all Shakespeare's action, takes fifteen minutes to perform, and has the audience rolling in the aisles.

→ SIR PHILIP SIDNEY

From *The Defense of Poesy* *c. 1581*

Sir Philip Sidney's remarks on comedy and tragedy offer one of the fullest analytical descriptions of the state of the two modes in the 1580s. The influence of classical models is apparent. Also notable is Sidney's devotion to the didactic function of comedy and tragedy, particularly their attention to folly and tyranny, respectively, and their power to urge audiences away from engaging in such behavior. The difference between the single tonality suggested in these excerpts and the multivocality of Shakespearean comedy and tragedy arises partly from the rapid development of English drama in the twenty years after the *Defense* was composed.

COMEDY

No, perchance it is the comic, whom naughty play-makers and stage-keepers have justly made odious. To the arguments of abuse I will answer after. Only thus much now is to be said, that the comedy is an imitation of the common errors of our life, which he representeth in the most ridiculous and scornful sort that may be, so as it is impossible that any beholder can be content to be such a one. Now, as in geometry the oblique must be known as well as the right, and in arithmetic the odd as well as the even, so in the actions of our life who seeth not the filthiness of evil wanteth a great foil to perceive the beauty of virtue. This doth the comedy handle so in our private and domestical matters, as with hearing it we get as it were an experience, what is to be looked for of a niggardly Demea, of a crafty Davus, of a flattering Gnatho, of a vainglorious Thraso [conventional characters in Roman comedy]; and not only to know what effects are to be expected, but to know who be such, by the signifying badge given them by the comedian. And little reason hath any man to say that men learn evil by seeing it so set out; since, as I said before, there is no man living but, by the force truth hath in nature, no sooner seeth these men play their parts, but wisheth them in *pistrinum* [flour mill, workhouse]; although perchance the sack of his own faults lie so behind his back that he seeth not himself dance the same measure; whereto yet nothing can more open his eyes than to see his own actions contemptibly set forth.

TRAGEDY

So that the right use of comedy will (I think) by nobody be blamed; and much less of the high and excellent tragedy, that openeth the greatest wounds, and showeth forth the ulcers that are covered with tissue; that maketh kings fear to be tyrants, and tyrants manifest their tyrannical humors; that with stirring the affects of admiration and commiseration teacheth the uncertainty of this world, and upon how weak foundations gilden roofs are builded; that maketh us know,

> Qui sceptra saevus duro imperio regit,
> Timet timentes, metus in auctorem redit.[1]

But how much it can move, Plutarch yieldeth a notable testimony of the abominable tyrant Alexander Pheraeus, from whose eyes a tragedy, well made and represented, drew abundance of tears, who without all pity had murdered infinite numbers, and some of his own blood, so as he that was not ashamed to make matters for tragedies yet could not resist the sweet violence of a tragedy. And if it wrought no further good in him, it was that he, in despite of himself, withdrew himself from hearkening to that which might mollify his hardened heart. But it is not the tragedy they do mislike; for it were too absurd to cast out so excellent a representation of whatsoever is most worthy to be learned.

[1]Seneca, *Oedipus*, 705–06: "The savage tyrant who sways his scepter with a heavy hand fears the subjects that fear him, and fear returns upon its creator."

→ **ELIZABETH CARY**

From *The Tragedy of Mariam, Fair Queen of Jewry*   *1613*

The first play written by a woman and published in England, *The Tragedy of Mariam* laments the restrictions on women's intellectual and religious freedom. It also reveals its author's familiarity with classical drama, specifically the doctrine of the unities. Taking her story from Jewish historical sources, Cary depicts a struggle for power in the court of Herod of Judea, a contest that ends when Herod, misled into executing his virtuous wife Mariam, discovers and mourns his mistake. Here in the Chorus's final speech, a summary of the play's action, Cary recapitulates the Sidneyan view that tragedy "teacheth the uncertainty of this world."

CHORUS:
    Whoever hath beheld with steadfast eye
    The strange events of this one only day;   260
    How many were deceiv'd, how many die,
    That once today did grounds of safety lay!
        It will from them all certainty bereave,
        Since twice six hours so many can deceive [mislead].

    This morning Herod held for surely dead,   265
    And all the Jews on Mariam did attend:
    And Constabarus rise from Salom's bed,
    And neither dream'd of a divorce or end.
        Pheroras joy'd that he might have his wife,
        And Babas' sons for safety of their life.   270

Tonight our Herod doth alive remain,
The guiltless Mariam is depriv'd of breath:
Stout Constabarus both divorc'd and slain,
The valiant sons of Babas have their death,
    Pheroras sure his love to be bereft,   275
    If Salome her suit unmade had left.

Herod this morning did expect with joy,
To see his Mariam's much belovèd face;
And yet ere night he did her life destroy,
And surely thought she did her name disgrace.   280
    Yet now again, so short do humours last,
    He both repents her death and knows her chaste.

Had he with wisdom now her death delay'd,
He at his pleasure might command her death:
But now he hath his power so much betray'd,   285
As all his woes cannot restore her breath.
    Now doth he strangely, lunaticly rave,
    Because his Mariam's life he cannot save.

This day's events were certainly ordain'd,
To be the warning to posterity: 290
So many changes are therein contain'd,
So admirably strange variety.
    This day alone, our sagest Hebrews shall
    In after times the school of wisdom call.

⇥ **ARISTOTLE**

From *Poetics*

fourth century B.C.
Translated by Richard McKeon

Although Aristotle's theory of tragedy was not well known in sixteenth-century England, his philosophical views had entered the culture indirectly through the ideas of humanist commentators. The analysis of tragic drama, excerpted here from a modern translation, has come to be extremely influential in modern treatments of Shakespearean and other forms of tragedy.

Let us proceed now to the discussion of Tragedy; before doing so, however, we must gather up the definition resulting from what has been said. A tragedy, then, is the imitation of an action that is serious and also, as having magnitude, complete in itself; in language with pleasurable accessories, each kind brought in separately in the parts of the work; in a dramatic, not in a narrative form; with incidents arousing pity and fear, wherewith to accomplish its catharsis of such emotions. Here by "language with pleasurable accessories" I mean that with rhythm and harmony or song superadded; and by "the kinds separately" I mean that some portions are worked out with verse only, and others in turn with song.

I. As they act the stories, it follows that in the first place the Spectacle (or stage-appearance of the actors) must be some part of the whole; and in the second Melody and Diction, these two being the means of their imitation. Here by "Diction" I mean merely this, the composition of the verses; and by "Melody," what is too completely understood to require explanation. But further: the subject represented also is an action; and the action involves agents, who must necessarily have their distinctive qualities both of character and thought, since it is from these that we ascribe certain qualities to their actions. There are in the natural order of things, therefore, two causes, Thought and Character, of their actions, and consequently of their success or failure in their lives. Now the action (that which was done) is represented in the play by the Fable or Plot. The Fable, in our present sense of the term, is simply this, the combination of the incidents, or things done in the story; whereas Character is what makes us ascribe certain moral qualities to the agents; and Thought is shown in all they say when proving a particular point or, it may be, enunciating a general truth. There are six parts consequently of every tragedy, as a whole (that is) of such or such quality, viz. a Fable or Plot, Characters, Diction, Thought, Spectacle, and Melody; two of them arising from the means, one from the manner, and three from the objects of the dramatic imitation; and there is nothing else besides these six. Of these, its formative elements, then, not a few of the dramatists have made due use, as every play, one may say, admits of Spectacle, Character, Fable, Diction, Melody, and Thought.

II. The most important of the six is the combination of the incidents of the story. Tragedy is essentially an imitation not of persons but of action and life, of happiness and misery. All human happiness or misery takes the form of action; the end for which we live is a certain kind of activity, not a quality. Character gives us qualities, but it is in our actions — what we do — that we are happy or the reverse. In a play accordingly they do not act in order to portray the Characters; they include the Characters for the sake of the action. So that it is the action in it, i.e., its Fable or Plot, that is the end and purpose of the tragedy; and the end is everywhere the chief thing. Besides this, a tragedy is impossible without action, but there may be one without Character. . . . The first essential, the life and soul, so to speak, of Tragedy is the Plot; and . . . the Characters come second — compare the parallel in painting, where the most beautiful colors laid on without order will not give one the same pleasure as a simple black-and-white sketch of a portrait. We maintain that Tragedy is primarily an imitation of action, and that it is mainly for the sake of the action that it imitates the personal agents. Third comes the element of Thought, i.e., the power of saying whatever can be said, or what is appropriate to the occasion. This is what, in the speeches in Tragedy, falls under the arts of Politics and Rhetoric; for the older poets make their personages discourse like statesmen, and the modern like rhetoricians. One must not confuse it with Character. Character in a play is that which reveals the moral purpose of the agents, i.e., the sort of thing they seek or avoid, where that is not obvious — hence there is no room for Character in a speech on a purely indifferent subject. Thought, on the other hand, is shown in all they say when proving or disproving some particular point, or enunciating some universal proposition. Fourth among the literary elements is the Diction of the personages, i.e., as before explained, the expression of their thoughts in words, which is practically the same thing with verse as with prose. As for the two remaining parts, the Melody is the greatest of the pleasurable accessories of Tragedy. The Spectacle, though an attraction, is the least artistic of all the parts, and has least to do with the art of poetry. The tragic effect is quite possible without a public performance and actors; and besides, the getting-up of the Spectacle is more a matter for the costumer than the poet.

Having thus distinguished the parts, let us now consider the proper construction of the Fable or Plot, as that is at once the first and the most important thing in Tragedy. We have laid it down that a tragedy is an imitation of an action that is complete in itself, as a whole of some magnitude; for a whole may be of no magnitude to speak of. Now a whole is that which has beginning, middle, and end. A beginning is that which is not itself necessarily after anything else, and which has naturally something else after it; an end is that which is naturally after something itself, either as its necessary or usual consequent, and with nothing else after it; and a middle, that which is by nature after one thing and has also another after it. A well-constructed Plot, therefore, cannot either begin or end at any point one likes; beginning and end in it must be of the forms just described. Again: to be beautiful, a living creature, and every whole made up of parts, must not only present a certain order in its arrangement of parts, but also be of a certain definite magnitude. Beauty is a matter of size and order, and therefore impossible either (1) in a very minute creature, since our perception becomes indistinct as it approaches instantaneity; or (2) in a creature of vast size — one, say, 1,000 miles long — as in that case, instead of the object being seen all at once, the unity and wholeness of it is lost to the beholder. Just in the same way, then, as a beautiful whole made up of parts, or a beautiful living creature, must be of some size, but a size to be taken in by the eye, so a story or Plot must be of some length, but of a length to be taken in by the memory. . . .

Tragedy, however, is an imitation not only of a complete action, but also of incidents arousing pity and fear. Such incidents have the very greatest effect on the mind when they occur unexpectedly and at the same time in consequence of one another; there is more of the marvelous in them then than if they happened of themselves or by mere chance. Even matters of chance seem most marvelous if there is an appearance of design as it were in them; as for instance the statue of Mitys at Argos killed the author of Mitys' death by falling down on him when a looker-on at a public spectacle; for incidents like that we think to be not without a meaning. A Plot, therefore, of this sort is necessarily finer than others.

• • •

Plots are either simple or complex, since the actions they represent are naturally of this twofold description. The action, proceeding in the way defined, as one continuous whole, I call simple, when the change in the hero's fortunes takes place without Peripety or Discovery; and complex, when it involves one or the other, or both. These should each of them arise out of the structure of the Plot itself, so as to be the consequence, necessary or probable, of the antecedents. There is a great difference between a thing happening *propter hoc* and *post hoc* ["because of this" and "after this"].

A Peripety is the change of the kind described from one state of things within the play to its opposite, and that too in the way we are saying, in the probable or necessary sequence of events; as it is for instance in *Oedipus:* here the opposite state of things is produced by the Messenger, who, coming to gladden Oedipus and to remove his fears as to his mother, reveals the secret of his birth [*Oedipus the King* 911–1085]. And in *Lynceus* [by Theodectes]: just as he is being led off for execution, with Danaus at his side to put him to death, the incidents preceding this bring it about that he is saved and Danaus put to death. A Discovery is, as the very word implies, a change from ignorance to knowledge, and thus to either love or hate, in the personages marked for good or evil fortune. The finest form of Discovery is one attended by Peripeties, like that which goes with the Discovery in *Oedipus*. There are no doubt other forms of it; what we have said may happen in a way in reference to inanimate things, even things of a very casual kind; and it is also possible to discover whether someone has done or not done something. But the form most directly connected with the Plot and the action of the piece is the first-mentioned. This, with a Peripety, will arouse either pity or fear — actions of that nature being what Tragedy is assumed to represent; and it will also serve to bring about the happy or unhappy ending. The Discovery, then, being of persons, it may be that of one party only to the other, the latter being already known; or both the parties may have to discover themselves. Iphigenia, for instance, was discovered to Orestes by sending the letter [*Iphigenia in Tauris* 727ff.]; and another Discovery was required to reveal him to Iphigenia.

Two parts of the Plot, then, Peripety and Discovery, are on matters of this sort. A third part is Suffering; which we may define as an action of a destructive or painful nature, such as murders on the stage, tortures, woundings, and the like. The other two have been already explained. . . .

The next points after what we have said above will be these: (1) What is the poet to aim at, and what is he to avoid, in constructing his Plots? and (2) What are the conditions on which the tragic effect depends?

We assume that, for the finest form of Tragedy, the Plot must be not simple but complex; and further, that it must imitate actions arousing fear and pity, since that is the distinctive function of this kind of imitation. It follows, therefore, that there are three forms of Plot to be avoided. (1) A good man must not be seen passing from happiness to misery, or (2) a bad man from misery to happiness. The first situation is not fear-inspiring or piteous, but simply odious to us. The second is the most untragic that can be; it has no one of the requisites of Tragedy; it does not appeal either to the human feeling in us, or to our pity, or to our fears. Nor, on the other hand, should (3) an extremely bad man be seen falling from happiness into misery. Such a story may arouse the human feeling in us, but it will not move us to either pity or fear; pity is occasioned by undeserved misfortune, and fear by that of one like ourselves; so that there will be nothing either piteous or fear-inspiring in the situation. There remains, then, the intermediate kind of personage, a man not preeminently virtuous and just, whose misfortune, however, is brought upon him not by vice and depravity but by some error of judgment, of the number of those in the enjoyment of great reputation and prosperity — e.g., Oedipus, Thyestes, and the men of note of similar families. The perfect Plot, accordingly, must have a single, and not (as some tell us) a double issue; the change in the hero's fortunes must be not from misery to happiness, but on the contrary from happiness to misery; and the cause of it must lie not in any depravity, but in some great error on his part; the man himself being either such as we have described, or better, not worse, than that. . . .

The tragic fear and pity may be aroused by the Spectacle; but they may also be aroused by the very structure and incidents of the play   which is the better way and shows the better poet. The Plot in fact should be so framed that, even without seeing the things take place, he who simply hears the account of them shall be filled with horror and pity at the incidents — which is just the effect that the mere recital of the story in *Oedipus* would have on one. To produce this same effect by means of the Spectacle is less artistic, and requires extraneous aid. Those, however, who make use of the Spectacle to put before us that which is merely monstrous and not productive of fear, are wholly out of touch with Tragedy; not every kind of pleasure should be required of a tragedy, but only its own proper pleasure.

✦ Title Page of *Richard III*   *1597* ➤

First Quarto

The title page pictured here (slightly reduced) indicates the problem of classifying early modern plays. What modern scholars call a history play was described to prospective buyers as a "tragedy." Early modern distinctions among dramatic modes were considerably less rigid than our own. One of the earliest of Shakespeare's plays to see print, *Richard III* was also one of the most popular; it was published seven times between 1597 and 1623.

THE TRAGEDY OF
King Richard the third.

Containing,
His treacherous Plots against his brother Clarence:
the pittiefull murther of his innocent nephewes:
his tyrannicall vsurpation: with the whole course
of his detested life, and most deserued death.

As it hath beene lately Acted by the
Right honourable the Lord Chamber-
laine his seruants.

AT LONDON
Printed by Valentine Sims, for Andrew Wise,
dwelling in Paules Chuch-yard, at the
Signe of the Angell.
1597.

→ WILLIAM LAMBARDE

From His Notes of a Conversation with
Queen Elizabeth I about *Richard II*   *1601*

William Lambarde, Queen Elizabeth's keeper of the records in the tower, recorded notes on his conversation with the queen in August 1601. The reference to Shakespeare's play concerns the earl of Essex's rebellion against Elizabeth, in preparation for which some of his supporters commissioned a performance of *Richard II*. The desired effect of such a performance would have been to figure Essex as the capable Bullingbrook and Elizabeth as the unfit Richard.

Her Majestie fell upon the reign of King Richard II, saying, "I am Richard II. Know ye not that?"

W. L.: "Such a wicked imagination was determined and attempted by a most unkind Gent [leman] the most adorned creature that ever your Majestie made."

HER MAJESTIE: "He that will forget God, will also forget his benefactor; this tragedy was played 40tie times in open streets and houses."

→ JOHN FLETCHER

From His Preface to *The Faithful Shepherdess*   *1608*

Shakespeare's occasional collaborator and successor as principal dramatist of the King's Men, John Fletcher helped to popularize the new Continental form of tragicomedy in England. This promotional description, from his prefatory remarks ("To the Reader") to his play *The Faithful Shepherdess* (1608), exhibits the influence of the Italian dramatist Giovanni Battista Guarini, whose tragicomedy *Il Pastor Fido* (The Faithful Shepherd) had received considerable attention. Along with one of his other collaborators, Francis Beaumont, Fletcher may have helped to shape the last phase of Shakespeare's career by developing the new form.

A tragicomedy is not so called in respect of mirth and killing, but in respect it wants deaths, which is enough to make it no tragedy, yet brings some near it, which is enough to make it no comedy: which must be a representation of familiar people, with such kind of trouble as no life be questioned, so that a God is as lawful in this as in a tragedy, and mean [lowly] people as in a comedy.

➜ THOMAS RYMER

From *A Short View of Tragedy* 1693

Thomas Rymer's *A Short View of Tragedy* offers a contemptuous dismissal of *Othello* and typifies a frequent neoclassical reaction to Shakespeare's innovations in the tragic mode. Although the nineteenth-century essayist Thomas Babington Macaulay referred to Rymer as "the worst critic that ever lived," his narrow views of *Othello* have often been repeated, if more delicately, in modern criticism of the play.

THE FABLE

Othello, a blackamoor captain, by talking of his prowess and feats of war, makes Desdemona, a senator's daughter, to be in love with him, and to be married to him without her parents' knowledge. And having preferred Cassio to be his lieutenant (a place which his ensign, Iago, sued for), Iago in revenge works the Moor into a jealousy that Cassio cuckolds him, which he effects by stealing and conveying a certain handkerchief which had, at the wedding, been by the Moor presented to his bride. Hereupon, Othello and Iago plot the deaths of Desdemona and Cassio; Othello murders her, and soon after is convinced of her innocence. And as he is about to be carried to prison, in order to be punished for the murder, he kills himself.

Whatever rubs or difficulty may stick on the bark, the moral, sure, of this fable is very instructive.

1. First, this may be a caution to all maidens of quality how, without their parents' consent, they run away with blackamoors. . . .

Secondly, this may be a warning to all good wives, that they look well to their linen.

Thirdly, this may be a lesson to husbands, that before their jealousy be tragical, the proofs may be mathematical.

CHAPTER 4

Performances, Playhouses, and Players

><

Going to a Play, Circa 1595

Let us imagine ourselves transported back to the London of Queen Eliza
beth, where we are attending the first performance of *Romeo and Juliet*. The
date is sometime in 1595 or 1596, probably in the autumn or summer, just
before two o'clock in the afternoon. We are seated on benches in a gallery of
the Theatre, one of the first permanent structures built for drama in England;
constructed in 1576 by James Burbage, it is located just north of the walls of the
City of London in a district called Shoreditch. The Curtain, another public
theater that stands nearby, was built a year later. We are not attending the
Globe because it has not yet been built. (All of these playhouses are indicated
on the map printed on p. 127.) Today's play was written by William Shakespeare, a poet (as dramatists are known) who has made his name with a series
of comedies (*The Comedy of Errors* and *Love's Labor's Lost* being two of his successes) and history plays based on the Wars of the Roses. The company
preparing to perform, resident at the Theatre, is known as the Lord Chamberlain's Men, a group of players who left other companies in 1594 to join under
the patronage of Henry Carey, Lord Hunsdon, and has rapidly become the most
successful troupe in England. William Shakespeare is a permanent member of
this company, a shareholder, as is its leading actor, Richard Burbage, son of the
carpenter-entrepreneur who built the Theatre. Musicians are warming up,
actors are rushing around in the *tiring-house* ("attiring house," or dressing room)
behind the stage, refreshments are being sold in the playhouse by vendors
who move among the crowd, and spectators — having paid their admission in
cash to *gatherers*, the early modern equivalent of ticket takers or ushers — are

filling the seats in the galleries or standing in the yard in front of the platform or stage. (Laurence Olivier's 1944 film version of *Henry V* opens with a visual reconstruction of this preperformance activity; *Shakespeare in Love* [1998] also gives a fair idea — except for the secret presence of the Queen — of what it might have been like to attend a performance in an Elizabethan amphitheater.)

Once the play has begun, we quickly notice that some of the conventions and performance practices common in the Elizabethan theater differ markedly from our own. To begin with, the stage is bare, without pictorial scenery; there is no souvenir program to introduce the characters; we must deduce such information as setting and time from the dialogue. The Prologue informs us that the play will last about two hours and that the action will occur in Verona. When the characters Sampson and Gregory enter, we know that they are outdoors because they are carrying swords and shields, which are customarily removed on entering a building. We gather that the area is public since they encounter their enemies, the Montagues ("I will frown as I pass by"), and citizens rush in with clubs and spears. The Prince's judgment confirms our conclusion: "If ever you disturb our streets again . . ." This first scene has much coming and going and falls into several sections, but it does not end until Romeo and Benvolio exit together at line 238, and the stage is momentarily empty. But only momentarily. Without delay *Enter* CAPULET, COUNTY PARIS, *and the Clown*" — they may even be entering from one door as Benvolio and Romeo go out the other — and the second scene begins. But we are not necessarily in the same place.

Scene in Elizabethan usage refers not so much to a unit of dramatic organization as to a location ("In fair Verona, where we lay our scene . . ."), a place where characters meet and converse: when the place changes, the scene changes. On occasion the scene will change — or slide to an adjoining location — even with characters still on the stage, as occurs between what modern texts call scenes 4 and 5 of the first act. In scene 4, the Montagues are clowning and listening to Mercutio's account of his Queen Mab dream in the street, presumably in front of the Capulet house; they then "*march about the stage*" and presumably stand to one side. Next the Capulet servants enter to prepare for the party (scene 5), and the host and guests enter at line 16; thus, the Montagues have crashed the party without moving. The indoor scene has come to them.

The point of all this detail is to demonstrate that the Elizabethan stage is what the great modern director Peter Brook, speaking of his ideal stage, refers to as "the Empty Space." Although large scenic properties such as beds, scaffolds, and tents were used, the public theaters did not employ backdrops or sets in the modern sense. There was no front curtain to raise and lower between scenes. The stage was bare so that it could be filled imaginatively and then instantaneously emptied and refilled. This nonpictorial theatrical style affords flexibility and a rapid pace. It also requires that the spectators activate and exercise their curiosity and intelligence, as the Prologue to *Henry V* states explicitly: "Suppose that you have seen," "O, do but think / You stand upon the rivage [shore] and behold a city. . . ," "Work, work your thoughts," and "eche out [supplement] our performance with your mind." As audience members we must participate by "playing along."

Such engagement also permits us to mark the passage of time. Since the drama is being performed in full daylight — this being London, full sunlight is infrequent — the dramatist gives verbal and visual codes for day and night. The play apparently begins in the morning — "You, Capulet, shall go along with me, / And, Montague, come you this afternoon" (1.1.99–100) — a point clarified by Benvolio's "But new strook nine" (161). If we are attentive, we can chart the passage of the day. As scene 2 begins, Capulet has already had his interview with the Prince, and perhaps Montague has too — "But Montague is bound as well as I, in penalty alike" — although the Prince may merely have promised Capulet that Montague would be so warned. In any case, we move through the day as the first act proceeds. Scene 3, the discussion of Juliet's possible marriage to Paris, ends with the Nurse's bawdy "Go, girl, seek happy nights to happy days." The women exit, whereupon night arrives immediately with scene 4: *Enter* ROMEO, MERCUTIO, BENVOLIO, *with five or six other* MASKERS; TORCH-BEARERS." Ironically, the illuminating presence of torches serves to indicate darkness on stage. Night continues through several scenes — during the Capulet party (1.5), as Romeo escapes from his friends after the party (2.1), as he enters the Capulet orchard and woos Juliet (2.2). There are more torches at the party ("she doth teach the torches to burn bright"); the Montagues very likely carry them in searching for Romeo, who in order to elude his pursuers does not carry one; perhaps one burns at Juliet's window. In a play that exploits the imagery of dark and light, day and night, and black and white, the presence of such stage props would enrich the text as well as serve as signals to the audience. At the end of Romeo and Juliet's "balcony scene" (2.2), morning approaches, or at least threatens to: "Good night, good night! Parting is such sweet sorrow, / That I shall say good night till it be morrow" (2.2.184–85). Four lines later, at the beginning of 2.3, the dawn has indeed arrived with Friar Lawrence's entrance: "The grey-ey'd morn smiles on the frowning night." The remainder of the play continues the pattern: we are told about the passage of time when it is helpful for us to know about it, but if such knowledge would be confusing, we are discouraged from thinking about the clock.

The bare stage is peopled with actors in sumptuous clothes. In fact, eye-popping costumes were one of the great attractions of the English stage, provoking comment from foreign visitors and Puritan critics. Wealthy citizens in their wills sometimes left their best clothing to favorite servants who, not legally allowed to wear it, sold it to the players. Clothing was so expensive that the Elizabethans carefully recycled it, creating a vigorous trade in secondhand apparel. The Prince in *Romeo and Juliet* would most likely wear rich robes of velvet or another plush fabric, trimmed perhaps in fox or rabbit or ermine; doublets were often embroidered in silver and gold; ladies' gowns were made of taffeta, silk, cloth of gold, and satin, and then finished with sleeves in complementary fabrics. Hats, gloves, boots, ruffs, cloaks, jerkins, chopines (high-heeled shoes), stockings, handkerchiefs, and other such accessories would be equally impressive.

Whether the costumes were appropriate to the Veronese setting of *Romeo and Juliet* appears to have been less important than their magnificence. In other words, credibility and cultural specificity were outweighed by the claims of spectacle for its own sake and the impracticality of faithfully representing the proper apparel of ancient Rome, ancient Greece, ancient Britain, Elsinore, Venice, the Forest of Arden, and Illyria. The crude sketch by Henry Peacham, reproduced on page 128, may represent a performance in an Elizabethan theater. One expert has very recently argued that the sketch shows a scene from another *Titus* play, not Shakespeare's *Titus Andronicus* as previously thought (see Schleuter). In either case, the drawing gives a sense of the visual eclecticism that must have characterized the staging of virtually any play with a non-English, noncontemporary setting. Apparel could be employed specifically, however, to fulfill the same semiotic function as torches and other props: nightgowns signified a late hour or surprised awakening, riding gear a journey, and various kinds of headwear the social or economic status of the wearer. Color could also be indicative, as we know from Hamlet's "customary suits of solemn black." The spectrum of colors reflected the rage for novelty characteristic both of the age of discovery and of fashion in most ages: popular hues included carnation, puke (dark brown), tobacco, and goose-turd green.

A theatrical troupe's wardrobe of magnificent costumes was one of its most valuable assets. Careful expense records were kept, as we know from the transcription of a handwritten list of costumes given on page 129. This inventory was prepared by Edward Alleyn, chief actor of the Lord Admiral's Men and son-in-law to Philip Henslowe, the theatrical manager. A glorious costume stolen by a disgruntled actor could be very costly to the company. For a production of Thomas Heywood's *A Woman Killed with Kindness* in 1603, the Lord Worcester's Men paid the author six pounds for the play, but spent six pounds, thirteen shillings, for the gown worn by the heroine (see Schoenbaum, *Shakespeare: His Life, His Language, His Theater* 52). The cost and brilliance of costumes served as a primary target of Puritan attacks on the stage, such as the ranting in William Prynne's *Histriomastix* (1633): "Those plays which are usually acted and frequently in over-costly effeminate, strange, meretricious, lust-exciting apparell, are questionlesse unseemely, yea unlawfull unto Christians" (qtd. in Barish 86). Into this assault on costume Prynne manages to smuggle a favorite complaint about the sexual indeterminacy associated with the theater: young men were wearing dresses in public.

Women did not act on the English stage until after the Restoration of Charles II in 1660. In our imaginary performance, the roles of Juliet, the Nurse, Lady Capulet, and Lady Montague, as well as some of the extras at the Capulet party and in the street, are probably being played by boys, although some scholars contend that certain female parts, especially older women, may have been taken by men. London offered a few theatrical companies made up exclusively of boys, referred to in the gossip between Hamlet and Rosencrantz and Guildenstern as the "little eyases" [unfledged hawks]. Some of these, like the company called Paul's Boys, were attached to schools or cathedrals and offered public performances intermittently over several decades. But in the major troupes most of the boy actors were apprenticed to members of the company and played women's roles until their voices changed or their physical growth made them no longer credible. This transvestite theater, as it has come to be known, had a palpable effect on the playwrights' creative choices; for example, it could limit the number of female parts called for and help to shape those roles. Moreover, it encouraged playwrights generally and Shakespeare in particular to develop the thematic possibilities of cross-dressing.

Writing with a certain group of actors in mind and with a financial stake in suiting his matter to his means, Shakespeare usually created only three or four female roles for each play. In *Julius Caesar* there are thirty-four men's roles, not counting messengers, senators, attendants, and spear-carriers, but only two women's parts. To some degree this paucity of female characters is a function not just of personnel but also of subject: historically, the assassination of Caesar was committed by men. And yet it may be that since the company consisted primarily of adult males Shakespeare dramatized stories without large numbers of female roles. Even in comedy, where the topic is courtship, men outnumber women: of the twenty-one named characters in *A Midsummer Night's Dream,* only four are female. If he had especially gifted boy actors, as he must have had in at least two phases of his professional career, Shakespeare exploited their talents by writing challenging parts for them. At the end of the 1590s, for example, the company probably included two exceptionally talented boys for whom Shakespeare wrote such parts as Portia and Nerissa (*The Merchant of Venice*), Beatrice and Hero (*Much Ado about Nothing*), and Rosalind and Celia (*As You Like It*). Then around 1606 he must have found an actor with star quality, one who partly inspired the creation of three of Shakespeare's greatest parts — Lady Macbeth, the irrepressibly talkative Volumnia in *Coriolanus,* and the monumental role of Cleopatra. Although these parts may have been performed by one or more adult males, the actor was probably a gifted juvenile. If so, his youth would have added even greater irony to the Egyptian queen's fears, expressed in her speech to Iras near the end of the play, of being taken captive to Rome and made to watch "Some squeaking Cleopatra boy my greatness / I' th' posture of a whore" (5.2.220–21).

The convention of boys dressed as girls led early modern playwrights to explore ideas of sexual roles and deceptive appearances. Often Shakespeare elected to return the boy actor to doublet and hose by disguising the female character as a boy, as when Rosalind in *As You Like It* disguises herself as Ganymede, taking the name of the beautiful, androgynous cupbearer of Jove. The layers of reality become dizzying in the wooing scenes of acts 3 and 4, where Rosalind as Ganymede plays Rosalind allowing herself to be courted by Orlando. Thus a boy actor plays a female character who plays a boy who pretends to be a girl. Recent scholarship has emphasized the homoerotic implications of these conventions, suggesting that the relationship between adult and apprentice actors may have been sexual, and that the dressing up of pretty boys as pretty girls had a frankly sexual appeal to the males in the audience.[1] Thus the Puritan opponents of the theater may have had a point in complaining about the erotic atmosphere and the "effeminacy" of stage practices. In *Twelfth Night*, Orsino describes his new manservant Cesario (actually Viola disguised) in erotic terms:

> For they shall yet belie thy happy years,
> That say thou art a man. Diana's lip
> Is not so smooth and rubious; thy small pipe [throat, voice]
> Is as the maiden's organ, shrill and sound,
> And all is semblative a woman's part.   (1.4.30–34)

Whatever the strength of the sexual charge, whether powerful or muted, Shakespeare was aware of it and eager to exploit the ironic discrepancies it generated. And modern directors have been quick to highlight these ironies as well. In Ian Judge's 1994 production of *Twelfth Night* at Stratford-upon-Avon, Orsino kissed Cesario on the lips at the end of act 2, scene 4, well before the public revelation of the character's gender in the final scene.

The Playhouses

As recently as 1989 a construction crew working on the south bank of the Thames, demolishing one office building to replace it with another, uncovered the architectural remains of the Rose Playhouse. What they found embedded in the mud was not much to look at: the foundations of pillarlike corner supports for the polygonal building's sides, the foundational outline of the original and the redesigned stage, a narrow trench or drip line made by rainwater falling off the thatched roof, bits of mortar and hazelnut shells that served as flooring in the yard in front of the stage, and evidence of a major reconstruction project apparently undertaken to increase the capacity of the building. A photograph of the foundations and a conjectural drawing of the outlines of the building are found on pages 132–33. This new tangible evidence, limited though it is, has been enormously helpful to scholars' efforts to ascertain the size and shape of the building before and after renovation, the dimensions of the stage, and other structural details that have a bearing on what the building looked like and how it was used for the presentation of stage plays. The original building was a fourteen-sided polygon about 72 feet in diameter, with an inner yard measuring not quite 50 feet in diameter; the stage was rather shallow, only about 15½ feet, and 35½ feet across at the rear, tapering to about 27½ feet at the downstage end. The roof was thatched.

The importance of the Rose find encouraged archeologists to dig just a few yards away, across Park Street, where they promptly unearthed (in October 1989) some of the remains of the Globe: a small section of outer wall, the foundations of a turret stairwell attached to that wall, and a small section of the

---

[1] See several of the essays in *Erotic Politics: Desire on the Renaissance Stage*, ed. Susan Zimmerman, particularly those by Lisa Jardine and Peter Stallybrass.

gallery wall (an inner wall facing onto the yard). More may yet be uncovered: some of the ruins seem to extend under existing buildings, which will have to be moved or removed before further excavation can occur. (The reconstruction of the Globe that opened on the South Bank in 1996 is slightly closer to the river than the original building was. For more on this re-creation, see pp. 372–73 in Chapter 10.) As incredible as it may seem, it took almost four hundred years to uncover the foundations of two of the most important buildings in British history. Now that we have studied them, we know considerably more about these structures and the plays that they housed than we did ten years ago; however, there is still much to learn. None of the public playhouses is still standing, and the archeological and pictorial evidence is sketchy and often conflicting.

The surviving drawings from the period, for example, often contradict what we know about the size of the theaters or seem inconsistent with recorded details of their structure. The Globe foundations discovered in Park Street are, after all, a physical record of the second Globe Playhouse, built immediately after the first Globe burned to the ground during a performance of Shakespeare's *Henry VIII* in June 1613. The second playhouse, about which we know a little, was said to have been built on the foundations of the first structure, in which many of Shakespeare's plays were originally performed, but we cannot be sure whether changes or improvements were introduced as the building was reconstructed. C. Walter Hodges's drawing on page 134 provides a conjectural view of the second Globe. The survey of the playhouses that follows, therefore, offers a useful lesson in the problems of theater history: much of it is speculative, details are still emerging, and even now there is detective work to be done.

In the 1590s several outdoor playhouses, what we tend to call public theaters, were operating around London. Indoor playhouses, or private theaters, had been in use in the 1570s and '80s; after the turn of the century they became increasingly important. (A leading theater historian, Andrew Gurr, regards the distinction between public and private as misleading, the main differences being the presence of a roof and the price of admission, so he calls the first type *amphitheaters* and the second *hall theaters*.) The outdoor playhouses were designed as theaters and located outside the City walls because they were thus beyond the reach of the London authorities, who tended to have Puritan sympathies and were therefore opposed to theatrical performances. The indoor playhouses were converted spaces within existing buildings. Their presence within the City was ambiguous, since the Blackfriars district where the main indoor playhouse stood was geographically within the walls but was legally known as a *Liberty*, a site not subject to City statutes.

The convenient notion that the Theatre was the first permanent playhouse in England — a sentimental choice, given its appropriate name and its connection with Shakespeare's plays — has recently been superseded by awareness that the Red Lion had been built as a playhouse for James Burbage almost ten years earlier. The principal outdoor playhouses were the Theatre (built 1576), the Curtain (1577), the Rose (1587), the Swan (1595), the Globe (1599), and the Fortune (1600). The Theatre and the Curtain, along with others such as the Fortune and the Red Bull (c. 1604), stood north of the City; the Rose, the Swan, and the Globe to the south just across the Thames, on the Bankside. A fascinating historical footnote concerns the connection between the Theatre and the Globe. In 1596 Burbage lost his lease on the property where the Theatre stood, and so the Lord Chamberlain's Men were unable to play in their accustomed place. After renting spaces and moving around for two seasons, the company devised a scheme: they hired workmen to dismantle the Theatre, hauled the timbers and ironwork across the river in January 1599, and engaged a contractor named Peter Street to use the materials to construct the Globe.

The major indoor playhouse was Blackfriars. It took its name from the old monastic neighborhood where in 1594 James Burbage purchased the Priory, a building that had been used as a theater between 1576 and 1584. His attempts to convert it for use by the Lord Chamberlain's Men were blocked by an early modern version of a neighborhood alliance that feared the effects of traffic and mischief. Over a decade later, in 1608, the space came into its own when the King's Men were authorized to use it as a theater. A year or so later they began to play there regularly while continuing to perform at the Globe.

Understanding the London playhouses and their function as performing spaces must begin with the so-called de Witt drawing of the Swan on page 135. The sketch we have was actually made circa 1596 by the Dutch scholar Arend van Buchell: he copied it into his notebook from a drawing sent him by his friend Johannes de Witt, who had just visited London. To some scholars the sketch raises more questions than it answers — the perspective is off, there are no spectators except perhaps a few above the stage, and there is no "inner stage"— but it does provide an introduction to sixteenth-century theater architecture and stagecraft. Another important picture that helps us to visualize these spaces is Wenceslas Hollar's 1644 engraving known as the *Long View of London* (p. 136), although one error in it demands correction: the arenas labeled "The Globe" and "Beere bayting [bearbaiting]" have been mistakenly reversed. Other relevant information comes from builders' contracts, financial details recorded in Henslowe's *Diary*, and the excavations of the last decade.

The amphitheater stage was elevated several feet and protruded into the center of the arena, jutting out from the housing that contained the backstage area and extended to the outside circular wall. The size of the stage at the Fortune was about 43 feet wide and 27 feet deep, larger than the Rose's platform described on page 114. Two columns on the stage itself supported a roof that partly covered the playing area; this canopy, known as the *heavens*, was adorned with paintings of the sun, moon, and stars visible from below. The *heavens* corresponded to the *hell* beneath the stage. A trapdoor in the stage gave access to the area beneath the stage so that in plays like Christopher Marlowe's *Doctor Faustus*, Faustus could be taken into hell. The hidden area under the stage platform also allowed for special effects: at a mysterious moment in *Antony and Cleopatra*, the stage directions stipulate that the "*Music of the hoboys [oboes] is under the stage*"; in *Hamlet*, the Ghost disappears through the trapdoor and then speaks from "the cellarage." Andrew Gurr has brilliantly concluded that, in the de Witt drawing, what appear to be curved trestles or pilings supporting the stage are in fact gaps in the curtains that concealed the below-stage area from the audience's view.

At the back of the stage were doors, through which entrances and exits were made. The number of doors is much disputed and may have varied from theater to theater. Some stage directions include the words "*at the other door,*" which would seem to specify two. On the other hand, certain texts obviously require a *discovery space* at the rear of the stage, an area hidden by a curtain or perhaps a door similarly covered: such a place could conceal Polonius when he hides behind the arras in the closet scene of *Hamlet,* or hide Desdemona's bed until it was thrust forward in the final scene of *Othello.* In other words, some playhouses may have had a middle door or hidden space; even in the Swan, with its two doors, such a concealed area could have been rigged up temporarily with curtains. Scholars still debate the existence and importance of the discovery space, but the most recent thinking suggests two kinds of spaces, one of them, according to Gurr, "permanent, a curtained alcove or discovery-space in the tiring-house wall, which served as a shop, tomb, cell, study or closet," the other "a special property, a raised platform, or even a curtained 'booth' set up on stage" that served as a tent (in the history plays) or Cleopatra's monument or an executioner's scaffold (*Shakespearean Stage* 149).

Above the stage in the de Witt drawing we see a gallery or a series of windows or rooms that may have served, like expensive boxes in a modern sports stadium, as private viewing rooms for the wealthy; known as the *tarras,* this section may also have been "the lords' rooms" referred to in a contemporary play script. One or more of these gallery rooms may have housed musicians for performances in which their services were wanted. The tarras was also used for plays in which two levels were specified, such as the balcony scene in *Romeo and Juliet.* Perhaps one of the above-stage rooms was reserved for such action in plays that required it, or perhaps the spectators were temporarily pushed aside. Higher still, above the tarras and the heavens, was the *hut,* an enclosed space that permitted hidden stagehands to create special effects, such as shaking sheets of metal for thunder, and to operate machinery for "flying" immortal or magical characters, such as Ariel in *The Tempest,* onto the stage. In the Swan drawing, a trumpeter makes use of a small platform attached to the hut, perhaps to announce the beginning of a performance. Most of the outdoor playhouses seem to have been constructed more or less according to this model, with minor variations. The key to theater architecture in this period is that its relative uniformity — a bare stage with heavens, hell, a trap, doors leading to the tiring-house, and a tarras — promotes the flexible, nonspecific nature of the staging implicit in the play texts that survive. In *Twelfth Night,* for example, the stage can represent a sumptuous room in Orsino's house at one moment, the deserted Illyrian seacoast at the next, and Olivia's garden immediately thereafter. In *Antony and Cleopatra,* the action moves fluidly back and forth among various indoor and outdoor locations from Egypt to Rome to Athens. The playing areas of the hall theaters may have been slightly smaller or different in detail, but they probably resembled those in the amphitheaters, for the King's Men performed the same repertory at both the Globe and Blackfriars.

What we call the *auditorium,* the area for the spectators, differed significantly in the outdoor and indoor theaters. The amphitheaters were large structures, much bigger than the faulty perspective of the Swan drawing suggests. The Globe was a polygon with perhaps as many as twenty sides (i.e., virtually round), a diameter of about 100 feet, and a capacity of some 3,000 spectators. The dimensions of the Swan were similar. The inside gallery walls were about 10 feet from the outer walls, which means that the diameter of the yard must have been about 80 feet (Gurr, *Shakespearean Stage* 143). The Rose, before its enlargement in 1592, was considerably smaller, about two-thirds the size of the Globe. Spectators would have entered at a single door and paid a gatherer one penny to be admitted to the yard, where they then stood around the base of the stage. Those who wanted to watch the play in greater comfort would have sought entry into one of the galleries, at the price of another penny; a seat in the higher galleries with a more expansive view would have cost a third penny. (See p. 8 in the Introduction as well as pp. 233–36 in Chapter 7 for contexts and equivalents of these prices.) The best seats in the house were located in the *lords' rooms,* those private portions of the gallery nearest the stage (and perhaps even over the stage itself) which cost sixpence. One benefit of the recent archeological discoveries is that they reveal the different forms of entry at the Rose and the Globe: at the Rose, a spectator entered the yard first and then the gallery; at the Globe, as the presence of outer stair turrets indicates, people entering the gallery did so directly from the back, without going through the yard (Gurr, *Shakespearean Stage* 134).

Who were the spectators entering the yard and the galleries? The makeup of the audience at the outdoor playhouses is much contested because such demographic information is hard to obtain. One view holds that Shakespeare's plays drew spectators from all but the lowest economic and social strata, that the audience was truly heterogeneous: merchants and their wives, aristocrats, whores, lawyers from the Inns of Court, laborers, visitors from the country and from abroad, apprentices, servants. Another account describes a more privileged crowd made up of people who could afford not only the price of admission but also time for pleasure in the middle of a workday. Such a view also relates attendance to literacy, noting that drama would have first attracted the educated, who would have been comparatively well-off. The repertories of particular theaters apparently drew different audiences: James Wright, writing a century later in 1699, reports that the Fortune and the Red Bull "were mostly frequented by Citizens, and the meaner sort [lower classes] of People" (qtd. in Gurr, *Playgoing in Shakespeare's London* 251). Whatever the majority at any given house, the evidence suggests that most social classes, from apprentices to gallants, were represented in the amphitheaters. If a woman was respectable, she was necessarily escorted by a man; if not, not. Men outnumbered women — once again literacy may be a factor — but there was a substantial number of women among the 3,000 people who packed the Globe for Shakespeare's most popular plays.

The indoor playhouses were considerably smaller, although the price of admission was higher, so they were at least as profitable to the companies as the larger amphitheaters. Blackfriars, the private theater about which we have the most information, comprised one large upper room in a large building, much like a giant ballroom or other public space at the top of a modern structure. The room's dimensions were about 66 feet by 46 feet. The stage stood at one of the smaller ends of the room, with a tiring-house behind it. Galleries curved around the length of the other three walls, with benches rather than standing places in the central area in front of the stage, here known as the *pit*. Whether there were boxes at the back of the Blackfriars stage is uncertain. In structure and detail, the stage apparently resembled that in the amphitheaters, with a trap, doors leading from the stage to the tiring-house, space for musicians, and a mechanism for flying.

The stage at Blackfriars had one feature that the amphitheaters probably lacked — spectators.[2] About ten stools around the edges could be hired by fashionable theatergoers who wished to see well and be seen. These gallants paid two shillings (twenty-four pence) for such a privilege. The price for entry into the hall, guaranteeing a place in an upper gallery, was sixpence. An additional shilling purchased a bench in the pit, and the expensive boxes, partitioned sections of the gallery, cost half a crown (two shillings and sixpence). These prices meant that ordinary citizens did not usually patronize the indoor theaters, and this exclusivity contributed, of course, to their popularity. Their location in town rather than in the suburbs or across the river also gave them special appeal for the socially and economically prominent (and those who coveted such prominence). Their sudden vogue was mainly attributable, however, to their location indoors, away from sources of natural light: since all illumination was supplied by candles and torches, it was possible to play at night.

Shakespeare appears to have noticed the prosperity and fashionability of his evening audiences. In *The Winter's Tale*, when Time, the Chorus, enters to announce the passage of some sixteen years, he also declares his familiarity with recent customs and modes of behavior.

> I witness to
> The times that brought them in; so shall I do
> To th' freshest things now reigning, and make stale
> The glistering of this present, as my tale
> Now seems to it. (4.1.11–15)

Thus Time asserts the irresistibility and constancy of change, and this passage may have had a particularly chilling effect on the sophisticated Blackfriars audience of 1610. Adorned in their most glittering clothing and jewelry, having paid dearly for their admission, and conscious of their superiority (whether

---

[2]Although some scholars believe that spectators may have sat on the stage at the Globe, the evidence is so far inconclusive.

social, political, or financial), the members of this chic crowd are warned that their days are numbered, that the darlings of fashion are always supplanted by others who are wealthier, more beautiful, more powerful. When Shakespeare began his career around 1590, these social considerations were not as meaningful as they unquestionably were by its end. The rise of indoor playing spaces helped to establish the link between attendance at the playhouse and social prominence, to give the theater the function that in some quarters it still maintains, that of social barometer.

The Companies

The fortunes of the London theatrical companies should probably be seen as an episode in the history of economics as well as the history of literature: a professional troupe was a company in both the financial and the theatrical senses. Groups of players had been touring the countryside and performing in town squares and London innyards since the fifteenth century; and as London grew in size and importance in the sixteenth century, the companies naturally began to gravitate toward it. Since actors were low on the social ladder, occupying the same level as vagabonds and beggars, the law required that troupes of players be sponsored by aristocratic patrons, men who accepted nominal responsibility for the companies (although in practice this connection was fairly remote). Throughout the 1570s, '80s, and '90s, many groups of professional players formed, merged, dissolved, and reconstituted themselves under a variety of patrons: Lord Strange's Men, Lord Pembroke's Men, Lord Worcester's Men, the Lord Admiral's Men, and the Lord Chamberlain's Men. (This list does not include the companies of boy actors, mentioned earlier, that were associated with educational institutions and that sometimes performed in the hall theaters.) By the middle of the 1590s, however, the many groups had distilled themselves down to two dominant companies, the Lord Admiral's Men and the Lord Chamberlain's Men. In 1598 an order from the Privy Council (the queen's executive committee) established these two as the only adult companies licensed to play in London.

Regular playing in a single location by the same group of actors is largely responsible for the maturing of English drama in this period and thus for the dramatic output of William Shakespeare. The success of these companies owes much to their connection with two strong theatrical families, headed by Philip Henslowe and James Burbage. The Lord Admiral's Men prospered thanks to the business acumen of Philip Henslowe, landlord, moneylender, theatrical promoter, and father-in-law of Edward Alleyn, the celebrated actor who originated heroic roles such as Marlowe's Tamburlaine and Doctor Faustus for the Admiral's Men. In 1587 Henslowe built the Rose, in partnership with John Cholmley, and then in 1592 enlarged it to increase profits. When the Lord Chamberlain's Men disassembled the Theatre north of town and opened the Globe in 1599 just next to the Rose on the Bankside, Henslowe responded to this competitive threat by arranging with the builder of the Globe, Peter

Street, to build a new theater, the Fortune, in the neighborhood just vacated by the Lord Chamberlain's Men.

Henslowe's passion for minute financial detail has been invaluable to theatrical historians. He kept a daily record of loans, expenditures, losses, money collected from performances, and the cost of business lunches. He also kept a log of plays performed on specific dates (see p. 137).[3] From Henslowe's *Diary* we learn, for example, that in the 1590s the usual fee paid to a playwright for a new play was five to eight pounds (the fee rose to ten to twelve pounds after 1600); that costumes were exceedingly expensive; that it generally took about three weeks from delivery of the manuscript for a company to mount a production of a play; that his company had among its properties "i [one] Hell mought [mouth]" (presumably for Faustus to be dragged into), "i bores head & Serberosse [Cerberus's] iii heads," and "i lyone; ii lyone heades; i great horse with his leages [legs]"; and that the average wage for a minor actor was ten shillings (or one-half of a pound) per week.

Henslowe's counterpart in the rival company was James Burbage, the carpenter-turned-impresario who arranged to build the Red Lion in 1567 and the Theatre in 1576, who purchased the Blackfriars building in 1595, and whose sons, Cuthbert and Richard, were his partners in his later theatrical dealings. Richard, the principal actor for the troupe, played such parts as Richard III, Shylock, and most of the great tragic figures from Brutus and Hamlet through Antony and Coriolanus. Links obtained among all the major theatrical figures and companies: Edward Alleyn had acted under Burbage's sponsorship at the Theatre in 1591 until the two fell out over money. James Burbage's principal achievement was probably the consolidation in 1594 of the Lord Chamberlain's Men from members of various other companies. This company became the greatest of all the early modern theatrical troupes and the vehicle for the production of all Shakespeare's plays from 1594 to the end of his career in 1612 or 1613. In 1603 the company came under royal patronage and was known thereafter as the King's Men. The company performed at court more than any of its rivals, in fact as often as all the other companies combined, and it continued its domination of the theatrical scene by producing the plays of Ben Jonson, John Webster, Thomas Middleton, and, after the retirement of Shakespeare, John Fletcher, Philip Massinger, John Ford, and James Shirley. Even after Shakespeare's death in 1616 and Richard Burbage's in 1619, the company carried on until the closing of the theaters in 1642.

Theatrical promoters like Henslowe and Burbage were influential but not all-important, for the permanent adult companies such as the Admiral's Men and the Chamberlain's Men were in fact cooperatively owned and run. The most important members were the shareholders, those men who held a financial interest in the company, jointly owned its assets (play texts, costumes, properties), and profited from its success. Being a shareholder in a London company was profitable, but it also entailed considerable responsibility: a

[3]Upon Henslowe's death these papers passed to Alleyn, who preserved them; they were discovered in the late eighteenth century by the great Shakespearean editor Edmond Malone and have been published in modern editions.

sharer had to commit his talents and services exclusively to the company, and could sell his share and leave the troupe only with the consent of his fellows. The company had eight shareholders in 1596, including William Shakespeare, Richard Burbage, the clown Will Kemp, Augustine Phillips, and John Heminges, one of the sponsors of the First Folio of Shakespeare's plays a quarter of a century later, in 1623. In 1603, when they became the King's Men, this number increased to twelve. The customary number for the major London companies seems to have been about ten. Although theatrical work was not a socially respectable profession, its financial rewards could provide a kind of social standing: in 1597, as we have seen in Chapter 1, Shakespeare used some of his shareholders' profits to buy the second-largest house in Stratford. In addition he invested in the Globe Theater as a property. Such financial backers were known as *housekeepers*. In the season of 1598–99 the Lord Chamberlain's Men turned the disaster of their eviction into a financial bonanza when they moved the timbers of the Theatre across the Thames and built the Globe. The costs for this venture, which must have been enormous, were shared by the two Burbage sons, who put up half the sum, and by five shareholders, who together raised the other 50 percent. Thenceforth, instead of having to turn over to the landlord half of the gallery receipts from each performance, the company in its new location was its own landlord; with anywhere from 500 to 3,000 spectators paying at least a penny (many of them more than that), the receipts were considerable (Gurr, *Shakespearean Stage* 44–45).

The sharers formed the core of each company, taking major parts (as in the case of Richard Burbage) and supplying scripts (as in the case of William Shakespeare), but they needed help with the multitude of tasks involved in theatrical work. Hired men, paid by the week, filled out the company, taking less important stage roles, playing musical instruments, assisting with properties and costumes, and serving as gatherers. (Interestingly, there is evidence that women sometimes worked as gatherers.) In addition there were the boys who played women's parts, some of whom would have been apprentices to the sharers. Some of Shakespeare's plays could have been performed by as few as a dozen or so actors, but most required considerably more. The average size of a full London company, counting apprentices, hired men, and musicians, was between twenty and thirty; for certain major productions even more performers and helpers were probably engaged; and on tour the number would have been reduced substantially. Actors in each company were almost certainly typed according to their specialties, and Shakespeare wrote with these actors in mind. (In fact, certain surviving printed texts refer to the character by the actor's name.) Burbage assumed the great tragic roles; the other great type was the Clown, for which Shakespeare's specialist changed. Until 1599 Will Kemp, a shareholder in the Lord Chamberlain's Men, acted the Clown's parts, and Shakespeare seems to have had him in mind in writing the roles of Dogberry in *Much Ado about Nothing*, Peter in *Romeo and Juliet*, and perhaps Bottom in *A Midsummer Night's Dream*. Kemp's decision to sell his share and leave the company coincided with Shakespeare's increasing attraction to tragedy and to the darker shades of comedy, and so the Clown's parts, now written for Robert

Armin, became more mordant and reflective, roles such as Feste in *Twelfth Night* and the Fool in *King Lear.*

The disproportionate number of characters to actors — the thirty-six parts in *Julius Caesar* and a company of perhaps twenty-four actors — meant that in virtually every play many actors performed several parts. A player taking a major role such as King Lear or Rosalind would not have acted another part in the same production, but other cast members would have. This convention of doubling, combined with the absence of scenery, the lack of artificial lighting in the amphitheaters, and the proximity of the audience, fostered what is known as the *presentational,* as opposed to the *representational,* style of performance. In presentational theater, the illusion of a fictional narrative is maintained at the same time that the audience is reminded that a fiction is being performed. In other words, there is no strict pretense that this is Hamlet striding the battlements at Elsinore; rather, the audience is conscious that they are watching Burbage playing Hamlet on the stage of the Globe. And doubling can augment the spectators' pleasure, first by multiplying the instances of representation (one actor playing several parts) on which drama is based, and, second, by increasing the sense of virtuosity that any good actor brings to any single part.

Whether sharers or hirelings, the actors worked very hard. The major companies played every day except during Lent and on major church holidays, and their repertories were immense. The Lord Admiral's Men, in the season of 1594–95 (autumn to summer), presented thirty-eight plays, twenty-one of them new (Gurr, *Shakespearean Stage* 103). Even great favorites were not repeated too often lest their potential popularity be damaged. Apparently a new play was added every couple of weeks or so. This repertory system required the actors to do a quick run-through of the scheduled play in the morning and then perform it in the afternoon. After a play had been running for some time, less rehearsal time would have been necessary; but with long gaps between performances, inevitable changes of personnel, and other unpredictable events, touch-up rehearsals must have been needed. Sometimes scripts were altered for revival: Ben Jonson was paid for additions to Thomas Kyd's *The Spanish Tragedy* some fifteen years after its initial run. And then new plays would have to be rehearsed as well. Naturally the company sharers would want to perform as often as possible, but they could not play in Lent, during epidemics of plague, or when vile weather made outdoor performance impossible.

The Theater and the Authorities

The municipal government and the Crown were both attentive to the growing popularity of the theater in Elizabethan London. Prohibitions against playing were issued by the Privy Council to defend against the spread of disease in periods of plague. Since medical science had not yet identified the cause of bubonic plague — bites from fleas spread by rats — it was assumed that the presence of crowds would contribute to contagion, and so the theaters were closed. Virulent outbreaks of plague ravaged London between 1592 and 1594 and again in 1603, when over 30,000 people died (in a population of just over 200,000), and in both cases the theaters were closed for over a year (see the plague bill reproduced on p. 33). The authorities also closed the playhouses during Elizabeth's final illness in 1603. In fact, during the first decade of the seventeenth century, public playing was forbidden repeatedly and for very lengthy periods: had it not been for handsomely rewarded performances at court and additional royal largesse, Shakespeare's company could have suffered financial ruin.

Had regulation of the theater been left to the London authorities, the playhouses would have been closed permanently. The members of the City Corporation, if not Puritans themselves, were responsive to the pressures of their Puritan constituencies, and the Puritans were increasingly antipathetic to actors, the practice of cross-dressing, colorful costume of any kind, the pretense or hypocrisy inherent in acting, and imaginative literature in general. But the theaters, located as they were in those dubious neighborhoods known as the Liberties, fell under the scrutiny of the Crown, not the City, and Elizabeth's and James's governments were more tolerant of the pleasures of playing and concerned that the municipal authorities of London not become too powerful. Government regulation was officially in the hands of the Privy Council, but the agency that executed the monarch's will in the sphere of public entertainment was the Revels Office headed by the Master of the Revels. Henry VIII had created this office to provide courtly performances, and it continued to fulfill that function under Elizabeth and the Stuarts, as well as to ensure that the Crown's interests were protected at all times. The Revels Office, like most bureaucratic agencies, was in an ambiguous position toward those it regulated. The Master found the players to be an easy and relatively cheap source of courtly entertainment: rather than having to devise and fund an elaborate performance himself, he could buy one ready-made by bringing the players to court for a royal performance.

The primary duty of the Master of the Revels was to license plays for performance, so the theatrical companies were required to submit a new script to the Revels Office to be checked for offensive material. The Master received a fee (seven shillings) for this service, and additional payment (five to ten shillings) for licensing the playhouse. During James's reign the Master was also responsible for checking and approving plays for print, again for a fee. The Master of the Revels, in other words, was the government censor, and material considered seditious or irreligious was removed from the text. A few surviving theatrical manuscripts bear the marks of censorship, and the occasional printed text reveals such cuts: *Richard II*, for example, was originally printed, almost certainly for political reasons, without the section in act 4, scene 1, in which the king is actually deposed.

On certain points the government could be extremely sensitive. In February 1601 the earl of Essex led his followers into London in an ill-organized and unsuccessful attempt at seizing the throne. The day before that uprising the

Lord Chamberlain's Men, paid specifically for the purpose by the supporters of Essex, mounted a performance of *Richard II*. Augustine Phillips, one of the shareholders of the company, was called before the Privy Council to explain. (An excerpt from his testimony is given on p. 140.) King James could be equally touchy. The satiric *Eastward Ho!*, a collaborative play by Ben Jonson, John Marston, and George Chapman, was presented in 1605 by a children's company at Blackfriars. It is full of topical jokes about the Scots, who had descended on England with their favorite son in 1603 and were purchasing knighthoods; it also ridicules City merchants and the Puritan economic ethic. The Crown was not amused, and Chapman and Jonson went briefly to jail, Marston having escaped arrest by leaving town. In 1606 Parliament passed legislation regulating the language of the stage, establishing a fine of ten pounds for anyone who should "jestingly or prophanely speake or use the holy name of God or of Christ Jesus, or of the Holy Ghoste or of the Trinitie." Although it could and sometimes did act punitively, the government for the most part maintained a hands-off policy toward the stage, and recently scholars have come to believe that this tolerance may itself have been a political act. In other words, by permitting a small degree of opposition to be expressed or enacted in the controlled space of the public playhouses, the government employed the theater as a kind of safety valve, an outlet for releasing political pressure before it increased to an explosion.

Governmental support of the theater had to do with pleasure as well as with politics: Elizabeth and James (and James's Queen Anne) liked plays. The monarch never attended the theater, however, no matter how fashionable it became or how aristocratic the audience. When the sovereign wished to see a performance, the players were summoned to the palace and paid for their services, as indicated in the records quoted on pages 140–41. The Lord Chamberlain's Men frequently performed Shakespeare's plays at the court of Elizabeth, and while we should be skeptical of the rumors to which the eighteenth and nineteenth centuries were susceptible — that Shakespeare wrote *The Merry Wives of Windsor* because Elizabeth wished to see Falstaff in love, or that Edward Alleyn returned to the stage after retirement because the Queen missed seeing him act — there is enough anecdotal evidence to suggest that Elizabeth encouraged the players not just because they were useful to her and to the Commonwealth but because she enjoyed their work. Scholars disagree on the extent to which James was engaged directly with the theatrical troupe that bore his name; J. Leeds Barroll has recently claimed that the company's connection with its patron was merely nominal (*Politics, Plague, and Shakespeare's Theater*). But whether or not James gave his players much thought, the company's participation in royal festivities increased markedly under the Stuarts, and court records attest that Shakespeare's plays were extremely popular at court. Performances during the holiday season — from early December through early February — were especially numerous. In addition, this was the age when the court masque flourished in the work of Ben Jonson and Inigo Jones. In such extravagant entertainments as *The Masque of Blackness* (1605) and *The Masque of Queens* (1609), players and dancers were often engaged to take minor roles, serving as foils to the mythical figures impersonated by Queen Anne and other noble members of the court. Whether Shakespeare participated in any of these royal performances is not known, but he was certainly aware of their visual magnificence, their immodest cost, and King James's fondness for the dancing that concluded the masques. This awareness may have stimulated him to develop the pageantry, music, and magic that characterize such late plays as *The Winter's Tale* and *The Tempest*.

The court, the amphitheaters, and the indoor theaters were the players' main performing locations, but there was one other venue — the provinces. The urban theatrical companies were descendants of the troupes of traveling players that moved from town to town throughout the fifteenth and sixteenth centuries; and even in the heyday of London theater, those actors who could not find work in town formed pickup groups that toured the countryside. Predictably, the major companies, having established themselves on the Bankside, in town, and at court, were not enthusiastic about returning to their peripatetic origins, as a letter from Edward Alleyn to his wife attests (p. 143). Road conditions were difficult, the number of spectators was reduced, and the profits were consequently smaller. Henslowe records paying an actor on tour half of what the man would have made in London. Sometimes, however, the players had no choice. The plague drove them out of London and into public squares or town halls. As is sometimes still the case today, the provinces probably didn't get quite the same show as the capital: the conditions of touring led to smaller casts and perhaps abbreviated scripts.

It is easy to imagine that in, say, 1595, when the threat of plague had subsided, Shakespeare and his fellows were gratified and relieved at having returned for a time to their commodious theater, its relatively urbane crowd, and a healthy box office. The actors playing Sampson and Gregory, the Capulets who begin *Romeo and Juliet,* must have felt particular relief and pleasure as they stepped onto the stage to deliver their bawdy puns.

THEATERS OF LONDON

City Wall

Boundary of area
within jurisdiction
of Guildhall

Halls and other
buildings used as
theaters

Other buildings

◅ Map Showing the Playhouses in Shakespeare's Time

This modern map of London circa 1600 indicates the location of the principal Elizabethan and Jacobean theaters. The major "public playhouses," or the outdoor arenas, are situated outside the City to the north and across the Thames River to the south.

→ HENRY PEACHAM

Sketch Accompanying Lines from *Titus Andronicus*

date uncertain

This sketch appears at the top of a manuscript page, above some transcribed lines from Shakespeare's *Titus Andronicus*. For many years scholars took it to represent a performance of the play, even though no such configuration of characters appears in Shakespeare's text. Recently, however, it has been suggested that the drawing actually illustrates a scene from *A Very Lamentable Tragedy of Titus Andronicus and the Haughty Empress,* a play that survives only in a German translation but that does contain an episode comparable to Peacham's illustration. English actors performed this play in Germany, so we are still probably safe in concluding that the drawing derives from the artist's experience of an actual stage production. The eclectic style of the costumes (both classical and Elizabethan) suggests a relaxed approach to historical authenticity on the Renaissance stage.

✦ Inventory of Theatrical Costumes

c. 1602

From Henslowe's Papers

This list of costumes, transcribed in the original spelling, was probably compiled about 1602. Most likely the apparel belonged to the Lord Admiral's Men, the troupe of players managed by Philip Henslowe, a theater owner and entrepreneur who kept meticulous records of his holdings and profits. The list is in the hand of Edward Alleyn, tragedian and Henslowe's son-in-law. Several items, indicated here by open parentheses at the left, are crossed out (in different ink) in the original.

1. A scarlett cloke wth ij [2] brode [broad] gould Laces: w^t [with] gould buttens of the sam downe the sids
2. A black velvett cloke
   A scarlett cloke Layd (the)[1] downe w^t silver Lace and silver buttens
4. A short velvett cap clok embroydered w^t gould and gould spangles
5. A watshod [watchet, light blue] sattins clok w^t v gould laces
6. A pur(l)pell sattin w^telted [welted, bordered] w^t velvett and silver twist
7. A bla*ck*[2] tufted cloke   cloke
8. A damask cloke garded cloke garded [guarded, trimmed] w^t velvett
   A longe blak tafata cloke
   A colored bugell [beaded cloak?] for aboye
   A scarlett w^t buttens of gould fact [faced, lined] w^t blew velvett
12. A scarlett fact w^t blak velvett
13. A stamell [red] cloke w^t (b)gould lace
14. blak bugell cloke

   Gownes
(1 hary ye viij gowne
2. the blak velvett gowne w^t wight fure
3. A crimosin Robe strypt w^t gould fact w^t ermin
4. on of wrought cloth of gould
5. on of red silk w^t gould butt*ens*
(6 a cardinalls gowne
7. wemens gowns
8. i blak velvett embroyde
9. w^t gould
10. i cloth of gould candish [Cavendish?, an actor or role] his stuf
11. blak velvett lact and drawne owt w^t wight sarsnett [silk fabric]
12. A black silk w^t red flush

---

[1]Parentheses indicate deletions or alterations.
[2]Italic letters indicate difficult readings, attenuated or blotted letters in the original.

13 A cloth of silver for pan [Parr?, an actor]

14 a yelow silk gowne

(15 a red silk gowne

(16 angels silk

17 ij blew calico gowns

Antik sutes [clown suits, motley]

1 a cote of crimosen velvett cutt in payns and embryderd in gould

2 i cloth of gould cote wᵗ grene bases [skirts]

3 i cloth of goul*d* cote wᵗ oraingtawny bases

4 i cloth of go<..>[3] silver cott wᵗ blewe silk & tinsell bases

5 i blew damask cote the more

6 a red velvett hors mans cote

7 A yelow tafata pd [?]

8 cloth of gould horsmans cote

9 cloth *of* bodkin [baudekin, rich fabric] hormans cote

10 orayngtany horsmans cot of cloth lact

11 daniels gowne

12 blew embroyderde bases

13 will somers [Will Summers, an actor] cote

14 wight embroyd bases

15 (g) gilt lether cot

16 ij hedtirs [head tires, tiaras] sett wᵗ stons

17

Jerkings and
dublets

1 A crymosin velvett pd wᵗ gould buttens & lace

2 a crymasin sattin case [fitted jacket] lact wᵗ gould lace all over

(3 A velvett dublett cut di*a*mond lact wᵗ gould lace and spang [small ornament]

4 a dublett of blak velvett cut [slashed ornamentally] on sillver tinsell

5 A ginger colored dublett

6 i wight sattin cute onwight

7 blak velvett wᵗ gould lace

8 green velvett

9 blak tafata cut on blak velvett lacte wᵗ bugell

---

[3]Angle brackets indicate letters or words that are illegible, mutilated, or cut away in the original.

10 blak velvett playne
11 ould wight sattin
12 red velvett for a boye
13 A carnation velvett lacte w^t silver
14 A yelow spangled case
15 red velvett w^t blew sattin sleves & case
16 cloth of silver Jerkin
17 faustus [Faustus, Marlowe's tragic character] Jerkin his clok

1 frenchose
blew velvett embr w^t gould paynes blew sattin scalin [unidentified garment]
2 silver paynes lact w^t carnation satins lact over w^t silver
3 the guises [masks]
(4 Rich payns [strips of cloth] w^t Long *stok*ins
5 gould payns w^t blak stript scalings of ca*nis* |?|
6 gould payns w^t velvett scalings
7 gould payns w^t red strypt scalings
8 black bugell
9 red payns for a boy w^t yelo scalins
10 pryams hoes [Priam's hose]
11 spangled hoes

venetians
(1 A purple velvett cut in dimonds Lact & spangels
2 red velved lact w^t gould spanish
(3 a purpell velvet emproydored w^t silver cut on tinse*l*
4 green velvett lact w^t gould spanish
5 blake velvett
6 cloth of silver
7 gren strypt sattin
8 cloth of gould for a boye

✦ Remains of the Rose Playhouse   *1989*

This photograph of the Rose foundations seen from above was taken in 1989, shortly after excavation. The group of pilings in the center should be ignored; they derive from a twentieth-century building.

✦ Two Plans of the Rose Playhouse

These modern sketches by John Orrell depict the ground plan of the original Rose Playhouse built in 1587 (top) and after its redesign in the spring of 1592 (bottom). The owner of the playhouse, Philip Henslowe, probably undertook the renovation to accommodate more spectators. At the northern end of the building, the stage and gallery walls were taken down and rebuilt farther back, thus extending the gallery and enlarging the size of the yard.

Rose Phase 1

Rose Phase 2

➔ C. WALTER HODGES

Illustration of the Second Globe

This modern speculative drawing by C. Walter Hodges indicates what the Globe probably looked like after its reconstruction in 1614. The original building burned to the ground on June 29, 1613, during a performance of Shakespeare's *Henry VIII*, when cannons set off during the play ignited the thatched roof. The event is recorded in a letter from Sir Henry Wotton dated July 2, 1613.

A   Main entrance
B   The yard
C   Entrances to lowest gallery
D   Position of entrances to staircase and upper galleries
E   Corridor serving the different sections of the middle gallery
F   Middle gallery ("twopenny rooms")
G   Position of "gentlemen's rooms" or "lords' rooms"
H   The stage
J   The hanging being put up round the stage
K   The "hell" under the stage
L   The stage trap leading down to the hell

M   Stage doors
N   Curtained "place behind the stage"
O   Gallery above the stage, used as required sometimes by musicians, sometimes by spectators, and often as part of the play
P   Backstage area (the tiring-house)
Q   Tiring-house door
R   Dressing rooms
S   Wardrobe and storage
T   The hut housing the machine for lowering enthroned gods, etc., to the stage
U   The "heavens"
W   Hoisting the playhouse flag

→ Copy of De Witt's Sketch of the Swan Playhouse 1596

This drawing, a copy of a sketch of the Swan Playhouse by Johannes de Witt, roughly suggests the structure of an Elizabethan outdoor playhouse. De Witt had visited London and included the original drawing in a letter to his friend Arend van Buchell, who copied it into his diary.

◄ WENCESLAS HOLLAR

Detail from *Long View of London*   *1644*

This detailed section from Wenceslas Hollar's engraving *Long View of London* depicts the south bank of the Thames River. The designations "The Globe" (over the amphitheater near the river) and "Beere bayting" (on the amphitheater to the left) are inaccurate and should be reversed.

→ PHILIP HENSLOWE   ➤

Log of Plays from His *Diary*   *1591/92*

This log of plays performed comes from the handwritten financial accounts of Henslowe's company, consisting of actors under the sponsorship of Lord Strange and the Lord Admiral. (The list is transcribed on p. 139.) The *Diary*, which lists plays and dates of performance, receipts collected at each performance, money lent to actors, fees paid to writers, and the costs of materials used in construction, is one of the most instructive and valuable documents in theater history. The sheet reproduced includes such notable titles as Christopher Marlowe's *The Jew of Malta* (*the Jewe of malltuse*), Thomas Kyd's *The Spanish Tragedy* (*Jeronymo*), and *Henry VI* (*harey the vj*), which may possibly be one of Shakespeare's three plays of that name.

The date at the top of Henslowe's page, February 19, 1591, corresponds to February 1592 in our modern calendar: in the sixteenth century, the New Year began on March 25. (To complicate matters further, Henslowe uses 1591 even past March 25 in these entries, failing to correct himself until April 24.)

The lines in the left margin signify Henslowe's division of the record into weeks. The word *ne* means new, indicating the first performance of a play. *Ester* is Easter. In the sums listed at the right, Henslowe indicates monetary amounts with Roman numerals. The abbreviations that follow the sums are as follows: *li* stands for pounds, *s* for shillings, and *d* for pence (from the Latin *libra, solidus,* and *denarius*).

In the name of god Amen 1591
begininge the 19 of febreary my
lord stranges mene A folowethe
1591

Rd at fryer bacone the 19 of febreary . . . . xvijs iij
Rd at mvlomvrco the 20 of febreary . . . . xxixs
Rd at orlando the 21 of febreary . . . . xvjs vjd
Rd at spanes comodye donne oracio the 23 of febreary . . . . xiij s vjd
Rd at syr John mandevell the 24 of febreary . . . . xij s viij d
Rd at harey of cornwell the 25 of febreary 1591 . . . . xxxij s
Rd at the Iewe of malta the 26 of febreary 1591 . . . . lvs
Rd at clorys & orgasto the 28 of febreary 1591 . . . . xviij s
Rd at mvlomvrco the 29 of febreary 1591 . . . . xxxiiij s
Rd at poope Ione the 1 of marche 1591 . . . . xv s
Rd at matchavell the 2 of marche 1591 . . . . xiiij s
Rd at harey the vj the 3 of marche 1591 . . . . iijll xvjs 8d
Rd at bendo & Richardo the 4 of marche 1591 . . . . xvjs
Rd at iijparts in one the 6 of marche 1591 . . . . xxxj s vjd
Rd at harey the vj the 7 of marche 1591 . . . . iij ll
Rd at the lockinglasse the 8 of marche 1591 . . . . vij s
Rd at senobia the 9 of marche 1591 . . . . xxij s vjd
Rd at the Iewe of malta the 10 of marche 1591 . . . . lvj s
Rd at harey the vj the 11 of marche 1591 . . . . xxxxvij s viij d
Rd at the comodey of doneoracio the 13 of marche 1591 . . . . xxviij s viij d
Rd at Ieronymo the 14 of marche 1591 . . . . xxxviij s viij d
Rd at harey the 16 of marche 1591 . . . . xxxxvj s viij d
Rd at molo molloco the 17 of marche 1591 . . . . xxviij s vij d
Rd at the Iewe of malta the 18 of marche 1591 . . . . xxxviij s
Rd at Ieronymo the 20 of marche 1591 . . . . xxxviij s
Rd at constantine the 21 of marche 1591 . . . . xij s
Rd at Iereconstable the 22 of marche 1591 . . . . xxiiij s
Rd at harey of cornwell the 23 of marche 1591 . . . . vij s vjd
Rd at fryer bacon the 25 of marche 1591 . . . . xvj s vjd
Rd at the lockinglasse the 27 of marche 1591 . . . . xvs
Rd at harey the vj the 28 of marche 1591 . . . . xxxxvij s viij d
Rd at mvlamvlloco the 29 of marche 1591 . . . . xxxiiij s
Rd at doneoracio the 30 of marche 1591 . . . . xxxxvij s
Rd at Ieronymo the 31 of marche 1591 . . . . iij ll
Rd at mandevell the 1 of aprell 1591 . . . . xiij s vj
Rd at matchevell the 2 of aprell 1591 . . . . xiij s
Rd at the Iewe of malta the 4 of aprell 1591 . . . . xxxxiij s
Rd at harey the vj the 5 of aprell 1591 . . . . xxxxj s
Rd at brandymer the 6 of aprell 1591 . . . . xxij s
Rd at Ieronymo the 7 of aprell 1591 . . . . xxvj s
Rd at mvlamvloco the 8 of aprell 1591 . . . . xxxxvj s

In the name of god A men 1591
beginge the 19 of febreary my
lord stranges mene A ffoloweth

1591

Rd at fryer bacvne the[1] 19 of febreary . . . satterdaye . . . . . xvij[s] iij[d] [2]

Rd at mvlomvr*co* the 20 of febreary . . . . xxix[s]

Rd at orlando th*e* 21 of febreary . . . . xvj[s] vj[d]

Rd at spanes comodye donne oracioe th*e* 23 of febreary . . xiij[s] vj[d]

Rd at sy[r] John mandevell th*e* 24 of febreary . . . . xij[s] vj[d]

Rd at harey of cornwell th*e* 25 of febreary 1591 . . . . xxxij[s]

Rd at the Jewe of malltuse th*e* 26 of febrearye 1591 . . . . l[s]

—— Rd at clorys & orgasto th*e* 28 of febreary 1591 . . . . xviij[s]

Rd at mvlamvlluco the 29 of febrearye 1591 . . . . xxxiiij[s]

Rd at poope Jone the 1 of marche 1591 . . . . xv[s]

Rd at matchavell the 2 of marche 1591 . . . . xiiij[s]

ne —— Rd at harey the vj the 3 of marche 1591 . . . . iij[li] xvj[s] 8[d]

Rd at bendo & Richardo th*e* 4 of marche 1591 . . . . xvj[s]

—— Rd at iiij playes in one th*e* 6 of marche 1591 . . . . xxxj[e] vj[d]

Rd at harey the vj the 7 of marche 1591 . . . . iiij[li]

Rd at the lockinglasse th*e* 8 of marche 1591 . . . . vij[s]

Rd at senobia the 9 of marche 1591 . . . . xxij[s] vj[d]

Rd at the Jewe of malta th*e* 10 of march*e* 1591 . . . . lvj[s]

Rd at harey the vj the 11 of marche 1591 . . . . xxxxvij[s] vj[d]

—— Rd at the comodey of doneoracio th*e* 13 march 1591–x– . . . xxviiij[e]

Rd at Jcronymo th*e* 14 of march 1591 . . . . iiij[li] xj[s]

Rd at harey the 16 of march*e* 1591 . . . . xxxj[s] vj[d]

Rd at mvlo mvllocco th*e* 17 of march*e* 1591 . . . . xxviij[s] vj[d]

Rd at the Jewe of malta th*e* 18 of march*e* 1591 . . . . xxxix[s]

—— Rd at Joronymo th*e* 20 of march*e* 1591 . . . . xxxviij[s]

Rd at constantine th*e* 21 of march*e* 1591 . . . . xij[s]

Rd at Q̲ Jerusallem the 22 of march*e* 1591 . . . . xviij[s]

Rd at harey of cornwell the 23 of march*e* 1591 . . . . xiij[s] vj[d]

Rd at fryer bacon the 25 of marche 1591 . . . . xv[s] vj[d]

Ester<.> Rd at the lockinglasse the 27 of march*e* 1591 . . . . lv[s]

Rd at harey the vj the 28 of marche 1591 . . . . iij[li] viij[s]

Rd at mvlimvlucko the 29 of march*e* 1591 . . . . iij[li] ij[s]

Rd at doneoracio the 30 of marche 1591 . . . . xxxix[s]

Rd at Joronymo th*e* 31 of march*e* 1591 . . . . iij[li]

Rd at mandefell the 1 of ap[r]ell 1591 . . . . xxx[s]

—— Rd at matchevell the 3 of ap[r]ell 1591 . . . . xxij[s]

Rd at the Jewe of malta th*e* 4 of ap[r]ell 1591 . . . . xxxxiiij[s]

Rd at harey the vj the 5 of ap[r]ell 1591 . . . . xxxxj[s]

Rd at brandymer th*e* 6 of ap[r]ell 1591 . . . . xxij[s]

Rd at Jeronymo th*e* 7 of ap[r]ell 1591 . . . . xxvj[s]

Rd at mvl*e* mvloco the 8 of ap[r]ell 1591. J. h.–01–10–00 . . . . xxiij[s]

---

[1]Italic letters indicate difficult readings, attenuated or blotted letters in the original.

[2]In this example, "xvij[s] iij[d]" equals seventeen shillings and three pence.

→ Testimony about a Performance of *Richard II*   *1600/01*

This excerpt from Elizabethan state papers describes the testimony of Augustine Phillips, a shareholder in the Lord Chamberlain's Men, who was summoned to account for the company's performance of *Richard II* in February 1600/01. Supporters of Robert Devereux, earl of Essex, commissioned the performance of a play in which a usurper takes the throne from a monarch deemed unfit to rule, arranging that it be performed the day before the earl's march on London in an attempted coup d'état.

The Examination of Augustyne Phillypps servant vnto the L Chamberlyne and one of hys players taken the xviij^{th} of Februarij 1600 vpon hys oth

He sayeth that on Fryday last was sennyght or Thursday Sr Charles Percy Sr Josclyne Percy and the L. Montegle with some thre more spak to some of the players in the presans of thys examinate [person being examined, i.e., Phillips] to have the play of the deposyng and kyllyng of Kyng Rychard the second to be played the Saterday next promysyng to gete them xl*s*. more then their ordynary to play yt. Wher thys Examinate and hys fellowes were determyned to have played some other play, holdyng that play of Kyng Richard to be so old & so long out of vse as that they shold have small or no Company at yt. But at their request this Examinate and his fellowes were Content to play yt the Saterday and had their xl*s*. more then their ordynary for yt and so played yt accordyngly

Augustine Phillips

→ Record of King James's Payment
to the King's Men   *1603/04–1604/05*

The Chamber Accounts kept by the Treasurer of the Chamber, one of the king's chief financial officers, record payments for performances at court by Shakespeare's company, as well as monetary gifts to support the company while the theaters were closed due to the plague.

116a   To Richard Burbadg one of his ma^{te} [majesty's] Comedians vppon the Councelle warraunte dated at Hamptoncourte viij° die [eighth day of] Februarij 1603 for the mayntenaunce and releife of himselfe and the rest of his Company being prohibited to p^rsente any playes publiquelie in or neere London by reason of greate perill that might growe throughe the extraordinary Concourse and assemblie of people to a newe increase of the plague till it shall please god to settle the Cittie in a more pfecte health by way of his Maties free gifte

xxx^{li} [30£]

116a   To Iohn Hemynge one of his ma^{te} players vppon the Councelle warraunte dated at the Courte at Whitehall vltimo die [last day of] Februar' 1603 for himselfe and the rest of his Company for two playes p^{r}sented before his ma^{tie} viz the one on Candelmas Day at night and the other on Shrouesonday at night the some of thirtene poundes six shilling and eight pence and[1] way of his ma^{te} rewarde for the same twoe playes six poundes thirteene shilling and iiij^{or} pence in all the some of

xx^{li}

137b To Iohn Hemynges one of his Ma^{te} players vppon the Counselle warraunte dated at the Courte at Whitehalle xxj^{mo} die \Ianuarij/1604 for the paines and expences of himselfe and his companie in playinge and presentinge of sixe Enterludes or plaies before his Matie viz on all Saintes daie at nighte the Sonday at nighte followinge beinge the iiijth of November 1604 S^t. Stephens daie at nighte Innocente day at nighte and on the vijth and viijth daies of Ianuarie for everie of the saide plaies accordinge to the usualle allowaunce of vj^{li} xiij^s iiij^d the peece xl^{li} and lxvj^s viij^d for everie plaie by waie of his Ma^{te} rewarde xx^{li} in all the some of

lx^{li}

[1]Scribal slip.

→ THOMAS HEYWOOD

From *An Apology for Actors* *1612*

Thomas Heywood was a playwright and popular writer who set about to answer the incessant religious attacks on the theater. He responds specifically to the various arguments about the immorality of stage plays, but he also defends the profession on the grounds that the theaters have always been among the ornaments of civilization, as is apparent in the great cities of the world.

The city of Rome ... grew to such height, that not Troy founded by Dardanus, Carthage laid by Dido, Tyrus built by Agenor, Memphis made by Ogdous, Thebes seated by Cadmus, nor Babylon reared by Semiramis were any way equal to this situation grounded by Romulus: to which all the discovered kingdoms of the earth after became tributaries. And in the noontide of their glory and height of all their honor, they edified theaters and amphitheaters: for in their flourishing commonweal their public comedians and tragedians most flourished, insomuch that the tragic and comic poets were all generally admired of the people and particularly every man of his private Mecenas.

In the reign of Augustus Christ was born, and as well in his days as before his birth these solemnities were held in the greatest estimation. In Julius Caesar's time, predecessor to Augustus, the famous honey-tongued orator Cicero flourished, who, amongst many other his eloquent orations, writ certain yet extant for the comedian Roscius (*Pro Roscio Comœdo*) of whom we shall speak more large hereafter. These continued in their honor till the reign of Tiberius Caesar, and under Tiberius Christ was crucified. To this end do I use this assertion because in the full and perfect time our Saviour sojourned on the earth, even in those happy and peaceful days the spacious theaters were in the greatest opinion amongst the Romans; yet neither Christ himself nor any of his sanctified apostles in any of their sermons, acts, or documents, so much as named them, or upon any abusive occasion touched them.

Therefore hence (methinks) a very probable and important argument may be grounded, that since they in their divine wisdoms knew all the sins abounding in the world before that time, taxed and reproved all the abuses reigning in that time, and foresaw all the actions and inconveniences (to the Church prejudicial) in the time to come. Since they (I say) in all their holy doctrines, books, and principles of Divinity were content to pass them over as things tolerated and indifferent, why should any nice and overscrupulous heads, since they cannot ground their curiousness either upon the Old or New Testament, take upon them to correct, control, and carp at that against which they cannot find any text in the sacred Scriptures?

In the time of Nero Caesar, the Apostle Paul was persecuted and suffered, Nero was then Emperor, Paul writ his Epistle to the Romans, and at the same time did the theaters most flourish amongst the Romans; yet where can we quote any place in his Epistles which forbids the Church of God, then resident in Rome, to absent themselves from any such assemblies?

To speak my opinion with all indifferency, God hath not enjoined us to wear all our apparel solely to defend the cold. Some garments we wear for warmth, others for ornament. So did the children of Israel hang earrings in their ears, nor was it by the law forbidden them. That purity is not looked for at our hands, being mortal and human, that is required of the Angels, being celestial and divine. God made us of earth, men; knows our natures, dispositions, and imperfections; and therefore hath limited us a time to rejoice, as he hath enjoined us a time to mourn for our transgressions. And I hold them more scrupulous than well advised that go about to take from us the use of all moderate recreations. Why hath God ordained for man variety of meats, dainties, and delicates if not to taste thereon? Why doth the world yield choice of honest pastimes, if not decently to use them? Was not the hare made to be hunted? the stag to be chased, and so of all other beasts of game in their several kinds? Since God hath provided us of these pastimes, why may we not use them to his glory? Now if you ask me: Why were not the theaters as gorgeously built in all other cities of Italy as Rome? And why are not playhouses maintained as well in other cities in England, as London? My answer is: It is not meet every mean esquire should carry the part belonging to one of the nobility, or for a nobleman to usurp the estate of a prince. Rome was a metropolis, a place whither all the nations known under the sun resorted. So is London, and being to receive all estates, all princes, all nations, therefore to afford them all choice of pastimes, sports, and recreations: yet were there theaters in all the greatest cities of the world, as we will more largely particularize hereafter.

→ EDWARD ALLEYN

Letter to His Wife

1593?

In August 1593, Edward Alleyn, the great tragedian and interpreter of Christopher Marlowe's heroic characters, wrote from Bristol to his wife in London while he was touring the provinces with the Lord Admiral's Men. The playhouses in the capital were closed for much of 1592 and 1593 owing to an epidemic of plague.

M_y good sweett mouse I comend me hartely
to yo^u And to my father my mother & my
sister bess hoping in god thought [though] the siknes
beround about you yett by his mercy itt may
escape yor house wch by y^e grace of god it
shall therfor vse this corse [course] kepe yor house
fayr and clean wch I knowe you will
and every evening throwe water before yor dore
and in yor bakcsid and haue in yor windowes
good store of rwe and herbe of grace and
w^t all the grace of god wch must be obtaynd
by prayers and so doinge no dout but ye lord
will mercyfully defend yo^u: now good mouse
I haue no newse to send you but this thatt
we haue all ou^r helth for wch the lord be praysed
I reseved yor letter att bristo [Bristol] by richard coulcy
for the wich I thank you   I haue sent yo^u by this
berer Thomas popes kinsman my whit [white]
wascote because it is a trobell to me to cary it
reseave it w^t this letter And lay it vp for
me till I com   if you send any mor letters
send to me by the cariers of shrowsbery or to west
chester or to york to be keptt till my lord
stranges players com and thus sweett hartt
w^t my harty comendā [commendations] to all o^r [our] frends I sess [cease]
from bristo this wensday after saynt Jams his day
being redy to begin the playe of hary of cornwall
mouse do my harty comend to m^r grigs his wif
and all his houshould and to my sister phillyps
      Yo^r Loving housband E Alleyn

mouse you send me no newes of any things
you should send of yor domestycall matters
such things as hapens att home as how yor
distilled watter proves or this or that or any
thing what you will

[*vertically in left-hand margin*]
and Jug I pray yo^u lett my orayng tawny stokins [stockings] of wolen
be dyed a very good blak against I com hom to wear in the
winter   yo^u sente me nott word of my garden but next tym you will
but remember this in any case that all that bed wch was parsley
in the month of september you sowe itt w^t spinage for then is the tym:
I would do it my self but we shall nott com hom till allholand tyd [All Saints'
      Day, November 1]
and so swett mouse farwell and broke [brook, endure] ou^r long Jorney w^t
      patienc

[*addressed:*]
This be delyvered
to m^r hinslo on [one] of the
gromes of hir ma͞ist [majesty's]
chamber dwelling
on the bank sid
right over against
the clink

CHAPTER 5

"I Loved My Books": *Shakespeare's Reading*

※

For almost four centuries Shakespeare has been stereotyped as the "natural" artist, the unlettered genius whose inspired creations owe hardly anything to learning and almost everything to inherent imaginative genius. Only fifteen years after Shakespeare's death John Milton, in "L'Allegro," commemorated his achievement by imagining a theater in which one might hear "sweetest Shakespeare, fancy's child, / Warble his native wood-notes wild." Milton here opposes Shakespeare's imaginative talents to the scholarly bent of his contemporary, Ben Jonson: Milton's alternative to the "native wood notes wild" is "Jonson's learned sock," a reference to the slipper worn by the classical actor of comedy. Even *native*, meaning English as opposed to Roman or Greek, is a code word for the nonclassical, the unpedantic.

In fact it was Jonson who, both during Shakespeare's lifetime and after his death, promulgated this distinction between learned playwrights like himself, devoted to classically sanctioned forms, and the natural and even barbarous creators of improbable fictions. These stereotypical oppositions cloud our understanding of what Shakespeare knew and how he came to know it. Surely what Shakespeare knew was not limited to the information he gathered from books, but because he made his living by the word, it seems worthwhile to consider what he was able to learn from other writers.

Scholars have meticulously studied the mass of material that the dramatist employed in composing his plays, from ancient comedies and tragedies to Italian novels and English narrative poems. In 1753–54 Charlotte Lennox published *Shakespeare Illustrated; or the Novels and Histories on which the Plays are founded,* a work that identified the sources of more than half the plays; as late as our own time, scholarly journals print articles with titles such as "A New Source for *Hamlet*, 1.3."

The simplest way to discover what Shakespeare read is to examine the printed sources of his work. This chapter begins with a review of the Greek and Roman literature that Shakespeare first encountered as a schoolboy ("Shakespeare and the Classics"). It then offers a brief catalogue ("Major Influences") of the principal literary influences. (The three books that Shakespeare used most extensively — Ovid's *Metamorphoses*, Plutarch's *Lives of the Noble Grecians and Romans*, and Holinshed's *Chronicles of England, Scotland, and Ireland* — are here mentioned briefly in the context of similar sources and then given special treatment at the end of the chapter.) These first two sections are designed to provide an overview of what Shakespeare found appealing and useful when he set to work.

But such a survey, if it did no more than describe the texts that Shakespeare certainly or probably or possibly consulted in writing a play, would surely be an inadequate register of Shakespeare's reading. To take the most obvious example, the Bible has a claim to being the most important book Shakespeare knew, even though it did not serve as a major source for any of his plots. So it is with Elizabethan poetry, some of which had a palpable effect on the development of his dramatic verse. It will be useful, in other words, to expand our definition of *source*, to look beyond the indisputable originals of the plays into less obviously influential books and especially into noncanonical forms of writing such as pamphlets and ballads. The Scriptures also complicate the definition of "reading." We know, for instance, that Shakespeare knew the Bible, but he need not have "read" it religiously or systematically. Law-abiding English citizens at the turn of the seventeenth century went to church every Sunday and on religious holidays, where they heard the Scriptures read from the pulpit and homilies based on biblical examples. Similarly, we know that Shakespeare knew the plays of Christopher Marlowe and Ben Jonson and other contemporary playwrights. Did he read them? Did he hear them spoken from the stage? Or did he learn them by heart, from the experience of acting in them? The third section of this chapter ("Indirect Sources") addresses some of these questions.

A few of Shakespeare's favorite books merit special attention, not only because it is fascinating to discover what the playwright particularly enjoyed reading but also because the nature of his artistic achievement is closely tied to his literary tastes. A work that he especially loved was Ovid's *Metamorphoses*, which he read in both the original Latin and in an Elizabethan translation by Arthur Golding (1567). Ovid's collection is valuable as an indicator of the kind of stories Shakespeare liked. He obviously relished the Roman poet's fantastic world of transformation and magic, but he also responded to the actual deeds of human heroes in the classical world. His basic text for such stories was Plutarch's *Lives of the Noble Grecians and Romans*. For accounts of colorful figures closer to his own time, Shakespeare turned repeatedly to Raphael Holinshed's recently published *Chronicles of England, Scotland, and Ireland*. A discussion of these works concludes the chapter ("Shakespeare's Favorites"). A brief analysis of their principal appeals will help to define the artistic sensibility that has endowed Shakespeare's work with its own enduring power.

Shakespeare was indisputably an enthusiastic and wide-ranging reader. But an investigation of his reading requires awareness that any conclusions we reach must be indefinite and partial. For example, we do not know where Shakespeare obtained the books he read or how many he owned — books were expensive. Perhaps at the beginning of his career he borrowed from a wealthy friend or patron, possibly the earl of Southampton, or had the use of his library. No one is sure about the extent to which the theatrical community intersected with the more conventional literary circles, and so information about Shakespeare's access to poetry and fiction in manuscript is uncertain. The temporal distance impedes our ability to discover the full range of his literary and nonliterary influences. Much of the printed material from the sixteenth and seventeenth centuries has perished. Moreover, it is not easy to draw absolute distinctions between printed and nonprinted texts: Shakespeare may have seen performances of many of the plays that nourished his work, but not read them. It is also important to remember that the world Shakespeare inhabited was much more of an oral culture than ours. But finally, even if we could identify all of Shakespeare's sources with absolute certainty, this knowledge would still be less important than recognition of his unparalleled capacity for adapting, combining, and transmuting what he read.

Shakespeare and the Classics

Shakespeare's command of the classics, those works of Greek and Roman antiquity reborn in England with the arrival of sixteenth-century humanism, was for a long time the subject of intense debate. A primary question was whether his connection was direct or oblique: did Shakespeare read the originals of the stories and dramas that he appropriated, or did he rely mainly on translations? Ben Jonson started the trouble, in his commemorative verses for the First Folio, when he declared that although Shakespeare had "small Latin and less Greek," such ignorance didn't matter because he still deserved to be ranked with the greatest classical authors. This debate was sustained throughout the eighteenth and nineteenth centuries by commentators who sought either to defend Shakespeare's learning and thus safeguard his artistic status, or else to defend his ignorance and thus emphasize his natural genius. In the second half of the eighteenth century, for example, a Cambridge University scholar named Richard Farmer was able, by means of verbal echoes in the plays, to identify the Elizabethan translations of Plutarch and Ovid that Shakespeare consulted. On the basis of these discoveries he insisted that the dramatist's learning did not include Greek and Latin originals: "He remembered perhaps enough of his schoolboy learning to put the *Hig, hag, hog* [the proper Latin is *hic, haec, hoc*] into the mouth of Sir Hugh Evans; and might pick up in the writers of the time, or the course of his conversation, a familiar phrase or two of French or Italian; but his *studies* were most demonstratively confined to *nature* and *his own language*" (qtd. in Halliday 162).

Modern scholarship has overturned these conclusions. We now know that while Shakespeare often used translations, he could and did read sources in Latin, French, and probably Italian. In scrutinizing a celebrated speech from Ovid that shows up in *The Tempest* as Prospero's "Ye elves of hills, brooks, standing lakes, and groves" (5.1.33ff), scholars have been able to demonstrate just how and where Shakespeare uses the translation and where he reverts to the original. Then what of Jonson's left-handed compliment? It needs to be put in context: Jonson was one of the most learned men of his age, a master of ancient and modern languages, a proud scholar who larded his classically derived tragedies with marginal quotations from and footnotes to the models and originals that he imitated. Compared to Jonson's mastery of Latin, Shakespeare's was perhaps "small." But considered on its own terms, Shakespeare's classical learning was respectable for the age in which he lived, and for the age in which *we* live, it was formidable.

Grammar schools in the sixteenth century were devoted to instruction in Latin grammar, and as a student at the King's New School in Stratford, Shakespeare would have spent much of his boyhood translating Latin. The Latin grammar text of William Lyly, grandfather of the playwright John Lyly, was supplemented by exercise books and composition manuals designed to inculcate the principles of rhetoric and style. Having mastered the fundamentals, pupils moved on to translation: for most of the day, six days a week, for about ten years, they rendered Latin texts into English and then retranslated the English back into Latin. The graduated curriculum of reading began with the relatively easy Latin of Aesop (translated from the original Greek) and Caesar. This introduction prepared them for the work of the great poets, historians, orators, and essayists: Cicero, Virgil, Ovid, Horace, Suetonius, Livy, Seneca. They also encountered Roman drama, especially the work of Terence, the favorite of the Renaissance humanists. The comedies of Plautus and tragedies of Seneca were studied less often in schools, but Shakespeare clearly read them, perhaps on his own.

The exact degree of Shakespeare's proficiency is difficult to ascertain, but we do know that he was able to read fairly sophisticated Latin in the original. In addition to the documented cases in which a Shakespearean passage departs from Arthur Golding's English version of the *Metamorphoses* in favor of a phrase or trope from the original, scholars have discovered other evidence. For example, in *The Rape of Lucrece* Shakespeare borrows certain details directly from a story in Ovid's *Fasti* that was available to him only in its Latin version. Apparently Shakespeare did not know Greek. It was less frequently studied than Latin in Renaissance England, and those who read the monuments of Greek literature usually depended on Latin translations. A major exception, Plutarch's *Lives,* was written in the author's native Greek (although composed during the Roman empire); it became widely known, however, through the English translation of Sir Thomas North, who used a French translation by Jacques Amyot. For the Renaissance reader, "classical" meant primarily Latin.

Major Influences

Not only was Shakespeare able to read Latin literature in the original, but he also seems to have liked it and to have decided that theater audiences would too. Thus Roman authors provided the material for many of his plays, early and late. Near the beginning of his career, about the time that he converted Ovid's story into *The Rape of Lucrece,* he turned to antiquity for what may have been his initial efforts in tragedy and comedy. Scrutiny of these classical texts and of the use Shakespeare made of them reveals two overriding characteristics of his practice as an adapter: first, his eclecticism, his genius for combining classical stories with other materials, both ancient and modern, to form new creations; and second, his ability to expand and multiply characters, episodes, and effects in order to surpass the classical models.

The plot of *Titus Andronicus* apparently derives from an English story of the Roman general and not from classical history. In order to represent its horrors more vividly, however, Shakespeare enriched the narrative with material taken from the *Thyestes* of Seneca, the Roman playwright whose vengeful ghosts and tormented heroes made him the acknowledged master of passion and violence; and he also drew on the *Metamorphoses,* adapting for his own story of rape and revenge Ovid's tale of Philomela, Tereus, and Procne. In creating *The Comedy of Errors,* Shakespeare combined two plays by the Roman dramatist Plautus: *Menaechmi,* an identity comedy in which twins are mistaken for each other; and *Amphitruo,* in which Jupiter, disguised as Amphitruo, assumes the husband's place in bed, while Mercury, disguised as Amphitruo's servant, shuts both husband and servant out of the house. Shakespeare immediately perceived the appeal of these plays and set about to reproduce and augment their attractions in his own farce: he re-creates Plautus's twins as the Antipholus brothers and then gives them twin servants, the Dromios, thus multiplying the opportunities for comic confusion. Having observed the effectiveness of this formula, he returned to it in his second twin comedy, *Twelfth Night.* There he developed romantic sentiments not present in Roman comedy, but he did not sacrifice delight in the hilarious consequences of mistaken identity. These Roman plays taught Shakespeare a great deal about dramatic construction and about the affective possibilities of comedy and tragedy. But he moved quickly to adapt other kinds of ancient writing, particularly Ovid's *Metamorphoses* and Plutarch's *Lives.* The influence of both these authors on Shakespeare is so pervasive that they demand separate treatment, along with Shakespeare's other favorite, Raphael Holinshed.

Holinshed's *Chronicles of England, Scotland, and Ireland,* however, is only one of the many books that fed Shakespeare's vision of England's past. Almost as influential was Edward Hall's *The Union of the Two Noble and Illustre Families of Lancaster and York* (second edition, 1548), particularly in the creation of Shakespeare's first group of history plays, the First Tetralogy *(Henry VI, Parts 1, 2, and 3* and *Richard III)*. The *Union* was the most ideologically pointed of the major sixteenth-century chronicles, for Hall frankly conceived of himself as an apologist for the Tudor monarchy. In dedicating the work to King Edward VI, he acknowledged previous historians' diligence but lamented their lack of moral purpose. To him the Wars of the Roses were a nightmare from which Henry VII, Edward's grandfather, had mercifully awakened his country; the villainous characterization of Henry's enemy, Richard III, is apparent in the excerpt given on page 163. Hall saw it as his duty to instruct his contemporaries in the causes and effects of the chaos, tyranny, and bloodshed that had afflicted England in the previous century.

Other historians also furnished Shakespeare with information or inspiration. Published in 1559 and often reprinted and expanded, *A Mirror for Magistrates* is an anthology of verse narratives in which notorious figures from classical and English history recount their tragic stories and anatomize the vices that accompany power. In 1595 Samuel Daniel published his long poem *The Civil Wars,* which was probably influenced by Shakespeare's First Tetralogy and in turn probably influenced the Second Tetralogy. The popular stage furnished historical dramas as well, such as the anonymous *Woodstock,* one of the sources for *Richard II,* and the (also anonymous) play called *The Famous Victories of Henry V.*

Just as the dramatists borrowed characters and details from the English chronicles, the historians — in the absence of modern copyright laws — did not hesitate to appropriate one another's work. Holinshed borrowed liberally from Hall's *Union,* just as Hall had relied on the narratives of his illustrious predecessors, particularly Sir Thomas More on the life of Richard III and Polydore Vergil, author of *Anglica Historia.* This kind of piggyback history sometimes makes it hard to determine which source Shakespeare was reading when he composed his history plays, although occasionally a textual quirk affords a cherishable picture of William Shakespeare sitting at his desk with a specific edition of a particular book open before him. In *Henry IV, Part 1,* for example, the opening scene presents King Henry's report on the prisoners taken by Hotspur at the battle of Holmedon, including "Mordake Earl of Fife and eldest son / To beaten Douglas" (1.1.71–72). Mordake actually was the son of the earl of Albany, but a punctuation error in Holinshed misled Shakespeare: "and of prisoners among other were these, Mordacke earle of Fife, son to the governour Archembald earle Dowglas, which in the fight lost one of his eies" (see Bullough 4: 183). The lack of a comma after "governour" is responsible for the error. Such glimpses into the compositional process are relatively rare, however, and usually it is difficult to tell which historian Shakespeare was reading.

All of these historians shared common purposes: the justification of the Tudor line, the condemnation of what they saw as tyranny, and the exposition of history's lessons. Hall's work is governed by his conviction that "wryting is the keye to enduce vertue, and represse vice" (Bullough 3: 10), so he is keen to demonstrate that the virtuous thrive and the wicked suffer. Although Holinshed does not moralize so overtly, he appears to share Hall's belief and his method. Not everyone does, however. Much later in literary history, when Miss Prism, the governess in Oscar Wilde's *The Importance of Being Earnest,* is asked to describe the ending of her romantic novel, she replies that "the good ended happily and the bad unhappily. That is what fiction means." As Shakespeare began the Second Tetralogy of histories, the great cycle including *Richard II, Henry IV, Parts 1 and 2,* and *Henry V,* he had come to accept the pessimism that underlies the Wildean irony, that only in books is virtue rewarded. Committed as he was to the value of order and the perils of discord, he nevertheless became increasingly conscious that the moral certainties of a Hall are not easy to sustain and that the writing of history, whether in dramatic or narrative form, is to a large extent a fictional enterprise. This is not to say that the First Tetralogy lacks irony about the transmission of historical events, as a quick reading of *Richard III* will attest. But the Second Tetralogy, particularly *Henry IV, Part 2,* urges a much more dubious view of the historian's task.

Another major literary group from which Shakespeare drew his plots was the fiction of his time, both European and English. These were mostly romances or adventure stories written in verse or prose. Many of them descend through various European languages from Greek originals, such as Apuleius's romance — actually an early version of a novel — called *The Golden Ass.* In a few cases, Shakespeare read translations of the Continental works; in other cases, he seems to have read the originals. Many of these narratives existed in multiple versions, having been retold in other forms and other languages, so Shakespeare's immediate source is not always obvious.

Romeo and Juliet offers a vivid example of Shakespeare's attraction to romantic tales that originated on the Continent and made their way into English. The play derives mainly from a long English poem, Arthur Brooke's *The Tragical History of Romeus and Juliet,* first printed about three decades earlier. Shakespeare knew this poem thoroughly (although he altered its thematic focus), but he may also have known the tale through its European sources, from which Brooke had derived his plot. Analogues of the story extend as far back as Greek romance of the third century, and several French and Italian versions, the details and themes of which vary widely, were produced in the hundred years before Shakespeare adapted it. In 1554 it appears in a form that we would recognize in Matteo Bandello's Italian prose *novella* (a long short story or a short novel, like its English equivalent); this version is retold by Boaistuau in French in 1559, and Brooke's three-thousand-line poem, a translation of Boaistuau, was published in 1562 and then reprinted in 1587. The flavor of Brooke's work can be suggested by a few of his couplets, which are written in "poulter's measure," a form in which lines of twelve and fourteen syllables alternate. Here is his account of the moment when Juliet discovers the dead Romeus:

> But when she neither could her swelling sorow swage,
> Ne yet her tender hart abyde her sickenes furious rage,

Falne on his corps, she lay long panting on his face,
And then with all her force and strength, the ded corps dyd embrace,
As though with sighes, with sobs, with force and busy payne,
She would him rayse, and him restore from death to lyfe agayne.   (2,725–30)

This passage provides a sample of the kind of writing that was popular in Elizabethan England and that Shakespeare found useful in seeking out dramatic subjects.

Such fictions from the Continent supplied the basis for several of Shakespeare's plays, comic, tragic, and tragicomic. *The Two Gentlemen of Verona*, one of his earliest comedies, derives from a Portuguese prose romance, *Diana Enamorada*, by Jorge de Montemayor. About 1603, in midcareer, Shakespeare seems to have been reading *Gli Hecatommithi*, an anthology of short fiction by the Italian Giovanni Battista Giraldi Cinthio. It contains the story of the lustful civic official that Shakespeare reproduces in *Measure for Measure* and the tale of the jealous captain that Shakespeare converts into *Othello*. An excerpt from Cinthio's anthology is found on page 169. At the end of his career Shakespeare returned to one of the fountainheads of this tradition, Giovanni Boccaccio, for the story of the wager in *Cymbeline*.

These European poets and romancers had English descendants who were working in the 1580s and '90s and whom Shakespeare also found stimulating and useful. In other words, he dramatized some of the most popular fiction of his own day. An appropriate analogy might be Hollywood: it is as if a screenwriter in our own time, unrestricted by laws of copyright, were to devise a script based on a novel by John Grisham or Stephen King. Thomas Lodge's *Rosalynde*, derived from a fourteenth-century English poem, was published in London in 1590, just as Shakespeare was beginning to write for the stage; about ten years later Lodge's prose pastoral served Shakespeare as a source for *As You Like It*, one of his experiments with romantic comedy. Sir Philip Sidney's *Arcadia*, also published in 1590, four years after the death of its author, was valuable to Shakespeare both directly and indirectly. As he wrote *King Lear*, developing the story of filial ingratitude and familial cruelty found in Holinshed, he perhaps remembered Sidney's tale of the Paphlagonian king abused by his monstrous son and converted it into the parallel subplot of the Gloucester family. Or it may be that his reading of that grim story in the *Arcadia* returned him to the old chronicle play, *King Leir*, that he then used, alongside Holinshed, for the main plot of his tragedy. The more significant influence of Sidney's fiction, however, is on Shakespeare's later work. The extravagance of romance, its episodic and assimilative tendencies, its pattern of quest and deferral, its geographical and temporal sprawl, its devotion to extremes of behavior and experience, its ultimately Protestant emphasis on the testing of human strength, its dependence on narrative and stylistic deviation or wandering — all of these qualities link the *Arcadia* with the romances of Shakespeare's final phase. In fact, late in his career Shakespeare seems to have been rereading a good deal of Elizabethan fiction. *The Winter's Tale* is a dramatization of a novella by Robert Greene called *Pandosto, or The Triumph of Time,* published in 1588 and then reprinted under a different title in 1607, three years before Shakespeare appropriated it. To read *Pandosto* alongside *The Winter's Tale* is to recognize Shakespeare's theatrical gift for transforming his sources: whereas Greene's heroine dies, Shakespeare teases his audience with uncertainty and then revises the original ending, creating one of the most effective final scenes in all of drama.

This multitude of works from a variety of traditions illuminates Shakespeare's characteristic mode of composition. He rarely made up his own plots but instead adapted them from fictions, biographies, dramas, and even current events that fired his imagination. Invention and imitation were not two distinct processes in Renaissance artistic theory. First-time readers are sometimes disappointed to learn that Shakespeare was not "original," in the sense of originating entirely new plots. But the knowledge that the raw materials are borrowed should not diminish our sense of Shakespeare's artistic ability; instead, it should allow us to appreciate more exactly the nature of his genius for choosing subjects, a talent involving three main skills. The first was his knack for recognizing a potentially effective theatrical story when he saw one, a talent so obvious as to require no elaboration here: that so many of his plots existed in so many languages and verse forms over so many centuries is sufficient evidence of his nose for what would sell.

Second, Shakespeare early exhibited a talent for synthesis, for combining unlikely pairs of tales into a unified whole. In *The Comedy of Errors,* for example, he surrounds the two Roman comedies with a frame story, the narrative of a merchant, Egeon, searching the Mediterranean for his lost son; it is taken from the ancient tale of Apollonius of Tyre as retold in the *Confessio Amantis,* a book of stories by the medieval English poet John Gower, a contemporary of Chaucer. This unusual alliance affords Shakespeare a variety of tonal effects: while the farcical errors produce scornful laughter, the old man's narrow escape and reunion with his family contribute a sense of comic empathy. Even those plays that derive from one principal source — as *All's Well That Ends Well* does from one of Boccaccio's stories — benefit from the playwright's voracious reading, his eye for meaningful details, and his tendency to prefer histrionic effect to historical fact.

Third, Shakespeare excelled at identifying the dramatic heart of a story and presenting it in a way that especially suited the conditions of the Elizabethan theater. This unfailing sense of a story's theatrical core is best illustrated by *Richard III,* another early effort. Whereas Hall's account of the life of Richard of Gloucester is the fairly predictable work of a political apologist, Shakespeare's theatrical version is a vivid and complex portrait of a charismatic psychopath. What Shakespeare succeeds in doing, as none of his predecessors managed, is to make his subject a compelling stage presence and a self-conscious actor. The soliloquy that opens the play ("Now is the winter of our discontent"), in which Richard takes the audience into his confidence and gleefully outlines his scheme for disposing of his rivals and taking the crown, is the first of Richard's many histrionic strategies: witty asides, privately hatched theatrical schemes ("Plots have I laid, inductions dangerous," 1.1.32), staged scenes designed for public consumption, and periodic reviews of his own performances. The source narratives of More, Hall, and Holinshed all hint at the connection between politics and theater — action and acting, plots and plots — but only Shakespeare brilliantly explores the psychology of political tyrant as theatrical superstar.

Indirect Sources

The list of works that Shakespeare directly used, large as it is, represents only a fraction of the writing he must have read, and we must exert some effort to locate other, subtler areas of his learning. The Bible is the most important of such texts. Stories from the Old and New Testaments are recalled by his characters; Christian doctrine is sometimes invoked as a context for interpreting dramatic action; and, perhaps most meaningfully, the cadences of the Elizabethan translations of the Bible are audible in his verse and prose. But Shakespeare's Bible was different from our own. The King James version (more properly called the Authorized Version) to our ears sounds "Shakespearean" because it was translated at the time that Shakespeare was writing. However, he could not have read it until he had virtually retired from the stage, for it was not published until 1611. Instead, he would have read the Geneva Bible (trans. 1560), an excerpt from which appears on page 167, or the Bishops' Bible (trans. 1568). The allusions in Shakespeare's work mostly echo these translations and sometimes their marginal notes as well. Into a similar category would fit *The Book of Common Prayer*, the guide to the rituals and sacraments of the Church of England composed in 1549; the public would have been almost as familiar with it as with the Scriptures themselves. (See "The Order for the Burial of the Dead" on p. 171.) A final, indispensable document of this Protestant culture was John Foxe's *Acts and Monuments* (first published in 1563), a history of Catholic persecution and reformist virtue that went through numerous editions, was placed officially in every parish church, and ended up next to the Bible in many private homes. (An excerpt appears on p. 174.)

Although no newspapers existed in Shakespeare's England — printing was still in an early stage, and cheap paper was scarce — people hungered for news. Consequently, balladeers exploited the sorts of topics featured in our tabloid press — natural disasters, monstrous crimes, success stories — rapidly converting newsworthy events into rhymed narratives. These crude verses were printed on *broadside* sheets (sizable pieces of paper), set to a familiar tune named on the sheet itself ("To the Tune of 'Greensleeves'") and offered for sale. Sometimes preceded or accompanied by pamphlets in prose reporting on the same events, the broadside ballads were a familiar and important means of communication in London and especially in the countryside. Shakespeare's amused attitude toward some of these balladeers and their wares can be seen in his portrait of Autolycus, the combination con man, peddler, and balladseller in *The Winter's Tale* who hawks incredible stories to the country rubes. Still, as C. H. Firth puts it, "The ballads . . . supply evidence on the character of Shakespeare's audience. These remnants of the popular literature of the time show how the people lived, and what they thought, the stories with which they were familiar, and the allusions which they could understand" (qtd. in Lee and Onions 2: 511).

Since printed ballads had to be noted in the Register of the Stationers' Company, we have a fairly accurate record of many of these crude poems, although as a result of their ephemeral nature, many are lost. The Stationers' Register records some twenty-four ballads on the defeat of the Spanish Armada in 1588; the various conspiracies against Queen Elizabeth and King James gave rise to rhymed accounts of the traitors and their crimes; and fires, floods, and other such cataclysms invariably inspired the creation of new ones. A few generalizations can be made about these ballads when they are looked at collectively. First, they reveal a fierce patriotism that combines national pride with religious fervor, directing scorn at France, Spain, and especially Catholicism, as the following title indicates:

A Letter to Rome, to Declare to the Pope
John Felton, His Friend, Is Hang'd in a Rope,
And Farther, Aright His Grace to Enform,
He Died a Papist and Seem'd Not to Turn.

Second, in addition to politics and religion, sex is a major topic. Autolycus entices prospective buyers with a salacious story about a frigid woman turned into a (cold) fish. Third, the balladeers often moralized the atrocities they announced, with fires or storms treated as proof of God's judgment on the wicked. (See "The True Form and Shape of a Monstrous Child," p. 178.) Finally, some ballads offered, instead of a version of current events, a crudely versified retelling of a famous biblical or ancient narrative.

The broadside form was also used for public information and governmental propaganda. Accounts of the horrifying executions of criminals were popular, and such ballads served the government's ideological needs. Often the regime employed broadsides officially for admonition or regulation, issuing proclamations concerning public behavior ("A Proclamation against Unlawful Assemblies"), dress codes, the carrying of weapons, the number of deaths from plague, price-fixing, border disputes, and other such social and economic problems. Sometimes important public figures, such as Robert Cecil, Elizabeth's secretary of state, arranged for their likenesses to be distributed in broadside form, although Elizabeth herself disliked her broadside portrait and issued a proclamation (in broadside) forbidding the representation of her in that manner (see Firth in Lee and Onions 2: 536). Later royal figures seem not to have objected, however: broadside portraits exist of King James's consort, Queen Anne, and their son Prince Henry.

News of the New World — this was, after all, the end of the age of exploration and the beginning of the age of colonization — was available to the reading public through travel literature that was sometimes published and sometimes circulated privately. In *Twelfth Night,* Maria ridicules Malvolio's self-satisfaction by complaining that "He does smile his face into more lines than is in the new map, with the augmentation of the Indies" (3.2.78–80). Richard Hakluyt (1552–1616), archdeacon of Westminster and self-appointed geographer to the nation, kept the public informed about the triumphs of English explorers and colonizers, publishing his *Divers Voyages Touching the Discovery of America* in 1582 (and dedicating it to Sir Philip Sidney) and his *Principal Navigations, Voyages, and Discoveries of the English Nation* in 1589 (enlarged to three volumes in 1598–1600). After his death his work was carried on by Samuel Purchas, whose *Purchas His Pilgrims* (1625) contains Sir William Strachey's account (written in 1610) of the terrible events suffered by a group of colonists on a voyage to North America (see the excerpt on p. 180). Apparently Shakespeare read Strachey's *True Reportory of the Wreck . . .* in manuscript just after it was written and long before it was published, since in many details the narrative resembles the experience of the shipwrecked courtiers in *The Tempest*.

Plays from the public theater and the children's companies belong in a discussion of Shakespeare's reading, although he would have seen rather than read many of them. As he began his career in the theater, the available offerings were extremely varied, from old-style morality plays to the mystery cycles (which he might have attended in Coventry near his hometown) to romantic or pastoral comedies by John Lyly and George Peele to "chronicle histories" (*The Troublesome Reign of John, King of England,* for example) to Kyd's sensational *Spanish Tragedy*. Shakespeare learned about structure, character, and other points of stagecraft from all of these types of drama, but his ear must have been especially enchanted by Christopher Marlowe's heroic speeches, delivered by Edward Alleyn from the stage of the Rose Playhouse. The words written for such outsized characters as Tamburlaine, Doctor Faustus, and Barabas, the Jew of Malta, lie behind Shakespeare's creation of his mesmerizing Richard III, Richard II, and Shylock. (A passage from one of Tamburlaine's speeches, taken from a facsimile of the 1590 edition of Marlowe's play, is found on p. 182). We know, too, that Shakespeare acted in two of Ben Jonson's plays, the comedy *Every Man in his Humour* in 1598 and then *Sejanus,* Jonson's attempt at classical tragedy, in 1603. In fact, Shakespeare's position as shareholder with the King's Men meant that he would have been well acquainted with the numerous plays in the company's repertory from about 1594 to about 1610.

If Shakespeare, like his contemporaries, had a taste for the outrageous and crude offerings of popular literature, he also took pleasure in more elusive, less popular writing, perhaps most significantly the *Essays* of the French thinker Michel de Montaigne. Montaigne's work might well be considered a major source, since the *Essays* directly influenced Shakespeare in the creation of the plays. However, I treat it here among the less obvious stimuli because Montaigne offered the playwright not stories or characters but ideas and philosophical viewpoints. Just before Shakespeare's rise to prominence, Montaigne was earning notice among European readers for his two volumes of essays published in 1580 and expanded in 1595. A few titles give a sense of his concerns: "That Our Intention Judgeth Our Actions," "Of the Force of Imagination," "Of Friendship," "A Consideration upon Cicero," "Of Thumbs." (An excerpt from Montaigne's essay "Of the Vanity of Words" appears on p. 63.) The tone of these reflections is elusive and complex: Montaigne's persona adopts a skeptical view of experience, an attitude that can vary from bitterness to mild irony to remote amusement. The distance from which Montaigne regards all mortal activity generates a tolerant affection for human creatures with all their failings, a balance that we also recognize in the mature Shakespeare. The playwright may have felt a philosophical kinship with Montaigne and may in fact have absorbed directly some of the Frenchman's perspectivism, his understanding that what we see depends on where we stand. Shakespeare had probably read Montaigne by about 1601 or so, for *Hamlet* seems to refer to one of the most ambitious and darkest of the essays, "An Apology of Raymond Sebond." Most likely Shakespeare read the essay in French, for the first English translation, by John Florio, was not published until 1603 (although Shakespeare might have seen the translation in manuscript). In any case, he certainly read Florio's version. In a later play, *The Tempest,* the old counselor, Gonzalo, describes his vision of the perfect society in language that echoes Florio's translation of the essay "Of the Cannibals." Shakespeare's skepticism, in this case, is more pervasive than Montaigne's: whereas the philosopher idealizes the savages and condemns their conquerors, the dramatist seems dubious about both groups. Other philosophical writers probably held Shakespeare's attention, although none so firmly as Montaigne.

As a poetic dramatist, however, Shakespeare was especially attracted to poetry, and the recent works of his contemporaries were always on his desk or in his head. He probably read Edmund Spenser's sonnets, published as the *Amoretti,* as well as his vast allegory, *The Faerie Queene,* issued in two parts, Books 1–3 in 1590, 4–6 in 1596. We know from references in the plays that he was familiar with the work of the lesser poets of the age, such as Samuel Daniel and Michael Drayton, and he may have been aware of the vigorous satires that young John Donne was writing at the end of the 1590s. Shakespeare's sonnets indicate an active interest in the tradition of sonnet sequences, the most celebrated of them being Sir Philip Sidney's *Astrophil and Stella,* written around 1580 but not published until 1591. (Two poems from that sequence appear on p. 183.) Sidney's brilliant lyrics very likely affected Shakespeare's efforts, both in the formal qualities of individual poems (wordplay, imagery, Petrarchan and anti-Petrarchan themes) and in the presence of a narrative loosely connecting the individual poems into a sequence, although the "characters" in *Astrophil and Stella* have proved less resistant to identification than the ghostly figures in Shakespeare's collection. The thematic reworkings and narrative mysteries of the 1609 Quarto are perhaps more comparable to, and may have stimulated, the sequence written by Sidney's niece, Lady Mary Wroth. In her *Pamphilia to Amphilanthus,* selections from which were circulating by 1612, Wroth inverts the conventional male–female struggle: Pamphilia is the female narrator lamenting the infidelities of the insensitive male lover. (See the two sonnets on p. 184.)

Other forms of writing popular in the period can only be mentioned. A primary source for poetry was the miscellany, an anthology of verses gathered by an editor or publisher and offered for sale under such titles as *A Gorgeous Gallery of Gallant Inventions* and *England's Helicon*. Probably the best known, *Songs and Sonnets*, the 1557 collection that we know as *Tottel's Miscellany*, receives a nod in *The Merry Wives of Windsor*, when the idiotic Slender wishes that he had brought his copy to impress the girl he hopes to win. Religious pamphleteers kept themselves busy, particularly in attacks on the theater like Stephen Gosson's *Plays Confuted in Five Actions*. The period saw major translations, such as Sir Thomas Hoby's rendering of Castiglione's elegant guide to aristocratic manners and success, *The Book of the Courtier*, and George Chapman's translations of Homer, which began to appear in 1598. Literary criticism appeared in such treatises as Sir Philip Sidney's *Defense of Poesy* and George Puttenham's *Art of English Poesy* (excerpts appear on pp. 99 and 68). And finally there were jokebooks, humorous equivalents to the poetic miscellanies, such as *A Hundred Merry Tales* and Robert Armin's *Nest of Ninnies*.

Shakespeare's Favorites

Most passionate readers have certain books to which they frequently return. For Shakespeare those books were Raphael Holinshed's *Chronicles*, Thomas North's translation of Plutarch's *Lives*, and Ovid's *Metamorphoses*. Each of these large, ambitious works involves the reader in a complete world — the realm of Britain from ancient to modern times, the two great European empires of Greece and Rome, and a prehistorical, mythological universe of deities and magic. Shakespeare valued each of these authors for different reasons, however, and it is important to notice those properties that attracted him to each of them.

Holinshed's *Chronicles of England, Scotland, and Ireland* was the most immediately helpful. It served as a source for a third of the plays — the ten histories as well as two tragedies (*King Lear* and *Macbeth*) and a romance (*Cymbeline*), all set in Britain. Shakespeare read the second edition of 1587 (the first appeared in 1577) and used it extensively. What was its attraction, and why did he compose with it open before him and return to it so often? Holinshed's prose is by no means distinguished, certainly not as elegant or vivid as North's rendering of Plutarch, for example. Nor did the historian arrange a compelling shape for most of the events he recounts, or for the episodic collection as a whole. What Holinshed did furnish was an absolutely comprehensive version of historical events that stimulated Shakespeare's imagination.

The scope of the *Chronicles* is captured in Stephen Booth's analysis of the length of the (enlarged) 1587 edition: "excluding blanks, scholarly apparatus, and seven title pages, the text runs to about three-and-a-half million words. That is roughly equal to the total of the Authorized Version of the Bible, the complete dramatic works of Shakespeare, *Clarissa*, Boswell's *Life of Johnson*, and *War and Peace* combined" (*The Book Called "Holinshed's Chronicles"* 1). The historical sweep afforded by such vast length can be thrilling, and apparently it excited Shakespeare, who seems not to have used the *Chronicles* merely as a reference tool but to have read widely and enthusiastically in it. In addition to range, Holinshed delivers mountains of detail. Much of this particularity results from the normal Tudor practice of incorporating and amplifying all the relevant work of one's professional predecessors. Shakespeare, by writing his dramas with the *Chronicles* before him, thus had access to the most recent and complete resources available, the latest model of the historian's product. The second edition of the *Chronicles*, published after Holinshed's death, had been augmented and annotated by (among others) Abraham Fleming, who added Latin tags to the margins and sought at every turn to put the recorded events in a moral context. Sometimes his moralizing squares with the episode to which it is attached; sometimes his interpretation seems flagrantly incompatible with the event. Fleming's prescriptive apparatus contributes yet another layer to the palimpsest of information and interpretation that Holinshed had devised.

Such complexity offered golden chances to a dramatist prospecting for theatrical conflict, and Shakespeare found it irresistible. The *Chronicles* should be regarded as a vast warehouse stuffed full of character studies, dates, details of battles, genealogical data, digressions on motives and consequences, Tudor political orthodoxy, and unintended subversions of that orthodoxy. Thus Shakespeare becomes a kind of shopper, a wholesale buyer passing up and down the aisles, scanning the displays and surveying the merchandise, choosing items that he can then polish up and offer to his own customers. Holinshed's book supplied the raw material to which Shakespeare gave theatrical shape, educing patterns and focusing ideas. For example, Holinshed only faintly delineates the parallelism that Shakespeare develops between Prince Hal and Hotspur in *Henry IV, Part 1*. Sometimes the dramatist wished to shroud rather than clarify the meaning of events, at least temporarily: in the opening scenes of the same play, the motives of the King and the Percy family are much less easy to discern than in the source. As the excerpt found on page 185 indicates, Holinshed emphatically establishes the "envy" of the Percy family and the King's fear of Mortimer's right to the throne. Shakespeare allows such emotions and motives to unfold slowly and indeterminately, as a means of investigating dramatically the ethics of rebellion, usurpation, and political loyalty. Similarly, he complicates the moral and political orthodoxy that emerges from the *Chronicles*, setting familiar conclusions against inconclusive facts and even prompting the audience to reflect on what it means to write history, in dramatic form or otherwise.

The historical biographies that make up Plutarch's *Lives of the Noble Grecians and Romans* offered the playwright heroic stories and characters, ready-made structures, and philosophical and stylistic pleasures. Shakespeare probably read the second edition (1595) of North's translation, using it as the basis for four tragedies: *Julius Caesar, Timon of Athens, Antony and Cleopatra,* and *Coriolanus*. Plutarch also contributed ideas about the classical world and innumerable historical details that turn up in other plays. Shakespeare compressed events, selected what he needed from the wealth of particulars, and drew on Plutarch's several versions of the episodes and persons, depending on what he needed at the moment. In composing *Julius Caesar,* for instance, he worked eclectically, choosing events that Plutarch records in three of his *Lives,* those of Brutus,

Mark Antony, and Caesar himself. Shakespeare is faithful to his Plutarchan source in a way that he never is with Holinshed or his other models, and for three reasons.

First, Plutarch's biographical accounts, focused narrowly as they are on individual lives rather than on a historical panorama, present concentration and potential dramatic shape, as Holinshed's narratives do not. Second, as many commentators have pointed out, Shakespeare seems to have responded to the intellectual issues that occupy Plutarch — the relation of purpose to accident, the nature of heroism in an unheroic world, the interpenetration of the personal and the political. Such ideas suggest affinities among Shakespeare's books, for Plutarch was a favorite not only of Shakespeare but also of Montaigne, who declared, "Plutarch is my man." Shakespeare might have said the same. Third, Shakespeare's affection for Plutarch probably owes most to the power and elegance of North's prose style. A comparison of Enobarbus's speech about Cleopatra's royal barge (*Antony and Cleopatra* 2.2) with North's prose account of the same subject will illustrate Shakespeare's admiration for and indebtedness to his source: the dramatic speech is more or less versified North, whose account is reprinted on page 186. As I have pointed out, Renaissance ideas about imitation and originality differed from our own. What to us might look like literary theft was to early modern writers the creative reproduction of a favorite passage. But Shakespeare made changes as well. To study his appropriation of North, both here and in other passages, is to discern a multitude of subtle but significant alterations that illustrate the difference between history and theater.

But his fidelity to Plutarch was not slavish, and *Antony and Cleopatra* furnishes a complicating example of his practice vis-à-vis his classical source. Plutarch, following the orthodoxy of his ancient predecessors, is unsympathetic, even harsh, in his portrayal of the Egyptian Queen. According to the Roman view, well set forth by Philo in the first speech of the play, Cleopatra is a kind of witch who has seduced and destroyed the heroic Antony. Shakespeare's representation of the story is much more nuanced, suggesting both the strengths and weaknesses of the two lovers. In fact, Shakespeare employs Plutarch's position as a foil, counting on the audience to enter the theater with the conventional (Roman) distaste for Cleopatra and then allowing her to beguile the audience with her imagination and wit. In leading the audience to such a complex and favorable assessment, Shakespeare may have been encouraged by the unusually sympathetic portrayal in *The Tragedy of Antonie*, a closet drama by Robert Garnier translated into English by Mary Sidney Herbert and published in 1592. (An excerpt from her translation appears on p. 187.)

Ovid is perhaps more important than either Holinshed or Plutarch, and it may even be true to say that the *Metamorphoses* was Shakespeare's favorite book. Ovidian originals influenced the two early narrative poems, *Venus and Adonis* and *The Rape of Lucrece*. Some of the comedies, notably *A Midsummer Night's Dream*, make explicit use of narrative material from the *Metamorphoses*. But Shakespeare did not regard Ovid's work as an object for slavish imitation; rather, it served as an imaginative stimulus, a source of inspiration. Shakespeare responded profoundly to the Roman mythographer's fantastic vision of human and divine experience, particularly to his all-encompassing theme of transformation. Sometimes Ovid's magical changes are for the better, as when Venus gratifies Pygmalion's yearning by giving life to the statue he has sculpted. Sometimes they are for the worse, as when Actaeon spies on the bathing Diana and is turned into a horned stag tormented by his own hounds. (See the sixteenth-century translation of this tale on p. 190.) Shakespeare invokes the Pygmalion myth at the end of *The Winter's Tale*, and the Actaeon story becomes Falstaff's humorous punishment in the final scene of *The Merry Wives of Windsor*. Ovid's presentation of change is fundamentally dramatic, and thus the transformational theme is to some extent responsible for shaping Shakespeare's theatrical structures. Finally, the allusive verbal texture of the plays is everywhere informed by Ovid's fantastic, memorable tales.

Ovid's shifting and elusive world appealed to and served Shakespeare in both his comic and tragic moods. The *Metamorphoses* lies behind Shakespeare's creation of a realm in which the impossible becomes possible, in which obstacles can be overcome and wishes fulfilled, in which change is beneficent and happiness attainable. For example, *The Taming of the Shrew*, packed with Ovidian references, depicts a world that seems constant in nothing but change. In the frame story, Christopher Sly is transformed into a rich lord and Bartholomew the page into his wife; in the play proper, "Tranio is changed into Lucentio" by means of disguise; Lucentio the student into Cambio the scholar; Hortensio the old suitor into Litio the music master; Petruchio on his wedding day into a kind of lunatic; an unsuspecting traveler into Vincentio, false father of the false Lucentio; Bianca the obedient daughter into an uncooperative wife; and, in the titular transformation, Katherina ("the curst") from an unhappy misfit into a seemingly contented spouse. Despite the heavy irony, these reversals and alterations intimate that human action is being guided by some providential force corresponding to Ovid's gods and goddesses. Conversely, Ovid's tales of disastrous alteration are consistent with the great Renaissance *topos* or theme of mutability, the impermanence of perfection. Thus his pattern of sudden decline informs the tragic reversal of fortune evident in, say, *Othello* and *King Lear*.

This attraction to metamorphosis is another manifestation of Shakespeare's commitment to the value of play, his pleasure in the beneficial effects of costumes, roles, impersonation, and all the other essentials and accidentals of the theater. To act is to inhabit the character of or to assume the persona of another in order to entertain, and the fictional realm created by performance affords the members of the audience, for the duration of the play, the chance to inhabit a world different from their own. Such a devotion to fiction accounts for Shakespeare's appreciation for the pleasures of storytelling, a taste satisfied by Ovid's compendium of exotic tales. Shakespeare's reverence for the theater and for fiction generally is part of a larger concern for the value of art in human affairs. In the Pygmalion section of book 10, Ovid asserts that "the best art . . . is that which conceals art." This insistence on the indistinguishability of the artificial and the natural, on art's equivalence and potential superiority to nature — the point of the Pygmalion episode — is a favorite Ovidian idea that pervades the Shakespearean canon as well. Always the idea is just beneath the surface, as in Shakespeare's sonnets, in Hamlet's instructions to Horatio to tell his story to future audiences, and in the comedies of identity, such as *As You Like It*. Occasionally that view breaks through the surface and declares itself explicitly. In *The Winter's Tale*, for example, it generates the debate between Perdita and Polixenes over the relative value of art and nature, and then later in the final scene when a statue comes to life.

The opposition of art and nature is only one of many that Shakespeare encourages his audience to consider, evaluate, and reevaluate, and his attachment to the principle of intellectual flexibility seems to reflect the Roman poet's fascination with various forms of transmutation. As he concludes the story of Diana and Actaeon with the voyeur's death, Ovid reports a divided reaction to Actaeon's fate:

> Much muttring was upon this fact. Some thought there was extended
> A great deale more extremitie than neded. Some commended
> *Dianas* doing: saying that it was but worthely
> For safegarde of hir womanhod. Eche partie did applie
> Good reasons to defende their case. (3.156–60, Golding translation)

Such conflicting assessments of dramatic action are built into Shakespeare's theatrical method: is *Henry V* a patriotic celebration of Christian kingship or a dark assault on militarism and royal vanity? Most sensitive readers see evidence for both claims, and this frequent Shakespearean opposition, known as *complementarity*, is likewise implicit in the *Metamorphoses*.

Much the same might be said of North's Plutarch and, perhaps to a lesser extent, the second edition of Holinshed's *Chronicles*. Shakespeare seems to have been drawn to stories and persons that were susceptible to plural and even contradictory readings. And having located such ambiguities, he exploited the inherent uncertainty of dramatic representation to develop them even further. He involved his audience in the complex process of interpretation to such an extent that interpretation becomes one of the principal themes of his plays.

Ultimately the study of Shakespeare's sources is the study of how Shakespeare treated his sources. What Keats refers to as Shakespeare's "negative capability," his gift for effacing himself entirely and entering imaginatively into the lives of his characters, is relevant to his transformation of his sources as well. He had an eye for the telling detail; he ignored history when necessary; he combined apparently incompatible narratives into something entirely new; he altered particulars that didn't suit him. But above all he had a genius for identifying the essence of a great story and retelling it theatrically. Some sixty versions of the Lear story were in circulation when Shakespeare set about to dramatize the tale of the old king in 1605. Nobody remembers these prior versions today. But *King Lear* continues to fill theaters.

→ EDWARD HALL

From *The Union of the Two Noble and Illustre Families of Lancaster and York* 1548

Edward Hall's *Union*, written during the reign of Henry VIII to promote the Tudor version of the nation's past, was one of Shakespeare's principal sources for the early history plays. This excerpt recounts Richard of Gloucester's plot to clear his path to the throne by arranging for James Tyrell to murder his nephews.

King Richard, after his coronation, taking his way to Gloucester to visit in his new honor the town of which he bare the name of old, devised as he rode [how] to fulfill that thing which he before had intended. And forasmuch as his mind gave him that his nephews living, men would not reckon that he could have right to the realm, he thought therefore without delay to rid them, as though the killing of his kinsmen might end his cause, and make him kindly [naturally] king. Whereupon he sent John Grene, whom he specially trusted, unto Sir Robert Brakenbury, constable of the Tower, with a letter and credence also, that the same Sir Robert in any wise should put the two children to death. This John Grene did his errand to Brakenbury, kneeling before our lady in the Tower, who plainly answered that he would never put them to death to die therefor. With the which answer Grene returned, recounting the same to King Richard at Warwick yet [still] on his journey, wherewith he took such displeasure and thought that the same night he said to a secret page of his: "Ah, whom shall a man trust? They that I have brought up my self, they that I went [weened, thought] would have most surely served me, even those fail me, and at my commandment will do nothing for me." "Sir," quoth the page, "there lieth one in the pallet-chamber [bedroom] without that I dare well say, to do your grace pleasure the thing were right hard that he would refuse," meaning this by [by this] James Tyrell, which was a man of goodly personage, and for the gifts of nature worthy to have served a much better prince, if he had well served God, and by grace obtained to have as much truth and good will, as he had strength and wit. The man had a high heart and sore longed upward, not rising yet so fast as he had hoped, being hindered and kept under by Sir Richard Ratcliff and Sir William Catesby . . . which thing this page had well marked and known: wherefore this occasion offered of very special friendship spied his time to set him forward, and such wise to do him good, that all the enemies that he had (except the devil) could never have done him so much hurt and shame, for upon the page's words, King Richard arose (for this communication had he sitting on a draft [a privy], a convenient carpet for such a counsel) and came out into the pallet-chamber, where he did find in bed the said James Tyrell and Sir Thomas Tyrell of person like and brethren of blood, but nothing of kin in conditions. Then said the king merely to them, "What, sirs, be you in bed so soon?" And called up James Tyrell, and broke to him secretly his mind in this mischievous matter, in the which he found him nothing strange [disaffected]. Wherefore on the morrow he sent him to Brakenbury with a letter by the which he was commanded to deliver to the said James all the keys of the Tower for a night, to the end that he might there accomplish the king's pleasure in such things as he there had given him in commandment. After which letter delivered and the keys received, James appointed the next night ensuing to destroy them, devising before and preparing the means. . . .

For James Tyrell devised that they should be murdered in their beds, and no blood shed. To the execution whereof he appointed Miles Forest, one of the four that before kept them, a fellow flesh-bred in murder before time. And to him he joined one John Dighton, his own horsekeeper, a big broad square and strong knave. Then all the other being removed from them, this Miles Forest and John Dighton about midnight, the sely [innocent] children lying in their beds, came into the chamber and suddenly lapped them up amongst the clothes [bedsheets] and so bewrapped them and entangled them, keeping down by force the featherbed and pillows hard unto their mouths, that within a while they smored [smothered] and stifled them, and their breaths failing, they gave up to God their innocent souls into the joys of heaven, leaving to the tormentors their bodies dead in the bed, which after the wretches perceived, first by the struggling with the pangs of death, and after long lying still, to be thoroughly dead, they laid the bodies out upon the bed, and fetched James Tyrell to see them, which when he saw them perfectly dead, he caused the murderers to bury them at the stair foot, meetly [appropriately] deep in the ground under a great heap of stones.

✦ From the Geneva Bible ➤ *1560*

Named for its place of publication, a center of Calvinist thought, the Geneva Bible was one of the earliest and most influential English translations of the Scriptures. There was fierce debate in the sixteenth century about whether the Bible should be translated into English at all, and the success of the Geneva version helped to settle the question. The title page and map, both reduced, are reprinted from a facsimile edition. The map, which precedes Paul's Epistle to the Romans, depicts the territory covered by the disciples on their missionary journeys. Some of the place names used by Shakespeare include Illyria (*Twelfth Night*), Siracuse (*The Comedy of Errors*), Cyprus and the Pontick Sea (*Othello*), and Phillipi (*Julius Caesar*).

The facsimile text (slightly enlarged) on page 167 is from chapter 5 of the Gospel According to Matthew and contains the first part of the Sermon on the Mount. A transcription of the entire chapter follows.

THE BIBLE

AND
HOLY SCRIPTVRES
CONTEYNED IN
THE OLDE AND NEWE
Testament.

TRANSLATED ACCOR-ding to the Ebrue and Greke, and conferred with the best translations in diuers langages.

WITH MOSTE PROFITABLE ANNOTA-tions vpon all the hard places, and other things of great importance as may appeare in the Epistle to the Reader.

FEARE YE NOT, STAND STIL, AND BEHOLDE the saluacion of the Lord, which he wil shewe to you this day. Exod. 14,13.

THE LORD SHAL FIGHT FOR YOU: THEREFORE holde you your peace, Exod. 14, vers.14.

AT GENEVA
PRINTED BY ROVLAND HALL
M.D.LX.

CHAP. V.

3 Christ teacheth who are blessed. 13 The salt of the earth & light of the worlde. 16 Good workes 17 Christ came to fulfil the Law. 21 What is ment by killing. 23 Reconciliation. 27 Adulterie. 31 Divorcement. 33 Not to sweare. 39 To suffer wrong. 43 To loue our enemies. 48 Perfection.

1 ANd when he sawe the multitude, he went vp into a mountaine: and whe he was set, his disciples came to him.

2 And he opened his mouthe and taught them, saying,

3 *Blessed are the poore in spirit, for theirs is the kingdome of heauen.

4 *Blessed are they that b mourne: for they shalbe comforted.

5 *Blessed are the meke: for they shal inherite the earth.

6 Blessed are they which d honger & thirst for righteousnes: for they shal be filled.

7 Blessed are the merciful: for thei shal obteine mercie.

8 Blessed are the*pure in heart: for they shal se God.

9 Blessed are the peace makers: for they shalbe called the e children of God.

10 Blessed are they *which suffer persecutio for righteousnes sake: for theirs is the kingdome of heauen.

11 *Blessed are ye when men reuile you, and persecute you, and say all maner of euil against you for my sake, falsely.

12 Reioyce and be glad, for great is your

rewarde in heauen: for so persecuted they the Prophets which were before you.

13 *Ye are the f salte of the earth: but if the salte haue lost his sauour, wherewith shal it be salted? It is thenceforthe good for nothing, but to be cast out, & to be troden vnder fote of men.

14 Ye are the light of the worlde. A citie that is set on an hill, can not be hid.

15 *Nether do men light a candel, and put it vnder a bushel, but on a candelsticke, & it giueth light vnto all that are in the house.

16 *Let your light so shine before men, that they may se your good workes, & glorifie your Father which is in heauen.

17 Thinke not that I am come to destroye the Law, or the Prophetes. h I am not come to destroye them, but to fulfil them.

18 *For truely I say vnto you, Til heauen and earth perish, one iote, or one title of the Law shal not scape, til i all things be fulfilled.

19 *Whosoeuer therefore shal breake one of k these least commandements, & teache men so, he shalbe called the least in the kingdome of heauen: but whosoeuer shal obserue and teache them, the same shal be called great in the kingdome of heauen.

20 For I say vnto you, except your righteousnes excede the righteousnes of y Scribes

and

CHAPTER 5

3 Christ teacheth who are blessed. 13 The salt of the earth and light of the world. 16 Good works. 17 Christ came to fulfill the Law. 21 What is meant by killing. 23 Reconciliation. 27 Adultery. 29 Offenses. 31 Divorce. 33 Not to swear. 39 To suffer wrong. 43 To love our enemies. 48 Perfection.

1 And when he saw the multitude, he went up into a mountain; and when he was set, his disciples came to him.

2 And he opened his mouth and taught them, saying,

3 "Blessed are the poor in spirit, for theirs is the kingdom of heaven.

4 Blessed are they that mourn, for they shall be comforted.

5 Blessed are the meek, for they shall inherit the earth.

6 Blessed are they which hunger and thirst for righteousness, for they shall be filled.

7 Blessed are the merciful, for they shall obtain mercy.

8 Blessed are the pure in heart, for they shall see God.

9 Blessed are the peace makers, for they shall be called the children of God.

10 Blessed are they which suffer persecution for righteousness sake, for theirs is the kingdom of heaven.

11 Blessed are you when men revile you and persecute you and say all manner of evil against you for my sake falsely.

12 Rejoice and be glad, for great is your reward in heaven; for so persecuted they the Prophets which were before you.

13 You are the salt of the earth; but if the salt has lost his savor, wherewith shall it be salted? It is thenceforth good for nothing but to be cast out and to be trodden under foot of men.

14   You are the light of the world. A city that is set on a hill cannot be hid.

15   Neither do men light a candle and put it under a bushel, but on a candlestick, and it giveth light unto all that are in the house.

16   Let your light so shine before men that they may see your good works and glorify your Father which is in heaven.

17   Think not that I am come to destroy the Law or the Prophets. I am not come to destroy them, but to fulfill them.

18   For truly I say unto you, Till heaven and earth perish, one iota, or one tittle of the Law shall not escape, till all things be fulfilled.

19   Whosoever therefore shall break one of these least commandments and teach men so, he shall be called the least in the kingdom of heaven; but whosoever shall observe and teach them, the same shall be called great in the kingdom of heaven.

20   For I say unto you, except your righteousness exceed the righteousness of the Scribes and Pharisees, you shall not enter into the kingdom of heaven.

21   You have heard that it was said unto them of the old time, 'Thou shalt not kill; for whosoever killeth shall be culpable of judgment.'

22   But I say unto you, whosoever is angry with his brother unadvisedly shall be culpable of judgment. And whosoever sayeth unto his brother, 'Raca,' [a term of insult] shall be worthy to be punished by the Council. And whosoever shall say, 'Fool,' shall be worthy to be punished with hell fire.

23   If then thou bring thy gift to the altar, and there remember that thy brother hath ought against thee,

24   Leave there thine offering before the altar and go thy way; first be reconciled to thy brother, and then come and offer thy gift.

25   Agree with thine adversary quickly while thou art in the way with him, lest thine adversary deliver thee to the judge, and the judge deliver thee to the sergeant, and thou be cast into prison.

26   Verily I say unto thee, thou shalt not come out thence till thou hast paid the utmost farthing.

27   You have heard that it was said to them of old time, 'Thou shalt not commit adultery.'

28   But I say unto you that whosoever looketh on a woman to lust after her hath committed adultery with her already in his heart.

29   Wherefore, if thy right eye cause thee to offend, pluck it out and cast it from thee; for better it is for thee that one of thy members perish than that thy whole body should be cast into hell.

30   Also if thy right hand make thee to offend, cut it off and cast it from thee; for better it is for thee that one of thy members perish than that thy whole body should be cast into hell.

31   It hath been said also, 'Whosoever shall put away his wife, let him give her a testimonial of divorce.'

32   But I say unto you, whosoever shall put away his wife (except it be for fornication) causeth her to commit adultery; and whosoever shall marry her that is divorced committeth adultery.

33   Again, you have heard that it was said to them of old time, 'Thou shalt not forswear thyself, but shalt perform thine oaths to the Lord.'

34   But I say unto you, Swear not at all, neither by heaven, for it is the throne of God,

35   Nor yet by the earth, for it is his foot stool, neither by Jerusalem, for it is the city of the great King.

36   Neither shalt thou swear by thine head, because thou canst not make one hair white or black.

37   But let your communication be: Yea, yea; Nay, nay. [Let your yes be yes and your no be no.] For whatsoever is more than these, cometh of evil.

38   You have heard that it hath been said, 'An eye for an eye, and a tooth for a tooth.'

39   But I say unto you, Resist not evil; but whosoever shall smite thee on thy right cheek, turn to him the other also.

40   And if any man will sue thee at the law and take away thy coat, let him have thy cloak also.

41   And whosoever will compel thee to go a mile, go with him two.

42   Give to him that asketh, and from him that would borrow of thee, turn not away.

43   You have heard that it hath been said, 'Thou shalt love thy neighbor and hate thine enemy.'

44   But I say unto you, Love your enemies; bless them that curse you; do good to them that hate you, and pray for them which hurt you and persecute you,

45   That you may be the children of your Father that is in heaven; for he maketh his sun to arise on the evil and the good and sendeth rain on the just and unjust.

46   For if you love them which love you, what reward shall you have? Do not the Publicans [tax collectors] even the same?

47   And if you be friendly to your brethren only, what singular thing do you? Do not even the Publicans likewise?

48   You shall therefore be perfect, as your Father which is in heaven is perfect."

➔   **GIOVANNI BATTISTA GIRALDI CINTHIO**

From *Gli Hecatommithi*   *1565*

The Principal Source for Othello   *Translated by Geoffrey Bullough*

Giovanni Battista Giraldi Cinthio's *Gli Hecatommithi* (1565) is an anthology of tales that Shakespeare apparently knew, probably in the original Italian. The passage reproduced here, in a modern translation by Geoffrey Bullough, is the story of the jealous captain that Shakespeare adapted as *Othello*. The use of Cinthio indicates that the playwright looked beyond his own nation and language for effective stories to dramatize.

Not long afterwards the Moor deprived the Corporal [the equivalent to Cassio] of his rank for having drawn his sword and wounded a soldier while on guard-duty. Disdemona was grieved by this and tried many times to reconcile the Moor with him. Whereupon the Moor told the rascally Ensign [the equivalent to Iago] that his wife importuned him so much for the Corporal that he feared he would be obliged to reinstate him. The evil man saw in this a hint for setting in train the deceits he had planned, and said: "Perhaps Disdemona has good cause to look on him so favourably!" "Why is that?" asked the Moor. "I do not wish," said the Ensign, "to come between man and wife, but if you keep your eyes open you will see for yourself." Nor for all the Moor's inquiries would the Ensign go beyond this: nonetheless his words left such a sharp thorn in the Moor's mind, that he gave himself up to pondering intensely what they could mean. He became quite melancholy, and one day, when his wife was trying to soften his anger towards the Corporal, begging him not to condemn to oblivion the loyal service and friendship of many years just for one small fault, especially since the Corporal had been reconciled to the man he had struck, the Moor burst out in anger and said to her, "There must be a very powerful reason why you take such trouble for this fellow, for he is not your brother, nor even a kinsman, yet you have him so much at heart!"

The lady, all courtesy and modesty, replied: "I should not like you to be angry with me. Nothing else makes me do it but sorrow to see you deprived of so dear a friend as you have shown that the Corporal was to you. He has not committed so serious an offence as to deserve such hostility.[1] But you Moors are so hot by nature that any little thing moves you to anger and revenge."

Still more enraged by these words the Moor answered: "Anyone who does not believe that may easily have proof of it! I shall take such revenge for any wrongs done to me as will more than satisfy me!" The lady was terrified by these words, and seeing her husband angry with her, quite against his habit, she said humbly: "Only a very good purpose made me speak to you about this, but rather than have you angry with me I shall never say another word on the subject."

The Moor, however, seeing the earnestness with which his wife had again pleaded for the Corporal, guessed that the Ensign's words had been intended to suggest that Disdemona was in love with the Corporal, and he went in deep depression to the scoundrel and urged him to speak more openly. The Ensign, intent on injuring this unfortunate lady, after pretending not to wish to say anything that might displease the Moor, appeared to be overcome by his entreaties and said: "I must confess that it grieves me greatly to have to tell you something that must be in the highest degree painful to you; but since you wish me to tell you, and the regard that I must have of your honour as my master spurs me on, I shall not fail in my duty to answer your request. You must know therefore that it is hard for your Lady to see the Corporal in disgrace for the simple reason that she takes her pleasure with him whenever he comes to your house. The woman has come to dislike your blackness."

[1] Cf. *Othello* 3.3.63–67.

→ From *The Book of Common Prayer*   *1559*

The Order for the Burial of the Dead

This work replaced the Catholic liturgy and served as the basis for services in the Church of England. The 1559 version was a carefully worded compromise between the versions of 1549 and 1552, the first of which was more nearly Roman, the second more radically Protestant. Since attendance at church was mandatory in Elizabethan England, the words of the services would have been familiar to Shakespeare and his audience.

The priest meeting the corpse at the church stile, shall say or else the priests and clerks shall sing, and so go either unto the church, or toward the grave.

I AM the resurrection and the life (saith the Lord): he that believeth in me, yea, though he were dead, yet shall he live. And whosoever liveth and believeth in me, shall not die forever. [John 11.]

I KNOW that my redeemer liveth, and that I shall rise out of the earth in the last day, and shall be covered again with my skin, and shall see God in my flesh: yea, and I myself shall behold him, not with other, but with these same eyes. [Job 19.]

WE brought nothing into this world, neither may we carry anything out of this world. The Lord giveth, and the Lord taketh away. Even as it hath pleased the Lord, so cometh things to pass: blessed be the name of the Lord. [1 Tim. 6. Job 1.]

When they come at the grave, whiles the corpse is made ready to be laid into the earth, the priest shall say, or the priest and clerks shall sing.

MAN that is born of a woman hath but a short time to live, and is full of misery. He cometh up and is cut down like a flower; he flieth as it were a shadow, and never continueth in one stay. [Job 14.] In the midst of life we be in death: of whom may we seek for succor but of thee, O Lord, which for our sins justly art displeased. Yet, O Lord God most holy, O Lord most mighty, O holy and most merciful savior, deliver us not into the bitter pains of eternal death. Thou knowest, Lord, the secrets of our hearts, shut not up thy merciful eyes to our prayers: but spare us Lord most holy, O God most mighty, O holy and merciful savior, thou most worthy judge eternal, suffer us not at our last hour for any pains of death to fall from thee.

Then while the earth shall be cast upon the body by some standing by, the priest shall say.

FORASMUCH as it hath pleased Almighty God of his great mercy to take unto himself the soul of our dear brother here departed: we therefore commit his body to the ground, earth to earth, ashes to ashes, dust to dust, in sure and certain hope of resurrection to eternal life, through our Lord Jesus Christ, who shall change our vile body that it may be like to his glorious body, according to the mighty working, whereby he is able to subdue all things to himself.

Then shall be said or sung.

I HEARD a voice from heaven saying unto me, Write, From henceforth blessed are the dead which die in the Lord. Even so saith the Spirit, that they rest from their labors. [Rev. 14:13.]

Then shall follow this Lesson, taken out of the fifteenth chapter to the Corinthians, the first Epistle.

CHRIST is risen from the dead, and become the first fruits of them that slept. For by a man came death, and by a man came the resurrection of the dead. For as by Adam all die, even so by Christ shall all be made alive. But every man in his own order: The first is Christ, then they that are Christ's at his coming. Then cometh the end, when he hath delivered up the kingdom to God the Father; when he hath put down all rule and all authority and power. For he must reign till he have put all his enemies under his feet. The last enemy that shall be destroyed is death. For he hath put all things under his feet. But when he saith all things are put under him, it is manifest that he is excepted, which did put all things under him. When all things are subdued unto him, then shall the Son also himself be subject unto him that put all things under him, that God may be all in all. Else what do they which are baptized over the dead, if the dead rise not at all? Why are they then baptized over them; yea, and why stand we alway then in jeopardy? By our rejoicing which I have in Christ Jesu our Lord, I die daily. That I have fought with beasts at Ephesus after the manner of men, what advantageth it me, if the dead rise not again? Let us eat and drink, for tomorrow we shall die. Be not ye deceived, evil words corrupt good manners. Awake truly out of sleep, and sin not. For some have not the knowledge of God. I speak this to your shame.

But some man will say, How arise the dead? With what body shall they come? Thou fool, that which thou sowest, is not quickened except it die. And what sowest thou? Thou sowest not that body that shall be, but bare corn, as of wheat or some other, but God giveth it a body at his pleasure, to every seed his own body. All flesh is not one manner of flesh, but there is one manner of flesh of men, and other manner of flesh of beasts, and other of fishes, another of birds. There are also celestial bodies, and there are bodies terrestrial. But the glory of the celestial is one, and the glory of the terrestrial is another. There is one manner glory of the sun, and another glory of the moon, and another glory of the stars. For one star differeth from another in glory: so is the resurrection of the dead. It is sown in corruption, it riseth again in incorruption. It is sown in dishonor, it riseth again in honor. It is sown in weakness, it riseth again in power. It is sown a natural body, it riseth a spiritual body. There is a natural body, and there is a spiritual body. As it is also written, The first man Adam was made a living soul, and the last Adam was made a quickening spirit. Howbeit, that is not first which is spiritual, but that which is natural, and then that which is spiritual. The first man is of the earth, earthy. The second man is the Lord from heaven, heavenly. As is the earthy, such are they that be earthy. And as is the heavenly, such are they that are heavenly. And as we have borne the image of the earthy, so shall we bear the image of the heavenly.

This say I brethren, that flesh and blood cannot inherit the kingdom of God, neither doth corruption inherit uncorruption. Behold, I show you a mystery. We shall not all sleep, but we shall all be changed, and that in a moment, in the twinkling of an eye by the last trump [trumpet]. For the trump shall blow, and the dead shall rise incorruptible, and we shall be changed. For this corruptible must put on incorruption, and this mortal must put on immortality. When this corruptible hath put on incorruption, and this mortal hath put on immortality, then shall be brought to pass the saying that is written, Death is swallowed up in victory. Death where is thy sting? Hell where is thy victory? The sting of death is sin; and the strength of sin is the law. But thanks be unto God, which hath given us victory, through our Lord Jesus Christ. Therefore my dear brethren, be ye steadfast and unmovable, always rich in the work of the Lord, forasmuch as ye know, how that your labor is not in vain in the Lord.

The Lesson ended, the priest shall say.

Lord have mercy upon us.
    Christ have mercy upon us.
Lord have mercy upon us.

Our Father which art in heaven, etc.
And lead us not into temptation.
Answer. But deliver us from evil. Amen.

The Priest.

Almighty God, with whom do live the spirits of them that depart hence in the Lord, and in whom the souls of them that be elected, after they be delivered from the burden of the flesh, be in joy and felicity: We give thee hearty thanks, for that it hath pleased thee to deliver this   N.   our brother out of the miseries of this sinful world; beseeching thee, that it may please thee of thy gracious goodness, shortly to accomplish the number of thine elect, and to haste thy kingdom, that we with this our brother, and all other departed in the true faith of thy holy name, may have our perfect consummation and bliss, both in body and soul, in thy eternal and everlasting glory. Amen.

The Collect

O merciful God, the Father of our Lord Jesus Christ, who is the resurrection and the life, in whom whosoever believeth, shall live though he die, and whosoever liveth and believeth in him, shall not die eternally; who also taught us (by his holy Apostle Paul) not to be sorry, as men without hope, for them that sleep in him: We meekly beseech thee (O Father) to raise us from the death of sin unto the life of righteousness, that when we shall depart this life, we may rest in him, as our hope is this our brother doth; and that at the general resurrection in the last day, we may be found acceptable in thy sight, and receive that blessing which thy well-beloved Son shall then pronounce to all that love and fear thee, saying, Come ye blessed children of my Father, receive the kingdom prepared for you from the beginning of the world. Grant this we beseech thee, O merciful Father, through Jesus Christ our mediator and redeemer. Amen.

→ JOHN FOXE

From *Acts and Monuments* 1563

One of the most popular books in Renaissance England, John Foxe's *Acts and Monuments* relates in abundant and colorful detail the stories of Christians who suffered persecution. Particularly popular were the histories of Protestants victimized during the reign of Queen Mary (1553–58), who restored Roman Catholicism to Britain after Henry VIII's break with Rome. The excerpt here describes the martyrdom of Nicholas Ridley and Hugh Latimer, burned at the stake as heretics at Oxford in 1555.

The Behavior of Doctor Ridley at His Supper
the Night before His Suffering

The night before he suffered, his beard was washed and his legs; and as he sat at supper the same night at Master Irish's (who was his keeper) he bade his hostess and the rest at the board to his marriage. "For," saith he, "tomorrow I must be married." And so showed himself to be as merry as ever he was at any time before. And wishing his sister at his marriage, he asked his brother (sitting at the table) whether she could find in her heart to be there or no, and he answered, "Yea, I dare say, with all her heart." At which word he said he was glad to hear of her so much therein. So at this talk Mistress Irish wept.

But Master Ridley comforted her and said, "O Mistress Irish, you love me not now, I see well enough. For in that you weep it doth appear you will not be at my marriage, neither are content therewith. Indeed, you be not so much my friend as I thought you had been. But quiet yourself; though my breakfast shall be something sharp and painful, yet I am sure my supper shall be more pleasant and sweet, etc." When they rose from the table, his brother offered him to watch all night with him. But he said, "No, no, that you shall not. For I mind, God willing, to go to bed and to sleep as quietly tonight as ever I did in my life." So his brother departed, exhorting him to be of good cheer and to take his cross quietly, for the reward was great, etc.

*The Behavior of Doctor Ridley and Master Latimer
at the Time of Their Death*

Upon the north side of the town, in the ditch over against Bailliol College, the place of execution was appointed; and for fear of any tumult that might arise to let [hinder] the burning of them, my Lord Williams [the officer of the guard] was commanded by the queen's letters and the householders of the city to be there assistant, sufficiently appointed. And when everything was in a readiness, they were brought to the stake by the mayor and bailiffs: Master Ridley in a fair black gown, such as he was wont to wear when he was bishop, with a tippet [scarflike garment covering the shoulders] of sables about his neck, nothing undressed; Master Latimer in a poor Bristol frieze frock [coarse woolen gown] all worn, with his buttoned cap and a kerchief on his head all ready to the fire, a new long shroud hanging over his hose down to his feet, which at the first sight stirred men's hearts to rue upon them, beholding on the one side the honor they sometime [formerly] had, on the other the calamity whereunto they were then descended.

Master Doctor Ridley, as he passed towards Bocardo, he looked up where Master Cranmer [formerly Archbishop of Canterbury, also burned at the stake] did lie, and belike he would have seen him at the glass window, to have spoken unto him. But then Master Cranmer was busy with Friar Soto and his fellows, disputing together, so that he could not see him through that occasion. Then Master Ridley, looking back, espied Master Latimer coming after. Unto whom he said, "O, be you there?" "Yea," said Master Latimer, "have after, as fast as I can follow." So he following a pretty way off, at length they came both to the stake one after the other, where first Doctor Ridley entering the place, marvelous earnestly holding up both his hands, looked towards heaven, etc., and with a glimpse of his eye aside espying Master Latimer, with a wonderful cheerful look ran unto him, and embraced and kissed him, and as they that stood near reported, comforted him, saying: "Be of good heart, brother, for God will either assuage the fury of the flame, or else strengthen us to abide it." With that went he to the stake, kneeled down by it, kissed it, most effectuously prayed, and behind him Master Latimer kneeled, as earnestly calling upon God as he. After they arose, the one talked with the other a little while, till they which were appointed to see the execution removed themselves out of the sun. What they said, I can learn of no man. Then Doctor Smith began his sermon to them upon this text of Saint Paul in the thirteenth chapter of the first Epistle to the Corinthians: *Si corpus meum tradam igni, charitatem autem non habeo, nihil inde utilitatis capio,* which is thus much in English: "If I yield my body to the fire to be burnt, and have not charity, I shall gain nothing thereby." Wherein he alleged that the goodness of the cause nor the holiness of the person should not be judged by the order of the death, which he confirmed by the examples of Judas, and of a woman in Oxford that of late hanged herself, for that then they and such like (as he or two or three other recited) might be adjudged righteous, which desperately sundered their lives from their bodies, as he feared that those men that stood before him would do.

But he cried still to the people to beware of them. For they were heretics and died out of the Church. And on the other side, he declared their diversity in opinions, as Lutherans, Oecolampadians [followers of Joannes Oecolampadius, German reformer and theologian], Zwinglians [followers of Huldreich Zwingli, Swiss theologian and reformer], of which sect they were, and that was the worst. But the old Church of Christ and the Catholic Faith believed far otherwise. At which place they lifted up both hands and their eyes to heaven, as it were calling God to witness of the truth.

The which countenance they made in many other places of his sermon, whereas they thought he spake amiss: he ended with a very short exhortation to them, to recant and come home again to the Church, and save their lives and souls, which else were condemned. His sermon was scant [hardly] in all a quarter of an hour.

Doctor Ridley said unto Master Latimer: "Will you begin to answer the sermon, or shall I?" Master Latimer said: "Begin you first, I pray you." "I will," said Master Ridley. Then the wicked sermon being ended, Doctor Ridley and Master Latimer kneeled down upon their knees, towards my Lord Williams of Tame, the vice-chancellor of Oxford, and divers [various] other commissioners appointed for that purpose, which sat upon a form [bench] thereby, unto whom Master Ridley said: "I beseech you, my lord, even for Christ's sake, that I may speak but two or three words," and whilst my lord bent his head to the mayor and vice-chancellor, as it appeared, to know whether he might give him leave to speak, the bailiffs and Doctor Marshall vice-chancellor ran hastily unto him, and with their hands stopped his mouth, and said: "Master Ridley, if you will revoke your erroneous opinions and recant the same, you shall not only have liberty so to do, but also the benefit of a subject, that is, have your life."

"Not otherwise?" said Master Ridley. "No," quoth Doctor Marshall. "Therefore if you will not do so, then there is no remedy but you must suffer for your deserts." "Well," quoth Master Ridley, "so long as the breath is in my body, I will never deny my Lord God and his known truth. God's will be done in me." And with that he rose up, and said with a loud voice: "Well, then, I commit our cause to Almighty God, which shall indifferently judge all." To whose saying Master Latimer added his old posy [motto], "Well, there is nothing hid but it shall be opened." And he said he could answer Smith well enough, if he might be suffered. Incontinently [immediately] they were commanded to make them ready, which they with all meekness obeyed. Master Ridley took his gown and his tippet, and gave it to his brother-in-law, Master Shepside, who all his time of imprisonment, although he might not be suffered to come to him, lay there at his own charges, to provide him necessaries, which from time to time he sent him by the sergeant that kept him. Some other of his apparel that was little worth he gave away; other the bailiffs took.

He gave away besides divers other small things to gentlemen standing by, and divers of them pitifully weeping, as to Sir Henry Lee he gave a new groat, and to divers of my Lord Williams' gentlemen some napkins, some nutmegs, and rasins [probably race, roots] of ginger, his dial, and such other things as he had about him to everyone that stood next him. Some plucked the points of his hose; happy was he that might get any rag of him. Master Latimer gave nothing, but very quietly suffered his keeper to pull off his hose and his other array, which to look unto was very simple. And being stripped into his shroud, seemed as comely a person to them that were there present as one should lightly [readily] see. And whereas in his clothes he appeared a withered and crooked sely [foolish] old man, he now stood bolt upright, as comely a father as one might lightly behold.

Then Master Ridley, standing as yet in his truss [close-fitting body garment], said to his brother: "It were best for me to go in my truss still." "No," quoth his brother, "it will put you to more pain; and the truss will do a poor man good." Whereunto Master Ridley said, "Be it in the name of God," and so unlaced himself. Then being in his shirt [undergarment], he stood upon the foresaid stone, and held up his hands, and said, "O heavenly Father, I give unto thee most hearty thanks for that thou hast called me to be a professor of thee, even unto death. I beseech thee, Lord God, take mercy upon this realm of England, and deliver the same from all her enemies."

Then the smith took a chain of iron and brought the same about both Doctor Ridley and Master Latimer's middles. And as he was knocking in a staple, Doctor Ridley took the chain in his hand, and shaked the same, for it did gird in his belly, and looking aside to the smith, said, "Good fellow, knock it in hard, for the flesh will have his course." Then his brother did bring him gunpowder in a bag, and would have tied the same about his neck. Master Ridley asked what it was; his brother said, "Gunpowder." Then said he, "I take it to be sent of God; therefore I will receive it, as sent of him. And have you any," said he, "for my brother?"— meaning Master Latimer. "Yea, sir, that I have," quoth his brother. "Then give it unto him," said he, "betime, lest you come too late." So his brother went and carried the same gunpowder unto Master Latimer. The meantime Doctor Ridley spake unto my Lord Williams and said, "My lord, I must be a suitor unto your lordship in the behalf of divers poor men, and especially in the cause of my poor sister. I have made a supplication to the queen's Majesty in their behalfs, I beseech your Lordship for Christ's sake to be a mean [mediator, advocate] to her Grace for them. My brother here hath the supplication and will resort to your Lordship to certify you thereof. There is nothing in all the world that troubleth my conscience, I praise God, this only excepted. Whiles I was in the See of London [religious office], divers poor men took leases of me and agreed with me for the same. Now I hear say the Bishop that now occupieth the same room will not allow my grants unto them made, but contrary unto all law and conscience hath taken from them their livings, and will not suffer them to enjoy the same. I beseech you, my Lord, be a mean for them. You shall do a good deed, and God will reward you."

Then brought they a faggot [stick] kindled with fire and laid the same down at Doctor Ridley's feet, and when he saw the fire flaming up towards him he cried with a wonderful loud voice, *"In manus tuas, Domine, commendo spiritum meum; Domine, recipe spiritum meum."* And after repeated this latter part often in English, "Lord, Lord, receive my spirit," Master Latimer crying as vehemently on the other side, "O Father of heaven, receive my soul," who received the flame as it were embracing it. After, as he had stroked his face with his hands, and as it were bathed them a little in the fire, soon died (as it appeared) with very little pain or none.

But Master Ridley, by reason of the evil making of the fire unto him, because the wooden faggots were laid about the gorse [prickly shrub], and over-high built, the fire burned first beneath, being kept down by the wood; which when he felt, he desired them for Christ's sake to let the fire come unto him. Which when his brother-in-law heard but not well understood, intending to rid him of his pain (for the which case he gave attendance), as one in such sorrow not well advised what he did, heaped faggots upon him that he clean covered him, which made the fire more vehement beneath, that it burned clean all his nether parts before it once touched the upper. And that made him leap up and down under the faggots, and often desire them to let the fire come unto him, saying "I cannot burn," which indeed appeared well. For after his legs were consumed by reason of his struggling with the pain (whereof he had no release, but only his contentation [contentment] in God) he showed that side toward us clean, shirt and all untouched with the flame. Yet in all this torment he forgot not to call unto God still, having in his mouth, "Lord, have mercy upon me," intermeddling this cry, "Let the fire come unto me, I cannot burn." In which pangs he labored till one of the standersby with his bill [blade or weapon] pulled off the faggots above, and where he espied the fire flame up, he wrested himself unto that side. And when the flame touched the gunpowder he was seen stir no more, but espied burning on the other side by Master Latimer. Which some said happened by reason that the chain loosed; others said that he fell over the chain, by reason of the poise of his body and the weakness of the nether limbs.

Some say that before he was like to fall from the stake, he defied them to hold him to it with their bills. Howsoever it was, surely it moved hundreds to tears, to behold the horrible sight. For I think there was none that had not clean exiled all humanity and mercy, which would not have lamented to behold the fury of the fire so rage upon their bodies. Signs there were of sorrow on every side.

✢ A Moralized Ballad   *1565*

"The True Form and Shape of a Monstrous Child" exemplifies the kind of macabre stories popular in early modern English culture. The original contains two drawings, beneath the title, giving front and rear views of the fused bodies. In the absence of newspapers, such ballads catered to the public taste for sensation, and many of them, like this one, justified their publication by offering a moral reading of the event. Shakespeare mocks such tales in the ballads sold by the peddler, Autolycus, in *The Winter's Tale*.

The True Form and Shape of a Monstrous Child which Was Born in Stony Stratford in Northamptonshire the Year of Our Lord MCCCCCLXV

This child was born on Friday, being the twenty-sixth day of January, betwixt six and seven of the clock in the morning, and lived two hours, and was christened by the midwife, and are both women children, having two bodies joining together, with four arms and four legs perfect, and from the navel upward one face, two eyes, one nose, and one mouth, and three ears, one being upon the backside of the head a little above the nape of the neck, having hair growing upon the head. Which child was born out of wedlock. The father's name is Richard Sotherne, who is now fled; and the mother is yet living in the same town. And this child was brought up to London where it was seen of divers worshipful men and women of the city, and also of the country. To witness that it is a truth and no fable, but a warning of God to move all people to amendment of life:

> You that do see this child disfigured here,
>   Two babes in one, disguised [unnaturally altered] to behold,
> Think with yourselves, when such things do appear,
>   All is not well, as wise heads may be bold.
> But God that can in secrets show the sign
> Can bring much more to pass by power divine.
>
> And we that live to see this wonder, how
>   The gaze is given to make this mervail [marvel] great,
> Let one by one that this beholdeth now
>   Be warned, as the wonder gives conceit,
> To live to mend the wondrous shape we see,
> Contrary much in all that ought to be.
>
> For as we find this figure seemeth strange
>   Because it shows proportion not in ure [in performance or
>   functions],
> So bear in mind how time can chop and change,
>   Disguising works in wills that be unsure [weak].
> From mean to more, from more to much excess,
> Where Nature wills desire should be less.
>   *Finis*
>
>   W[illiam] Elderton

Imprinted at London in Fleet Street beneath the
Conduit at the sign of St. John Evangelist
by Thomas Colwell

→ SIR WILLIAM STRACHEY

From *A True Reportory of the Wreck and Redemption of Sir Thomas Gates* 1610

A Source for The Tempest

Sir William Strachey's *A True Reportory of the Wreck and Redemption of Sir Thomas Gates, Knight, upon and from the Islands of the Bermudas, His Coming to Virginia, and the Estate of That Colony* was not published until 1625, but the account was written in July 1610 about an episode that occurred in the previous year. It exemplifies the marvelous tales brought back to England by travelers, especially those who had journeyed to the New World. Shakespeare seems to have read Strachey's report in manuscript and to have relied on it in composing *The Tempest*.

During all this time, the heavens looked so black upon us, that it was not possible the elevation of the Pole might be observed: nor a star by night, nor sun beam by day was to be seen. Only upon the Thursday night Sir George Summers, being upon the watch, had an apparition of a little round light, like a faint star, trembling, and streaming along with a sparkling blaze, half the height upon the mainmast, and shooting sometimes from shroud to shroud [a set of ropes], tempting to settle as it were upon any of the four shrouds; and for three or four hours together, or rather more, half the night it kept with us, running sometimes along the main-yard to the very end, and then returning. At which, Sir George Summers called divers about him, and showed them the same, who observed it with much wonder, and carefulness: but upon a sudden, towards the morning watch, they lost the sight of it, and knew not what way it made. The superstitious sea-men make many constructions of this sea-fire, which nevertheless is usual in storms: the same (it may be) which the Grecians were wont in the Mediterranean to call Castor and Pollux, of which, if one only appeared without the other, they took it for an evil sign of great tempest. The Italians, and such who lie open to the Adriatic and Tyrrhenian Sea, call it (a sacred Body) Corpo sancto; the Spaniards call it Saint Elmo, and have an authentic and miraculous legend for it. Be it what it will, we laid other foundations of safety or ruin, then in the rising or falling of it, but could it have served us now miraculously to have taken our height by, it might have strucken amazement and a reverence in our devotions, according to the due of a miracle. But it did not light us any whit the more to our known way, who ran now (as do hoodwinked men) at all adventures, sometimes north, and northeast, then north and by west, and in an instant again varying two or three points, and sometimes half the compass. East and by south we steered away as much as we could to bear upright, which was no small carefulness nor pain to do, albeit we much unrigged our ship, threw overboard much luggage, many a trunk and chest (in which I suffered no mean loss), and staved many a butt of beer, hogsheads of oil, cider, wine, and vinegar, and heaved away all our ordnance [ammunition or weapons] on the starboard side, and had now purposed to have cut down the mainmast, the more to lighten her, for we were much spent, and our men so weary, as their strengths together failed them with their hearts, having travailed now from Tuesday till Friday morning, day and night, without either sleep or food; for the leakage taking up all the hold, we could neither come by beer nor fresh water; fire we could keep none in the cookroom to dress any meat, and carefulness, grief, and our turn at the pump or bucket were sufficient to hold sleep from our eyes. . . . And from Tuesday noon till Friday noon, we bailed and pumped two thousand ton, and yet do what we could, when our ship held least in her (after Tuesday night second watch) she bore ten foot deep, at which stay our extreme working kept her on eight glasses, forbearance whereof had instantly sunk us, and it being now Friday, the fourth morning, it wanted little but that there had been a general determination to have shut up hatches and, commending our sinful souls to God, committed the ship to the mercy of the sea. Surely, that night we must have done it, and that night had we then perished; but see the goodness and sweet introduction of better hope, by our merciful God given unto us. Sir George Summers, when no man dreamed of such happiness, had discovered and cried "Land." Indeed the morning now three quarters spent, had won a little clearness from the days before, and it being better surveyed, the very trees were seen to move with the wind upon the shore side: whereupon our governor commanded the helmsman to bear up, the boatswain sounding at the first, found it thirteen fathom, and when we stood a little in seven fathom; and presently heaving his lead the third time, had ground at four fathom, and by this, we had got her within a mile under the southeast point of the land, where we had somewhat smooth water. But having no hope to save her by coming to an anchor in the same, we were enforced to run her ashore, as near the land as we could, which brought us within three quarters of a mile of shore, and by the mercy of God unto us, making out our boats, we had ere night brought all our men, women, and children, about the number of one hundred and fifty, safe into the island.

We found it to be the dangerous and dreaded island, or rather islands, of the Bermuda: whereof let me give your Ladyship a brief description, before I proceed to my narration. And that the rather, because they be so terrible to all that ever touched on them, and such tempests, thunders, and other fearful objects are seen and heard about them, that they be called commonly The Devils Islands, and are feared and avoided of all sea travelers alive, above any other place in the world. Yet it pleased our merciful God to make even this hideous and hated place both the place of our safety, and means of our deliverance.

And hereby also, I hope to deliver the world from a foul and general error: it being counted of most, that they [the islands] can be no habitation for men, but rather given over to devils and wicked spirits. Whereas indeed we find them now by experience to be as habitable and commodious as most countries of the same climate and situation; insomuch as if the entrance into them were as easy as the place itself is contenting, it had long ere this been inhabited, as well as other islands. Thus shall we make it appear, that Truth is the Daughter of Time, and that men ought not to deny everything which is not subject to their own sense.

The Bermudas be broken islands, five hundred of them in manner of an archipelago (at least if you may call them all islands that lie, how little soever into the sea, and by themselves) of small compass, some larger yet than other, as time and the sea hath won from them, and eaten his passage through, and all now lying in the figure of a crescent, within the circuit of six or seven leagues at the most, albeit at first it is said of them that they were thirteen or fourteen leagues, and more in longitude, as I have heard. For no greater distance is it from the northwest point to Gates's Bay, as by this map your Ladyship may see, in which Sir George Summers, who coasted in his boat about them all, took great care to express the same exactly and full, and made his draft perfect for all good occasions, and the benefit of such, who either in distress might be brought upon them, or make sail this way.

→ CHRISTOPHER MARLOWE

From *Tamburlaine the Great*   *1590*

This famous speech from Christopher Marlowe's play *Tamburlaine the Great* is reproduced (enlarged slightly) from the 1590 Quarto. (A transcription of the speech follows.) The incantatory power of the verse and the hero's "high astounding terms" could be heard in the public playhouses shortly after Shakespeare's arrival in London. Verse such as this helped to shape the development of Shakespeare's poetic style.

> 𝕹ature that fram'd vs of foure Elements,
> 𝖂arring within our breasts for regiment,
> 𝕯oth teach vs all to haue aspyring minds:
> 𝕺ur soules,whose faculties can comprehend
> 𝕿he wondrous Architecture of the world:
> 𝕬nd measure euery wandring plannets course.
> 𝕾till climing after knowledge infinite,
> 𝕬nd alwaies moouing as the restles Spheares.
> 𝖂ils vs to weare our selues and neuer rest.
> 𝖀ntill we reach the ripest fruit of all.
> 𝕿hat perfect blisse and sole felicitie.
> 𝕿he sweet fruition of an earthly crowne.

> Nature that framed us of four elements,
> Warring within our breasts for regiment,
> Doth teach us all to have aspiring minds.
> Our souls, whose faculties can comprehend
> The wondrous architecture of the world
> And measure every wandering planet's course,
> Still climbing after knowledge infinite,

5

And always moving as the restless spheres,
Wills us to wear [push] ourselves and never rest
Until we reach the ripest fruit of all,   10
That perfect bliss and sole felicity,
The sweet fruition of an earthly crown.

➜ SIR PHILIP SIDNEY

Two Sonnets from *Astrophil and Stella*   *c. 1579*

Sir Philip Sidney's sonnet sequence was written about 1579 and published for the first
time in 1591, five years after the author's death. Shakespeare appears to have known the
sequence and to have been influenced by it in the composition of his own sonnets, particularly by Sidney's playfully skeptical response to Petrarchan conventions.

SONNET 2

Not at first sight, nor with a dribbed [feeble, missed] shot,
    Love gave the wound which, while I breathe, will bleed;
    But known worth did in mine of time proceed,
    Till by degrees it had full conquest got.
I saw and liked, I liked but loved not,   5
    I loved, but straight did not what Love decreed.
    At length to Love's decrees I, forc'd, agreed,
    Yet with repining at so partial lot.
Now even that footstep of lost liberty
    Is gone, and now, like slave-born Muscovite,   10
    I call it praise to suffer tyranny;
And now employ the remnant of my wit
    To make myself believe that all is well,
    While, with a feeling skill, I paint my hell.

SONNET 7

When Nature made her chief work, Stella's eyes,
    In color black why wrapp'd she beams so bright?
    Would she in beamy black, like painter wise,
    Frame daintiest luster mix'd of shades and light?
Or did she else that sober hue devise   5
    In object best to knit and strength our sight,
    Lest, if no veil those brave gleams did disguise,
    They, sunlike, should more dazzle than delight?

Or would she her miraculous power show,
   That, whereas black seems beauty's contrary,   10
   She even in black doth make all beauties flow?
Both so, and thus she, minding Love should be
   Placed ever there, gave him this mourning weed
   To honor all their deaths who for her bleed.

→ **LADY MARY WROTH**

Two Sonnets from
Pamphilia to Amphilanthus   *comp. 1612?; pub. 1621*

Niece of Sir Philip Sidney and one of the most accomplished women of her time, Lady Mary Wroth extended the English sonnet tradition in ways comparable to those found in Shakespeare's 1609 sequence. Her narrator is female and suffers from the neglect and unkindness of a faithless lover. Her poems teem with imagery of darkness and light, and the references in Sonnet 22 to black skin and to the sunburnt Indians reflect her participation in Jonson's *Masque of Blackness,* a work commissioned by Queen Anne and performed at court in 1605.

SONNET 8

Led by the power of grief, to wailings brought
   By false conceit of change fallen on my part,
   I seek for some small ease by lines, which bought,
   Increase the pain; grief is not cured by art.
Ah! how unkindness moves within the heart   5
   Which still is true, and free from changing thought;
   What unknown woe it breeds, what endless smart
   With ceaseless tears, which causelessly are wrought.
It makes me now to shun all shining light,
   And seek for blackest clouds me light to give,   10
   Which to all others only darkness drive;
   They on me shine, for sun disdains my sight.
Yet though I dark do live, I triumph may,
Unkindness, nor this wrong, shall love allay.

SONNET 22

Like to the Indians scorched with the sun,
   The sun which they do as their god adore,
   So am I used by love; for evermore
   I worship him, less favors have I won.

Better are they who thus to blackness run,   5
    And so can only whiteness' want deplore,
    Than I, who pale and white am with grief's store,
    Nor can have hope but to see hopes undone.
Besides their sacrifice received in sight
    Of their chose saint, mine hid as worthless rite,   10
    Grant me to see where I my offerings give,
Then let me wear the mark of Cupid's might
    In heart, as they in skin of Phoebus' light,
    Not ceasing offerings to love while I live.

→ RAPHAEL HOLINSHED

From *The Chronicles of England, Scotland, and Ireland*   *1587*

Second Edition

First published in 1577 and then amplified and revised a decade later, Raphael Holinshed's monumental history drew heavily on previous Tudor accounts. The 1587 version was a source for Shakespeare's plays on English history, as well as for *Macbeth, King Lear,* and parts of *Cymbeline.* The excerpt provided here describes the conflict between the recently crowned Henry IV and the members of the Percy family, events dramatized at the beginning of *Henry IV, Part 1.*

Henry, earl of Northumberland, with his brother Thomas, earl of Worcester, and his son, the lord Henry Percy, surnamed Hotspur, which were to King Henry in the beginning of his reign both faithful friends and earnest aiders, began now to envy his wealth and felicity; and especially they were grieved, because the king demanded of the earl and his son such Scottish prisoners as were taken at Holmedon and Nesbit: for of all the captives which were taken in the conflicts fought in those two places, there were delivered to the king's possession only Mordake, earl of Fife, the duke of Albany's son, though the king did divers and sundry times require deliverance of the residue, and that with great threatenings. Wherewith the Percys being sore offended, for that they claimed them as their own proper prisoners, and their peculiar preies [preys], by the counsel of the lord Thomas Percy, earl of Worcester, whose study was ever (as some write) to procure malice, and set things in a broil, came to the king unto Windsor (upon a purpose to prove [test] him) and there required of him that either by ransom or otherwise, he would cause to be delivered out of prison Edmund Mortimer, earl of March, their cousin germane [first cousin], whom (as they reported) Owen Glendower kept in filthy prison, shackled with irons, only for that he took his [the king's] part, and was to him faithful and true.

The king began not a little to muse at this request, and not without cause: for indeed it touched him somewhat near, sith [since] this Edmund was son to

Roger, earl of March, son to the lady Phillippa, daughter of Lionel, duke of Clarence, the third son of King Edward the Third; which Edmund, at King Richard's going into Ireland, was proclaimed heir apparent to the crown and realm, whose aunt, called Elianor, the lord Henry Percy had married; and therefore King Henry could not well hear that any man should be earnest about the advancement of that lineage. The king, when he had studied on the matter, made answer that the earl of March was not taken prisoner for his cause, nor in his service, but willingly suffered himself to be taken, because he would not withstand the attempts of Owen Glendower and his complices, and therefore he would neither ransom him, nor relieve him.

The Percys with this answer and fraudulent excuse were not a little fumed [angered], insomuch that Henry Hotspur said openly: "Behold, the heir of the realm is robbed of his right, and yet the robber with his own will not redeem him." So in this fury the Percys departed, minding nothing more than to depose King Henry from the high type [summit] of his royalty, and to place in his seat their cousin Edmund, earl of March, whom they did not only deliver out of captivity, but also (to the high displeasure of King Henry) entered in league with the foresaid Owen Glendower. Herewith, they by their deputies in the house of the archdeacon of Bangor, divided the realm amongst them, causing a tripartite indenture to be made and sealed with their seals, by the covenants whereof, all England from Severn and Trent, south and eastward, was assigned to the earl of March; all Wales, and the lands beyond Severn westward, were appointed to Owen Glendower; and all the remnant from Trent northward, to the lord Percy.

→ PLUTARCH

From *Lives of the Noble Grecians and Romans*   *Translated by Sir Thomas North, 1579*

Thomas North's version of Plutarch was Shakespeare's major source for the classical tragedies. This excerpt records Cleopatra's appearance on the barge; the parallel passage in *Antony and Cleopatra* is Enobarbus's speech in act 2, scene 2. Shakespeare has versified North's prose and made numerous subtle changes, but many similarities of diction and imagery are apparent.

Therefore when she was sent unto by divers letters, both from Antonius himself, and also from his friends, she made so light of it, and mocked Antonius so much, that she disdained to set forward otherwise, but to take her barge in the river of Cydnus, the poop whereof was of gold, the sails of purple, and the oars of silver, which kept stroke in rowing after the sound of the music of flutes, oboes, citherns [guitars], viols, and such other instruments as they played upon in the barge. And now for the person of herself: she was laid under a pavilion of cloth of gold of tissue, appareled and attired like the goddess Venus, commonly drawn in picture; and hard by her, on either hand of her, pretty fair boys appareled as painters do set forth god Cupid, with little fans in their hands, with the which they fanned wind upon her. Her ladies and gentle-women also, the fairest of them were appareled like the nymphs Nereides (which are the mermaids of the waters) and like the Graces, some steering the helm, others tending the tackle and ropes of the barge, out of the which there came a wonderful passing sweet savor of perfumes, that perfumed the wharf's side, pestered with innumerable multitudes of people. Some of them followed the barge all alongst the river's side: others also ran out of the city to see her coming in. So that in the end, there ran such multitudes of people one after another to see her, that Antonius was left post alone [entirely alone] in the marketplace, in his Imperial seat to give audience: and there went a rumor in the people's mouths, that the goddess Venus was come to play with the god Bacchus, for the general good of all Asia. When Cleopatra landed, Antonius sent to invite her to supper to him. But she sent him word again, he should do better rather to come and sup with her. Antonius, therefore, to show himself courteous unto her at her arrival, was contented to obey her, and went to supper to her: where he found such passing sumptuous fare, that no tongue can express it.

→ MARY SIDNEY HERBERT, COUNTESS OF PEMBROKE

From Her Translation of *The Tragedy of Antonie* by Robert Garnier   *1592*

Translation was one of the literary vehicles available to women who wished to publish their writing, although the rendering of psalms and other religious material was deemed most suitable. The countess of Pembroke, sister to Sir Philip Sidney, had arranged for the publication of much of his work after his death in 1586, and in 1592 she published her translation (from the French) of a closet drama on the life of Marc Antony. It is distinguished by its sympathetic representation of Cleopatra, a portrait that contradicted the orthodox negative view derived from the Romans. Shakespeare in his play (c. 1607) later encouraged a similarly complex response in his audience. The passage printed below is the final movement of the play, after the death of Antony. Surrounded by her attendants, Cleopatra imagines herself joined with him in death and, in the act of suicide, achieves a kind of heroic eloquence given to few female characters in the period.

ERAS:
    Alas, yet let us weep, lest sudden death
    From him our tears and those last duties take,
    Unto his tomb we owe.
CHARMION:
               Ah, let us weep
    While moisture lasts, then die before his feet.
CLEOPATRA:
    Who furnish will mine eyes with streaming tears,
    My boiling anguish worthily to wail?

120

Wail thee Antony, Antony my heart?
Alas, how much I weeping liquor want!
Yet have mine eyes quite drawn their conduits dry   125
By long beweeping my disastered harms.
Now reason is, that from my side they suck
First vital moisture, then the vital blood.
Then let the blood from my sad eyes outflow,
And smoking yet with thine in mixture grow.   130
Moist it, and heat it new, and never stop;
All wat'ring thee, while yet remains one drop.

CHARMION:
Antony take our tears; this is the last
Of all the duties we to thee can yield
Before we die.

ERAS:
            These sacred obsequies,   135
Take, Antony, and take them in good part.

CLEOPATRA:
O Goddess, thou whom Cyprus doth adore,
Venus of Paphos, bent to work us harm
For old Iulus' brood, if thou take care
Of Caesar, why of us tak'st thou no care?   140
Antony did descend, as well as he,
From thine own son by long enchainèd line;
And might have ruled, by one and self same fate
True Trojan blood, the stately Roman state.
    Antony, poor Antony, my dear soul,   145
Now but a block, the booty of a tomb,
Thy life, thy heat is lost, thy colour gone,
And hideous paleness on thy face hath seized.
Thy eyes, two suns, the lodging place of love,
Which yet for tents to warlike Mars did serve,   150
Locked up in lids (as fair day's cheerful light
Which darkness flies) do winking hide in night.
    Antony by our true loves I thee beseech —
And by our hearts' sweet sparks have set on fire
Our holy marriage, and the tender ruth   155
Of our dear babes, knot of our amity —
My doleful voice thy ear let entertain,
And take me with thee to the hellish plain,
Thy wife, thy friend. Hear Antony, O hear
My sobbing sighs, if here thou be, or there.   160
    Lived thus long, the wingèd race of years
Ended I have as destiny decreed,
Flourished and reigned, and taken just revenge
Of him who me both hated and despised.

Happy, alas too happy — if of Rome   165
Only the fleet had hither never come.
And now of me an image great shall go
Under the earth to bury there my woe.
What say I? Where am I? O Cleopatra,
Poor Cleopatra, grief thy reason reaves.   170
No, no, most happy in this hapless case,
To die with thee, and dying thee embrace;
My body joined with thine, my mouth with thine,
My mouth, whose moisture-burning sighs have dried
To be in one self tomb, and one self chest,   175
And wrapped with thee in one self sheet to rest.
    The sharpest torment in my heart I feel,
Is that I stay from thee, my heart, this while;
Die will I straight now, now straight will I die,
And straight with thee a wand'ring shade will be,   180
Under the cypress trees thou haunt'st alone,
Where brooks of hell do falling seem to moan.
But yet I stay, and yet thee overlive,
That ere I die due rites I may thee give,
    A thousand sobs I from my breast will tear,   185
With thousand plaints thy funerals adorn;
My hair shall serve for thy oblations;
My boiling tears for thy effusions;
Mine eyes thy fire, for out of them the flame
(Which burnt thy heart on me enamored) came.   190
    Weep my companions, weep, and from your eyes
Rain down on him of tears a brinish stream.
Mine can no more, consumèd by the coals
Which from my breast, as from a furnace, rise.
Martyr your breasts with multiplièd blows,   195
With violent hands tear off your hanging hair,
Outrage your face. Alas, why should we seek
(Since now we die) our beauties more to keep?
    I spent in tears, not able more to spend,
But kiss him now, what rests me more to do?   200
Then let me kiss you, you fair eyes, my light,
Front seat of honor, face most fierce, most fair!
O neck, O arms, O hands, O breast where death
(O mischief) comes to choke up vital breath.
A thousand kisses, thousand, thousand more   205
Let you my mouth for honor's farewell give,
That in this office weak my limbs may grow,
Fainting on you, and forth my soul may flow. [*She dies.*]

➔ OVID

From *Metamorphoses* *Translated by Arthur Golding, 1567*

The Roman poet's collection of mythological stories was written in Latin, circa 1 A.D. The story of Diana and Actaeon is presented here in a sixteenth-century translation by Arthur Golding, which Shakespeare knew. Shakespeare found Ovid useful less as a source of dramatic plots than as a storehouse of allusion and an inspiration for the ideas of transformation that inform the comedies.

Now *Thebes* stood in good estate, now *Cadmus* might thou say
　That when thy father banisht thee it was a luckie day.
To joyne aliance both with *Mars* and *Venus* was thy chaunce,
Whose daughter thou hadst tane to wife, who did thee much advaunce,
Not only through hir high renowne, but through a noble race　　　　5
Of sonnes and daughters that she bare: whose children in like case
It was thy fortune for to see all men and women growne.
But ay the ende of every thing must marked be and knowne,
For none the name of blessednesse deserveth for to have,
Unlesse the tenor of this life last blessed to his grave.　　　　10
Among so many prosprous happes that flowde with good successe,
Thine eldest Nephew was a cause of care and sore distresse.
Whose head was armde with palmed hornes, whose own hounds in yᵉ wood
Did pull their master to the ground and fill them with his bloud.
But if you sift the matter well, ye shall not finde desart [deserving]　　15
But cruell fortune to have bene the cause of this his smart.
For who could doe with oversight? Great slaughter had bene made
Of sundrie sortes of savage beastes one morning, and the shade
Of things was waxed verie short. It was the time of day
That mid betweene the East and West the Sunne doth seeme to stay;　　20
When as the Thebane stripling thus bespake his companie,
Still raunging in the waylesse woods some further game to spie.
Our weapons and our toyles are moist and staind with bloud of Deare:
This day hath done inough as by our quarrie may appeare.
Assoone as with hir scarlet wheeles next morning bringeth light,　　25
We will about our worke againe. But now *Hiperion* bright
Is in the middes of Heaven, and seares the fieldes with firie rayes.
Take up your toyles, and ceasse your worke, and let us go our wayes.
They did even so, and ceast their worke. There was a valley thicke
With Pinaple and Cipresse trees that armed be with pricke.　　30
Gargaphie hight this shadie plot, it was a sacred place
To chast *Diana* and the Nymphes that wayted on hir grace.
Within the furthest end thereof there was a pleasant Bowre
So vaulted with the leavie trees, the Sunne had there no powre:
Not made by hand nor mans devise, and yet no man alive,　　35
A trimmer piece of worke than that could for his life contrive.

With flint and Pommy [lava] was it wallde by nature halfe about,
And on the right side of the same full freshly flowed out
A lively spring with Christall streame: whereof the upper brim
Was greene with grasse and matted herbes that smelled verie trim.   40
When *Phebe* [Diana] felt hir selfe waxe faint, of following of hir game,
It was hir custome for to come and bath hir in the same.
That day she having timely left hir hunting in the chace,
Was entred with hir troupe of Nymphes within this pleasant place.
She tooke hir quiver and hir bow the which she had unbent,   45
And eke hir Javelin to a Nymph that served that intent.
Another Nymph to take hir clothes among hir traine she chose,
Two losde [loosened] hir buskins from hir legges and pulled of hir hose.
The Thebane Ladie *Crocale,* more cunning than the rest,
Did trusse hir tresses handsomly which hung behind undrest.   50
And yet hir owne hung waving still. Then *Niphe* nete and cleene
With *Hiale* glistring like the grash [grass] in beautie fresh and sheene,
And *Rhanis* clearer of hir skin than are the rainie drops,
And little bibling *Phyale,* and *Pseke* that pretie Mops,
Powrde water into vessels large to washe their Ladie with.   55
Now while she keepes this wont, behold, by wandring in the frith [game
    preserve]
He wist not whither (having staid his pastime till the morrow)
Comes *Cadmus* Nephew to this thicke: and entring in with sorrow
(Such was his cursed cruell fate) saw *Phebe* where she washt.
The Damsels at the sight of man quite out of countnance dasht,   60
(Bicause they everichone were bare and naked to the quicke.)
Did beate their handes against their brests, and cast out such a shricke,
That all the wood did ring thereof: and clinging to their dame
Did all they could to hide both hir and eke themselves fro shame.
But *Phebe* was of personage so comly and so tall,   65
That by the middle of hir necke she overpeerd them all.
Such colour as appeares in Heaven by *Phebus* broken rayes
Directly shining on the Cloudes, or such as is alwayes
The colour of the Morning Cloudes before the Sunne doth show,
Such sanguine colour in the face of *Phœbe* gan to glowe   70
There standing naked in his sight. Who though she had hir gard
Of Nymphes about hir: yet she turnde hir bodie from him ward [away].
And casting backe an angrie looke, like as she would have sent
An arrow at him had she had hir bow there readie bent:
So raught [reached] the water in hir hande, and for to wreake the spight,   75
Besprinckled all the heade and face of the unluckie Knight,
And thus forespake the heavie lot that should upon him light.
Now make thy vaunt among thy Mates, thou sawste *Diana* bare.
Tell if thou can: I give thee leave: tell heardly: doe not spare.
This done, she makes no further threates, but by and by doth spread   80
A payre of lively olde Harts hornes upon his sprinckled head.

She sharpes his eares, she makes his necke both slender, long and lanke.
She turnes his fingers into feete, his armes to spindle shanke.
She wrappes him in a hairie hyde beset with speckled spottes,
And planteth in him fearefulnesse. And so away he trottes,   85
Full greatly wondring to him selfe what made him in that cace
To be so wight [agile] and swift of foote. But when he saw his face
And horned temples in the brooke, he would have cryde alas,
But as for then no kinde of speach out of his lippes could passe.
He sight [sighed] and brayde: for that was then the speach that did remaine,   90
And downe the eyes that were not his, his bitter teares did raine.
No part remayned (save his minde) of that he earst [formerly] had beene.
What should he doe? turne home againe to *Cadmus* and the Queene?
Or hyde himselfe among the Woods? Of this he was afrayd,
And of the tother ill ashamde. While doubting thus he stayd: 95
   His houndes espyde him where he was, and Blackfoote first of all
   And Stalker speciall good of sent began aloud to call.
This latter was a hound of *Crete*, the other was of *Spart*.
Then all the kenell fell in round, and everie for his part,
Dyd follow freshly in the chase more swifter than the winde,   100
Spy, Eateal, Scalecliffe, three good houndes comne all of *Arcas* kinde.
Strong Kilbucke, currish Savage, Spring, and Hunter fresh of smell,
And Lightfoote who to lead a chase did beare away the bell.
Fierce Woodman hurte not long ago in hunting of a Bore
And Shepeheird woont to follow sheepe and neate [cattle] to fielde afore.   105
And Laund a fell [savage] and eger bitch that had a Wolfe to Syre:
Another brach [bitch] callde Greedigut with two hir Puppies by hir.
And Ladon gant as any Greewnd [greyhound] a hownd in *Sycion* bred,
Blab, Fleetewood, Patch whose flecked skin wᵗ sundrie spots was spred:
Wight, Bowman, Royster, beautie faire and white as winters snow,   110
And Tawnie full of duskie haires that over all did grow,
With lustie Ruffler passing all the resdue there in strength,
And Tempest best of footemanshipe in holding out at length.
And Cole, and Swift, and little Woolfe, as wight as any other,
Accompanide with a *Ciprian* hound that was his native brother,   115
And Snatch amid whose forehead stoode a starre as white as snowe,
The resdue being all as blacke and slicke as any Crowe,
And shaggie Rugge with other twaine that had a Syre of *Crete*,
And dam of *Sparta:* Tone [th' one] of them callde Jollyboy, a great
And large flewd [with large flews or jaws] hound: the tother Chorle who ever
   gnoorring [growling] went,   120
And Ringwood with a shyrle [shrill] loud mouth the which he freely spent,
With divers mo whose names to tell it were but losse of tyme.
This fellowes over hill and dale in hope of pray doe clyme.
Through thick and thin and craggie cliffes where was no way to go,
He flyes through groundes where oftentymes he chased had ere tho,   125
Even from his owne folke is he faine (alas) to flee away.

He strayned oftentymes to speake, and was about to say,
I am *Acteon:* know your Lorde and Mayster sirs I pray.
But use of wordes and speach did want to utter forth his minde.
Their crie did ring through all the Wood redoubled with the winde.   130
First Slo did pinch him by the haunch, and next came Kildeere in,
And Hylbred fastned on his shoulder, bote [bit] him through the skinne.
These came forth later than the rest, but coasting thwart a hill,
They did gainecope [trap] him as he came, and helde their Master still,
Untill that all the rest came in, and fastned on him to.   135
No part of him was free from wound. He could none other do
But sigh, and in the shape of Hart with voyce as Hartes are woont,
(For voyce of man was none now left to helpe him at the brunt)
By braying show his secret grief among the Mountaynes hie,
And kneeling sadly on his knees with dreerie teares in eye,   140
As one by humbling of himselfe that mercy seemde to crave,
With piteous looke in stead of handes his head about to wave.
Not knowing that it was their Lord, the huntsmen cheere their hounds
With wonted noyse and for *Acteon* looke about the grounds.
They hallow who could lowdest crie still calling him by name   145
As though he were not there, and much his absence they do blame,
In that he came not to the fall, but slackt to see the game.
As often as they named him he sadly shooke his head,
And faine he would have beene away thence in some other stead,
But there he was. And well he could have found in heart to see   150
His dogges fell deedes, so that to feele in place he had not bee.
They hem him in on everie side, and in the shape of Stagge,
With greedie teeth and griping pawes their Lord in peeces dragge.
So fierce was cruell *Phebes* wrath, it could not be alayde,
Till of his fault by bitter death the raunsome he had payde.   155
    Much muttring was upon this fact. Some thought there was extended
A great deale more extremitie than neded. Some commended
Dianas doing: saying that it was but worthely
For safegarde of hir womanhod. Eche partie did applie
Good reasons to defende their case.   160

CHAPTER 6

"What Is Your Text?"

———————————— >-<‹ ————————————

Because Shakespeare has become, for many who study him and even for many who do not, an object of veneration or a cultural idol, his works have almost assumed the status of religious documents. A quick look at two modern editions of Shakespeare, however, will reveal variations in this sacred text, numerous and sometimes major differences in the words that constitute it. In the 1986 Oxford edition of *Hamlet*, for example, Hamlet in his first soliloquy wishes that his "too too solid flesh would melt, / Thaw, and resolve itself into a dew"; in the Riverside edition, that flesh is "too too sallied" (*sallied* is a variation of *sullied*, meaning "stained"). This inconsistency, a famous instance of a textual *crux*, or problem, raises a question that every student of Shakespeare needs to be aware of: how can we tell what Shakespeare wrote? Whether we read from a collection of the complete works such as *The Riverside Shakespeare* or *The Complete Pelican Shakespeare*, or a single-play volume from a popular series such as the Folger or Signet editions, the excellence and familiarity of modern Shakespeare texts have made it easy to read the plays. But this same convenience distances us from the difficulties of the original texts and protects us from the problems and uncertainties attendant on the laborious process of establishing that text. It is worthwhile to spend some time defamiliarizing our modern books, to move away from them temporarily so as to examine the nature and origins of the Shakespearean text. What is it, and how did it get to be the way that it is?

What Is a Shakespearean Text?

The central problem in textual scholarship is one of authority, a problem related, as the etymology suggests, to that of authorship. Textual scholars seek to establish as accurately as possible the words that the author wrote. But as anyone who has ever used a word processor to produce a revised version of a document will recognize, this is not an easy matter. Is it immediately clear which is the original and which the revision? Is there a longhand version against which the printed copies can be checked? For works composed some four hundred years ago, these difficulties are compounded, and there are different problems as well. No manuscripts for any of Shakespeare's plays have survived. (The British Library possesses a handwritten set of additions to a collaborative play called *Sir Thomas More*. One section of these four sheets has been identified as Shakespeare's and is said to be in his hand, a claim that has won surprisingly wide acceptance. However, textual experts have recently become increasingly dubious about the attribution.) His plays have come down to us in the form of books printed from lost manuscripts, either authorial drafts or copies of them. Furthermore, the printing process that gave us those books was in a relatively early state of development, making its products highly vulnerable to error. Even the author who supervised the printing of his works and checked proofs directly from the press, which Shakespeare apparently did not do for his plays, found that mistakes inevitably made their way into the final versions. Spelling and punctuation were flexible and irregular: the surviving signatures imply that Shakespeare spelled even his own name in different ways.

But the problems associated with textual authority derive not only from an evolving orthographic system and an imperfect mechanical process. An even greater source of confusion is the genre in which Shakespeare wrote. Of all forms of writing, drama is probably the one in which the author's identity is hardest to establish because theater, as we observed in Chapters 1 and 4, is essentially a collaborative art. An Elizabethan lyric poet's words may have been accidentally misread in the printing house, but the dramatist's words were subject to modification well before the printing process even began. The scribe who copied out the parts for the actors, for example, may have misunderstood the author's penmanship and thus introduced errors. An actor may have found a particular line difficult to deliver and requested a change — or simply made the change himself. Actors frequently misremember or alter lines, and sometimes these erroneous versions become a permanent part of the play text. The prompter, or "book-keeper," needing more time to get an actor on stage, may have contributed a line or two himself to stall the action until the required character could appear. If the play were running overtime in rehearsal, the author or perhaps the book-keeper might have made cuts. The rehearsal scenes in *A Midsummer Night's Dream,* in which the mechanicals prepare their play *Pyramus and Thisbe* for Duke Theseus, humorously depict how changes might have been introduced into a theatrical script.

Still another obstacle to textual authority is Shakespeare's apparent indifference to publishing. Only about half of his plays were printed during his lifetime, and he seems not to have been directly involved in their publication. However, he may have overseen the printing of his early narrative poems, *Venus and Adonis* and *The Rape of Lucrece*. As strange as it may seem to us, such authorial distance was not uncommon in the theater of early modern England. To a Renaissance playwright, "publication" meant presentation of the work to the public on a stage; it did not necessarily imply preservation in the form of a printed book. Copyright laws as we know them did not exist, and prevailing notions of intellectual or artistic property had little to do with the author. Normally a play belonged to the dramatic company, the Lord Admiral's Men or the King's Men, for example, that produced it on the stage, or else to the bookseller or printer who had purchased it from that company.

When a playwright finished a script, he delivered it to the theatrical company for which he worked (or which had commissioned or purchased it) and thus relinquished his rights to the play. ("He" is the appropriate pronoun: there were no female professional playwrights.) Only one or two complete copies of the script existed, the author's original and perhaps another copy; one of these served as "the book of the play," the master copy used for the stage production. Transcripts were expensive to produce, of course, since the entire play had to be copied over by hand with quill pen and ink. Actors were never given complete versions of the script, as is the practice in the modern theater, but were provided with only their own parts, known as *sides*, consisting of their lines with cues and instructions for entrances and exits. (In the second scene of *A Midsummer Night's Dream*, the mechanicals' first rehearsal, Peter Quince distributes the "parts" to the actors and urges them to learn their lines.) A theatrical company carefully guarded its copies of the script to prevent theft and subsequent performance of the play by another theatrical troupe. After a number of performances, when a play had ceased to draw audiences and was to be taken out of the repertory, the company may have sold the script to a publisher, who then printed and sold copies to the public. It was not in a company's interest to publish a popular play that might warrant revival, since the fewer copies in circulation the better.

The record of publication for Shakespeare's plays during his active career offers some insight into the economics of the Renaissance theatrical companies and their dramatic properties. The first of his plays to be published was *Titus Andronicus* in 1594; as the title page (reproduced on p. 211) reveals, the author went unnamed. At about the same time there appeared a version of one of the *Henry VI* plays — unattributed, with a different title, and textually very different from the one we know. From 1597, when Shakespeare was becoming one of the most popular and productive dramatists in London, more and more of his plays began to see print: *Richard II* in 1597; *Love's Labor's Lost* and *Henry IV, Part 1* in 1598; *A Midsummer Night's Dream*, *The Merchant of Venice*, *Much Ado about Nothing*, and *Henry IV, Part 2* in 1600. In addition, versions of *Romeo and Juliet* and *Henry V* that differ substantially from those printed later were issued in 1598 and 1600 respectively. During the second decade of Shakespeare's career, however, fewer of his plays appeared in bookshops: some of those we rank among his most important (*As You Like It, Julius Caesar, Twelfth Night, Macbeth, Antony and Cleopatra, The Winter's Tale,* and *The Tempest*) were printed only after his death, in the 1623 collected edition known as the First Folio. (See the title page and catalogue reproduced on pp. 212–13.) This publishing record suggests that as Shakespeare became famous and a potential source of income for the new theatrical troupe that he and his associates had established in 1594, some of his scripts were sold to publishers in an effort to capitalize on his name and the popularity of his recent work. As their principal playwright's reputation grew and as the King's Men consolidated their theatrical sovereignty in Jacobean London, the frequency of publication began to diminish, as if the company no longer needed to make a few pounds off old scripts and was less inclined to dispose of them.

The complexities of this route from playwright to actors to printer, and the number of stops along the way, make it extremely difficult for modern scholars to determine the accuracy of a Shakespearean text. Some of the most perplexing questions arise from the existence of different texts for some plays. The First Folio contains thirty-six plays; of these, eighteen had already been printed in single-play editions called quartos. Thus, for about half of the plays we have two versions, and for some of these we have multiple versions because the quartos were reprinted to meet demand. It is important to keep in mind that reprinting in the Renaissance meant something different from what it does now, when a popular text can simply be copied photographically. At the turn of the seventeenth century, reprinting a play meant starting over, perhaps correcting mistakes found in the earlier version and probably introducing new errors. Thus a reprinted Renaissance text may actually be a new version of the play. In some cases, notably *King Lear,* the differences between the two texts, the Quarto of 1608 and the Folio of 1623, are so numerous and significant that the hazards of reprinting alone cannot account for them; as we shall see, some scholars now believe that Shakespeare himself may have revised his initial version, which if true would make both texts "authorial."

When you open a modern edition of *King Lear,* which text are you reading? How will you know? Which one is "Shakespeare's"? Who decided? On what grounds? Does it matter? What is at stake in the attempt to certify the text as "Shakespeare's" alone, rather than Shakespeare's and Nicholas Rowe's, or Alexander Pope's, or David Bevington's, or one of the many other editors who have attempted to establish the text over the past four centuries? To such questions this chapter will attempt to provide at least partial answers, but the effort to do so has been complicated by recent developments in critical theory. The postmodern urge to think of authorship as collective rather than individual and the concomitant challenge to authorial intention have altered the entire enterprise of textual scholarship. In particular, uncertainty about definitions of authorship makes it virtually impossible to establish an authoritative text. In the face of such complications, it makes sense to gather as many facts as possible, and thus a brief introduction to the printing process at the turn of the seventeenth century is in order.

From Pen to Press: The Printing of Renaissance Plays

An account of early modern printing must begin with the author's original manuscript. A dramatist who wrote a play did so in longhand, producing a manuscript sometimes known as the author's *foul papers*. Before the play was submitted for performance, either the dramatist himself or a professional scribe probably made a transcript suitable for theatrical use. This second manuscript is now known as a *fair copy*. Then a member of the company marked up that copy, specifying theatrical business that the author might have left unclear and attending to textual details that affected the process of theatrical realization. This adjusted version became known as *the book of the play,* and to the company that owned it, it was the most valuable form of the text. Of these three manuscript versions — foul papers, fair copy, or the book of the play — one (and sometimes more than one) was used by the publisher as the copy text for printing; all were in different ways problematic. The paradigm I have described is necessarily simplified. Numerous variations of these three categories of handwritten texts probably existed. And as Paul Werstine reminds us, "These texts were open to penetration and alteration not only by Shakespeare himself and by his fellow actors but also by multiple theatrical and extra-theatrical scriveners, by theatrical annotators, adapters and revisers (who might cut or add), by censors, and by compositors and proofreaders" (86).

Foul papers probably represented the version closest to the author's intentions, although such a manuscript might not include authorial changes introduced into the fair copy or, during the course of rehearsal, into the book of the play. Foul papers, as the name connotes, were often difficult to read. The penmanship, what is known as secretary hand, is not easy for the modern eye to decipher; and while a contemporary reader would have had less trouble than we do, the writing still exhibits certain orthographic features that could make it confusing even to the practiced reader. Foul papers by definition offer an early version of the play and would have contained deletions, marginal and interlinear additions, and other instances of second thoughts or false starts. Inconsistencies, as we know from the rough drafts of our own papers, were manifold: in one of the early printed versions of *Romeo and Juliet,* which appears to have been set from foul papers, the stage directions refer to Juliet's mother variously as "Mother," "Capulet's Wife," "Lady," and "Lady of the house"; the prefixes to the character's speeches vary from "Wife" to "Mo." to "M." to "La." to "Capu. Wi." to "Cap. Wi." to "Old La." Some of the speech prefixes in manuscript originals even shift from the name of the character to the name of the actor for whom Shakespeare wrote the part.

Fair copy might be easier to read and thus to transcribe and set into type, but it, too, would presumably contain mistakes, especially if it were made not by the author but by a hired copyist. Mistakes aside, the copyist's own linguistic and orthographic biases could intrude. Ralph Crane, a professional scribe whose transcripts of several plays were used in the printing of the First Folio, had certain preferences in punctuation (he appears to have been inordinately fond of parentheses, for example) that have made their way into our modern texts but probably do not reflect Shakespeare's practice. The book of the play can be especially perplexing because it may remove us even further from the author's original script. Again, however, the term *original* is indefinite and unreliable when used in reference to a dramatic text, given its collaborative nature. It is difficult to know whether certain characteristics of a text deriving from the book of the play result from an author's design or from the conditions of a theatrical process with which the author may have had little or even nothing to do. Any of these potentially faulty documents might have served as copy text for the printer who made the play available for public sale and thus preserved it for posterity. And still more errors would be introduced in the print shop.

For understanding the printing of Renaissance books the first important term to grasp is *sheet*, denoting the large piece of paper with which the printer began and which was pressed onto the inked type. (This sheet was probably at least 18 by 14 inches in size; paper was handmade, and the size of printing sheets may have varied. Moreover, it is difficult to speculate based on existing folios: these vary significantly in size, and many would have been cut down for purposes of binding and perhaps cut down again years later for rebinding.) To make a folio — the large form used for the collected edition of Shakespeare's plays — the printer folded the sheet once, making two leaves, or four pages front and back; the book was thus about 9 by 14 inches. To make a quarto — the form in which a single play was usually published — the printer folded the sheet twice, making four leaves (hence the name *quarto*), or eight pages front and back; this book was thus about 7 by 9 inches, or the size of a large modern paperback. For a folio, the folded sheets were gathered into groups and sewn together. With the First Folio, they were gathered "in sixes," that is, three folded sheets were placed within one another at the fold, producing a *gathering*, or *quire*, of six leaves, or twelve pages. For a quarto, the single folded sheet, producing eight pages, was the unit of sewing. The folding, sewing, and binding were the last steps in the process.

Whatever the size of the book, folio or quarto, pages were not printed in numerical order. One entire sheet was placed flat onto the printing press, first on one side and then on the other. The printing was done according to the size of the gathering, so that for a folio-in-sixes, twelve pages (or three sheets, front and back) were prepared for a single gathering. This system required that the pages be set up according to the way the sheet would finally be folded: with the folio format, for example, pages one and twelve were printed on one side of a sheet, and then pages two and eleven on the reverse side (see the illustration on page 200). Two compositors would have set the type simultaneously, one of them beginning on page six and working backward to page one, the second beginning on page seven and working forward to page twelve. Thus the side of the sheet containing pages six and seven was set first and printed first, and then the other side (pages five and eight) was set and printed. As awkward as the process may seem, this was the most economical way to print a text. Beginning not at the beginning but in the middle of a gathering that contained three entire sheets, or twelve pages of a finished book, the

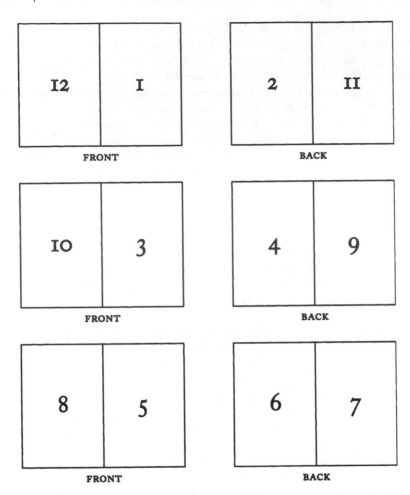

Illustration of the folding and printing process for a gathering of twelve folio pages, reproduced from G. B. Harrison, Introducing Shakespeare, *p. 208*

printer had to estimate the amount of text that would fill each of the twelve pages. This process of estimation was called *casting off* copy.

Once the copy had been cast off, normally by an experienced printer accustomed to the task, the compositors (from *com-pose,* or "put together") began the process of setting type. Reading the portion of the manuscript assigned to them by the person who had cast it off, they selected pieces of metal type, taking each one from large cases divided into small boxes containing each letter and punctuation mark. They then placed the pieces of type, formed into the words of the text, into the frame that was locked into the bed of the press. (A seventeenth-century illustration of a print shop is found on p. 214.) The blank sheet was pressed onto the bed and imprinted; it was then removed and proofread, after which the pieces of type were extracted from the frame and sorted and returned to their cases.

This process of casting off copy and then printing pages out of numerical order saved time and type, but it could also create serious problems for the printing house. For example, the last page of the Quarto text of *King Lear* (1608), shown on page 215, presents a case in which the printer apparently had to squeeze text onto the last page available to him. Consequently we see evidence of corner-cutting: two short speeches are run together on the same line; the Duke of Albany's sympathetic tribute to Lear is converted from verse to prose, which takes less space. The need for economy may also explain why a word is dropped ("great" in "this great decay") and the stage direction for Lear's death omitted. These and other such compromises saved the printer the expense of having to use another sheet.

The chaos that must have reigned in the London print shops of the late sixteenth century is hard to exaggerate. To start with, the noise emanating from the machinery must have been overwhelming, as the wooden and iron parts of the printing presses banged against each other in the process of setting paper to type. Printing was a dirty job as well, considering the quantities of ink required. The leather print balls used to apply the ink had to be kept supple, so English pressmen soaked the leather overnight in human urine. It is thus likely that the print shops were plagued with flies. Sometimes compositors were working on more than one book at a time; likewise, portions of a single book were sometimes printed by various houses and then bound together. The organizational challenges must have been enormous. In view of these physical difficulties, it is to be expected that errors would appear in the printed versions of Shakespeare's plays — dropped lines, perhaps even larger omissions, the misreading of handwriting, the wrong letter substituted for the right one, blunders in casting off copy. We should be surprised only that the texts we have do not contain more obvious mistakes than they do.

Shakespeare's Plays in Print

Of the eighteen Shakespeare plays printed in quarto, a majority were printed more than once. Some of these reprints signify the popularity of a particular play: it was reprinted because the first printing sold out and a demand for it still existed. Some of the plays, however, may have been reprinted because the first issue represented an unusually faulty text. These peculiar and problematic versions are sometimes known as "bad quartos." Many of them may have been published illicitly, a result of theft or some other irregularity; and in a few cases the appearance of a bad quarto seems to have stimulated Shakespeare's company to arrange for the printing of a more accurate version of the text.

Hamlet is the classic instance of such a scenario. The first printed version, or First Quarto (Q1), appeared in 1603, and it differs radically from the version we read now. In Q1 the text is very short, about half the length of the later versions; scenes and speeches are placed in an order different from the sequence we know; the figure familiar to us as Polonius is called Corambis; and certain well-known passages are barely recognizable. Consider the beginning of the play's most famous speech:

> To be, or not to be, I [ay] there's the point,
> To Die, to sleepe, is that all? I all:
> No, to sleepe, to dreame, I mary there it goes . . .

As these three lines attest, the differences between this passage and the familiar Folio (F) version are not minor, and additional variations appear in the complete versions of the speech from Q1 and F on pages 216 and 217. Once the Quarto text had appeared for sale in London, the King's Men evidently arranged for a corrected version to be made available. Q2, published in 1604 (although some copies read 1605), is advertised as being "Newly imprinted and enlarged to almost as much againe as it was, according to the true and perfect Coppie."

The status of such different versions is now the subject of fierce debate. Some textual scholars believe that a bad quarto derived from a reconstructed version of the play by a person or persons only slightly familiar with it; some of these pirated texts are thought to have been concocted by actors who had played small parts in the production and who then sought, with varying degrees of success, to re-create the play from memory. Thus the poor texts of the bad quartos are said to result from "memorial reconstruction." Although this theory is sometimes disputed on the grounds that evidence is slim, nineteenth-century theatrical practice attests to feats of memory no less impressive. Moreover, the Spanish playwright Lope de Vega, a contemporary of Shakespeare, speaks of professional dramatic pirates who went to the theater deliberately to memorize and reproduce plays for print (see Potter 21). In the case of *Hamlet*, it looks as if the text was recited to a scribe by the actor who played the tiny parts of Marcellus and Lucianus. Some form of memorial reconstruction appears to be the most plausible way of accounting for the wildly discrepant texts of certain plays.

Strong resistance has arisen to the pejorative nature of the term *bad quarto*, and some scholars argue that modern editors have been too quick to dismiss these versions as corrupt and un-Shakespearean. One new theory — actually an old theory revived — came to prominence in the 1970s and '80s: that some of the bad quartos may in fact be early Shakespearean versions of the plays, akin to rough drafts, and that the differences between two texts of a play are attributable to Shakespeare's own rewriting of the initial version. The controversy over the two texts of *King Lear*, described below, has prompted scholars to reassess several quarto texts formerly condemned as inferior, such as the 1597 Quarto of *Richard III* and the 1602 Quarto of *The Merry Wives of Windsor;* Steven Urkowitz, whose arguments about the revision of *King Lear* have gained considerable favor, has sought to rehabilitate even the bad quarto of *Hamlet*. According to one witty scholar, there is now no such thing as a bad quarto, only a misunderstood quarto or an unloved quarto.

Most of those who stop short of attributing to Shakespeare the peculiar version of "To be or not to be" found in Q1 of *Hamlet* will admit the legitimacy of two Shakespearean versions of *King Lear*. The existence of two different texts of *King Lear*, the 1608 Quarto and the 1623 Folio, has always puzzled scholars, who naturally want to know which was the "real," the authoritative, the "Shakespearean" form of the play. Although the 1608 printing has not generally been considered a bad quarto, the discrepancies between it and the Folio often led editors to posit the existence of a prior ideal text. Now, however, both versions are held to be legitimate and authorial, the Folio constituting Shakespeare's later revision of the Quarto. Q is a relatively good text, and it contains certain lines and episodes that do not appear in F but that seem indisputably Shakespearean, not the invention or the faulty recollection of a pirate reporter. F contains about one hundred lines absent from Q, while Q contains about three hundred lines not found in F. Until recently most modern editors of *King Lear*, believing each text to be a corruption of a lost original, combined Q and F, even though such a synthesis creates some redundancy. Even more troubling, such a conflation offers the reader a dramatic work Shakespeare apparently never conceived. The revision theory has Shakespeare himself revising Q into F, expanding the earlier text in some places but also cutting so as to achieve greater speed in the second half of the play. These scholarly debates have begun to have a significant impact on what we read: the Oxford edition of the complete works, prepared in the 1980s by editors who fueled the debate over *King Lear*, prints both versions as if they were separate plays. Even the original titles vary, one being *The Historie of King Lear* (Q), the other *The Tragedie of King Lear* (F).

Uncertainties about the alternative versions of a play point to an important shift in modern thinking about textual scholarship and what it can achieve. Shortly after the beginning of the twentieth century, bibliographical scholars such as W. W. Greg, R. B. McKerrow, and, later, Fredson Bowers and Charlton Hinman began to study the process by which Shakespeare's texts came into physical being and thus to develop the tools of analytical bibliography, methods that have taught us how to judge the texts that have survived. Professor Hinman, who published his detailed investigations in *The Printing and Proof-Reading of the First Folio of Shakespeare*, compared each page of fifty-five copies of the First Folio at the Folger Shakespeare Library and even identified individual pieces of type that had become damaged in the printing process. He and other scholars distinguished the work of five compositors who set the pages of the First Folio, discerning their spelling preferences, propensity for certain kinds of errors, and varying degrees of skill. Compositor B, for example, a thorough professional, set over half the pages of the book. Compositor E, on the other hand, was an apprentice, probably a teenager, who joined the project late, worked mainly on the tragedies, and made an enormous number of mistakes in reading copy and setting type. The spelling practices of Compositors A and B are illustrated in the facsimiles on page 218.

The precision of this research and the fascinating historical picture it produced imparted a spirit of optimism and potential certainty to the enterprise of textual scholarship. Fredson Bowers, writing in 1958, articulated the guiding principles of textual criticism:

> May we not lay this down as a doctrine? In all cases when a definitive
> edition is proposed for a dramatist, or other author, of no matter what
> century, we should insist (*a*) that it be critically edited, and (*b*) that in its
> texture of accidentals, as well as in its words, it conform to the closest
> approximation to the author's own linguistic and orthographic character-
> istics that can be recovered.   (141)

At the risk of oversimplifying, we can say that this first wave of twentieth-
century textual criticism was based on two assumptions: that an ideal text of a
Shakespeare play did exist, and that a scientific approach would permit the
scholar, with persistence and luck, to recover that text as the author wrote it.

Postmodern editing has rejected the first of these premises. It is now generally conceded that there was no such thing as a final perfected version of, say,
Hamlet; that Shakespeare probably reworked and altered the text continuously
during its theatrical life; and that the problem of dramatic authorship, with
actors, prompters, and scribes all contributing to the creation of the play,
makes it naive to fetishize a single text. Such thinking can be taken too far: it
is probably wrongheaded to defend Q1 of *Hamlet* as just one among several
legitimate versions. Nevertheless, these doubts about the perfect text point us
in the right direction. They remind us that the words before us, as solid and
authoritative as they may look, are unstable and open to question, and they
should lead us to recognize that we cannot approach any Shakespeare play
fairly without being aware of the complex and curious process by which it
came into existence.

The Folio seems more solid and reliable than many of the quartos (especially the bad ones), and whatever its inherent textual problems, it is the only
source we have for almost half of the plays. As a volume of collected works, it
was very nearly anticipated by another publisher three years after the playwright's death. Thomas Pavier, a Londoner who had obtained the rights to a
few of the plays already in print, made a shady effort to amass and sell a volume
of previously published quartos. His scheme was foiled by defensive action on
the part of the King's Men (although a few Pavier quartos were printed and
sold). It is unclear whether Shakespeare's former colleagues had already planned
such a book, or whether Pavier's entrepreneurial efforts stimulated them to
undertake a collected edition. (Furthermore, we are not certain whether the
primary impetus was commemorative, and so initiated by the players, or commercial, and so initiated by the publishers; almost certainly the motives were
mixed.) Whatever the sequence, two of Shakespeare's fellow actors, John
Heminges and Henry Condell, joined with the London publishers Edward
Blount and Isaac Jaggard to produce a volume that contained not only the
plays already in print but most of the hitherto unprinted works as well. They
sought to acquire the rights to the plays already in print — these texts were
owned by the men who had registered and then printed them — and to
assemble usable manuscripts of those never published. This was a formidable
task, and the contents of the volume were determined by whether rights could
be secured. In the case of *Troilus and Cressida,* for example, it appears that the
two people who had registered and published the Quarto of 1609, at first

unwilling to yield their rights to the play, came to terms at the eleventh hour, when the Folio was almost completely printed; when they did agree, the contents were rearranged slightly in order to facilitate the last-minute inclusion of *Troilus*. The negotiations were concluded so hastily and late that a few copies of the Folio seem to have been sewn and placed on sale before *Troilus and Cressida* was entirely printed and bound into the book.

The Folio, known now as the First Folio, was offered for sale in London in November 1623 for one pound. (For a complicated set of reasons, there may have been some flexibility in the price.) It contains thirty-six plays, eighteen of which had never seen print before, some of them among Shakespeare's greatest achievements (e.g., *Macbeth, Twelfth Night,* and *The Tempest*). Not every play in which Shakespeare had a hand is present. Two on which he worked with John Fletcher, *The Two Noble Kinsmen* (printed later in quarto) and *Cardenio* (now lost), are absent, as is *Pericles*, a late play with similarly uncertain authorship. Yet *Henry VIII,* also a late collaboration with Fletcher, does appear in the volume. Considering that the playwright was dead when the Folio project was begun and that some of the plays had been printed before, the vital question concerns the nature of the various materials that were to be printed in it. To ascertain as exactly as possible the words that Shakespeare wrote, it is important to know what sources the printers used as copy to set the type for each play in the Folio.

The sources for the works printed in the Folio are: (1) Shakespeare's own manuscripts, (2) scribal transcripts of those manuscripts, some of them from the playhouse, (3) quarto versions already in print, or (4) some combination of these. For plays already printed in reasonably accurate form, the quarto version was used as copy text, often corrected or annotated with reference to a manuscript, either authorial or scribal, of the same play. *A Midsummer Night's Dream,* for example, falls into this category, having been printed from Q2 but supplemented with readings from another copy. For plays never printed, different kinds of manuscripts were consulted. Sometimes Shakespeare's own draft (foul papers) was used as the source: *The Comedy of Errors* exhibits characteristics that indicate a direct authorial origin. Sometimes the source is a scribal transcript prepared with the aim of achieving a clean, legible copy, although for whom the transcript was prepared is not always clear (the acting company? the printers themselves?). Manuscripts prepared by Ralph Crane (the professional scribe) served as copy texts for several plays in the Folio, such as *The Two Gentlemen of Verona* and *The Tempest.* Occasionally a copy that had been used as the book of the play became the basis for the Folio text, as with *Macbeth;* this may explain why the Scottish play is notably shorter than most of the tragedies, since the book of the play may have been a transcript designed for a particular kind of performance. Or it may be that *Macbeth* is brief because Shakespeare's artistic sense so dictated.

All these complexities are germane to the inescapable question of textual authority. To approach the problem microscopically, how can we be sure that the word we admire in a favorite speech was written by Shakespeare and not supplied by a scribe who could not decipher the original, or invented by a stage manager whose place in the text was smudged and who needed a word right away, or mistakenly set down by a compositor who was momentarily wool-gathering? To put the matter in macroscopic terms, if a New York publishing house wishes to offer a modern-spelling edition of *Hamlet* and engages an editor to prepare it, which early version should be used for copy text? The problematic Q1 might be dismissed easily, except that it contains one scene (between the Queen and Horatio, near the end of act 4) found in no other contemporary text. What about the second Quarto, which has been thought to derive from authorial foul papers? It is usually considered the best choice. But then the Folio version contains many useful directions for stage practice absent from Q2: should some of these be included? Shouldn't the editor simply choose the readings that seem most authoritative from each version and combine them into a single text? But what is the basis for deciding on "the readings that seem most authoritative"? And isn't the *Hamlet* produced by such compromises the creation of the editor more than the author? But once again, in the case of early modern plays, what is an author?

Some Examples of Textual Instability

A glance at some famous textual problems in Shakespeare transports us quickly from the abstract to the concrete and reveals how contingent and problematic our texts can be. Here is the conclusion of *Titus Andronicus*, Shakespeare's earliest tragedy, as printed in the Folio of 1623:

> See Iustice done on *Aaron* that damn'd Moore,
> From whom, our heauy happes had their beginning:
> Then afterwards, to Order well the State,
> That like Euents, may ne're it Ruinate.

Many readers have condemned these last four lines — as heavy-handed morally as they are poetically — as too crude to be worthy of the world's most celebrated playwright. At the same time, however, all of *Titus* has struck many readers and audiences as coarse and un-Shakespearean, and the lines are consistent with its raw theatricality (hands cut off; severed heads exhibited onstage; a tongue cut out; and, at a banquet near the end of the play, a mother invited to feast on a pie made with the flesh of her two sons). Indeed, the play seems to have been composed by a young dramatist still learning his craft and responsive to the sensational revenge plays of the early 1590s. So it is with this last verse passage, which strikes the ear perhaps as crude but not completely uncharacteristic, not unlike, for example, the two lines that precede these in the Folio: "Her life was Beast-like, and deuoid of pitty, / And being so, shall have like want of pitty." As it turns out, these two lines are authentic, but the last four lines were in fact not written by Shakespeare at all — they appear to have been composed by a printer.

Using the techniques of analytical bibliography, scholars have determined that the Folio text of *Titus Andronicus* was prepared from the third Quarto

(1611) of the play, which was reprinted from the second Quarto of 1600. All of these texts are substantially alike, and all contain (with minor variations) the last four lines about Aaron's villainy and the restoration of order in Rome. In 1904, however, the textual picture changed radically with the discovery in Sweden of a copy of the first printing of *Titus Andronicus*, Q1 (1594). (Still the world's only surviving copy, it now resides in the Folger Shakespeare Library in Washington, D.C.) What is important here is that Q1 does not contain the four lines quoted above, and scholarly detective work has thus created a fascinating story of how the new ending of *Titus Andronicus* came into being.

The evidence suggests that the text for Q2 — the basis for the Folio and all subsequent texts until this century — was prepared from a copy of Q1, but that the physical book used as the source was defective, with the last three leaves damaged at the bottom and the words obscured. G. Blakemore Evans describes what must have happened as the printer approached the end of his job and found himself confronted with defective copy:

> Instead of obtaining another copy of Q1, somebody (almost certainly in the printing house) "restored" the missing words or lines as best he could by guesswork. On the last page (sig. K4v) he outdid himself. Misled by the fact that the text as he found it did not fill out the page and by the chance that the original compositor of Q1 had placed the final *Exeunt* (now missing because of the damage to the leaf) two lines below the last line of the play, he invented four new and feeble lines relating to Aaron and the disposing of the state. (*Riverside Shakespeare* 1051)

Modern editions therefore omit these last lines. The end of the play provides a rare glimpse at how spurious lines made their way into a Shakespeare text and, until new information became available, were considered authorial. The text, in other words, is never definitive, and it is possible that additional facts will surface and cause us to alter our assumptions about other passages, perhaps even cherished lines in familiar plays.

In the case of *Titus Andronicus* it is relatively easy to decide which text is more nearly Shakespearean, but other conflicts between a quarto and the Folio versions of a play are less easy to resolve. *A Midsummer Night's Dream*, for example, appeared in quarto in 1600, four or five years after the initial stage performances. In the Quarto text, Egeus, Hermia's angry father who resists her marriage to Lysander, is overruled by the Duke and leaves the stage in act 4 without having agreed to her marriage or having blessed it. He does not appear again for the wedding festivities in act 5. In the Folio, however, Egeus does reemerge in act 5, scene 1, to present Theseus with the list of proposed after-dinner entertainments, a task assigned in the Quarto to Philostrate, the master of the revels. Whether Egeus attends or does not attend his daughter's wedding feast need not seriously alter the ending of the play, but his presence there can augment the sense of reconciliation and harmony and thus lighten the tone of the final scene. Did Shakespeare revise the play with this conciliatory motive? Possibly, but an alternative explanation is practical or financial. The Folio text may derive from a theatrical prompt-book, thus opening a window onto theatrical history: in his first appearance in act 1, scene 1, Philostrate doesn't speak and isn't strictly necessary to the action. It could be that the company gave Philostrate's lines in the last act to Egeus and thus managed with one fewer actor by doubling the two parts. There is a textual lesson here: in attempting to establish the authority of Shakespeare's lines, it is sometimes helpful to check the bottom line.

One of the most famous textual cruxes is the conflict in *Hamlet* between F's "too too solid flesh" and Q2 through Q4's "too too sallied flesh," mentioned at the beginning of this chapter. (Q1 prints "too much griev'd and sallied flesh.") The crux results from competing texts: Q2 and F both have some claim to authority. The choice is not only between Q2's "sallied" and F's "solid," how-ever. "Sallied" appears to be an early version of "sullied," or stained, and there-fore editors usually select either "sullied" or "solid." Some editors — such as Irving Ribner in his revision of Kittredge's edition (1936) — have chosen the Folio's "too too solid," possibly because it seems logically consistent with "melt, thaw, and resolve" in the following line. On the other hand, the second Quarto apparently represents the version of the play closest to Shakespeare's own manuscript — if there was only one manuscript version — so other editors (Harbage in the Pelican [1969], Barnet in the Signet [1972], and Bevington in the complete HarperCollins edition [1992]) print "sullied," the modernized form of Q2's "sallied." Stanley Wells and Gary Taylor, in the recent Oxford edition (1986), use Q2 as their copy text but depart from it to print "solid." In cases like this, the choice is very technical, depending on the editor's view of the competing authority of the early texts, and so modern readers have little choice but to trust the editor while remaining aware that decisions are being made for them.

An even trickier case occurs when a play exists in only one early text and yet a reading seems to demand emendation. In the third scene of *Measure for Measure*, the Duke explains to a Friar his own failure to enforce Viennese laws against fornication:

> We have strict statutes and most biting laws,
> The needful bits and curbs to headstrong weeds,
> Which for this fourteen years we have let slip;   (1.3.19–21)

The problem here is the word "weeds" or, as the Folio spells it, "weedes." The statutes and laws are described figuratively as bits and curbs designed to rein in or control human passion or desire, here expressed as weeds. This reads suspi-ciously like a mixed metaphor: it requires no extraordinary literary sensibility to recognize that bits and curbs have little effect on weeds. What can it mean that "weeds" have been "let slip"? Or have the bits and curbs been allowed to slip? There is no quarto, no alternative text, against which to check the Folio reading. The apparent imagistic incompatibility led Lewis Theobald, the eighteenth-century editor, to alter the word on logical grounds, so "weeds" became "steeds." Not satisfied with either F's original or with Theobald's pro-posed substitution, later editors have made other suggestions: "wills," which mediates between the figurative and the literal (since "will" is a synonym for sexual desire in the period); and "jades," meaning horses, which (like "steeds") is logically consonant with the metaphorical context.

Which of these did Shakespeare write? Considerations of figurative language would seem to call for "steeds" or "jades," and yet "weeds" may have a poetic claim: it has been pointed out that in at least two other plays Shakespeare metaphorically associates "curbs" with "weeds." (See Wells and Taylor, *William Shakespeare: A Textual Companion* 470.) Moreover, "weeds" would seem to have the paleographic edge. Elizabethan handwriting is difficult to decipher and risky to make judgments about, but it is unlikely that a compositor or scribe would have misread so badly as to print "w" when "st" or "j" was written in the manuscript, especially since "steeds" or "jades" seems so immediately appropriate.

Which of these should a modern editor print? The Riverside edition retains "weeds," as does the Norton; the Pelican and the Arden editors emend to "jades"; Kittredge chooses "steeds," as does a recent editor, David Bevington. In brief, the theoretical question is this: when, and on what grounds, should the editor emend? Or, how bad must the poetry be before an alternative reading is sought? Bibliographical history is crammed with editors, particularly in the eighteenth century, who disgraced themselves by attempting to tidy up what seemed to them messy or irregular and therefore unacceptable texts; in the attempt to enforce scientific principles, it is easy to forget that irregularity is a characteristic of genius.

Yet sometimes emendation is unavoidable. In fact, many of the same editors who emended mistakenly also made an inspired guess that suddenly clarified an obscure passage. For the Hostess's tearful narration of the death of Falstaff in *Henry V,* Lewis Theobald (again) offered just such a brilliant reading. In the Folio text — the only text, since the Quarto omits the questionable line — the Hostess describes the dying man as follows: "for after I saw him fumble with the Sheets, and play with Flowers, and smile vpon his fingers end, I knew there was but one way: for his Nose was as sharpe as a Pen, and a Table of greene fields." That last phrase, "and a Table of greene fields," seems hopelessly puzzling until one sees, as Theobald suggested, that "a" is a sixteenth-century contraction (*'a*) of "he" — it also appears earlier in the speech — and that "Table" is probably an error in transmission for "babbled." Thus the green fields represent the heavenly region, the Elysian Fields that the Hostess imagines Falstaff preparing to enter. Gary Taylor, in his recent Oxford edition of *Henry V,* briefly summarizes the four reasonable alternatives: "to retain the Folio reading, to emend *and* to *on* (Collier) [so that the Pen lies on a green Table], emend *Table* to *talkd* (as proposed by Theobald's anonymous 'gentleman sometime deceased'), or to emend *Table* to *babeld* (Theobald)" (293). Should an editor print "babbled"? Almost certainly; like virtually all modern editors, Taylor does. It is true that to do so is to tamper with a text, but in these lines the case for accepting Theobald's guess seems nearly irresistible.

Shakespeare's Texts and the General Reader

The problems of textual transmission can seem absurdly pedantic and of interest only to specialists. But I hope it is clear that an awareness of this process is vital to an understanding of Shakespeare's plays and of "Shakespeare" as a cultural presence. The optimism of editorial theory in the first half of the twentieth century, marked by confidence that a text of each of Shakespeare's plays could be established and trusted, has yielded in recent times to skepticism in the face of multiple versions, the apparent irrecoverability of authorial intention, and the recognition that every text, even the earliest quartos and Folio, is an edited text. Although scholars need access to all the available versions of a play, no matter how minute the differences, the complexities and frustrations caused by these variations should not incapacitate the non-specialist. To extend the multiplicity theory too far, printing every collected edition of Shakespeare with two texts of *King Lear,* three of *Hamlet,* and competing versions of other plays, would be self-defeating. At some point an editor must choose which reading of a line to print, and an actor must decide which word to speak. For the general reader, the appropriate response to textual uncertainty should combine skepticism and faith.

↝ **Title Page of** *Titus Andronicus* *1594*

First Quarto

The first of Shakespeare's plays to appear in print, though without his name on the title page, was the Roman tragedy *Titus Andronicus*. Only one copy of the Quarto survives. It was discovered in Sweden in 1904 and is now housed in the Folger Shakespeare Library in Washington, D.C.

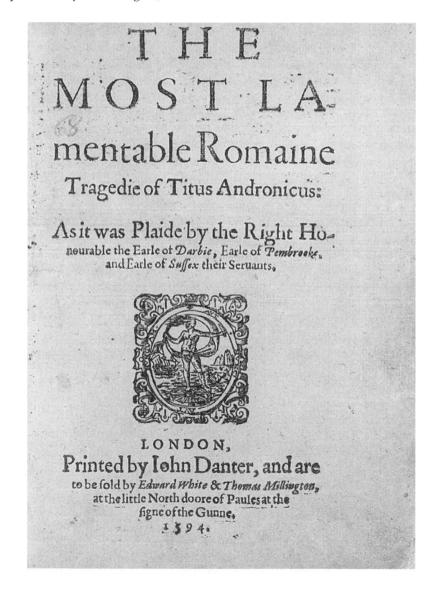

→ Title Page and Catalogue of the First Folio   *1623*

Seven years after Shakespeare's death, a collected edition of his plays, the book we know as the First Folio, was published in London through the cooperation of a group of his former colleagues. It should be noted that the plays are grouped into just three categories: comedies, histories, and tragedies. Modern editions classify *Cymbeline, The Winter's Tale,* and *The Tempest* (along with *Pericles,* not published in the Folio) as romances. *Troilus and Cressida* was not originally listed in the catalogue but appears to have been added late; it is placed between *Henry VIII* and *Coriolanus. The Two Noble Kinsmen,* a collaboration with John Fletcher, is not included in the collection; nor are the sonnets, lyrics, or the narrative poems, *Venus and Adonis* and *The Rape of Lucrece.*

A CATALOGVE

of the seuerall Comedies, Histories, and Tragedies contained in this Volume.

COMEDIES.

The Tempest.	Folio 1.
The two Gentlemen of Verona.	20
The Merry Wiues of Windsor.	38
Measure for Measure.	61
The Comedy of Errours.	85
Much adoo about Nothing.	101
Loues Labour lost.	122
Midsommer Nights Dreame.	145
The Merchant of Venice.	163
As you Like it.	185
The Taming of the Shrew.	208
All is well, that Ends well.	230
Twelfe-Night, or what you will.	255
The Winters Tale.	304

HISTORIES.

The Life and Death of King John.	Fol. 1.
The Life & death of Richard the second.	23
The First part of King Henry the fourth.	46
The Second part of K. Henry the fourth.	74
The Life of King Henry the Fift.	69
The First part of King Henry the Sixt.	96
The Second part of King Hen. the Sixt.	120
The Third part of King Henry the Sixt.	147
The Life & Death of Richard the Third.	173
The Life of King Henry the Eight.	205

TRAGEDIES.

The Tragedy of Coriolanus.	Fol. 1.
Titus Andronicus.	31
Romeo and Juliet.	53
Timon of Athens.	80
The Life and death of Julius Cæsar.	109
The Tragedy of Macbeth.	131
The Tragedy of Hamlet.	152
King Lear.	283
Othello, the Moore of Venice.	310
Anthony and Cleopater.	346
Cymbeline King of Britaine.	369

→ **Illustration of a Seventeenth-Century Print Shop** *1620*

Frontispiece to Edmund Rive's Twelve Rules Introducing to the Art of Latin

This illustration provides a view of the major tools and duties involved in early modern printing. The press stands in the center, and the man in the middle forces the platen down onto a rectangular frame, pressing the paper over a form containing inked type. The man on the left holds the leather balls used to apply the ink; the man seated at the back, the compositor, sets type for the next pages by selecting letters from the multi-sectioned case.

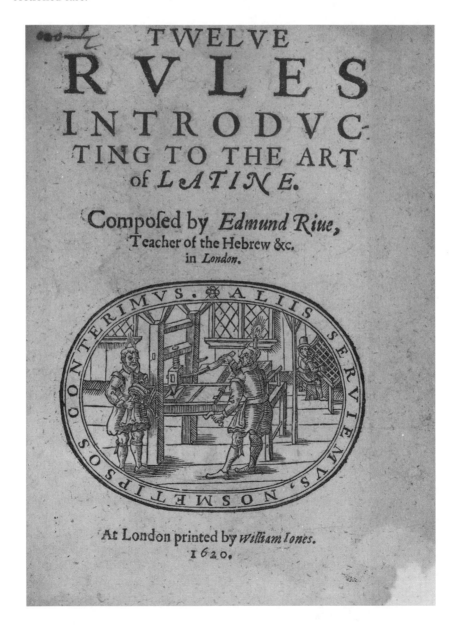

First Quarto

This facsimile of the last page of *King Lear* shows the printer's attempt to crowd text onto the page so as not to have to use another sheet. Some lines are crowded together, for example, and subsequent texts suggest, in their more complete version of the scene, that the compositor of this first printing may have been forced to omit lines. (See p. 201 for a more detailed discussion of this textual matter.) The cuts could have resulted, however, from authorial revision.

The Historie of King Lear.

Kent. That from your life of difference and decay,
Haue followed your sad steps.   *Lear.* You'r welcome hither.
    Kent. Nor no man else, als chearles, darke and deadly,
Your eldest daughters haue foredoome themselues,
And desperatly are dead.   *Lear.* So thinke I to.
    Duke. He knowes not what he sees, and vaine it is,
That we present vs to him,   *Edg.* Very bootlesse.   *Enter*
Capt. Edmund is dead my Lord.   *Captaine.*
    Duke. Thats but a trifle heere, you Lords and noble friends,
Know our intent, what comfort to this decay may come, shall be
applied : for vs we wil resigne during the life of this old maiesty,
to him our absolute power, you to your rights with boote, and
such addition as your honor haue more then merited, all friends
shall tast the wages of their vertue, and al foes the cup of their de-
seruings, O see, see.
    Lear. And my poore foole is hangd, no, no life, why should a
dog, a horse, a rat of life and thou no breath at all, O thou wilt
come no more, neuer, neuer, neuer, pray you vndo this button,
thanke you sir, O, o,o,o.   *Edg.* He faints my Lord, my Lord.
    Lear. Breake hart, I prethe breake.   *Edgar.* Look vp my Lord.
    Kent. Vex not his ghost, O let him passe,
He hates him that would vpon the wracke,
Of this tough world stretch him out longer,
    Edg. O he is gone indeed.
    Kent. The wonder is, he hath endured so long,
He but vsurpt his life.
    Duke. Beare them from hence, our present busines
Is to generall woe, friends of my soule, you twaine
Rule in this kingdome, and the goard state sustaine.
    Kent. I haue a iourney sir, shortly to go,
My maister cals, and I must not say no.
    Duke. The waight of this sad time we must obey,
Speake what we feele, not what we ought to say,
The oldest haue borne most, we that are yong,
Shall neuer see so much, nor liue so long.

FINIS.

✢ Facsimile of "To be or not to be" from
Hamlet, Prince of Denmark   *1603*

First Quarto

This version of "To be or not to be" differs radically from the speech that modern actors usually perform, which derives from later published versions (1604 and 1623). Scholars are uncertain about the origins of the differences, although most attribute them to a faulty copy text for the 1603 Quarto.

To leaue vs here?
 Que. With all my hart.   *exit.*
 Cor. And here *Ofelia,* reade you on this booke,
And walke aloofe, the King fhal be vnfeene.
 Ham. To be,or not to be, I there's the point,
To Die, to fleepe, is that all? I all:
No, to fleepe, to dreame, I mary there it goes,
For in that dreame of death, when wee awake,
And borne before an euerlafting Iudge,
From whence no paffenger euer retur'nd,
The vndifcouered country, at whofe fight
The happy fmile, and the accurfed damn'd.
But for this, the ioyfull hope of this,
Whol'd beare the fcornes and flattery of the world,
Scorned by the right rich, the rich curffed of the poore?
            The

  Prince of Denmarke
The widow being oppreffed, the orphan wrong'd,
The tafte of hunger, or a tirants raigne,
And thoufand more calamities befides,
To grunt and fweate vnder this weary life,
When that he may his full *Quietus* make,
With a bare bodkin, who would this indure,
But for a hope of fomething after death?
Which pufles the braine, and doth confound the fence,
Which makes vs rather beare thofe euilles we haue,
Than flie to others that we know not of.
I that, O this confcience makes cowardes of vs all,
Lady in thy orizons, be all my finnes remembred.
 Ofel. My Lord, I haue fought opportunitie, which now
I haue, to redeliuer to your worthy handes, a fmall remem-
brance, fuch tokens which I haue receiued of you.
 Ham. Are you faire?
 Ofel. My Lord.
 Ham. Are you honeft?

The Harlots Cheeke beautied with plaiſt'ring Art
Is not more vgly to the thing that helpes it,
Then is my deede, to my moſt painted word.
Oh heauie burthen!

Pol. I heare him comming, let's withdraw my Lord.

Exeunt.

Enter Hamlet.

Ham. To be, or not to be, that is the Queſtion:
Whether 'tis Nobler in the minde to ſuffer
The Slings and Arrowes of outragious Fortune,
Or to take Armes againſt a Sea of troubles,
And by oppoſing end them: to dye, to ſleepe
No more; and by a ſleepe, to ſay we end
The Heart-ake, and the thouſand Naturall ſhockes

That Fleſh is heyre too? 'Tis a conſummation
Deuoutly to be wiſh'd. To dye to ſleepe,
To ſleepe, perchance to Dreame; I, there's the rub,
For in that ſleepe of death, what dreames may come,
When we haue ſhuffel'd off this mortall coile,
Muſt giue vs pawſe. There's the reſpect
That makes Calamity of ſo long life:
For who would beare the Whips and Scornes of time,
The Oppreſſors wrong, the poore mans Contumely,
The pangs of diſpriz'd Loue, the Lawes delay,
The inſolence of Office, and the Spurnes
That patient merit of the vnworthy takes,
When he himſelfe might his *Quietus* make
With a bare Bodkin? Who would theſe Fardles beare
To grunt and ſweat vnder a weary life,
But that the dread of ſomething after death,
The vndiſcouered Countrey, from whoſe Borne
No Traueller returnes, Puzels the will,
And makes vs rather beare thoſe illes we haue,
Then flye to others that we know not of.
Thus Conſcience does make Cowards of vs all,
And thus the Natiue hew of Reſolution
Is ſicklied o're, with the pale caſt of Thought,
And enterprizes of great pith and moment,
With this regard their Currants turne away,
And looſe the name of Action. Soft you now,
The faire *Ophelia?* Nimph, in thy Orizons
Be all my ſinnes remembred.

Ophe. Good my Lord,

Facsimile of
"To be or not to be"
from *Hamlet,
Prince of Denmark*
1623 Folio

This familiar version of "To be or not to be," printed in the Folio, more nearly resembles the speech as it appeared in all printings except the first. This is also substantially the version of the speech printed in the Second Quarto of 1604, which appears to have been published as a corrective to the problematic Q1.

wit.

Rich. I,good leaue haue you, for you will haue leaue,
Till Youth take leaue,and leaue you to the Crutch.

King. Now tell me, Madame, doe you loue your
Children ?

Wid. I,full as dearely as I loue my felfe.

King. And would you not doe much to doe them
good ?

Wid. To doe them good, I would fuftayne fome
harme,

King. Then get your Husbands Lands, to doe them
good.

Wid. Therefore I came vnto your Maieftie.

King. Ile tell you how thefe Lands are to be got.

Wid. So fhall you bind me to your Highneffe feruice.

King. What feruice wilt thou doe me,if I giue them?

Wid. What you command,that refts in me to doe.

King. But you will take exceptions to my Boone.

Wid. No,gracious Lord,except I cannot doe it.

King. I,but thou canft doe what I meane to aske.

Wid. Why then I will doe what your Grace commands.

Rich. Hee plyes her hard, and much Raine weares the

Prouoke vs hither now,to flaughter thee.

Cla. If you do loue my Brother,hate not me :
I am his Brother,and I loue him well.
If you are hyr'd for meed, go backe againe,
And I will fend you to my Brother Gloufter :
Who fhall reward you better for my life,
Then *Edward* will for tydings of my death.

2 You are decciu'd,
Your Brother Gloufter hates you.

Cla. Oh no,he loues me, and he holds me deere :
Go you to him from me.

1 I fo we will.

Cla. Tell him,when that our Princely Father Yorke,
Bleft his three Sonnes with his victorious Arme,
He little thought of this diuided Friendfhip :
Bid Gloufter thinke on this, and he will weepe,

1 I Milftones,as he leffoned vs to weepe.

Cla. O do not flander him,for he is kinde.

1 Right,as Snow in Harueft :
Come, you deceiue your felfe,
'Tis he that fends vs to deftroy you heere.

Cla. It cannot be, for he bewept my Fortune,

A Comparison of the Work of Compositors A and B on the 1623 Folio

The two passages reproduced here from Peter Blayney's *The First Folio of Shakespeare* (1991) exhibit the different spelling habits of two of the printers, or compositors, who set type for the Folio. Scholars have been able to use the idiosyncrasies of early modern spelling and other such clues to ascertain a great deal of information about the printing of Shakespeare's plays.

The passage above, from Henry VI, Part 3 *(Histories, page 159), was set by Compositor A and shows a cluster of his characteristic* doe *spellings. Neither* goe *nor* here *is illustrated (neither word is used as often as* do*), but A's preference for using an "a" in* deare *or* dearely *is also shown.*

The passage on the left, from Richard III *(Histories, page 181), was set by Compositor B and includes four of his best-documented preferential spellings:* do, go, heere, *and* deere.

CHAPTER 7

Town and Country:
Life in Shakespeare's England

———————————— >*< ————————————

Several scenes in the first two acts of *Henry IV, Part 1* are given over to a robbery. The Prince and his companion Ned Poins are expected to participate but instead play a trick on Falstaff by failing to join in the heist and then robbing him of the loot. The robbery itself is preceded by a short scene (2.1) set at the inn where the travelers who will be robbed have been spending the night and are now preparing to get on the road. Although it does little to advance the action and so is often cut in performance, the episode explores in a socially specific context the problems of loyalty and betrayal that are central to the play's political concerns: King Henry is accused of having stolen the crown. A more unusual function of the scene, however, is as a window onto the daily life of working people in sixteenth-century England. Devoted as it is not to kings but to laborers and criminals, the inn scene provides a useful introduction to the topics to be considered in this chapter — daily life (both urban and rural) in Shakespeare's England, the occupations of the populace, the geography of the London in which Shakespeare lived and worked, clothing, diet, travel, recreation, money, and other such features of Elizabethan culture. These are vast subjects, impossible to cover adequately. But my purpose is not to construct a social history of Tudor and Stuart England. Rather, it is to offer some perspectives on the material world that informed Shakespeare's work and to familiarize the modern reader with some early modern cultural contexts.

The time is early morning, before dawn. The place is the yard, or loading area, of an inn on the road to London, probably in the town of Rochester. (This is the equivalent of a truck stop between the eastern coastal towns and the metropolis.) In the first half of the scene, the two characters who share the stage are carriers, men who are transporting goods from the country to be sold in the city. One carries turkeys in a large basket, while another transports bacon and ginger. The second carrier is taking his provisions to Charing Cross, the area that in Shakespeare's time was a small village between the City of London and the royal palaces of Whitehall and Westminster.

These workers begin their day very early, at about two in the morning, although the first carrier, making a guess based on the position of the constellations in the sky, fears that it is already four o'clock and that he is running late. They are trying to get on the road but receive no assistance from the new ostler, the keeper of the horses at the inn. The old one, recently dead, was much more helpful: ". . . This house is turn'd upside down since Robin ostler died. . . . What, ostler! A plague on thee! hast thou never an eye in thy head? Canst not hear?" (2.1.10–11, 27–28). They complain not only about the service but also about the provisions at the inn. The fodder for the animals is moldy and makes them sick, and the carriers themselves fare no better. Because the management at the inn won't provide chamber pots, the guests have to urinate in the fireplace, a practice that the travelers believe breeds the fleas that have infested the house. The carriers are anxious about crime, too. When Gadshill enters and asks to borrow a lantern to find his horse, the carriers scornfully refuse, apparently knowing a thief when they see one. Thus they remain tight-lipped about their route or schedule:

GADSHILL: Sirrah carrier, what time do you mean to come to London?
SECOND CARRIER: Time enough to go to bed with a candle, I warrant
     thee.   (2.1.41–44)

The remainder of the scene depicts a private conversation between Gadshill and the Chamberlain, an attendant at the inn, who is on the take: the Chamberlain is acting as informant for Gadshill and his band of thieves, identifying the guests who are carrying large sums of money and thus setting up the highway robbery to come. Gadshill is the name both of the highwayman and of the spot where Falstaff's robbery will take place. To Shakespeare's contemporaries, the term was synonymous with danger to travelers.

Travel was a strenuous and potentially dangerous business in sixteenth-century England, as Shakespeare himself would have been aware from his frequent journeys on horseback between Stratford and London. The roads connecting the capital with the rest of the kingdom were fairly primitive, designed for pedestrians or single riders; coaches were seldom used outside London at this period. Whether on foot or on horseback, travelers were dependent on the inn for rest and refreshment and vulnerable to the numerous uncertainties that still afflict those who take to the road: miserable weather, unreliable roads, bad food, poor service, and highway robbery (whether literal or figurative). An excerpt from William Harrison's *Description of England* (see p. 237) outlines some of those perils in terms that are particularly germane to Shakespeare's portrait of the inn at Rochester. As Harrison's description indicates, the travelers coming down the hill in act 2, scene 2, of *Henry IV, Part 1*, could not have been completely surprised to hear the shouts of Falstaff and his cronies. To any traveler, a safe arrival in London must have been a relief.

London

To a first-time visitor from the country, arrival in London must have been an overwhelming experience. At the end of the sixteenth century, London had reached a population of about two hundred thousand. *London,* however, is a problematic term. Strictly speaking, the City of London was a relatively small area bounded on three sides by ancient walls, dating from Roman times, and by the Thames River on the fourth side. At various points along the walls were gates (such as Moorgate and Newgate) that allowed access into the City itself from outlying villages and fields. By the sixteenth century the walls no longer served a defensive function. Rather, they helped to define the central commercial, residential, and judicial district, which contained the Tower of London (built on a fortress begun in Roman times), St. Paul's Cathedral (although not the same building that stands on the site now), the guildhalls of tradesmen and merchants, the Inns of Court housing the lawyers, the offices of the municipal government, Sir Thomas Gresham's Royal Exchange (the newest public building in Elizabethan London), and the principal markets and shopping streets. The metropolitan area was considerably larger, however, and the City as it exists today has assimilated and still retains the names of places such as Charing Cross, Covent Garden, and Islington that in Shakespeare's day were villages or suburban areas only loosely connected to the City of London. In the early seventeenth century, for example, Hyde Park and St. James's Park, two of the green areas that today offer relief from the crowds and concrete of modern London, were forests in which King James hunted deer.

St. Paul's Cathedral was the social center of the City. It was not located in the geographical middle of town, however, but closer to the western wall and thus to Westminster, toward which London was expanding. St. Paul's was not only a house of worship but also a popular place for meeting friends, making deals, hearing gossip, hiring help, finding employment, picking pockets, leaving messages, and buying books. As a site for various kinds of social interaction, the nave of St. Paul's appears frequently in the drama and prose of Shakespeare's contemporaries, particularly in the London comedies of Ben Jonson. Although Falstaff reports that he contracted for the services of Bardolph in the aisle of St. Paul's, such a reference is rare for Shakespeare because he doesn't write about contemporary London in the ways that playwrights such as Jonson and Thomas Dekker and Thomas Middleton do. Since the Middle Ages the impropriety of such commerce in the main church had made the city fathers anxious, and sporadic efforts were made to control or relocate it. But convenience and tradition triumphed over law. Most of the urban traffic would have been on foot, as people went about their daily business of buying and selling, carrying water, visiting friends, feeding themselves, and seeking various kinds of entertainment. Those who had to travel from one end of town to the other might have taken one of the water taxis on the Thames, a popular and rapid system of transportation mentioned by a Swiss visitor, Thomas Platter, in his record of his travels (see p. 241). Although coaches were becoming an increasingly frequent form of urban transportation, they were available only to aristocrats and wealthy merchants. For most Londoners, the area around St. Paul's served as a natural and traditional meeting place.

The business districts of the City of London were divided loosely according to merchandise or service, with the divisions to some extent grounded in the practical requirements of the business. To buy fresh fish, for example, the householder or housewife went to Bridge Street, near Billingsgate, a gate or pier on the banks of the Thames where the fish could be easily unloaded from skiffs, small boats that transferred to shore the catch from larger seagoing ships. But dried fish were sold elsewhere, a couple of blocks away in Thames Street. Such places as Shoe Lane or Poultry proclaim their function, and some of these streets and alleys survive even in modern London. Yet it is worth noting that as early as Shakespeare's day fowl were no longer sold in Poultry, having been displaced by other marketable goods. As John Stow records in his *Survey of London* (1598), commercial London was a dynamic place, with shops and services changing locations as the metropolis grew and neighborhoods changed (see p. 238). Isabella Whitney's poem "The Manner of Her Will, and What She Left to London" effectively conveys the size and energy of the city as the speaker moves from place to place, identifying buildings, naming streets, and describing various shopkeepers and merchants, from grocers and sellers of "knacks" to gun dealers (see the excerpt on p. 239).

One determinant of the geography of commercial London was the influence of the twelve great guilds: Mercers (dealers in expensive cloth), Grocers, Drapers (makers of or dealers in lesser fabrics), Fishmongers, Goldsmiths, Skinners, Merchant-Tailors, Haberdashers, Salters (makers of or dealers in salt), Ironmongers, Vintners, and Clothworkers. Their codes for supply, marketing, and training gave each group a kind of unity and spirit that helped to foster concentration in a particular location. This grouping by district was not absolute, as Stow's description indicates, and larger and less specialized markets had grown up in some of the wider thoroughfares such as Cheapside — one Elizabethan map illustrates temporary stalls placed in the center of the street — and on London Bridge itself. The merchants and tradesmen were a significant part of the newly prosperous urban class in Elizabethan London, and to some degree their economic prosperity was stimulated and protected by Elizabeth's and the City Aldermen's (or Elder-men's) political policy. The enforcement of church rules about meatless days, for example — Fridays, certain holidays, and Lent, that period of abstinence extending from late winter through Easter — was motivated as much by economics as by religion. As Harrison's *Description* records, the statutes served to protect the thriving fishing industry and all its attendant trades, such as river-carriers, wholesale and retail fishmongers, and shipbuilders.

A London merchant owned or leased the building in which his shop was located. The ground floor served as the place of business, with goods displayed indoors and perhaps outdoors on tables under an awning made of light wood. The merchant and his family lived behind and above the shop, together with his servants and apprentices. If the house were large enough, lodgers might be taken in: Shakespeare seems to have rented a room in the Cripplegate area from a French family, the Mountjoys, who were tire-makers (creators of ladies' headdresses). (See the map on p. 35.) Some merchants' houses even had gardens behind them. This combination of business and residence led to the crowding, bustle, and noise for which London was famous to visitors from the country and abroad. Most of the streets were narrow and seemed even narrower because the upper stories of the houses overhung the ground floor. This invasion of public air space gave the householder more square footage than he had paid for, but it also shut out sunlight from the street.

Most of the streets were intended for pedestrian traffic, although horses and carts and even small herds of animals used them as well. Horse-drawn coaches, which were becoming more common as the city prospered, were probably confined to the larger thoroughfares and to the main roads leading out of town. Certain intersections had conduits, or fountainlike spigots, from which water was collected by water-carriers — Ben Jonson depicts a colorful example of such a figure in his play *Every Man in his Humour* — and delivered in large wooden containers to customers throughout the city. Many streets had a gutter or channel in the center down which wastewater and sometimes sewage ran into ditches and then into the Thames.

On the margins of the City, however, there was more room, both for building and for recreational spaces. Along the river were impressive mansions — palaces, in some cases — built by great families as town houses and known by the familial names: Essex House, Arundel House, Somerset House. (Some of the later buildings that replaced these mansions have retained their names: Somerset House, for example, rebuilt in 1776 on the site of the original Tudor building and then renovated in the 1980s to contain the Courtauld collection of paintings, is located on the corner of the Strand and Waterloo Bridge, looking across the river to the present site of the National Theatre.) Occupying the northern (City) side of the Thames and extending from the western walls toward Westminster, these great houses were set back from the river, surrounded by grounds planted with trees and gardens, and fitted with private docks or piers for convenient access to transportation. To the north of the City was Moorfields, an open area planted as a kind of park and used for archery and other outdoor pastimes. And just to the north of Moorfields along Bishopsgate Street was the area known as Shoreditch, the site of two important early playhouses: the Theatre, built in 1576, and the Curtain, erected a year or two later.

On the western edge of the City of London were the Inns of Court, the buildings and grounds that served as home for the legal profession. The Inns were multifunctional, serving as graduate school, dormitory, library, dining hall, office building, social club, site of plays and revels, and legal center. Beyond the Inns lay the route to Westminster, the home of the monarch, the court, and Parliament: regular traffic flowed between the palaces of Westminster and Whitehall, on the one hand, and the City of London on the other. When Shakespeare's King Henry IV laments that his son, the Prince of Wales, is wasting his time in "barren pleasures" and "rude society," he is objecting to Hal's drinking in one of the taverns a couple of miles down the road at

Eastcheap, in the center of London proper. This movement between town and court along the Strand led to major commercial and residential development, notably the construction of the Cockpit theater in Drury Lane in 1616; such growth would make this area the center of London life in the eighteenth century. But in Shakespeare's day it was semirural. Along the way was a garden once associated with a disbanded convent, the "convent garden" (or Covent Garden); the Church of St. Martin in the Fields, now facing the crowds of Trafalgar Square, was located in actual fields; and St. Martin's Lane was a small passage leading from the Thames to the countryside north of the suburbs. The quickest route between Westminster and London was the river. The monarchs had royal barges to transport themselves and important courtiers and visitors, while the boatmen mentioned in Platter's account stood ready to take ordinary citizens upstream ("Westward Ho!"), downstream ("Eastward Ho!"), or across the river, perhaps to the Bankside to see a play.

London Bridge in the sixteenth century was much more than a means of crossing the Thames, although, except for boats, it was the only way across. Like the medieval bridge across the Arno River that still survives in Florence, London Bridge was a virtual neighborhood in itself, the site of shops, houses, and street life. Above the archway leading onto the bridge the authorities mounted the decapitated heads of traitors and left them there to rot, as a warning against treason. John Stow in his *Survey of London* recounts the history of London Bridge and then describes its appearance in 1598:

> To conclude of this bridge over the said river of Thames, I affirm, as in other my descriptions, that it is a work very rare, having with the drawbridge twenty arches made of squared stone, of height sixty feet, and in breadth thirty feet, distant from one another twenty feet, compact and joined together with vaults and cellars; upon both sides be houses built, so that it seemeth rather a continual street than a bridge; for the fortifying whereof against the incessant assaults of the river, it hath overseers and officers, viz., wardens, as aforesaid, and others. (25–26)

London Bridge was vital in connecting the capital with the countryside and agricultural riches of the southern counties; indeed, it offered virtually the only practical land access to the southeastern quadrant of England. (See the extract from Lupold von Wedel's *Journey through England and Scotland*, p. 241.)

The Suburbs

More immediately London Bridge connected the urban center with one of its liveliest and most notorious suburbs. The borough of Southwark and the Bankside contained prisons (the Clink), hospitals, taverns (the Tabard Inn, where Chaucer's pilgrims begin their journey), playhouses and other centers of entertainment such as gambling houses, brothels ("the stews"), and the arena for bearbaiting, the Bear Garden. This neighborhood, one of the several outlying districts known as the "Liberties" because they were beyond the jurisdiction of the City authorities until 1608, served as a haven for criminals, drifters (known as "masterless men"), the unemployed, the ill (particularly lepers), prostitutes, and others with a dubious relation to the law. In Queen Elizabeth's time, the Liberties on the Bankside were legally answerable to the bishop of Winchester, but in practice the "government" of all these areas — including some former monastic sites within the City itself — was negligible. The Liberties were useful to the City authorities as semidetached ghettos for crime and disease. Steven Mullaney has described the topographical and cultural ambiguities of such suburbs in early modern London.

> Whatever could not be contained within the strict bounds of the community found its place here, making the Liberties the preserve of the anomalous, the unclean, the polluted, and the sacred. Like the French *banlieux*, London's Liberties were places of exile, yet the banishment enacted in them was of a more ambivalent order. What was lodged outside the city was excluded, yet retained; denied a place within the community, yet not merely exiled. The licentious, dangerous, unclean, or polluted was cast out of the city, but was then maintained as such and even placed on public display. (22)

Although some urban historians consider Mullaney's claims overstated, it is nonetheless true that the Liberties functioned as a safety zone for the socially marginal.

Before Henry VIII abolished the Roman Catholic religious houses in the 1530s, Southwark had contained a number of abbeys and priories ("the sacred" in Mullaney's description), as well as the homes of some powerful men, religious and secular. The dissolution of the abbeys increased the instability of the borough, but it had always been a rough neighborhood, and the authorities made periodic efforts, sometimes vigorous, sometimes halfhearted, to close the brothels and clean up the area. These attempts were of limited success and duration, however, and the records of the time indicate awareness and official toleration of what amounted to London's red-light district. (Thomas Nashe's *Christ's Tears over Jerusalem* registers outrage at the immorality of the London brothels; see p. 242.) It is worth emphasizing that the theaters that produced some of the greatest works of the English stage, the Rose and the Globe, were identified geographically (and, by some, morally) with prostitution, criminality, and excessive "liberty." (See the map of sixteenth-century theaters on p. 127.)

The Countryside

My description of London and its suburbs has concentrated on the arts we associate with civilization and urban life — architecture, commerce, government, theater, and various forms of petty crime, or con-artistry. It is axiomatic that to shift to the countryside takes us closer to nature, but this division between town and country is not as sharp as it might at first appear. While admiring the natural glories of the English countryside, with its pastures, farming lands, great forests, and wild coastline, we must remember that the bounty and to some extent the beauty of these lands have for centuries depended on the agricultural arts. Rural life, in other words, was also highly organized, arranged into patterns calculated through centuries of experience to take advantage of climate, soil, and the cycles of marketable crops. Careful management of land was essential to the survival of the individual family as well as the collective national family.

In the second act of *A Midsummer Night's Dream*, Titania deplores the consequences of her quarrel with Oberon: discord in the fairy realm results in horrible weather in the mortal world. The winds and rain have been so fierce that

> The ox hath therefore stretch'd his yoke in vain,
> The ploughman lost his sweat, and the green corn
> Hath rotted ere his youth attain'd a beard.
> The fold stands empty in the drowned field,
> And crows are fatted with the murrion flock.   (2.1.93–97)

As a possible source for this description, scholars look to the summer of 1593, a year or two before *A Midsummer Night's Dream* was probably written, in which abnormal weather ruined crops and brought hardship to much of the English economy. But whether or not the lines refer to a particular summer, they speak to the direct connection between bad weather and economic disaster. In Titania's description, the rains have inundated the fields, undoing the work of the oxen, who would have pulled the farmer's plow and thus prepared the ground for the planting of seed. All this water has destroyed the crops on the stalk: the "green corn" that has been ruined is the young, unripe grain, probably wheat or barley (not the grain that North Americans call corn). The sheep, unable to graze the sodden pastures, are dying from the disease of sheep and cattle known as murrain, the only beneficiaries being the scavenger birds. Titania goes on to complain that the seasons have become indistinguishable from one another and to lament the effect on humankind. Even so brief a passage illustrates the correspondence between the seasonal cycles and human needs, which has come to seem less immediate to us thanks to the conveniences of modern life.

In *Henry IV, Part 2*, when the Hostess reflects sentimentally on her acquaintance with Falstaff, "I have known thee these twenty-nine years, come peasecod-time" (2.4.382–83), she indicates the way that certain times of the year were naturally and familiarly associated with the growth of certain foods. Fruit became available in the spring and early summer and continued to be available through the fall, berries and other early varieties giving way to cherries, apples, and other orchard fruits; vegetables were likewise restricted according to season. A notable exception to this rule was grain, particularly winter wheat and rye, which could be sown from August through November and then harvested in the winter months. Domestic animals were born in the spring and slaughtered in the autumn and winter to supply food in the barren months of January, February, and March. Very little of the meat was eaten fresh; rather, meat was mostly dried or smoked for later use. (There was, however, conspicuous consumption of meat and game by members of the nobility and, aping them, the wealthy citizens of the town.) As with meat, certain fruits, nuts, and vegetables were preserved and stored for use during the winter (importing exotic or unseasonal produce from warmer climates was practiced only by the most privileged). Sugar was a rare and precious commodity. Winter weather could also make the roads impassable and therefore hamper the transportation of meat and other provisions from the countryside to the city. The government's ban on meat during Lent and on holidays may have remained in force as long as it did not only for reasons of religious doctrine and for encouragement of the fishing industry, but also for practical reasons. In other words, it may have been a realistic response to the limited availability of meat. Awareness of such a correspondence between season and supply offers a revealing context for the numerous seasonal episodes and references that we find in Shakespeare's plays.

Our response to the sheepshearing festival in *The Winter's Tale*, for example, depends on our awareness of the festivity that resulted from the sense of abundance and fulfillment. (The time of the scene in the play is uncertain: the shearing of sheep usually took place in July, but this party seems later than that. Whatever the date, the emphasis on reward for labor and fulfillment after privation is unmistakable.) After months of shortage and expectation, the country people have shorn the sheep, collected and sold the wool, and are now spending the profits on edible treats and other pleasures. As Shakespeare's young shepherd makes his way to the market to purchase supplies for the festival, he counts his money and consults his list:

> Let me see: every 'leven wether tods [eleven sheep make one tod, or twenty-eight pounds of wool], every tod yields pound and odd shilling; fifteen hundred shorn, what comes the wool to? . . . I cannot do't without compters [counters, or metal disks for doing arithmetic]. Let me see: what am I to buy for our sheep-shearing feast? Three pound of sugar, five pounds of currants, rice — what will this sister of mine do with rice? But my father hath made her mistress of the feast, and she lays it on. She hath made me four and twenty nosegays for the shearers. . . . I must have saffron to color the warden [winter pear] pies; mace; dates, none — that's out of my note; nutmegs, seven; a race [root] or two of ginger, but that I may beg; four pounds of pruins, and as many of raisins o' th' sun.
>
> (4.3.32–49)

With each tod worth a little over a pound sterling, the profits amount to some 140 pounds. When we consider that the average wage for a laborer was perhaps 7 pounds a year, it becomes clear that this is a very prosperous year for the Clown and his family. And even for those whose profits were not so high, the end of work gave way to a festive atmosphere and such luxuries and delights as holiday foods, flowers, singing, dancing, and buying from peddlers, the rural equivalent of shopping.

The Bohemian festival represented in *The Winter's Tale* may or may not be a historically accurate portrayal of English country life at the beginning of the seventeenth century, but it helps to introduce the values and routines of the rural existence that Shakespeare must have been exposed to while growing up in a small town in Warwickshire. Elizabethan towns and villages differed from one another according to their location and the natural resources associated with their geographical situation. The sheep farming in an inland area such as the Cotswolds, for example, would have produced villages that looked quite different from those in the coal mining districts of the northeastern coast. But certain features were probably common to most of them, such as those structures necessary to the conduct of community life: a parish church (with graveyard), a tavern or inn, a manor house and surrounding park for the local commanding gentry, a municipal hall of some kind, a village green for meeting neighbors, a mill for grinding wheat, a partly open marketplace, perhaps a schoolhouse, and common land for grazing. Since Stratford-upon-Avon was a market town, its population would have swelled on market days, as people gathered to trade in secondary goods and services (meals, beer, entertainment) as well as primary products such as food and clothing. In addition to the regular markets held in such towns, special bazaars and fairs sprang up throughout the country, the largest of them devoted to the sale of items beyond daily needs. In effect these fairs were wholesale markets offering grain in large quantities, animals, and other kinds of agricultural "stock." The setting for Ben Jonson's *Bartholomew Fair* is just such a mart in the London suburb of Smithfield, and a quick look at that play reveals that the fairgoers hardly limit their activities to the buying and selling of necessities.

Rural Life

Whatever the commercial emphasis of a given village or town, some kind of farming would have occupied virtually every country family. Most of the villagers would have been tenant farmers, a term that requires some explanation. English agriculture, like the English language, the English church, and virtually everything else at the end of the sixteenth century, was in a state of flux. The medieval feudal system, in which most of the populace worked land owned by the lord of the manor for the primary benefit of that lord, had more or less dissolved by Shakespeare's day, but it had not yet developed into the private system of the family farm with which we are familiar. Some of the citizens in country towns had become extremely successful, and many towns saw the building of large new houses by those country farmers and merchants who, through entrepreneurial skill or good luck, had managed to take advantage of bountiful harvests or the strength of the emerging economy. (See the extract from Gervase Markham's *The English Husbandman*, p. 243.) Despite the private successes of certain families in every town, most of the land in a given parish legally was still owned by the lord of the manor, who received rent for its use, sometimes in cash and sometimes in goods. But practically speaking, this property was held in common and managed by the citizens who worked it.

Rural communities by the end of the sixteenth century had devised a fairly complicated system for the productive use of the common land. Some of the property, often that bordering a river, was designated as meadowland and reserved for grazing sheep and cattle — livestock, unlike crops, could be moved in the event of a flood. The brushy areas, or thickets, near the forests were not especially desirable, but they served their purpose. According to R. E. Prothero,

> These wastes and woods supplied many village wants. They provided heather and fern for thatching, or bedding for the cattle, or light fuel for brewing or baking; they fed the swine with beech-mast or acorns; in winter their trimmings and loppings helped to keep the half-starved stock alive; they furnished bushes to stop gaps as well as wood for movable fences, hop poles, and implements of husbandry.
>
> ("Agriculture and Gardening" 1:351)

As for the arable (or farmable) land, the most important principle in the system of management was rotation, and usually the available farmland was divided into three sections: one-third given over to rye or wheat, the principal grains cultivated for the making of bread; one-third to lesser grains such as barley, oats, and beans, some of which went for human consumption but most for silage; and one-third to lying fallow, so as to prevent depletion of the soil's nutrients.

Each villager was given a six-acre portion in each of these three areas, for a total of eighteen acres, only twelve of which he would use in any one year. Each six-acre assignment was not in one plot, but was made up of smaller portions, scattered through the field and demarcated by small strips of grass. This crazy-quilt arrangement ensured a fair distribution of the choicest land among all the tenants. Each farmer was thus responsible for and benefited from his own plots of this land, although certain functions, such as guarding the seeded land against birds, were performed by a villager assigned to the task and paid by the group. I have radically simplified the description of this system of agriculture; as economic historians have demonstrated, there were exceptions and variations in every village (see Coleman 31–34). Even those towns in which the use of land was most democratically organized contained private fields or pastures enclosed for the cultivation of domestic animals by a few well-to-do yeomen, or freeholders. Many areas in the south of England had been virtually privatized for some time, with hedges and fences separating the available land into individual plots. The village model set forth here was less common in the northern counties, simply because the region was sparsely populated and the land less suited to producing grain. Some citizens of a town or village did not participate as tenants but worked as laborers or servants to those who did. And scattered throughout the country were a few freeholders who owned their land and employed several farmhands. In other words, the English agricultural economy was varied.

It was also undergoing momentous changes. From time to time the lord of a manor sought to raise rents and thus make the land more profitable, although the lord's long-standing affiliations with the community usually kept greed in check. The more serious threat was the sale of property to merchants or other newly prosperous men from London who wished to consolidate the lands into larger, more productive farms and whose distance could easily insulate them from local hardship and complaint. There was constant tension between private and public rights to the arable lands and pastures. Likewise, disputes arose over the opposing claims of shepherds and tillers, conflicts similar to those between ranchers and farmers in the settling of the American West.

Such problems are best represented by the disputes over enclosure that became more and more frequent and violent in the sixteenth and early seventeenth centuries. As the wool trade expanded, stimulated partly by foreign demand for English cloth, much of the land that had been used for growing grain was being converted to pastureland for sheep and thus was being fenced, or enclosed. One of the primary effects of this conversion was unemployment. Sheepherding was far less labor-intensive than farming, and many of those people associated with agriculture — not only farmers and their helpers but related laborers, such as millers — lost their means of supporting their families. (See the excerpt from John Moore's *A Target for Tillage,* p. 245, which speaks to this problem.) According to D. C. Coleman, "What mattered was the extinction of common rights. . . . Sometimes it was the pasturing on the commons of large numbers of cattle or sheep, by bigger farmers, thus making life more difficult for the smaller husbandman; sometimes it was the loss of ancient rights in the woodlands — to cut underwood, to run pigs" (40). Who had the ultimate claim on the land around the village? The lord to whom it had been legally entrusted by the Crown centuries before, or the villagers who had used it for farming and pasture down through those centuries? When grain shortages occurred, as they often did in the late sixteenth and early seventeenth centuries, many people understandably laid the blame on the enclosers. In several cases these tensions erupted into angry protest, with villagers taking shovels and other tools and leveling the fences erected by the enclosers. Such uprisings — like an important one that occurred in the Midlands in 1607 — may be reflected in the class disputes of *Coriolanus.*

Countrywomen worked ceaselessly at what we might call "keeping house," except that the term encompasses far more than it does today. The *huswife* or housewife — a term in common use at this period — spent her days baking bread, making butter and cheese, minding the poultry, brewing beer, gathering wood for the fire, tending the household garden, cooking meals, spinning yarn, making cloth, sewing clothes, washing clothes, making candles, fashioning tools of various kinds, supervising any servants, and all the while keeping one eye on the children. Although some items could be purchased in shops in larger villages and at fairs, most household goods were homemade, and because the husband was usually working in the field, it was up to the wife to make and maintain her own equipment. (See the passage from Sir Anthony Fitzherbert's *The Book of Husbandry,* p. 246.) Women also worked in the fields, especially at times of urgent need, such as harvest or planting season, and even children had regular duties in and outside the home, such as carrying messages, carding wool, scaring crows or other predators away from the crops, and caring for the younger children.

The Daily Routine

Whether in the city or the country, the English day began early, the rhythms of daily life influenced above all by the rising and setting of the sun. The northern longitude of England means that the summer days are very long, the winter days very short. Before daybreak, someone in the household had to rise and prepare the house for the business of the day. A successful merchant in London would have assigned the job to a servant living in the household. In less prosperous houses, a member of the family, perhaps an older child, performed this task. In winter it meant stoking or relighting the fires needed for warmth; in summer it meant at least readying the fire in the stove for the morning meal. In all seasons water was needed for morning face washing and other such preparations: in the country, it came from a well or river; in the city, from one of the public conduits or wells, although the wealthy could afford to have their water delivered. Breakfast consisted of bread and butter, and perhaps cheese or fruit, or maybe both. There was no coffee or tea in Shakespeare's England: ale or beer was the main beverage, taken at all hours of the day. By the time the sun came up people were ready for business, with the farmer already in the field and the shopkeeper opening his doors and displaying merchandise in front of the shop.

With such an early start to the day, lunch was welcome when it came, just at the noon hour. This was the principal meal, when meat was served, if it was available, and the family assembled for conversation and an hour away from labor. (See the excerpt from Harrison's *Description*, p. 248.) In the city, the workday usually ended around five or so; in the country, sundown determined the end of work. Closing time or quitting time was followed by a light supper and, in the winter, prayers and bed. There may have been time for reading, if the family could afford books, but since candles were expensive, as was firewood, going to bed early was not only healthy but also economical. In summer, of course, the hours before sunset (9 or 10 P.M. throughout most of England) allowed time for recreation: perhaps walking in the meadows outside the City walls or along the river away from the village; making music or dancing; playing games, both card games and physical sports such as tag, ball games, or archery (see Mulcaster's *Positions*, p. 248); drinking with friends at a tavern and perhaps smoking a pipe of tobacco, a recent import from the New World; and, of course, talking about who was walking and dancing and playing and drinking with whom.

Clothing

The state of English dress at this period is too broad and complex to be covered adequately in a paragraph or two, but no topic so effectively introduces the dynamic and unfixed nature of English culture at the end of the sixteenth century. Fashion statements are hardly new, and the subjects of Elizabeth I could not resist making them — about their newfound wealth and the jewels it could buy, about their savvy in locating an exotic fabric, about the sophistication of their tailor (whose latest pattern for trunk hose [breeches] attested to his eye for novelty and his Continental connections), about the number of different garments in which they could afford to appear. Thanks to increasing prosperity and exchange with Europe, English fashions were changing rapidly and becoming ever more elaborate and various, so much so that the winds of fashion became a favorite topic both for Puritan outrage and for dramatic satire around the turn of the seventeenth century. The wealthy spent immense sums of money on clothing: a fine outfit for a man or a woman, even without jewelry and other such embellishments, might cost fifty to sixty pounds or more, perhaps ten times the annual wages of a laborer. When we consider that some of the most notable dramatists of the day were paid five pounds or so for a new play, we get a sense of how expensive clothing could be and how it could serve as a badge of economic or social success. (See Harrison's *Description* on p. 250 for an eloquent complaint about sartorial extravagance in the sixteenth century.)

The major articles of clothing for prosperous, fashionable men were the following: leather shoes; knitted stockings, which gave greater definition to the leg than the sewn leggings they replaced; short trousers, called trunk hose, in various shapes (a popular style being the Spanish pumpkin-shaped breeches stuffed with wool or even with bran), which were worn over tight-fitting thigh leggings much like our spandex bicycle shorts; a codpiece, often ornamented, to connote masculinity; a doublet or jacket, with several pairs of detachable sleeves; a rich shirt of linen or silk, worn under the doublet but peeking out from it; a ruff made of stiff white lace to set off the face and head; perhaps an earring; and sometimes a hat made of velvet or other luxurious fabric and adorned with feathers and jewels. Prosperous, fashionable women wore high-heeled shoes and stockings; an elaborate dress or skirt in a choice of voluminous styles, all of them designed to minimize the size of the waist by augmenting the hips; to support the skirt, an elaborate underframe called a farthingale, made of bone or wood, or in the simplest form, a padded cylinder like a child's inner tube wrapped around the hips and known as a bum roll; a jacket augmented with shoulder pads and nipped in at the waist; sleeves, separate from the bodice, secured with lace, and often puffed out with batting or other stuffing; sometimes openwork or a piece of sheer gauze to display part of the breasts; a ruff, perhaps supplemented with starched gauze wings behind the head; and, for the head, jewels, a small hat, a cloth covering, or an elaborate hairstyle. Cosmetics were worn, mostly in red and white, to achieve contrast between lips, cheeks, and the rest of the face. The popularity of makeup became a frequent target of dramatic satire, as in Hamlet's remarks to Ophelia ("God hath given you one face, and you make yourselves another" [3.1.143–44]) and to the skull of Yorick ("Now get you to my lady's chamber, and tell her, let her paint an inch thick, to this favor she must come" [5.1.192–94]).

Because for centuries differences in dress had been a reliable register of the hierarchies of class and position, the blurring of these distinctions and the rapid changes in fashion were alarming to political authorities. The social order depended on knowing who belonged in what slot, and in an age when the complete attire of a gentleman was available to anyone with the cash to purchase or the wit to steal it, the complications of dress were seen as a threat to that social order. Consequently, Tudor authorities occasionally sought to enforce the codes regulating dress, known as sumptuary laws, that had been on the books for decades but were only intermittently observed. Legally, rich materials such as fur and silk were to be worn only by earls, dukes, and other members of the aristocracy; the amount of fabric allowed for a man's pants (the trunk hose) was restricted to a yard and three-quarters; servants' clothing, usually dyed blue to identify the wearer's position in service, was to be without ornament. But these statutes conflicted with social practices. In their wills, great men often left their clothing to favorite servants as a sentimental gesture; these servants soon began to discover (unsentimentally) that they could make a profit by selling this rich apparel. Sometimes they sold it to the acting companies who needed fabulous costumes for the portrayal of royalty. (Puritan opponents of the theater fixed their moral outrage on this technical violation of decorum.) Alternatively, some servants found that by wearing their deceased masters' suits themselves, they could pass for persons of rank in society. The hangman, too, was entitled to receive the clothing of those who were executed. For all these reasons, a thriving trade arose in used clothing. As merchants began to prosper, their social ambitions led them to emulate the apparel of the aristocracy. At the beginning of Elizabeth's reign, in 1559, the government got tough, intending to preserve these sartorial boundaries by punishing violators, but the crackdown was a failure. Other restrictive efforts followed, all of them unsuccessful, so finally in 1604 Parliament admitted the impossibility of legislating style and repealed the sumptuary laws.

Getting and Spending

Implicit in this discussion of food and clothing has been the fact that there was much more to buy in England in 1600 than there had been in 1500, owing partly to the growth of London as a commercial center, the development of trade with the Continent, and a substantial increase in population. In other words, a sophisticated cash economy had begun to emerge. Although Shakespeare doesn't set his plays in contemporary London, those of some of his theatrical colleagues dramatize the emergence of the capitalist economy in the first decades of the seventeenth century. They also reveal, often with considerable scorn, some of the social consequences of new wealth and the desire to consume: unscrupulous merchants, squandered fortunes, stolen purses, swindlers and scam artists, commodity schemes. This last phenomenon was a scam whereby a needy borrower had to take his loan not in cash but in cloth or some other kind of goods, which he was then forced to sell at a loss. The proliferation of shops invited the moneyed classes to indulge in the pleasures of shopping, and increasing traffic between Europe and the New World filled those shops with an abundance and variety of imported goods. Advertising, aided by the printing press, began to develop into a sophisticated enterprise. In Jonson's *The Alchemist* the tobacconist Abel Drugger seeks help in devising a sign for his shop, one that will magically attract wealthy customers. The expansion of the English wool trade, a cause and effect of rural enclosure, made fabrics available as never before. But urban sharks stood ready to take advantage, especially of the gawker from the country: Thomas Middleton in his *Michaelmas Term* creates two cloth-sellers called Falselight and Shortyard, whose names indicate their shady practices. Hats, ruffs, tobacco, imported fruit, books (particularly devotional literature), jewelry, spices — suddenly there seemed almost no limit to what one might purchase. (See the advertisement by John Murrell on p. 252.) Especially in the city, people had money in their purses.

But what kind of money did people have, and how much? The English used a wide range of coins (paper money was to come later) and gave these coins a variety of names, both formal and slang. Shakespeare refers casually to numerous units of currency, often exploiting them for wordplay: pounds, shillings, marks, angels, nobles, florins, crowns, half-crowns, groats, pence, ha'pennies. To the modern American ear, these words and the distinctions they signify are perplexing, although the modern analogues (bucks, two bits, nickels, and dimes) give no trouble. The terms may be unfamiliar even to Britons who have grown up since 1971, when the monetary system in the U.K. was simplified to pounds and pence.

In Shakespeare's day, a pound was worth twenty shillings, each shilling worth twelve pence, thus 240 pence in the pound. A mark equaled two-thirds of a pound; an angel-noble (or angel or noble), ten shillings and sixpence; a crown, five shillings or a quarter of a pound; a half-crown, two-and-a-half shillings; and a florin, two shillings. New coins were introduced from time to time, but old ones remained in circulation. With a little explanation, most of these nouns make sense: for example, the angel, in circulation from the mid–fifteenth to the mid–seventeenth century, got its name from the image with which it was stamped, a picture of the archangel Michael defeating a dragon. Sometimes coins were identified by the name of the monarch in whose reign they were issued and whose picture they bore (e.g., a "James shilling" or an "Elizabeth groat"). Finally, a significant distinction between the early modern monetary system and our own is that coins were not merely tokens of value but valuable in themselves for the precious metals they contained. Thus, when Mercutio accuses Romeo of having given him "the slip," the joke turns on a pun for a counterfeit coin.

Early modern nomenclature, if unfamiliar, can at least be learned, but the system of prices and values represented is much more elusive. As I indicated in the Introduction, any attempt to translate sixteenth-century wages and costs into modern terms will be thwarted by such problems as inflation and the altered values of goods and services. We will do better to consider a few examples of what people earned and what they had to pay for certain goods (for many of these figures I have relied on William Ingram's *The Business of Playgoing* 36ff.). The first rule is that the pound was a substantial sum of money. An unskilled laborer earned perhaps five or six pence per day, which would amount to something like seven pounds per year. Around 1600 "hired men" in the theater, those actors who did not own a share of the company, were paid ten shillings per week, or about half a pound. But this rate cannot simply be multiplied into an annual income of twenty-five pounds, since playing times were seasonal and affected by variables such as the plague. Prices of consumable goods are similarly hard to interpret, since much food was raised and prepared at home. A loaf of bread cost a penny, which was also the price of a portion of ale in a tavern. The principle of supply and demand — not to mention the difference between early modern and modern pricing — is apparent in the relative costs of a chicken (two pence) and a lemon (six pence). Given these figures, the fifty-pound price on a smart suit of clothing makes Harrison's satiric analysis easy to understand.

Admission to the playhouse cost a penny, and entrance to the gallery (that is, the right to a seat) cost another penny. When the play being staged was published, it could be purchased in quarto form from the booksellers near St. Paul's at the price of six pence. In 1623 the Folio collection of Shakespeare's works went on sale there: the price (unbound) was about one pound. As a shareholder in his theatrical company, Shakespeare earned substantially more than the standard five- or six-pound fee for a script by collecting a percentage of the profits from performances. In 1597 he bought New Place, the imposing house in Stratford to which he retired. Legal records show that he paid William Underhill sixty pounds in silver but do not indicate if this was the total purchase price. By the standards here described, Shakespeare had become a wealthy man in his first decade in show business.

That players were making money was a source of outrage to many religious moralists and social critics who railed against money wasted on theatergoing. In *Vertues Commonwealth: or The High-way to Honour,* Henry Crosse complained of the "many poor, pinched, needy creatures, that live off alms, and that have scarce neither cloth to their back nor food for the belly, yet will make hard shift [will do anything] but they will see a play, let wife and children beg, languish in penury, and all they can rape and rend is little enough to lay upon such vanity" (qtd. in Ingram 41). This is a more serious version of Trinculo's remark, in *The Tempest,* about English values: "When they will not give a doit to relieve a lame beggar, they will lay out ten to see a dead Indian" [2.2.31–33]. Such polemics as Crosse's remind us that many English people were desperately poor and without skills or other means of improving their lot. Such official assistance as existed was sporadic and locally organized: the parish church, for example, was responsible for ministering to the poor in its neighborhood. London writers comment repeatedly on the problem of masterless men, ne'er-do-wells without family or work who support themselves by crime or begging and who thus threaten the social order. Poverty in the countryside was even more common, if perhaps less conspicuous. While some people subsisted in misery, some thrived by virtue of commercial ingenuity or hard work or the misuse of others. Philip Henslowe, often mentioned in these pages for the theatrical acumen he displayed in managing the Lord Admiral's Men, apparently made less money from his theaters than from his brothels and his money-lending.

In describing the culture in which Shakespeare moved, I have fixed my attention almost entirely on the occupations and preoccupations of merchants, farmers, housewives, and others near the middle of the social and economic scale, those who were neither aristocrats nor beggars. Shakespeare himself was born into the middle class and became through his success a member of what we would probably call the upper middle class. But Shakespeare's own upward mobility aside, the rise of the middle class is arguably the most important historical phenomenon in the late sixteenth century. As I indicated in Chapter 2 on Shakespeare's dramatic language, the age of Elizabeth was a period of linguistic transition, in which a discourse that we recognize as "modern" and more or less like our own emerged from the less familiar conventions of Middle and Old English. Similar instabilities and fluctuations characterize the economic and social spheres, as England moved from feudalism to precapitalism, from a medieval to a modern society. What we witness in England and in Europe generally at the end of the sixteenth century is, for better or worse, the emergence of the culture of success. Most of the features of English life that I have described, from the growth of London to the struggles over enclosure to the power of fashion, are a function of this familiar modern phenomenon. And so, we might add, is the career of the young man who left the small town to make his fortune in the city and returned at the end of that career a famous and wealthy playwright.

➔ **WILLIAM HARRISON**

From *The Description of England* 1587

The Conditions of English Inns and Overnight Travel

Printed as a part of the second edition of Raphael Holinshed's *Chronicles of England, Scotland, and Ireland,* William Harrison's *Description* is an encyclopedic survey not only of topography and other physical features of England but also of its social and political structures and the manners and habits of its people.

If the traveler have a horse, his bed doth cost him nothing, but if he go on foot he is sure to pay a penny for the same; but whether he be horseman or footman, if his chamber be once appointed he may carry the key with him, as of his own house, so long as he lodgeth there. If he lose aught whilst he abideth in the inn, the host is bound by a general custom to restore the damage, so that there is no greater security anywhere for travelers than in the greatest inns of England. Their horses in like sort [manner] are walked, dressed, and looked unto by certain hostlers or hired servants, appointed at the charges of the goodman of the house, who in hope of extraordinary reward will deal very diligently, after outward appearance, in this their function and calling. Herein, nevertheless, are many of them blameworthy, in that they do not only deceive the beast oftentimes of his allowance by sundry means — except their owners look well to them — but also make such packs with slipper merchants [con men] which hunt after prey (for what place is sure from evil and wicked persons?) that many an honest man is spoiled of his goods as he traveleth to and fro, in which feat also the counsel of the tapsters or drawers of drink and chamberlains is not seldom behind or wanting. Certes [certainly] I believe not that chapman [merchant] or traveler in England is robbed by the way without the knowledge of some of them; for when he cometh into the inn, and alighteth from his horse, the hostler forthwith is very busy to take down his budget [leather pouch] or capcase [small traveling bag] in the yard from his saddle-bow, which he peiseth [weighs] slyly in his hand to feel the weight thereof: or if he miss of this pitch [trick], when the guest hath taken up his chamber, the chamberlain that looketh to the making of the beds will be sure to remove it from the place where the owner hath set it, as if it were to set it more conveniently somewhere else, whereby he getteth an inkling whether it be money or other short wares [less valuable things], and thereof giveth warning to such odd guests as haunt the house and are of his confederacy, to the utter undoing of many an honest yeoman as he journeyeth by the way. The tapster in like sort for his part doth mark his behavior and what plenty of money he draweth when he payeth the shot [bill] to the like end, so that it shall be a hard matter to escape all their subtle practices. Some think it a gay matter to commit their budgets at their coming to the goodman of the house: but thereby they oft betray themselves. For albeit their money be safe for the time that it is in his hands (for you shall not hear that a man is robbed in his inn), yet after their departure the host can make no warrantise [guarantee] of the same, since his protection extendeth no further than the gate of his own house, and there cannot be a surer token unto such as pry and watch for those booties, than to see any guest deliver his capcase in such manner.

→ JOHN STOW

From *Survey of London*   *1598*

The Location of Tradesmen in London

A dedicated historian and collector of manuscripts, John Stow (1525?–1605) produced several accounts of English political history, but his most important work is surely the *Survey*, one of the great records of the growth of a great city. He offers abundant detail about the physical appearance of the city — its walls, bridges, monuments, markets, and neighborhoods — and here identifies the locations of the various tradesmen in the London of the 1590s.

Men of trades and sellers of wares in this city have often times since changed their places, as they have found their best advantage. For whereas mercers [dealers in expensive cloth] and haberdashers used to keep their shops in West Cheap, of later time they held them on London Bridge, where partly they yet remain. The goldsmiths of Guthertons [Gutter] Lane and Old Exchange are now for the most part removed into the south side of West Cheap, the peppers and grocers of Sopers Lane are now in Bucklesbury, and other places. The drapers of Lombard Street and of Cornhill are seated in Candlewick Street and Watheling Street; the skinners from St. Mary Pellipers, or at the Axe, into Budge Row and Walbrooke; the stockfishmongers [sellers of dried fish] in Thames Street; wet fishmongers in Knightriders Street and Bridge Street; the ironmongers, of Ironmongers Lane and Old Jewry, into Thames Street; the vintners from the Vinetree [Vintry] into divers places. But the brewers for the more part remain near to the friendly water of Thames; the butchers in Eastcheap and St. Nicholas Shambles; the hosiers [makers or sellers of stockings] of old time in Hosier Lane, near unto Smithfield, are since removed into Cordwainer Street, the upper part thereof by Bow Church, and last of all into Birchoveris [Birchin] Lane by Cornhill; the shoemakers and curriers of Cordwainer Street removed, the one to St. Martins le Grand, the other to London Wall near unto Moorgate; the founders [casters of metal] remain by themselves in Lothbury; cooks or pastlers [bakers] for the more part in Thames Street, the other dispersed into divers parts; poulterers of late removed out of the Poultry betwixt the stocks and great conduit in Cheap, into Grass Street and St. Nicholas Shambles; bowyers [bow makers], from Bowyers Row by Ludgate into divers places, and almost worn out with the fletchers [arrow makers]; Pater Noster bead-makers and text-writers are gone out of Pater Noster Row into Stationers [booksellers' area] of Pauls Churchyard; patten makers [makers of clogs or overshoes] of St. Margaret, Pattens Lane, clean worn out; laborers every workday are to be found in Cheap, about Sopers Lane end; horse coursers [dealers or brokers] and sellers of oxen, sheep, swine, and such like, remain in their old market of Smithfield, etc.

→ **ISABELLA WHITNEY**

From "The Manner of Her Will, and What She Left to London" *1573*

Whitney published *A Sweet Nosegay*, her second book, in 1573. A miscellany of poems, verse epistles, and other forms, it contains the poem excerpted below. (For more on Whitney, see Chapter 8, p. 257.) In these poignant verses Whitney creates a speaker who bequeathes to London — and to her readers — the pleasures and disappointments to be found in the city.

And now let me dispose such things
    As I shall leave behind,
That those which shall receive the same
    May know my willing mind.
I first of all to London leave,   25
    Because I there was bred,
Brave buildings rare, of churches store,
    And Paul's to the head.
Between the same, fair streets there be
    And people goodly store;   30
Because their keeping craveth cost,
    I yet will leave him more.
First for their food, I butchers leave,
    That every day shall kill;
By Thames you shall have brewers store   35
    And bakers at your will.
And such as orders do observe
    And eat fish thrice a week,
I leave two streets full fraught therewith;
    They need not far to seek.
Watling Street and Canwick Street   40
    I full of woollen leave,
And linen store in Friday Street,

If they me not deceive.
And those which are of calling such   45
   That costlier they require,
I mercers leave, with silk so rich
   As any would desire.
In Cheap, of them they store shall find,
   And likewise in that street,   50
I goldsmiths leave with jewels such
   As are for ladies meet,
And plate to furnish cupboards with
   Full brave there shall you find,
With purl [thread] of silver and of gold   55
   To satisfy your mind;
With hoods, bongraces [shades], hats or caps
   Such store are in that street
As, if on t'one side you should miss,
   The t'other serves you feat [nicely].   60
For nets of every kind of sort
   I leave within the Pawn,
French ruffs, high purls [ruffs or bands], gorgets [wimples], and sleeves
   Of any kind of lawn [fine linen].
For purse or knives, for comb or glass,   65
   Or any needful knack,
I by the Stocks have left a boy
   Will ask you what you lack.
I hose do leave in Birchin Lane
   Of any kind of size,   70
For women stitched, for men both trunks
   And those of Gascoyne guise.
Boots, shoes, or pantables [slippers] good store
   St Martin's hath for you;
In Cornwall, there I leave you beds   75
   And all that longs [belongs] thereto.
For women shall you tailors have,
   By Bow the chiefest dwell;
In every lane you some shall find
   Can do indifferent well.   80
And for the men few streets or lanes
   But body-makers [tailors] be,
And such as make the sweeping cloaks
   With guards [borders] beneath the knee.
Artillery at Temple Bar   85
   And dags [pistols] at Tower Hill;
Swords and bucklers of the best
   Are nigh the Fleet until.

➜ THOMAS PLATTER

From *Travels in England* 1599
The Thames River *Translated by Clara Williams*

Thomas Platter was a well-educated Swiss printer who traveled extensively and kept a detailed journal of his experiences. This brief excerpt records his impressions of the Thames.

It is customary to cross the water or travel up and down the town as at Lyons and elsewhere by attractive pleasure craft, for a number of tiny streets lead to the Thames from both ends of the town; the boatmen wait there in great crowds, each one eager to be the first to catch one, for all are free to choose the ship they find most attractive and pleasing, while every boatman has the privilege on arrival of placing his ship to best advantage for people to step into. . . .

➜ LUPOLD VON WEDEL

From *Journey through England and Scotland* 1584–85
A Visit to the Bearbaiting Arena *Translated by Gottfried von Bulow*

Lupold von Wedel describes his journey across London Bridge and into Southwark, finishing with his report on the entertainment known as bearbaiting, in which a large dog was made to fight with a bear (often tied to a stake).

The Thames is crossed by a bridge, leading to another town on the other side of the water called Sedorck [Southwark]. This bridge is built of stone, 470 paces long, but its upper part has not the appearance of a bridge, being entirely set with fine houses filled with all kinds of wares, very nice to look at. . . .

On the 23rd we went across the bridge to the above-mentioned town. There is a round building three stories high, in which are kept about a hundred large English dogs, with separate wooden kennels for each of them. These dogs were made to fight singly with three bears, the second bear being larger than the first, and the third larger than the second. After this a horse was brought in and chased by the dogs, and at last a bull, who defended himself bravely. The next was that a number of men and women came forward from a separate compartment, dancing, conversing, and fighting with each other; also a man who threw some white bread among the crowd, that scrambled for it. Right over the middle of the place a rose was fixed, this rose being set on fire by a rocket: suddenly lots of apples and pears fell out of it down upon the people standing below. Whilst the people were scrambling for the apples, some rockets were made to fall down upon them out of the rose, which caused a great fright but amused the spectators. After this, rockets and other fireworks came flying out of all corners, and that was the end of the play.

→ THOMAS NASHE

From *Christ's Tears over Jerusalem*   1592
The Brothels of Suburban London

Thomas Nashe (1567–1601) was a colorful figure in the London literary world. Playwright, satirist, pamphleteer, and writer of prose fiction, Nashe often indulged in a bitter and polemical assault on the manners and morals of the day. This passage, excerpted from the 1613 edition, specifically attacks the toleration of the brothels of suburban London.

London, what are thy suburbs but licensed stews? Can it be so many brothel-houses of salary sensuality and six-penny whoredom (the next door to the magistrate's) should be set up and maintained, if bribes did not bestir them? I accuse none, but certainly justice somewhere is corrupted. Whole hospitals of ten-times-a-day dishonested strumpets have we cloistered together. Night and day the entrance unto them is as free as to a tavern. Not one of them but hath a hundred retainers. Prentices and poor servants they encourage to rob their masters. Gentlemen's purses and pockets they will dive into and pick, even whiles they are dallying with them.

No Smithfield ruffianly swashbuckler will come off with such harsh hell-raking oaths as they. Every one of them is a gentlewoman, and either the wife of two husbands, or a bed-wedded bride before she was ten years old. The speech-shunning sores, and sight-irking botches of their unsatiate intemperance, they will unblushingly lay forth, and jestingly brag of, wherever they haunt. To church they never repair. Not in all their whole life would they hear of God, if it were not for their huge swearing and forswearing by him. . . .

Great cunning do they ascribe to their art, as the discerning (by the very countenance) a man that hath crowns in his purse; the fine closing in with the next justice or alderman's deputy of the ward; the winning love of neighbors round about, to repel violence, if haply their houses should be environed or any in them prove unruly (being pilled and polled [stripped, shaved, or fleeced] too unconscionably). They forecast [scout] for back doors to come in and out by undiscovered. Sliding windows also, and trap-boards in floors, to hide whores behind and under, with false counterfeit panes in walls, to be opened and shut like a wicket [gate]. Some one gentleman generally acquainted [having many friends], they give his admission unto sans fee, and free privilege thenceforward in their nunnery, to procure them frequentance. Awake your wits, grave authorized law-distributors, and show yourselves as insinuative subtle, in smoking this city-sodoming trade out of his starting-holes, as the professors of it are in underpropping it. . . .

Monstrous creatures are they; marvel is it fire from heaven consumes not London, as long as they are in it. A thousand parts better were it to have public stews than to let them keep private stews as they do. The world would count me the most licentiate loose strayer under heaven, if I should unrip but half so much of their venereal machiavellism [sexual deceitfulness] as I have looked into. We have not English words enough to unfold it. Positions and instructions have they to make their whores a hundred times more whorish and treacherous than their own wicked affects [inclinations] (resigned to the devil's disposing) can make them. Waters and receipts [drinks and recipes; medicines] have they to enable a man to the act after he is spent, dormative potions to procure deadly sleep, that when the hackney [hired woman] he hath paid for lies by him, he may have no power to deal with her, but she may steal from him, whiles he is in his deep memento [reverie or doze], and make her gain of three or four other [customers].

→ GERVASE MARKHAM

From *The English Husbandman*   *1613*
Rural Domestic Architecture and Interior Design

A versatile man of letters who wrote plays and poetry and may have moved in the same circles as William Shakespeare, Gervase Markham (1568–1637) is best remembered today for his pamphlets and advice on country life. This passage from one such pamphlet offers a description of a design for a modest country house.

Here you behold the model of a plain country man's house, without plaster or imbosture [embellishment], because it is to be intended that it is as well to be built of stud and plaster, as of lime and stone; or if timber be not plentiful, it may be built of coarser wood, and covered with lime and hair; yet if a man would bestow cost in this model, the four inward corners of the hall would be convenient for four turrets, and the four gavel [gable] ends, being thrust out with bay windows might be formed in any curious manner: and where I place a gate and a plain pale [fence], might be either a terrace, or a gatehouse, of any fashion whatsoever; besides all those windows which I make plain, might be made bay windows, either with battlements or without: but the scope of my book tendeth only to the use of the honest husbandman and not to instruct men of dignity, who in architecture are able wonderfully to control me; therefore that the husbandman may know the use of this facsimile, he shall understand it by this which followeth.

A. Signifieth the great hall.
B. The dining parlor for entertainment of strangers.
C. An inward closet within the parlor for the mistress's use, for necessaries.

D. A stranger's lodging within the parlor.

E. A staircase into the rooms over the parlor.

F. A staircase into the goodman's rooms over the kitchen and buttery [room for storing provisions].

G. The screen in the hall.

H. An inward cellar within the buttery, which may serve for a larder.

I. The buttery.

K. The kitchen, in whose range may be placed a brewing lead [a vessel for brewing], and convenient ovens, the brewing vessels adjoining.

L. The dairy house for necessary business.

M. The milkhouse.

N. A fair sawn pale [well-cut fence] before the foremost court.

P. A place where a pump would be placed to serve the offices of the house.

 This figure signifieth the doors of the house.

This figure signifieth the windows of the house.

This figure signifieth the chimneys of the house.

Now you shall further understand that on the south side of your house, you shall plant your garden and orchard, as well for the prospect thereof to all your best rooms, as also your house will be a defense against the northern coldness, whereby your fruits will much better prosper. You shall on the west side of your house, within your inward dairy and kitchen court, fence in a large base court, in the midst whereof would be a fair large pond, well stoned and graveled in the bottom, in which your cattle may drink, and horses when necessity shall urge be washed; for I do by no means allow washing of horses after instant labor. Near to this pond you shall build your dovecote, for pigeons delight much in the water; and you shall by no means make your dove-house too high, for pigeons cannot endure a high mount, but you shall build it moderately, clean, neat, and close, with water pentisses [penthouses, or overhangs] to keep away vermin. On the north side of your base court you shall build your stables, ox-house, cow-house, and swinecotes, the doors and windows opening all to the south. On the south side of the base court, you shall build your hay barns, corn barns, pullen-houses for hens, capons, ducks, and geese; your French kiln, and malting floors, with such like necessaries: and over cross betwixt both these sides you shall build your bound hovels [connected shacks], to carry your peas, of good and sufficient timber, under which you shall place when they are out of use your carts, wains, tumbrels [dung wagons], plows, harrows, and such like, together with plow-timber and axletrees [frames and axles], all which would very carefully be kept from wet, which of all things doth soonest rot and consume them. And thus much of the husbandman's house, and the necessaries thereto belonging.

> JOHN MOORE

From *A Target for Tillage* 1613

A Leicestershire parson, Moore captures in his polemic the anger of many Jacobean villagers over the enclosure of farmland. Greedy landowners had begun to seek greater profits in the wool trade by grazing sheep on their fields. Moore uses theological language to identify the farmer, or tiller, with God's plan for earthly abundance and human contentment, and to attack the advocates of enclosure as predatory and even monstrous. A "target" is a shield, and his book is thus a defense of the old ways of farming.

M an, I confess, lives not by bread alone. Yet as the end of God's providence is that man should live, so the means of his providence is that man should live by bread, which bread must needs be got by his travail [labor] and tillage. A corporal substance is to be maintained by corporal sustenance, and as man at the first was taken out of the earth, so will God have the fruits of the earth to be his food as the fruit of his travail, that so by the bread of the earth our bodies of earth may be nourished and relieved. Our mortal life is upholden by earthly means, and as meats are ordained for the belly, and the belly for meats, so death shall dissolve both it and them to earth again.

The consideration whereof . . . reproveth and condemneth all such as hinder this abundance of God's blessings, by intercepting or utterly abolishing this mystery of tillage, to wit, all such persons as decay both houses and husbandries, that lay the land waste and labor to make it a wilderness in regard of men, fit only for a few such monsters in men's shape, and all kind of their cattle which they desire to keep; having rooted out men (the image of the eternal God), turned houses into bushes, and poor people into sheep, preferring the fellowship of beasts before the society of men, made like to God. Such kind of spoilers of their country may instead of their neighbors (whom they have rooted out) salute their oxen, sheep, and horses, which they have nourished and increased. A fearful woe is pronounced against all such as dwell alone with the destruction of their brethren: joining house to house, and field to field, till there be no place for the poor, that so they may be placed by themselves in the midst of the earth. This is in mine ears (saith the Lord of Hosts) and for this shall their own houses one day be desolate, and their great and stately palaces without inhabitant. These are wasters of their country, who delight rather in Abimelech's plow, to sow the land with salt (as he did the city) to make it barren and fruitless [see Judges 9:45], than with good seed of corn and grain for the plentiful provision of food for God's people; and take greater pleasure to sow the soil with the innocent blood of their poor brethren than in procuring the means of abundance of bread by good husbandry and tillage; and so in God's account do make their possessions fields of blood, purchased in effect with the hazard of the lives of God's inheritance, for the want of food.

→ SIR ANTHONY FITZHERBERT

From *The Book of Husbandry*   *1523*

What Works a Wife Should Do

Sir Anthony Fitzherbert (1470–1538), justice of the court of common pleas, wrote an important summary of English law and a treatise on the rights of landlords and tenants. *The Book of Husbandry* is a practical manual designed to instruct farmers in the principles of agriculture and their wives in the domestic arts.

First, in the morning when thou art waked and purpose to rise, lift up thy hand and bless thee and make a sign of the Holy Cross, *In nomine patris et filii et spiritus sancti. Amen.* In the name of the Father, the Son, and the Holy Ghost. And if thou say a *Pater Noster* [the Our Father], an *Ave* [the Hail Mary], and a *Credo* [the Creed], and remember thy Maker, thou shalt speed much the better. And when thou art up and ready, then first sweep thy house, dress up thy dishboard, and set all things in good order within thy house. Milk thy kie [kine, or cows], suckle thy calves, sile up [strain] thy milk, take up thy children and array them, and provide for thy husband's breakfast, dinner, supper, and for thy children and servants; and take thy part with them. And . . . ordain [set aside a portion of] corn [grain] and malt to the mill to bake and brew withal when need is. And mete [measure] it to the mill and from the mill, and see that thou have thy measure again besides the toll [charges] or else the miller dealeth not truly with thee, or else thy corn is not dry as it should be. Thou must make butter and cheese when thou may. Serve thy swine both morning and evening, and give thy pullen [poultry] meat [food] in the morning. And when time of year cometh, thou must take heed how thy hens, ducks, and geese do lay, and to gather up their eggs, and when they wax broody to set them there as no beasts, swine, nor other vermin hurt them. And thou must know that all whole-footed fowl will sit a month and all cloven-footed fowl will sit but three weeks except a peahen and such other great fowls as cranes, bustards [large birds], and such other. And when they have brought forth their birds to see that they be well kept from the gleyd [kites], crows, fully martes [foumarts, i.e., polecats], and other vermin.

And in the beginning of March, or a little before, is time for a wife to make her garden and to get as many good seeds and herbs as she can, and specially such as be good for the pot and for to eat. And as oft as need shall require, it must be weeded, for else the weed will overgrow the herbs. And also in March is time to sow flax and hemp, for I have heard old housewives say that better is March hurds than April flax, the reason appeareth [hurds are the tough part of flax; i.e., better to plant in March regardless of the product]. But how it should be sown, weeded, pulled, rippled [combed], watered, washed, dried, beaten, braked [crushed], tawed [softened], hackled [hacked], spun, wound, wrapped, and woven, it needed not for me to show, for they be wise enough. And thereof may they make sheets, boardcloths [tablecloths], towels, shirts, smocks, and such other necessaries. And therefore let thy distaff [stick for spinning wool or flax] be always ready for a pastime that thou be not idle. . . .

It may fortune sometime that thou shalt have so many things to do that thou shalt not well know where is best to begin. Then take heed which thing should be the greatest loss if it were not done and in what space it would be done; and then think what is the greatest loss and there begin. . . .

It is a wife's occupation to winnow all manner of corns, to make malt [for brewing beer], wash and wring, to make hay, to shear corn, and in time of need to help her husband to fill the muck wain or dung cart, drive the plow, to load hay, corn, and such other. Also to go or ride to the market to sell butter, cheese, milk, eggs, chickens, capons, hens, pigs, geese, and all manner of corn. And also to buy all manner of necessary things belonging to a household, and to make a true reckoning and account to her husband what she hath received and what she hath paid. And if the husband go to the market to buy or sell (as they oft do), he then to show his wife in like manner. For if one of them should use [practice] to deceive the other, he deceiveth himself, and he is not like to thrive, and therefore they must be true either to other.

→ WILLIAM HARRISON

From *The Description of England* 1587
Dining Customs

William Harrison's record of English eating habits affords a specific picture of when people took their meals. As with other customs, the time when people dined was to some extent determined by the class to which they belonged.

With us the nobility, gentry, and students do ordinarily go to dinner at eleven before noon, and to supper at five, or between five and six at afternoon. The merchants dine and sup seldom before twelve at noon, and six at night, especially in London. The husbandmen dine also at high noon, as they call it, and sup at seven or eight; but out of the term in our universities the scholars dine at ten. As for the poorest sort they generally dine and sup when they may, so that to talk of their order of repast, it were but a needless matter. I might here take occasion also to set down the variety used by antiquity in their beginnings of their diets, wherein almost every nation had a several [distinct] fashion, some beginning of custom (as we do in summer time) with salads at supper, and some ending with lettuce, some making their entry with eggs, and shutting up their tables with mulberries, as we do with fruit and conceits [fancy trifles, sweets] of all sorts. Divers (as the old Romans) began with a few crops [sprouts] of rue, as the Venetians did with the fish called gobius; the Belgians with butter (or as we do yet also) with butter and eggs upon fish days [Fridays or Lent]. But whereas we commonly begin with the most gross food, and end with the most delicate, the Scot, thinking much [i.e., fearing] to leave the best for his menial servants, maketh his entrance at the best, so that he is sure thereby to leave the worst.

→ RICHARD MULCASTER

From *Positions . . . for the Training Up of Children* 1581
Chapter 27, "Of the Ball"

One of the great educators of Elizabethan London, Richard Mulcaster (1530?–1611) was headmaster of two major London schools for upper-middle-class children rather than aristocrats. His other major work, *The Elementarie* (1582), concerns itself chiefly with language. The section of *Positions* from which the following excerpt is taken is devoted to sports, asserting the physical benefits of ball-playing but cautioning against quarreling and injury. Throughout Mulcaster promotes the humanist ideal, derived from the ancients, of a sound mind in a sound body.

The play at the ball seemeth compound because it may be used both within doors and without. Whereof good writers have delivered us thus much: that in the old time there were divers kinds of balls and divers kinds of exercise therewith, according to the divers use of the ball either small or great, both amongst the Romans and Greeks, whose names I use so much because they were best acquainted both with the things and with the right use thereof. . . .

The little hand ball whether it be of some softer stuff, and used by the hand alone, or of some harder, and used with the racket, whether by tennis play with another, or against a wall alone, to exercise the body with both the hands, in every kind of motion, that concerneth any, or all the other exercises, is generally noted to be one of the best exercises and the greatest preservations of health. Insomuch as Galen [the Greek physician] bestoweth a whole treatise upon the use and praise of it, wherein he compareth it with other exercises, and preferreth it before all, for parability [easily prepared, i.e., easy to get up a game], to be all men's game; for profitableness, to do all men good; for pleasantness, to quick all men's spirits, and in short knits up the sum of his conclusion thus: that the use of the little ball doth plant in the mind courage, in the body health, in all the limbs a trim and well proportionate constitution, so it be moderately and advisedly executed. Playing at the ball in general is a strong exercise, and maketh the body very nimble, and strengtheneth all the vital actions. The little handball is counted to be a swift exercise, without violence, and therefore the racketers in tennis play, if they use it in that kind which is thought to be most healthful, must show themselves nimble without straining, and yet it falleth out most commonly contrary, while desire to win some wager makes the winners lose a benefit, which they wish for more, and would gladly get to better their health by [i.e., sometimes competition can interfere with the therapeutic value of the game]. This playing abateth [diminishes] grossness and corpulence, as all other of the same sort do: it maketh the flesh sound and soft; it is very good for the arms, the green [young] and growing ribs, the back, and by reason the legs are mightily stirred thereby; it is a great furtherer to strength; it quickeneth the eyes by looking now hither, now thither, now up, now down; it helpeth the ridgebone [spine] by stooping, bending and coursing about; it is very good for bellies and stomachs, that be troubled with wind [gas] or any pain which proceedeth from the cold. Now to the contrary it is not good for ill and blear eyes, raw stomaches, undigested meat, which have more need of rest than stirring, and for such as will soon be turnsick [dizzy], which the oft turning about of the head and eyes cannot but cause. The playing at tennis is more costly and straining to answer an adversary, but the playing against the wall is as healthful and the more ready because it needeth no adversary, and yet practiseth every kind of motion, every joint of the body, and all without danger. Children use this ball diversly, and every way healthfully, in regard of the exercise. If accidentary faults fall out among children, in the use of play, the parties must bear the blame and not the play [i.e., quarreling is the fault of the contestants, not the game itself].

The second kind I make the football play, which could not possibly have grown to this greatness [popularity] that it is now at, nor have been so much used as it is in all places, if it had not had great helps both to health and strength, and to me the abuse of it is a sufficient argument that it hath a right use: which being revoked to his primitive [i.e., returned to its original form or use] will both help, strength, and comfort nature: though as it is now commonly used, with thronging of a rude multitude, with bursting of shins and breaking of legs, it be neither civil, neither worthy the name of any train [means] to health. Wherein any man may evidently see the use of the training master: for if one stand by which can judge the play [i.e., a referee], and is judge over the parties, and hath authority to command in all the place, all those inconveniences have been, I know, and will be I am sure very lightly redressed, nay they will never intermeddle in the matter, neither shall there be complaint, where there is no cause. Some smaller number with such overlooking, sorted into sides and standings, not meeting with their bodies so boisterously to try their strength, nor shouldering or shuffing on another so barbarously and using to walk after, may use football for as much good to the body, by the chief use of the legs, as the armball, for the same, by the use of the arms. And being so used, the football strengtheneth and brawneth the whole body, and by provoking superfluities [unnecessary fluids] downward, it dischargeth the head and upper parts, it is good for the bowels, and to drive down the stone and gravel from both the bladder and the kidneys. It helpeth weak hams by much moving, beginning at a mean [moderately], and simple shanks by thickening of the flesh, no less than riding doth. Yet rash running and too much force oftentimes breaketh some inward conduit, and bringeth ruptures.

→ WILLIAM HARRISON

From *The Description of England* 1587
Fashion

Such detailed commentary on fashion is fascinating for the pictorial details it provides about what English men and women wore in sixteenth-century London. It is also instructive for its assault on sartorial folly and excess. Actors often came under attack for the impropriety of their costumes — as "vagabonds" they were not entitled to such splendor — and for the convention of cross-dressing.

The fantastical folly of our nation, even from the courtier to the carter, is such that no form of apparel liketh [pleases] us longer than the first garment is in the wearing, if it continue so long and be not laid aside, to receive some other trinket newly devised by the fickle-headed tailors, who covet to have several tricks in cutting, thereby to draw fond customers to more expense of money. For my part, I can tell better how to inveigh against this enormity than describe any certainty of our attire; since such is our mutability that today there is none to [nothing comparable to] the Spanish guise, tomorrow the French toys [trinkets] are most fine and delectable, ere long no such apparel as [i.e., except] that which is after the high Alman [German] fashion, by and by the Turkish manner is generally best liked of, otherwise the Morisco [Moorish] gowns, the Barbarian sleeves, the mandilion [a cape with sleeves] worn to Colley-Weston-ward, and the short French breeches make such a comely vesture that, except it were a dog in a doublet, you shall not see any so disguised as are my countrymen of England. And as these fashions are diverse, so likewise it is a world to see the costliness and the curiosity, the excess and the vanity, the pomp and the bravery [splendor], the change and the variety, and finally the fickleness and the folly, that is in all degrees, insomuch that nothing is more constant in England than inconstancy of attire. Oh, how much cost is bestowed nowadays upon our bodies, and how little upon our souls! How many suits of apparel hath the one, and how little furniture hath the other! How long time is asked in decking up of the first, and how little space left wherein to feed the latter! How curious [hard to satisfy], how nice [fastidious] also, are a number of men and women, and how hardly can the tailor please them in making it fit for their bodies! How many times must it be sent back again to him that made it! What chafing, what fretting, what reproachful language doth the poor workman bear away! And many times when he doth nothing to it at all, yet when it is brought home again, it is very fit and handsome; then must we put it on, then must the long seams of our hose be set by a plumb-line, then we puff, then we blow, and finally, sweat till we drop, that our clothes may stand well upon us.

I will say nothing of our heads, which sometimes are polled [cut short], sometimes curled, or suffered to grow at length like woman's locks, many times cut off above or under the ears round, as by [using] a wooden dish. Neither will I meddle with our variety of beards, of which some are shaven from the chin like those of Turks, not a few cut short like to the beard of Marquis Otto, some made round like a rubbing brush, other with a *pique de vant* [a short, pointed Vandyke beard] (oh, fine fashion!) or now and then suffered to grow long, the barbers being grown to be so cunning in this behalf as the tailors. And therefore, if a man have a lean and straight face, a Marquis Otto's cut will make it broad and large; if it be platterlike, a long slender beard will make it seem the narrower; if he be weasel-beaked, then much hair left on the cheeks will make the owner look big, like a bowdled [ruffled] hen, and so grim as a goose. . . . Many old men do wear no beards at all. Some lusty courtiers also and gentlemen of courage do wear either rings of gold, stones, or pearl in their ears, whereby they imagine the workmanship of God not to be a little amended. But herein they rather disgrace than adorn their persons, as by their niceness [luxuriousness] in apparel, for which I say most nations do not unjustly deride us, as also for that we do seem to imitate all nations round about us, wherein we be like to the *polypus* [octopus] or chameleon; and thereunto bestow most cost upon our asses, and much more than upon all the rest of our bodies, as women do likewise upon their heads and shoulders.

In women also it is most to be lamented that they do now far exceed the lightness [lasciviousness] of our men (who nevertheless are transformed from the cap even to the very shoe), and such staring attire as in time past was supposed meet for none but light hussies only, is now become an habit for chaste and sober matrons. What should I say of their doublets with pendant codpieces on the breast, full of jags and cuts, and sleeves of sundry colors? their galligaskins [loose breeches] to bear out their bums and make their attire to fit plum round (as they term it) about them? their farthingales and diversely colored nether stocks of silk, jersey, and such like, whereby their bodies are rather deformed than commended? I have met with some of these trulls [loose women] in London so disguised, that it hath passed my skill to discern whether they were men or women.

Thus it is now come to pass that women are become men and men transformed into monsters.

→ JOHN MURRELL

From *A Delightful Daily Exercise for Ladies and Gentlewomen* *1621*

The full title page of Murrell's book reads as follows: *A Delightful Daily Exercise for Ladies and Gentlewomen, Whereby is set forth the secret mysteries of the purest preservings in glasses and other confrictionaries, a making of breads, pastes, preserves, suckets, marmalades, tartstuffs, rough candies, with many other things never before in print. Whereto is added a Book of Cookery, by John Murrell Professor thereof. London. Printed for Thomas Dewe, and are to be sold at his shop in St. Dunstan's Churchyard in Fleet Street, 1621.* The second leaf after the title page is devoted entirely to the following sentence: "If any of you are desirous of any of the moulds mentioned in the book you may inquire at the shop of Thomas Dewe in St. Dunstan's Churchyard in Fleet Street, where you may have them." This may be one of the earliest examples of "integrated shopping," a store selling both the recipes and the equipment for making the dishes.

TO MAKE ENGLISH BISKET

Take eight new-laid eggs, taking away the whites of four of them, beat the eight yolks and the other four whites in a fair bowl the fourth part of an hour, then take a pound of fine flour being dried in an earthen pot close covered. Then take eight ounces of hard sugar beaten fine, and beat them into your eggs with the end of a rolling pin, and beat it so very hard for the space of an hour but by no means let it stand still, always beating it. Then have an oven as hot as for manchet [fine wheat bread] ready clean, having some saucers of flat plates or little tin coffins [i.e., bread moulds] buttered over with a feather as thin as you can strike it over. Then put into your foresaid paste coriander seed, sweet fennel seed, and caraway seed, of each the fourth part of an ounce. When you have beaten these into your paste, put it into your saucers and set them presently into the oven, and when you see it rise up and look white, you may take down your lid, and in a quarter of an hour they will be made. Then box it up and keep it all the year.

CHAPTER 8

Men and Women: Gender, Family, Society

Statements about gender, family, and society in the sixteenth and seventeenth centuries must be qualified by considerations of economics, geography, class, and other such shaping factors. The Puritan cloth-seller and his wife who kept shop together in London should not be lumped together with the Catholic family living on a vast landed estate near the Scottish border nor with the widowed tenant farmer struggling to subsist on a small plot of land in the West country. Most of what we know about courtship, marital relations, child rearing, inheritance, and the organization of the early modern household derives from the families of property owners, a group that expanded dramatically between 1500 and 1600. As these prosperous people became more numerous and conspicuous, they tended to emulate the social and familial behaviors of the group just above them, the landed gentry descended from the ruling elites of the fourteenth and fifteenth centuries. Thus, some generalizations will apply to more than one distinct group, but we should keep in mind that early modern England comprised many social practices and experiences. In the pages that follow, the customs of distinct social and economic classes are frequently elided, and yet such inevitable distortions are the price of establishing historical difference, of explaining clearly how the lives of early modern men and women and their families do and do not resemble our own.

The Situation of Women

England was ruled by a brilliant and strong-willed woman in the second half of the sixteenth century, but the monarchy was not a career option for women. The normal occupation for women at the time was marriage and motherhood.

This is not to say, however, that women did not work. On the contrary, the wife's job of running a household and rearing children was all-consuming, at least as demanding as, if not more so than, the corresponding duties of the husband. Upper-class women had servants to help with these tasks, while women of the lower social and economic strata did more of the actual labor themselves. But only a handful of very wealthy women were entirely at leisure. The comparative freedom of modern women to fulfill themselves in a variety of ways, with marriage and procreation as alternatives that may be embraced, postponed, combined with other professional pursuits, or rejected altogether, makes the limited options for women in early modern culture seem oppressive and unjust. While we deplore such restrictions, there is little point in what Stephen Booth calls "accusing the past of having been the past" (265). Instead, we must add to our disapproval an effort to appreciate the historical, economic, and philosophical causes of these constraints.

That women occupied a position subordinate to men in the early modern period is beyond dispute; that this was the "natural" state of affairs was almost beyond dispute. Although the idea is repugnant to modern sensibilities, most thinkers in the sixteenth century took it as axiomatic that men are superior to women. This is hardly the place to explore the ancient origins of gender hierarchies, but it is worth spending a moment to mention the cooperation of biology and philosophy in the creation of traditional roles for men and women. In primitive societies the greater physical strength of males led to a corresponding distribution of duties: the man killed the bear, the woman cooked it. Aristotle, much revered by humanist writers in early modern Europe, had offered a biological account of gender difference (see the passage on p. 278); and medieval theorists of the body developed and illustrated his ideas. Reading and rereading (and retranslating) Galen, the Greek writer on physiology, they and their humanist descendants articulated the doctrines of the elements and the humours.

Each of the four elements was composed of a mixture of qualities. Air was thought to be hot and wet; fire was hot and dry; earth was cold and dry; and water, cold and wet. Each of these elements was in turn associated with one of the *humours,* or bodily fluids — the sanguine (blood), the phlegmatic (phlegm), the choleric (choler), and the melancholic (black bile). The warmer elements were appropriate to masculinity. Thus, Shakespeare's Cleopatra asserts her transcendence of her female body when in the act of suicide she declares, "I am fire and air; my other elements / I give to baser life" (5.2.289–90). The apparent superiority of the masculine qualities was not absolute, however, for men were vulnerable to the fault of excessive heat. Nonetheless, the female body was thought to be less capable than the male of keeping the humours and elements in balance, owing partly to the fact of menstruation. According to the Dutch medical writer Levinus Lemnius in 1658,

> a woman's mind is not so strong as a mans. . . . If any man desires a natural reason for it, I answer him thus, that a womans flesh is loose, soft, and tender, so that the choler being kindled presently spreads all the body over, and causeth a sudden boyling of the blood about the heart. . . .

If any man would more neerely have the cause of this explain'd and desires a more exact reason; I can find no nearer cause that can be imagined,
than the venim and collections of humours that she every month heaps
together, and purgeth forth by the course of the moon; For when she
chanceth to be angry, as she will presently be, all that sink of humours
being stirred fumeth, and runs through the body, so that the Heart and
Brain are affected with the smoky vapours of it, and the Spirits both vitall
and animal, that serve those parts are inflamed . . . reason being but weak
in them, and their judgment feeble, and minds not well order'd, they are
sharply enraged, and cannot rule their passions.   (Qtd. in Schoenfeldt 36)

This attempt to justify the perceived inferiority of the female is representative
of the physiological and psychological theories prevalent in early modern
Europe. (A clear explanation of the doctrine of the humours is found in
Vaughan's *Directions for Health*, p. 279.)

From the ancient world through the Middle Ages and into the Renaissance, physical differences between men and women generated a hierarchy
that came to be "naturalized" in early examples of social theory. Greater physical strength was linked with greater intellectual ability and more profound
capacity for feeling. In the second act of *Twelfth Night*, Orsino lectures Viola
(disguised as a male) on the inferiority of female affection:

There is no woman's sides
Can bide the beating of so strong a passion
As love doth give my heart; no woman's heart
So big, to hold so much; they lack retention.
Alas, their love may be call'd appetite,
No motion of the liver, but the palate . . .   (2.4.93–98)

Shakespeare, of course, is mocking Orsino's male ego, since his pupil is a
woman who loves the Duke more profoundly and constantly than he loves the
hard-hearted Olivia. But such constructions of male and female abilities and
roles led to the orthodoxy of male dominance. In medieval and early modern
Europe, these "scientific" justifications of female subordination were reinforced by Christian doctrine in both its Catholic and Protestant forms. The
Pauline commitment to the husband as the head of the wife, as Christ is the
head of the church, represents the standard viewpoint. Eve, having been created second, was thought to be further removed from God than Adam.
Finally, the traditional association of woman with home and hearth was
enforced by a fact of medical history: the absence of any reliable or consistently practiced form of contraception meant that women gave birth to children who had to be taken care of. And in order to ensure social stability, the
traditional place of woman was developed by moralists and social theorists
into an ideology of subordination and domestic responsibility.

Such physiological and ideological restrictions limited independence of
action among women, but they did not suppress it entirely. There was at least
some actual resistance to the social roles prescribed for women. One of the
most notorious examples from the first decade of the seventeenth century was

a London character named Mary Frith, also known as Moll Cutpurse, who wore men's clothes, carried a sword, and smoked a pipe. She attracted enough attention to become the subject of a play by Thomas Middleton and Thomas Dekker known as *The Roaring Girl,* which was performed at the Fortune theater with Moll herself in attendance. A few women even paraded through the streets of London wearing men's clothing, a practice that seriously disturbed King James and led to sermons against sartorial disorder. But such unconventionality was exceptional. It is telling that Mary Frith flourished in London, for cities have always tolerated greater freedom of behavior. Similarly, the more significant kind of female independence grew out of the mercantile culture of London. Married women became involved in their husbands' business enterprises by assisting in the shop and keeping accounts, and even though women could not legally own property by themselves, widows of shopkeepers and craftsmen sometimes assumed ownership and control of the business after the husband's death. A well-provided-for widow probably enjoyed the greatest freedom of any early modern woman. Moreover, a substantial number of English women seem to have entered the marketplace on their own, doing laundry, working in the cloth trade, or selling fruit or baked goods and other provisions. Ben Jonson's comedy, *Bartholomew Fair* (1614), presents an unforgettable entrepreneur in the person of Ursula the Pig Woman, who runs what amounts to an outdoor lunch counter specializing in pork and who also seems, as a kind of pimp, to sell female human flesh. At this point we verge on the kind of commerce represented by prostitutes and other social outcasts who populated the brothels, or *stews,* in Southwark. In *Pericles,* a late play, Shakespeare mordantly depicts the business practices of the brothel owners (male and female) and their kind, but those scenes also encourage sympathy for young women who, by various accidents, might have found themselves engaged in such a trade. (See the excerpt from Thomas Nashe's *Christ's Tears over Jerusalem,* p. 242.)

If ideology and law limited independence of action, they exerted less influence over freedom of thought. Education became increasingly available to the middle classes, an effect of the spread of Continental humanism, the arrival of a print-based culture, and the Protestant belief that individual Christians ought to be permitted and able to read the Bible in their own language. Such expanded opportunities did not effect an immediate change in literacy, however. Although statistics are sketchy and probably unreliable, it appears that less than 50 percent of males could read and write at the turn of the seventeenth century, and boys were schooled more frequently than girls. Still, the number of readers vastly increased during the sixteenth century, and the widening pedagogical system began to produce greater numbers of literate and, in the highest reaches of society, extremely learned women. Some aristocratic women wrote verse, translated the Scriptures or classical literature, or produced philosophical treatises. Lady Mary Wroth, the niece of Sir Philip Sidney, wrote poetry — a sonnet sequence — and a long prose romance called *The Countess of Montgomery's Urania;* apparently she was the first English woman to produce either of these forms. Elizabeth Cary, viscountess of Falkland, composed a play, *The Tragedy of Mariam*. Although apparently not performed, it was the first published play by an Englishwoman (1613). Scholars have recently turned their attention to other *closet dramas,* plays composed not for public performance but for reading or private presentation, written by women of noble families. Mary Sidney Herbert's translation of Robert Garnier's *Tragedy of Antonie* (see p. 187) falls into this category. Her status as countess of Pembroke allowed her to serve, along with other aristocratic women such as Lucy Harrington Russell, countess of Bedford, as literary patron to a number of male writers. Her role in English letters was then carried on by her niece, Lady Mary Wroth. And a final notable figure in this context is Lady Anne Southwell, whose witty epistolary defense of poetic art is found on page 279.

One of the first women in England to write original verse and publish it was Isabella Whitney (born circa 1548), and what is especially remarkable is that she was a member not of the nobility but of the gentry, what we would call the upper-middle class. Whitney moved to London to serve in the household of an aristocrat, perhaps as a companion to the lady of the family; when illness deprived her of her position, she began to write various kinds of poetry. After publishing *The Copy of a Letter, lately written in meter, by a young Gentlewoman to her unconstant Lover* (1567), she brought out *A Sweet Nosegay* (1573), a collection that begins with this poignant address to the reader:

This harvest time, I harvestless,
    and serviceless also,
And subject unto sickness, that
    abroad I could not go.

Thus, she says, she began to read and write, and the book consists of various kinds of poetry — versified moral maxims, verse letters, replies to those, and the poem excerpted in Chapter 7 (see p. 239).

In the next generation we find one of the most fascinating women in Renaissance England, Aemilia Lanyer (1569–1645), whose social status is somewhat ambiguous. Daughter of an Italian court musician and an English mother, she was mistress of Lord Hunsdon (the patron of Shakespeare's company) but married another court musician (the marriage hastily arranged to cover Hunsdon's illegitimate child). Acquainted with Queen Elizabeth and later royal figures, she was a client of the astrologer Simon Forman, who is the source of much of what we know about her: "she was paramour to my old Lord Hunsdon that was Lord Chamberlain and was maintained in great pride; being with child she was for colour married to a minstrel." Lanyer is a leading candidate (although there is virtually no proof) for the role of Shakespeare's "dark lady." She is now acknowledged as an accomplished poet and an eloquent apologist for the dignity of women. In *Salve Deus Rex Judaeorum* ("Hail, God, King of the Jews"), she reflects poetically on the biblical account of the Passion, using the story to enter the contemporary debate over misogyny and female independence. The second section of the poem, "Eve's Apology in Defense of Women," is excerpted on page 281.

The uncomfortable situation of educated women appears vividly in the case of Arbella Stuart (1575–1615), certainly one of the most learned and impressive women of her time. Child of a noble family and possessor of what some — herself included — considered a reasonable claim to the English throne, Stuart's aristocratic advantages make her atypical but nonetheless worthy of notice. Queen Elizabeth treated her properly but kept her under virtual house arrest, fearing her potential political strength; when her cousin James became king in 1603, he brought her to court but watched her closely. Stuart consoled herself by studying. She knew French, Italian, Latin, Greek, Hebrew, and perhaps Spanish; she was adept at music, dancing, embroidery, and other arts considered suitable for females; she also mastered skills usually reserved for males, such as hunting, hawking, and the keeping of accounts. She did not, however, regard these accomplishments as commensurate with her abilities and ambitions. In privately pursuing her monarchical claim, attempting to retrieve her ancestral properties, and seeking to arrange a canny political marriage, she was forced to maneuver at some distance from the actual center of power. Consequently, she produced a fascinating series of letters that, taken together, constitute a record of female independence and learning put to imaginative use. In the words of Barbara Lewalski, "her letters are noteworthy for their witty and ironic comments on Elizabethan and Jacobean court society; for their unconscious self-representation combined with highly conscious self-fashioning; and for their rhetorical strategies of self-defense, ranging from obfuscation to self-abasement to insistent self-justification. . . . In them, Arbella Stuart works out a rhetoric of concealment as a strategy for retaining some limited power of self-determination in a repressive milieu" (67).

The education of women stimulated a broader range of thought about gender roles, and such discourse in turn generated powerful cultural anxiety about potential disruption of the social order. In short, what we regard as progress was seen by some in the Renaissance as monstrous or dangerous, and a number of writers responded to such social changes with misogynistic polemics. One of the most frequent forms of abuse directed against educated women was the equation of eloquence and promiscuity: looseness of tongue came to symbolize looseness of body and spirit. Such conventional attacks on female speech were taken over from the Middle Ages, specifically from such church fathers as St. John Chrysostom, St. Jerome, and others, and then expanded to fit the circumstances of free-thinking women. In 1615 Joseph Swetnam published his *Arraignment of Lewd, Idle, Froward, and Unconstant Women;* it was reprinted nine times in twenty years. The word *froward* (forward or aggressive) appears repeatedly in contemporary antifeminist discourse: women are charged with being "unruly," "shrewish," "disorderly," and "monstrous." Some of Shakespeare's outspoken women endure mockery for using their tongues. Volumnia, the mother of Coriolanus, is accused of being "mankind," that is, masculine, for speaking incessantly and in an unladylike way, and Paulina in *The Winter's Tale* is called "a mankind witch," "a callet [scold] of boundless tongue," and "Dame Partlet [a clucking hen]" for daring to tell the king the truth. The attempt of women to rule over their husbands, when the opposite is the "natural" relation, is one of the frequent themes of the misogynist tradition, as is evident in John Taylor's versified form of the complaint:

Ill fares the hapless family that shows
A cock that's silent, and a Hen that crows.
I know not which live more unnatural lives,
Obedient husbands, or commanding wives.   (Qtd. in Underdown 118)

The abundance of such angry discourse suggests that the earliest hints of emancipation among women were producing a backlash among defenders of the status quo.

Patriarchy

Patriarchy has become a familiar term in recent critical discourse, and yet its familiarity, its status as a buzzword, can be an obstacle to a full understanding of its historical, economic, religious, and social implications. The origins of the concept are biblical, the etymological root being derived from the leaders of the twelve tribes of Israel described in the Pentateuch and closely associated with divine law. In the ancient world and down through the Middle Ages, the patriarch tended to be the leader of a clan or tribe or large group of kinfolk, sometimes the chief of all the people in a certain region or even the head of a nation. Sir Robert Filmer's historical treatise entitled *Patriarcha, or The Natural Power of Kings*, written in the middle of the seventeenth century, develops the analogy between the primitive tribe, the monarchical state, and the English family:

> . . . not only Adam, but the succeeding Patriarchs had, by right of fatherhood, royal authority over their children. . . . I see not then how the children of Adam, or of any man else, can be free from subjection to their parents. And this subordination of children is the only fountain of all regal authority, by the ordination of God himself.

However, with the emergence of the modern state — and England under Henry VIII and Elizabeth I represents a primary stage of this development — came the simultaneous rise of the smaller family. The consolidation of power in the monarch reduced the influence of the feudal families and the lords that headed them, and a concomitant effect of this shift from patron to sovereign was a dispersal of authority from a few powerful lords to the male partner of each conjugal unit. England in the sixteenth and seventeenth centuries is the site of origin for many modern notions about the structure and function of the family, particularly the role of the father, for out of these developments the nuclear family took its shape. (For a more extensive excerpt from *Patriarcha*, see p. 283.)

Authority in the early modern family rested finally with the father. Wives had authority over children and servants, but the principle that the woman was "the weaker vessel" and consequently dependent on the superior judgment

and ability of her husband — a doctrine derived from St. Paul and his interpreters — gave the father uncontested rule over his wife and all members of
the household. Writing in 1571, Edmund Tilney puts the doctrine in the
mouths of two of his characters in a dialogue:

> Ye say well, Madam, quoth M. *Erasmus*. For in deede both divine, and
> humaine lawes, in our religion giveth the man absolute aucthoritie, over
> the woman in all places.
>
> And, quoth the Lady *Julia*, as I sayde before, reason doth confirme the
> same, the man being as he is, most apt for the soveraignetie being in gov-
> ernement, not onely skill, and experience to be required, but also capacity
> to comprehende, wisdome to understand, strength to execute, solicitude
> to prosecute, pacience to suffer, meanes to sustayne, and above all a great
> courage to accomplishe, all which are commonly in a man, but in a
> woman very rare.   (*The Flower of Friendship* 134)

Wives, in other words, were to yield to their husbands. According to the
Homily of the State of Matrimony, a widely disseminated sermon intended for
delivery at the conclusion of the marriage service, "St. Paul expresseth it in this
form of words: *Let women be subject to their husbands, as to the Lord; for the husband is the head of the woman, as Christ is the head of the Church* [Ephesians
5:22–23]. Here you understand that God hath commanded that ye should
acknowledge the authority of the husband and refer to him the honor of obedience." As the language of this passage discloses, paternal dominion in the
home was reinforced by the emphases and particularly the imagery of Elizabethan political and religious discourse. As God the Father was to all creation
and the monarch to the state, so was the father to the household. (A generous
portion of the homily is found on p. 285.) Some historians believe that the reason the homily was read so often is that masculine authority in the domestic
sphere was increasingly under threat. According to Susan Amussen, "No one
questioned women's subordination to their husbands — they just sometimes
refused to give it" (210).

The Pauline insistence on female submission is grounded in the creation
account recorded in Genesis 2 and 3, in which man is created first and then
woman is formed from a rib taken from man. This passage, which develops
the story of the serpent and the tree of knowledge, culminates in the punishment of Adam and Eve for the sin of disobedience: "Unto the woman he said,
I will greatly increase thy sorrows, and thy conceptions. In sorrow shalt thou
bring forth children, and thy desire *shall be subject* to thine husband, and he
shall rule over thee" (Genesis 3:16, Geneva). Commentators in the sixteenth
and seventeenth centuries, echoing the arguments of the medieval church
fathers, made much of this hierarchical relation. William Gouge, author of a
number of influential marriage manuals, asserted that the family was "a school
wherein the first principles and grounds of government and subjection are to
be learned . . . inferiors that cannot be subject in a family . . . will hardly be
brought to yield such subjection as they ought in Church or Commonwealth"

(qtd. in Amussen 200). (See p. 290 for Gouge's comparison between marriage and the social order.) The analogy between the marriage contract and the social contract, family and commonwealth, was useful to both political and domestic theorists because it was reversible. The challenges to the monarchy that became more frequent under the Stuarts and culminated in the English Civil Wars and the execution of King Charles (1649) meant that such commentary tended to be more abundant in the seventeenth century than in the sixteenth, when the doctrine of divinely given order was less open to question. Husbands, like monarchs, were expected to be conscious of their duty to their subjects and were exhorted not to behave tyrannically toward their wives, children, and servants.

Genesis contains another account of creation, however, one found in the first chapter and preceding the story of the rib. "Furthermore God said, Let us make man in our image according to our likeness, and let them rule over the fish of the sea, and over the fowl of the heaven, and over the beasts, and over all the earth, and over every thing that creepeth and moveth on the earth. Thus God created the man in his image: in the image of God created he him: he created them male and female" (1:26–27, Geneva). This alternative version of the creation of the race is consistent with the assertion appended to the story of the creation of woman out of man: "Therefore shall man leave his father and his mother, and shall cleave unto his wife: and they shall be one flesh" (Genesis 2:24). This emphasis on conjugal oneness is the source of a theme common to many writers on domestic ideology, the belief in mutuality and even equality. Throughout commentary on the relations of husbands and wives and the proper ordering of rights and responsibilities between them, the "natural" authority of the husband in the household is modified by an increasingly important Protestant religious doctrine: the principle of companionate marriage.

The basis for conjugal mutuality was the doctrine of spiritual equality among men and women, a belief that emerged in the humanist writings of the early sixteenth century and that, strangely enough, was derived also from St. Paul: "For all ye that are baptized into Christ, have put on Christ. There is neither Jew nor Grecian: there is neither bond nor free: there is neither male nor female: for ye are all one in Christ Jesus" (Galatians 3:27–28, Geneva). This text seems incompatible with the apostle's insistence, in the Letter to the Ephesians (5:22) and cited in the homily on marriage, on the natural subjection of wives to their husbands, and in fact this conflict between subjection and equality is replicated throughout the marriage manuals and domestic treatises. Many writers recommend that husband and wife ideally should bring to their marriage similarity in age, class, and economic status. But some commentators offer even bolder statements of the doctrine of equality that directly contradict the hegemony of the husband. For example, Tilney's *Flower of Friendship*, cited earlier on the topic of male superiority, also presents a statement of resistance to that argument based on the spiritual status of the wife and the strength of ancient example:

There is another great mainteyner of the *Flower*, and that is the goodly grace of obedience. For reason it is that we obey our Husbandes. God commaundeth it, and we are bounde so to doe.

I know not, quoth the Lady *Isabella*, what we are bound to do, but as meete is it, that the husband obey the wife, as the wife the husband, or at the least that there be no superioritie betwene them, as the auncient philosophers have defended. For women have soules as wel as men, they have wit as wel as men, and more apt for procreation of children than men. What reason is it then, that they shall be bound, whom nature hath made free?   (133)

"For women have soules as wel as men" is a powerful — and irrefutable — claim, and yet in Tilney's fictional dialogue the young woman who makes this assertion is overruled. In fact, the statement of male superiority cited earlier is Lady Julia's refutation of her daughter's protofeminist claims. But the characters' dispute is especially useful in exposing the contradictions inherent in early modern thinking about gender and power. These conflicts seem particularly meaningful when we consider that Tilney's dialogue on female submission is dedicated "To the Noble and most Vertuous Princesse, Elizabeth, by the Grace of God, of England, Fraunce, and Irelande, Queene, defender of the Faith. Etc." and was published in London in 1568, at a point when the question of Elizabeth's marriageability was a topic of national concern.

The early humanists had developed the ideal of companionate marriage, and Puritan pressure on English thought magnified its importance. Reformed theology promoted not only the doctrine of Grace as given indiscriminately to men and women but also the supremacy of the individual conscience in matters of salvation; both of these principles served to elevate the status of women in relation to all mortal creatures, even their husbands. Moreover, the increasingly forceful emphasis among Puritan preachers on the Christian's freedom from the unjust control of secular authority, a tenet that would receive its strongest literary expression in the writings of John Milton, tended to complicate the traditional hierarchy, civilly sanctioned and enforced, between husband and wife. If, as radical Protestants believed, the individual soul was to be governed only by its perception of the divine will, then this principle posed a contradiction to the dominion of the spouse and cleared the way for the doctrine of companionate marriage. The same contradiction could be seen in the larger political arena. In other words, Milton's antiroyalism is perfectly consistent with his endorsement of divorce. While these generalizations are not meant to suggest anything as improbable as Miltonic feminism, it is nevertheless true that the Puritan devotion to conscience and individual salvation conflicted with the ideology of subjection that linked the family and the state in discussions of domestic and political order and obedience. The ideal of companionate marriage based on conjugal sympathy and even equality developed slowly throughout the seventeenth century and came to fruition in the eighteenth, but its origins can be heard resounding from the Reformed pulpit and Protestant pamphlets as early as Elizabeth's reign. Further, a version of it is both audible and visible in at least some of Shakespeare's comedies. Despite the traditions of masculine authority in the family, it seems quite clear at the end of *Much Ado about Nothing* that Benedick will not succeed in dominating Beatrice.

Primogeniture

In the second scene of *King Lear,* the illegitimate son of the Earl of Gloucester confides to the audience his conviction that he deserves to inherit his father's property and title because he is more capable than his legitimate older brother.

> Wherefore should I
> Stand in the plague of custom, and permit
> The curiosity of nations to deprive me,
> For that I am some twelve or fourteen moonshines
> Lag of a brother?   (1.2.2–6)

Edmund's argument proceeds from his belief in his own strength. He considers himself smarter and more aggressive than Edgar, attributing these qualities to the passion that stimulated the liaison in which he was conceived. His contempt for the niceties of social convention expresses itself in his wordplay, his toying with the various forms of *bastard* and particularly his mockery of the word *legitimate.*

> Well then,
> Legitimate Edgar, I must have your land.
> Our father's love is to the bastard Edmund
> As to th' legitimate. Fine word, "legitimate."
> Well, my legitimate, if this letter speed
> And my invention thrive, Edmund the base
> Shall top th' legitimate.   (1.2.15–21)

Legitimate comes from the Latin for *law (lex, legis),* and Edmund's worrying of the word calls attention to its pertinence to the subject of the speech, the rights of heredity that customarily belong to the legally recognized eldest son. In seeking to substitute a biological or natural privilege — "Now, gods, stand up for bastards!" (1.2.22) — Edmund assails one of the foundations of English law, the convention of primogeniture. The passage from Sir Thomas Smith on page 292 provides a sixteenth-century justification of the practice.

Primogeniture (first-born) refers to the right of the eldest son to inherit the family property, and some of the early modern writers on politics and economics associate it specifically with the patriarchal transmission of governmental authority from tribal leaders down to contemporary rulers, whether of kingdoms or households. Taking hold as it did in the feudal practices of England in the Middle Ages, primogeniture was calculated to protect the property of large families, to keep estates from being dismantled or divided into a number of small and therefore weaker units. In the Renaissance the head of an important household was normally regarded as a caretaker of the family property, one to whom the ancestors had entrusted the health and prosperity of the family holdings. Thus the well-being of the group took precedence over that of any individual member, including the heir himself. Even when primogeniture worked as it was supposed to do, keeping estates from being broken up and land from being dispersed into smaller parcels, the price of the system could be ruinous for virtually all members of the family.

The eldest son, despite his apparent advantage, was in a sense trapped, having no real option but to await the death of his father so that he could succeed to guardianship of the estate. The younger children fared much worse, dependent as they were on the goodwill of their father to provide for them. In the case of daughters, this meant money for a dowry with which to attract a husband; in the case of younger sons, an education or a living, or at least the means to marry well. But sometimes goodwill was hindered by a lack of resources. Owing to financial hardships or entails (legal restrictions deriving from earlier wills that controlled the use of property or income), some apparently wealthy fathers were unable to provide for their younger children. A younger son was sometimes regarded as insurance against the death of the eldest son — Lawrence Stone compares such a boy to "a kind of walking sperm bank" — and many of these young men attended the university and became clergymen. But the problem was pervasive enough in England in the 1590s for Falstaff to joke about drafting the "younger sons of younger brothers," men who were at the bottom of the economic ladder and hadn't a shilling to give in the way of a bribe to escape military service.

The system of inheritance was complicated to start with and grew more so in the Renaissance. Even now English property laws are notoriously complex, one source being the movement from the feudal system, by which *land*-lords (the word needs defamiliarizing) held Crown properties in tenancy, to the modern system, by which a larger number of individuals own outright or hold in tenancy smaller units of land. (In England today, much of the land is still legally held by aristocratic estates rather than by the people who own houses or flats on that property.) The sixteenth century saw the beginnings of this shift, but it also introduced a host of other problems. The transformation of England's state religion from Catholicism to Protestantism, for example, led to the dissolution of religious houses such as monasteries and convents; one effect of this policy was a rise in the number of marriageable women, daughters who might have gone (cheaply) into convents but who now had to be provided for. Next, the significant increase in population between 1500 and 1600, with twice as many people occupying the same finite amount of land, created major economic and social dislocation. And the expansion of commerce produced cash that merchants and others wished to secure by investing in land. Shakespeare himself turned his London theatrical earnings into real estate investments in his hometown.

The social tensions inherent in the system of primogeniture find expression not only in diaries and court records but also in the theater of the period, where familial anxiety becomes the basis for dramatic conflict. In Thomas Middleton's *Your Five Gallants*, a character encounters a group of fashionable young men and greets them with, "Why so merry, gentlemen, are your fathers dead?" Such rivalry existed not only between fathers and children but also between widowed mothers and sons and among some siblings. One historian has suggested that the familial relationship least likely to suffer damage from the problems of inheritance was that between brother and sister, because the female's secondary legal status meant that property was not an issue. It was certainly an issue between brothers. At the beginning of *As You Like It*, Orlando bitterly complains of being misused by his elder brother, Oliver, and cheated of his small inheritance:

> OLIVER: Know you where you are, sir?
>
> ORLANDO: O, sir, very well; here in your orchard.
>
> OLIVER: Know you before whom, sir?
>
> ORLANDO: Ay, better than him I am before knows me. I know you are my eldest brother, and in the gentle condition of blood you should so know me. The courtesy of nations allows you my better, in that you are the first born, but the same tradition takes not away my blood, were there twenty brothers betwixt us. I have as much of my father in me as you. . . . (1.1.40–50)

This is different from Edmund's mockery of primogeniture. Orlando objects not to the system of inheritance ("the courtesy of nations") but to his brother's abuse of it in failing to honor their dead father's provision for Orlando. The drama of the period contains a sufficient number of such scenes and references to intimate that inheritance was becoming a widespread social concern. Indeed, on a national scale, the question of succession was of paramount importance at the turn of the seventeenth century, since Queen Elizabeth had no firstborn to inherit her throne. In the Shakespeare family, William, as the eldest son, was the beneficiary of primogeniture, inheriting in 1601 the Henley Street property, where his aunt Joan continued to live. We may remark in passing that he had a younger (legitimate) brother, also an actor, named Edmund.

Marriage and Money

Early modern matrimonial customs may seem cold-blooded, but it is important that we study them from a sixteenth-century point of view. Social historians such as Lawrence Stone and Ann Jennalie Cook have demonstrated that the ideas about romantic love and personal choice that govern our concepts of marriage are effects of social and attitudinal changes that took place in the eighteenth and nineteenth centuries. Stone urges that we "rid ourselves of three modern Western culture-bound preconceptions": (1) that marriage for love or personal attraction is morally superior to marriage for money or power, and that the categories are easily separable; (2) that authentic union must be underwritten by emotional attachment, or else the resulting marriage is the equivalent of commerce or prostitution; and (3) that personal autonomy or individual desire in the selection of a marriage partner should outweigh the claims of the family or the larger social group. As he argues, "Marriage among the property-owning classes in sixteenth-century England was, therefore, a collective decision of family and kin, not an individual one" (*Family* 85–87).

In the words of a sixteenth-century proverb, "More belongs to marriage than four bare legs in a bed." Marriage was part of a system of inheritance and economics so ingrained and pervasive that the emotional affections or physical desires of a man and woman diminished in importance. This was especially true among the upper classes, where the amount of property being inherited could be substantial, and where marriage was regarded as a convenient instrument for joining or ensuring peace between two powerful families, for consolidating land holdings, or for achieving other familial, financial, or even political ends. Once a marriage was agreed on, certain fiscal transactions took place. The bride's family promised to give to the married couple a *dowry* made up of property, valuables (silver and jewelry, for example), and cash. This was also called the bride's *portion*, and it was paid at the time of the wedding or soon after, occasionally in installments. If a young man could find a young woman whose family could afford a substantial dowry, then he could look forward to living comfortably. Moreover, his parents might be able to save some of their holdings to settle on their other children, perhaps their own daughters. The groom's family agreed to provide the couple with money to live on, to specify exactly what the groom would inherit at his father's death, and to guarantee a *dower* (the parallel term to dowry), the sum that the bride would inherit should the groom die before her. Another guaranteed sum called the *jointure* protected the bride in case her husband's property was seized (e.g., for treason). In fact, it is useful to think of all of these settlements as a form of security, both for the couple being married and for the families sending them out into the world. The monetary arrangements I have described were designed to guarantee that the couple would live comfortably, and that if one partner should die the other would not be penniless or a drain on his or her family.

The complexities and permutations of this system were considerable, of course, but a few generalizations can be made about practices of the sixteenth and seventeenth centuries. It was better to have sons than daughters. Because primogeniture ensured that an estate was passed on intact from father to eldest son, that young man's prospects were very bright. His parents sought the daughter of a prominent or wealthy family whose dowry would be worthy of the inheritance he would receive. If his parents were dead, he presented himself to the family of an appropriate partner, as Petruchio does in *The Taming of the Shrew*. Indeed, consciousness of these economic and social customs makes such Shakespearean suitors as Petruchio and Claudio in *Much Ado about Nothing* look less like fortune hunters and more like prudent conservators of their familial legacy.

If the estate was extremely large, the father normally made financial arrangements for the daughters and younger sons; if it was extremely small, these younger children might be so disadvantaged that they would have to remain unmarried. For younger sons in particular, this was considered a reasonable option, for they could find ways of supporting themselves — by teaching, taking religious orders, or even going to sea. Daughters, though, could serve as a serious drain on a family's estate. The father would need to provide a dowry for each in order to get them married and out of his house, and women lacked the alternatives to marriage that young men had. Although daughters could be costly to provide for, an heiress could improve a family's fortune by attracting the son of a prominent landed family. This system of financial reciprocity meant that the upper classes tended to marry at a younger age than the middle and lower classes because the size of the estates involved was a primary consideration. Marriages might be arranged even in the infancy of the couple concerned and confirmed when the prospective bride and groom reached puberty. Our nearest contact with this system is the complex set of negotiations that still attend the wedding of a member of the royal family in Britain or Japan. Practically speaking, ending a marriage through divorce was not an option in the early modern period, although on those rare occasions when it did occur (for reasons of sexual impotence, for instance), great care was taken about the financial consequences.

These arrangements applied to the wealthiest and most prominent members of society, but the middle and even the lower classes, insofar as they could, emulated these contractual practices in order to protect their offspring and guarantee financial stability. Parents had authority over their children in matters of marriage, certainly until the young person reached adulthood and, in some cases, as long as the parents lived. The dowry system required that a young man or woman receive parental approval, and sometimes even then the marriage could not go forward until certain obstacles were removed: property might need to be sold or cash might need to be raised, a process that could take some time; a suitable house might have to be found for the couple; a groom might have to wait until the end of his apprenticeship. Conversely, a match proposed by parents might have to wait until the couple themselves could be made to agree to it. A Shakespearean version of this scenario is Capulet's trouble with his recalcitrant teenage daughter in the fourth act of *Romeo and Juliet*.

The primacy of money in the matrimonial process raises the question of attraction or "love." Although the emotions of the young couple were not the main consideration in courtship, they were not utterly irrelevant, and the evidence suggests that then, as now, parents wanted to accommodate a child's desires while doing what they thought best for the child's future happiness. The passage from George Whetstone's *Heptameron of Civil Discourses* (p. 292) indicates an awareness of the value of free choice. At the risk of overgeneralizing, we can say that the more money was at stake, the less personal affection counted in the business of courtship. Shakespeare's comedies often turn on the question of who will decide on a suitable marriage partner. In *A Midsummer Night's Dream*, when Egeus insists on his power to select his daughter's mate — "she is mine, and all my right of her / I do estate unto Demetrius" (1.1.97–98) — his diction, particularly the possessive pronouns and the verb *estate*, indicates the importance of property and his conception of his daughter as a possession. In *Much Ado about Nothing,* the young woman named Hero is an heiress who is a most eligible marriage partner, and when it appears that Don Pedro ("the Prince") will ask for her hand, her father appears ready to give her a choice: "I will acquaint my daughter withal, that she may be the better prepar'd for an answer" (1.2.21–22). It may be, however, that he is merely engaging in a formality, that he will instruct her to be prepared to accept. Two scenes later her cousin Beatrice exposes the potential conflict of will:

> ANTONIO [*to Hero*]: Well, niece, I trust you will be rul'd by your father.
> BEATRICE: Yes, faith, it is my cousin's duty to make cur'sy and say, "Father, as it please you." But yet for all that, cousin, let him be a handsome fellow, or else make another cur'sy and say, "Father, as it please me." (2.1.50–56)

In fact, Don Pedro acts as a go-between and asks for Hero's hand on behalf of Claudio, whose social rank (Count) satisfies her father and whose appearance satisfies her. Like most writers of comedy, Shakespeare usually sympathizes with the daughter. But in reality, as opposed to the reality portrayed on stage, the clash between a parent's wishes and those of a son or daughter was usually decided in favor of the parent.

Where huge fortunes were not in the balance — that is, among the vast majority of young people in England — personal autonomy carried greater weight. Other considerations increased in importance, matters such as age, companionship, emotional sympathy, and sexual attraction. Also, there was apparently more time for choice. While among the upper classes the need to make financial arrangements as early as possible meant that they tended to marry their children in their teens, many English people waited until their midtwenties to marry. There are several reasons for this delay. In the early modern period, owing mainly to nutrition, children reached puberty somewhat later than they do now, perhaps a year or maybe even two or three years later, and this fact may have postponed slightly the physical urge to mate. But, as usual, the main causes were financial. A young man without family resources had to work for some time to afford the cost of marriage, which consisted at least of a dwelling for him and his bride and the establishment of a steady income to support her and the children who would follow. The effect of these circumstances was that most people put off getting married: in England in the sixteenth century, the average age for marriage was twenty-seven for men and twenty-four for women (see Laslett). In *Romeo and Juliet,* Shakespeare deliberately takes years off the age of the heroine in the sources (in one source she is seventeen, in another fifteen) for a variety of theatrical reasons, chiefly to magnify the drama of Juliet's progress from innocence to lovestruck girlhood to marriage to courageous suicide. But Romeo and Juliet should not be taken as typical candidates for marriage in sixteenth-century England. Although Shakespeare himself was eighteen on his wedding day, his wife was about twenty-six, and their surviving children, Susanna and Judith, did not marry until they were twenty-four and thirty-one.

Family Life

Most people got married, and most people had children, but family life in the Renaissance was different from our experience. Juliet's nurse, in her conversation with Juliet and Lady Capulet, offers a glimpse of one of the principal differences:

> But as I said,
> On Lammas-eve at night shall she be fourteen,
> That shall she, marry, I remember it well.
> 'Tis since the earthquake now aleven years,
> And she was wean'd — I never shall forget it —
> Of all the days of the year, upon that day;
> For I had then laid wormwood to my dug,
> Sitting in the sun under the dove-house wall.
> My lord and you were then at Mantua —
> Nay, I do bear a brain — but as I said,
> When it did taste the wormwood on the nipple
> Of my dug and felt it bitter, pretty fool,
> To see it teachy and fall out wi' th' dug!   (1.3.20–32)

This character is called Nurse because she nursed Juliet as an infant, and here she describes how she weaned the toddler from her breast milk by applying a bitter substance to her nipple. Although *Romeo and Juliet* is set in Italy in an unspecified century, this scene at least reflects conventional practice in sixteenth-century England: most well-to-do mothers did not nurse their babies, but instead turned them over to a wet nurse who suckled them after having weaned her own children. Although resistance to the practice began to manifest itself in the medical discourse of the late sixteenth century, wet nursing was still the rule for those who could afford it. Even the countess of Lincoln, whose treatise on the necessity of a mother's suckling her own children is excerpted on page 293, confesses at the end of her argument that as a young mother she herself was misled into employing a wet nurse, and she cautions other women against the practice.

Juliet's Nurse apparently lives in the Capulet household, but most English parents who could afford to do so gave up the child into the keeping and the household of the nurse, visiting it from time to time and then receiving it again into their home when the child was weaned. The choice of a proper nurse was important, as Gail Kern Paster, the most recent authority on the topic, points out.

> In hiring her services, parents leased exclusive rights to her lactating breasts and their milk. During the period of hire, the wet nurse was expected not to suckle another child and to maintain an adequate supply of milk. She was expected not to menstruate, not to become pregnant, and if she did, to notify her nurse-child's parents.   (199)

Paster goes on to add that "nurses' moral and ethical qualities mattered since these were believed to be transmitted through the milk" (200). Naturally these expectations put the nurse in an ambiguous position. Some nurses violated these strictures by nursing more than one child; likewise, some fathers disposed of a bastard child by giving it to a careless, overworked wet nurse who could be counted on to neglect it (Dolan 124–25). In other words, the marginality of the nurse's position could lead to exploitation, chicanery, and suspicion, especially given the cultural anxieties attending such matters as legitimacy and lineage. Contemporary records disclose accusations of baby switching, accidental and deliberate, and even of infanticide. To us the idea of wet nursing may seem heartless and even barbaric, but it continued in Britain until well into the nineteenth century.

Similarly alien to most of us is the practice of sending one's children away for education or apprenticeship. The most prominent members of the nobility engaged live-in tutors for their children as a substitute for formal schooling. Some villages had grammar schools for the sons of prosperous citizens, and some educated women ran *dame schools*, the equivalent of the modern preschool, in which a few very young local boys and girls were taught to read and write. But many parents who could afford to do so sent their sons away for education. Sons and daughters of the nobility and gentry were often placed in the houses of other aristocrats to serve as companions. In *Twelfth Night*, Olivia's lady-in-waiting, Maria, may represent such a practice, as may Beatrice in *Much Ado about Nothing*, who is Hero's cousin and who seems to be parentless. Less prosperous or prominent families often put their children in service or apprenticed the boys to artisans or tradesmen who taught them a skill.

Such patterns meant that many children actually lived with their parents for a relatively short period of time: in the case of wealthy children, from the time they returned from the wet nurse until they went away to school. Most children seem to have left home by their early teens, as apprenticeship or training for domestic service began around age fourteen. Evidence of these practices has led some historians to conclude that early modern family relations were characterized by a lack of affection, that mothers and fathers did not bind themselves emotionally to their children in the way that modern parents do. Childhood was brief — so the argument goes — and infant mortality high, so people sought to protect themselves from separation by means of emotional distance (Stone, *Family* 5). But such conclusions have recently been vigorously challenged. There is no question that the structure of the family was different from its modern counterpart, that the emphasis on parents and children bound closely into a separate unit did not fully develop until the eighteenth and nineteenth centuries. But ample evidence exists of parental attachment to children, such factors as wet nursing and early apprenticeship notwithstanding. For an especially poignant example, see Ben Jonson's poem "On My First Son," page 295.

One distinguishing trait of the early modern family was a relative absence of privacy in virtually all classes of society. Among the poor and the small property owners, interior space was at a minimum, and even large families lived in houses with a few rooms that were shared by all. The notion of a private chamber for each person is a much later development; in the Renaissance, it was not uncommon for all members of an immediate family to sleep in the same room, and for several children to occupy the same bed. In such circumstances, activities like sexual intercourse and relieving oneself in the chamber pot were performed with a minimum of privacy and perhaps none at all. At inns and other such public accommodations, travelers routinely shared beds with strangers, as the passage from a French manual on manners indicates (see p. 295). Enforced intimacy among family members was one of the factors that influenced early modern notions of community, and it is not too much to suggest that this absence of privacy helped to delay the emergence of "the individual" as a psychological category. Parents, siblings, other relatives, and even near neighbors were much more closely involved in one another's daily lives than is customary in our experience. Among the wealthy, too, the presence of servants diminished privacy, and personal servants often lived in virtually the same room as their masters. Finally, the architecture of large houses at the time — rooms connected to rooms rather than to a central corridor, making it necessary to go through others' rooms as one moved through the house — meant that the sense of personal space and separation from others was at a minimum. Adjustments were made to modify such openness, such as the use of curtained beds, but the notion of the personal and the private is largely a post-Enlightenment phenomenon.

The Renaissance offers exceptions to this paradigm of family life, the Virgin Queen being the most famous, but generally speaking the ideology of the family was inescapable. Elizabeth (at least publicly) considered herself married to her people, the head of a vast national family. Some people did not marry, such as younger sons who perhaps could not afford to set up housekeeping or daughters who found themselves without a dowry and thus unable to attract a suitor. But such nonparticipation in the experience of family life was considered not so much a choice as a misfortune. The practice of arranged marriage, especially in the upper classes, led some people (both male and female) to seek physical pleasure outside matrimony. During his marriage to Catherine of Aragon, Henry VIII had an illegitimate son, Henry Fitzroy, whom the king acknowledged and arranged to have reared on the margins of the court. The innumerable jokes about cuckolds in Renaissance dramatic texts, combined with the sermonizing against adultery, suggest that marital infidelity was a familiar and troublesome social problem.

Nor is sexual activity before marriage a twentieth-century invention. Even though adolescents reached puberty later than they do now, the relatively late age for getting married meant that young people's sexual urges had to be either postponed or satisfied illicitly. In some parts of the culture, especially among the rural poor, sexual intercourse for a betrothed couple and even their cohabitation were quietly tolerated. The Church of England recognized the validity of several kinds of "irregular" marriages. A couple who promised before witnesses to marry each other in the future and who then consummated the agreement sexually were considered legally wed, whether or not a church ceremony ever took place. This was called a marriage contract *per verba de futuro*. Likewise, a couple who declared to each other before witnesses a phrase such as "I hereby take you as my husband/wife" were considered married; their words constituted the contract. This was called a marriage contract *per verba de praesenti*. Such agreements, known variously as *spousals, handfasts,* and *precontracts,* play a minor role in many of Shakespeare's plays. In *Twelfth Night,* Olivia calls Sebastian her "husband" on the basis of a verbal agreement in the presence of a priest, but before a religious or legal ceremony has taken place. Spousals play a major role in *Measure for Measure,* where the making and breaking of marriage contracts is a source of conflict among four of the major and two of the minor characters. Of the randy Lucio, we learn that "Mistress Kate Keepdown was with child by him in the Duke's time; he promis'd her marriage. His child is a year and a quarter old . . ." (3.2.198–201).

Ecclesiastical regulations were frequently incompatible with civil law, which required a church ceremony, and the intricacy and variety of these matrimonial arrangements attest to the difficulty of aligning the legal system and the human heart, not to mention the libido. Questions of property and paternity attendant on these marriages were tried mostly in the ecclesiastical courts or, as they were more familiarly known for obvious reasons, the "bawdy courts," and they offer some helpful evidence on sexual mores in the period. But these records and the statistics they supply reflect only a fraction of the actual practice. We know that between 1550 and 1600 more than one in five brides — including Shakespeare's wife — were pregnant at the altar, that the actual ratio was almost certainly even higher, and that the frequency of premarital sexual activity was much higher than that (Stone, *Family* 610).

What about homosexuality in the Renaissance? This is a complex topic, embracing everything from King James's private affections to early modern medical theory to Shakespeare's sonnets. But recent critical studies of homosexuality have helped to shed some light on an issue that has often been misunderstood, repressed, or delicately ignored. One result of these recent investigations has been the recognition that "the homosexual" as a human category is fairly recent, and that the term *homosexuality* did not come into currency until the nineteenth century. As Bruce Smith, the author of the best book on this topic, notes, "No one in England during the sixteenth and seventeenth centuries would have thought of himself as 'gay' or 'homosexual' for the simple reason that those categories of self-definition did not exist" (11–12). The absence of a category or label does not imply, of course, that people did not engage in sexual activity with members of their own sex until the reign of Queen Victoria. From the beginnings of recorded time, from Sodom to Lesbos to Athens, men and women have done so. But ways of thinking about such sexual behavior have changed. Legally and religiously, homosexual acts were forbidden in Renaissance England (see the excerpt from Sir Edward Coke's *Institutes,* p. 296). But the language used to describe them — *buggery* and *sodomy* — was vague and also covered bestiality, child molestation, and certain heterosexual acts considered improper. It seems clear that homosexual acts were widely practiced in Renaissance England and that the legal penalty of death was exacted only in extreme cases, such as the rape of a child.

When homosexual desires and acts were discussed, they were condemned, notably by Puritan divines and writers, as part of the general depravity to which man's carnal nature was vulnerable. Mostly, however, they were not discussed. Still, it is clear that men had erotic feelings for other men and sometimes acted on them, and one of the primary sources for such information is the imaginative literature of the period. (See the excerpt from Richard Barnfield's *The Tears of an Affectionate Shepherd* on p. 298.) Even less is known about lesbian desire in the early modern period: it is not even acknowledged in most legal writing on sexual offenses, and since most imaginative literature was written by men, the subject is rarely addressed. Recently, however, Valerie Traub and a few other scholars have begun to investigate the homosocial and potential sexual implications of female friendship.

In poetry and drama, male homosexual behavior was associated with the ancient tradition of friendship, which the Renaissance valued and which finds eloquent expression in Michel de Montaigne's essay "On Friendship." Military or naval service often generated a sense of comradeship that represents one aspect of this tradition: we might recall the devotion of the seafaring Antonio to the handsome young Sebastian in *Twelfth Night*. To many writers in Renaissance Europe, such affections appear to have been less culturally threatening than a corresponding obsession with women, a pursuit believed to make effeminate the men who fell victim to it. As for homosexual acts, the tension between prohibition and practice is puzzling. Again Bruce Smith is helpful:

> The one salient fact about homosexuality in early modern England, as in early modern Europe generally, is the disparity that separates the extreme punishments described by law and the apparent tolerance, even positive valuation, of homoerotic desire in the visual arts, in literature, and, . . . , in the political power structure. What are we to make of a culture that could consume popular prints of Apollo embracing Hyacinth and yet could order hanging for men who acted on the very feelings that inspire that embrace? (13–14)

Christopher Marlowe's *Edward II* depicts in its protagonist a king who suffers an amorous obsession for a beautiful young man. A significant number of Shakespeare's sonnets are erotically charged with homosexual passion. But there is little profit in asking whether Shakespeare or Marlowe was "a homosexual." The point is that writers, like other people, did not define themselves in such terms.

The Social Structure

Even today commentators insist that to understand twenty-first-century England it is necessary to admit the pervasiveness and depth of the class system, and the hierarchies that influence social practice in our time are a legacy of the distinct levels of status that obtained in the sixteenth and seventeenth centuries. Discrete and workable categories for the different groups that populated early modern England are difficult to establish, however. Lawrence Stone describes the problem as follows:

> If the historian is to reduce his evidence to intelligible order he is obliged to use abstract concepts and collective nouns. In discussing society he deals in groups labelled peasants, yeomen, gentry and aristocracy; or tenants and landlords, wage-labourers and capitalists; or lower class, middle class and upper class; or Court and Country; or bourgeois and feudal. Some of these categories, like titular aristocracy, are status groups; some, like capitalists, are economic classes with similar incomes derived from similar sources; some, like "Court," describe groups whose income, interests and geographical location are all temporarily based on a single institution. Every individual can be classified in many different ways, and the problem of how to choose the most meaningful categories is particularly difficult when dealing with mobile societies like that of seventeenth-century England.   (*Causes* 33)

These subtleties notwithstanding, it is true that in the sixteenth and seventeenth centuries a man or woman was born into a family that inhabited one of several levels of society, and that people did not easily move from one class to another.

For purposes of outlining the social system in Shakespeare's England, we may divide the population into the following groups. Aristocracy: persons of noble birth who possessed large estates in the country but who also often took their place in London at court or in Parliament. Gentry, sometimes known as minor gentry: descendants of the aristocracy whose holdings were smaller but who still possessed considerable wealth, as well as persons who through commercial enterprise (such as ownership of a monopoly) had managed to amass property and prestige and thus were entitled to be called gentlemen. Citizens: mostly urban tradesmen or shopkeepers, who either made products for public consumption or sold them, e.g., leather goods, books, cloth, dairy products, wheels for carriages, and the like (this group would probably also include innkeepers). Yeomen: the rural equivalent of citizens, who owned (or in some cases had the use of) agricultural or grazing lands from which they made more than a subsistence wage — sometimes even handsome profits. Servants, laborers, or peasants: persons who owned little but made their living working for others, either on farms or in households (those who lived in the city tended to be better off financially than their rural counterparts). The indigent: beggars and others who, from geographical or social circumstances, injury, or personal temperament, found themselves unable to work. As the historian's reservations suggest, these groupings are inadequate. Where do we put lawyers, for example? A small professional class was emerging, but by 1600 it was not large enough to be reckoned significant. How to classify prostitutes? Or sailors? Or criminals? Finally, there were small, marginal categories such as "masterless men" or vagrants, some of them ex-soldiers, who moved from place to place picking up work as they could, stealing, or preying on the gullible. Among those who defied easy categorization, actors — "players" — were foremost. In fact, their dubious position necessitated that they put themselves under the nominal protection of an aristocratic patron.

Social conditioning tended to keep people in their places, and one aspect of the patriarchy that reinforced class boundaries was the paternalistic treatment of the lower classes by the upper. Theoretically, aristocrats took it as their duty to behave charitably and humanely toward those considered their social inferiors. As Derek Hirst has pointed out, most people did not seem to object to the class system per se, but rather to the injustices that it could breed. Even in food riots that occurred in the late sixteenth and early seventeenth centuries, the participants complained not so much about the wealth of their neighbors as about such abuses as grain hoarding or price gouging, about, in other words, the attempt to take unfair advantage (51). But social ordering was not merely traditional and psychological: laws existed to enforce social order, as a glance at royal proclamations from any five-year period between 1540 and 1640 will reveal (see pp. 299 and 301). Of such strictures, the sumptuary laws described in Chapter 7 are perhaps the most fascinating. In theory, a person's clothing revealed at a glance the social class to which he or she belonged: for example, only countesses and ladies above that rank could wear purple silk. But the regulatory statutes were frequently broken. Finally, the lack of easy geographical mobility helped to keep the population in place literally, for one could not simply decide to move from one part of the country to the other. An exception to this rule was London, which attracted a large number of industrious people hoping to make their fortunes, including William Shakespeare himself.

It is not surprising that the class system, despite its long history and the conditioning that helped to enforce it, was the source of tension and resentment. From the royal court to the alehouse, people objected to the behavior of others on grounds of status: either the adversary was called unworthy of the class represented, or the plaintiff thought himself equally important. Because, practically speaking, people were most immediately affected by local government, they had fairly direct means of redress against perceived injustices, and object they did. The records of local courts teem with complaints against others for what amount to violations of the social order. Public drunkenness, abusing the right to public land, quarreling, disputes about preferential seating in church — many of these common complaints involve issues of status and importance in the community, and the rhetoric in which these complaints were recorded attests to a colorful repertoire of class-based insults. "Henry Weavers claimed superiority when he told Mr. Miles Lynn, a parson, in 1613, that 'I am a better man than thou art, knave parson, a turd in thy teeth'" (qtd. in Amussen 212). Such class-connected language provides a useful context for Kent's contemptuous speech to Oswald in the second act of *King Lear*.

How fixed were these social structures? It is difficult to give an all-purpose answer, but to some extent the boundaries between classes became more permeable as the sixteenth century passed into the seventeenth. Apprenticeship was one means of social and economic ascent. A bright and industrious young man from a poor family or the younger son of a gentleman could apprentice himself to a craftsman and eventually set himself up in that trade. If the master had no children, the young man might inherit the business. The increasing availability of education also made for social and economic mobility. Once again the cardinal example is William Shakespeare, who parlayed his grammar school education into a career in the theater, a coat of arms for his family, and substantial real estate holdings in the town of his birth. For women the opportunities for social advancement were more limited, although some women were occasionally apprenticed in what were considered appropriate trades. In the city, where social lines were quicker to disintegrate, young women from humble backgrounds were able to better themselves economically (although less often socially) through advantageous marriages. Movement up the social and economic scale was not easy, but the history of the Tudor and Stuart period indicates that changes were occurring at large. As the yeomanry grew in number, as merchants began to exploit the possibilities of consumption, as the aristocracy began to lose its grip on real estate and similar financial resources, and as the population continued to increase, the rigid social boundaries were put under pressure and the familiar lines began to blur. The old feudal order that had dominated England until the end of the fifteenth century was gradually being supplanted by an early capitalist system that depended more heavily on individual ownership and allowed greater mobility largely on the basis of financial success.

Economically, England was heterogeneous. Racially, it was not. In the Middle Ages the Celtic tribes that had originally populated the island intermarried with the Europeans who immigrated there, beginning with the Romans and then with the Saxons and Scandinavians. The Norman Conquest of 1066 produced an influx of the French, who were eventually assimilated. The English nation in the sixteenth and seventeenth centuries, therefore, was largely made up of the descendants of Northern Europeans. Representatives of other races and nations were comparatively rare. The island's geographical isolation created a cultural insularity, and even xenophobia, unique in Europe. The Spanish and Portuguese had had commerce of various kinds with the African continent for hundreds of years, England for less than a century. Jews had been cast out of England in 1290, and while some Jews did manage to live and work in Shakespeare's London — the law was inconsistently enforced — the prohibition was not lifted until 1655, at the instigation of Oliver Cromwell. Londoners (although probably not their country cousins) were occasionally exposed to visiting Africans and American natives. Their status as objects of curiosity is implicit in Trinculo's joke, in *The Tempest*, about what the English will pay to see "a dead Indian" (2.2.31–33). That foreigners were so regarded is indicative of the racial homogeneity of the culture as well as of the cultural anxieties strangers tended to generate. The reality of this prejudice appears in an edict issued by Elizabeth I in 1601, in which she is said "to be highly discontented to understand the great number of Negroes and blackamoors which (as she is informed) are carried into this realm . . ." and "hath given a special commandment that the said kind of people shall be with all speed avoided [expelled] and discharged out of this her majesty's realms" ("Licensing Casper van Senden," qtd. in Hughes and Larkin 3:221). (See the similar edict issued in July 1596, p. 302).

Shakespeare plays upon these anxieties in his depiction of such characters as Shylock the Jewish moneylender in *The Merchant of Venice*, Aaron the Moor in *Titus Andronicus*, and, most memorably, Othello. Other characters throughout the canon are described as "dark" or "tawny," but the terms probably refer to hair color and relatively dark Caucasian complexions rather than to African skin tones. The Dark Lady of the sonnets is usually thought to fall into this category, although Jonathan Crewe has wondered how our perceptions of Shakespeare might be changed if "instead of always genteelly speaking of Shakespeare's Dark Lady sonnets, we could bring ourselves to call them the Black Woman sonnets" (120). Was Shakespeare himself a racist? Strictly speaking, almost certainly. The culture that produced him had little acquaintance with and little sympathy for what modern cultural theorists have come to call the Other. And yet some of these theatrical representatives of Otherness, particularly Shylock and Othello, are portrayed with a high degree of sympathy. It appears that Shakespeare took theatrical advantage of his audience's cultural racism by presenting exotic figures who can behave barbarously and yet who command respect and sympathy, figures who, as Shylock points out, bleed when pricked and laugh when tickled.

Conclusion: The Body Politic

In the opening scene of *Coriolanus*, the aged and sage Menenius, a patrician member of the Roman establishment, gives an impromptu lecture, "The Fable of the Belly," to a group of hungry and rebellious plebeians in which he symbolically represents the proper functioning of society. The sources of the fable (in Plutarch and Sir Philip Sidney) would have been familiar to the educated auditors around 1607, and the rhetoric would have been familiar to all. The analogy between a well-ordered society and a healthy body was a commonplace in English social and political thought. The playwright's retelling of "The Fable of the Belly" represents a sophisticated and ambiguous move because one finds it difficult to decide whether Shakespeare is mocking or approving the old Roman's moral story about social order. And this difficulty is itself salutary in helping us to think about Shakespeare's ambiguous representation of the social, familial, and political structures that have served as the focus of this chapter. Clearly Shakespeare was no revolutionary. Far from challenging the systems with which he grew up, he exploited them, perhaps even reinforced them, for his own professional advantage. And yet neither was he a blind reactionary. Capable of seeing through the "robes and furred gowns" that King Lear deplores, those rich conventions that conceal inequity and corruption, Shakespeare asked his audience to think critically about the fundamental arbitrariness of the English — indeed, of any — social system. His questions are still relevant.

→ ARISTOTLE

From *Historia Animalium*

fourth century B.C.
Translated by Richard Cresswell

Although Aristotle's work was not as well known in early modern England as it is now, his thought had filtered into the culture through the writings of other ancient writers who had depended on his philosophical and scientific treatises. This passage, distinguishing between male and female characteristics in the animal kingdom, represents the ancient system of hierarchies on which Renaissance thinkers drew.

And in all animals in which there is a distinction of the sexes nature has given a similar disposition to the males and to the females. This is most conspicuous in man, and the larger animals, and in viviparous quadrupeds; for the disposition of the female is softer, and more tameable and submissive, and more ingenious; as the females of the Lacedemonian dog are more gentle than the males. . . .

The females of all animals are less violent in their passions than the males, except the female bear and pardalis [panther], for the female of these appears more courageous than the male. In other animals the females are more soft and insidious, less simple, more petulant, and more active in the care of their young. The disposition of the males is opposed to this; for they are more passionate and fierce, more straightforward, and less invidious. The vestiges of these dispositions exist, as we may say, in all, but are more conspicuous in those which have the strongest moral habits, and most of all in mankind; for the nature of the human subject is the most complete, so that these habits appear more conspicuous in mankind than in other animals.

Wherefore women are more compassionate and more readily made to weep, more jealous and querulous, more fond of railing, and more contentious. The female also is more subject to depression of spirits and despair than the male. She is also more shameless and false, more readily deceived, and more mindful of injury, more watchful, more idle, and on the whole less excitable than the male. On the contrary, the male is more ready to help, and, as it has been said, more brave than the female; and . . . if the sepia [cuttlefish] is struck with a trident, the male comes to help the female, but the female makes her escape if the male is struck.

→ **WILLIAM VAUGHAN**

From *Natural and Artificial Directions for Health*   *1600*

William Vaughan, described on the title page of his book as "Master of Arts and Student in the Civil Law," explains the doctrine of the humours in a question-and-answer format. The subtitle of the work, "Derived from the best philosophers, as well modern as ancient," gestures at the roots of the humoural theory in the medical works of Galen, the celebrated ancient Greek physician.

CHAPTER 2. OF THE FOUR HUMOURS

What is an humour?   An humour is a moist and running body, into which the meat in the liver is converted, to the end that our bodies might be nourished by them.

What is the nature of the sanguine humour?   The sanguine humour is hot, moist, fatty, sweet, and seated in the liver because it watereth all the body and giveth nourishment unto it; out of which likewise issue the vital spirits, like unto small and gentle winds that arise out of rivers and wells.

What is the phlegmatic humour?   The phlegmatic humour is of color white, brackish like unto sweat, and properly placed in the kidneys, which draw to themselves the water from the blood, thereby filling the veins instead of [i.e., with] good and pure blood.

What is the choleric?   The choleric humour is hot and fiery, bitter, and like unto the flower of wine [scum formed in fermentation]. It serveth not only to clean the guts of filth, but also to make the liver hot and to hinder the blood from putrefaction.

What is the melancholic humour?   The melancholic humour is black, earthly, resembling the lees of blood, and hath the spleen for a seat assigned unto it. Howbeit physicians say that there be three kinds of melancholy. The first proceedeth from the annoyed brain; the second cometh whenas the whole constitution of the body is melancholic; the third springeth from the bowels, but chiefly from the spleen and liver.

→ **LADY ANNE SOUTHWELL**

Letter on Poetry   *1627*

The following letter by Lady Anne Southwell (1574–1636) to her friend Cicely MacWilliams, Lady Ridgeway, provides a glimpse into the private literary culture in which many women participated during the Tudor and Stuart periods. Particularly interesting is Southwell's desire to situate poetic expression in the context of God's creation of the elements and humours.

How falls it out (noble lady) that you are become a sworn enemy to poetry? It being so abstruse an art as it is that I may say the other arts are but bases and pedestals, unto the which this is the capital; the mere [complete] herald of all ideas; the world's true vocal harmony, of which all other arts are but parts. Or rather, may I justly say, it is the silk thread that strings your chain of pearl which, being broken, your jewels fall into the rushes [floor coverings], and the more you seek for it, the more it falls into the dust of oblivion. You say you affect prose, as your ancestors did. Error is not to be affected for antiquity.[1] Therefore (noble and witty lady) give me your hand: I will lead you up the stream of all mankind. Your great-great-grandfather had a father, and so the last, or rather the first father, was God, whose never-enough-to-be-admired creation was poetically confined to four general genuses: earth, air, water, and fire. The effects which give life unto his verse were hot, cold, moist, and dry, which produce choler, melancholy, blood, and phlegm. By these just proportions, all things are propagated. Now being thus poetically composed, how can you be at unity with your self and at odds with your own composition?

It may be, you will say, that poesy is a fiction, and fiction is a lie. O but Rahab's concealing the spies was more to be approved than Doeg's truth.[2] But herein, poesy seems to do more for nature than she is able to do for her self, wherein it doth but lay down a pattern what man should be, and shows that imagination goes before reality. But he is not worthy the name of a physician but of an empiric [i.e., a mere pharmacist] only, that gives one potion to all manner of diseases. For it is as great an error to give purges to one in a consumption as it is to give cordials to one in a repletion [state of being fed to excess]. Therefore it is necessary to know how the humour abounds, that so we may the boldlier apply. Then, since all are either fools or physicians, to escape the former I will take upon me to know what hath so distasted your palate against this banquet of souls, divine poesy.

Some wanton Venus or Adonis hath been cast before your chaste ears, whose evil attire, disgracing this beautiful nymph, hath unworthied her in your opinion.[3] And will you, because you see a man mad, wish yourself without melancholy, which humour is the hand of all the soul's faculties? All exorbitant things [i.e., things out of their orbit] are monstrous, but bring them again to their orbicular form and motion and they will retain their former beauties. Our reason ought to be the stickler in this case: who would not scornfully laugh with Micholl, to see the old prophet dance?[4] But when we know he danced before the ark, must we not think the host of heaven was in exultation with him, as well as that of Jerusalem? To hear a Hero and Leander or some such other busy nothing might be a means to scandalize this art. But

---

[1] I.e., the antiquity or familiarity of a practice doesn't justify our continuation in error.
[2] Old Testament examples of Rahab's clever falsehood (Joshua 2 and 6) and Doeg's foolish truth-telling (1 Samuel 21:7–9).
[3] Here, as with the reference to Marlowe's *Hero and Leander* below, Southwell seems to disapprove of Elizabethan erotic narratives.
[4] "Micholl" (Michal), the daughter of Saul and wife of David, mocked the latter's ecstatic dancing before God (2 Samuel 6:16ff).

can a cloud disgrace the sun? Will you behold poesy in perfect beauty? Then see the kingly prophet, that sweet singer of Israel [King David], explicating the glory of our god, his power in creating, his mercy in redeeming, his wisdom in preserving, making these three as it were the comma, colon, and period to every stanza. Who would not say the musical spheres did yield a cadency to his song, and in admiration cry out, "O never-enough-to-be-admired divine poesy"? It is the subject that commends or condemns the art. But noble lady, I will trouble you no further now, yet when I have your honorable word of reconciliation, I will then delineate out every limb of her and how she is enveloped up with the rest of the arts. In the mean time I rest more than thankful for your noble loving letter, as the lover of your virtues.

→ AEMILIA LANYER

From *Salve Deus Rex Judaeorum*   *1611*

Lanyer's poem ("Hail, God, King of the Jews") is an original mix of devotional meditation, Passion narrative, biblical hermeneutics, and feminist apologia. The passage below is her defense of Eve and of women in general, an argument spoken by the wife of Pontius Pilate, the judge who authorized the crucifixion of Jesus.

Till now your indiscretion sets us free,
And makes our former fault much less appear;[1]
Our Mother *Eve,* who tasted of the Tree,
Giving to *Adam* what she held most dear,
Was simply good, and had no power to see,   765
The after-coming harm did not appear:
    The subtle serpent that our sex betrayed,
    Before our fall so sure a plot had laid.

That undiscerning Ignorance perceived
No guile or craft that was by him [the serpent] intended;   770
For had she known of what we were bereaved,
To his request she had not condescended.
But she (poor soul) by cunning was deceived,
No hurt therein her harmless heart intended.
    For she alleged [answered with] God's word, which he denies,   775
    That they should die, but even as gods, be wise.

But surely *Adam* cannot be excused;
Her fault, though great, yet he was most to blame;
What weakness [i.e., Eve] offered, strength [Adam] might have refused,
Being Lord of all, the greater was his shame: 780

[1] Having condemned Jesus, you men, in your poor judgment, diminish the significance of Eve's fault of having yielded to the serpent.

Although the serpent's craft had her abused,
God's holy word ought all his actions frame,
    For he was lord and king of all the earth,
    Before poor *Eve* had either life or breath.

Who being framed by God's eternal hand, 785
The perfect'st man that ever breathed on earth,
And from God's mouth received that strait [strict] command,
The breach whereof he knew was present death:
Yea, having power to rule both sea and land,
Yet with one apple won to lose that breath 790
    Which God had breathèd in his beauteous face,
    Bringing us all in danger and disgrace.

And then to lay the fault on Patience [Eve, and all women] back,
That we (poor women) must endure it all;
We know right well he did discretion [good judgment] lack, 795
Being not persuaded thereunto at all;
If *Eve* did err, it was for knowledge sake,
The fruit being fair persuaded him to fall:
    No subtle serpent's falsehood did betray him;
    If he would eat it, who had power to stay him? 800

Not *Eve*, whose fault was only too much love,
Which made her give this present to her dear,
That what she tasted, he likewise might prove,
Whereby his knowledge might become more clear;
He never sought her weakness to reprove 805
With those sharp words, which he of God did hear:
    Yet men will boast of knowledge, which he took
    From *Eve's* fair hand, as from a learnèd book.

If any evil did in her remain,
Being made of him, he was the ground of all; 810
If one of many worlds could lay a stain
Upon our sex, and work so great a fall
To wretched man, by Satan's subtle train [deception, traps],
What will so foul a fault amongst you all?
    Her weakness did the serpent's words obey, 815
    But you in malice God's dear son betray.

Whom, if unjustly you condemn to die,
Her sin was small to what you do commit;
All mortal sins that do for vengeance cry,
Are not to be comparèd unto it. 820
If many worlds would altogether try,
By all their sins the wrath of God to get,
    This sin of yours surmounts them all as far
    As doth the sun another little star.

Then let us have our liberty again,   825
And challenge [attribute] to yourselves no sov'reignty:
You came not in the world without our pain,
Make that a bar against your cruelty;
Your fault being greater, why should you disdain
Our being your equals, free from tyranny?   830
  If [i.e., Even if] one weak woman simply did offend,
  This sin of yours hath no excuse, nor end.

→ **SIR ROBERT FILMER**

From *Patriarcha, or The Natural Power of Kings*   *c. 1630*

Sir Robert Filmer's treatise, although written after Shakespeare's death and not published until even later in the seventeenth century, provides an exceptionally detailed statement of early modern orthodoxy concerning familial, social, and political organization. This passage insists on the biblical origins of the analogy between fathers and kings.

It may seem absurd to maintain that kings now are the fathers of their people, since experience shows the contrary. It is true, all kings be not the natural parents of their subjects, yet they all either are or are to be reputed the next heirs to those first progenitors who were at first the natural parents of the whole people, and in their right succeed to the exercise of supreme jurisdiction; and such heirs are not only lords of their own children but also of their brethren and all others that were subject to their fathers. And therefore we find that God told Cain of his brother Abel, "His desires shall be subject unto thee, and thou shalt rule over him." Accordingly, when Jacob bought his brother's birthright, Isaac blessed him thus, "Be lord over thy brethren, and let the sons of thy mother bow before thee."

As long as the first fathers of families lived, the name of Patriarchs did aptly belong unto them; but after a few descents, when the true fatherhood itself was extinct and only the right of the father descended to the true heir, then the title of prince or king was more significant to express the power of him who succeeds only to the right of that fatherhood which his ancestors did naturally enjoy. By this means it comes to pass that many a child, by succeeding a king, hath the right of a father over many a gray-headed multitude, and hath the title of *Pater Patriae* [father of the fatherland].

It may be demanded what becomes of the right of fatherhood, in case the crown does escheat for want of an heir [in case there is no apparent successor to the throne]? Whether doth it not then devolve to the people? The answer is, it is but the negligence or ignorance of the people to lose the knowledge of the true heir. For an heir there always is. If Adam himself were still living, and now ready to die, it is certain that there is One Man, and but one in the world, who is next heir, although the knowledge who should be that one One Man be quite lost.

This ignorance of the people being admitted, it doth not by any means follow that for want of heirs the supreme power is devolved to the multitude and that they have power to rule and choose what rulers they please. No, the kingly power escheats in such cases to the prime and independent heads of families. For every kingdom is resolved into those parts whereof at first it was made. By the uniting of great families or petty kingdoms, we find the greater monarchies were at the first erected, and into such again as into their first matter many times they return again. And because the dependency [sequence] of ancient families is oft obscure or worn out of knowledge, therefore the wisdom of all or most princes have thought fit to adopt many times those for heads of families and princes of provinces whose merits, abilities, or fortunes have ennobled them or made them fit and capable of such regal favors. All such prime heads and fathers have power to consent in the uniting or conferring of their fatherly right of sovereign authority on whom they please. And he that is so elected claims not his power as a donative [gift] from the people, but as being substituted properly by God, from whom he receives his royal charter of an universal father, though testified by the ministry of the heads of the people.

If it please God, for the correction of the prince or punishment of the people, to suffer princes to be removed and others to be placed in their rooms, either by the factions of the nobility or rebellion of the people, in all such cases the judgment of God, who hath power to give and take away kingdoms, is most just. Yet the ministry of men who execute God's judgments without commission is sinful and damnable. God doth but use and turn men's unrighteous acts to the performance of his righteous decrees.

In all kingdoms or commonwealths in the world, whether the prince be the supreme father of the people or but the true heir of such a father, or whether he come to the crown by usurpation or by election of the nobles or of the people or by any other way whatsoever, or whether some few or a multitude govern the commonwealth — yet still the authority that is in any one, or in many, or in all these, is the only right and natural authority of a supreme father. There is and always shall be continued to the end of the world a natural right of a supreme father over every multitude, although by the secret will of God many at first do most unjustly obtain the exercise of it.

To confirm this natural right of regal power, we find in the decalogue [the Ten Commandments] that the law which enjoins obedience to kings is delivered in the terms of "Honor thy father," as if all power were originally in the father. If obedience to parents be immediately due by a natural law, and subjection to princes but by the mediation of an human ordinance, what reason is there that the laws of nature should give place to the laws of men, as we see the power of the father over his child gives place and is subordinate to the power of the magistrate?

If we compare the natural rights of a father with those of a king, we find them all one, without any difference at all, but only in the latitude or extent of them. As the father over one family, so the king as father over many families extends his care to preserve, feed, clothe, instruct, and defend the whole commonwealth. His war, his peace, his courts of justice, and all his acts of sovereignty tend only to preserve and distribute to every subordinate and inferior father and to their children their rights and privileges, so that all the duties of a king are summed up in an universal fatherly care of his people.

→ From *An Homily of the State of Matrimony*   1563

This and other homilies, read from the pulpit during the Anglican Church service, were useful to Elizabeth's and James's government as instruments of political edification and social control. The *Homily of the State of Matrimony* constitutes the central Elizabethan statement on the duties of husbands and wives, the biblical mandate for these duties, and their implications for order in the state.

The word of almighty God doth testify and declare whence the original beginning of matrimony cometh and why it is ordained. It is instituted of God to the intent that man and woman should live lawfully in a perpetual friendly fellowship, to bring forth fruit, and to avoid fornication. By which means a good conscience might be preserved on both parties in bridling the corrupt inclinations of the flesh within the limits of honesty. For God hath straightly forbidden all whoredom and uncleanness and hath from time to time taken grievous punishments of [grievously punished] this inordinate lust, as all stories and ages hath declared. Furthermore, it is also ordained that the Church of God and his kingdom might by this kind of life be conserved and enlarged, not only in that God giveth children by his blessing, but also in that they be brought up by the parents godly in the knowledge of God's word, that this, the knowledge of God and true religion, might be delivered by succession from one to another, that finally many might enjoy that everlasting immortality.

Wherefore, forasmuch as matrimony serveth as well to avoid sin and offense as to increase the kingdom of God, you, as all other which enter that state, must acknowledge this benefit of God with pure and thankful minds, for that he hath so ruled your hearts that you follow not the example of the wicked world, who set their delight in filthiness of sin, where both of you stand in the fear of God and abhor all filthiness. For that is surely the singular gift of God, where the common example of the world declareth how the devil hath their hearts bound and entangled in divers snares so that they in their wiveless state run into open abominations without any grudge [remorse] of their conscience. Which sort of men that liveth so desperately and filthily, what damnation tarrieth for them? Saint Paul describeth it to them, saying: "Neither whoremongers, neither adulterers shall inherit the kingdom of God." This horrible judgment of God you be escaped through his mercy, if so be that you live inseparately [together] according to God's ordinance. But yet

I would not have you careless, without watching. For the devil will assay to attempt all things to interrupt and hinder your hearts and godly purpose, if you will give him any entry. For he will either labor to break this godly knot once begun betwixt you, or else at the least he will labor to encumber it with divers griefs and displeasures.

And this is his principal craft, to work dissension of hearts of the one from the other, that whereas now there is pleasant and sweet love betwixt you, [he] will in the stead thereof bring in most bitter and unpleasant discord. And surely that same adversary of ours doth, as it were from above, assault man's nature and condition. For this folly is ever from our tender age grown up with us, to have a desire to rule, to think highly by our self, so that none thinketh it meet to give place to another. That wicked vice of stubborn will and self-love is more meet to break and dissever the love of heart than to preserve concord. Wherefore married persons must apply their minds in most earnest wise to concord, and must crave continually of God the help of his holy spirit so to rule their hearts and to knit their minds together that they be not dissevered by any division of discord.

This necessity of prayer must be oft in the occupying and using of married persons, that oft time the one should pray for the other lest hate and debate do arise betwixt them. . . .

But to this prayer must be joined a singular diligence, whereof St. Peter giveth his precept, saying: "You husbands deal with your wives according to knowledge, giving honor to the wife, as unto the weaker vessel, and as unto them that are heirs also of the grace of life that your prayers be not hindered." This precept doth particularly pertain to the husband. For he ought to be the leader and author of love in cherishing and increasing concord, which then shall take place if he will use measurableness [temperance] and not tyranny, and if he yield some things to the woman. For the woman is a weak creature, not endued with like strength and constancy of mind. Therefore they be the sooner disquieted and they be the more prone to all weak affections and dispositions of mind more than men be, and lighter they be, and more vain in their fantasies and opinions. These things must be considered of the man, that he be not too stiff, so that he ought to wink at some things, and must gently expound all things, and to forbear. . . .

Now as concerning the wife's duty. What shall become her? Shall she abuse the gentleness and humanity of her husband and at her pleasure turn all things upside down? No surely, for that is far repugnant against God's commandment. For thus doth St. Peter preach to them: "You wives, be you in subjection to obey your own husband." To obey is another thing than to control or command, which yet they may do to their children and to their family. But as for their husbands, them must they obey and cease from commanding and perform subjection. For this surely doth nourish concord very much when the wife is ready at hand at her husband's commandment, when she will apply herself to his will, when she endeavoreth herself to seek his contentation [contentment] and to do him pleasure, when she will eschew all things that might offend him. For thus will most truly be verified the saying of the poet: "A good wife, by obeying her husband, shall bear the rule," so that he shall have a delight and a gladness the sooner at all times to return home to her. But on the contrary part, when the wives be stubborn, froward, and malapert [impudent], their husbands are compelled thereby to abhor and flee from their own houses, even as they should have battle with their enemies.

Howbeit, it can scantly [hardly] be but that some offenses shall sometime chance betwixt them, for no man doth live without fault, specially for that the woman is the more frail part. Therefore let them beware that they stand not in their faults and willfulness, but rather let them acknowledge their follies and say: "My husband, so it is that by my anger I was compelled to do this or that. Forgive it me, and hereafter I will take better heed." Thus ought women the more readily to do, the more they be ready to offend. And they shall not do this only to avoid strife and debate, but rather in the respect of the commandment of God as St. Paul expresseth it in this form of words: "Let women be subject to their husbands, as to the Lord; for the husband is the head of the woman, as Christ is the head of the Church." Here you understand that God hath commanded that ye should acknowledge the authority of the husband and refer to him the honor of obedience. And St. Peter saith in that same place afore rehearsed that "holy matrons did sometimes deck themselves, not with gold and silver, but in putting their whole hope in God" and in "obeying their husbands, as Sara obeyed Abraham, calling him Lord, whose daughters you be" (saith he) "if you follow her example." This sentence is very meet for women to print in their remembrance.

Truth it is, that they must specially feel the griefs and pains of their matrimony in that they relinquish the liberty of their own rule, in the pain of their travailing [labor of childbirth], in the bringing up of their children, in which offices they be in great perils and be grieved with great afflictions, which they might be without if they lived out of matrimony. But St. Peter saith that this is the chief ornament of holy matrons, in that they set their hope and trust in God, that is to say, in that they refused not from marriage for the business thereof, for the griefs and perils thereof, but committed all such adventures to God in most sure trust of help, after that they have called upon his aid. O woman, do thou the like, and so shalt thou be most excellently beautified before God and all his angels and saints, and thou needest not to seek further for doing any better works. For, obey thy husband, take regard of his requests, and give heed unto him to perceive what he requireth of thee, and so shalt thou honor God, and live peaceably in thy house. And beyond this, God shall follow thee with his benediction that all things shall well prosper both to thee and to thy husband, as the Psalm saith, "Blessed is the man which feareth God and walketh in his ways. Thou shalt have the fruit of thine own hands, happy shalt thou be, and well shall it go with thee. Thy wife shall be as a vine plentifully spreading about thy house. Thy children shall be as the young springs [shoots or sprigs] of the olives about the table. Lo, thus shall that man be blessed" (saith David) "that feareth the Lord."

This let the wife have ever in mind, the rather admonished thereto by the apparel of her head, whereby is signified that she is under covert [the protection] and obedience of her husband. And as that apparel is of nature so appointed to declare her subjection, so biddeth St. Paul that all other of her raiment should express both shamefastness and sobriety. For if it be not lawful for the woman to have her head bare, but to bear thereon the sign of her power [protector] wheresoever she goeth, more is it required that she declare the thing that is meant thereby. And therefore these ancient women of the old world called their husbands lords, and showed them reverence in obeying them. . . .

Let not therefore the woman be too busy to call for the duty of her husband where she should be ready to perform her own, for that is not worthy any great commendation. And even so again let not the man only consider what [be]longeth to the woman and to stand so earnestly gazing thereon, for that is not his part or duty. But as I have said, let either parties be ready and willing to perform that which belongeth specially to themselves. For, if we be bound to hold out our left cheek to strangers which will smite us on the right cheek, how much more ought we to suffer an extreme and unkind husband?

But yet I mean not that a man should beat his wife. God forbid that, for that is the greatest shame that can be, not so much to her that is beaten, as to him that doth the deed. But, if by such fortune thou chancest upon such an husband, take it not too heavily, but suppose thou that thereby is laid up no small reward hereafter and in this lifetime no small commendation to thee if thou canst be quiet. But yet to you that be men, thus I speak. Let there be none so grievous fault to compel you to beat your wives. But what, say I, your wives? No, it is not to be borne with that an honest man should lay hands on his maidservant to beat her. Wherefore, if it be a great shame for a man to beat his bound servant, much more rebuke it is to lay violent hands upon his free-woman. And this thing may we well understand by the laws which the paynims [pagans] hath made, which doth discharge her any longer to dwell with such an husband, as unworthy to have any further company with her, that doth smite her. For it is an extreme point thus so vilely to entreat [treat] her like a slave that is fellow to thee of thy life and so enjoined unto thee beforetime in the necessary matters of thy living. And therefore a man may well liken such a man (if he may be called a man rather than a wild beast) to a killer of his father or his mother. And whereas we be commanded to forsake our father and mother for our wives' sake, and yet thereby do work them none injury but do fulfill the law of God, how can it not appear then to be a point of extreme madness to entreat her despitefully for whose sake God hath commanded thee to leave parents? Yea, who can suffer such despite? Who can worthily express the inconvenience that is, to see what weepings and wailings be made in the open streets when neighbors run together to the house of so unruly an husband as to a Bedlam man [madman] who goeth about to overturn all that he hath at home? Who would not think that it were better for such a man to wish the ground to open and to swallow him in than once ever after to be seen in the market?

But peradventure thou wilt object that the woman provoketh thee to this point. But consider thou again that the woman is a frail vessel and thou art therefore made the ruler and head over her, to bear the weakness of her in this her subjection. And therefore study thou to declare the honest commendation of thine authority, which thou canst no way better do than to forbear to utter [treat badly] her in her weakness and subjection. For even as the king appeareth so much the more noble, the more excellent and noble he maketh his officers and lieutenants, whom, if he should dishonor and despise the authority of their dignity, he should deprive himself of a great part of his own honor. Even so, if thou dost despise her that is set in the next room beside thee, thou dost much derogate and decay the excellency and virtue of thine own authority. Recount all these things in thy mind, and be gentle and quiet. Understand that God hath given thee children with her and are made a father and by such reason appease thyself.

Dost not thou see the husbandmen, what diligence they use to till that ground which once they have taken to farm, though it be never so full of faults? As for an example, though it be dry, though it bringeth forth weeds, though the soil cannot bear too much wet, yet he tilleth it and so winneth fruit thereof. Even in like manner, if thou wouldst use like diligence to instruct and order the mind of thy spouse, if thou wouldst diligently apply thyself to weed out by little and little the noisome weeds of uncomely manners out of her mind with wholesome precepts, it could not be but in time thou shouldst feel the pleasant fruit thereof to both your comforts.

Therefore, that this thing chance not so, perform this thing that I do here counsel thee. Whatsoever any displeasant matter riseth at home, if thy wife hath done aught amiss, comfort her and increase not the heaviness. For, though thou shouldst be grieved with never so many things, yet shalt thou find nothing more grievous than to want the benevolence of thy wife at home. What offense soever thou canst name, yet shalt thou find none more intolerable than to be at debate with thy wife. And for this cause most of all oughtst thou to have this love in reverence. And if reason moveth thee to bear any burden at any other men's hands, much more of thy wife's. For if she be poor, upbraid her not; if she be simple, taunt her not, but be the more courteous. For she is thy body and made one flesh with thee.

But thou peradventure wilt say that she is a wrathful woman, a drunkard, a beastly, without wit and reason. For this cause, bewail her the more. Chafe not in anger, but pray to almighty God. Let her be admonished and holpen [helped] with good counsel, and do thou thy best endeavor that she may be delivered of all these affections. But if thou shouldst beat her, thou shalt increase her evil affections, for frowardness [aggression] and sharpness is not amended with frowardness but with softness and gentleness. Furthermore, consider what reward thou shalt have at God's hand. For, where thou mightst beat her and yet for the respect of the fear of God thou wilt abstain and bear patiently her great offenses, the rather in respect of that law which forbiddeth that a man should cast out his wife, what fault soever she be cumbered with, thou shalt have a very great reward and before the receipt of that reward thou shalt feel many commodities, for by this means she shall be made the more obedient and thou for her sake shalt be made the more meek. It is written in a story of a certain strange philosopher which had a cursed wife [Socrates and Xanthippe], a froward, and a drunkard. When he was asked for what consideration he did so bear her evil manners, he made answer: "By this means" (said he) "I have at home a schoolmaster and an example how I should behave myself abroad. For I shall" (saith he) "be the more quiet with other, being thus daily exercised and taught in the forbearing of her." Surely it is a shame that paynims should be wiser than we, we I say, that be commanded to counterfeit angels or rather God himself through meekness. And for the love of virtue, this said philosopher Socrates would not expel his wife out of his house. Yea, some say that he did therefore marry his wife to learn this virtue by that occasion. . . .

Therefore give thanks to God for his great benefit in that you have taken upon you this state of wedlock and pray you instantly that almighty God may luckily defend and maintain you therein, that neither you be overcomed with any temptation nor with any adversity. But before all things take good heed that you give no occasion to the devil to let and hinder your prayers by discord and dissension. For there is no stronger defense and stay in all our life than is prayer, in the which we may call for the help of God and obtain it, whereby we may win his blessing, his grace, his defense, and protection, so to continue therein to a better life to come. Which grant us he that died for us all, to whom be all honor and praise, for ever and ever. Amen.

→ WILLIAM GOUGE

From *Of Domestical Duties: Eight Treatises*   *1634*

William Gouge's work is a handbook on the theory and practice of Christian marriage, offering advice to husbands and wives, analysis of potential problems between spouses, and emphasis (derived from Puritan doctrine) on mutuality in spousal relationships. This excerpt from the third edition develops the familiar analogy between the marriage relationship and the social order.

COMMON-MUTUAL DUTIES BETWIXT MAN AND WIFE

Of the vices contrary to a joint care of governing the Family

The mind and practice of many, both husbands and wives, is contrary to this duty.

Many a husband because the wife's office is especially to abide at home will put off all government to the wife: leaving it to her not only to order the things in the house but also to bring in all needful things, to order and govern the children both young and old, yea even to provide for them also, to take in, to put out, to use all sorts of servants as pleaseth her. Yea, if servants shall be stubborn and stout against her, he will take no notice of it, nor endure to be told of it, much less afford her his assistance, but suffer her to be disgraced and despised. As for religious duties, he will no way meddle with them. Oh base-minded men, unworthy to be husbands and heads of wives! Shall your wives who were made to be a help to you have no help from you, no, not in those things which especially belong to your charge? Shall the weaker vessels bear all the burden? Assuredly as the man carrieth away the greatest reputation and honor when a family is well governed (though it be by the joint care and wisdom of his wife) so lieth he most open to the judgment of God, if the government thereof be neglected, and through the neglect thereof, children and servants grow impious: instance Eli, and David. For as in a Commonwealth the greatest honor of good government, victorious battles, happy peace, and prosperity, and the greatest dishonor and damage of the contrary, redoundeth to the King, so to the man who is chief governor in a family: for it is presupposed that all which do any good are instruments of the highest governor; if any evil or mischief fall out, that it is through his negligence.

On the other side, because the husband is the most principal, many wives think that the government of the family nothing at all appertains to them, and thereupon are careless of the good thereof and will not stir their least finger to order any thing aright: but if any thing be amiss lay all the blame on their husbands. Do not such pervert that main end for which God made them, even *to be an help?* Do they not carry themselves most unworthy of the place wherein God hath set them, namely, to be joint-governors with their husbands, and partakers of their dignities? As by their negligence they make themselves accessary to all the evil which falleth out in the family, so assuredly shall they have their part in those judgments which are executed on the head thereof.

Most contrary to the fore-named duty is the practice of such as are hindrances one to another in governing the family: as when wives are not only negligent themselves in coming to religious exercises, but keep back children and servants, and so are a great grief unto their religious husbands; or when they use any of the children or servants to be instruments of iniquity; or are themselves disquiet and troublesome in the house, like to her of whom Solomon speaketh in this proverb, "It is better to dwell in the corner of the house top, than with a contentious woman in a wide house."

Husbands also are oft an hindrance to that good government which their wives would help forward, when they scoff and scorn at that good counsel which their wives give them for that purpose; or when they will not suffer their wives to meddle with any thing at all, nor endure that they should find any fault, much less take in hand to redress any thing that is amiss. These and such like perverse dispositions are in husbands and wives, whereby it cometh to pass that they who were joined together to be a mutual help each to other prove heavy, yea, intolerable burdens.

→ SIR THOMAS SMITH

From *De Republica Anglorum: The Manner of Government or Policy of the Realm of England* 1583
Of Children

Sir Thomas Smith (1513–1577) was an important Tudor legal scholar and theorist. His political treatise draws heavily on the traditions informing English law and social practice, many of which were inherited from the ancients. Here he explains the system of primogeniture as practiced in England in the sixteenth century.

The testator disposeth in his last will his moveable goods freely as he thinketh meet and convenient without controlment of wife or children. And our testaments for goods moveable be not subject to the ceremonies of the civil law, but made with all liberty and freedom. . . . Of lands as ye have understood before, there is difference: for when the owner dieth, his land descendeth only to his eldest son, all the rest both sons and daughters have nothing by the common law, but must serve their eldest brother if they will, or make what other shift they can to live: except that the father in life time do make some conveyance and estates of part of his land to their use, or else by devise, which word amongst our lawyers doth betoken a testament written, sealed, and delivered in the life time of the testator before witness: for without those ceremonies a bequest of lands is not available. But by the common law if he that dieth hath no sons but daughters, the land is equally divided among them, which portion is made by agreement or by lot. Although as I have said ordinarily and by the common law, the eldest son inheriteth all the lands, yet in some countries all the sons have equal portion, and that is called gavelkinde, and is in many places in Kent. In some places the youngest is sole heir: and in some places after an other fashion. But these being but particular customs of certain places and out of the rule of the common law, do little appertain to the disputation of the policy of the whole realm, and may be infinite. The common wealth is judged by that which is most ordinarily and commonly done through the whole realm.

→ GEORGE WHETSTONE

From *An Heptameron of Civil Discourses* 1582
Household Laws to Keep the Married in Love, Peace, and Amity

George Whetstone's treatment of the conditions necessary for satisfactory marriage (as "reported by Segnior Phyloxenus") examines the complementary claims of parents ("foresight") and children ("fancy") in the selection of a marriage partner. Such conflicts are obviously relevant to Shakespeare's plays in which betrothals are opposed by parents or by participants, notably *A Midsummer Night's Dream, Othello,* and *The Merry Wives of Windsor.*

The satisfaction of fancy is the source of joy in marriage. But there be many means to dam up the course of delight between the married, if the match be not made as well by foresight, as free choice.

The office of foresight is to prevent following [later] mischances and (advisedly) to consider if present ability will support a household, and (according to their calling) leave a portion to their posterity.

In this point, the experience of the parents is to be preferred before the rash imaginations of the son. For the aged married by proof know that in time many accidents of mischance will hinder the endeavors of the best husbands.

The office of foresight is likewise to consider of the equality in years, lest the one growing and the other declining in perfection, after a while repent, when remedy comes too late: the rose full blown seemeth fair for a time, but withereth much sooner than the tender bud.

It is the office of foresight to consider of the equality of bringing up, lest a diversity in manners between the married make a division of desires. For spaniels and curs hardly live together without snarling.

And it is the office of foresight to see that there be a consent in religion between the married, for if their love be not grafted in their souls, it is like[ly] their marriage will be infirmed with the defects of the body.

The office of free choice is the root or foundation of marriage, which consisteth only in the satisfaction of fancy. For where the fancy is not pleased, all the perfections of the world cannot force love, and where the fancy delighteth, many defects are perfected or tolerated among the married.

→ ELIZABETH CLINTON

From *The Countess of Lincoln's Nursery* 1628

According to the Preface, "the general consent of too many mothers in an unnatural practice," that is, the use of wet nurses for the feeding of infants, "hath caused one of the noblest and fairest hands in this land to set pen to paper." The author begins by citing a number of biblical examples to support her thesis that women ought to breast-feed their own children, and then proceeds to answer possible objections.

Because it hath pleased God to bless me with many children and so caused me to observe many things falling out to mothers and to their children, I thought good to open my mind concerning a special matter belonging to all child-bearing women seriously to consider of, and to manifest my mind the better, even to write of this matter so far as God shall please to direct me. In sum, the matter I mean, *is the duty of nursing due by mothers to their own children.* . . .

By his word it is proved, first by examples, namely the example of Eve. For who suckled her sons Cain, Abel, and Seth, etc., but herself? Which she did not only of mere necessity, because yet no other woman was created, but especially because she was their mother and so saw it was her duty, and because she had a true natural affection, which moved her to do it gladly. Next the example of Sarah, the wife of Abraham. For she both gave her son Isaac suck, as doing the duty commanded of God, and also took great comfort and delight therein, as in a duty well pleasing to herself, whence she spake of it as of an action worthy to be named in her holy rejoicing. Now if Sarah, so great a princess, did nurse her own child, why should any of us neglect to do the like, except (which God forbid) we think scorn to follow her, whose daughters it is our glory to be, and which we be only upon this condition, that we imitate her well-doing. Let us look therefore to our worthy pattern, noting withal that she put herself to this work when she was very old and so might the better have excused herself than we younger women can, being also more able to hire and keep a nurse than any of us. But why is she not followed most in the practice of this duty? Even because they want [lack] her virtue and piety. This want is the common hindrance to this point of the woman's obedience. For this want makes them want love to God's precepts, want love to his doctrine, and like stepmothers, want due love to their own children. . . .

To proceed, take notice of one example more, that is, of the blessed Virgin: as her womb bare our blessed Savior, so her paps gave him suck. Now who shall deny the own mother's suckling of their own children to be their duty since every godly matron hath walked in these steps before them? . . .

Oh, consider, how comes our milk? Is it not by the direct providence of God? Why provides he it, but for the child? The mothers then that refuse to nurse their own children, do they not despise God's providence? Do they not deny God's will? Do they not as it were say, "I see, O God, by the means thou has put into me that thou wouldst have me nurse the child thou hast given me, but I will not do so much for thee." Oh impious, and impudent unthankfulness, yea monstrous unnaturalness, both to their own natural fruit born so near their breasts and fed in their own wombs, and yet may not be suffered to suck their own milk. . . .

It is objected that it is troublesome, that it is noisome to one's clothes, that it makes one look old, etc. All such reasons are uncomely and un-Christian to be objected, and therefore unworthy to be answered. They argue unmotherly affection, idleness, desire to have liberty to gad from home, pride, foolish fineness, lust, wantonness, and the like evils. Ask Sarah, Hannah, the blessed Virgin, and any modest, loving mother what trouble they accounted it to give their little ones suck? Behold most nursing mothers and they be as clean and sweet in their clothes and carry their age and hold their beauty as well as those that suckle not. And most likely are they so to do because, keeping God's ordinance, they are sure of God's blessing, and it hath been observed in some women that they grew more beautiful and better favored by very nursing their own children.

→ BEN JONSON

On My First Son   *1603*

Historians have established convincingly that relationships between parents and children were different in the early modern period than they are now. For example, the practices of sending infants out to nurse or of binding young boys as apprentices to a craftsman suggest a degree of emotional distance that we might find strange. Nevertheless, such practices do not signify an absence of emotional ties, as Ben Jonson's poetic lament for the death of his child will readily indicate.

Farewell, thou child of my right hand, and joy;
My sin was too much hope of thee, loved boy:
Seven years thou wert lent to me, and I thee pay,
Exacted by thy fate, on the just day.
O could I lose all father now! For why
Will man lament the state he should envy,
To have so soon 'scaped world's and flesh's rage,
And, if no other misery, yet age?
Rest in soft peace, and asked, say, "Here doth lie
Ben Jonson his best piece of poetry."
For whose sake henceforth all his vows be such
As what he loves may never like too much.

→ # Excerpts from Conduct Books   *1555–1774*

These three passages from manuals of behavior describe proper bedroom conduct with regard to strangers. It was accepted practice for guests in inns to share rooms and even beds with one another.

From Of Good Manners and Proper Behavior *(1555) by Pierre Broë*

If you share a bed with another man, keep still.
Take care not to annoy him or expose yourself by abrupt movements.
And if he is asleep, see that you do not wake him.

From The Rules of Decency and Christian Manners
(1749 Edition) by Jean Baptiste de la Salle

You ought . . . neither to undress nor go to bed in the presence of any other person. Above all, unless you are married, you should not go to bed in the presence of anyone of the other sex.

It is still less permissible for people of different sexes to sleep in the same bed, unless they are very young children. . . .

If you are forced by unavoidable necessity to share a bed with another person of the same sex on a journey, it is not proper to lie so near him that you disturb or even touch him; and it is still less decent to put your legs between those of the other. . . .

It is also very improper and impolite to amuse yourself with talk and chatter. . . .

When you get up you should not leave the bed uncovered, nor put your nightcap on a chair or anywhere else where it can be seen.

From The Rules of Decency and Christian Manners
(1774 Edition) by Jean Baptiste de la Salle

It is a strange abuse to make two people of different sex sleep in the same room. And if necessity demands it, you should make sure that the beds are apart, and that modesty does not suffer in any way from this commingling. Only extreme indigence can excuse this practice. . . .

If you are forced to share a bed with a person of the same sex, which seldom happens, you should maintain a strict and vigilant modesty. . . .

When you have awakened and had sufficient time to rest, you should get out of bed with fitting modesty and never stay in bed holding conversations or concerning yourself with other matters . . . nothing more clearly indicates indolence and frivolity; the bed is intended for bodily rest and for nothing else.

→ SIR EDWARD COKE

From *The Third Part of the Institutes of the Laws of England*   1644

Of Buggery or Sodomy

Sir Edward Coke (1552–1634) was chief justice of the King's Bench and crown prosecutor in the trials of the earl of Essex and the perpetrators of the Gunpowder Plot. His *Institutes* (published posthumously) outlines and explains the principal tenets of the English legal system; the following selection from the third edition sets forth the nature of the crime — "buggery," or sodomy — and gives the official view of the criminality of homosexual acts.

Buggery is a detestable and abominable sin, amongst Christians not to be named, committed by carnal knowledge against the ordinance of the Creator and order of nature, by mankind with mankind, or with brute beast, or by womankind with brute beast.

Bugeria is an Italian word, and signifies so much as is before described. *Paederastes* or *Paiderastes* is a Greek word, *Amator puerorum* [lover of boys], which is but a *Species* of Buggery: and it was complained of in Parliament, that the Lumbards had brought unto the Realm the shameful sin of Sodomy that is not to be named, as there it is said. Our ancient authors do conclude, that it deserveth death, *ultimum supplicium* [the final punishment], though they differ in the manner of punishment. *Britton* saith, that Sodomites and Miscreants shall be burnt: and so were the Sodomites by Almighty God. *Fleta* saith, *Pecorantes & Sodomitae in terra vivi confodiantur* [buggerers and sodomites should be buried alive]: and therewith agreeth the *Mirror, pur le grand abomination* [concerning the great abomination]; and in another place he saith, *Sodomitae est crime de Majestie vers le Roy celestre* [sodomy is a crime of *lesemajeste* against the King of Heaven]. But (to say it once for all) the judgment in all cases of felony is, that the person attainted be hanged by the neck until he or she be dead. But in ancient times in that case, the man was hanged and the woman was drowned, whereof we have seen examples in the reign of R[ichard].I. And this is the meaning of ancient Franchises granted *de Furca and Fossa,* of the Gallows and the Pit, for the hanging upon the one and drowning in the other: but *Fossa* is taken away, and *Furca* remains.

Cum masculo non commiscearis coitu foemineo, quia abominatio est. Cum omni pecore non coibis, nec maculaberis cum eo. Mulier non succumbet jumento, nec miscebitur ei, quia scelus est, etc. [Thou shalt not lie with mankind, as with womankind: it is abomination. Neither shalt thou lie with any beast to defile thyself therewith; neither shall any woman stand before a beast to lie down thereto: it is confusion, etc. (Leviticus 18:22–23, King James version).]

The Act of 25 H[enry].8.[chapter 6] hath adjudged it felony, and therefore the judgment for felony doth now belong to this offense, viz. to be hanged by the neck till he be dead. He that readeth the Preamble of this Act, shall find how necessary the reading of our ancient Authors is. The statute doth take away the benefit of Clergy from the Delinquent. But now let us peruse the words of the said description of Buggery.

Detestable and abominable.] These just attributes are found in the Act of 25 H[enry].8.[chapter 6].

Amongst Christians not to be named.] These words are in the usual Indictment of this offense, and are in effect in the Parliament Roll of 50 E[dward].3. *Ubi supra, nu. 58.*

By Carnal knowledge, etc.] The words of the Indictment be, *Contra ordinationem Creatoris and naturae ordinem, rem habuit veneream, dictumque puerum carnaliter cognovit, etc.* [against the ordinance of the Creator and the order of Nature, he had sexual intercourse and had carnal knowledge of the said boy]. So as there must be *penetratio,* that is, *res in re* [the thing in the thing], either with mankind or with beast, but the least penetration maketh it carnal knowledge. See the indictment of *Stafford,* which was drawn by great advice, for committing Buggery with a Boy; for which he was attainted and hanged.

The Sodomites came to this abomination by four means, viz. by pride, excess of diet, idleness, and contempt of the poor. *Otiosus nihil cogitat, nisi de ventre and venere* [the idle think of nothing but the belly and fornication]. Both the agent and consentient are felons: and this is consonant to the law of

God, *Qui dormierit cum masculo coitu foemineo, uterque operatus est nefas, and morte moriatur* [If a man also lie with mankind, as he lieth with a woman, both of them have committed an abomination: they shall surely be put to death . . . (Leviticus 20:13, KJV)]. And this accordeth with the ancient Rule of law, *Agentes and consentientes pair poena plecentur* [the doers and those consenting to the doing alike deserve punishment].

Emissio seminis [ejaculation] maketh it not Buggery, but is an evidence in case of Buggery of penetration: and so in Rape the words be also *carnaliter cognovit* [had carnal knowledge], and therefore there must be penetration: and *emissio seminis* without penetration maketh no Rape. . . . If the party buggered be within [beneath] the age of discretion, it is no felony in him, but in the agent only. When any offense is felony either by the Common law, or by statute, all Accessories both before and after are incidentally included. So if any be present, abetting and aiding any to do the act, though the offense be personal and to be done by one only, as to commit Rape, not only he that doth the act is a principal, but also they that be present, abetting and aiding the misdoer, are principals also; which is a proof of the other case of Sodomy.

Or by woman.] This is within the Purvien [Purview] of this Act of 25 *H[enry].8.[chapter 6].* For the words be, *if any person, etc.* which extend as well to a woman as to a man, and therefore if she commit Buggery with a beast, she is a person that commits Buggery with a beast, to which end this word [*person*] was used. And the rather, for that somewhat before the making of this Act, a great Lady had committed Buggery with a Baboon, and conceived by it, etc.

There be four sins in holy Scripture called *Clamantia peccata*, crying sins, whereof this detestable sin is one, expressed in this *Distichon*,

> *Sunt vox clamorum, vox sanguinis, and Sodomorum,*
> *Vox oppressorum, merces detenta laborum.*

> [They are the voice of shouts, the voice of blood, and of Sodomites, the voice of the oppressed, when punishment is withheld.]

➔ RICHARD BARNFIELD

From *The Tears of an Affectionate Shepherd Sick for Love, or The Complaint of Daphnis for the Love of Ganymede* 1594

The following brief excerpt from Barnfield's poem is a fairly explicit instance of the homoerotic strain in much Elizabethan verse, including Shakespeare's sonnets. Although the conventions of the pastoral may have served to distance and aestheticize somewhat the emotions expressed, the speaker's theme is unmistakable. "Ganymede," the name of Jove's cupbearer, was the archetype of the beautiful boy, and thus Rosalind takes that name when she disguises herself as a boy in *As You Like It.*

Scarce had the morning star hid from the light
Heaven's crimson canopy with stars bespangled,
But I began to rue th'unhappy sight
Of that fair boy that had my heart entangled;
    Cursing the time, the place, the sense, the sin;   5
    I came, I saw, I viewed, I slippèd in.

If it be sin to love a sweet-faced boy,
(Whose amber locks trussed up in golden trammels
Dangle adown his lovely cheeks with joy,
When pearl and flowers his fair hair enamels),   10
    If it be sin to love a lovely lad,
    Oh then sin I, for whom my soul is sad. . . .

Oh would to God he would but pity me,
That love him more than any mortal wight,
Then he and I with love would soon agree,
That now cannot abide his suitor's sight.
    O would to God (so I might have my fee)   95
    My lips were honey, and thy mouth a Bee.

Then shouldst thou suck my sweet and my fair flower
That now is ripe, and full of honey berries;
Then would I lead thee to my pleasant bower
Filled full of grapes, of mulberries, and cherries,   100
    Then shouldst thou be my wasp or else my bee,
    I would thy hive, and thou my honey be.

I would put amber bracelets on thy wrists,
Crownets of pearl about thy naked arms,
And when thou sitst at swilling Bacchus' feasts,   105
My lips with charms should save thee from all harms.
    And when in sleep thou tookst thy chiefest pleasure,
    Mine eyes should gaze upon thine eyelids' treasure.

➔   QUEEN ELIZABETH I

List of Royal Proclamations   *1596–1601*

These titles of the proclamations issued by Elizabeth I in a five-year period provide a glimpse of some of the chief concerns of her government at the end of the sixteenth century. The proclamation is the early modern equivalent of the executive order and was used to control a wide range of economic, social, and political problems.

February 11, 1596	Enforcing Statutes against Vagabonds and Rogues
April 1596	Regulating Chester Wages
May 3, 1596	Ordering Punishment of Persons with Forged Credentials
May 29, 1596	Enforcing Statutes for Winding of Wool
July 31, 1596	Enforcing Orders for Marketing Grain; Prohibiting Unlicensed Manufacture or Sale of Starch
August 20, 1596	Ordering Peace Kept on Scottish Border
September 29, 1596	Licensing Collections for Marshalsea Prisoners
November 2, 1596	Enforcing Orders against Dearth; Ordering Hospitality Kept in Country, and Defenses Maintained
April 8, 1597	Regulating Chester Wages
July 6, 1597	Enforcing Statutes and Proclamations of Apparel
July 23, 1597	Dispensing Certain Persons from Statutes of Apparel
August 13, 1597	Ordering Peace Kept on Scottish Borders
September 15, 1597	Defending Lord Mayor from Slander; Ordering Grain to Markets
September 27, 1597	Granting Letters of Marque against Spanish Shipping
1597	Enforcing Statute for Making Caps
January 9, 1598	Ordering Deportation of Hanse Merchants [draft]
February 26, 1598	Enforcing Abstinence from Meat
May 20, 1598	Granting Monopoly for Starch
August 23, 1598	Enforcing Former Statutes, Proclamations, and Orders against Forestalling Grain
September 9, 1598	Placing London Vagabonds under Martial Law
February 8, 1599	Prohibiting Piracy against Allied Shipping
March 31, 1599	Declaring Reason for Sending Army into Ireland
January 14, 1600	Establishing Commission for Concealed Lands
January 14, 1600	Enforcing Statutes on Abstinence from Meat, Ale Houses, and Vagabonds
March 18, 1600	Enforcing Statutes against Export of Gold and Silver
March 28, 1600	Ordering Imprisonment of Persons Sowing Woad
June 2, 1600	Defending Lord Treasurer from Libels; Ordering Grain Hoarders Punished
December 21, 1600	Enforcing Statutes against Handguns
c. January 1601	Licensing Casper van Senden to Deport Negroes [draft]
c. 1600 (uncertain)	Authorizing Copper Coinage [draft]
January 9, 1601	Granting Patent for Customs on Silk, Lawn, Taffeta, etc.
February 7, 1601	Mitigating Statutes for Wool Cloth Manufacture
February 9, 1601	Announcing Arrest of Earl of Essex
February 15, 1601	Placing London Vagabonds under Martial Law
April 5, 1601	Offering Reward for Information on Libels against the Queen
July 3, 1601	Enforcing Statutes against Transporting English Coin to Ireland
November 28, 1601	Reforming Patent Abuses

→ QUEEN ELIZABETH I

Royal Proclamation against Vagabonds and Unlawful Assemblies

September 9, 1598

Rogues and vagabonds constituted an intractable social evil in early modern London, at least in the eyes of the authorities. This royal proclamation represents one effort in an ongoing program to control vagrancy, begging, and crime.

BY THE QUEENE

The Queen's Majesty's proclamation for suppressing of the multitudes of idle vagabonds, and for staying of all unlawful assemblies, especially in and about the City of London, and for orders to punish the same.

Forasmuch as it is seen that notwithstanding the good laws provided for the restraining of idle people and vagabonds, yet for want of due execution thereof by the justices of peace and other ministers authorized thereunto, there are in many parts of the realm and specially about the city of London and her majesty's court manifestly seen wandering in the common highways, to the annoyance of the common people both in their goods and lives, multitudes of able men, neither impotent nor lame, exacting money continually upon pretense of service in the wars without relief, whereas many of them never did serve, and yet such as have served, if they were maimed or lamed by service, are provided for in the countries by order of sundry good laws and statutes in that behalf made and provided: For reformation whereof her majesty straightly commandeth all justicers and officers to have better regard than heretofore they have had and to appoint upon certain days in the week monthly (for some convenient season) watches and privy searches in places needful, and thereby to attach and imprison such idle vagabonds, and to send the lame and maimed into the countries according to the said statutes; and doth further notify hereby to all her subjects that because the disorder of those vagrant persons is, through neglect of her ordinary officers of justice, grown to such unruliness and undutifulness, that there hath been of late divers routs and unlawful assemblies of rogues and vagabonds, coloring their wandering by the name of soldiers lately come from the wars, who, arming themselves with shot and other forbidden weapons, have not only committed robberies and murders upon her majesty's people in their travel from place to place, but also resisted and murdered divers constables and others that have come to the rescue. Her majesty therefore, being compelled to look with the eye of severity into these growing outrages, and being minded to provide for her good and dutiful subjects by cutting off in the beginning such lewd and notorious offenders, meaneth for that purpose to appoint a provost marshal with sufficient authority to apprehend all such as shall not be readily reformed and corrected by the ordinary officers of justice, and them without delay to execute upon the gallows by order of martial law. And these her majesty's commandments she willeth to be duly observed upon pain of her indignation. Given at her Majesty's Manor of Greenwich, the ninth day of September 1598, in the fortieth year of Her Highness' reign.

→ QUEEN ELIZABETH I

Edict Arranging for the Expulsion from England of Negroes and Blackamoors   *July 18, 1596*

Concerned about what she considered the excessive number of "blackamoors" in the realm, the queen licensed Casper van Senden, who had delivered to England eighty-nine prisoners held by the Spanish, to transport to Spain and Portugal the same number of black slaves living in England. The order is explained as repayment of a personal debt to van Senden, as well as in larger economic terms: these slaves were taking work away from Englishmen.

An open warrant to the Lord Mayor of London and to all vice-admirals, mayors, and other public officers whatsoever to whom it may appertain. Whereas Casper van Senden, a merchant of Lubeck, did by his labor and travel procure eighty-nine of her majesty's subjects that were detained prisoners in Spain and Portugal to be released, and brought them hither into this realm at his own cost and charges, for the which his expenses and declaration of his honest mind toward those prisoners he only desireth to have license to take up so much blackamoors here in this realm and to transport them into Spain and Portugal. Her majesty in regard of the charitable affection the suppliant hath showed, being a stranger [foreigner], to work the delivery of our countrymen that were there in great misery and thralldom and to bring them home to their native country, and that the same could not be done without great expense, and also considering the reasonableness of his requests to transport so many blackamoors from hence, doth think it a very good exchange, and that those kind of people may be well spared in this realm, being so populous and numbers of able persons, the subjects of the land and Christian people, that perish for want of service, whereby through their labor they might be maintained. They are therefore in their lordships' names required to aid and assist him to take up such blackamoors as he shall find within this realm with the consent of their masters, who we doubt not, considering her majesty's good pleasure to have those kind of people sent out of the land and the good deserving of the stranger toward her majesty's subjects, and that they shall do charitably and like Christians rather to be served by their own countrymen than with those kind of people, will yield those in their possession to him.

CHAPTER 9

Politics and Religion:
Early Modern Ideologies

>—<

Consideration of political and religious ideology and practice in the early modern period necessarily begins with Queen Elizabeth I, who ruled England for most of Shakespeare's lifetime. The foundation of Elizabeth's authority was laid a century before her prime, however, with the assumption of power by her grandfather, King Henry VII, who defeated Richard III at the battle of Bosworth Field in 1485. The first of the Tudor monarchs, Henry VII immediately and single-mindedly set about to consolidate power in the Crown so as to avoid the civil strife that had plagued the nation throughout most of the fifteenth century. His son, Henry VIII, followed his example by further strengthening the power of the monarchy, and that son's most celebrated daughter, Elizabeth I, perfected the strategy. (Her successor, James I, employed it less effectively thanks to his recklessly authoritarian style.) When Henry VIII took the throne in 1509 at the age of seventeen, one of his first public actions was to execute two councillors who had served his father loyally but angered the people. Elizabeth acted with similar determination when she was crowned in 1558, although the unsettled national mood — her half-sister, Mary, had brought England near to civil war during her brief reign by restoring Catholicism as the state religion — made her wary and deliberate. Throughout Elizabeth's forty-five-year reign she ruthlessly adhered to the principles of royal privilege and authority, managing both to check the influence of Parliament and to restrain the powerful noble families whose jostling for power had historically led to unrest and bloodshed. In terms of internal politics, the reign of Elizabeth was stable, if not entirely free of strife. And since the queen was de facto head of the Church of England as well as head of state, she managed to impose a similar balance in the religious sphere.

An Absolute Monarchy?

England was an absolutist state in Shakespeare's day and would remain so until the middle of the seventeenth century. The term *absolutist* requires some definition, however, for it was disagreement over the exact meaning of the word — how much power did the monarchy legitimately hold? — that, when magnified and backed with force, led to the Civil Wars of the 1640s. (The excerpt from Sir Thomas Smith's *De Republica Anglorum* on p. 326 addresses the problem of royal versus parliamentary authority.) At Runnymede in the thirteenth century, a group of powerful English nobles had forced King John to acknowledge in the *Magna Carta* that the supremacy of the monarch was conditional, thus creating the basis for what would become the "mixed constitution" of England, the system under which authority was held and exercised by the monarch, the House of Lords, and the House of Commons. Despite the faintly democratic sound of this arrangement, central political authority actually rested in the hands of a very few people. During the sixteenth and early seventeenth centuries the balance of power continually shifted among monarch and councillors and important members of the aristocracy. These fluctuations usually corresponded to the popularity and political savvy of the monarch. Elizabeth, an unfailing pragmatist, exhibited a genius for apparent consultation and compromise among disputing constituencies, a talent that paradoxically secured and increased her own power, whereas James I, who fancied himself a political theorist, loudly adopted a more dogmatic line about the unimpeachable sovereignty of the king and thus contributed ultimately to the diminution of that authority. (See the extended passage from James's speech to Parliament on p. 328.)

The absolute power of the monarch was limited to certain political areas, however, and sometimes limited even within those areas. Taxation — it will come as no surprise to the modern reader — was one of the most potentially volatile topics in early modern England, and in this sphere particularly the sovereign's power was dependent on the will of others, usually the most powerful members of the landed aristocracy who asserted themselves through Parliament. The expenses of running the government, and the means of covering those expenses, were considerably different in the sixteenth and seventeenth centuries than they are in modern times because government was a very different enterprise than it is now. To take the most immediate and costly examples, there were no standing military forces to support (although individual campaigns had to be funded from time to time), and comparatively few social services (the Poor Laws for the relief of the indigent were financed at the parish level). The costs of government arose mostly from the maintenance of the monarch and the accompanying expenses of the royal household, and though these budgets were not trivial, they amounted to a fraction of the expenditures associated with the modern state. The revenues needed to finance the royal establishment were obtained from two major sources: the profits from Crown lands, which were considerable, and the customs tax on imports (chiefly wine) and exports (chiefly wool), income that had benefited the monarch since the fourteenth century. Under normal circumstances, other forms of royal subsidy, which had to be approved by Parliament, were unnecessary. But normal circumstances were often disrupted by national and international problems in the second half of the sixteenth century, notably the high rate of inflation and the conflicts with Spain, and so the direct taxation of landowners and workers that was supposed to be exceptional became, as Elizabeth's reign progressed, more like the rule. Parliament jealously guarded its authority over taxation. It usually acceded to the requests of Elizabeth and her ministers, but after 1603, under the Stuarts, the royal demand for ever greater subsidies became an increasing source of friction between the kings and their Parliaments.

If England was an absolutist state and its people subject to the will of the monarch, then what was the role of Parliament? As the etymology of the word implies (from the French *parler*, to speak), the main function of Parliament was to discuss policy, not to make it. Officially it met to authorize taxation and to endorse important acts of state; frequent and fierce debate arose over whether its powers extended any further than this. The Crown retained the right to call the members into session, which it did mainly when it required money or official support for national or international policy. Toward the end of Elizabeth's reign Parliament was called frequently, to confront the various crises of the 1580s and 1590s, but "frequently" in this context means every few years, and not necessarily for long periods of time. As J. P. Kenyon points out, these various meetings "were all separate parliaments, and their sessions were brief; men still spoke of 'this parliament' or 'the parliaments,' not of 'Parliament' in general" (*Stuart England* 32).

Although the representational function of Parliament was often proclaimed, the assembly was hardly responsive to the people in the way that the modern legislative body has theoretically become. Wealthy landowners came to town to represent themselves, particularly to safeguard their economic interests; and even though the population of London had increased faster than the population of the nation as a whole, the makeup of Parliament was still heavily weighted toward the countryside. Sometimes members took it upon themselves to advise the monarch, as when one of Elizabeth's early parliaments urged her to marry and produce an heir. At one point in James's reign there was even serious debate over the relative sovereignty of king and Parliament when in 1610 the House of Commons declared that the English government ought to be described as consisting of "King in Parliament." But such instances of self-assertion were unusual, and from the Elizabethan era through the outbreak of the English Revolution, the monarchs tended to use Parliament when possible and otherwise to ignore or tolerate it. The concern that emerges from such Elizabethan and Jacobean plays as *Richard II* and *Coriolanus* over the proper origins and uses of political power attests to profound anxiety about the tension between popular and monarchical authority.

The day-to-day workings of government were carried out by executive officers and bureaucrats under the supervision of the monarch's principal ministers and councillors, who were also members of Parliament. As will become clear, Elizabethan and Jacobean government was a decentralized system, with most of the responsibility for decision making and judicial administration resting in the hands of magistrates and councils at the level of the town, the county, and the parish. Apart from religion — a very large exception, as we shall see — the main business of government was international, and the monarchs devoted a large portion of their time to international affairs. Upon taking the throne in 1558, Queen Elizabeth regularly presented herself as a possible partner in marriage. Using the prospect of royal alliance as international leverage, she welcomed suitors (or their brokers) from Spain, France, Denmark, and other European states for over two decades. King James played the same game with his children, Prince Henry, Princess Elizabeth, and then, unexpectedly, Prince Charles (after Henry's early death in 1612, at the age of eighteen). England was not immune to the turmoil that afflicted Europe in the second half of the sixteenth century: Spanish adventurism under Philip II, the religious strife that split the French nation between Catholics and Protestants and seriously affected the European balance of power, the vulnerable position of the Netherlands, the uncertain role of Scotland and its unpredictable Queen Mary Stuart, and papal opposition to the Anglican Church. Elizabeth remained constantly alert to this European instability, seeking to capitalize on opportunities and forestall perils. By the time of her death the configuration of power on the Continent had changed, and King James, conceiving of himself as pacifist and diplomat, devoted much energy to negotiating settlements with Spain and other former and prospective enemies.

Councillors

Foreign affairs and those national and local problems the Crown chose to address were conducted by the monarch with the assistance of a small group of influential advisers. The most powerful and trusted of these advisers comprised the Privy Council. In Elizabeth's circle the principal minister was Sir William Cecil, knighted in 1551 by her brother, Edward VI, and raised to the peerage as Baron Burghley by Elizabeth twenty years later. Serving the queen in various offices, including Secretary of State and Lord Treasurer, from her accession until his death in 1598, Burghley also groomed his son, Robert Cecil, to assist and follow him in office. Elizabeth's other chief ministers were colorful men as well. Sir Thomas Gresham, the financial genius who looked after economic affairs, borrowed money in Antwerp and other European financial centers and built the Royal Exchange. Robert Dudley, earl of Leicester and Master of the Horse, was a particular favorite of Elizabeth, so much so that in the 1560s he was regularly mentioned as a likely husband for her. But Dudley presented two liabilities: first, the inconvenient fact that he was married already, and second, the scandal that ensued when, as his relations with the queen became more intimate, his wife was found dead, having apparently fallen to the bottom of a flight of stairs. Another major player, Francis Walsingham, was appointed principal secretary (one of two) in 1573, under the sponsorship of Burghley. Educated as was Burghley in the Protestant circles at

Cambridge, Walsingham had fled the country in the 1550s in reaction to Mary Tudor's militant Catholicism; when he took his place in the Privy Council some fifteen years after his return, residual zeal made him probably the most radical of Elizabeth's advisers. Walsingham was also the genius behind the regime's sophisticated system of intelligence, the father, in short, of the early modern spy network. His web of informants and double agents paid its most handsome dividends in the entrapment of Mary, Queen of Scots, in a plot to assassinate Elizabeth. (This is not to say that Mary was innocent of conspiracy, but government moles certainly helped her along.) Further, Walsingham's men were present in a tavern at Deptford in 1593 when the playwright Christopher Marlowe was killed in a brawl, stabbed through the eye. There is evidence that Marlowe himself did some spying on the Continent, but whether his death was a political murder is still a matter of debate.

Robert Cecil, very short and very ambitious, provided continuity between Elizabeth's and James's reigns. Succeeding his father in 1596 as the queen's Secretary of State, he privately initiated and supervised the process by which the Scottish king assumed the English throne. This was a tricky business. The queen, aged and ill, resolutely refused (at least publicly) to name her successor, fearing that to do so would imperil her own security. James VI of Scotland was the most likely candidate, his claim resting on his descent from Margaret Tudor, the sister of Henry VIII and Elizabeth's aunt. So as early as March of 1601, two years before the old queen's death, Cecil entered into clandestine negotiations to arrange for James's succession when the time came, as the letter on page 331 indicates. For Cecil, a primary benefit of such an arrangement was that he could remain as Secretary of State; indeed, he prospered under the new king, who immediately made him Lord Cecil of Essendine and later earl of Salisbury and who endowed him with more and more political responsibility until Cecil's death in 1612. Another of James's chief officers was the philosopher and literary figure Francis Bacon, who served as Solicitor General, Attorney General, Lord Keeper, and Lord Chancellor, although his public career ended badly in 1621 when he was convicted, removed from office, and sentenced to prison for taking bribes.

If some of the most vivid figures in Elizabeth's time were her potential suitors, something similar might be said of the reign of King James. Although married (to Anne of Denmark) and the father of several children, James was famously susceptible to the attractions of good-looking young men, and so the Stuart court was adorned by the presence of such royal favorites as Robert Carr, earl of Somerset, and the last and most powerful, George Villiers, duke of Buckingham. (See James's letter to Buckingham on p. 332.) Undoubtedly these personal affections influenced James's domestic and international policies, but it is also important to remember that the Stuart regime was managed by a secretariat that was firmly Elizabethan in origin and disposition and that went about its business without too much concern for the king's most recent beau.

But description of those people who advised Elizabeth and James and who carried on the everyday business of government conveys an inadequate image of what the courts of the two monarchs were actually like. Elizabeth's father and grandfather had vastly increased the sophistication and glitter of the English court, attracting writers like Sir Thomas More and painters like Hans Holbein and making the royal households around London worthy of comparison with the more established European cultural centers. Elizabeth herself was intelligent and charismatic. She dominated the scene at court partly by mastering the arts of self-representation. Attending her until he lost favor and retired to his country home was the brilliant Sir Philip Sidney — courtier, sonneteer, fiction writer, soldier, and literary theorist. James I deliberately set about to make his court the envy of Europe, spending enormous sums on courtly entertainments, and to some extent he achieved that goal. But he also elicited ridicule for his practice of knighting multitudes of Scots who descended on London after his accession, and many of his subjects — see Sir John Harington's report on a famous courtly party on page 333 — were aware and critical of Jacobean extravagance.

The Monarchs

Elizabeth and James were symbolic figures, as the portraits reproduced on pages 309 and 310 indicate. As Louis Adrian Montrose puts it in speaking of "The Queen," "here I mean not the person of Elizabeth Tudor but rather the whole field of cultural meanings personified in her" ("Elizabethan Subject" 303). Montrose's distinction is important because it represents the emphasis of much recent interpretation, which has tended to favor the cultural over the personal. Mindful of royal symbolism, we may still find it fascinating to learn something about the two human beings who personify these meanings. If I have more to say about Elizabeth and her court than about James and his, it is because, speaking structurally or bureaucratically, much of what was true in 1590 was still true in 1610. And Shakespeare lived three times as long a subject of Elizabeth as he did of James.

The twentieth-century reputation of Queen Elizabeth offers a lesson in the extremes of historical evaluation. One school of thought, led by Sir John Neale, the author of a major biography published in 1934 that is still influential, has come near to canonizing Elizabeth. According to this view she was bright, independent, cautious, able to distinguish the essential from the temporary. She was also circumspect by nature and experience, her prudence deriving from an enormous sense of royal responsibility. She used apparent indecision strategically, to purchase time in order to gain advantage from delay. Her negotiation of a *via media*, or middle way, between Catholics and reformers was a brilliant act of diplomacy. The disappointments and crises of her reign — the execution of the Scottish queen, the military conflicts in France and the Netherlands, the fierce monetary inflation at the end of the century — all these were probably inevitable, not her fault. Predictably, such a hagiographic approach has generated its negative complement, to wit: the queen was capricious, bull-headed, vacillating, out of touch with reality. Her uncertainty was a function of monstrous personal vanity, which exaggerated her fear of making a mistake. Whatever the motives, her unwillingness to make decisions disabled any attempt at consistent policy. The religious accommodation was an unsatisfactory compromise that did not resolve conflict but merely postponed it. The disappointments and crises of her reign — diplomatic, military, and economic — were all her fault.

These two positions are interpretations, responses to evidence that may itself be interpretive, shaped by the conditions of its transmission. But whether historians emphasize the positive or negative valence, they are responding to the irreducible fact that Elizabeth was both brilliant and difficult. She spoke

The "Ermine Portrait" of Elizabeth I.

Portrait of James I, by Paul van Somer.

several languages (including French, Italian, and Spanish), translated Latin for pleasure, played the virginal (a forerunner of the piano), wrote verse, and impressed the diplomatic corps from other nations with her wit and force of personality. Having lived a virtual prisoner during the five-year reign of her sister Mary, she was wary, alert to potential betrayal, and slow to commit herself to a course of action. Although the name of Niccolò Machiavelli had become a byword for treachery in Shakespeare's England, much of Elizabeth's maneuvering might have come from the pages of the Italian's provocative and ironic political handbook, *The Prince*. (See the excerpt on p. 334.) For good or ill, she was a consummate politician.

No one ever described James I as brilliant. Despite his learning and his philosophical ambitions, it has become permissible and even customary to think of the first Stuart king as something of a fool. This extreme characterization is probably a result of the gap between his conception of his own talents and achievements and the judgment that history has rendered. His high opinion of his powers of intellect led him to compose political treatises, such as the *Basilikon Doron* of 1594 (see p. 336), a kind of political manual addressed to his son, in which he expatiated philosophically on the divine right of kings and its importance in a parliamentary monarchy. His diplomatic ambitions led him to seek glory in the wide and perilous theater of Continental politics. But it seems clear that such efforts constituted a kind of showboating, that in reality James was an indolent, self-satisfied man who preferred to spend the day hunting rather than wrangling over the quotidian details of political policy. While his tastes were extravagant, his gift for finances was practically nil. One of his contemporaries put it this way: "He was very liberal of what he had not in his own grip, and would rather part with £100 he never had in his keeping than one twenty-shilling piece within his own custody" (qtd. in Kenyon, *The Stuarts* 39–40). It is vital to remember that, as a Scot, James was a foreigner in England — in the seventeenth century the difference between the two cultures was immense. The king had great difficulty dealing with Parliament. He also hated crowds. According to J. P. Kenyon, quoting the Jacobean courtier Sir John Harington, "The demonstrativeness of the English people soon palled — 'The access of the people made him so impatient that he often dispersed them with frowns, that we may not say with curses,' and on being told that they only wanted to look upon his face he cried out in a tantrum, 'God's wounds! I will pull down my breeches and they shall also see my arse!'" (*The Stuarts* 42).

For all his faults, James had one virtue that redeems him: he supported the theater. As king of Scotland, he had summoned players from England to celebrate his marriage in 1589, and when he arrived in London to ascend the English throne in 1603 he became the patron of Shakespeare's company, renaming them the King's Men and inviting them frequently to perform at court. Some have attributed the expansion and success of theater under James to the inclinations of his wife, Queen Anne, who seems to have relished taking part in courtly performances. Whoever the chief sponsor was, devotion to the drama was part of the larger Stuart taste for spectacle, which manifested itself in the lavish royal entertainment known as the court masque, an elaborate mixture of poetry, scenery, and dance (the last being the king's favorite part of the show). As a form, the masque was developed by Ben Jonson (the poet) and Inigo Jones (the designer) from the fairly modest courtly exercises performed during Elizabeth's time into an expensive and sophisticated celebration of Jacobean power, virtue, and royalty. Although professional actors were sometimes paid to swell the scene, the main performers were favorite courtiers and members of the royal family itself. In *The Masque of Queenes* of 1609, players may have taken the parts of the witches who open the show and are then banished, but the climax of the evening was the spectacular entry of Queen Anne and her attendants bejeweled and costumed as great ladies of history, from Cleopatra to Boadicea. We get a glimpse of what the court masque might have been like in *The Tempest,* in the masque of Ceres with which Prospero honors the espousal of Ferdinand and Miranda.

Queen Elizabeth also took pleasure in plays. Although the story that Shakespeare composed *The Merry Wives of Windsor* because the queen had been captivated by the character of Falstaff in the two *Henry IV* plays and wanted to see Falstaff in love is probably apocryphal, court records attest that she saw several of Shakespeare's plays performed at court by the Lord Chamberlain's Men. Her real passion, however, was the theater of politics. There she was the principal thespian, the star performer ever conscious of her effect on her courtly and popular audiences. It might be said that a gift for the histrionic was the source of her political genius and survival. Her pattern of vacillation and postponement, which frustrated her ministers and which modern historians have seen as a cornerstone of her policy, involved such theatrical strategies as poses and deception and a highly developed sense of timing. As she herself acknowledged in 1586, "We princes, I tell you, are set on stages, in sight and view of all the world" (qtd. in Levin 129).

The execution of Mary, Queen of Scots, in 1587 reveals the complicated interplay of histrionics and sincerity that characterized Elizabeth's style. When, thanks to Walsingham and his spies, Mary was convicted of involvement in the Babington conspiracy to murder Elizabeth and take the English throne, Elizabeth found herself in a serious dilemma. There was no precedent for trying a prince under English law, and so Elizabeth appointed a royal commission to investigate the charges. It pronounced Mary's guilt emphatically, whereupon Parliament formally demanded her execution and reacted angrily to the queen's unwillingness to proceed. Elizabeth wanted to be rid of her troublesome kinswoman but hesitated to take responsibility for killing a fellow monarch. She was also vexed by the potential impact on foreign relations: Scotland, France (Mary was the widow of King Francis II), and Spain (Mary was Catholic) could be expected to respond angrily, perhaps even militarily, to the execution of Mary. The queen procrastinated, arguing that Parliament would receive only "an answer answerless." Like Henry IV at the end of Shakespeare's *Richard II,* she appears to have hinted that she would welcome an unauthorized murder. Ultimately she signed Mary's death warrant but refused to release it so that it could be acted upon.

After more than eight weeks of torturous deliberation and uncertainty, Burghley and other cabinet ministers took action. Meeting in secret at Burghley's house on the third of February 1587, they agreed to send the warrant and execute Mary without the queen's knowledge. When the deed was done and word reached the capital, people celebrated by lighting bonfires, ringing bells, and feasting for a week. Before the execution, Elizabeth's irresolution seems to have been made up of both moral reservations and concern for appearances; after the fact, her actions imply a high degree of theatricality. She did not celebrate Mary's death. On the contrary, apparently distraught with grief, the queen dressed herself in mourning and commanded that a royal funeral be held publicly in the cathedral at Peterborough. She fulminated against the Privy Council and for a full month refused to see Burghley at all. William Davison, the secretary who had released the warrant without her permission, was committed to the Tower, kept there for a year and a half, and subjected to punishing fines. But these fines were later forgiven and Davison continued to receive his fees as secretary for the remainder of his life — a hint that these broad gestures were moves in a performance intended for audiences both domestic and international, and calculated to distance the queen from the execution.

Such a sense of performance was crucial to Elizabeth's success, as the accounts of various ambassadors and courtiers attest. In August 1588, just after the defeat of the Spanish Armada, but while the nation was still under threat of invasion from the duke of Parma, Elizabeth made a triumphant appearance among the English troops gathered at Tilbury. Disregarding the advice of those who feared for her safety, she arrayed herself in armor, rode boldly through the assembled militia, and inspiringly addressed the cheering men (see the text of the speech on p. 328). In the Tilbury speech, Elizabeth accentuates the positive, and such a stance was a familiar part of her style of government, at least as far as the public was concerned. Leaving ministers and lackeys to censure, to punish, to refuse, she dwelt on the affirmative themes of unity, forgiveness, and affection for her people, and doing so with graciousness and majesty, she thereby won their hearts. So apparent was this style in all her dealings, according to Sir John Harington, that she "convert[ed] her reign, through the perpetual love-tricks that passed between her and her people, into a kind of romance" (qtd. in Lockyer 210). The excerpt from Simon Forman's *Diary*, page 339, provides an astonishing example of this mode of thought. But what about more conventional amours? She employed the same "love-tricks" with the various suitors who, earlier in her reign, had come calling from the courts of Europe and the great houses of England. Apart from Robert Dudley, the most prominent suitors were the Austrian Archduke Charles, brother of the Holy Roman Emperor, and two Frenchmen, the duke of Anjou (who became King Henry III) and the duke of Alençon. Elizabeth seriously considered the first two candidates fairly early in her reign, in the 1560s and in 1571–72 respectively. She very nearly married Alençon in 1579, when she was forty-five, in what many considered a last attempt, at the end of her childbearing years, to settle the question of the succession. But doubt among her ministers was compounded by mounting opposition among the people, particularly those with Puritan leanings who feared Catholic encroachment, and so inertia won the day. Ultimately Queen Elizabeth rejected all suitors in favor of a corporate spouse, the English people at large. William Shakespeare, connoisseur of the theatrical, and professional analyst of monarchy, living as he did in the capital in the last fifteen years of Elizabeth's reign and performing before her at court, must have observed and to some degree appreciated these tactics.

Elizabeth was entering her late sixties at the end of the 1590s, and by that time her willfulness, short temper, and habit of playing one courtier against another had created a fractious and risky atmosphere at court. Although Robert Cecil and other advisers continued to perform their duties with a mixture of genuine service and self-interest, a final favorite had captured the queen's eye. Attractive, courageous, reckless, perhaps even unbalanced, Robert Devereux, earl of Essex, had been a member of Elizabeth's court for over a decade, but his heroic performance at the siege of Cadiz against the Spanish in 1596 made him something of a national, as well as a royal, favorite. The unusual and uncertain nature of the relationship between a glamorous young courtier and a vain and aged female monarch has proved endlessly fascinating to historians, not to mention Italian composers (Gaetano Donizetti's opera of 1836, *Roberto Devereux*) or Hollywood scriptwriters (the 1939 film with Bette Davis and Errol Flynn, *The Private Lives of Elizabeth and Essex*). To what extent was their friendship amorous or sexual? We cannot say for sure. Given Elizabeth's fondness throughout her reign for attractive young men, one of the most intensely debated questions about her is whether the Virgin Queen actually preserved her virginity.

What we do know about the Essex affair is that it ended badly and to some degree blotted the last years of the Elizabethan age. Essex actively encouraged not only the affections of his sovereign but also of the people. He attracted the loyalty of a group of young aristocrats in London, including Shakespeare's one-time patron, the earl of Southampton, and there was even cautious talk that Essex should be king. In 1598 Elizabeth sent Essex to Ireland to quell the rebels gathered under the earl of Tyrone. Disregarding the queen's explicit orders for managing the campaign, he failed in his mission, returned to England, and presented himself (unannounced) in the queen's bedchamber to justify his actions. Spooked by his popular appeal and swayed by his enemies, notably the Cecil faction, Elizabeth placed him under house arrest. Then, in 1601, Essex gambled and lost. Claiming mistreatment by the queen and slander by the Cecils, he mounted what was in effect a coup d'état, a march on London intended, Essex said, to correct the mistreatment he had suffered, and calculated, others said, to remove Elizabeth from the throne and replace her either with James VI of Scotland or with Essex himself. Essex had a few powerful supporters; as the excerpt on page 140 indicates, the day before his march on the palace, some of them sponsored the Lord Chamberlain's Men in a performance of Shakespeare's *Richard II*, the play in which a king is deposed. But the coup was poorly planned and immediately put down, and Essex was executed on a wintry morning in 1601. Elizabeth had not seen him since his wild return from Ireland.

The Church

Religion and politics were virtually inseparable in the sixteenth century, and the greatest danger facing Elizabeth on her accession in 1558 was the religious crisis. Mary Tudor, her half sister who had ruled England for the previous five years, had swiftly reversed the ecclesiastical reforms initiated by Henry VIII and Edward VI and reinstituted Catholicism as the state religion, thus bringing the nation close to civil war. Worse still to many minds was that Queen Mary had married Philip II of Spain. Hundreds of Protestant activists had fled the land for Holland, the German principalities, and the Calvinist enclave at Geneva, and among many who remained at home the resistance to a reconciliation with Rome was formidable. The conflict between the new regime and a number of intransigent Protestant bishops appointed by Henry and Edward led to the persecution of heretics under Mary — hence the queen's nickname "Bloody Mary." The most famous incident occurred at Oxford in October 1555 when Hugh Latimer and Nicholas Ridley were burned at the stake. (See John Foxe's account on p. 174.) Although these two clergymen were celebrities, most of those executed were laypeople. These violent consequences of royal succession were still fresh in the English consciousness when Elizabeth was crowned in November of 1558, and people naturally wanted to know where the young queen stood on the issues of the mass, the administration of the sacraments, whether *The Book of Common Prayer* should be used (and which version?), priestly marriage, the former monastic properties, and other fiercely debated questions. Such disputes, with their potentially deadly outcomes, form the background for Shakespeare's obsession, in the English histories and tragedies such as *King Lear*, with "the division of the kingdom."

In negotiating a smooth transition back to Anglican practice, the young queen succeeded because she was a pragmatist. Her compromise, known as the Elizabethan Settlement, did not completely and permanently eliminate the animosity between Catholic and Protestant zealots, but its terms managed to accommodate most reasonable leaders of the opposing factions. Elizabeth from the beginning had sought to maintain what was called the *via media*, the middle way, wanting to preserve the more or less Catholic elements of ritual that had survived Henry's break with Rome, while at the same time adhering in most matters to the doctrines that had motivated the European reformers. At Mary's death, many influential Protestants returned from the Continent fired with the radical enthusiasm of John Calvin and his followers, and some of these men took seats in Parliament. One of the first problems was the need to agree on an acceptable version of *The Book of Common Prayer*. The radical reformers wanted the 1552 edition, which reflects a more vigorous anti-Catholic ideology. For example, it treats the Communion service not as transubstantiation, a sacrament in which the bread and wine are actually changed into the body and blood of Christ, but rather as a symbolic representation. Moreover, it includes a petition that God should deliver the Christian from "the Bishop of Rome and all his detestable enormities." Elizabeth and her advisers favored the earlier, more nearly Roman document, and so a compromise was reached in which the 1552 Protestant book was approved but with a series of major revisions tempering its reformist ideology. The appurtenances of Roman ritual were mostly discarded, and yet the priests of the Church of England were instructed to wear white surplices and special dress for the serving of Holy Communion. Neither hard-line Marian Catholics nor radical Protestants were pleased, but almost everyone to the center of these two positions was able to live with the Elizabethan Settlement.

These religious controversies never disappeared; zealots on both sides repeatedly challenged Elizabeth's efforts to maintain the middle way. Catholicism was mostly kept in check, since Catholics were forbidden by the Act of Uniformity (1559) to practice their faith and in fact were obliged to attend the Anglican service every Sunday or be fined. But there was considerable pressure from the Continent. In 1570 Pius V issued a papal bull titled *Regnans in excelsis* excommunicating Elizabeth; his successor, Pope Gregory XIII, went so far as to encourage true Christians to assassinate the "Jezebel" who ruled England, offering to absolve them in advance. Missionary Jesuit priests sent secretly to England, treasonous plots on behalf of the Scottish queen, and war (or rumors of war) with Spain combined to foster stronger enforcement of anti-Catholic measures. For the most part, Elizabeth saw to it that private faith was not threatened: the law required attendance at the Anglican service, but the queen resolutely opposed legislation that would have made the taking of Communion compulsory. Governmental policy was aimed at suppressing Catholicism in its more public and evangelical forms. For example, anyone saying mass was subject to a huge monetary fine and a year in prison; similarly, those attempting to make converts were treated harshly. These statutes had some effect, but the government's most valuable instrument was the passage of time. Legitimate Catholic services could be conducted only by an ordained priest, and as the years went by such a figure became harder and harder to find. As one historian has pointed out, by the time of Elizabeth's death no more than a dozen or so Catholic priests survived from Mary's reign, and the authorities had strictly enforced the prohibition against Catholic immigration. Fewer priests meant fewer services and fewer Catholics; by the end of the sixteenth century England had outlasted the Roman peril (see Guy 300–01).

The more insidious threat to Elizabeth's desire for religious balance came from Protestant ideologues or, as they came to be called toward the end of the century, Puritans. Vigorous scholarly debate has arisen over the term *Puritan* because it has been employed too loosely, invoked to describe people who were philosophically and chronologically diverse, from violent anti-Catholics of the 1560s to Cromwellian anti-Royalists of the 1650s. (Jonas A. Barish, quoting the historian Christopher Hill to the effect that "the word Puritan . . . is an admirable refuge from clarity of thought," goes on to defend his use of the noun: "Nevertheless, the term has come to stand, with some justice, for a complex of attitudes best represented by those strictly designated as Puritans . . ." [82n].) I use it here to describe those members of the Church of England who, especially in the late years of Elizabeth's reign, sought to purify the English church of the residual evidence of Roman practice in the liturgy and ceremony of the Anglican service — the wearing of vestments, the adoration of the cross, kneeling, elaborate music. Under the influence of Calvin and his followers in Geneva, many Protestants had come to regard salvation as more personal and internal. The reformers thus sought to remake the hierarchical system of church government, returning greater authority to individual congregations. They urged a greater emphasis on preaching and, in certain quarters, "prophesying." The hatred of Elizabeth in the Catholic capitals of Europe gave strength to the cause of radical Protestantism in England, and the queen's own inner circle contained several advisers with Puritan sympathies, men trained at Cambridge who had absorbed elements of radical Genevan theology. (See p. 340 for an instance of Puritan polemics.)

Elizabeth herself, however, was uncompromisingly middle of the road. John Whitgift, professor of divinity at Cambridge who was appointed Archbishop of Canterbury in 1583, attempted in 1595 to supplant the Thirty-nine Articles that governed the Church of England with a more Calvinist set of principles; the sharp-eyed queen thwarted the attempt, however, instructing Cecil to inform Whitgift that "she mislikes much that any allowance hath been given by your Grace of any points to be disputed of predestination (being a matter tender and dangerous to weak, ignorant minds) and thereupon requireth your Grace to suspend them" (qtd. in Lockyer 202). By means of such vigilance Elizabeth managed to check the extremists in both camps. She commissioned Richard Hooker to write a philosophical defense of the Anglican Church and its system of church government. *The Laws of Ecclesiastical Polity*, printed in multiple volumes beginning in 1593, differentiated the English church from the radical Calvinist system of individually organized ecclesiastical units (see the excerpt on p. 349). As one distinguished historian puts it, Hooker "supplied a learned and reasoned basis for the theological position of the church of England, and commended the *via media*, not as a convenient halfway house between Rome and Geneva, but as the true, if reformed, descendant of the primitive church" (Davies 68). Elizabeth's commitment to the middle way gave the Protestant cause forty-five years to set down deep roots, and by the time James took the throne, the Church of England, its root system firmly in place, had flowered.

It was not without natural enemies, however. At the death of Elizabeth, the underground Catholic community in England appealed to the new king in the hope that they might be granted greater liberty and toleration, but militant Protestants resisted these efforts and managed to win James to their side. (See the excerpts from *The Catholics' Supplication* and *An Answer to the Catholics' Supplication* beginning on p. 343.) When statutes aimed at discouraging the practice and especially the spread of Catholicism were reenacted in 1604, and persecution, particularly of Jesuit priests, continued, the reaction took a violent course. In 1605 the Catholic opponents of James's religious policy attempted a fatal strike at the monarch, with a conspiracy known as the Gunpowder Plot. A group of dissidents, including Robert Catesby, a Jesuit priest named Father Henry Garnet, and the trigger man, Guy Fawkes, had rented space beneath the houses of Parliament (not the grand nineteenth-century structure as we know it, but its more modest predecessor), packed it with explosives, and planned to blow up the building on the occasion of the king's visit to open Parliament on November 5. The scheme was exposed at the last moment and the conspirators hanged, but the Gunpowder Plot was a national scandal that shattered James's image of himself as beloved leader and conciliator. Shakespeare was clearly affected by it. *Macbeth*, a play about a Scottish political assassination written for a Scottish king about 1606, seems to refer to Father Garnet and his notoriously ambiguous responses at his trial. After the murder of Duncan, the Porter imagines himself the keeper of the gates of Hell and welcomes such a devious speaker: "Faith, here's an equivocator, that could swear in both the scales against either scale, who committed treason enough for God's sake, yet could not equivocate to heaven" (2.3.8–11). Predictably, this terrorist act led to further suspicion and surveillance of Catholics.

But Puritans were discontented as well. James attempted to defang the fiercest of the radical reformers by convening and personally chairing a royal symposium on religious practice, the Hampton Court Conference of 1604, although he did not accede to most of their extreme Protestant demands. (It was this conference that led to the retranslation of the Bible published in 1611, the one we know as the King James Bible, or Authorized Version.) As I have indicated, a crux of religious contention at this stage of the English Reformation was church government. Among Puritans the Calvinist insistence on independence and local authority in church government carried over into secular politics, creating among many English people a protodemocratic and antiauthoritarian climate intolerable to King James. For his part, the king had begun to relish his authority as head of the Anglican Church, particularly after his relative insignificance in Scotland's radically reformed presbyterian structure. It is this linkage of hierarchy in church government with hierarchy in politics that marks one of James's most cherished principles, that expressed in his axiom "No bishop, no king." In other words, in James's view the religious principle of episcopacy, of authority vested in the bishop, also underwrote the structure of monarchy. Many Englishmen, especially some members of Parliament, passionately contested such ideology, and the conflict was never entirely resolved. In fact, failure to resolve it was one of the causes, some forty years later, of the English Revolution.

The Ideology of Order

In pressing the identification of religious with political sovereignty, King James hardly offered the world a new idea but instead adopted and exaggerated a familiar tenet of sixteenth-century thought. Because less than half the male population, and still less of the female, could read, and because books were expensive and newspapers nonexistent, a primary source of intellectual and philosophical guidance was the Sunday sermon. The government saw to it that such a forum did not go to waste. Elizabeth and her ministers were ever conscious of their power to use the pulpit for political ends, and they did so by encouraging the clergy to promulgate an ideology of order and obedience. As the sixteenth century drew to its close and the practices of Protestantism began to take firm hold in the Anglican Church, the Sunday sermon became an increasingly dominant feature of the divine service — the more Puritan the congregation, the more central was preaching — and frequently the sermon became a vehicle for the promotion of political values acceptable and advantageous to the Elizabethan regime. In those parishes where the priest was not licensed to preach, other ways were devised of acquainting the public with official political doctrine. One such maneuver was the use of the homily, a formal exhortation read from the pulpit to promote the interests of the state: it served to link the spiritual and the political into an ideological program of order and fear.

One of the most significant, *An Homily against Disobedience and Willful Rebellion,* was issued in 1570 in answer to the Northern Rebellion, the uprising of the previous year in support of Mary, Queen of Scots. A brief paragraph expresses the tenor of the piece, with an extended excerpt reprinted on page 345.

> Thus do you see that neither heaven nor paradise could suffer any rebellion in them, neither be places for any rebels to remain in. Thus became rebellion, as you see, both the first and greatest, and the very root of all other sins, and the first and principal cause both of all worldly and bodily miseries — sorrows, diseases, sicknesses and deaths — and, which is infinitely worse than all these, as is said, the very cause of death and damnation eternal also.

The identification established here between political and religious disobedience, sedition and sin, is one of the defining characteristics of ideology in early modern England. To lose one's life in political conflict could be construed as honorable, even glorious — the cardinal example in Shakespeare is Hotspur in *Henry IV, Part 1* — but to lose one's soul is another matter. Thus the policymakers in Elizabeth's government saw to it that rebellion was invested with grave spiritual consequences. Moreover, they made the Bible a political instrument, particularly the Old Testament with its morally charged narratives of disobedience to an angry God and its record of a people for whom religion and government were one and the same.

The official commitment to order and obedience was intimately connected to the cultural doctrine that we know as the Great Chain of Being. This theory of cosmic organization, which came down to the Elizabethans from the religious and political thinkers of the Middle Ages, held that God had created the universe according to a system of hierarchies, that every living creature and even every inanimate object occupied its ordained place in an elaborate interlocking scheme, and that awareness of that scheme and one's place in it was a precondition for the peaceful and productive operation of society. Moreover, the elaborate specificity of the system meant that it produced a vast system of analogies. The sun was chief among heavenly bodies, the king chief among men, the lion among beasts, the rose among flowers, and so on. In the fifteenth century Sir John Fortescue had written a disquisition on natural law that insists upon the naturalness of hierarchical authority:

> In this order hot things are in harmony with cold, dry with moist, heavy with light, great with little, high with low. In this order angel is set over angel, rank upon rank in the kingdom of heaven; man is set over man, beast over beast, bird over bird, and fish over fish, on the earth in the air and in the sea: so that there is no worm that crawls upon the ground, no bird that flies on high, no fish that swims in the depths, which the chain of this order does not bind in most harmonious concord. Hell alone, inhabited by none but sinners, asserts its claim to escape the embraces of this order. . . . God created as many different kinds of things as he did creatures, so that there is no creature which does not differ in some respect from all other creatures and by which it is in some respect superior or inferior to all the rest. So that from the highest angel down to the lowest of his kind there is absolutely not found an angel that has not a superior and inferior; nor from man down to the meanest worm is there any creature which is not in some respect superior to one creature and inferior to another. So that there is nothing which the bond of order does not embrace.   (Qtd. in Tillyard 26–27)

The utility of such a hierarchical philosophy for the governments of Elizabeth and James is obvious. As the doctrine made its way into English law, its effect was to criminalize extreme forms of ambition and social disruption.

Internal unrest that occurred despite this ideology, such as the Northern Rebellion of 1569 mentioned above, was suppressed by the raising of local militia on an as-needed basis. For other kinds of crime — theft, murder, treason, or other individual transgressions — justice was enforced by a system of freelance officers, local constables, justices of the peace, and a tough system of penalties. In some cases offenders were tortured with special instruments. Prisons were used chiefly as a holding tank while decisions were made about guilt or appropriate sentencing (except in the case of debtors, who were imprisoned at their own expense). Punishment was for the most part corporal, involving public whipping, dismemberment, and death. By law, stealing even a small sum of money, anything over two shillings, was considered a capital crime, although courts often intentionally undervalued goods in order to protect the petty thief from execution. In theory, the Elizabethan system of justice was severe; in fact, enforcement was hit or miss. From Hamlet's lament about "the law's delay" to the endless and inconclusive interrogation of Pompey in *Measure for Measure,* Shakespeare's plays repeatedly allude to the imperfections of human judicial systems.

Imperfect or not, the Elizabethan judicial system could function swiftly and fiercely. Executions were usually public and often celebratory. In 1579, as the queen seriously considered marriage to the French duke of Alençon, a Puritan gentleman named John Stubbs published a pamphlet titled "The Discovery of a Gaping Gulf whereinto England is like to be swallowed by another

French marriage, if the Lord forbid not the banns by letting her Majesty see the sin and punishment thereof." Stubbs considered himself a patriot, a concerned citizen looking out for his monarch's safety. For this offense, he and his publisher were taken to the scaffold. Sir John Neale describes what happened there:

> At the scaffold, each made a loyal speech to the people, Stubbs ending with a pun: "Pray for me," he begged, "now my calamity is at hand"; and when his right hand had been cut off, he took his hat from his head with his left, cried "God save the Queen!" and swooned. The publisher lifted his bloody stump; "I have left there a true Englishman's hand," he cried, and went away very stoutly and with great courage. A deep silence pervaded the multitude of spectators.   (246)

Such public displays of royal power were not infrequent. In the first few years of James's reign, his government executed some seventy persons each year in London, a city of fewer than 250,000 occupants (see Wotton 25). That there were not more is a testimony to the orthodoxy of hierarchy and order.

Another proof of the pervasiveness of this doctrine is the absence of a police force or a standing army in England in the sixteenth and early seventeenth centuries. The most compelling explanation is financial: Elizabeth preferred not to tax her people in order to support a professional militia, and her foreign policy was not expansionist. But the nation did not escape foreign entanglements. Since her predecessor had lost the English foothold in France, the town of Calais, Elizabeth sought to regain control of it or another French port. More than once she dispatched money and soldiers to the Netherlands to aid the Dutch in their struggles with Spain. (In one of these campaigns, Sir Philip Sidney was wounded in the leg and consequently died.) The rebellious Irish repeatedly threatened English hegemony there, and the occupation was costly. Militarily, Elizabeth's tightfistedness was aided by geography: isolation helped to protect the populace from external threat. In *Richard II*, John of Gaunt figuratively refers to England as

> this little world,
> This precious stone set in the silver sea,
> Which serves it in the office of a wall,
> Or as a moat defensive to a house,
> Against the envy of less happier lands.   (2.1.45–49)

In other words, the island nation was spared the need for an army. Substantial sums were spent on naval operations, however, which not only provided defense but also promoted exploration and colonization. After the execution of Mary, Queen of Scots, Spain attempted to invade England, but the effort was thwarted by the superior artillery of the English ships and the brilliant seamanship of Sir Francis Drake, whose forces defeated the Spanish Armada in July 1588. Occasional conflicts continued to erupt during the remainder of Elizabeth's reign and into James's, but as the Stuart kings (both James and Charles) began to misuse and lose their authority, external conflict gave way to civil war.

Shakespeare's Theater and the Problem of Authority

Shakespeare provides a clear statement of the ideology of order, one that depends on many of the same images and analogies found in the major philosophical expositions of the idea. In the first act of *Troilus and Cressida,* as the Greeks lament the length of the Trojan War and deplore Achilles' sulking in his tent, Ulysses delivers an extended speech in which he assigns responsibility for the impasse to the dissolution of authority and degree in his own camp.

> Troy, yet upon his bases, had been down,
> And the great Hector's [the Trojan champion's] sword had lack'd a
>   master,
> But for these instances:
> The specialty of rule hath been neglected,
> And look how many Grecian tents do stand
> Hollow upon this plain, so many hollow factions.
> When that the general is not like the hive
> To whom the foragers shall all repair,
> What honey is expected? Degree being vizarded [covered],
> Th'unworthiest shows as fairly in the mask.
> The heavens themselves, the planets, and this centre
> Observe degree, priority, and place,
> Insisture, course, proportion, season, form,
> Office, and custom, in all line of order;
> And therefore is the glorious planet Sol
> In noble eminence enthron'd and spher'd
> Amidst the other; whose med'cinable eye
> Corrects the ill aspects of planets evil,
> And posts like the commandment of a king,
> Sans check, to good and bad. But when the planets
> In evil mixture to disorder wander,
> What plagues and what portents, what mutiny!
> What raging of the sea, shaking of earth!
> Commotion in the winds! frights, changes, horrors
> Divert and crack, rend and deracinate [uproot]
> The unity and married calm of states
> Quite from their fixure! O, when degree is shak'd,
> Which is the ladder of all high designs,
> The enterprise is sick. How could communities,
> Degrees in schools, and brotherhoods in cities,
> Peaceful commerce from dividable shores,
> The primogenity and due of birth,
> Prerogative of age, crowns, sceptres, laurels,
> But by degree stand in authentic place?
> Take but degree away, untune that string,
> And hark what discord follows. Each thing meets
> In mere oppugnancy [complete opposition]: the bounded waters
> Should lift their bosoms higher than the shores,

And make a sop of all this solid globe;
Strength should be lord of imbecility,
And the rude son should strike his father dead;
Force should be right, or rather, right and wrong
(Between whose endless jar justice resides)
Should lose their names, and so should justice too!
Then every thing include itself in power,
Power into will, will into appetite,
And appetite, an universal wolf
(So doubly seconded with will and power),
Must make perforce an universal prey,
And last eat up himself. Great Agamemnon,
This chaos, when degree is suffocate,
Follows the choking,
And this neglection of degree it is
That by a pace goes backwards with a purpose
It hath to climb. The general's disdain'd
By him one step below, he by the next,
That next by him beneath; so every step,
Exampled by the first pace that is sick
Of his superior, grows to an envious fever
Of pale and bloodless emulation [rivalry],
And 'tis this fever that keeps Troy on foot,
Not her own sinews. To end a tale of length,
Troy in our weakness stands, not in her strength.   (1.3.75–137)

The rhetoric Ulysses employs did not originate with Shakespeare. The imagery in particular — the beehive, the planetary system of concentric spheres, the ladder, the musical scale, the sun, the king, the boundaries of sea and shore, chaos, cannibalism, fever — derives from the same tradition that produced the standard contemporary works on the subject of political and divine order, such as Hooker's *Laws of Ecclesiastical Polity* and Sir Thomas Elyot's *The Book Named the Governor.* Ulysses' speech is a powerful denunciation of those who neglect degree and fail to observe the divinely inscribed system of hierarchies, but we should remember that it is the speech of a fictional character whose political ends and distaste for Achilles require that he take this stand and who can scarcely be heard over the grinding of his ax.

Is it also an expression of Shakespeare's own position? Many readers over the past four centuries have thought so. As I have suggested, Shakespeare has often been considered a willing spokesman for the orthodoxy of his age, a loyal monarchist with a hatred for disorder and a contempt for political rebellion and disobedience. E. M. W. Tillyard opens his chapter on "Order" in *The Elizabethan World Picture* by quoting Ulysses' speech and implying that it is an expression of Shakespeare's own personal views. According to this early critical orthodoxy, the history plays constitute a warning against political division and opportunism, and *King Lear* represents a passionate exposition of the danger of breaking what Sir John Fortescue over a century earlier had called the "bond of order."

Other students of the period have taken a contrary position. While acknowledging the average Elizabethan's familiarity with the Chain of Being, they dispute Tillyard's assertion that it was universally regarded as natural and divinely ordained. Rather, they consider the paradigm a political tool employed by the state, particularly through the pulpit, to legitimate existing political structures and justify unjustifiable social and economic conditions. Some of these critics also credit Shakespeare (along with more outspoken dissenters of his age) with great intellectual liberty. Cultural materialists, most of them British followers of the Marxist cultural critic Raymond Williams, believe that Shakespeare's theater presented a deliberate threat to established authority in representing the means by which the government deployed its power and repressed opposing voices. Jonathan Dollimore, for example, sees *Measure for Measure* as sexually subversive, as sympathetic to the marginalized claims of deviant sexuality — specifically prostitution — and as a challenge to those forces of Jacobean authority that would attempt to regulate desire ("Transgression and Surveillance" 84).

Even more sophisticated readings of these political and theatrical conflicts are available. Certain American literary critics known as new historicists, influenced heavily by the French theorist Michel Foucault, insist that Shakespeare's theatrical enterprise was an unwitting instrument of state power, that it contributed paradoxically to the maintenance of the dominant political ideology. Stephen Greenblatt contends that the plays written for the public theater, especially Shakespeare's, generate subversive ideas about Elizabethan and Jacobean political authority but then reabsorb those subversive energies so that the critique of authority is contained within the theatrical system. His reading of the Great Tetralogy is characteristic: "the Henry plays confirm the Machiavellian hypothesis that princely power originates in force and fraud even as they draw their audience toward an acceptance of that power" (65). In other words, the theater functioned as a safety valve: it created and released a performed version of political dissidence while reinforcing the very powers that it challenged.

The Stage and Its Opponents

The view that the Crown tolerated the public theaters because they offered a sanitized form of resistance is made more plausible by the presence of a fierce antitheatricalism among the most extreme Puritan factions. The location of the public theaters, in the Liberties outside the walls of the City of London, was a result of opposition to the stage on the part of the City authorities, many of whom were themselves Puritans or were influenced by the heavy concentration of Puritans within their precincts. This compromise represents one instance of détente in a larger struggle between the monarch and the civic powers. Elizabeth and James not only put up with the acting companies but actually sponsored them and paid them to perform at court, and both monarchs' taste for "play" enraged the most fervent of the Protestant reformers.

Beginning in the 1570s and continuing into the seventeenth century, fierce attacks on the practices of the stage began to appear in print, a function of the professionalization of the theater, the construction of the permanent play-houses, and the increasing popularity of theatergoing among the people. Stephen Gosson published the vitriolic *Plays Confuted in Five Actions* in 1582, and though Gosson himself was not a Puritan, there is evidence that his polemic was commissioned by the City authorities. The following year Philip Stubbes, a Puritan zealot and furious opponent of the stage, produced a simi-lar assault on the immorality of the theater called *The Anatomy of Abuses,* and it was subsequently reprinted (see p. 351). These antitheatrical arguments are grounded in the Protestant abhorrence of ceremony and spectacle, and related to the more general suspicion of representation of any sort. Stubbes makes much of the etymological connection between "actor" and "hypocrite," and a corollary argument deplores the erasure of social and class distinctions in stage performances. (Ulysses' speech on social order reflects this position: "Degree being vizarded, / Th'unworthiest shows as fairly in the mask" [*Troilus and Cressida*, 1.3.83–84].) His other major complaint involves cross-dressing, or men taking women's parts:

> Our Apparell was given us as a signe distinctive to discern betwixt sex and sex, and therfore one to weare the Apparel of another sex is to participate with the same, and to adulterate the veritie of his own kinde. Wherefore these Women may not improperly be called *Hermaphroditi,* that is, Mon-sters of bothe kindes, half women, half men.   (Stubbes sig. F5v)

All of these contentions are linked by a distaste for transgression and fear that boundaries might be blurred.

Shakespeare himself survived these vehement assaults on his livelihood. He mostly avoided topical representation of contemporary controversy and so had little to say artistically about the Puritan detractors, unlike his colleague Ben Jonson, who in *The Alchemist* created a devastating portrait of two Puritan zealots, the wild-eyed Ananias and his elder and more sinister associate, Tribulation Wholesome. Shakespeare's treatments of the stage and of the imag-ination generally tend to be affirmative and oblique, displaced in the plays-within-plays in *Love's Labor's Lost, A Midsummer Night's Dream, Hamlet,* and *The Tempest.* But in one case he permitted himself a swipe at the antitheatrical faction. In *Twelfth Night,* Maria, describing the sober and hypocritical Malvo-lio, says that "sometimes he is a kind of puritan." Although she does not specifically identify him with a particular sect of religious reformers, Maria does glance disapprovingly at the self-righteousness and antifestivity charac-teristic of Protestant zeal. In the last moments of the play, tricked and humili-ated by a comic scheme, Malvolio leaves the stage with a parting resolution: "I'll be reveng'd on the whole pack of you" (5.1.378). History made the line prophetic. Less than fifty years later Oliver Cromwell, leading the descen-dants of the Elizabethan Puritans, deposed and executed Charles I, abolished the monarchy, took control of the state, and closed the playhouses.

→ SIR THOMAS SMITH

From *De Republica Anglorum: The Manner of Government or Policy of the Realm of England* 1583

Of Parliament and the Monarchy

Sir Thomas Smith's posthumously published work describes the respective functions of Parliament and the monarchy. Although Smith does not seem to acknowledge a potential conflict, the relationship between these two institutions became increasingly fractious after the death of Elizabeth I.

Book 2, Chapter 1

Of the Parliament and the Authority Thereof

The most high and absolute power of the realm of England consisteth in the Parliament. For as in war where the King himself in person, the nobility, the rest of the gentility, and the yeomanry are, is the force and power of England; so in peace and consultation where the Prince is to give life, and the last and highest commandment, the barony for the nobility and higher, the knights, esquires, gentlemen, and commons for the lower part of the commonwealth, the bishops for the clergy be present to advertise, consult, and show what is good and necessary for the commonwealth, and to consult together, and upon mature deliberation every bill or law being thrice read and disputed upon in either house, the other two parts first each a part, and after the Prince himself in presence of both the parties doth consent unto and alloweth. That is the Prince's and whole realm's deed: whereupon justly no man can complain, but must accommodate himself to find it good and obey it.

That which is done by this consent is called firm, stable, and *sanctum* [holy], and is taken for law. The Parliament abrogateth old laws, maketh new, giveth orders for things past, and for things hereafter to be followed, changeth rights and possessions of private men, legitimateth bastards, establisheth forms of religion, altereth weights and measures, giveth forms of succession to the crown, defineth of doubtful rights whereof is no law already made, appointeth subsidies, tails [a kind of tax], taxes, and impositions, giveth most free pardons and absolutions, restoreth in blood and name as the highest court, condemneth or absolveth them whom the Prince will put to that trial. And to be short, all that ever the people of Rome might do either in *Centuriatis comitiis* or *tributis* [Roman representative assemblies] the same may be done by the Parliament of England, which representeth and hath the power of the whole realm both the head and the body. For every Englishman is intended to be there present, either in person or by procuration and attorneys, of what preeminence, state, dignity, or quality soever he be, from the Prince (be he King or Queen) to the lowest person of England. And the consent of the Parliament is taken to be every man's consent.

Book 2, Chapter 3

Of the Monarch King or Queen of England

The Prince whom I now call (as I have often before) the Monarch of England, King or Queen, hath absolutely in his power the authority of war and peace, to defy what Prince it shall please him, and to bid him war, and again to reconcile himself and enter into league or truce with him at his pleasure or the advice only of his privy council. His privy council be chosen also at the Prince's pleasure out of the nobility or barony, and of the knights, and esquires, such and so many as he shall think good, who doth consult daily, or when need is of the weighty matters of the realm, to give therein to their Prince the best advice they can. The Prince doth participate to them all, or so many of them as he shall think good, such legations and messages as come from foreign Princes, such letters or occurrents [news] as be sent to himself or to his secretaries, and keepeth so many ambassades [messages] and letters sent unto him secret as he will, although these have a particular oath of a councillor touching faith and secrets administered unto them when they be first admitted into that company. So that herein the kingdom of England is far more absolute than either the dukedom of Venice is, or the kingdom of the Lacedemonians [Spartans] was. In war time, and in the field the Prince hath also absolute power, so that his word is a law, he may put to death, or to other bodily punishment, whom he shall think so to deserve, without process of law or form of judgment. This hath been sometime used within the realm before any open war in sudden insurrections and rebellions, but that not allowed of wise and grave men, who in that their judgment had consideration of the consequence and example, as much as of the present necessity, especially, when by any means the punishment might have been done by order of law. This absolute power is called martial law. . . .

To be short the Prince is the life, the head, and the authority of all things that be done in the realm of England. And to no Prince is done more honor and reverence than to the King and Queen of England, no man speaketh to the Prince nor serveth at the table but in adoration and kneeling; all persons of the realm be bareheaded before him: insomuch that in the chamber of presence where the cloth of estate is set, no man dare walk, yea though the Prince be not there, no man dare tarry there but bareheaded. This is understood of the subjects of the realm.

→ QUEEN ELIZABETH I

The Tilbury Speech

1588

Although historians debate whether the words that have come down to us are actually those spoken at Tilbury, most accept the speech as genuine. Elizabeth was described on this occasion by a contemporary as "full of princely resolution and more than feminine courage" and as having "passed like some Amazonian empress through all her army" (Neale 302). The armor she wore, the speech, the audacity of her being there at all — these declare her acute sense of audience and her understanding of how to make the spectators adore her.

My loving people, I have been persuaded by some that are careful of my safety to take heed how I committed myself to armed multitudes, for fear of treachery. But I tell you that I would not desire to live to distrust my faithful and loving people. Let tyrants fear: I have so behaved myself that under God I have placed my chiefest strength and safeguard in the loyal hearts and good-will of my subjects. Wherefore I am come among you at this time but for my recreation and pleasure, being resolved in the midst and heat of the battle to live and die amongst you all, to lay down for my God and for my Kingdom and for my people mine honor and my blood even in the dust. I know I have the body but of a weak and feeble woman, but I have the heart and stomach of a king and of a king of England too — and take foul scorn that Parma or any prince of Europe should dare to invade the borders of my realm. To the which rather than any dishonor shall grow by me, I myself will venter [risk] my royal blood; I myself will be your general, judge, and rewarder of your virtue in the field. I know that already for your forwardness you have deserved rewards and crowns, and I assure you in the word of a prince you shall not fail of them. In the meantime, my lieutenant general shall be in my stead, than whom never prince commanded a more noble or worthy subject. Not doubting but by your concord in the camp and valor in the field and your obedience to myself and my general, we shall shortly have a famous victory over those enemies of my God and of my kingdom.

→ KING JAMES I

From *A Speech to the Lords and Commons of the Parliament at Whitehall*

March 21, 1610

James's insistence on the monarch's supremacy to Parliament draws on the familiar imagery of divinity (kings as gods), paternity (kings as fathers), and biology (kings as heads of bodies). The timing of this speech is significant: some six years after James's assumption of the English throne, Parliament was becoming disillusioned with the king's authoritarian attitude and, as a result, increasingly recalcitrant.

The state of monarchy is the supremest thing upon earth. For kings are not only God's lieutenants upon earth, and sit upon God's throne, but even by God himself they are called gods. There be three principal similitudes that illustrates the state of monarchy. One taken out of the word of God, and the two other out of the grounds of policy and philosophy. In the Scriptures kings are called gods, and so their power after a certain relation compared to the divine power. Kings are also compared to fathers of families, for a king is truly *parens patriae,* the politic father of his people. And lastly, kings are compared to the head of this microcosm of the body of man.

Kings are justly called gods for that they exercise a manner or resemblance of divine power upon earth. For if you will consider the attributes to God, you shall see how they agree in the person of a king. God has power to create, or destroy, make, or unmake at his pleasure, to give life, or send death, to judge all, and to be judged nor accountable to none; to raise low things, and to make high things low at his pleasure, and to God are both soul and body due. And the like power have kings. They make and unmake their subjects; they have power of raising and casting down, of life and of death; judges over all their subjects, and in all cases, and yet accountable to none but God only. They have power to exalt low things and abase high things, and make of their subjects like men at the chess: a pawn to take a bishop or a knight, and to cry up or down any of their subjects, as they do their money. And to the king is due both the affection of the soul and the service of the body of his subjects. . . .

As for the father of a family, they had of old under the law of nature *patriam potestatem* [ancestral power], which was *potestatem vitae et necis* [power of life and death] over their children or family. I mean such fathers of families as were the lineal heirs of those families whereof kings did originally come, for kings had their first original from them who planted and spread themselves in colonies through the world. Now a father may dispose of his inheritance to his children at his pleasure: yea, even disinherit the eldest upon just occasions, and prefer the youngest, according to his liking; make them beggars or rich at his pleasure; restrain, or banish out of his presence, as he finds them give cause of offence, or restore them in favor again with the penitent sinner. So may the king deal with his subjects.

And lastly, as for the head of the natural body, the head has the power of directing all the members of the body to that use which the judgment in the head thinks most convenient. It may apply sharp cures, or cut off corrupt members, let blood in what proportion it thinks fit, and as the body may spare, but yet is all this power ordained by God *ad aedificationem, non ad destructionem* [for constructive, not destructive use]. For though God have power as well of destruction as of creation or maintenance, yet will it not agree with the wisdom of God to exercise his power in the destruction of nature and overturning the whole frame of things, since his creatures were made that his glory might thereby be the better expressed. So were he a foolish father that would disinherit or destroy his children without a cause, or leave off the careful education of them. And it were an idle head that would in place of physic so poison or phlebotomize [bleed] the body as might breed a dangerous distemper or destruction thereof.

But now in these our times we are to distinguish between the state of kings in their first original, and between the state of settled kings and monarchs that do at this time govern in civil kingdoms. For even as God, during the time of the Old Testament, spake by oracles and wrought by miracles, yet how soon it pleased him to settle a Church which was bought and redeemed by the blood of his only Son, Christ, then was there a cessation of both, he ever after governing his people and Church within the limits of his revealed will. So in the first original of kings, whereof some had their beginning by conquest, and some by election of the people, their wills at that time served for law. Yet how soon kingdoms began to be settled in civility and policy, then did kings set down their minds by laws, which are properly made by the king only, but at the rogation [formal request] of the people, the king's grant being obtained thereunto. And so the king became to be *lex loquens* [a speaking law], after a sort, binding himself by a double oath to the observation of the fundamental laws of his kingdom: tacitly, as by being a king; and so bound to protect as well the people as the laws of his kingdom, and expressly, by his oath at his coronation. So as every just king in a settled kingdom is bound to observe that paction [contract] made to his people by his laws, in framing his government agreeable thereunto, according to that paction which God made with Noah after the deluge: "Hereafter seed-time and harvest, cold and heat, summer and winter, and day and night shall not cease, so long as the earth remains." And therefore a king governing in a settled kingdom leaves to be a king, and degenerates into a tyrant, as soon as he leaves off to rule according to his laws. In which case the king's conscience may speak unto him as the poor widow said to Philip of Macedon: "Either govern according to your law, *aut ne rex sis* [or you are no king]." And though no Christian man ought to allow any rebellion of people against their prince, yet does God never leave kings unpunished when they transgress these limits. For in that same psalm where God says to kings *vos dii estis* [you are gods], he immediately thereafter concludes, "But ye shall die like men." The higher we are placed, the greater shall our fall be. *Ut casus sic dolor* [As the fall is, so is the grief]: the taller the trees be, the more in danger of the wind; and the tempest beats sorest upon the highest mountains. Therefore all kings that are not tyrants, or perjured, will be glad to bound themselves within the limits of their laws; and they that persuade them the contrary are vipers and pests, both against them and the commonwealth. For it is a great difference between a king's government in a settled state and what kings in their original power might do in *individuo vago* [as unrestrained individuals]. As for my part, I thank God I have ever given good proof that I never had intention to the contrary. And I am sure to go to my grave with that reputation and comfort, that never king was in all his time more careful to have his laws duly observed, and himself to govern thereafter, than I.

I conclude then this point touching the power of kings with this axiom of divinity: that as to dispute what God may do is blasphemy, but *quid vult deus* [what God wishes], that divines may lawfully and do ordinarily dispute and discuss, for to dispute *a posse ad esse* [from potential to actual] is both against logic and divinity, so is it sedition in subjects to dispute what a king may do in the height of his power. But just kings will ever be willing to declare what they will do, if they will not incur the curse of God. I will not be content that my power be disputed upon. But I shall ever be willing to make the reason appear of all my doings, and rule my actions according to my laws. . . .

But I would wish you to be careful to avoid three things in the matter of Grievances.

First, that you do not meddle with the main points of government. That is my craft: *tractent fabrilia fabri* [let craftsmen take care of their craft]; to meddle with that were to lesson me. I am now an old king, for six and thirty years have I governed in Scotland personally, and now have I accomplished my apprenticeship of seven years here; and seven years is a great time for a king's experience in government. Therefore there would not be too many Phormios to teach Hannibal. I must not be taught my office.

Secondly, I would not have you meddle with such ancient rights of mine, as I have received from my predecessors, possessing them *More Maiorum* [by the custom of our ancestors]: such things I would be sorry should be accounted for Grievances. All novelties are dangerous as well in a politic as in a natural body. And therefore I would be loath to be quarreled in my ancient rights and possessions. For that were to judge me unworthy of that which my predecessors had and left me.

And lastly, I pray you beware to exhibit for Grievance any thing that is established by a settled law, and whereunto (as you have already had a proof) you know I will never give a plausible answer. For it is an undutiful part in subjects to press their king, wherein they know beforehand he will refuse them. Now, if any law or statute be not convenient, let it be amended by Parliament, but in the mean time term it not a Grievance: for to be grieved with the law is to be grieved with the king, who is sworn to be the patron and maintainer thereof. But as all men are flesh, and may err in the execution of laws, so may you justly make a Grievance of any abuse of the law, distinguishing wisely between the faults of the person and the thing itself.

→ KING JAMES I

Secret Letter to Sir Robert Cecil
c. 1602

This is one of a series of private exchanges between James VI of Scotland (later James I of England) and Elizabeth's chief minister. Since the aging queen refused to name her successor, and since James's lineage gave him the most plausible claim, Cecil initiated a secret plan to insure James's succession to the English throne after the death of Elizabeth. Note the numerical code by which the various persons are denoted (Cecil is 10, Elizabeth is 24, James is 30). Another remarkable feature is the Scottish sound of James's spelling (here not modernized).

My dearest 10 [Sir Robert Cecil], I ame ashamed that I can as yett by no other meanes uitnesse my thankefulnes for youre daylie so honorable iudiciouse and painfull labouris for the furtherance of my greatest hoapes, then by baire inke and paper, and that youre trauellis of so great uorthe and inæstimable ualew shoulde be repayed uith so poore a recompence, but the best excuse is that these paperis are but uitnessis of that treasure of gratitude quhiche by youre goode desairtis is daylie noorished in my hairte.

I ame not a lytle encouraged by the letre of 24 [Queen Elizabeth] quhiche discoveris a great integritie in her affection, and plainnes in her dealing; quhom I oucht to thanke for her goode temper, ye may easilie guesse. I haue ansourid her in the best sorte I coulde, as by the coppie thairof ye will persaue, and that ye maye haue proofe that my confidence is fullie setlid upon you, I haue sent you the substance of tuo messages that Sir Antonie Shurley hath latelie sent me, uithout keeping up one iote thairof, quhose errouris appeare rather to proceide from ignorance then malice. Ye can not doe me a greatter seruice then to moue 24 [Queen Elizabeth] to continew this inuarde and privie forme of intelligence, quhairby I hoape ye shall in the ende proue a honest and happie minister.

To faithfull 8 [Mr. Edward Bruce] his lettir I remitte all particulairs, and speciallie my opinion hou ye shall behaue youre self in that maitter, quhiche, god knowis, is more greeuouse unto me then any temptation that satan by goddis permission coulde haue deuysed to haue aflicted me uith. But heir I ende, with the assurance of the continuance of my constant loue to my most faithfull 3 [Lord Henry Howard], assuring him that, as I ame infinitelie sorie for that defluxion fallin upon his eye, so uoulde I thinke ane hospitall a reuairde that uolde keepe no proportion, ather for a kings honoure to giue, or by him for so uell meriting seruices to be receaued. And thus, my dearest 10 [Sir Robert Cecil], I bidde both you and 3 [Lord Henry Howard] most hairtelie fair uell.

Your moste louing and assurid freind
30 [KING JAMES].

→ KING JAMES I

Letter to George Villiers, Duke of Buckingham   *c. December 1623*

Written less than two years before James's death, the letter expresses the profundity of the king's affection for his handsome young courtier. Buckingham was the most important in a long line of royal favorites.

I cannot content myself without sending you this present [letter], praying God that I may have a joyful and comfortable meeting with you and that we may make at this Christmas a new marriage ever to be kept hereafter; for, God so love me, as I desire only to live in this world for your sake, and that I had rather live banished in any part of the earth with you than live a sorrowful widow's life without you. And so God bless you, my sweet child and wife, and grant that you may ever be a comfort to your dear dad and husband.

→ SIR JOHN HARINGTON

Letter Describing the Revels at King James's Court   *1606*

Godson of Queen Elizabeth and a witty observer of court manners, Sir John Harington (1561–1612) describes the revels at James's court on the occasion of the visit of Queen Anne's brother, King Christian of Denmark. The excesses of the court noticed here were a subject of fierce satire in the period. Although Shakespeare usually avoids such concrete satire, the performance of his plays at court on similar evenings must have made him aware of this type of behavior.

One day, a great feast was held, and after dinner the representation of Solomon, his temple, and the coming of the Queen of Sheba was made, or (as I may better say) was meant to have been made, before their Majesties, by device of the Earl of Salisbury and others. — But, alas! as all earthly things do fail to poor mortals in enjoyment, so did prove our presentment hereof. The lady who did play the queen's part did carry most precious gifts to both their Majesties; but forgetting the steps arising to the canopy, overset her caskets into his Danish Majesty's lap and fell at his feet, though I rather think it was in his face. Much was the hurry and confusion; cloths and napkins were at hand, to make all clean. His Majesty then got up and would dance with the Queen of Sheba; but he fell down and humbled himself before her, and was carried to an inner chamber and laid on a bed of state; which was not a little defiled with the presents of the queen which had been bestowed on his garments; such as wine, cream, jelly, beverage, cakes, spices, and other good matters. The entertainment and show went forward, and most of the presenters went backward, or fell down, wine did so occupy their upper chambers. Now did appear, in rich dress, Hope, Faith, and Charity. Hope did assay to speak, but wine rendered her endeavors so feeble that she withdrew, and hope the king would excuse her brevity: Faith was then all alone, for I am certain she was not joined with good works, and left the court in a staggering condition. Charity came to the king's feet and seemed to cover the multitude of sins her sisters had committed; in some sort she made obeisance and brought gifts, but said she would return home again, as there was no gift which heaven had not already given his Majesty. She then returned to Hope and Faith, who were both sick and spewing in the lower hall. Next came Victory, in bright armor, and presented a rich sword to the king, who did not accept it, but put it by with his hand; and, by strange medley of versification, did endeavor to make suit to the king. But Victory did not triumph long, for after much lamentable utterance, she was led away like a silly captive and laid to sleep in the outer steps of the antechamber. Now did Peace make entry, and strive to get foremost to the king; but I grieve to tell how great wrath she did discover unto those of her attendants; and much contrary to her semblance, most rudely made war with her olive branch, and laid on the pates of those who did oppose her coming.

I have much marveled at these strange pageantries, and they do bring to my remembrance what passed of this sort in our queen's days; of which I was sometime an humble presenter and assistant, but I never did see such lack of good order, discretion, and sobriety, as I have now done. I have passed much time in seeing the royal sports of hunting and hawking, where the manners were such as made me devise the beasts were pursuing the sober creation, and not man in quest of exercise or food. I will now, in good sooth, declare to you, who will not blab, that the gunpowder fright [the Gunpowder Plot of 1605, a Catholic attempt to assassinate King James] is got out of all our heads, and we are going on, hereabouts, as if the devil was contriving every man should blow up himself by wild riot, excess, and devastation of time and temperance. The great ladies do go well-masked, and indeed it be the only show of their modesty, to conceal their countenance; but, alack, they meet with such countenance to uphold their strange doings that I marvel not at aught that happens. The lord of the mansion is overwhelmed in preparations at Theobalds, and doth marvelously please both kings, with good meat, good drink, and good speeches. I do often say (but not aloud) that the Danes have again conquered the Britons, for I see no man, or woman either, that can command himself or herself. I wish I was at home: — *O rus, quando te aspiciam?* [O fields, when will I see you?"] — And I will; before the Prince Vaudemont cometh.

I hear the uniting the kingdoms is now at hand; when the Parliament is held more will be done in this matter. Bacon is to manage all the affair, as who can better do these state jobs? My cousin, Lord Harington of Exton, doth much fatigue himself with the royal charge of the princess Elizabeth; and midst all the foolery of these times, hath much labor to preserve his own wisdom and sobriety. If you would wish to see how folly doth grow, come up quickly; otherwise, stay where you are, and meditate on the future mischiefs of those our posterity, who shall learn the good lessons and examples held forth in these days. I hope to see you at the Bath and see the gambols you can perform in the hot waters very speedily, and shall rest your assured friend in all quiet enjoyments and hearty good affections.

→ NICCOLÒ MACHIAVELLI

From *The Prince*   *1513*

Translated by Daniel Donno

When Shakespeare's Richard of Gloucester boasts that he could "set the murtherous Machivel to school" (*3 Henry VI* 3.2.193), he invokes the image of the treacherous Italian politician associated with the author of *The Prince,* one of the most influential books in sixteenth-century Europe. The chapter reprinted here, "In What Way

Princes Should Keep Their Word," is probably the most provocative of all in its endorsement of equivocation and its exploration of the link between language and power.

CHAPTER XVIII — IN WHAT WAY PRINCES SHOULD KEEP THEIR WORD

How praiseworthy it is that a prince keeps his word and governs by candor instead of craft, everyone knows. Yet the experience of our own time shows that those princes who had little regard for their word and had the craftiness to turn men's minds have accomplished great things and, in the end, have overcome those who governed their actions by their pledges.

You must recognize that there are two ways of fighting: by means of law, and by means of force. The first belongs properly to man, the second to animals; but since the first is often insufficient, it is necessary to resort to the second. Therefore, a prince must know how to use both what is proper to man and what is proper to beasts. The writers of antiquity taught rulers this lesson allegorically when they told how Achilles and many other ancient princes were sent to be nurtured by Chiron the centaur, so that he would train them in his discipline. Their having a creature half-man and half-beast as tutor only means that a prince must know how to use both the one and the other nature, and that the one without the other cannot endure.

Since a prince, then, is required to know how to assume a beastlike nature, he must adopt that of the fox and that of the lion; for a lion is defenseless against snares, and a fox is defenseless against wolves. Hence a prince ought to be a fox in recognizing snares and a lion in driving off wolves. Those who assume the bearing of the lion alone lack understanding. It follows, then, that a wise prince cannot and should not keep his pledge when it is against his interest to do so and when his reasons for making the pledge are no longer operative. If all men were good, this would be a bad precept, but since they are evil and would not keep a pledge to you, then you need not keep yours to them. Nor did a prince ever lack legitimate reasons by which to color his bad faith. One could cite a host of modern examples and list the many peace treaties, the many promises that were made null and void by princes who broke faith, with the advantage going to the one who best knew how to play the fox. But one must know how to mask this nature skillfully and be a great dissembler. Men are so simple and so much inclined to obey immediate needs that a deceiver will never lack victims for his deceptions. Of recent examples proving this, there is one I will not omit. Pope Alexander VI never gave thought to anything but deception and never lacked someone on whom to practice it. There never was a man who made promises more persuasively or swore to them more solemnly and kept so few of them as he. Yet his tricks always brought the results he desired, for he knew this side of the world well.

Therefore a prince will not actually need to have all the qualities previously mentioned, but he must surely seem to have them. Indeed, I would go so far as to say that having them all and always conforming to them would be harmful, while appearing to have them would be useful. That is, it will be well for him to seem and, actually, to be merciful, faithful, humane, frank, and religious. But he should preserve a disposition which will make a reversal of conduct possible in case the need arises. It must be understood, however, that a prince — especially a prince who has but recently attained power — cannot observe all of those virtues for which men are reputed good, because it is often necessary to act against mercy, against faith, against humanity, against frankness, against religion in order to preserve the state. Thus he must be disposed to change according as the winds of fortune and the alterations of circumstance dictate. As I have already said, he must stick to the good so long as he can, but, being compelled by necessity, he must be ready to take the way of evil.

Hence a prince must take care never to utter a word that is not implicit with the five above-mentioned qualities; and he must never appear to be anything but the very soul of clemency, faithfulness, frankness, humanity, and religion to all who see and hear him. But of all the qualities he must seem to have, none is more important than the last. Generally, men judge by the eye rather than the hand, for all men can see a thing, but few come close enough to touch it. All men will see what you seem to be; only a few will know what you are, and those few will not dare to oppose the many who have the majesty of the state on their side to defend them. In all men's acts, and in those of princes most especially, it is the result that renders the verdict when there is no court of appeal. Let the prince conquer a state, then, and preserve it; the methods employed will always be judged honorable, and everyone will praise them. For the mob is always impressed by appearances and by results; and the world is composed of the mob. The few cannot prevail when the many have someone to rely upon. A certain ruler of our time, whom it is better not to name, preaches nothing but peace and faith, yet he is the extreme enemy of both; and if he had been true to either of them, he would more than once have lost either power or reputation.

→ KING JAMES I

From *Basilikon Doron* 1594

Almost ten years before assuming the throne of England, James VI of Scotland wrote *Basilikon Doron*, an analysis of the proper practice of monarchy addressed to his infant son, Prince Henry. James also wrote treatises on witchcraft and on tobacco.

And therefore to return to my purpose anent [concerning] the government of your subjects, by making and putting good laws to execution, I remit the making of them to your own discretion, as you shall find the necessity of new-rising corruptions to require them. For *ex malis moribus bonae leges natae sunt* [from evil customs are born good laws]; besides, that in this country, we have already more good laws than are well executed, and am only to insist in your form of government anent their execution. Only remember, that as parliaments have been ordained for making of laws, so you abuse not their institution, in holding them for any men's particulars. For as a parliament is the honorablest and highest judgment in the land (as being the king's head court) if it be well used, which is by making of good laws in it, so is it the injustest Judgment-seat that may be, being abused to men's particulars: irrevocable decreits [decrees] against particular parties being given therein under color of general laws, and ofttimes the estates [parliamentary body] not knowing themselves whom thereby they hurt. And therefore hold no parliaments, but for necessity of new laws, which would be but seldom: for few laws and well put in execution are best in a well-ruled commonweal. As for the matter of fore-faltures [forcing nobles to forfeit land or title], which also are done in parliament, it is not good tigging [meddling] with these things. But my advice is, you fore-fault none but for such odious crimes as may make them unworthy ever to be restored again; and for smaller offenses, you have other penalties sharp enough to be used against them.

And as for the execution of good laws, whereat I left, remember that among the differences that I put betwixt the forms of the government of a good king and an usurping tyrant, I show how a tyrant would enter like a saint while he found himself fast underfoot, and then would suffer his unruly affections to burst forth. Therefore be you contrary, at your first entry to your kingdom, to that *Quinquennium Neronis* [the first five years (benevolent ones) of Nero's reign], with his tender-hearted wish, *Vellem nescirem literas* ["I wish I had not learned to write," Nero's response to signing a death warrant], in giving the law full execution against all breakers thereof but exception. For since you come not to your reign *precariò* [by anyone's permission], nor by conquest, but by right and due descent, fear no uproars for doing of justice, since you may assure yourself, the most part of your people will ever naturally favor justice, providing always that you do it only for love to justice, and not for satisfying any particular passions of yours, under color thereof. Otherwise, how justly that ever the offender deserve it, you are guilty of murder before God. For you must consider that God ever looketh to your inward intention in all your actions.

And when you have by the severity of justice once settled your countries and made them know that you can strike, then may you thereafter all the days of your life mix justice with mercy, punishing or sparing, as you shall find the crime to have been willfully or rashly committed, and according to the by-past behavior of the committer. For if otherwise you kyth [make known] your clemency at the first, the offenses would soon come to such heaps, and the contempt of you grow so great, that when you would fall to punish, the number of them to be punished would exceed the innocent, and you would be troubled to resolve whom-at to begin: and against your nature would be compelled then to wrack [injure] many, whom the chastisement of few in the beginning might have preserved. But in this, my over dear bought [costly] experience may serve you for a sufficient lesson. For I confess, where I thought (by being gracious at the beginning) to win all men's hearts to a loving and willing obedience, I by the contrary found the disorder of the country and the loss of my thanks to be all my reward.

But as this severe justice of yours upon all offenses would be but for a time (as I have already said), so is there some horrible crimes that you are bound in conscience never to forgive: such as witch-craft, willful murder, incest (especially within the degrees of consanguinity), sodomy, poisoning, and false coin. As for offenses against your own person and authority, since the fault concerneth yourself, I remit to your own choice to punish or pardon therein, as your heart serveth you, and according to the circumstances of the turn, and the quality of the committer.

Here would I also eke [add] another crime to be unpardonable, if I should not be thought partial: but the fatherly love I bear you will make me break the bounds of shame in opening it unto you. It is, then, the false and unreverent writing or speaking of malicious men against your parents and predecessors: you know the command in God's law, "Honor your Father and Mother." And consequently, since you are the lawful magistrate, suffer not both your princes and your parents to be dishonored by any; especially sith the example also toucheth yourself, in leaving thereby to your successors, the measure of that which they shall mete out again to you in your like behalf. I grant we have all our faults, which, privately betwixt you and God, should serve you for examples to meditate upon, and mend in your person; but should not be a matter of discourse to others whatsoever. And sith you are come of as honorable predecessors as any prince living, repress the insolence of such, as under pretense to tax a vice in the person, seek craftily to stain the race, and to steal the affection of the people from their posterity. For how can they love you, that hated them whom-of you are come? Wherefore destroy men innocent young sucking wolves and foxes, but for the hatred they bear to their race? And why will a colt of a courser of Naples give a greater price in a market than an ass-colt, but for love of the race? It is therefore a thing monstrous to see a man love the child and hate the parents: as on the other part, the infaming and making odious of the parents is the readiest way to bring the son in contempt. And for conclusion of this point, I may also allege my own experience: for besides the judgments of God, that with my eyes I have seen fall upon all them that were chief traitors to my parents, I may justly affirm I never found yet a constant biding by me in all my straits by any that were of perfect age in my parents' days, but only by such as constantly bode by them. I mean specially by them that served the queen my mother: for so that I discharge my conscience to you, my son, in revealing to you the truth, I care not what any traitor or treason-allower think of it.

And although the crime of oppression be not in this rank of unpardonable crimes, yet the overcommon use of it in this nation, as if it were a virtue, especially by the greatest rank of subjects in the land, requireth the king to be a sharp censurer thereof. Be diligent therefore to try and awful to beat down the horns of proud oppressors. Embrace the quarrel of the poor and distressed, as your own particular, thinking it your greatest honor to repress the oppressors. Care for the pleasure of none, neither spare you any pains in your own person, to see their wrongs redressed: and remember of the honorable style given to my grandfather of worthy memory, in being called *the poor man's King*. And as the most part of a king's office standeth in deciding that question of *meum* and *tuum* [mine and thine], among his subjects; so remember when you sit in judgment that the throne you sit on is God's, as Moses saith, and sway neither to the right hand nor to the left, either loving the rich, or pitying the poor. Justice should be blind and friendless: it is not there you should reward your friends or seek to cross your enemies.

→ SIMON FORMAN

From His *Diary* *January 1597*

On a Dream about an Encounter with Queen Elizabeth

Simon Forman (1552–1611), astrologer and pseudophysician, here privately describes a dream about Queen Elizabeth. The language and details of the entry suggest the underside of the "romance" between queen and subjects that Elizabeth sought to maintain.

Dreamt that I was with the Queen, and that she was a little elderly woman in a coarse white petticoat all unready. She and I walked up and down through lanes and closes, talking and reasoning. At last we came over a great close where were many people, and there were two men at hard words. One of them was a weaver, a tall man with a reddish beard, distract of his wits. She talked to him and he spoke very merrily unto her, and at last did take her and kiss her. So I took her by the arm still, and then we went through a dirty lane. She had a long white smock very clean and fair, and it trailed in the dirt and her coat behind. I took her coat and did carry it up a good way, and then it hung too low before. I told her she should do me a favor to let me wait on her, and she said I should. Then said I, "I mean to wait *upon* you and not under you, that I might make this belly a little bigger to carry up this smock and coat out of the dirt." And so we talked merrily; then she began to lean upon me, when we were past the dirt and to be very familiar with me, and methought she began to love me. When we were alone, out of sight, methought she would have kissed me.

→ JOHN FIELD AND THOMAS WILCOX(?)

From *An Admonition to the Parliament* 1572

Attributed to John Field and Thomas Wilcox, this document is an early attack on the corruption of the Anglican Church. It captures the tenor of reformist ideology and serves as a guide to the direction of Puritan thought in the last decades of the sixteenth century.

May it therefore please your wisdoms to understand, we in England are so far off from having a church rightly reformed according to the prescript of God's word, that as yet we are not come to the outward face of the same. For to speak of that wherein all consent, and whereupon all writers accord: the outward marks whereby a true Christian church is known, are preaching of the word purely, ministering of the sacraments sincerely, and ecclesiastical discipline which consisteth in admonition and correction of faults severely. Touching the first, namely the ministry of the word, although it must be confessed that the substance of doctrine by many delivered is sound and good, yet herein it faileth, that neither the ministers thereof are according to God's word proved, elected, called, or ordained: nor the function in such sort so narrowly looked unto, as of right it ought and is of necessity required. For whereas in the old church a trial was had both of their ability to instruct and of their godly conversation also, now by the letters commendatory of some one man, noble or other, tag and rag, learned and unlearned, of the basest sort of the people (to the slander of the Gospel in the mouths of the adversaries) are freely received. In those days no idolatrous sacrificers or heathenish priests were appointed to be preachers of the Gospel: but we allow and like well of popish mass-mongers, men for all seasons, King Henry's priests, King Edward's priests, Queen Mary's priests, who of a truth (if God's word were precisely followed) should from the same be utterly removed. Then they taught others; now they must be instructed themselves, and therefore like young children they must learn catechisms. Then election was made by the common consent of the whole church: now every one picketh out for himself some notable good benefice, he obtaineth the next advowson [right of office] by money or by favor, and so thinketh himself to be sufficiently chosen. Then the congregation had authority to call ministers; instead thereof now they run, they ride, and by unlawful suit and buying, prevent other suitors also. Then no minister [was] placed in any congregation but by the consent of the people; now that authority is given into the hands of the bishop alone, who by his sole authority thrusteth upon them such as they many times as well for unhonest life, as also for lack of learning, may and do justly dislike. Then none [was] admitted to the ministry, but a place was void before hand to which he should be called; but now bishops (to whom the right of ordering ministers doth at no hand appertain) do make 60, 80, or a 100 at a clap, and send them abroad into the country like masterless men. Then after just trial and vocation they were admitted to their function, by laying on of the hands of the company of the eldership only; now

there is (neither of these being looked unto) required an alb, a surplice, a vest-
ment, a pastoral staff, beside that ridiculous, and (as they use it to their new
creatures) blasphemous saying, "Receive the holy ghost." Then every pastor
had his flock, and every flock his shepherd, or else shepherds; now they do not
only run fisking [scampering] from place to place (a miserable disorder in
God's church) but covetously join living to living, making shipwreck of their
own consciences, and being but one shepherd (nay, would to God they were
shepherds and not wolves) have many flocks. Then the ministers were preachers; now bare readers. And if any be so well disposed to preach in their own
charges, they may not without my Lord's license. In those days known by
voice, learning, and doctrine; now they must be discerned from other by
popish and Antichristian apparel, as cap, gown, tippet, etc. Then, as God gave
utterance they preached the word only; now they read homilies, articles,
injunctions, etc. Then it was painful; now gainful. Then poor and ignomin-
ious; now rich and glorious. And therefore titles, livings, and offices by
Antichrist devised are given to them, as Metropolitan, Archbishop, Lord's
Grace, Lord Bishop, Suffragan, Dean, Archdeacon, Prelate of the Garter,
Earl, County Palatine, Honor, High Commissioners, Justices of Peace and
Quorum, etc. All which, together with their offices, as they are strange and
unheard of in Christ's church, nay plainly in God's word forbidden, so are they
utterly with speed out of the same to be removed. Then ministers were not
tied to any form of prayers invented by man, but as the spirit moved them, so
they poured forth hearty supplications to the Lord. Now they are bound of
necessity to a prescript order of service and book of common prayer in which a
great number of things contrary to God's word are contained, as baptism by
women, private Communions, Jewish purifyings, observing of holy days, etc.,
patched (if not all together, yet the greatest piece) out of the Pope's portuis
[manual]. Then feeding the flock diligently; now teaching quarterly. Then
preaching in season and out of season; now once in a month is thought sufficient, if twice, it is judged a work of supererogation. Then nothing taught but
God's word; now princes' pleasures, men's devices, popish ceremonies, and
Antichristian rites in public pulpits defended. Then they sought them; now
they seek theirs.

These, and a great many other abuses are in the ministry remaining, which
unless they be removed and the truth brought in, not only God's justice shall
be poured forth, but also God's church in this realm shall never be built. For if
they which seem to be workmen are no workmen in deed, but in name, or else
work not so diligently and in such order as the workmaster commandeth, it is
not only unlikely that the building shall go forward, but altogether impossible
that ever it shall be perfected. The way therefore to avoid these inconveniences
and to reform these deformities is this: your wisdoms have to remove advow-
sons, patronages, impropriations, and bishops' authority, claiming to themselves thereby right to ordain ministers, and to bring in that old and true
election, which was accustomed to be made by the congregation. You must
displace those ignorant and unable ministers already placed, and in their
rooms appoint such as both can and will by God's assistance feed the flock.

You must pluck down and utterly overthrow without hope of restitution the Court of Faculties, from whence not only licenses to enjoy many benefices are obtained, as pluralities, trialities, totquots [licenses for multiple benefices], etc., but all things for the most part, as in the court of Rome are set on sale, licenses to marry, to eat flesh in times prohibited, to lie from benefices and charges, and a great number beside of such like abominations. Appoint to every congregation a learned and diligent preacher. Remove homilies, articles, injunctions, a prescript order of service made out of the mass book. Take away the lordship, the loitering, the pomp, the idleness, and livings of bishops, but yet employ them to such ends as they were in the old church appointed for. Let a lawful and a godly seignorie look that they preach, not quarterly or monthly, but continually: not for filthy lucre's sake, but of a ready mind. So God shall be glorified, your consciences discharged, and the flock of Christ (purchased with his own blood) edified.

Now to the second point, which concerneth ministration of sacraments. In the old time, the word was preached before they were ministered; now it is supposed to be sufficient if it be read. Then, they were ministered in public assemblies; now in private houses. Then by ministers only; now by midwives, and deacons, equally. But because in treating of both the sacraments together we should deal confusedly: we will therefore speak of them severally. And first for the Lord's Supper, or Holy Communion.

They had no introit, for Celestinus a pope brought it in about the year 430. But we have borrowed a piece of one out of the mass book. They read no fragments of the Epistle and Gospel; we use both. The Nicene Creed was not read in their Communion; we have it in ours. There was then accustomed to be an examination of the communicants, which now is neglected. Then they ministered the Sacrament with common and usual bread; now with wafer cakes, brought in by Pope Alexander, being in form, fashion, and substance like their god of the altar. They received it sitting; we kneeling, according to Honorius' decree. Then it was delivered generally, and indefinitely, "Take ye and eat ye"; we particularly, and singularly, "Take thou, and eat thou." They used no other words but such as Christ left; we borrow from papists, "The body of our Lord Jesus Christ which was given for thee, etc." They had no "Gloria in excelsis" in the ministry of the Sacrament then, for it was put to afterward; we have now. They took it with conscience; we with custom. They shut men by reason of their sins, from the Lord's Supper; we thrust them in their sin to the Lord's Supper. They ministered the Sacrament plainly; we pompously with singing, piping, surplice and cope wearing. They simply as they received it from the Lord; we, sinfully, mixed with man's inventions and devices. And as for Baptism, it was enough with them, if they had water, and the party to be baptised faith, and the minister to preach the word and minister the sacraments.

Now we must have surplices devised by Pope Adrian, interrogatories ministered to the infant, godfathers, and godmothers, . . . holy fonts invented by Pope Pius, crossing and such like pieces of popery, which the church of God in the apostles' times never knew (and therefore not to be used), nay (which we are sure of) were and are man's devices, brought in long after the purity of the primitive church. To redress these, your wisdoms have to remove (as before) ignorant ministers, take away private communions and baptisms, to enjoin deacons and midwives not to meddle in ministers' matters; if they do, to see them sharply punished. To join assistance of elders and other officers, that seeing men will not examine themselves, they may be examined, and brought to render a reason of their hope. That the statute against wafer cakes may more prevail than an injunction. That people be appointed to receive the Sacrament rather sitting, for avoiding of superstition, than kneeling, having in it the outward show of evil, from which we must abstain. . . . That both the Sacrament of the Lord's Supper and Baptism also may be ministered according to the ancient purity and simplicity. . . . And finally, that nothing be done in this or any other thing but that which you have the express warrant of God's word for.

✦ From *The Catholics' Supplication* and *An Answer to the Catholics' Supplication*   *1603*

When James I succeeded to the throne in 1603, English Catholics approached the new king with a plea for toleration, appealing particularly to his memory of the execution (or martyrdom) of his mother, Mary, Queen of Scots. The appearance of *The Catholics' Supplication* was immediately followed by the publication of Christopher Muriel's *Answer*, a point-by-point refutation of the Catholic plea.

THE CATHOLICS' SUPPLICATION

The main of this realm, if we respect religion (setting petty sects aside), consisteth upon four parts: Protestants, who have domineered all the former Queen's days; Puritans, who have crept up apace among them; Atheists or Politicians, who were bred upon their brawls and contentions in matters of faith; and Catholics, who as they are opposite to all, so are they detested of all, because Error was ever an enemy to Truth. Hardly all, or any of the first, two, three can be suppressed, and therefore we beseech your majesty to yield us as much favor as others of contrary religion (to that which shall be publicly professed in England) shall obtain at your hands. For if our fault be like, or less, or none at all, in equity our punishment ought to be like, or less, or none at all. . . . Questionless, dread Sovereign, the kingdom of England, by cruel persecution of Catholics, hath been almost odious to all Christian nations: trade and traffic is decayed, wars and blood hath seldom ceased, subsidies and taxes never so many, discontented minds innumerable, all which your majesty's princely connivency to your humble suppliants, the afflicted Catholics, will easily redress, especially at your highness' ingress. . . .

How grateful will it be to all Catholic princes abroad, and honorable to your majesty, to understand how Queen Elizabeth's severity is changed into your royal clemency, and that the lenity of a man reedified that which the misinformed anger of a woman destroyed. . . . We request no more favor at your grace's hands, than that we may securely profess that Catholic religion which all your happy predecessors professed, from Donaldus the first converted unto your majesty's peerless mother last martyred. A religion venerable for antiquity, majestical for amplitude, constant for continuance, irreprehensible for doctrine, inducing to all kind of virtue and piety, dissuading from all sin and wickedness. A religion beloved by all primitive pastors, established by all ecumenical councils, upheld by all ancient doctors, maintained by the first and most Christian emperors, recorded almost alone in all ecclesiastical histories, sealed with the blood of millions of martyrs, adorned with the virtues of so many confessors, beautified with the purity of thousands of virgins, so conformable to natural sense and reason and finally so agreeable to the sacred text of God's word and gospel. The free use of this religion we request, if not in public churches, at least in private houses; if not with approbation, yet with toleration, without molestation. . . .

Your sacred majesty's most devoted servants,
The Catholics of England

An Answer to the Catholics' Supplication

. . . and as for the religion that was professed in those days [the early days of the Christian church] and long before Constantine's time, it was the same religion that we in England do now profess [i.e., the Church of England]. And it is for certain that the heathenish and infidel emperors, both long before Constantine's days and long since, did persecute the now professed religion in England, and that it was sealed with the blood of many martyrs, adorned with the virtues of many thousand confessors, beautified with the blood of the pure and immaculate virgins; neither were the bishops of Rome in those days freed from the said persecutions. But when infidel emperors by God's divine providence ceased their tyranny, then the Luciferian popes by degrees and steps climbing the highest staff of the ladder of pride did so far exceed in haughtiness of heart, insolency, and tyranny, that they first did shake off the lawful authority of emperors in the electing and admitting the pope, and then presently after they did domineer and tyrannize over emperors, kings, and all degrees of persons spiritual and temporal, so that it is to be doubted whether the heathenish emperors in their time or the irreligious popes in their time have persecuted and tormented to death the greater number of faithful Christians and the saints of God. It is superfluous to rehearse the stories of these things, seeing they be recorded in all ecclesiastical histories, and in the chronicles of all kingdoms. And we are persuaded that your grace hath both seen and read the history of these bloody tragedies. But of late time the pope hath been well plumed of his borrowed feathers, and his Luciferian pride somewhat depressed. Yet if the papists will so be content, we will join with them to procure that several and free counsel may be held in Christendom, whereunto both Papists and Protestants may freely repair, that thereby the Church of Christ may have peace, and the ignorant may be confirmed in the true faith. And to this purpose hath one of our learned divines offered himself to dispute with any papists whosoever (and many other will do the like) so that [provided that] his person may be secured from peril. This I pray God that it may be effected, and that he that is the true God may be worshipped of all, and that Baal may be utterly forgotten, that all Christian kingdoms agreeing in true doctrine and sincere truth may jointly acknowledge one verity, one faith, one baptism, one religion, and one only God in trinity, and trinity in unity, the Father, the Son, and the Holy Ghost, Amen. . . .

These Romanists have sugared words, but their hearts be full of deadly poison, for although they be a generation of vipers, yet they can change their shape into an Angel of light to deceive the very elect, if it were possible. The world can testify that the manifold treasons and conspiracies of the papists were sufficient testimonies of their demerit. And if they must needs be "tormented in soul and conscience for their least prevarication," needs must thousands of their souls and consciences be tormented for their many treasons and conspiracies against their late anointed queen now deceased. But whatsoever they profess in words it is impossible so long as they profess in the Romish religion to be faithful subjects unto your grace. . . .

Therefore whatsoever they profess in words, they cannot serve God and the devil, neither can they truly serve and obey you and the Pope. Two so great contrarieties cannot concur in one subject. And thus I conclude, praying to God, as our bounden duty requireth, that of his great goodness he will vouchsafe to bless, preserve, and defend your royal majesty, our noble queen, and all your princely children from all your enemies both foreign and domestical, spiritual and temporal, and from the treasons and conspiracies of all Romanists. That your sacred Majesty and your posterity may live and reign over us in the fear of God, and to his honor and glory in regal dignity, happy prosperity, godly peace and unity, and that after this life you may have celestial felicity in the life to come forevermore, Amen.

Your Majesty's most humble and dutiful subject,

Christopher Muriel, Senior

→ From *An Homily against Disobedience and Willful Rebellion* 1570

One of the most influential of the homilies read from the pulpit during Anglican Church services, the *Homily against Disobedience* was a direct response to the Northern Rebellion of 1569. It represents the Crown's attempts to use the church as a means of social control by identifying political with religious ideology: political rebellion was not only illegal but also sinful, a cause for spiritual damnation.

Obedience is the principal virtue of all virtues, and indeed the very root of all virtues, and the cause of all felicity. But as all felicity and blessedness should have continued with the continuance of obedience, so with the breach of obedience and breaking in of rebellion, all vices and miseries did withal break in and overwhelm the world. The first author of which rebellion, the root of all vices and mother of all mischiefs, was Lucifer, first God's most excellent creature and most bounden subject, who, by rebelling against the majesty of God, of the brightest and most glorious angel is become the blackest and most foulest fiend and devil, and from the height of heaven is fallen into the pit and bottom of hell.

Here you may see the first author and founder of rebellion, and the reward thereof. Here you may see the grand captain and father of all rebels, who, persuading the following of his rebellion against God their creator and lord, unto our first parents, Adam and Eve, brought them in high displeasure with God, wrought their exile and banishment out of Paradise, a place of all pleasure and goodness, into this wretched earth and vale of all misery, procured unto them sorrows of their minds, mischiefs, sickness, diseases, death of their bodies, and, which is far more horrible than all worldly and bodily mischiefs, he had wrought thereby their eternal and everlasting death and damnation, had not God by the obedience of his son, Jesus Christ, repaired that which man by disobedience and rebellion had destroyed, and so of his mercy had pardoned and forgiven him. Of which all and singular the premises the Holy Scriptures do bear record in sundry places. Thus you do see that neither heaven nor paradise could suffer any rebellion in them, neither be places for any rebels to remain in. Thus became rebellion, as you see, both the first and greatest, and the very root of all other sins, and the first and principal cause both of all worldly and bodily miseries — sorrows, diseases, sicknesses, and deaths — and, which is infinitely worse than all these, as is said, the very cause of death and damnation eternal also. After this breach of obedience to God and rebellion against his majesty, all mischiefs and miseries breaking in therewith and overflowing the world, lest all things should come unto confusion and utter ruin, God forthwith, by laws given unto mankind, repaired again the rule and order of obedience thus by rebellion overthrown, and, besides the obedience due unto his Majesty, he not only ordained that in families and households the wife should be obedient unto her husband, the children unto their parents, the servants unto their masters, but also, when mankind increased and spread itself more largely over the world, he by his Holy Word did constitute and ordain in cities and countries several and special governors and rulers, unto whom the residue of his people should be obedient.

As in reading of the Holy Scriptures we shall find in very many and almost infinite places, as well of the Old Testament as of the New, that kings and princes, as well the evil as the good, do reign by God's ordinance, and that subjects are bound to obey them; that God doth give princes wisdom, great power, and authority; that God defendeth them against their enemies, and destroyeth their enemies horribly; that the anger and displeasure of the prince is as the roaring of a lion, and the very messenger of death; and that the subject that provoketh him to displeasure sinneth against his own soul; with many other things concerning both the authority of princes and the duty of subjects.

But here let us rehearse two special places out of the New Testament, which may stand in stead of all other. The first out of Saint Paul's Epistle to the Romans, and the thirteenth chapter, where he writeth thus unto all subjects: "Let every soul be subject unto the higher powers, for there is no power but of God, and the powers that be are ordained of God. Whosoever therefore resisteth the power, resisteth the ordinance of God. And they that resist, shall receive to themselves damnation. For princes are not to be feared for good works, but for evil. Wilt thou then be without fear of the power? Do well, so shalt thou have praise of the same, for he is the minister of God for thy wealth; but if thou do evil, fear. For he beareth not the sword for naught, for he is the minister of God to take vengeance upon him that doth evil. Wherefore you must be subject, not because of wrath only, but also for conscience sake. For, for this cause you pay also tribute, for they are God's ministers, serving for the same purpose. Give to every man therefore his duty; tribute, to whom tribute belongeth; custom, to whom custom is due; fear, to whom fear belongeth; honor, to whom you owe honor." Thus far are Saint Paul's words. The second place is in St. Peter's first Epistle, and the second chapter, whose words are these: "Submit yourselves unto all manner [i.e., kinds of] ordinance of man for the Lord's sake, whether it be unto the king, as unto the chief head, either unto rulers, as unto them that are sent of him for the punishment of evildoers, but for the cherishing of them that do well. For so is the will of God, that with well doing you may stop the mouths of ignorant and foolish men: as free, and not as having the liberty for a cloak of maliciousness, but even as the servants of God. Honor all men, love brotherly fellowship, fear God, honor the king. Servants, obey your masters with fear, not only if they be good and courteous, but also though they be froward." Thus far out of Saint Peter.

By these two places of the Holy Scriptures it is most evident that kings, queens, and other princes (for he speaketh of authority and power, be it in men or women) are ordained of God, are to be obeyed and honored of their subjects; that such subjects as are disobedient or rebellious against their princes disobey God and procure their own damnation, that the government of princes is a great blessing of God given for the commonwealth, specially of the good and godly; for the comfort and cherishing of whom God giveth and setteth up princes; and on the contrary part, to the fear and for the punishment of the evil and wicked. Finally that if servants ought to obey their masters, not only being gentle, but such as be froward, as well and much more ought subjects to be obedient, not only to their good and courteous but also to their sharp and rigorous princes. It cometh therefore neither of chance and fortune (as they term it) nor of the ambition of mortal men and women climbing up of their own accord to dominion, that there be kings, queens, princes, and other governors over men being their subjects; but all kings, queens, and other governors are specially appointed by the ordinance of God. And as God himself, being of an infinite majesty, power, and wisdom, ruleth and governeth all things in heaven and in earth, as the universal monarch and only king and emperor over all, as being only able to take and bear the charge of all: so hath he constituted, ordained, and set earthly princes over particular kingdoms and dominions in earth, both for the avoiding of all confusion, which else would be in the world if it should be without such governors, and for the great quiet and benefit of earthly men their subjects, and also that the princes themselves in authority, power, wisdom, providence, and righteousness in government of people and countries committed to their charge, should resemble his heavenly governance, as the majesty of heavenly things may by the baseness of earthly things be shadowed and resembled. And for that similitude that is between the heavenly monarchy and earthly kingdoms well governed, our savior Christ in sundry parables saith that the kingdom of heaven is resembled unto a man a king, and as the name of the king is very often attributed and given unto God in the Holy Scriptures, so doth God himself in the same Scriptures sometime vouchsafe to communicate his name with earthly princes, terming them gods: doubtless for that similitude of government which they have or should have not unlike unto God their king. Unto the which similitude of heavenly government, the nearer and nearer that an earthly prince doth come in his regiment, the greater blessing of God's mercy is he unto that country and people over whom he reigneth: and the further and further that an earthly prince doth swerve from the example of the heavenly government, the greater plague he is of God's wrath, and punishment by God's justice, unto that country and people over whom God for their sins hath placed such a prince and governor. . . .

What shall subjects do then? Shall they obey valiant, stout, wise, and good princes, and condemn, disobey, and rebel against children being their princes, or against undiscreet and evil governors? God forbid. For first, what a perilous thing were it to commit unto the subjects the judgment [as to] which prince is wise and godly, and his government good, and which is otherwise. As though the foot must judge of the head, an enterprise very heinous, and must needs breed rebellion. For who else be they that are most inclined to rebellion, but such haughty spirits? From whom springeth such foul ruin of realms? Is not rebellion the greatest of all mischiefs? And who are most ready to the greatest mischiefs, but the worst men? Rebels therefore the worst of all subjects are most ready to rebellion, as being the worst of all vices, and furthest from the duty of a good subject. As on the contrary part, the best subjects are most firm and constant in obedience, as in the special and peculiar virtue of good subjects. What an unworthy matter were it then to make the naughtiest subjects, and most inclined to rebellion and all evil, judges over their princes, over their government, and over their councillors, to determine which of them be good or tolerable, and which be evil and so intolerable that they must needs be removed by rebels, being ever ready as the naughtiest subjects, soonest to rebel against the best princes, specially if they be young in age, women in sex, or gentle and courteous in government, as trusting by their wicked boldness easily to overthrow their weakness and gentleness, or at the least so to fear the minds of such princes, that they may have impunity of their mischievous doings. But whereas indeed a rebel is worse than the worst prince, and rebellion worse than the worst government of the worst prince that hitherto hath been: both are rebels unmeet ministers, and rebellion an unfit and unwholesome medicine to reform any small lacks in a prince, or to cure any little griefs in government, such lewd remedies being far worse than any other maladies and disorders that can be in the body of a commonwealth. But whatsoever the prince be, or his government, it is evident that for the most part those princes whom some subjects do think to be very godly and under whose government they rejoice to live, some other subjects do take the same to be evil and ungodly and do wish for a change. If therefore all subjects that mislike of their prince should rebel, no realm should ever be without rebellion. It were more meet that rebels should hear the advice of wise men, and give place unto their judgment, and follow the example of obedient subjects, as reason is that they whose understanding is blinded with so evil an affection, should give place to them that be of sound judgment, and that the worse should give place to the better: and so might realms continue in long obedience, peace, and quietness. But what if the prince be undiscreet, and evil indeed, and it also evident to all men's eyes that he so is? I ask again, what if it be long of [a result of] the wickedness of the subjects, that the prince is undiscreet or evil? Shall the subjects both by their wickedness provoke God for their deserved punishment to give them an undiscreet or evil prince, and also rebel against him, and withal against God, who for the punishment of their sins did give them such a prince? Will you hear the Scriptures concerning this point? "God," say the Holy Scriptures, "maketh a wicked man to reign for the sins of the people." Again: "God giveth a prince in his anger (meaning an evil one) and taketh away a prince in his displeasure," meaning specially when he taketh away a good prince for the sins of the people, as in our memory he took away our good Josias, King Edward, in his young and good years for our wickedness. And contrarily the Scriptures do teach that God giveth wisdom unto princes, and maketh a wise and good king to reign over that people whom he loveth, and who loveth him.

→ RICHARD HOOKER

From *Of the Laws of Ecclesiastical Polity*   *1593*

A staunch defender of Anglican doctrine against the growing power of Puritan thought and practice, Richard Hooker develops the principle of natural law in his massive eight-volume *Laws*. He spent most of the 1590s working on the project, and five books were published before his death in 1600, with the others appearing later; the entire work was finally published in 1662. The following excerpt from Book I demonstrates Hooker's brilliant command of English prose.

I am not ignorant that by "law eternal" the learned for the most part do understand the order, not which God hath eternally purposed himself in all his works to observe, but rather that which with himself he hath set down as expedient to be kept by all his creatures, according to the several condition wherewith he hath indued them. They who thus are accustomed to speak apply the name of law unto that only rule of working which superior authority imposeth; whereas we, somewhat more enlarging the sense thereof, term any kind of rule or canon whereby actions are framed a law. Now that law which, as it is laid up in the bosom of God, they call eternal, receiveth according unto the different kinds of things which are subject unto it different and sundry kinds of names. That part of it which ordereth natural agents we call usually nature's law; that which angels do clearly behold and without any swerving observe is a law celestial and heavenly; the law of reason, that which bindeth creatures reasonable in this world, and with which by reason they may most plainly perceive themselves bound; that which bindeth them, and is not known but by special revelation from God, divine law; human law, that which out of the law either of reason or of God men probably gathering to be expedient, they make it a law. All things, therefore, which are as they ought to be are conformed unto this second law eternal; and even those things which to this eternal law are not conformable are notwithstanding in some sort ordered by the first eternal law. For what good or evil is there under the sun, what action correspondent or repugnant unto the law which God hath imposed upon his creatures, but in or upon it God doth work according to the law which himself hath eternally purposed to keep; that is to say, the first law eternal? So that a two-fold law eternal being thus made, it is not hard to conceive how they both take place in all things.

Wherefore to come to the law of nature: albeit thereby we sometimes mean that manner of working which God hath set for each created thing to keep; yet forasmuch as those things are termed most properly natural agents which keep the law of their kind unwittingly, as the heavens and elements of the world, which can do no otherwise then they do; and forasmuch as we give unto intellectual natures the name of voluntary agents, that so we may distinguish them from the other; expedient it will be that we sever the law of nature observed by the one from that which the other is tied unto. Touching the former, their strict keeping of one tenure, statute, and law is spoken of by all, but hath in it more than men have as yet attained to know, or perhaps ever shall attain, seeing the travail of wading herein is given of God to the sons of men, that perceiving how much the least thing in the world hath in it more than the wisest are able to reach unto, they may by this means learn humility. Moses, in describing the work of creation, attributeth speech unto God: "God said, Let there be light; let there be a firmament; let the waters under the heaven be gathered together into one place; let the earth bring forth; let there be lights in the firmament of heaven." Was this only the intent of Moses, to signify the infinite greatness of God's power by the easiness of his accomplishing such effects without travail, pain, or labor? Surely it seemeth that Moses had herein besides this a further purpose, namely, first to teach that God did not work as a necessary but a voluntary agent, intending beforehand and decreeing with himself that which did outwardly proceed from him; secondly, to show that God did then institute a law natural to be observed by creatures, and therefore, according to the manner of laws, the institution thereof is described as being established by solemn injunction. His commanding those things to be which are, and to be in such sort as they are, to keep that tenure and course which they do, importeth the establishment of nature's law. This world's first creation, and the preservation since of things created, what is it but only so far-forth a manifestation by execution what the eternal law of God is concerning things natural? And as it cometh to pass in a kingdom rightly ordered that after a law is once published it presently takes effect far and wide, all states framing themselves thereunto; even so let us think it fareth in the natural course of the world. Since the time that God did first proclaim the edicts of his law upon it, heaven and earth have heark'ned unto his voice, and their labor hath been to do his will. He "made a law for the rain." He gave his "decree unto the sea, that the waters should not pass his commandement." Now if nature should intermit her course and leave altogether, though it were but for a while, the observation of her own laws; if those principal and mother elements of the world, whereof all things in this lower world are made, should loose [let go] the qualities which now they have; if the frame of that heavenly arch erected over our heads should loosen and dissolve itself; if celestial spheres should forget their wonted motions, and by irregular volubility turn themselves any way as it might happen; if the prince of the lights of heaven, which now as a giant doth run his unwearied course, should, as it were through a languishing faintness, begin to stand and to rest himself; if the moon should wander from her beaten way, the times and seasons of the year blend themselves by disordered and confused mixture, the winds breathe out their last gasp, the clouds yield no rain, the earth be defeated of heavenly influence, the fruits of the earth pine away as children at the withered breasts of their mother no longer able to yield them relief; — what would become of man himself, whom these things now do all serve? See we not plainly that obedience of creatures unto the law of nature is the stay of the whole world?

→ PHILIP STUBBES

From *The Anatomy of Abuses* 1583

One of the most vocal and intemperate of Puritan social and religious critics, Philip Stubbes (c. 1555–c. 1610) here attacks the immorality in and around the public playhouses. He typically associates actors with various forms of sexual and social crime and develops the argument that plays exemplify and encourage immoral behavior.

Do they not maintain bawdry, insinuate foolery, and renew and remembrance of heathen idolatry? Do they not induce whoredom and uncleanness and nay, are they not rather plain devourers of maidenly virginity and chastity? For proof whereof, but mark the flocking and running to theaters and curtains, daily and hourly, night and day, time and tide, to see plays and interludes, where such wanton gestures, such bawdy speeches, such laughing and fleering [ridiculing], such kissing and bussing, such clipping and culling, such winking and glancing of wanton eyes and the like is used, as is wonderful to behold. Then the godly pageants being done, every mate sorts to his mate, every one brings another homeward of their way very friendly, and in their secret conclaves (covertly) they play the Sodomites, or worse. And these be the fruits of plays and interludes, for the most part. And whereas, you say, there are good examples to be learned in them.

Truly, so there are. If you will learn falsehood, if you will learn cozenage; if you will learn to play the hypocrite; to cog, lie, and falsify; if you will learn to jest, laugh, and fleer, to grin, to nod, and mow [jest]; if you will learn to play the vice, to swear, tear, and blaspheme both heaven and earth. If you will learn to become a bawd, unclean, and to devirginate maids, to deflower honest wives; if you will learn to murder, slay, kill, pick, steal, rob, and rove; if you will learn to rebel against princes, to commit treasons, to consume treasures, to practice idleness, to sing and talk of bawdy love and venery; if you will learn to deride, scoff, mock, and flout, to flatter and smooth; if you will learn to play the whoremaster, the glutton, drunkard, or incestuous person; if you will learn to become proud, haughty, and arrogant; and finally, if you will learn to contemn God and all his laws, to care neither for heaven nor hell, and to commit all kind of sin and mischief, you need to go to no other school, for all these good examples may you see painted before your eyes in interludes and plays. . . .

Therefore I beseech all players and founders of plays and interludes, in the bowels of Jesus Christ, as they tender the salvation of their souls, and others, to leave off that cursed kind of life and give themselves to such honest exercises and godly mysteries as God hath commanded them in his word to get their livings withal. For who will call him a wise man that playeth the part of a fool and a vice? Who can call him a Christian who playeth the part of a devil, the sworn enemy of Christ? Who can call him a just man that playeth the part of a dissembling hypocrite? And to be brief, who can call him a straight-dealing man, who playeth a cozener's trick? And so of all the rest. Away therefore with this so infamous an art, for go they never so brave [no matter how splendid they appear], yet are they counted and taken but for beggars. And is it not true? Live they not upon beggings of every one that comes? Are they not taken by the laws of the realm for rogues and vagabonds? I speak of such as travel the countries with plays and interludes, making an occupation of it, and ought to be punished, if they had their deserts.

CHAPTER 10

From Bracegirdle to Branagh:
Shakespeare in Performance
from 1660 to the Present

>‹

In London in the autumn of 1912, a young director named Harley Granville Barker staged radically simplified productions of *The Winter's Tale* and *Twelfth Night*, sweeping away the extravagance of the nineteenth century performance tradition with a stroke of modernity. Determined to challenge a public accustomed to elaborate, realistic scenery and a stage full of extras — as many as 250 in a performance of *Julius Caesar* — Granville Barker engaged only about 15 actors and placed them in simple, stylized settings. The significance of his achievement was not immediately and universally acknowledged, but before long almost everybody saw what prescient viewers perceived at once, that the old, grandiose style of staging was finished. What had been praised as opulence was now condemned as clutter.

The history of Shakespeare in performance is marked by actions, reactions, and countermovements as theater people search for new ways of selling the plays to the public. Sometimes the turn takes decades to arrive, but eventually the entire enterprise of Shakespearean staging is reconceived and a new mode of performance comes to dominate the theatrical scene. This oscillation between extremes comprises most major elements of production: the style of acting, the size of the house, the shape of the acting area, the furnishing of the stage, the treatment of the text. Often what looked like an innovation at the time was not new at all but a device that had fallen out of favor years or decades before and was unfamiliar to theatergoers at the time of its revival. This is not to say that there is nothing new under the sun: the admission of actresses onto the stage in 1660 counts as a major change, and technology has frequently created new theatrical opportunities and even new modes of performance, such as film at the end of the nineteenth century and television in the twentieth. But the twenty-first-century playgoer who is delighted with an original stage effect or a brilliant new line reading may be further surprised to discover that it was apparently introduced by Mrs. Siddons at the end of the eighteenth century and may not have been original with her.

The staging of Shakespeare's plays seems to have changed relatively little from the time of his retirement in 1616 to the suspension of public theatrical performance during the English Civil Wars and the Interregnum — that is, from 1642 to 1660. Since those theatrical practices are treated in Chapter 3, this account of the history of Shakespearean performance properly begins with the reopening of the London theaters upon the restoration of Charles II in 1660. But it is worth pausing to interrogate received wisdom about the Puritan shutting of the playhouses. The edict of 1642 outlawing theatrical performance was at first simply an emergency measure, a Parliamentary attempt at crowd control during the hectic early days of the Great Rebellion. Some troupes of players continued to perform in London until a more stringent ban was announced in 1648. During a performance of *Rollo, Duke of Kent* at the Phoenix by the remnants of the King's Men, antiroyalist soldiers entered the playhouse and hustled the actors, still in costume, off to jail. That moment would seem to have put a period on dramatic performance, but in fact the public ban did not eradicate theatrical activity in England. Although the official prohibition means that records of theatrical activity are sketchy, some troupes of actors went into the provinces, where the movement of a tour afforded them liberty unavailable in London. In town, drama went underground: private performances were given in aristocratic homes and in such semiprivate gathering places as the Inns of Court, and William Davenant even managed to open a public theater for a short time in 1656. Plays were not only acted but also written during the Interregnum. When the monarch regained the throne in 1660, the ban was rescinded, two major producers obtained licenses to arrange public performances, and both initiated the construction of new playhouses. The demand for material to perform meant that a number of Shakespeare's plays, although considered old-fashioned and of questionable commercial value, were dusted off and readied for public presentation.

Innovations, Technical and Theatrical

Although the Restoration theatrical scene produced some colossal personalities who helped to shape the modern English theater, the importance of these individuals fades in light of three major changes in performance practice occurring shortly after 1660. All three were to have a profound effect on the future of Shakespearean production. First, actresses were introduced onto London's public stages. This major innovation may owe something to King Charles's well-known admiration for the female figure, or perhaps to his fifteen-year residence on the Continent, where actresses regularly performed alongside their male counterparts. Whatever the cause, when old plays were revived women now took the roles that had been written for boys, and Restoration playwrights scampered to create new works for such attractive and talked-about performers as Nell Gwynne (King Charles's mistress) and Anne Brace-girdle, referred to in the title of this chapter. This new pool of talent meant that older works could be selected with an eye to their showing off the new performers most alluringly, and some of Shakespeare's romantic comedies (e.g., *Twelfth Night* and *As You Like It*) provided ready-made vehicles for exhibiting the actresses' legs.

A second milestone was the movement indoors. The earlier Stuart theater had been performed in both the outdoor amphitheaters and the indoor "hall" theaters, but the leaders of the two companies that were licensed upon the return of the monarch leased indoor spaces and fitted them out for theatrical performance. The commitment to indoor theater had a powerful influence on the nature of performance, the composition of the audience, and the cultural position of theater as an institution. In short, theater became a little less "popular," a little more elite, more thoroughly respectable than before the Revolution. Sir William Davenant (1608–1667), Shakespeare's own godson, was one of King Charles's licensees. He converted an old tennis court in Lincoln's Inn Fields into an indoor theater, and his arrangement of the interior space brought a third new feature to the theatrical experience.

That development was the addition of physical scenery. Davenant and his builders retained the thrust stage familiar from the Elizabethan playhouse, but they also constructed a very large box — a room, really — behind the stage. In this upstage area, painted flats could be placed as a setting or background for the action played in front. This shutter-and-wing system, as it was known, employed a series of horizontal grooves cut across the floor of the backstage area. The narrow troughs held the thin flats, or "scenes," made of board or canvas and painted perspectivally to resemble a city street, a domestic interior, or another familiar or appropriate location. The key to this system was that the grooves allowed stagehands to slide the flats from the wings across the back of the stage, and to do it quickly: in a performance of *A Midsummer Night's Dream*, for example, they might dazzle the audience by whisking away the "walls" of the Duke's palace to reveal the painted underbrush in the "Wood outside Athens." These three phenomena changed the essential nature of theatrical performance, making it a more expensive and thus a more patrician entertainment.

The impact of these changes on the production of Shakespeare's plays was powerful because they led directly to the alteration of texts. This is especially true of the use of scenery. With physical "scenes" to orient the audience, stage managers or directors could eliminate lines in which the author engages in poetic scene-painting. A brief Shakespearean episode might be eliminated altogether so as not to require the construction of an additional set of flats. The increased sophistication of stage machinery, of which the shutter-and-wing system was a part, created opportunities for using flying contraptions and other such devices. More business led to more cutting, and so for perhaps the first time in the English public theater spectacle came to be at odds with text. (The contest between visual and poetic effects had arisen earlier in the rrel between Ben Jonson and Inigo Jones about priorities in their masques for the Stuart court, and it is still with us: witness the complaints of New York critics in the last quarter of the twentieth century about the tyranny of the visual, epitomized by the falling chandelier in *The Phantom of the Opera* or the helicopter that lands onstage in *Miss Saigon*.) The spectacle was not only mechanical, however. The introduction of actresses meant an increase in opportunities for music and dance, delights that consumed stage time and thus could require the additional trimming of scripts. The need to accommodate the spectacle was not the only motive for the alteration of Shakespeare's plays, however. Producers were always on the lookout for commercial novelty, some means of drawing customers to the new and improved version of a famous story. The title page of Davenant's 1674 adaptation of an old play advertises *Macbeth: A Tragedy: with all the alterations, amendments, additions, and new songs; as it is now acted at the Duke's Theatre.*

The story of Restoration Shakespeare is a narrative of texts transformed. Thanks to the labors of John Dryden and others, Shakespeare was seen more commonly in adaptations than in the "original" texts on which we now tend to insist. (Throughout this chapter the adjective in the phrase "original texts" is used provisionally: it refers to those versions published in quarto during and just after Shakespeare's lifetime, and in the Folio of 1623. It means, in other words, the first published versions of the plays Shakespeare wrote, as opposed to the adaptations that began to appear in the Restoration.) Sometimes a play was altered to enlarge the role of a favorite minor character. In 1663 Grumio in *The Taming of the Shrew* became a Scotsman who gave his name to the newly titled play, *Sauny the Scot,* with the Italian setting shifted to London in the present and Shakespeare's action drastically reduced. Occasionally a play would be amplified to provide roles for favorite performers. Thomas Shadwell revised *Timon of Athens,* which has only two tiny female roles, by adding two major female characters, one for his wife and one for the celebrated Mary Betterton. Sometimes the adaptor transformed the original into an essentially different work. Dryden, for example, converted *Antony and Cleopatra* into *All for Love,* smoothing over the competing tones of Shakespeare's tragedy in favor of a dominant mood of heroism and romance, and domesticating the infinitely various Cleopatra. The new emphasis sounds clearly in the subtitle, *The World Well Lost.*

Such additions and interpolations were not frowned upon as tampering or vandalism, as they would have been at other moments in history. Shakespeare was thought by some to be rather outmoded anyway: in the 1660s the plays of Jonson and Fletcher seem to have been more popular, and companies catered to audiences who wanted to see new twists on some of the old, familiar tales. Often the revisions attest to the growing neoclassical taste for symmetry and balance. When Dryden remade *The Tempest* into *The Enchanted Island* (1667), for example, he augmented the spectacle by introducing more songs and substantially increasing the size of the cast: Miranda and Caliban each gain sisters; Ariel finds a female love interest; and in the most flagrant effort at harmony and parallelism, Shakespeare's Miranda, who has never seen a man until she meets Ferdinand, is matched with a new character named Hippolito, a man who, until he falls for Miranda's sister, has never seen a woman. These additions are purchased at the cost of Shakespeare's subplot: King Alonso's brother Sebastian disappears, and with him the assassination plot against Alonso. And Dryden's revisions were appropriated and extended by Thomas Shadwell, who added so much more music that the play was virtually transformed into an opera. Such alterations were not atypical. Colley Cibber adapted *Richard III,* for example, and many other plays were reworked and well received. Not until well into the next century did the pendulum begin to swing back toward the Shakespearean originals.

Perhaps the most notorious instance of textual alteration is Nahum Tate's version of *King Lear* (1681). The reviser made free with language, characters — the Fool is eliminated, for example — and plot episodes; so creative was he that his dénouement bears scant resemblance to the one we know. Scrapping the events that lead to the Folio's heartbreaking stage direction, *Enter Lear with Cordelia in his armes,* Tate arranges Cordelia's rescue, marries her to Edgar, installs them on the English throne together, and permits the old king to survive and enjoy their loving ministrations. (An excerpt from this scene appears on p. 383.) The rewrite is not in itself shocking, especially given the cultural norms of the day, and many of Shakespeare's plays have endured more radical reconstruction. What is astonishing is that some form of Tate's adaptation was virtually the *only* version in which *The Tragedy of King Lear,* by William Shakespeare, was played on the English stage for almost a century and a half, until Macready's nearly thorough restoration of the Shakespearean text in 1838. Even Doctor Johnson records that he preferred Tate's ending. But the wheel would turn again: one of the great services provided by the actor-managers of the nineteenth century was their reclamation of Shakespeare's texts. These later restorations of Shakespearean originals were seldom as pure as their promoters suggested, but the motive for "authenticity" in the nineteenth century was the same as for adaptation in the seventeenth and eighteenth centuries to sell the public something new.

Actors and Their Roles

The most superficial acquaintance with English stage history teaches that the star system is not an invention of Hollywood. Burbage, Betterton, Bracegirdle, Garrick, Siddons, Kean, Irving, Terry, Gielgud, Olivier, Dench — the history of Shakespearean performance can be charted by following the line of great actors and actresses from the age of Elizabeth to our own time. To study these artists and their way with language or character is to see recapitulated the pattern of displacement I have described. The public likes what it knows; thus, charismatic performers who become public favorites can sometimes retain that status longer than their artistic achievements might warrant. Yet the public also craves novelty: ultimately fashions change and the former darling is forgotten. Of the many theatrical celebrities in the Restoration, Sir Thomas

Betterton (1635–1710) was the idol of the day. His professional lineage from Shakespeare himself was nearly direct: when the actor-manager Sir William Davenant, Shakespeare's godson, died in 1668, Betterton took charge of his company. Before long he had established himself as the great tragedian of the age. He first played Hamlet in 1661 at the age of 26; he last played it in 1709, at the age of 74. Of the latter performance, *The Tatler* reported that "he acted *youth;* and by the prevalent power of proper manner, gesture, and voice, appeared throughout the whole drama a *young* man of great expectation, vivacity, and enterprise" (Wells 18; italics mine). Betterton's longevity in his tragic roles suggests the tendency of audiences to stick with what they know and to want what they know they like. But such an aged Hamlet would also seem to invite an alternative, and though it took some time, a replacement finally arrived to seize the imagination of the theatergoing public.

The eighteenth century offers an unmistakable example of the paradoxical tension between old and new, between sameness and novelty, that persists in the history of Shakespearean production and, more generally, the history of theatrical taste. The public wants innovation but doesn't know it wants it. Audiences worship the familiar above all things, and they can be made to reject what they know only by a radical who scorns it and offers them something entirely new. Although other Hamlets and Richard IIIs followed Betterton in the early 1700s, notably Colley Cibber (1671–1757) and James Quin (1693–1766), their performances seem to have reproduced or to have modified only a little the rather formal, oratorical style of the previous age. Thus by the 1740s the public was ready, perhaps without knowing it, for a theatrical iconoclast to capture its attention and reinvigorate Shakespearean performance. In October of 1741 David Garrick (1717–1779) made his entrance as Richard III. He was so young and unknown that the producer billed him, almost truthfully, as "a gentleman who never appeared on any stage," but shortly he established himself as the most important Shakespearean actor of the century. (See the portrait of Garrick as King Lear on p. 383.) Performer, producer, promoter, and friend of such luminaries as Dr. Johnson, the playwright Richard Brinsley Sheridan, and the painter Sir Joshua Reynolds — Garrick was part beneficiary, part cause of the "Shakespeare boom" that exploded in Georgian London. Possessed of a talent for publicity as well as for performance, Garrick not only rejected the declamatory style of Cibber and his successor James Quin but loudly advertised his iconoclasm. He appointed himself Shakespeare's chief advocate for the age. Publicizing his commitment to "authenticity," a tactic that has seldom gone out of fashion, he implied that he alone was seeking to realize Shakespeare's intentions. He restored to *King Lear* much of what Tate had expunged, but without going so far as to reinstate the Fool or Shakespeare's own ending. Always Garrick considered the playability of a line or scene, altering the text frequently according to his intuition and sense of public taste. (See Holland, "The Age of Garrick," in Jackson and Bate 72.) In 1769 he helped to organize a Jubilee celebration at Stratford-upon-Avon. Never mind that the Jubilee, apart from Garrick's presentation of a new ode to Shakespeare, was something of a fiasco: no Shakespeare play was performed, torrential rains washed out most of the activities, and the locals charged piratical prices for food and lodging. Still the event counts as one of the first ceremonies in the history of Bardolatry and is the forerunner of many modern Shakespeare festivals.

Garrick's success owes something to the rapid growth of journalism and printing in the eighteenth century, an enterprise that the theatrical profession was able to exploit for publicity, and even today Garrick seems a more significant figure than a Davenant or Betterton because we know more about him. But celebrity alone cannot sustain a career, and Garrick gave the press much real substance to write about. One of his most effective instruments was his body, particularly his willingness to move it. Garrick broke the stasis of the actor that had accompanied the older, monumental style and replaced it with a kinetic approach to the great roles. In the early scenes of *King Lear,* for example, a contemporary reports that he "displayed all the force of quick transition from one passion to another: he had, from the most violent rage, descended to sedate calmness; had seized, with unutterable sensibility, the various impressions of terror, and faithfully represented all the turbid passions of the soul" (Thomas Davies, qtd. in Wells 23). In other words, he cannily engaged the audience in his character's passage from one mood to another. Given the preferences then in vogue, this mercurial method seemed revolutionary, apparently pointing the way toward what we might call, if we use the words cautiously, "realism," or a more "naturalistic" style. Such an impact is confirmed by some reviewers' complaints about Garrick's disrespect for the poetry, his willingness to sacrifice music to feeling.

His successor, predictably, took the opposite tack. In the wake of Garrick's animation and individuality, John Philip Kemble (1757–1823) opted for stillness and gentility, all in an effort to propound the universality of the action represented. Although it is difficult to make fine discriminations on nothing more than reported evidence, it seems that Kemble's formality differed somewhat from the kind of acting popular before Garrick. The paintings of Reynolds and Gainsborough suggest the decorum and stasis considered appropriate for the production of Shakespeare at the end of the eighteenth century, and it was at this time that theatrical practices became highly codified. Performers were expected to deliver the familiar gesture. The art was to be found in the execution of the conventional turn, not in the invention of a new one. Each of the major roles in the major plays was freighted with established forms of pose, gesture, and vocal inflection that audiences came to observe and evaluate. Ingenuity or originality was unwanted: playgoers arrived at the Theater Royal, Drury Lane, curious to see how well Mrs. So-and-So would present the established vocal and physical turns in Ophelia's mad scene.

Kemble was celebrated and admired, but he was finally less significant than his sister, Sarah Siddons (1755–1831). Mrs. Siddons, as she was always referred to in her day, was probably the most venerated of all Shakespearean actresses, and her most famous performance was as Lady Macbeth (see her portrait on p. 386). As she prepared the role, a rumor gradually leaked out into the theatrical community that she intended to change one of the habitual actions performed by all Lady Macbeths in recent memory. Whereas her forebears had held a candle throughout the sleepwalking scene, Mrs. Siddons proposed to put it down so that she could appear to wash blood from her hands. Before the performance there was outrage; afterward, ovations. Her way with language was also original and sensitive to nuance, as indicated in Robert Speaight's summary of some contemporary reports:

> Much of the detail and emphasis has come down to us. The long pause — Mrs. Siddons could pause as long as Kemble, though with better reason — on "made themselves ――――― air"; the sudden energy on "*shalt be* what thou art promised"; the association of "*my* spirits in your ear" with the spirits she has just invoked; the downward and decisive inflection on "We *fail*"; the triumph in her voice on "Great Glamis! worthy Cawdor," and its supernatural timbre, with the staring eyes and hollowed hands, as she called upon the "sightless substances" that "wait on nature's mischief"; the sharp significance of "Tomorrow — as he *purposes*"; the slow insinuation of "be the serpent under 't"; the tenderness of "I have given suck" transformed into the fiendish cruelty of "plucked my nipple from its boneless gums"; the deadly whispering of the colloquy following the murder; the authority of "Give *me* the daggers," which caused more than one member of the audience to start out of their seat. "Not all the perfumes of Arabia" came like the whispered echo from a hollow grave; and the final "Oh, oh, oh" was a shudder rather than a sigh, with an undertone of imbecility, at once pathetic and horrifying.   (41)

Without violating the formality and decorum of the stage, Mrs. Siddons succeeded in giving her roles an individual stamp. Byron, speaking of George Frederick Cooke and John Philip Kemble and Edmund Kean, said that Mrs. Siddons "was worth them all put together."

As the eighteenth century gave way to the nineteenth, changes in the theater mimicked larger cultural transformations. As romanticism supplanted classicism, so passionate, individualistic acting dethroned the stately tableaux and ossified gestures of Kemble and his tribe. Nineteenth-century England brought forth at least five theatrical geniuses — Edmund Kean (1787–1833), William Charles Macready (1793–1873), Henry Irving (1838–1905), Ellen Terry (1848–1928), and Sir Herbert Beerbohm Tree (1853–1917) — as well as a number of minor titans — Charles Kemble (younger brother of John Philip) and his daughter Fanny, Samuel Phelps, Charles Kean (son of Edmund), and many other popular performers. It is tempting to recount in detail the specific techniques and distinctive gifts of each of the major actors, doubly so because some of them, Edmund Kean in particular, inspired the praise of such writers as John Keats, the poet Leigh Hunt, and the essayist William Hazlitt. Lacking space for such treatment, I direct readers curious about these performers and their talents to the supplementary reading list for contemporary reviews and biographies. A more efficient way of telling their story is to concentrate on the distinctive features of nineteenth-century theater generally, remembering that the performance of Shakespeare was the touchstone for virtually all histrionic activity.

First is the figure of the actor-manager. Except for Edmund Kean, whose passionate acting and persona made him appear sublimely oblivious to such mundane considerations as contracts and leases, most of the great nineteenth-century actors also supervised the business end of their operations. Granted, since the days of Burbage, himself a shareholder in the King's Men, many leading actors had also taken charge of their companies. But this occupation becomes practically institutionalized in the nineteenth century, when their work offstage becomes as important as their acting: selecting and preparing the texts, arranging them into a "season," leasing a theater, casting other actors, determining the style of production, arranging for the decor and costumes, commissioning or choosing music, and other such administrative duties. The character of Vincent Crummles in Dickens's *Nicholas Nickelby* is a second-rank, provincial version of this actor-manager, one whose modest talents keep him and his company on tour and mostly out of London. The capital welcomed such figures as Macready and Irving, however, as did America: Irving and his troupe made four American tours. Their home theater was the Lyceum in London, and the pairing of Irving and Terry made them the sensation of the later Victorian era, particularly as Benedick and Beatrice, the Macbeths, Hamlet and Ophelia, and Shylock and Portia. The whole town talked about Irving and his company, George Bernard Shaw and Henry James wrote about him, painters of the day captured him and Terry in many of their great parts, and he was the first actor in England to be knighted.

The actor-manager had a lot to manage, for Romantic and Victorian Shakespeare was nothing if not spectacular. Not surprisingly, the scenery that had been introduced in the 1660s became more abundant, elaborate, and sophisticated over the next two centuries so that many Victorian audiences considered decoration to be of paramount importance. The move toward verisimilitude reached its apex in the extravaganzas of Irving at the Lyceum and of his successor Sir Herbert Beerbohm Tree, the last of the Shakespearean ringmasters. Pictorial detail, splendor, and especially variety, all congruent with the growth of photography and the Victorian taste for amplitude, were the desired theatrical effects at the close of the century. One theatrical phenomenon of the late 1700s was an increasing enthusiasm for setting a play in the time and place represented in the action. The empty platform at the original Globe had made the locations imaginary, of course, and the costumes of the Lord Chamberlain's Men were, as far as we can tell, more or less Elizabethan. By contrast, Kemble and other producers took pride in the achievement of historical accuracy or geographical specificity, making sure that costumes were properly Roman or that the dressed stage resembled an actual wood outside Athens. The mechanical capacities of the great Victorian theaters meant that representational specificity could be achieved as never before in the history of the stage.

It might be said that the dominant feature of the Victorian theater building was the proscenium arch. The enormous stage could accommodate a huge quantity of flats and constructed sets, there was room for an orchestra in front of the stage and for troupes of dancers on it, hundreds of extras could be engaged to fill out the crowd scenes, and the use of a front curtain allowed for the shifting of ever more elaborate backdrops and constructed sets, as well as for thrilling the crowd with a sudden change of scene. All this activity was framed by the lines of the proscenium arch. The virtuosity of the actor was now matched by the expertise of the scene painter: the more different scenes, the better; the more elaborate, the better. "Scene painter" rather than "set designer" is the appropriate term because the desired result was pictorial. Shakespeare having given Lady Macbeth a letter from her husband to read aloud on her very first entrance, Ellen Terry read it by the light of a roaring fire, with a visual effect much like that of a Pre-Raphaelite painting (Jackson 123). Probably, however, Terry did not make an "entrance," since the front curtain would have risen to reveal her kneeling before the fire. (See the portrait of Terry as Lady Macbeth on p. 387.)

Whereas Shakespeare's company performed many of his plays with no more than 12 to 15 actors, Victorian producers hired as many people as they could afford and as their enormous stages could accommodate. Some Titanias in *A Midsummer Night's Dream* commanded bands of fairies that numbered as many as 150 rather than the 4 with speaking roles stipulated in the text. (An illustration of the last scene of Charles Kean's 1856 production, p. 396, suggests the grandiosity of the Victorian style.) Throughout much of the nineteenth century, public scenes were peopled with hordes of extras (supernumeraries, or "supers"), particularly in the Roman plays, and the outdoor climaxes — the funeral in *Julius Caesar,* the banishment of Coriolanus — were meant to be visually and aurally overwhelming. Battle scenes also were fortified with crenelated battlements, ranks of soldiers, and an arsenal of impressive, "authentic" weaponry. If Shakespeare did not offer such a scene in the chosen play, the actor-manager might supply it so as to achieve the maximum in variety and spectacle. The thinking went as follows: had Shakespeare in the sixteenth century had access to the technical means available in the nineteenth, he would certainly have dramatized those episodes.

One of the most famous interpolations occurred in Charles Kean's spectacular production of *Richard II* in 1852. In the text the Duke of York describes to his wife Henry IV's glorious entrance into London, followed by the mocked and deposed Richard; Kean staged the reported scene, riding a horse triumphantly across the stage in front of Tudor houses to the cheers of hundreds of extras. (Published engravings suggest that the setting was Elizabethan rather than fourteenth-century; sometimes the historical accuracy was not total.) Tree inserted into his *King John* a tableau in which the king is made to sign the Magna Carta. These fin-de-siècle productions cost thousands of pounds, obviously, but there were other kinds of costs. In order to make time for such pageantry, for cumbersome scene changes, and for music and dance, the actor-manager was obliged to trim the text, and sometimes a huge portion had to be omitted. The use of the front curtain had other textual consequences: Shakespeare often ended his scenes on an informal, conversational note, as two actors left the stage and were immediately replaced by others in a new scene, but Irving needed definite, preferably climactic endings. So he wrote them. And

Tree invented a final tableau for his *Tempest* that depicted Caliban posed on a promontory, stretching out his arms toward the ship carrying Prospero and company away from the island.

Such lavishness almost always provokes a reaction, and soon the spectacular histrionic style would become as outdated as Victorian decoration or morality. A few dissenters had raised their voices (or pens) early against the grandiose theater of Irving and Tree. George Bernard Shaw was one such Jeremiah, concerned about the suffocation of the verse by the emphasis on pictures, and other artistic and cultural forces (to be taken up below) would bring about the end of representational extravagance. Surely the most important factor in the death of nineteenth-century Shakespeare was the intervention of World War I. But rather than proceed directly to the "modern," we must cross the Atlantic to consider Shakespeare's conquest of Cassius's "nations yet unborn."

American Shakespeare

The United States and Canada have taken Shakespeare thoroughly to heart in the last two centuries, but it is worth recalling that the earliest English settlers in the New World were enemies of the English theatrical tradition, not participants in it. The library of a New England gentleman in the seventeenth century would have been more likely to contain a copy of Stephen Gosson's *Plays Confuted in Five Actions* or William Prynne's *Histriomastix*, one of the antitheatrical polemics, than a quarto edition of one of Shakespeare's plays. The Puritan legacy governed intellectual life and entertainment in the colonies throughout the seventeenth century and even later. In 1687 Increase Mather, the Massachusetts minister and member of the famous colonial family, published a book in London entitled *Testimony Against Several Prophane and Superstitious Customs Now Practised by Some in New-England.* The customs were gambling, health-drinking — that is, the drinking of toasts — the celebration of Christmas, and other such evils. Mather cautions the reader that in the time since he began composing the book "there is much discourse of beginning stage-plays in New England" and therefore he is obliged to compose a Preface demonstrating that "Stage-Plays had their Original from those Devil-Gods whom the Gentiles Worshiped," that "'Tis the usual practice of *Stage-Players* to make themselves and others merry with the Vices and Wickedness of Men," that "The Natural Effects of *Stage-Plays* have been very pernicious," and that "The generality of good Men, both in former and in latter Ages, have looked upon *Stage-Plays* as abominable Vanities" (13–16). New England, God's country, was to be preserved from such abominations.

Mather, echoing the complaints of his Tudor and Stuart predecessors, was fighting a rear-guard action, and the winds began to shift in the middle of the eighteenth century. The first recorded performance of a Shakespeare play in the colonies occurred in 1750, when a troupe of English players traveled from the West Indies to New York and presented *Richard III.* They also performed in Williamsburg, Virginia, and returned to New York and Philadelphia over the next several years. That company would soon be joined by others. As the colonists became more numerous, more prosperous, and more diverse philosophically, Shakespeare began to make his way into the culture, often as a kind of social marker. Companies made up mostly of traveling English actors began to stage a range of plays in the major urban centers, particularly Philadelphia and New York, where George Washington attended a performance of *Hamlet* in the spring of 1773. There was still resistance, however: Washington's apparent sanction notwithstanding, Boston authorities in 1792 closed a production of *Hamlet* on moral grounds.

That educated people in colonial America possessed at least a minimal acquaintance with some of the major Shakespearean speeches and characters is apparent from the following parody, published in 1770 in a newspaper called *The Massachusetts Spy:*

> Be taxt or not be taxt — that is the question,
> Whether 'tis nobler in our minds to suffer
> The sleights and cunning of deceitful statesmen
> Or to petition 'gainst illegal taxes
> And by opposing end them?   (Dunn 108)

American politicians are still fond of invoking the name or appropriating the words of Shakespeare, a tactic that we see has a distinguished historical precedent. In fact, the intelligentsia in the late 1700s and early 1800s hoped to enrich and dignify the young nation with the cultural authority of British imports, and even at this relatively early point, few names served this purpose better than Shakespeare.

Some of the early nineteenth-century English actors — notably Edmund and Charles Kean and William Charles Macready — made triumphant tours of the United States, where they found receptive audiences and commanded immense fees. Later in the century Irving and Tree toured America frequently with full companies and splendid productions. Acting not only in the cities but also in small towns, they sometimes made do with primitive halls, makeshift stages, and impromptu seating: sometimes spectators brought their own chairs. (In this sense early American Shakespeare may have resembled Elizabethan more than Victorian staging.) And the tours were not confined to the East Coast. Charles Kean and his wife Ellen Tree played a season in San Francisco in 1865, offering sixty performances of six different plays, including *Hamlet, Othello,* and *Much Ado about Nothing.* These guest artists were venerated for the professionalism they brought to the rough new world, and they were well remunerated: for their California engagement Kean and company collected the enormous sum of $30,000.

Before long the "authentic" Shakespearean performers began to feel competition from local talent. Many of the earliest "American" actors and actresses had immigrated to the United States: Adelaide Nelson from England, Ada Rehan from Ireland, and Helena Modjeska from Poland. The most notable of the early immigrants was Junius Brutus Booth, whose significance lay not so much in his tragic acting as in his siring of a theatrical dynasty. One of his sons, Edwin Booth, dominated American stages in the second half of the nineteenth century by playing Romeo, Hamlet, Lear, Benedick, and Petruchio. Many theater historians consider him the greatest American stage actor to date. Edwin had two brothers, Junius Brutus Booth Jr. and John Wilkes Booth, who shot President Lincoln in Ford's Theater. Six months before the assassination, in November of 1864, the three brothers appeared together in New York in a benefit performance of *Julius Caesar* (see the playbill advertising that performance on p. 389). On that occasion John Wilkes Booth did not take the role of Brutus, the murderer, but of Mark Antony, defender of the fallen leader.

One extraordinary American actor of the period was Ira Aldridge, an African American born in the United States in 1807. After acting briefly in New York, Aldridge went to Scotland to study at the University of Glasgow. He turned up later in London working in the theater as a gofer, then acting, then assuming larger parts. Edmund Kean saw him act and engaged him for Othello, a role audiences were accustomed to seeing played by a white actor as a tanned North African (see the portrait of Aldridge as Othello on p. 388). Kean, of course, performed Iago. Aldridge was also in demand for Aaron, Shakespeare's villainous Moor in *Titus Andronicus,* but he took roles in contemporary plays as well. As American actors gained experience, achieved fame, and established a distinctive style, the rivalry between Old- and New-World Shakespeare began to intensify. This was not merely a question of Yankee jingoism but a contest between high and low art, between gentility and manly vigor. In New York City in 1854 the competition exploded into a melee, an actual street riot in Astor Place between the fans of Edwin Forrest and those of William Macready. Forrest was a brash, physical American actor who deliberately opposed his histrionic vigor and masculinity to the more polished and elegant — the more English — mode of Macready. As enemies of Macready swarmed outside the theater denouncing the "bloody British actor," and as part of the audience attempted to stop his performance as Macbeth, soldiers arrived to keep the peace. They ended up firing into the crowd, and ultimately thirty-one people died, with many more wounded.

The lucrative San Francisco season of Charles Kean and company mentioned previously was not a fluke. Improbable as it may seem, the American West was for a time one of the most hospitable territories in the world for the performance of Shakespeare. Not only did touring players act the plays, but the settlers and prospectors who had raced to California for the Gold Rush of the 1850s seem to have studied, memorized, declaimed, lampooned, and enjoyed them in various forms. Sizable communities such as Sacramento and San Francisco constructed theaters, and even though they were repeatedly destroyed by the fires to which such towns were vulnerable, the citizens quickly rebuilt them. In the smaller towns and outposts, a stage was often fitted into the back room of a saloon; if that arena was unavailable, then barns, wagons, or other improvised settings were rigged up for the touring companies whose visit added a welcome flash of glamour to a laborious and hazardous life. Although the more renowned performers confined themselves mainly to the cities, the camps and remote areas welcomed pickup groups, theatrical families, or one semifamous name surrounded by a few supporting actors. Junius Brutus Booth went West, and his son Edwin, still a teenager and some years away from stardom, apprenticed by playing all the major tragic roles with a patched-together California troupe.

The larger and more organized groups performed complete plays in the larger towns: *Richard III* was always popular, and the tragedies, particularly *Hamlet* and *Othello,* tended to draw more than the comedies. Complete performances were often followed by a short farce or other kind of spoof, and the farther away from the towns the companies got, the more likely was the bill also to consist of songs, burlesques, well-known scraps from plays, and virtuoso performances on the banjo. We should not, however, be too quick to accept a mental image of cultivated British thespians orating and emoting before a mob of hayseeds and brutes. Many of the miners, as well as the grocers and saddlers and loggers who supplied them, were decently educated, and the almost universal familiarity with the King James Bible would have made Shakespeare's language much more accessible to most Americans of that period than to their modern counterparts. (And it is important to note that in England during the same period performances often included what we might call warm-up acts or sideshows, interjected songs or speeches, and sometimes a short farce to close off the evening.) No doubt many of the stories about the popularity of Shakespeare's plays in the midst of the California Gold Rush are exaggerated — instances of the Western taste for the tall tale — but still it is clear that by 1850 the Shakespearean empire extended west of the Mississippi to the Pacific. And further too: when Charles Kean and his company visited San Francisco for the first time, they were on their way home from performing in Australia, and one of the California actresses took herself and her husband off to Hawaii.

Twentieth-Century Stages, Modern and Postmodern

In T. S. Eliot's *Old Possum's Book of Practical Cats,* Gus, the aged theater cat, is famous among his younger colleagues because "he has acted with Irving, / He has acted with Tree." In other words, Gus is a relic of the past, and everybody knows it. Just as Kean and the other romantic actors had consciously rebelled against the stately and conventional style of the late eighteenth century, so the twentieth century sought its own distinctive mode for interpreting the plays, and a few important markers denote the birth of the modern style. Our familiarity with the modernist aesthetic makes it easy to see that twentieth-century theatrical reforms were consonant with the artistic revolution in painting, sculpture, music, poetry, fiction, fashion, and other arts and crafts. Speaking broadly, we can say that the primary impulse was to simplify. The protests raised by Shaw and others against Victorian and Edwardian excess were shared by the theatrical reformer William Poel (1852–1934), who preached loud and long against the tyranny of the pictorial and the accretions of tradition.

Poel was a fundamentalist, one who wished to recreate the physical conditions of Shakespeare's own theater and thus to effect an "Elizabethan revival." He mounted a number of productions in the hope that the virtues of his dogma would be self-evident to the public, yet though his ideas generated some theoretical interest, finally his approach came to be regarded as a kind of curiosity. And textually, Poel was not as pure as his doctrine would imply, since he monkeyed with the texts almost as much as the Victorians he challenged. The more enduring contribution to modern Shakespeare was made by a designer, Edward Gordon Craig.

Son of the quintessential nineteenth-century actress, Ellen Terry, with a point of view determined by his immersion in symbolism and other Continental artistic movements, Craig (1872–1966) reimagined the Shakespearean scene with the help of the contemporary enthusiasm for abstraction or expressionism. Beginning as both director and designer in small venues where he exerted absolute control, Craig first came to public notice with his London staging of *Much Ado about Nothing* in 1903. Although he conceived a production that would permit him to realize his complete vision, the actual show was a hybrid that clearly registers the passage from the Victorian to the modern stage. Much was old-fashioned. Time and money were so short that costumes were not created but borrowed from previous stagings, and the same may be said of the characterizations. Terry played Beatrice, as she had with Irving in 1882, and she had no intention of altering her conception, even for her visionary son. But Craig's designs, owing partly to his extraordinary ideas and partly to the low budget, were like nothing that had been seen before. The church scene, in which Claudio shames Hero, made a tremendous impact by virtue of its visual restraint. The atmosphere of solemnity and dread was generated by a stage draped with fabric, the extensive use of candles, and the projection of colored lights onto an altar. Craig later went to Russia to join forces with the great director Konstantin Stanislavsky of the Moscow Art Theatre, where they collaborated on a production of *Hamlet* in front of massive abstract screens. The effort was crippled by strife between Craig and the Russian company, who weren't able to implement the designer's vision. Arrogant and idealistic, Craig was so committed to his lofty imaginary stage that before long he withdrew entirely from the practical world of the theater. Self-exiled in the south of France, he continued to disseminate his modernist tenets in print, and his influence was far-reaching. One of his most gifted disciples was the American designer Robert Edmond Jones. Jones's expressionistic set for John Barrymore's *Hamlet* is reproduced on page 391.

The other major player in the rejection of the literal was Harley Granville Barker, playwright, director, and passionate spokesman for social and artistic change. In 1912 at the Savoy Theatre, the house built by Richard D'Oyly Carte for Gilbert and Sullivan's operettas, the thirty-five-year-old Granville Barker directed his wife Lillah McCarthy in revolutionary productions of *The Winter's Tale* (in September) and *Twelfth Night* (in November). The keynote for both was simplicity of design, a brisk tempo, and careful attention to language. Both texts, even *The Winter's Tale,* a very long play, were performed virtually uncut. Whereas Poel had for decades been evangelizing about plain Shakespeare, Granville Barker seized the essence of Poel's idea while discarding the antiquarian, pedantic dogma. Audiences were accustomed to the lavishness of Tree's *Twelfth Night,* in which Malvolio was accompanied through the hyper-realistic greenery of Olivia's garden by four subordinate Malvolios, junior stewards dressed exactly like their master. Granville Barker, on the other hand, employed as few actors as the script permitted, reverted to the Folio texts, and amazed the eye with Norman Wilkinson's stylized scenery and costumes. (See the photograph of Lillah McCarthy as Viola in Wilkinson's fancifully abstract garden on p. 390.) This pair of productions was followed in 1914 by *A Midsummer Night's Dream,* similar in spirit and design, and equally audacious. (Granville Barker's *Prefaces to Shakespeare,* written much later, are both brilliant and reasonable, a practical and theoretical treasury for anyone interested in the performance of Shakespeare.) My emphasis on Granville Barker's originality should not be taken to mean that the theatrical world changed overnight. Many old-timers still preferred the realism on which they were reared, and plenty of directors were content to satisfy such tastes. Nineteenth-century Shakespeare endured well into the twentieth century, and had the war not intervened, the elaborate style would probably have lasted even longer.

The chaos in Europe after World War I brought new life and ideas to British theater. A thorough accounting of the birth of modern Shakespeare, like the birth of twentieth-century theater generally, would have to give notice to the theoretical ideas of Stanislavsky, to the visual influence of the Russian constructivists, to the detailed and prescient direction of Max Reinhardt in Berlin, to the Polish Futurist (and Craig disciple) Leon Schiller, and to other Continental influences, both theoretical and practical. These fascinating topics lie outside the purview of this chapter, but it should be said that the most far-reaching European directors appropriated for Shakespeare the techniques of abstraction and expressionism that were changing the other arts. And while English experiments were perhaps not as bold as that, the twenty-year period between the wars was a time of theatrical transition, with experimentation appearing in various places and in several forms. For example, Barry Jackson, ingenious director of the Birmingham Repertory Theatre, sought to give what we might call "relevance" to the too familiar Shakespearean script. Beginning his tenure before World War I, he began to be noticed in the 1920s for producing the plays in modern dress and for cultivating in his performers a more "natural," less obviously poetic speech. British audiences were not accustomed to cigarettes, cocktail shakers, and plus-fours in *Hamlet, Prince of Denmark.* Jackson was hardly the first to employ modern dress. A look at the illustrations of Garrick or Mrs. Siddons suggests that the eighteenth century did much of its Shakespeare in "modern dress," and the German theater in the first decade of the twentieth century made moves in this direction. But Jackson's desire to shock the spectator with a self-consciously contemporary look *was* new and influential, and some of his productions were transferred to London, where they stimulated considerable comment.

The 1920s, '30s, and '40s witnessed a contest between the novel and the traditional. Granville Barker's influence was apparent in that more and more productions were staged with a unit set: the three women who made up the design team called Motley were pioneers in this practice, notably in the 1935 *Romeo and Juliet* at the New Theatre in London. Their simple setting allowed "fluency of action as the Elizabethan stage would have afforded" (Anthony Davies in Jackson and Bate 148). Once again, innovation was a return to an older style. At the Shakespeare Memorial Theatre in Stratford-upon-Avon, the Russian emigré Theodore Komisarjevsky surprised audiences accustomed to more conventional stagings, infusing very familiar plays with freshness and ingenuity. His innovation was felt especially in texts with an established performing tradition: for *The Merchant of Venice* (1932) he comically distorted the perspective of the set, desentimentalized Shylock, and played Bach in the background. Today such eclecticism has become routine and unremarkable, but many theatergoers at the time found it bewildering and revolutionary. At the same time, tradition persisted, particularly in the performances of some great actors, notably John Gielgud (great-nephew of Ellen Terry), Ralph Richardson, Peggy Ashcroft, Edith Evans, and Laurence Olivier, who carried with them the aura of the nineteenth-century theatrical stars. That 1935 *Romeo and Juliet* dazzled audiences with Peggy Ashcroft as Juliet and with Gielgud and Olivier alternating in the roles of Romeo and Mercutio. A decade later, in the productions of Olivier and Richardson at the New Theatre, visual effects took second place to the virtuosity of the acting, and in general the two men charted a middle way between the conventional and the radical. (See the excerpt from Kenneth Tynan on p. 401.) And at the Old Vic, a nineteenth-century house just south of the Thames, a dynamo named Lilian Baylis mounted seasons of Shakespeare for some forty years, attempting to produce all the plays on a more or less regular cycle and engaging some of England's most talented directors and actors. The success of this venture had much to do with the brilliance of the Belfast-born director Tyrone Guthrie, whose energy and ingenuity made him a fit successor to Barker and Jackson.

Three phenomena characterize Shakespearean performance after the Second World War: the rise of institutional theater, the reconception of theatrical space, and the dominance of the director. To some extent it might be said that Shakespeare had already become institutionalized. Irving's tenure at the Lyceum or Tree's at the Haymarket constituted a semipermanent enterprise, and performances had been given annually at Stratford-upon-Avon since the opening of the Shakespeare Memorial Theatre in 1879. But in the postwar years of the 1950s, as public funding of the arts in Britain became more dependable and substantial, and as North American communities began to support their local Shakespeare festivals, the cultural significance of Shakespeare and those who performed him began to change.

A sign of this development was the founding of the Royal Shakespeare Company in 1960–61. Peter Hall, fresh from Cambridge and newly appointed director of the Shakespeare Memorial Theatre in Stratford, wanted an ensemble of actors who could work together in play after play over a period of years. He argued successfully that government support for a core group of actors, directors, designers, and technicians would afford financial security, artistic liberty, and the kind of ease that generates imaginative experiment. Hall had already exhibited an uncommon sensitivity to tonal complexity in his own productions, notably a *Coriolanus* with Olivier (1959), and he managed to generate popular excitement at the same time that he earned artistic respect. He also possessed a genius for keeping the company in the news. The initial triumph was Hall and John Barton's ambitious production of the first history cycle in 1963, *The Wars of the Roses*. The acting was extraordinary: Peggy Ashcroft entered as the teenage bride of Henry VI newly come from France, and ended as mad Margaret, the usurped crone in *Richard III* who exits vowing to return to France. Such bravura performances were strikingly framed in the designs of John Bury, whose spare iron set and gray leather uniforms revealed the influence of Berthold Brecht and the Berliner Ensemble. And the textual approach was adventurous: not only were the three *Henry VI* plays consolidated into two, but some of the resulting gaps were bridged by blank verse that John Barton himself had written based on episodes from Holinshed's *Chronicles*. In this respect the modern insistence on textual fidelity bowed slightly to the eighteenth- and nineteenth-century tradition of textual manipulation. It was a heady time in the English theater, and within a few years the Royal Shakespeare Company (RSC) had made itself an indispensable feature of English theatrical life.

Such an achievement would have been impossible without state sponsorship, and the continuation of that support allowed the company to grow. The RSC now occupies three theaters in Stratford-upon-Avon, not only the Shakespeare Memorial Theatre but also the Swan, a medium-sized house paid for by an American donor, and The Other Place, a small space suitable for "chamber Shakespeare" and especially for new plays. The company also performs for much of the year in three theaters in London. A measure of the stability Peter Hall established is that the RSC has had only four artistic directors — Hall, Trevor Nunn, Terry Hands, and Adrian Noble — in forty years, an amazing record for a public theatrical enterprise. Success and growth have not been without pains, however. The demands of producing all Shakespeare's plays on a four- or five-year rotation, of filling six theaters for eight performances a week, of arranging tours to perform in places other than Stratford and London, of engaging major actors who will commit themselves to a year or more away from London, of training newcomers whose vocal and physical range have been stunted by acting for television, of pleasing both critics and tourists, and of being scrutinized and hyped and attacked by the press — all these have made for some difficult days. But there have been artistic triumphs too. For better or worse, the RSC dominated the production of Shakespeare in Britain in the last half of the twentieth century.

The RSC was not the only beneficiary of the Arts Council in the 1960s. In London, Laurence Olivier, by now Sir Laurence, used his fame to bring into being the National Theatre that had been desired and debated and planned and delayed since the days of George Bernard Shaw. Although the company had no building and thus played at the Old Vic, although rehearsal and administrative conditions were minimal, and although doing Shakespeare was not its principal charge, the National Theatre in its early days mounted some extraordinary stagings of his plays. Three of its most notable were John Dexter's *Othello* (1964) with Olivier and Maggie Smith; Clifford Williams's *As You Like It* (1967) with an exclusively male cast and a contemporary setting, all Mylar and sixties fashions; and Jonathan Miller's Victorian *Merchant of Venice* (1970), a showcase for Olivier's Shylock. Olivier led the company for a decade, acting occasionally but also reinventing himself as an administrator and helping to plan the new building on the South Bank of the Thames, just next to Waterloo Bridge.

This looming concrete structure — forbidding without, comfortable within — has not improved in appearance since it opened in 1975, but it contains three superb performing spaces, a black-box theater known as the Cottesloe, a proscenium stage called the Lyttleton, and an amphitheater-style house modeled after the Greek theater at Epidaurus and named, appropriately, the Olivier. Shortly before the move into the new building Olivier ceded his directorship to Peter Hall, who held the position for sixteen years. (The vicissitudes of Hall's tenure at the National — strikes, funding disputes with the Thatcher government, the difficulties of overseeing a massive operation and sustaining quality throughout — are chronicled in his *Diaries*, which the famously energetic director was able to keep in the midst of the chaos.) Hall was succeeded by Richard Eyre, director from 1988 to 1996, and Eyre by Trevor Nunn, who had been Hall's successor at the RSC. All of these directors have given the public some memorable Shakespeare: Hall's *Antony and Cleopatra* (1977) in the Olivier, with Anthony Hopkins and Judi Dench; Eyre's intimate production of *King Lear* (1996), with Ian Holm; and Trevor Nunn's production of *The Merchant of Venice* (1999–2000) with Henry Goodman as Shylock, a production that opened in the Cottesloe and had such a success that it was restaged in the Olivier to accommodate demand.

Beyond the major subsidized companies and commercial houses is the phenomenon known as the Fringe, a term referring to the many companies that operate on the margins of the theatrical establishment. Generally these are small, nonprofit groups performing in neighborhood theaters, social halls, and pubs. Budgets are low, schedules are irregular, and performances are not always polished. But the Fringe can provide such rare qualities as intimacy, youthful vigor, and the spirit of the underdog, and some exceptional performers and organizations have emerged from this milieu. One of the most successful Fringe companies was Declan Donnellan's Cheek by Jowl, which operated throughout the 1980s and 1990s and did some memorable work, notably an all-male *As You Like It* that dazzled critics and audiences around the world. One Fringe theater that has become a powerful, mainstream organization is the Almeida Theatre, which stages the works of Shakespeare and other dramatists, often with celebrated film actors: Ralph Fiennes played Hamlet, Richard II, and Coriolanus for the Almeida. Kenneth Branagh founded his

Renaissance Theatre Company in 1987 with a pickup group of seasoned players; it was neither Fringe nor establishment. Such enterprises continue to do imaginative theater, but the major subsidized companies have come to dominate the field and have taken the place of what until 1960 or so was West End classical theater.

Enthusiasts in Canada and the United States, although without much governmental aid, have delivered Shakespeare to millions of spectators through a series of festivals and permanent or semipermanent institutions. The most ambitious and successful of these is the Shakespeare festival in the small town of Stratford, Ontario. It was begun by Tyrone Guthrie with two productions in a tent in 1953, and in a brilliant stroke that looked back to the popular successes of the nineteenth century, he persuaded the film star Alec Guinness to lead the company as Richard III. A new, permanent building was completed within a few years, an old movie theater was also appropriated for other kinds of plays, and a third stage is now in use as well. Guthrie departed after only a few years to found a theater in Minneapolis, Minnesota, but his successors at Stratford have managed to sustain quality and variety, despite the incessant financial problems.

In the United States the most nearly comparable venture is the festival at Ashland, Oregon, boasting an excellent indoor house, an outdoor Elizabethan-style theater, and experimental space as well. On the other coast, in New York City, Joseph Papp began to present free Shakespeare from a movable truck in the 1950s. This enterprise grew into a branch of the New York Public Theater, the New York Shakespeare Festival, which each summer offers two productions in Central Park performed without charge. Some famous actors have played against the backdrop of trees and distant skyscrapers: Meryl Streep, Sam Waterston, Kevin Kline, Tracy Ulmann, and James Earl Jones are the most familiar. For a time in the 1960s and 1970s the Shakespeare Theatre in Stratford, Connecticut, achieved artistic and popular success with its productions. Many other states have nurtured festivals that play mostly in the summer and have earned exceptional loyalty among their patrons, notably the Alabama, Colorado, Utah, and North Carolina Shakespeare festivals. The Shakespeare Theater in Washington, D.C., under the direction of Michael Kahn, has grown from a branch of the Folger Shakespeare Library to a major cultural force in the U.S. capital, presenting four or five Shakespeare plays per year with a permanent company supplemented by other actors. The Shenandoah Shakespeare Express, a young company based in Staunton, Virginia, performs at home and also tours the nation, playing largely at schools and colleges. From the smallest of these festivals to the Royal Shakespeare Company itself, permanent institutions specializing in the production of Shakespeare's plays are a relatively new phenomenon, the twentieth century's distinctive contribution to the Shakespearean branch of theater history.

The most recent English entry into the Shakespeare game is the re-creation of the Globe Theatre in the Southwark district of London, very near where the original building stood. The dream of the American actor Sam Wanamaker, the project gathered strength in the 1980s and was finally realized thanks to the financing of some influential people, the interest of many in the academic community, and — above all — a subsidy from the National Lottery. Working from archival records and supervised by scholars familiar with the most recent information about Elizabethan practices (the kind of material set out in Chapter 3), the builders have done their best to replicate the space that Shakespeare and his actors and audience occupied. Construction of the building was done, insofar as possible, according to sixteenth-century principles, with thatching for the roof and oak dowels in the timbered frame, although historical fidelity necessarily yielded to modern fire and safety codes. The most noticeable concession to custom is the set of floodlights affixed to the thatched roof, a compromise that permits the company to perform at night as well as in the afternoon. Opening with a preliminary season in 1996, the theater now houses a company under the direction of Mark Rylance and produces about three plays per year, from May to September. Shakespeare is the primary attraction, but works of his contemporaries have been performed also, and the space has been made available for play readings, brief runs by small visiting companies, and other such educational endeavors. Much is still uncertain: there is debate, for example, about the dimensions and height of the stage, the location and size of the pillars that support the roof, and other such architectural features, and scholars hope that use of the building may suggest answers to some of these intractable problems. One thing is certain: the enterprise has been a huge success with the public, and the supervisors hope to be able soon to recreate a Jacobean indoor theater on the premises.

Thanks partly to the rise of the permanent or semipermanent Shakespeare company, the twentieth century altered the history of Shakespearean performance when it introduced the second major phenomenon mentioned above, the redefinition of the performing space. As theatrical taste and practice developed from the seventeenth to the nineteenth centuries, theater architecture gradually changed with it. By the middle of the nineteenth century, Shakespeare's wooden platform with the audience positioned on three sides had become a proscenium stage, the picture-frame structure built for the painterly style of representation. Some prophets around 1900 lamented the tyranny of this immutable arrangement, but not until the second half of the century was someone able to do something about it. Directors in the Royal Shakespeare Memorial Theatre at Stratford have attempted to modify the stage somewhat, pushing it slightly into the auditorium or putting galleries on the sides of the stage to connect spectator and actor. Yet any solution is an unsatisfactory compromise because, as Trevor Nunn put it, "the actors are in one room and the audience in another." Thus Tyrone Guthrie, in leading his Canadian company from tent to permanent home, insisted on a stage that resembled a Greek amphitheater, with the audience surrounding the playing area on three sides. Thanks to his insistence and to the cooperation of his designer, Tanya Moiseiwitsch, the Festival Theater in Stratford, Ontario, is so constructed. Other theater architects have taken note, and for the most part their aim has been to enhance contact between audience and actor. The Swan Theatre in Stratford-upon-Avon puts the audience in a U on three sides of the actors, and many other spaces — The Other Place in Stratford, the Cottesloe in the National, The Pit in the Barbican, the Frank Patterson Theatre in Canada, the Mitzi Newhouse at Lincoln Center — can be configured according to the requirements of the text. "Chamber Shakespeare," "black-box Shakespeare," "promenade Shakespeare" — many novel configurations are now available.

A final development of the last half of the twentieth century is the sovereignty of the director. So far as we know, the Tudor and Stuart companies mounted plays without one: there seems to have been a stage manager, and the author may have been present to supervise blocking or offer assistance of other kinds, but there is no record of a person with the authority and responsibility of the modern director. In the eighteenth and nineteenth centuries the actor was supreme, and people spoke of Kean's Richard III or Irving's Shylock. These superstars in effect directed their supporting players. (Irving famously nabbed for himself the red cloak that Ellen Terry as Lady Macbeth had planned to wear over her celebrated beetle-wing dress, shown on p. 387.) But in none of these eras was there a company member whose only job was to direct. In the increasingly complex world of the modern and postmodern theater, with the need to coordinate set and costume designers, lighting designers, composers and music masters, textual consultants, and star actors, the director has emerged as the central figure in the mounting of a Shakespeare play. Today we may still refer to an actor's role — say, Ralph Fiennes's Hamlet or Anthony Sher's Richard III — but we are more likely to speak of the Peter Brook *Midsummer Night's Dream* or the John Barton *Twelfth Night* or the Deborah Warner *Titus Andronicus*. After Granville Barker and Max Reinhardt, one of the first figures to enlarge the role of director was Orson Welles, whose Mercury Theater productions in New York in the 1930s depended very much on his brilliant and audacious way with the text. His famous "Voodoo *Macbeth*," set in nineteenth-century Haiti and performed by a black cast in a theater in Harlem, may be the first case in which a play was deliberately removed from its own fictional period and transferred to an entirely different setting (Kennedy 145).

In England Peter Brook did much to magnify the director's role. He was a *wunderkind*, as directors often seem to be. At Stratford in 1946 he was given responsibility for *Love's Labor's Lost*, a play that was not in particular favor and that can be difficult to sell. The twenty-one-year-old Brook not only directed it, designed sets and costumes in the style of a Watteau painting, and composed the music, but he also staged it so imaginatively that it was a surprise hit. In the mid-1950s he revived Shakespeare's earliest tragedy, *Titus Andronicus*, a play that had never been taken seriously, with Laurence Olivier and Vivien Leigh. After the opening, it was taken very seriously. The effect of the tragedy was unexpectedly powerful, so much so that spectators sometimes fainted in the bloodier scenes. A well-read, cosmopolitan, and imaginative director, Brook drew inspiration from a variety of sources: under the influence of the Polish critic Jan Kott, he directed Paul Scofield in *King Lear* (Stratford, 1963; filmed, 1970) as if it were a text from the theater of the absurd, something like Samuel Beckett's *Endgame*.

If he had staged nothing else, his *Midsummer Night's Dream* for the Royal Shakespeare Company (1970) would qualify him as one of the most influential directors of the twentieth century. Indeed it is probably the most famous single Shakespeare production of the century. Contemptuous of Victorian pictorialism — of gossamer fairies and live bunnies and fake romance — Brook banished all such trappings from his stage. Taking his cue from Theseus's notion, in reference to the "Pyramus and Thisbe" play, that the audience must use its imagination, the director and his designer, Sally Jacobs, challenged the imaginative faculty of their audience, setting the play against three white walls, in a space that resembled a handball court. (The photograph of Jacobs's set on p. 397 conveys the visual starkness of the production.) Oberon and Puck supervised (literally) the nocturnal confusion from trapezes; a metal plate twirled on a stick stood for the magic plant and its love-lotion; Titania's bower was a giant red feather suspended in the midst of the white space; the trees were coils of metal that descended to entangle the lovers. The only hint of tradition was a joke: some of the "Wedding March" from Mendelssohn's familiar score was played mockingly to accompany Bottom's erection as he succumbed to Titania. Such spare and original staging was calculated to emphasize the words, which were beautifully spoken. (I can still recall after thirty years the tone of Sara Kestleman's imperious declaration to Bottom, "I am a spirit of no common rate"). Audiences, journalists, scholars — everyone was electrified, and the production toured to New York, to Paris, to Moscow, to Japan. (See Robert Speaight's review of Brook's production on p. 398.) Although he directed other Shakespeare plays for the Royal Shakespeare Company after his *Dream*, Brook has mostly concentrated his energies on his theatrical ensemble in Paris, where he still pursues experimental and multicultural projects.

Other directors might be mentioned — Nicholas Hytner and Sam Mendes, like Peter Hall and Trevor Nunn before them, went directly from Cambridge University into the role of director, and their names are commonly mentioned as theatrical leaders in the twenty-first century. But the phenomenon that really is new, a welcome offshoot of directors' theater, is the emergence of the female director. To date the major figure in this category is indisputably Deborah Warner, whose production of *Titus Andronicus* in the Swan Theatre in Stratford (1987) remains one of the most successful and significant productions of the last two or three decades. Warner came to the mainstream from the Fringe after starting her own company, Kick Theater, in the early '80s and creating some powerful productions with limited resources. She has gone on to other directorial successes, particularly in the opera house. Her memorable Shakespeares have included a fascinating *King John* at Stratford, a *King Lear* at the National in 1990, and an unconventional *Richard II* (also for the National) in which Fiona Shaw played the title part.

Warner's assistant director on *Titus Andronicus* was Katie Mitchell, who has gone on to do some very exciting work for several companies. Her production of *Henry VI, Part 3* at Stratford (1994), performed by young actors on a dirt floor, brought youth, intensity, and contemporaneity to the Wars of the Roses:

Richard of Gloucester stalked through The Other Place as a kind of skinhead, a particularly sullen member of an aggressive young family on the move. And yet, outside the theater at the interval, veteran theatergoers complained about the loss of poetry ("You should have heard Alan Howard's Henry in the late '70s") and it did little good to remind them that the same complaint had been lodged against Olivier at the beginning of his career and even against Garrick in the eighteenth century. Before long, a new actor or director or technician will appear and make us see and hear Shakespeare in an entirely new light.

Shakespeare Screened

The formidable topic of Shakespeare on film can only be gestured at in these pages. Almost as soon as motion pictures were conceived as a popular form of entertainment, Shakespeare was deemed an appropriate and potentially rich source of material. The first bit of filmed Shakespeare consisted of scenes from Beerbohm Tree's stage production of *King John* (1899), and throughout the silent-movie era, or roughly the next thirty years, the novelty of the medium (and the absence of dialogue) gave great latitude for experiment. Naturally, the early cinema was related to the spectacular visual style of the nineteenth-century theater, but new filmmakers produced a range of types: documents of stage performances, favorite scenes from familiar plays, star vehicles, adaptations. Our conventional ninety or so minutes had not yet become the standard, a fact that left room for originality. Many of the earliest films were Italian and French, with a few British and American efforts as well, and one obvious directorial strategy was to use the authority of Shakespeare, already the world's dramatist, to legitimize the new medium.

Tree was brought to Hollywood by D. W. Griffith and was paid a vast sum for playing the lead in *Macbeth* (1916), but the film failed with the public and no copies survive. On the other coast, Vitagraph Studios in New York made a series of ten-minute films, known as one-reelers, of scenes from plays from *Richard III* to *Twelfth Night* to *Julius Caesar*. And the European expressionist movement in the arts led to some fascinating silent efforts. In Germany the director Svend Gade made *Hamlet, the Drama of Vengeance* (1920), a film starring the popular, versatile actress Asta Nielsen and taking its cue from the eccentric theory proposed in 1881 that Hamlet was actually a woman in disguise. In American movies the treatment of Shakespeare was usually more conventional. Even before the film industry agreed upon Hollywood as its center of operations, the early producers attempted to give themselves and their studios "class" by appropriating the "classiest" of scriptwriters for their bankable stars. That they were aware of the nakedness of their attempt to buy authority and prestige is suggested by the famous credit line in the first Shakespearean talkie, the Mary Pickford-Douglas Fairbanks *Taming of the Shrew* (1929): "By Sam Taylor with additional dialogue by William Shakespeare." (Pickford bankrolled the film, and it may be that she insisted on having her part amplified.) The facetious line was attacked by critics as presumptuous and subsequently removed from the print.

The attempt to transfer to film the practices of the stage sometimes made for damaging or risible incongruities. For centuries *Romeo and Juliet* had been performed in the theater by "mature" actors and actresses who were in some cases even three or four times as old as the lovers, and thanks to the conventions of theatrical illusion audiences accepted this kind of falsification. But on film, where "realism" or at least the appearance of verisimilitude is a basic requirement, such discrepancies were more glaring. Thus, in George Cukor's 1936 film of the play, produced by Irving Thalberg, Juliet was played by Norma Shearer, aged thirty-four and (not coincidentally) Mrs. Irving Thalberg; Romeo was Leslie Howard (most familiar as Ashley Wilkes in *Gone with the Wind*), aged forty-one. To our eyes, the hairstyles and costumes of the 1930s conspire to make the two stars look even older, and this is not to mention the fifty-four-year-old John Barrymore as Tybalt. As the medium grew up, awareness of such problems led to more credible attempts at representation, and thus when Franco Zeffirelli filmed the play in 1968, his Juliet was the sixteen-year-old Olivia Hussey. Naturally most of us are inclined toward those versions nearest to our own day, where the prevailing style is familiar to us, but many of the older films can still be viewed not just as historical curiosities but with real pleasure, and a number of them are masterpieces. The sumptuous silvery tones in Max Reinhardt's black-and-white *A Midsummer Night's Dream* (1935), for example, would justify repeated viewings even without the pleasures of Mickey Rooney's Puck or James Cagney's Bottom.

Midway through the twentieth century, two distinct traditions of filmed Shakespeare began to emerge: the first might be called the "popular" or "naturalistic" model of Laurence Olivier and later Franco Zeffirelli; the second is the more abstract, obviously artful work of directors such as Orson Welles and Grigori Kozintsev. Olivier's immense energy and theatrical authority advanced the medium of filmed Shakespeare in three major productions. His first experience with Shakespeare and the camera was as an actor, playing Orlando in Paul Czinner's British *As You Like It* (1936), although *Highlights from As You Like It* might be a more apt title, since the film is barely 1½ hours long. As a director, Olivier began with a famously patriotic *Henry V* (1944), produced during World War II and dedicated to the troops who participated in the Normandy landings on D-Day. Understandably, King Henry is the scarcely blemished war hero, the strong-jawed and severely barbered patriot who thrashes the superior French army at Agincourt and marries their charming princess. (See the photograph of Olivier as Henry V on p. 400.) An original feature of the film was its setting the opening scenes in a reconstruction of the Globe and then proceeding into an apparently familiar cinematic mode for the action in France. In fact, however, the mise-en-scène is cleverly manipulated so as to resemble the illustrations in the medieval Book of Hours. Angles are skewed, colors heightened, and the entire production has the look of a fairy tale come to life. Only toward the latter part of the film, particularly the battle at Agincourt, does the style become "realistic."

After the war, Olivier followed his success with the even more ambitious *Hamlet* (1948), for which he won an Academy Award as Best Actor. Filmed in black and white and influenced by the Freudian interpretation of Ernest Jones, the film famously opens with a voice-over telling viewers what to think: "This is the story of a man who could not make up his mind." The film is also notable for the peculiar casting of the twenty-eight-year-old Eileen Herlie as Gertrude. Although she was transformed into a matron, the fact that she was thirteen years younger than her celluloid son helped to bolster the Oedipal subtext. The last of Olivier's cinematic projects preserved his bravura performance in the title role of *Richard III,* his characterization supported by a number of famous theatrical colleagues, including Gielgud, Richardson, and Claire Bloom as Lady Anne.

Olivier's cinematic mantle was taken by the Italian stage and opera director Franco Zeffirelli, whose sumptuous, colorful style gave his films, especially those with Italian settings, a rich and "authentic" feel. His *Taming of the Shrew* (1966), with Elizabeth Taylor and Richard Burton romping their way through an idealized but very detailed Padua, exploited the notoriously stormy married life of the two stars. (The Pickford–Fairbanks *Taming of the Shrew* of four decades earlier had done much the same thing.) This was followed shortly by *Romeo and Juliet* (1968), cast with handsome young actors and accompanied by Nino Rota's highly romantic musical score. The film was a great popular success, engaging as it did with the themes of the culture of the 1960s, generational strife, youthful independence, and — in the era of Vietnam — the premature death of young people. Zeffirelli's next Shakespeare was by way of Verdi, a film of the opera *Otello* (1986) with Placido Domingo as the hero. Then in 1990 he presented Mel Gibson, known more for his Mad Max movies than for Renaissance tragedy, as an active rather than a contemplative Prince Hamlet.

Zeffirelli represents the link between the popular realism of Olivier and the current steward of that tradition, Kenneth Branagh, and it is not surprising that films in this mode have often derived from particular stage productions: examples include Olivier's *Richard III* and Zeffirelli's *Romeo and Juliet.* Similarly, Branagh's first entry as film director followed his much-praised performance as Henry V in Adrian Noble's 1984 production for the Royal Shakespeare Company. His film of *Henry V* (1989) raised eyebrows because of the director's young age (twenty-eight) and his attempt on the same text as Olivier's famous version. Although Branagh's film still celebrates English power, he deliberately supplements Olivier's patriotism with an emphasis on the costs of victory. (It is fascinating that theater directors have begun to take note of their cinematic predecessors: Matthew Warchus's stage version of *Henry V* for the RSC contained unmistakable visual "quotations" from both Olivier and Branagh.) Branagh has gone on to become something of a phenomenon, with productions of an idyllic Tuscan *Much Ado about Nothing* (1993), an uncut and luxuriously cast *Hamlet* (1997), and a musical *Love's Labor's Lost* (2000). One clever tactic that links Branagh to his great theatrical ancestors is the integration into his cast of a few popular film stars not known for their classical acting: Keanu Reeves and Michael Keaton in *Much Ado about Nothing,*

Robin Williams and Billy Crystal in *Hamlet*, Alicia Silverstone and Nathan Lane in *Love's Labor's Lost*.

Parallel to this tradition, however, is the more experimental and audacious style of directors such as Orson Welles, Grigori Kozintsev, Akira Kurosawa, and a few other auteurs. Welles made three Shakespeare films and did so almost singlehandedly, raising the money by begging wherever he could and by taking acting roles in second-rate films or television productions, borrowing locations, cutting the script, directing, and playing the lead. Each time it was catch-as-catch-can. *Macbeth*, for example, was filmed (in twenty-one days!) partly on the defunct set of a Western mining town donated by a studio. His *Othello* was shot over a period of years: he would raise enough money to shoot a few minutes of film, exhaust that stash, and then suspend production until he could raise more funds. This practice required inventive solutions for problems in continuity: for some essential shots the original actor was no longer available, and so Welles used doubles or filmed from a distance so as to disguise the substitution. His masterpiece is *Chimes at Midnight*, a conflation of *Parts 1 and 2 of King Henry IV*, in which Welles plays Falstaff alongside several distinguished stage actors, among them John Gielgud as King Henry. Welles's films are characterized by a distinctive, expressionistic look: all are filmed in sharply contrasted black and white, with inventive camera angles and other technical efforts to enhance the meanings of the text or to conceive cinematic equivalents for Shakespeare's theatrical effects. Kozintsev is responsible for two of the most impressive Shakespeare films ever made, *Hamlet* (1964) and *King Lear* (1970), each using Boris Pasternak's Russian translation of Shakespeare's text. They feature immensely moving performances by Innokenti Smoktunovsky as Hamlet and Yuri Yarvet, a fierce-looking Lithuanian actor, as Lear. The director's Marxist readings made for an original approach, but still the films were so sophisticated as to be disturbing: the *Hamlet*, for example, was withdrawn from circulation in the last days of the Soviet regime. Kurosawa had a genius for adaptation, taking a Shakespearean story and transposing it into a Japanese setting and another era: *Throne of Blood* (1957) places the story of the brutal Macbeths in a Samurai culture, while *Ran* (1985), meaning "chaos," is *King Lear* revised into the story of an old man and his sons. *Ran* was made in color, and the brilliance of the cinematic surface contrasts pointedly with the bleakness of Kurosawa's narrative vision.

The first bit of televised Shakespeare was a single scene from *As You Like It*, telecast by the British Broadcasting Company from 3:55 to 4:06 on the afternoon of February 6, 1937. Other transmissions of Shakespeare to millions followed over the next four decades, notably an American *Macbeth* (1954) with Maurice Evans and Judith Anderson, produced for the program known as *Hallmark Hall of Fame*. At the end of the 1970s the BBC, in concert with Time-Life Television Productions and America's Public Broadcasting Service, initiated a project called *The Shakespeare Plays*, in which the entire canon would be taped and presented on television at a rate of some four a year. Unfortunately, the comprehensiveness of the enterprise and the sense of "permanence" associated with a filmed performance led the producers to rein in their directors, to discourage experimentation, and to strive for a normative or "straight" reading of each text. When, for example, would the world be offered another film of *Pericles*? This one, then, had to be "canonical" and clear. The series offers some very fine performances, preserving Anthony Quayle's justly famous Falstaff, first seen at Stratford-upon-Avon in the 1950s, and presenting a young Kate Nelligan as a passionate Isabella in *Measure for Measure*. Too often timidity and limitation made for dull readings, however, and thus, for plays that exist in other versions, the BBC's are rarely anyone's favorite performances. Still, the series boasts some indisputable successes, notably Jonathan Miller's *Taming of the Shrew* (with John Cleese of *Monty Python* as Petruchio), Miller's *All's Well That Ends Well*, and *Richard II* with Derek Jacobi.

The BBC tapes survive in video libraries, and another minor category of filmed Shakespeare is also mainly available on video: taped stage productions that pretend to be little more than a document of the theatrical performance. Stuart Burge's film of the National Theatre's *Othello* (1965) records the titanic performance by Olivier in the title role, with a young Maggie Smith as Desdemona. The National's Victorian *Merchant of Venice* (1973) was also taped, this time for television rather than for theatrical release. In 1988 Branagh's much-praised staging of *Twelfth Night* at the Riverside Studios in London was taped for television. With youthful, giddy principals but also with considerable pathos for the nasty treatment of Malvolio, the production explores a wide range of tones, helped immensely by Paul McCartney's memorable score. It ends with a very melancholy Feste shutting the gates of Olivia's estate as the snow falls. Among the strongest examples of such "documentary" Shakespeare is the video of Trevor Nunn's *Macbeth* (1976), a small-scale production originally done in The Other Place at Stratford and filmed with little alteration. Ian McKellen and Judi Dench are thrilling as the Macbeths (see the photograph of Dench as Lady Macbeth on p. 387), and an obvious motive of the film was to preserve two classic performances. As one critic put it, the large number of close-ups indicated that this *Macbeth* was about the speaking of verse.

By far the most significant development in filmed Shakespeare at the end of the twentieth and beginning of the twenty-first centuries is the creative approach to setting, usually a transfer to a time and place nearer the present. This new approach might be regarded as the cinematic equivalent of the Birmingham Rep's "modern dress" productions in the 1920s, an attempt to freshen the familiar text by making it contemporary. Theater audiences became accustomed to unusual settings decades ago, but the medium of film allows for an infinitely more elaborate and detailed sense of place, and also for greater directorial invention. Although the scripts are of necessity heavily cut, the original language is retained, and rather than fear the dissonance between Shakespearean verse and an up-to-the-minute milieu, directors have begun to play with and exploit the parallels and differences. In Michael Almereyda's version of *Hamlet* (2000), "Denmark" is a corporation headquartered in contemporary Manhattan, with Claudius its new CEO; Ethan Hawke as Hamlet delivers "To be or not to be" while roaming the Action aisle of a Blockbuster video store.

The most commercially successful of these modern re-settings is probably the Australian Baz Luhrmann's *William Shakespeare's ROMEO + JULIET* (1996), with the teen idols Leonardo DiCaprio and Claire Danes as the lovers. Having set the play in a very violent modern city à la Miami, Luhrmann performs some ingenious turns on the text. Shakespeare's Prologue becomes an African American television newswoman; Gregory, Samson, and the other Capulets and Montagues are gang members who brandish not rapiers but guns (a "Sword 381"); the fight is stopped by the arrival of Captain Prince, the police officer who substitutes for Shakespeare's Prince; Mercutio's Queen Mab speech is a drug-induced hallucination; Romeo lingers alone in an amusement park called the "Grove of Sycamore"; during the balcony scene the couple end up happily falling into the Capulet pool; Mantua, to which Romeo is banished, becomes a kind of desert trailer park; and when Friar Laurence decides to "send post-haste to Romeo," a Federal Express–like truck ("Post-Haste Delivery") drops off a letter that lies unnoticed on the stoop of a trailer overnight.

The price of such visual innovation is — as it was on the Restoration stage with which we began — a radical trimming of the text. All cinematic versions of Shakespeare plays (except for Branagh's complete *Hamlet*) cut a significant quotient of lines, the average being something like 60 percent, but *William Shakespeare's ROMEO + JULIET* cuts even more severely. What is especially noticeable is that the theatrical inexperience of his two stars prompted Luhrmann to distill most of the major speeches down to three or four lines. The character of the Nurse remains but speaks almost not at all. The same radical pruning of language occurs in Richard Loncraine's *Richard III* (1995) with Ian McKellen, an updating to the 1930s with Richard of Gloucester as a Fascist upstart: the film was based on Richard Eyre's 1990 production for the National Theatre. This *Richard III* has a running time of 107 minutes, and the fact that no line is spoken until 11 minutes into the film attests to the director's devotion to visual rather than verbal considerations. But the images are brilliant and include references to Darth Vader, Indiana Jones, action films, and familiar television commercials. Julie Taymor's eclectic *Titus* (1999), featuring Anthony Hopkins and Jessica Lange and based on Shakespeare's bloody first tragedy, mixes elements of ancient and modern Rome — chariots and motorcycles, Roman orgies and video games, a microphone with an SPQR logo. (See a still from the film on page 405.) Taymor retains a much higher percentage of the text than most directors do, an act of fidelity that makes the film run longer than most commercial movies. Even more outlandish adaptations have been created, often by eliminating the text altogether and using only the story: the 1956 science fiction film *Forbidden Planet* is a version of *The Tempest*, for example; *Men of Respect* (1991) rewrites *Macbeth* in the realm of the Mafia; and *10 Things I Hate about You* (1999) relocates *The Taming of the Shrew* to an American high school.

Considering this abundance of productions and adaptations, it should not surprise us that in the year 2000, William Shakespeare was named Man of the Millennium in a number of surveys, besting such competitors as Thomas

Jefferson, Wolfgang Amadeus Mozart, and Albert Einstein. Such polls mean little, perhaps, but the results attest to the power of the human imagination, the lure of language artfully arranged, and the delights of play. Shakespeare's domination of the theater and his increasingly important presence on movie screens show no signs of diminishing in the first part of the twenty-first century. The Bard is big business. School groups perform *Julius Caesar* in bedsheets, publishers distribute new editions of the plays, Oxfordians strain to discredit the man from Stratford, film actors make huge financial sacrifices to play juicy roles on stage, readers struggle valiantly with esoteric footnotes, advertisers appropriate famous lines to hawk a variety of products, directors choose unlikely settings to freshen familiar stories, scholars convene to debate interpretations, tourists swarm to the birthplace in Henley Street, college students read a Shakespeare *Companion*. I suspect that Shakespeare, even with his uncanny understanding of human beings and their ways, would be surprised at the extent of the modern Shakespeare industry.

✦ David Garrick as King Lear   *1761*

After a Painting by Benjamin Wilson

David Garrick (1717–1779) was the most famous actor of the eighteenth century. He revolutionized the conventions of English acting by moving in the direction of naturalism and contributed greatly to the phenomenon known as Bardolatry, or Shakespeare worship, by organizing the first Shakespeare Jubilee at Stratford-upon-Avon. In this engraving by Jo McArdell, Garrick is shown as King Lear, one of his greatest roles, in the storm scene.

✦ NAHUM TATE

From *The History of King Lear*   *1681*

Nahum Tate (1652–1715) radically revised Shakespeare's texts to accord with the standards and sensibilities of Restoration culture. Rejecting the bleakness of the Shakespearean tragic vision, Tate eliminated the fool, ennobled the virtuous characters, and softened and sentimentalized the ending. Not only does Lear survive, but Cordelia also escapes death and marries Edgar, who assumes the throne. This is the version that replaced Shakespeare's on the stage for almost 150 years. Following are the last few moments of Tate's final scene.

LEAR:
    . . . Where is my Kent, my Cajus?
KENT: Here, my liege.
LEAR:
    Why I have news that will recall thy youth.
    Ha! didst thou hear't, or did th'inspiring gods
    Whisper to me alone? Old Lear shall be
    A king again.   105
KENT:
    The prince, that like a god has power, has said it.
LEAR:
    Cordelia then shall be a queen, mark that:
    Cordelia shall be queen. Winds, catch the sound
    And bear it on your rosy wings to heaven.
    Cordelia is a queen.   110

Re-enter Edgar with Gloster.

ALBANY:
    Look, sir, where pious Edgar comes
    Leading his eyeless father. O my liege!
    His wondrous story will deserve your leisure:
    What he has done and suffered for your sake,
    What for the fair Cordelia's.   115
GLOSTER:
    Where is my liege? Conduct me to his knees to hail
    His second birth of empire. My dear Edgar
    Has, with himself, revealed the king's blest restoration.
LEAR:
    My poor dark Gloster.
GLOSTER:
    O let me kiss that once more sceptered hand!   120
LEAR:
    Hold, thou mistak'st the majesty, kneel here.
    Cordelia has our power, Cordelia's queen.
    Speak, is not that the noble suffering Edgar?
GLOSTER:
    My pious son, more dear than my lost eyes.
LEAR:
    I wronged him too, but here's the fair amends.   125
EDGAR:
    Your leave, my liege, for an unwelcome message.
    Edmund (but that's a trifle) is expired.
    What more will touch you, your imperious daughters
    Gonerill and haughty Regan, both are dead,
    Each by the other poisoned at a banquet.   130
    This, dying, they confessed.

CORDELIA:
O fatal period of ill-governed life!
LEAR:
Ingrateful as they were, my heart feels yet
A pang of nature for their wretched fall.
But, Edgar, I defer thy joys too long.   135
Thou served'st distressed Cordelia; take her crowned,
Th'imperial grace fresh blooming on her brow.
Nay, Gloster, thou hast here a father's right,
Thy helping hand t'heap blessings on their heads.
KENT:
Old Kent throws in his hearty wishes too.   140
EDGAR:
The gods and you too largely [generously] recompense
What I have done; the gift strikes merit dumb.
CORDELIA:
Nor do I blush to own myself o'erpaid
For all my sufferings past.
GLOSTER:
Now, gentle gods, give Gloster his discharge.   145
LEAR:
No, Gloster, thou hast business yet for life.
Thou, Kent and I, retired to some cool cell,
Will gently pass our short reserves of time
In calm reflections on our fortunes past,
Cheered with relation of the prosperous reign   150
Of this celestial pair. Thus our remains [remaining life]
Shall in an even course of thought be passed;
Enjoy the present hour, nor fear the last.
EDGAR:
Our drooping country now erects her head,
Peace spreads her balmy wings, and Plenty blooms.
Divine Cordelia, all the gods can witness   155
How much thy love to empire I prefer!
Thy bright example shall convince the world
(Whatever storms of Fortune are decreed)
That truth and virtue shall at last succeed.   160

Exeunt omnes.

FINIS

✦ Three Lady Macbeths

Sarah Siddons   *c. 1814*

Sarah Siddons (1755–1831), a member of the Kemble family of actors and producers, is one of the most important actresses in English stage history. Mrs. Siddons, as she was invariably known, caused a sensation as Lady Macbeth by violating the conventions of gesture and movement that audiences had come to expect. Even after her retirement she made public appearances to do readings of the part. Her gown reflects the elegant, neoclassical style of the period, a costume deemed appropriate even for a Scottish lady.

Ellen Terry 1889

(Alice) Ellen Terry (1847–1928) dominated the late Victorian stage alongside her male counterpart, Henry
Irving. Unlike her predecessor, Sarah
Siddons, who had shown no gift for
comedy, Terry was a famous Portia,
Beatrice, and Imogen, as well as a
superb tragedienne. This painting by
John Singer Sargent shows her in her
beetle-wing dress, one of the most
famous costumes in theatrical history.
According to Oscar Wilde, Terry as
Lady Macbeth "evidently patronises
local industries for her husband's
clothes and the servants' liveries, but
she takes care to do all her own shopping in Byzantium."

Judi Dench 1976

Dame Judi Dench (b. 1934) is the
reigning Shakespearean actress of our
day, the latest in a line of performers
that stretches back through Peggy
Ashcroft and Ellen Terry to Fanny
Kemble, Sarah Siddons, and Anne
Bracegirdle. She has triumphed in
many roles, comic (Viola, Titania,
Beatrice) and tragic (Juliet, Cleopatra,
Volumnia). Dench is shown here in
Trevor Nunn's production of *Macbeth*
at The Other Place, the converted-
barn theater in Stratford-upon-Avon.
The spareness of her costume is characteristic of modern black-box Shakespeare.

→ Ira Aldridge as Othello   *1852*

Ira Aldridge (1807–1867), reputed to be the grandson of a chieftain of Senegal, was the first major African American actor. Born in the United States, Aldridge attended the African Free School in New York and, after moving to Scotland, entered the world of the professional theater, acting in London and Dublin. Edmund Kean, the principal English tragedian of the day, engaged him to play Othello to Kean's Iago: such casting was a significant innovation because audiences had to this point regarded Othello not as a sub-Saharan African but rather as a North African or Arab, i.e., a light-skinned African. In the 1850s Aldridge toured Europe, playing such roles as Richard III and Macbeth. This illustration of Aldridge as Othello derives from a tour in 1852.

→ Playbill Advertising a Gala Performance of *Julius Caesar* 1864

Featuring the Three Booth Brothers

Junius Brutus Booth, an English actor who emigrated to America in 1821, fathered a theatrical dynasty: three sons all found careers in the theater. Junius Brutus Booth Jr. worked mainly as a manager; Edwin Booth became America's greatest nineteenth-century actor. The third son was also an actor — John Wilkes Booth. The playbill shown here, a rare piece of Shakespearean Americana now in the collection of the Folger Shakespeare Library in Washington, D.C., advertises a special gala performance of *Julius Caesar* in which the three Booth brothers performed together. Less than six months before the assassination of President Lincoln, John Wilkes Booth played Marc Antony, the Roman who condemns Caesar's assassins.

The potential spectator is advised that no one will profit from the special performance; rather, the gala evening is to be a benefit for the Shakespeare Statue Fund. Nineteenth-century audiences expected the kind of varied program described here: the playbill promises orchestral excerpts from operas by Bellini, Halevy, Meyerbeer, and Wagner.

→ Norman Wilkinson's Set Design for *Twelfth Night*   *1912*

For Harley Granville Barker's 1912 production of *Twelfth Night* at the Savoy Theatre in London, Norman Wilkinson created a severely stylized setting. Lillah McCarthy, who was married to Barker at the time, is shown here as Viola/Cesario in Olivia's garden. The abstract shrubbery was a deliberate and radical challenge to the prevailing realism inherited from the Victorian stage. The same team also produced *The Winter's Tale* (1912) and *A Midsummer Night's Dream* (1914).

✦ Robert Edmond Jones's Set Design for John Barrymore's *Hamlet*

1922, 1925

New York and London

Reflecting the influence of the visionary English designer Edward Gordon Craig, Jones's design for Barrymore's *Hamlet* represents the style known as expressionism. In dwarfing the famous actor (and, by extension, the character), the steps and distant arch do not merely locate the action: they also offer, in their immensity of scale, an interpretation of the text. As the photograph suggests, Jones was adept at using stage lighting to enhance his designs.

↱ John Barrymore's Script for *Hamlet*   1922

Directed by Arthur Hopkins

This plan for the blocking of the sword fight between Hamlet and Laertes in the final scene of *Hamlet* was handwritten on the last few pages of Barrymore's script, which is now in the Folger Library in Washington, D.C. It indicates the precision and detail ("Ham taps floor") with which stage combat is conceived and executed.

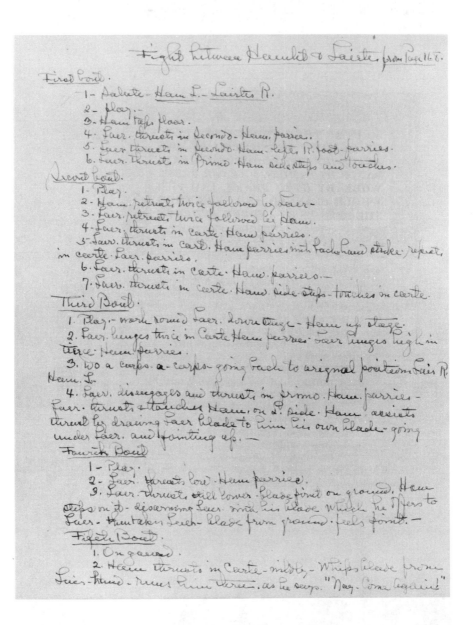

→ WILLIAM HAZLITT

Review of *A Midsummer Night's Dream* 1816

From The Examiner, *January 21, 1816*

William Hazlitt, essayist and cultural critic, describes the elaborate style of nineteenth-century Shakespeare production in his review of Frederic Reynolds's staging of *A Midsummer Night's Dream*. He also reveals the tension in Romantic thought about dramatic representation. On the one hand, the public relished such spectacular performances as that described here and (later in the century) those of Charles Kean and Henry Irving (see the illustration of Kean's production of *A Midsummer Night's Dream* on p. 396). On the other, many nineteenth-century writers, including Hazlitt and Charles Lamb, considered the physical stage inhospitable to Shakespeare's genius, believing that the ideal performance existed only in one's own imagination. As Hazlitt puts it, "the regions of fancy and the boards [i.e. the stage] of Covent Garden are not the same thing."

We hope we have not been accessory to murder, in recommending a delightful poem to be converted into a dull pantomime; for such is the fate of the *Midsummer Night's Dream*. We have found to our cost, once for all, that the regions of fancy and the boards of Covent Garden are not the same thing. All that is fine in the play, was lost in the representation. The spirit was evaporated, the genius was fled; but the spectacle was fine: it was that which saved the play. Oh, ye scene-shifters, ye scene-painters, ye machinists and dressmakers, ye manufacturers of moon and stars that give no light, ye musical composers, ye men in the orchestra, fiddlers and trumpeters and players on the double drum and loud bassoon, rejoice! This is your triumph; it is not ours: and ye full-grown, well-fed, substantial, real fairies, Messieurs Treby, and Truman, and Atkins, and Misses Matthews, Carew, Burrell, and MacAlpine, we shall remember you: we shall believe no more in the existence of your fantastic tribe. Flute the bellows-mender, Snug the joiner, Starveling the tailor, farewell! you have lost the charm of your names; but thou, Nic Bottom, thou valiant Bottom, what shall we say to thee? Thou didst console us much; thou didst perform a good part well; thou didst top the part of Bottom the weaver! He comes out of thy hands as clean and clever a fellow as ever. Thou art a person of exquisite whim and humour; and thou didst hector over thy companions well, and fall down flat before the Duke, like other Bullies, well; and thou didst sing the song of the Black Ousel well; but chief, thou didst noddle thy ass's head, which had been put upon thee, well; and didst seem to say, significantly, to thy new attendants, Peaseblossom, Cobweb, Moth, and Mustard-seed, "Gentlemen, I can present you equally to my friends, and to my enemies!"

All that was good in this piece (except the scenery) was Mr. Liston's Bottom, which was an admirable and judicious piece of acting. Mr. Conway was Theseus. Who would ever have taken this gentleman for the friend and companion of Hercules? Miss Stephens played the part of Hermia, and sang several songs very delightfully, which, however, by no means assisted the progress or interest of the story. Miss Foote played Helena. She is a very sweet girl, and not at all a bad actress; yet did anyone feel or even hear her address to Hermia? To show how far asunder the closet and the stage are, we give it here once more entire:

> Injurious Hermia! most ungrateful maid!
> Have you conspir'd, have you with these contriv'd
> To bait me with this foul derision?
> Is all the counsel that we two have shar'd,
> The sister-vows, the hours that we have spent,
> When we have chid the hasty-footed time
> For parting us, O! is it all forgot?
> All school-days' friendship, childhood innocence?
> We, Hermia, like two artificial gods,
> Created with our needles both one flower,
> Both on one sampler, sitting on one cushion,
> Both warbling of one song, both in one key,
> As if our hands, our sides, voices, and minds,
> Had been incorporate. So we grew together,
> Like to a double cherry, seeming parted,
> But yet an union in partition;
>
> . . . . . .
>
> And will you rent our ancient love asunder,
> To join with men in scorning your poor friend?
> It is not friendly, 'tis not maidenly:
> Our sex, as well as I, may chide you for it,
> Though I alone do feel the injury.

In turning to Shakespeare to look for this passage, the book opened at the *Midsummer Night's Dream*, the title of which half gave us back our old feeling; and in reading this one speech twice over, we have completely forgot all the noise we have heard and the sights we have seen. Poetry and the stage do not agree together. The attempt to reconcile them fails not only of effect, but of decorum. The *ideal* has no place upon the stage, which is a picture without perspective; everything there is in the foreground. That which is merely an airy shape, a dream, a passing thought, immediately becomes an unmanageable reality. Where all is left to the imagination, every circumstance has an equal chance of being kept in mind, and tells according to the mixed impression of all that has been suggested. But the imagination cannot sufficiently qualify the impressions of the senses. Any offence given to the eye is not to be got rid of by explanation. Thus Bottom's head in the play is a fantastic illusion, produced by magic spells: on the stage it is an ass's head, and nothing more; certainly a very strange costume for a gentleman to appear in. Fancy cannot be represented any more than a simile can be painted; and it is as idle to attempt it as to personate Wall or Moonshine. Fairies are not incredible, but fairies six feet high are so. Monsters are not shocking, if they are seen at a proper distance. When ghosts appear in midday, when apparitions stalk along Cheapside, then may the *Midsummer Night's Dream* be represented at Covent Garden or at Drury Lane; for we hear that it is to be brought out there also, and that we have to undergo another crucifixion.

Mrs. Faucit played the part of Titania very well, but for one circumstance — that she is a woman. The only glimpse which we caught of the possibility of acting the imaginary scenes properly, was from the little girl who dances before the fairies (we do not know her name), which seemed to show that the whole might be carried off in the same manner — by a miracle.

→ # Two Productions of *A Midsummer Night's Dream* ➤

Charles Kean, London   *1856*

Peter Brook, Stratford-upon-Avon   *1970*

The two productions of *A Midsummer Night's Dream* pictured here illuminate radically different ways of presenting Shakespeare. Charles Kean's version typified the pictorialism and inflated scale characteristic of the Victorian stage. In this portrayal of the final scene, scores of fairies and Athenians stand before a Greek temple representing Theseus's palace. Peter Brook's production was perhaps the most famous Shakespeare production of the twentieth century. Seventeen actors played the text before three white walls, with a minimum of properties and no change of set. Brook believed that the audience's imagination should supply the forest and the magic. (See Robert Speaight's review of the production on p. 398.) Although Brook consciously set out to annihilate nineteenth-century extravagance and literalism, it might be said that his production was, in its minimalist way, as flamboyant as Kean's.

Charles Kean, London, 1856

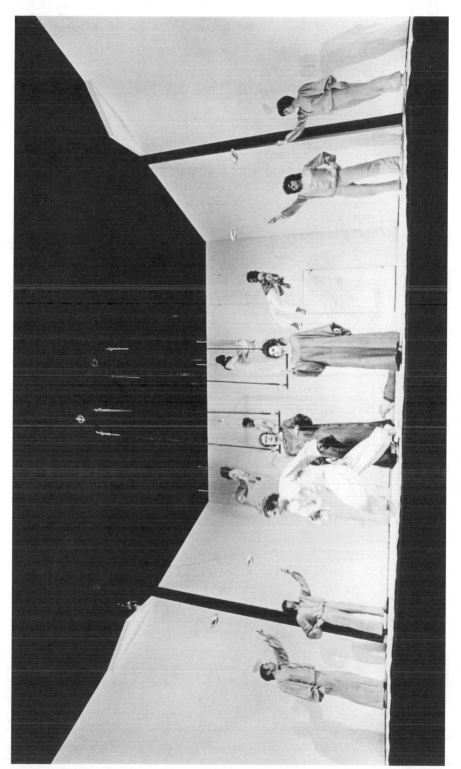

Peter Brook, Stratford-upon-Avon, 1970

→ ROBERT SPEAIGHT

Review of Peter Brook's *A Midsummer Night's Dream*   1970

From Shakespeare Quarterly

This review of Peter Brook's *Dream* by Robert Speaight reveals how shocking the production was to audiences at the time. Seeking to scrape away the encrustations of the nineteenth-century performance tradition, the director worked at length with his actors on emphasizing words over visual effects and allowing the text to speak directly to the spectator's imagination. The production ultimately ran for 535 performances in thirty-six cities and towns, from Stratford-upon-Avon to New York City and Tokyo.

It was eight years since Mr. Brook had directed a play at Stratford, and one assumed that he would not have directed the *Dream* unless he had something very particular to say about it. In fact, he forced one to forget — not, let me emphasize, the play itself — but anything one had seen done with it, or imagined being done with it, in the theatre. He swept the mind of the spectator as clear as he had swept his stage, allowing the text of the play, beautifully and deliberately spoken, to play upon you with the freshness of words seen for the first time upon the printed page. He persuaded you to forget a century of theatrical tradition, with its conventions and its clichés; and commanded you into a frame of mind where the very notion of magic, of supernatural agency, had to be created afresh. You could, if you chose, harbour a reminiscence of *Alice in Wonderland,* but of nothing else. The French have a phrase which communicates the peculiar, the explosively original, quality of this production. They speak of a *mystère en pleine lumière,* and this suggests the brilliant white light that Mr. Brook threw upon his staring white stage, with only Titania's bright red feather bed to relieve it.

One saw nothing remotely resembling a tree — only coils of wire played out from a fishing rod over the iron railings which encircled the décor from above. One saw nothing remotely resembling a fairy — but then we were not supposed to have been brought up on fairies. Puck, who was also Philostrate, might have reminded you a little of Pierrot; Theseus dreamt himself into Oberon, and Titania dreamt herself into Hippolyta. There was much play with steel ladders and spinning tops; and if you asked yourself how Mr. Brook was getting away with it all, you might have answered: "Marry, how, *trapsically*" — because Oberon and Puck descended from the skies on swings with an acrobatic agility. Indeed the virtuosities of the circus gave one a clue to Mr. Brook's translation of midsummer magic into surrealism. Yes, one might object, but how can a play spun out of cobwebs and gossamer, and drenched in the morning dew, stand up to a treatment so metallic and so apparently defiant of mystery? The answer is that the mystery was all the deeper because it was seen so clearly — as clearly, no doubt, as it was once seen on the bare platform of the Globe. Because the words had no visual counterpart, they seized the imagination the more surely. The play was recognized as timeless, because it was neither brought up, nor brought back, to date. Mr. Brook's audacious originality compelled respect, because he himself, in his recreation of a play about which everything had seemed to be said, had allowed it, in the last analysis, to stand gravely and lyrically, and also very amusingly, on its own feet. Utterly novel, it was still endearingly familiar. The laughs came in the right place, and when the poetry soared you caught your breath. This production was no brilliant exercise in cerebration; the pit of the stomach responded to it. Of course it would have been intolerable if the text had not been treated like the Ark of the Covenant, but here I can imagine Mr. Brook saying — "'Night's swift dragons cut the clouds asunder,' don't ask me to assist a line like *that* with stage lighting."

The humours of the play were safe — and indeed traditionally secure — with Mr. Waller as Bottom principally in charge of them. No one I have seen since Ralph Richardson has played the part as well — and that was nearly forty years ago. Mr. Locke's Quince was exquisitely muted to a kind of saintly (and no doubt celibate) simplicity, although why he should have doubled the part with Aegeus I could not quite understand. Miss Kestelman's Titania was as easy to look at as to listen to. But the production was ruled, as it should be, by its Oberon and its Puck. Mr. Kane salted his mischief with a Gallic wit, which I found a welcome relief from the conventional caperings, and spoke his verse as well as I have ever heard it spoken. Mr. Alan Howard combined a patrician charm with an effortless authority, and justified his doubling of the part with Theseus, for alone in this play Theseus and Oberon are rulers. Each untangles the knot which others have tied. Mr. Howard's luminously clear handling of the verse was never so labored that it disturbed the melodic line. At a time when black magic is the only magic that most people any longer believe in, there was much excuse for a production of the *Dream* where the magic was as white as the Arctic snows or the swan's down on the Avon; and there was never a moment's doubt after the opening performance that this one had taken its place in history.

→ Laurence Olivier as Henry V   *1944*

Arguably the greatest classical actor of the twentieth century — his chief competitor would probably be John Gielgud, who sometimes performed with him — Laurence Olivier filmed his *Henry V* in an effort to boost British morale near the end of World War II. In the scene pictured here, as King Henry prepares his troops for the battle of Agincourt, he rides before a backdrop designed to look like a medieval Book of Hours. Olivier also directed films of *Hamlet* (1948) — for which he won Academy Awards for Best Actor and Best Picture — and *Richard III* (1954), and he acted in other productions that were filmed, notably John Dexter's *Othello* (1964) and Jonathan Miller's *The Merchant of Venice* (1970).

From *He That Plays the King*   *1950*

In 1945 Laurence Olivier and Ralph Richardson led a company of actors in performances of *Henry IV, Part 1* and *Henry IV, Part 2* at the New Theatre in London. Richardson played Falstaff in both parts, while Olivier took the major role of young Hotspur in the first and, in the second, the supporting role of old Justice Shallow. Kenneth Tynan, whose passion for the theater and stylistic brilliance made him one of the great critics of the twentieth century, here captures the distinctive gifts of these two great performers. In the 1960s, when Olivier was named head of the new National Theatre, he hired Tynan as chief literary advisor for the company.

From a production so unobtrusive that at times it looked positively mousy, three very great pieces of acting emerged. The Old Vic was now at its height: the watershed had been reached, and one of those rare moments in the theatre had arrived when drama paused, took stock of all that it had learnt since Irving, and then produced a monument in celebration. It is surprising, when one considers it, that English acting should have reached up and seized a laurel crown in the middle of a war, and that the plays in which the prize was won should have been plays of battle, tumult, conspiracy and death, as the histories are. There was a bad atmosphere then amongst the acting clubs of London — an atmosphere such as one finds in the senior common-rooms of the women's colleges at Oxford: an air of pugnacious assurance and self-sufficiency mixed with acrid misogyny. There were roughly two groups of actors: the elder, who seemed to be suffering from thyroid deficiency, a condition which induces a blunt and passive sedentariness in the sufferer: and the very young ones, afflicted by the opposite sickness, thyroid excess, whose symptoms are emaciation and nervous constriction. The good, mature players were silent: the state of society had tied their hands, and they tied their own tongues. It was left to Richardson and Olivier to sum up English acting in themselves; and this was what, in *Henry IV,* they achieved.

Richardson's Falstaff was not a *comic* performance: it was too rich and many-sided to be crammed into a single word. The humour of it, as in Max Beerbohm's prose, was in the texture: there were no deliberate farcical effects. This was the down-at-heel dignity of W. C. Fields translated into a nobler language: here was a Falstaff whose principal attribute was not his fatness but his knighthood. He was Sir John first, and Falstaff second, and let every cock-a-hoop young dog beware. The spirit behind all the rotund nobility was spry and elastic: that, almost, of what Skelton in a fine phrase called "friskajolly younkerkins"; there was also, working with great slyness but great energy, a sharp business sense: and, when the situation called for it, great wisdom and melancholy ("Peace, good Doll! do not speak like a death's-head: do not bid me remember my end" was done with most moving authority). Each word emerged with immensely careful articulation, the lips forming it lovingly and then spitting it forth: in moments of passion, the wild white halo of hair stood angrily up and the eyes rolled majestically: and in rage one noticed a slow meditative relish taking command: "Marry, there is another indictment upon thee, for suffering flesh to be eaten in thy house, contrary to the law; for the which I think — thou — wilt — howl": the last four words with separate thrice-chewed pungency. Richardson never rollicked or slobbered or staggered: it was not a sweaty fat man, but a dry and dignified one. As the great belly moved, step following step with great finesse lest it overtopple, the arms flapped fussily at the sides as if to paddle the body's bulk along. It was deliciously and subtly funny, not riotously so: from his height of pomp Falstaff was chuckling at himself: it was not we alone, laughing at him. He had good manners and also that respect for human dignity which prevented him from openly showing his boredom at the inanities of Shallow and Silence: he had only recently sunk from the company of kings to the company of heirs-apparent. None of the usual epithets for Falstaff applied to Richardson: he was not often jovial, laughed seldom, belched never. In disgrace, he affected the mask of a sulky schoolboy, in the manner of Charles Laughton: in command, he would punch his wit at the luckless heads of his comrades, and their admiration would forbid response. The rejection scene at the end of Part 2 came off heartrendingly well: with his back to the audience Richardson thumped forward to welcome the new king, his whilom jackanapes: and after the key-cold rebuke which is his answer, the old man turned, his face red and working in furious *tics* to hide his tears. The immense pathos of his reassuring words to Shallow even now wets my eyes: "I shall be sent for soon at night." He hurried, whispered through the line very energetically, as if the whole matter were of no consequence: the emptiness of complete collapse stood awfully behind it. It was pride, not feasting and foining, that laid this Falstaff low: the youthful, hubristic heart inside the corporeal barrel had flown too high, and must be crushed. Cyril Connolly might have been speaking of this performance when he said: "Imprisoned in every fat man a thin one is wildly signalling to be let out" — let out, and slaughtered. Beside this Falstaff, Nicholas Breton's picture of a drunkard seems almost blasphemous: "a tub of swill, a spirit of sleep, a picture of a beast and a monster of a man."

Enough has already been written of Olivier's Hotspur, that ferocious darling of war. With the roughness and heedlessness of the warrior chieftain, he mixed the heavyhanded tenderness of the very virile husband: and knotted the performance into a unity by a trick, the stammer which prefaced every word beginning with the letter "w." This clever device fitted perfectly with the over-anxiousness, the bound-burstingness, the impotent eagerness of the character. The long speech of explanation to the king about the unransomed prisoners, beginning "My liege, I did deny no prisoners," is essentially an apology: for this Hotspur it was an aggressive explosion of outraged innocence:

> . . . for it made me *mad* [almost a shriek]
> To see him shine so brisk and smell so sweet
> And talk so like a waiting-gentlewoman
> Of guns and drums and w— w—

(Here the face almost burst for frenzy: the actor stamped the ground to loosen the word from his mouth. Finally, in a convulsion of contempt, it sprang out)

w-*wounds* — God save the mark!

This impediment dovetailed so well with Hotspur's death that one could not escape concluding that Olivier had begun his interpretation of the part at the end and worked backwards: the dying speech ends thus:

. . . no, Percy, thou art dust,
And food for —
HENRY: For worms, brave Percy.

I need not add that Olivier died in the throes of uttering that maddening, elusive consonant.

The most treasurable scenes in these two productions were those in Shallow's orchard: if I had only half an hour more to spend in theatres, and could choose at large, no hesitation but I would have these. Richardson's performance, coupled with that of Miles Malleson as Silence, beak-nosed, pop-eyed, many-chinned and mumbling, and Olivier as Shallow, threw across the stage a golden autumnal veil, and made the idle sporadic chatter of the lines glow with the same kind of delight as Gray's *Elegy*. There was a sharp scent of plucked crab-apples, and of pork in the larder: one got the sense of life-going-on-in-the-background, of rustling twigs underfoot and the large accusing eyes of cows, staring through the twilight. Shakespeare never surpassed these scenes in the vein of pure naturalism: the subtly criss crossed counterpoint of the opening dialogue between the two didderers, which skips between the price of livestock at market and the philosophic fact of death ("Death, saith the Psalmist, is certain; all must die"), is worked out with fugal delicacy: the talk ends with Shallow's unanswered rhetorical question: "And is old Double dead?" No reply is necessary: the stage is well and truly set, and any syllable more would be superfluous. The flavour of sharp masculine kindness Olivier is adept in: for me the best moment in his "Hamlet" film was the pat on the head for the players' performing dog which accompanied the line: "I am glad to see thee well." And it was in the very earth of this Gloucestershire orchard. Olivier was the Old Satyr in this Muses' Elizium; "Through his lean chops a chattering he doth make, which stirs his staring, beastly-drivell'd beard." This Shallow (pricked with yet another nose, a loony apotheosis of the hook-snout he wore as Richard) is a crapulous, paltering scarecrow of a man, withered up like the slough of a snake; but he has quick, commiserating eyes and the kind of delight in dispensing food and drink that one associates with a favourite aunt. He pecks at the lines, nibbles at them like a parrot biting on a nut; for all his age, he darts here and there nimbly enough, even skittishly; forgetting nothing, not even the pleasure of Falstaff's page, that "little tiny thief." The keynote of the performance is old-maidishness, agitated and pathetically anxious to make things go with a swing: a crone-like pantomime dame, you might have thought, were it not for the beady delectation that steals into his eyes at the mention of sex. (Shallow was, as Falstaff later points out, "as lecherous as a monkey.") His fatuous repetitions are those of importunate female decrepitude: he nags rather than bores. Sometimes, of course, he loses the use of one or more of his senses: protesting, over the table, that Falstaff must not leave, he insists, emphasizing the words by walking his fingers over the board: "I will not excuse you, sir; you shall not be excused; excuses shall not be admitted; there is no excuse shall serve; you shall not be excused" — and after his breathless panic of hospitality, he looks hopefully up: but Falstaff has long since gone. Shallow had merely forgotten to observe his departure: and the consequent confusion of the man, as he searches with his eyes for his vanished guest, is equaled only by his giggling embarrassment at finding him standing behind him.

Of all the wonderful work Olivier did in this and the previous Old Vic season, I liked nothing more than this. A part of this actor's uniqueness lies in the restricted demands he makes on his audience's rational and sensual capacities. Most actors invite the spectator either to pass a *moral* judgment on the characters they are representing; or to pass a *physical* judgment on their own appearance. A normal actor playing a moderately sympathetic part will go all out to convince the audience that he is a thoroughly good man, morally impeccable; playing a villain, he will force them to see the enormity of the man's sins. He will translate the character into the terms of a bad nineteenth-century novel. An attractive actor playing the part of a *jeune premier* [young leading man] will try primarily to arouse the admiration of the women and the envy of the men; a player of farce will rely chiefly on grotesque make-up to establish the character for him. But most actors do insist on a judgment of one kind or another: and they are better or worse actors according to the degree to which it is obvious that they are *insisting*. Olivier makes no such attempts to insist, and invites no moral response: simply the thing he is shall make him live. It is a rare discretion, an ascetic tact which none but he dares risk.

Titus *1999*

Directed by Julie Taymor

Julie Taymor's film of Shakespeare's first tragedy, *Titus Andronicus*, represents a trend that seems likely to continue in the twenty-first century. While respecting Shakespeare's language — and managing to include more of the text than most film directors do — she alters the setting to stimulate the audience's imagination with more-familiar cultural signals. Her *Titus* takes place in a kind of mythical Rome, one that is both primitive and sophisticated. In the scene pictured here, for example, Jessica Lange (as the villainous Tamora) wears a dress suggestive of an ancient breastplate, while Alan Cumming (as the emperor Saturninus) is dressed in a modern dinner jacket.

Bibliography

⊁

The Bibliography is divided into two parts, "Works Cited" and "Suggestions for Further Reading." The first part contains all primary and secondary works quoted or discussed in the text or excerpted at the end of each chapter. Titles of primary texts have been modernized. The second part is an extremely selective list of materials that will be of use to the student wishing to know more about Shakespeare's art and culture. It is subdivided into six broad categories: "Miscellaneous Resources"; "Contexts: Intellectual, Social, Ideological"; "Shakespearean Performance"; "Text and Language"; "Dramatic Forms and Influences"; and "Critical and Theoretical Works." With one or two exceptions, a book or article that appears in "Works Cited" is not recorded again under "Suggestions for Further Reading." Thus, both lists should be consulted.

Works Cited

Amussen, Susan D. "Gender, Family, and the Social Order, 1560–1725." Fletcher and Stevenson 196–217.

Aristotle. *Historia Animalium.* Trans. Richard Cresswell. London, 1883.

———. *The "Poetics."* See Halliwell.

Ascham, Roger. *The Schoolmaster.* London, 1570.

Barish, Jonas A. *The Antitheatrical Prejudice.* Berkeley: U of California P, 1981.

Barnfield, Richard. *The Tears of an Affectionate Shepherd Sick for Love, or The Complaint of Daphnis for the Love of Ganymede.* London, 1594.

Barroll, J. Leeds. *Politics, Plague, and Shakespeare's Theater: The Stuart Years.* Ithaca: Cornell UP, 1991.

Bate, Jonathan, and Russell Jackson. *Shakespeare: An Illustrated Stage History.* Oxford: Oxford UP, 1996.

Bentley, Gerald Eades. *Shakespeare: A Biographical Handbook.* New Haven: Yale UP, 1961.

Blayney, Peter W. M. *The First Folio of Shakespeare.* Hanover, Md.: Folger Library Publications, 1991.

The Book of Common Prayer 1559. Ed. John E. Booty. Charlottesville: U of Virginia P for the Folger Shakespeare Library, 1976.

Boose, Lynda E. *"The Taming of the Shrew,* Good Husbandry, Enclosure." *Shakespeare Reread: The Texts in New Contexts.* Ed. Russ McDonald. Ithaca: Cornell UP, 1994. 193–225.

Booth, Stephen. "The Function of Criticism at the Present Time and All Others." *Shakespeare Quarterly* 41 (1990): 262–68.

Bowers, Fredson. *Textual and Literary Criticism.* Cambridge: Cambridge UP, 1959.

Brooke, Arthur. *The Tragical History of Romeus and Juliet.* London, 1562.

Bullough, Geoffrey. *Narrative and Dramatic Sources of Shakespeare.* 8 vols. London: Methuen, 1957–75.

Cary, Elizabeth. *The Tragedy of Mariam, Fair Queen of Jewry.* London, 1613.

Castiglione, Baldassare. *The Book of the Courtier.* Trans. George Bull. Harmondsworth: Penguin, 1967.

Chambers, E. K. *William Shakespeare: A Study of Facts and Problems.* 2 vols. Oxford: Oxford UP, 1930.

Cinthio, Giovanni Battista Giraldi. *Gli Hecatommithi.* 1565. Bullough 7:239–52.

Clinton, Elizabeth. *The Countess of Lincoln's Nursery.* London, 1628.

Coke, Sir Edward. *The Third Part of the Institutes of the Laws of England.* 3rd ed. London, 1644.

Coleman, D. C. *The Economy of England 1450–1750.* Cambridge: Cambridge UP, 1977.

Cook, Ann Jennalie. *Making a Match: Courtship in Shakespeare and His Society.* Princeton: Princeton UP, 1991.

Crewe, Jonathan. *Trials of Authorship: Anterior Forms and Poetic Reconstruction from Wyatt to Shakespeare.* Berkeley: U of California P, 1990.

Crosse, Henry. *Vertues Commonwealth: or The High-way to Honour.* London, 1603.

Culler, Jonathan, ed. *On Puns: The Foundation of Letters.* Oxford: Blackwell, 1988.

Daniel, Samuel. *Musophilus.* London, 1599.

Dasent, John R., et al., eds. *Acts of the Privy Council of England, 1452–1628.* 32 vols. London, 1890–1907.

Davies, Godfrey. *The Early Stuarts, 1603–1660.* 2nd ed. Oxford: Oxford UP, 1959.

Dolan, Frances E. *Dangerous Familiars: Representations of Domestic Crime in England, 1550–1700.* Ithaca: Cornell UP, 1994.

Dollimore, Jonathan. "Transgression and Surveillance in *Measure for Measure.*" Dollimore and Sinfield 72–87.

Dollimore, Jonathan, and Alan Sinfield. *Political Shakespeare.* Ithaca: Cornell UP, 1985.

Elias, Norbert. *The Civilizing Process: The Development of Manners.* Trans. Edmund Jephcott. New York: Urizen, 1978.

Elizabeth I, queen of England. "Edict Arranging for the Expulsion from England of Negroes and Blackamoors." Dasent et al. 26:22.

———. "Proclamation Placing London Vagabonds under Martial Law." Hughes and Larkin 3:196–97.

———. "Open Warrant to the Lord Mayor of London." Dasent et al. 26:20.

———. "The Tilbury Speech." August 1588. *Elizabeth I: Collected Works.* Ed. Leah S. Marcus, Janel Mueller, and Mary Beth Rose. Chicago: U of Chicago P, 2000.

Elyot, Sir Thomas. *The Book Named the Governor.* 2nd ed. London, 1553.

Erasmus, Desiderius. Foreword to the Third Edition of the Latin New Testament. 1522. Trans. Robert P. Adams. *The Praise of Folly and Other Writings.* New York: Norton, 1989.

Evans, G. Blakemore, ed. *The Riverside Shakespeare.* Boston: Houghton, 1974.

Farmer, Richard. *An Essay on the Learning of Shakespeare.* Cambridge, 1767.

Felperin, Howard. *Shakespearean Romance.* Princeton: Princeton UP, 1972.

Field, John, and Thomas Wilcox (?). *An Admonition to the Parliament.* London, 1572.

Fielding, Henry. *Tom Jones.* Ed. George Sherburn. New York: Random, 1950.

Filmer, Sir Robert. *Patriarcha, or The Natural Power of Kings.* London, 1680. See also Sommerville 6–7.

Firth, C. H. "Ballads and Broadsides." Lee and Onions 2:511–38.

Fitzherbert, Sir Anthony. *The Book of Husbandry.* London, 1523.

Fletcher, Anthony, and John Stevenson. *Order and Disorder in Early Modern England.* Cambridge: Cambridge UP, 1985.

Fletcher, John. "To the Reader." *The Faithful Shepherdess.* London, c. 1609.

Forman, Simon. From His *Diary.* In *Simon Forman: Sex and Society in Shakespeare's Age.* Ed. A. L. Rowse. London: Weidenfeld and Nicolson, 1974.

Fortescue, Sir John. *Works.* Trans. Chichester Fortescue. Ed. Lord Clermont. London, 1869. 1:322. See Tillyard 26–27.

Foxe, John. *Acts and Monuments of These Latter and Perilous Days.* London, 1563.

Frere, W. H., and C. E. Douglas. *Puritan Manifestoes: A Study of the Origin of the Puritan Revolt.* 1907. Rpt. London: Church Historical Society, 1954.

Frisbee, George. *Edward de Vere, A Great Elizabethan.* London: Cecil Palmer, 1931.

Frye, Northrop. *Anatomy of Criticism.* Princeton: Princeton UP, 1957.

The Geneva Bible. A facsimile of the 1560 edition with an introduction by Lloyd E. Berry. Madison: U of Wisconsin P, 1969.

Gosson, Stephen. *Plays Confuted in Five Actions.* London, 1582.

Gouge, William. *Of Domestical Duties: Eight Treatises.* 2nd ed. London, 1626.

Greenblatt, Stephen. *Shakespearean Negotiations.* Oxford: Oxford UP, 1988.

Gurr, Andrew. *Playgoing in Shakespeare's London.* Cambridge: Cambridge UP, 1987.

———. *The Shakespearean Stage.* 3rd ed. Cambridge: Cambridge UP, 1992.

Guy, John. *Tudor England.* Oxford: Oxford UP, 1988.

Hall, Edward. *The Union of the Two Noble and Illustre Families of Lancaster and York.* 2nd ed. London, 1548.

Halliday, F. E. *A Shakespeare Companion.* Rev. ed. Harmondsworth: Penguin, 1964.

Halliwell, Stephen, ed. *The "Poetics" of Aristotle: Translation and Commentary.* Chapel Hill: U of North Carolina P, 1987.

Harbage, Alfred, ed. *The Complete Pelican Shakespeare.* Harmondsworth: Penguin, 1969.

Harington, Sir John. "To Secretary Barlow." July 1606. Letter 44 of *The Letters and Epigrams of Sir John Harington.* Ed. Norman Egbert McClure. Philadelphia: U of Pennsylvania P, 1930.

Harrison, G. B. *Introducing Shakespeare.* Rev. ed. Harmondsworth: Penguin, 1964.

Harrison, William. *The Description of England.* 2nd ed. London, 1587.

Hazlitt, William. Rev. of *A Midsummer Night's Dream,* prod. Frederic Reynolds. *The Examiner* 21 Jan. 1816. Rpt. in *Hazlitt on Theatre.* Ed. William Archer and Robert Lowe. London, 1895.

Henslowe, Philip. *Henslowe's Diary*. Ed. R. A. Foakes and R. T. Rickert. Cambridge: Cambridge UP, 1961.

Herbert, Mary Sidney, trans. *The Tragedy of Antonie*. By Robert Garnier. London, 1592.

Heywood, Thomas. *An Apology for Actors*. London, 1612.

Hinman, Charlton. *The Printing and Proofreading of the First Folio of Shakespeare*. Oxford: Oxford UP, 1966.

Hirst, Derek. *Authority and Conflict, 1603–1658*. Cambridge, Mass.: Harvard UP, 1985.

Holinshed, Raphael. *The Chronicles of England, Scotland, and Ireland*. 2nd ed. London, 1587.

An Homily against Disobedience and Willful Rebellion. London, 1570.

An Homily of the State of Matrimony. In *The Second Tome of Homilies*. London, 1563.

Hooker, Richard. *Of the Laws of Ecclesiastical Polity*. London, 1593.

Hoskyns, John. *Directions for Speech and Style*. Ed. Hoyt H. Hudson. Princeton: Princeton UP, 1935.

Hughes, Paul L., and James F. Larkin. *Tudor Royal Proclamations*. 3 vols. New Haven: Yale UP, 1964–69.

Ingram, William. *The Business of Playing: The Beginnings of the Adult Professional Theater in Elizabethan London*. Ithaca: Cornell UP, 1992.

James I, king of England. *Basilikon Doron*. McIlwain 3–52.

———. "To George Villiers, Duke of Buckingham." December 1623(?). Letter 218 in *Letters of King James VI & I*. Ed. G. P. V. Akrigg. Berkeley: U of California P, 1984.

———. "A Speech to the Lords and Commons of the Parliament at Whitehall." March 21, 1610. McIlwain 306–25.

Johnson, Samuel. *The Works of Samuel Johnson*. Ed. Arthur Sherbo. New Haven: Yale UP, 1968. 7:74.

Jonson, Ben. "On His First Son." In *Works*. London, 1616.

Kenyon, J. P. *Stuart England*. Harmondsworth: Penguin, 1978.

———. *The Stuarts*. Rpt. London: Fontana, 1966.

Klein, Joan Larsen. *Daughters, Wives, and Widows: Writings by Men about Women and Marriage in England, 1500–1640*. Urbana: U of Illinois P, 1992.

Lanham, Richard. *A Handlist of Rhetorical Terms*. Berkeley: U of California P, 1968.

Lanyer, Aemilia. *Salve Deus Rex Judaeorum*. London, 1611.

Laslett, Peter. *The World We Have Lost: England before the Industrial Age*. 3rd ed. New York: Scribner's, 1984.

Leary, Penn. *The Cryptographic Shakespeare: A Monograph Wherein the Poems and Plays Attributed to William Shakespeare are Proven to Contain the Enciphered Name of the Concealed Author, Francis Bacon*. Omaha, Neb.: Westchester, 1987.

Lee, Sidney, and C. T. Onions. *Shakespeare's England: An Account of the Life and Manners of His Age*. 2 vols. Oxford: Clarendon, 1916.

Lennox, Charlotte. *Shakespeare Illustrated: or the Novels and Histories on which the Plays Are Founded*. London, 1753–54.

"A Letter to Rome . . ." [Ballad]. London, 1571(?).

Lever, Ralph. *The Art of Reason, Rightly Termed Witcraft*. London, 1573.

Levin, Carole. *"The Heart and Stomach of a King": Elizabeth I and the Politics of Sex and Power*. Philadelphia: U of Pennsylvania P, 1994.

Lewalski, Barbara. *Writing Women in Jacobean England*. Cambridge, Mass.: Harvard UP, 1993.

Lewis, C. S. *English Literature in the Sixteenth Century*. Oxford: Clarendon, 1954.

Lockyer, Roger. *Tudor and Stuart Britain, 1471–1714*. New York: St. Martin's, 1964.

Machiavelli, Niccolò. *The Prince.* 1513. Trans. Daniel Donno. New York: Bantam, 1966.

Mahood, M. M. *Shakespeare's Wordplay.* London: Routledge, 1957.

Markham, Gervase. *The English Husbandman.* London, 1613. Sigs. A4v–B1v.

Marlowe, Christopher. *Tamburlaine the Great.* London, 1590.

McCarthy, Cormac. *The Crossing.* New York: Knopf, 1994.

McIlwain, Charles Howard, ed. *The Political Works of James I.* Cambridge, Mass.: Harvard UP, 1918.

Meres, Francis. *Palladis Tamia: Wit's Treasury.* London, 1598. Chambers 2:193–95.

Middleton, Thomas. *Your Five Gallants.* London, 1608(?).

A Mirror for Magistrates. "Caius Julius Caesar." 1587 edition. Bullough 5:168–73.

Montaigne, Michel de. *The Complete Works of Montaigne: Essays, Travel Journals, Letters.* Trans. Donald M. Frame. Stanford: Stanford UP, 1958.

———. "Of the Vanity of Words." Trans. John Florio. London, 1603.

Montrose, Louis Adrian. "The Elizabethan Subject and the Spenserian Text." *Literary Theory/Renaissance Texts.* Ed. Patricia Parker and David Quint. Baltimore: Johns Hopkins UP, 1986.

———. "'Shaping Fantasies': Figurations of Gender and Power in Elizabethan Culture." *Representations* 2 (1983): 61–94.

Moore, John. *A Target for Tillage.* London, 1613.

Moryson, Fynes. *An Itinerary.* London, 1617.

Moxon, Joseph. *Mechanic Exercises.* London, 1683.

Mulcaster, Richard. *Positions . . . for the Training Up of Children.* London, 1581.

Mullaney, Steven. *The Place of the Stage: License, Play, and Power in Renaissance England.* Chicago: U of Chicago P, 1988.

Muriel, Christopher. *An Answer unto the Catholics' Supplication . . . Whereunto Is Annexed the Supplication of the Papists.* London, 1603.

Murrell, John. *A Delightful Daily Exercise for Ladies and Gentlewomen . . . Whereunto Is Added a Book of Cookery.* London, 1621.

Nashe, Thomas. *Christ's Tears over Jerusalem.* Rev. ed. London, 1613.

Neale, John. *Elizabeth I.* Rpt. Harmondsworth: Penguin, 1990.

Ovid [Publius Ovidius Naso]. *The xv Books of P. Ovidius Naso, entitled Metamorphosis.* Trans. Arthur Golding. London, 1567.

———. *Metamorphoses.* Trans. Rolfe Humphries. Bloomington: Indiana UP, 1955.

Paster, Gail Kern. *The Body Embarrassed: Drama and the Disciplines of Shame in Early Modern England.* Ithaca: Cornell UP, 1993.

A Plague Bill. London, 1609.

Platter, Thomas. *Travels in England.* Trans. Clare Williams. London: Jonathan Cape, 1937.

Plutarch. *The Lives of the Noble Grecians and Romans.* Trans. Thomas North. London, 1579.

Potter, Lois. "Reconstructing Shakespeare." *Times Literary Supplement* 7 Apr. 1995: 21.

Preston, Thomas. *A Lamentable Tragedy, Mixed Full of Pleasant Mirth, Containing the Life of Cambyses, King of Persia.* London, 1569(?).

Prothero, R. E. "Agriculture and Gardening." Lee and Onions 1:346–80.

Prynne, William. *Histriomastix: The Players' Scourge.* London, 1633.

Puttenham, George. *The Art of English Poesy.* London, 1589.

Rabkin, Norman. "Rabbits, Ducks, and *Henry V.*" *Shakespeare Quarterly* 28 (1977): 279–96. Rpt. in *Shakespeare and the Problem of Meaning.* Chicago: U of Chicago P, 1981.

Reynolds, Richard. *A Book Called the Foundation of Rhetoric.* London, 1563.

Rhetorica Ad Herennium. Qtd. in Lanham.

Righter [Barton], Anne. *Shakespeare and the Idea of the Play.* Harmondsworth: Penguin, 1961. Rpt. Westport: Greenwood, 1977.

Rive, Edmund. *Twelve Rules Introducting to the Art of Latin.* London, 1620.

Rymer, Thomas. *A Short View of Tragedy.* London, 1693.

Schleuter, June. "Rereading the Peacham Drawing." *Shakespeare Quarterly* 50 (1999): 171–84.

Schoenbaum, Samuel. *Shakespeare: His Life, His Language, His Theater.* New York: Signet, 1990.

———. *William Shakespeare: A Compact Documentary Life.* Oxford: Oxford UP, 1977.

Schoenfeldt, Michael. *Bodies and Selves in Early Modern England: Physiology and Inwardness in Spenser, Shakespeare, Herbert, and Milton.* Cambridge: Cambridge UP, 1999.

Shakespeare, William. *Mr. William Shakespeare's Comedies, Histories, & Tragedies.* F1. London, 1623.

———. *The Most Lamentable Roman Tragedy of Titus Andronicus.* Q1. London, 1594.

———. *The Riverside Shakespeare.* Ed. G. Blakemore Evans. Boston: Houghton Mifflin, 1974.

———. *The Tragedy of King Richard the Third.* Q1. London, 1597.

———. *The Tragical History of Hamlet, Prince of Denmark.* Q1. London, 1603.

———. *Mr. William Shakespeare, His True Chronicle History of the Life and Death of King Lear and His Three Daughters.* Q1. London, 1608.

Sidney, Sir Philip. *Astrophil and Stella.* London, 1598.

———. *The Defense of Poesy.* London, 1595.

Sinfield, Alan. *Faultlines: Cultural Materialism and the Politics of Dissident Reading.* Berkeley: U of California P, 1992.

Skura, Meredith. *Shakespeare the Actor and the Purposes of Playing.* Chicago: U of Chicago P, 1993.

Smith, Bruce. *Homosexual Desire in Shakespeare's England.* Chicago: U of Chicago P, 1991.

Smith, Sir Thomas. *De Republica Anglorum: The Manner of Government of England.* London, 1583.

Sommerville, Johann B., ed. *Patriarcha and Other Writings.* Cambridge: Cambridge UP, 1991.

Southwell, Lady Anne. "Letter on Poetry." 1621. *The Southwell-Sibthorpe Commonplace Book.* Folger Ms. V.b.198. Ed. Jean Klene. Tempe, Ariz.: Medieval & Renaissance Texts & Studies, 1997.

Speaight, Robert. "Shakespeare in Britain." Rev. of *A Midsummer Night's Dream,* dir. Peter Brook. *Shakespeare Quarterly* 21 (1970): 439–49.

———. *Shakespeare on the Stage: An Illustrated History of Shakespearian Performance.* Boston: Little, 1973.

Stone, Lawrence. *The Causes of the English Revolution, 1529–1642.* New York: Harper, 1972.

———. *The Family, Sex and Marriage in England, 1500–1800.* New York: Harper, 1977.

Stow, John. *A Survey of London.* London, 1598.

Strachey, Sir William. *A True Reportory of the Wreck and Redemption of Sir Thomas Gates.* Bullough 8:275–94.

Stubbes, Philip. *The Anatomy of Abuses.* London, 1583.

Swetnam, Joseph. *Arraignment of Lewd, Idle, Froward, and Unconstant Women.* London, 1615.

Tate, Nahum. *The History of King Lear.* London, 1681.

Taylor, Gary. Introduction. *Henry V.* By William Shakespeare. Oxford: Oxford UP, 1982.

Taylor, Gary, and Michael Warren, eds. *The Division of the Kingdoms: Shakespeare's Two Versions of "King Lear."* Oxford: Clarendon, 1983.

Tillyard, E. M. W. *The Elizabethan World Picture.* New York: Random House, n.d.

Tilney, Edmund. *The Flower of Friendship.* Ed. Valerie Wayne. Ithaca: Cornell UP, 1992.

"The True Form and Shape of a Monstrous Child." [Ballad]. London, 1565.

Tynan, Kenneth. *He That Plays the King.* London: Longman's, Green, 1950.

Underdown, David. "The Taming of the Scold: The Enforcement of Patriarchal Authority in Early Modern England." Fletcher and Stevenson 116–36.

Urkowitz, Steven. *Shakespeare's Revision of "King Lear."* Princeton: Princeton UP, 1980.

Vaughan, William. *Natural and Artificial Directions for Health.* London, 1602.

Ward, John. From his *Diary.* Chambers 2:249–50.

Wedel, Lupold von. *Journey through England and Scotland Made by Lupold von Wedel in the Years 1584 and 1585.* Ed. Gottfried von Bulow. *Transactions of the Royal Historical Society* ns 9 (1895): 228–30, 267.

Wells, Stanley, and Gary Taylor, with John Jowett and William Montgomery. *William Shakespeare: A Textual Companion.* Oxford: Clarendon, 1987.

Werstine, Paul. "Narratives about Printed Shakespeare Texts: 'Foul Papers' and 'Bad Quartos.'" *Shakespeare Quarterly* 41 (1990): 65–86.

Whetstone, George. *An Heptameron of Civil Discourses.* London, 1582.

Whitney, Isabella. "The Manner of Her Will, and What She Left to London." London, 1573.

Wilde, Oscar. *The Importance of Being Earnest.* In *Plays.* Harmondsworth: Penguin, 1954.

Wilson, Thomas. *The Art of Rhetoric.* London, 1553.

Wotton, David, ed. *Democracy and Divine Right.* Harmondsworth: Penguin, 1986.

Wright, George T. *Shakespeare's Metrical Art.* Berkeley: U of California P, 1988.

Wroth, Lady Mary. *Pamphilia to Amphilanthus.* London, 1621.

Zimmerman, Susan, ed. *Erotic Politics: Desire on the Renaissance Stage.* London: Routledge, 1992.

Suggestions for Further Reading

MISCELLANEOUS RESOURCES

Allen, M. J. B., and Kenneth Muir, eds. *Shakespeare's Plays in Quarto: A Facsimile Edition.* Berkeley: U of California P, 1981.

Andrews, John F. *William Shakespeare: His World, His Work, His Influence.* 3 vols. New York: Scribner's, 1985.

Bentley, Gerald Eades. *The Jacobean and Caroline Stage.* 7 vols. Oxford: Oxford UP, 1966.

Berger, Thomas L., William C. Bradford, and Sidney L. Sondergard. *An Index of Characters in Early Modern English Drama: Printed Plays, 1500–1660.* Cambridge: Cambridge UP, 1998.

Bergeron, David, and Geraldo U. de Sousa. *Shakespeare: A Study and Research Guide.* 3rd ed. Lawrence: U of Kansas P, 1995.

Bevington, David. *The Goldentree Bibliography of Shakespeare.* Arlington Heights, Ill.: AHM, 1978.

Bulman, James C., J. R. Mulryne, and Margaret Shewring. *Shakespeare in Performance Series.* Manchester: Manchester UP, 1982–.

Callaghan, Dympna. *A Feminist Companion to Shakespeare.* Oxford: Blackwell, 2000.

Cerasano, S. P., and Marion Wynne-Davies. *Readings in Renaissance Women's Drama: Criticism, History, and Performance, 1594–1998.* London: Routledge, 1998.

Chambers, E. K. *The Elizabethan Stage.* 4 vols. Oxford: Oxford UP, 1923.

Engle, Ron, Felicia Hardison Londré, and Daniel J. Watermeier. *Shakespeare Companies and Festivals: An International Guide.* Westport, Conn.: Greenwood, 1995.

Harbage, Alfred, Samuel Schoenbaum, and Sylvia S. Wagonheim. *Annals of English Drama, 975–1700.* Rev. ed. London: Routledge, 1989.

Hinman, Charlton. *The Norton Facsimile: The First Folio of Shakespeare.* New York: Norton, 1968.

Honan, Park. *Shakespeare: A Life.* Oxford: Oxford UP, 1998.

Hunter, G. K. *English Drama 1586–1642: The Age of Shakespeare.* Oxford: Oxford UP, 1997.

McManaway, James G., and Jeanne Addison Roberts. *A Selective Bibliography of Shakespeare: Editions, Textual Studies, Commentary.* Charlottesville: U of Virginia P for the Folger Shakespeare Library, 1975.

O'Brien, Peggy, ed. *Shakespeare Set Free.* 3 vols. New York: Washington Square, 1993–95.

Schoenbaum, Samuel. *William Shakespeare: A Documentary Life.* Oxford: Oxford UP, 1975.

Spevack, Marvin. *A Complete and Systematic Concordance to the Works of Shakespeare.* 9 vols. Hildesheim, Ger.: Georg Olms, 1969–80.

———. *The Harvard Concordance to Shakespeare.* Cambridge, Mass.: Harvard UP, 1973.

Vickers, Brian. *English Renaissance Literary Criticism.* Oxford: Clarendon, 1999.

Wells, Stanley. *The Cambridge Companion to Shakespeare Studies.* Rev. ed. Cambridge: Cambridge UP, 1986.

———. *Shakespeare: A Bibliographical Guide.* Oxford: Oxford UP, 1990.

Williams, Gordon. *A Glossary of Shakespeare's Sexual Language.* London: Athlone, 1997.

Collected Editions

Alexander, Peter, ed. *William Shakespeare: The Complete Works.* London: Collins, 1951.

Barnet, Sylvan, ed. *The Complete Signet Classic Shakespeare.* New York: Harcourt, 1972. Also issued in single-play paperback editions.

Bevington, David, ed. *The Complete Works of Shakespeare.* New York: HarperCollins, 1992.

Evans, G. Blakemore, ed. *The Riverside Shakespeare.* Boston: Houghton, 1974.

Greenblatt, Stephen J., gen. ed. *The Norton Shakespeare.* New York: Norton, 1997.

Kittredge, George Lyman, ed. *The Complete Works of Shakespeare.* Boston: Ginn, 1936. Rev. ed. by Irving Ribner, 1971.

Wells, Stanley, and Gary Taylor, with John Jowett and William Montgomery, eds. *William Shakespeare: The Complete Works.* Oxford: Oxford UP, 1986.

Single-Play Editions

Bevington, David, ed. *The Bantam Shakespeare.* New York: Bantam, 1980.

Braunmuller, Albert, and Brian Gibbons, gen. eds. *The New Cambridge Shakespeare.* Cambridge: Cambridge UP, 1984–. Replaces *The New Cambridge Shakespeare.* Gen. ed. John Dover Wilson and Arthur Quiller-Couch.

Carroll, William C., ed. *Macbeth: Texts and Contexts.* Boston: Bedford, 1999.

Dolan, Frances E., ed. *The Taming of the Shrew: Texts and Contexts.* Boston: Bedford, 1996.

Hodgdon, Barbara, ed. *The First Part of King Henry the Fourth: Texts and Contexts.* Boston, Bedford, 1997.

Kastan, David Scott, Richard Proudfoot, and Ann Thompson, gen. eds. *The Arden Shakespeare.* 3rd ed. London: Routledge, 1994–. Replaces *The New Arden Shakespeare.* Gen. ed. Harold F. Brooks and Harold Jenkins.

Mowat, Barbara, and Paul Werstine, gen. eds. *The New Folger Library Shakespeare.* New York: Washington Square, 1990–. Replaces *The Folger Shakespeare.* Ed. Louis B. Wright and Virginia LaMar.

Orgel, Stephen, and A. R. Braunmuller, gen. eds. *The Pelican Shakespeare.* New York: Penguin, 1999–. Replaces *The Pelican Shakespeare.* Ed. Alfred Harbage et al. 1969.

Paster, Gail Kern, and Skiles Howard, eds. *A Midsummer Night's Dream: Texts and Contexts.* Boston: Bedford, 1999.

Smith, Bruce, ed. *Twelfth Night, or What You Will: Texts and Contexts.* Boston, Bedford, 2001.

Spencer, T. J. B., gen. ed. *The New Penguin Shakespeare.* Harmondsworth: Penguin, 1967–.

Wells, Stanley, and Gary Taylor, gen. eds. *The New Oxford Shakespeare.* Oxford: Oxford UP, 1982–.

Other

Booth, Stephen, ed. *Shakespeare's Sonnets, edited with analytic commentary.* New Haven: Yale UP, 1977.

Journals

Shakespeare Jahrbuch (Germany). 1946–.
Shakespeare Newsletter. 1951–.
Shakespeare Quarterly. 1950–.
Shakespeare Studies. 1965–.
Shakespeare Survey (England). 1948–.

CONTEXTS: INTELLECTUAL, SOCIAL, IDEOLOGICAL

Baker, Herschel. *The Wars of Truth.* Cambridge, Mass.: Harvard UP, 1952.

Bakhtin, Mikhail. *Rabelais and His World.* Trans. Helene Iswolsky. Bloomington: Indiana UP, 1984.

Beilin, Elaine V. *Redeeming Eve: Women Writers of the English Renaissance.* Princeton: Princeton UP, 1987.

Belsey, Catherine. *Shakespeare and the Loss of Eden: The Construction of Family Values in Early Modern Culture.* New Brunswick: Rutgers UP, 1999.

Black, J. B. *The Reign of Elizabeth, 1558–1603.* 2nd ed. Oxford: Oxford UP, 1959.

Bristol, Michael. *Carnival and Theater: Plebeian Culture and the Structure of Authority in Renaissance England.* London: Routledge, 1985.

Bruster, Douglas. *Drama and the Market in the Age of Shakespeare.* Cambridge: Cambridge UP, 1992.

Byrne, Muriel St. Clare. *Elizabethan Life in Town and Country.* 8th ed. Boston: Houghton, 1961.

Carroll, William C. *Fat King, Lean Beggar: Representations of Poverty in the Age of Shakespeare.* Ithaca: Cornell UP, 1996.

Craig, Hardin. *The Enchanted Glass: The Elizabethan Mind in Literature*. New York: Oxford UP, 1936.

Cressy, David. *Literacy and the Social Order: Reading and Writing in Tudor and Stuart England*. Cambridge: Cambridge UP, 1980.

Ferguson, Margaret, Maureen Quilligan, and Nancy J. Vickers, eds. *Rewriting the Renaissance: The Discourses of Sexual Difference in Early Modern Europe*. Chicago: U of Chicago P, 1986.

Frye, Roland M. *Shakespeare and Christian Doctrine*. Princeton: Princeton UP, 1963.

Garber, Marjorie, ed. *Cannibals, Witches, Divorce: Estranging the Renaissance*. Baltimore: Johns Hopkins UP, 1987.

Gillies, John. *Shakespeare and the Geography of Difference*. Cambridge: Cambridge UP, 1994.

Greenblatt, Stephen. *Learning to Curse: Essays in Early Modern Culture*. London: Routledge, 1990.

———. *Renaissance Self-Fashioning: More to Shakespeare*. Chicago: U of Chicago P, 1980.

Hall, Kim F. *Things of Darkness: Economics of Race and Gender in Early Modern England*. Ithaca: Cornell UP, 1996.

Haydn, Hiram. *The Counter-Renaissance*. New York: Scribner's, 1950.

Hendricks, Margo, and Patricia Parker. *Women, "Race," and Writing in the Early Modern Period*. London: Routledge, 1994.

Howell, Wilbur. *Logic and Rhetoric in England, 1500–1700*. Princeton: Princeton UP, 1956.

Jankowski, Theodora. *Pure Resistance: Queer Virginity in Early Modern English Drama*. Philadelphia: U of Pennsylvania P, 2000.

———. *Women in Power in the Early Modern Drama*. Urbana: U of Illinois P, 1992.

Jardine, Lisa. *Still Harping on Daughters. Women and Drama in the Age of Shakespeare*. 1983. 2nd ed. New York: Columbia UP, 1989.

Jordan, Constance. *Renaissance Feminism: Literary Texts and Political Models*. Ithaca: Cornell UP, 1990.

Kahn, Coppélia. *Roman Shakespeare: Warriors, Wounds, and Women*. London: Routledge, 1997.

Kantorowicz, Ernst. *The King's Two Bodies*. Princeton: Princeton UP, 1957.

Kinney, Arthur. *Humanist Poetics*. Amherst: U of Massachusetts P, 1986.

Kristeller, Paul Oscar. *Renaissance Thought and Its Sources*. Ed. Michael Mooney. New York: Columbia UP, 1979.

Laqueur, Thomas. *Making Sex: Body and Gender from the Greeks to Freud*. Cambridge, Mass.: Harvard UP, 1990.

Levin, Harry. *The Myth of the Golden Age in the Renaissance*. Bloomington: Indiana UP, 1969.

Levy, F. J. *Tudor Historical Thought*. San Marino: Huntington Library, 1967.

Lovejoy, Arthur O. *The Great Chain of Being: A Study of the History of an Idea*. Cambridge, Mass.: Harvard UP, 1936.

Marcus, Leah S. *The Politics of Mirth: Johnson, Herrick, Milton, Marvell, and the Defense of Old Holiday Pastimes*. Chicago: U of Chicago P, 1986.

Montrose, Louis Adrian. *The Purpose of Playing: Shakespeare and the Cultural Politics of the Elizabethan Theatre*. Chicago: U of Chicago P, 1996.

Orgel, Stephen. *Impersonations: The Performance of Gender in Shakespeare's England*. Cambridge: Cambridge UP, 1996.

Peck, Linda Levy, ed. *The Mental World of the Jacobean Court*. Cambridge: Cambridge UP, 1991.

Popkin, Richard H. *The History of Skepticism from Erasmus to Spinoza*. Berkeley: U of California P, 1979.

Quinones, Ricardo J. *The Renaissance Discovery of Time*. Cambridge, Mass.: Harvard UP, 1972.

Shuger, Debora Kuller. *Habits of Thought in the English Renaissance: Religion, Politics, and the Dominant Culture*. Berkeley: U of California P, 1990.

Siraisi, Nancy G. *Medieval and Early Renaissance Medicine: An Introduction to Knowledge and Practice*. Chicago: U of Chicago P, 1990.

Stone, Lawrence. *The Crisis of the Aristocracy, 1558–1641*. Oxford: Oxford UP, 1965.

Tawney, R. H. *Religion and the Rise of Capitalism*. Rpt. Gloucester, Mass.: Peter Smith, 1962.

Thomas, Keith. *Religion and the Decline of Magic*. Rpt. Harmondsworth: Penguin, 1973.

Underdown, David. *Revel, Riot, and Rebellion: Popular Politics and Culture in England, 1603–1660*. Oxford: Oxford UP, 1985.

Watson, Robert N. *The Rest Is Silence: Death as Annihilation in the English Renaissance*. Berkeley: U of California P, 1994.

Woodbridge, Linda. *Women and the English Renaissance*. Urbana: U of Illinois P, 1984.

Wright, Louis B. *Middle-Class Culture in Elizabethan England*. Rpt. Ithaca: Cornell UP for the Folger Shakespeare Library, 1958.

SHAKESPEAREAN PERFORMANCE

Beckerman, Bernard. *Shakespeare at the Globe*. New York: Columbia UP, 1962.

Bentley, Gerald Eades. *The Professions of Dramatist and Player in Shakespeare's Time, 1590–1642*. Princeton: Princeton UP, 1986.

Buchman, Lorne. *Still in Movement: Shakespeare on Screen*. Oxford: Oxford UP, 1991.

Bulman, James C., ed. *Shakespeare, Theory, and Performance*. London: Routledge, 1996.

Bulman, James C., and Herbert Coursen. *Shakespeare on Television: An Anthology of Essays and Reviews*. Hanover, N.H.: UP of New England, 1988.

Cook, Ann Jennalie. *The Privileged Playgoer of Shakespeare's London, 1576–1642*. Princeton: Princeton UP, 1981.

Crowl, Samuel. *Shakespeare Observed: Studies in Performance on Stage and Screen*. Athens: U of Ohio P, 1992.

Desmet, Christy, and Robert Sawyer. *Shakespeare and Appropriation*. London: Routledge, 1999.

Dessen, Alan C. *Elizabethan Stage Conventions and Modern Interpreters*. Cambridge: Cambridge UP, 1984.

Fischlin, Daniel, and Mark Fortier. *Adaptations of Shakespeare: A Critical Anthology of Plays from the Seventeenth Century to the Present*. London: Routledge, 2000.

Goldman, Michael. *Shakespeare and the Energies of Drama*. Princeton: Princeton UP, 1972.

Granville-Barker, Harley. *Prefaces to Shakespeare*. Rev. ed. 4 vols. Princeton: Princeton UP, 1946–47.

Greg, W. W. *Dramatic Documents from the Elizabethan Playhouses*. 2 vols. Oxford: Oxford UP, 1931.

Gurr, Andrew. *The Shakespearian Playing Companies*. Oxford: Clarendon, 1996.

Hodgdon, Barbara. *The Shakespeare Trade: Performances and Appropriations*. Philadelphia: U of Pennsylvania P, 1998.

Holland, Peter. *English Shakespeares: Shakespeare on the English Stage in the 1990s*. Cambridge: Cambridge UP, 1997.

Jackson, Russell, Robert Smallwood, and Philip Brockbank, eds. *Players of Shakespeare*. 3 vols. to date. Cambridge: Cambridge UP, 1986–93.

Joseph, B. L. *Elizabethan Acting*. 2nd ed. Oxford: Oxford UP, 1964.

Kennedy, Dennis. *Foreign Shakespeare: Contemporary Performance*. Cambridge: Cambridge UP, 1993.

———. *Looking at Shakespeare: A Visual History of Twentieth-Century Performance*. Cambridge: Cambridge UP, 1993.

Kiernan, Pauline. *Staging Shakespeare at the New Globe*. New York: St. Martin's, 1999.

Levine, Laura. *Men in Women's Clothing*. Cambridge: Cambridge UP, 1993.

McMillin, Scott, and Sally-Beth MacLean. *The Queen's Men and Their Plays*. Cambridge: Cambridge UP, 1998.

Novy, Marianne. *Transforming Shakespeare: Contemporary Women's Re-Visions in Literature and Performance*. New York: St. Martin's, 1999.

Orgel, Stephen. *The Illusion of Power: Political Theater in the English Renaissance*. Berkeley: U of California P, 1975.

Shattuck, Charles H. *Shakespeare on the American Stage*. 2 vols. Washington: Folger Shakespeare Library, 1976–87.

Styan, J. L. *Shakespeare's Stagecraft*. Cambridge: Cambridge UP, 1967.

Wells, Stanley, ed. *Shakespeare in the Theatre: An Anthology of Criticism*. Oxford: Oxford UP, 1997.

Worthen, W. B. *Shakespeare and the Authority of Performance*. Cambridge: Cambridge UP, 1997.

TEXT AND LANGUAGE

Abbott, E. A. *A Shakespearian Grammar*. Rpt. New York: Haskell House, 1966.

Blake, N. F. *Shakespeare's Language: An Introduction*. London: Methuen, 1983.

Clemen, Wolfgang. *The Development of Shakespeare's Imagery*. London: Methuen, 1951.

De Grazia, Margreta. *Shakespeare Verbatim*. Oxford: Clarendon, 1990.

De Grazia, Margreta, and Peter Stallybrass. "The Materiality of the Shakespearean Text." *Shakespeare Quarterly* 44 (1993): 255–83.

Edwards, Philip, Inga-Stina Ewbank, and G. K. Hunter, eds. *Shakespeare's Styles*. Cambridge: Cambridge UP, 1980.

Greg, W. W. *The Shakespeare First Folio: Its Bibliographical and Textual History*. Oxford: Clarendon, 1955.

Halliday, F. E. *The Poetry of Shakespeare's Plays*. London: Duckworth, 1954.

Houston, John Porter. *Shakespearean Sentences: A Study in Style and Syntax*. Baton Rouge: Louisiana State UP, 1988.

Joseph, Sister Miriam. *Shakespeare's Use of the Arts of Language*. New York: Columbia UP, 1947.

Kokeritz, Helge. *Shakespeare's Pronunciation*. New Haven: Yale UP, 1953.

Lanham, Richard. *The Motives of Eloquence: Literary Rhetoric in the Renaissance*. New Haven: Yale UP, 1976.

Magnusson, Lynne. *Shakespeare and Social Dialogue*. Cambridge: Cambridge UP, 1999.

Maguire, Laurie E. *Shakespearean Suspect Texts: The "Bad" Quartos and Their Contexts*. Cambridge: Cambridge UP, 1996.

Marcus, Leah S. *Unediting the Renaissance: Shakespeare, Marlowe, Milton*. London: Routledge, 1996.

McKerrow, R. B. *An Introduction to Bibliography for Literary Students*. Oxford: Clarendon, 1927.

Onions, C. T. *A Shakespeare Glossary*. Rev. Robert D. Eagleson. Oxford: Oxford UP, 1986.

Parker, Patricia. *Literary Fat Ladies: Rhetoric, Gender, Property*. London: Methuen, 1987.

———. *Shakespeare from the Margins: Language, Culture, Context*. Chicago: U of Chicago P, 1996.

Partridge, Eric. *Shakespeare's Bawdy*. Rev. ed. London: Routledge, 1969.

Spurgeon, Caroline F. E. *Shakespeare's Imagery and What It Tells Us*. Cambridge: Cambridge UP, 1935.

Vickers, Brian. *The Artistry of Shakespeare's Prose*. London: Methuen, 1968.

Willbern, David. *Poetic Will: Shakespeare and the Play of Language*. Philadelphia: U of Pennsylvania P, 1997.

Williams, George Walton. *The Craft of Printing and the Publication of Shakespeare's Works*. Washington: Folger Books, 1985.

DRAMATIC FORMS AND INFLUENCES

Baldwin, T. W. *William Shakespeare's Five-Act Structure*. Urbana: U of Illinois P, 1947.

Barber, C. L. *Shakespeare's Festive Comedy*. Princeton: Princeton UP, 1959.

Bate, Jonathan. *Shakespeare and Ovid*. Oxford: Clarendon, 1993.

Belsey, Catherine. *The Subject of Tragedy: Identity and Difference in Renaissance Drama*. London: Methuen, 1985.

Bevington, David. *From "Mankind" to Marlowe*. Cambridge, Mass.: Harvard UP, 1962.

Booth, Stephen. *"King Lear," "Macbeth," Indefinition, and Tragedy*. New Haven: Yale UP, 1983.

Bradbrook, Muriel. *The Growth and Structure of Elizabethan Comedy*. London: Chatto and Windus, 1955.

Bradley, A. C. *Shakespearean Tragedy*. Rpt. New York: St. Martin's, 1967.

Campbell, L. B. *Shakespeare's "Histories": Mirrors of Elizabethan Policy*. San Marino: Huntington Library, 1947.

———. *Shakespeare's Tragic Heroes: Slaves of Passion*. Cambridge: Cambridge UP, 1930.

Carroll, William C. *The Metamorphoses of Shakespearean Comedy*. Princeton: Princeton UP, 1985.

Charney, Maurice. *Shakespeare's Roman Plays*. Cambridge, Mass.: Harvard UP, 1961.

Colie, Rosalie. *The Resources of Kind: Genre Theory in the Renaissance*. Ed. Barbara K. Lewalski. Berkeley: U of California P, 1973.

Danson, Lawrence. *Shakespeare's Dramatic Genres*. Oxford: Oxford UP, 2000.

Doran, Madeleine. *Endeavors of Art: A Study of Form in Elizabethan Drama*. Madison: U of Wisconsin P, 1954.

Evans, Bertrand. *Shakespeare's Comedies*. Oxford: Oxford UP, 1960.

———. *Shakespeare's Tragic Practice*. Oxford: Oxford UP, 1979.

Foakes, R. A. *Shakespeare: The Dark Comedies to the Last Plays*. Charlottesville: U of Virginia P, 1971.

Frye, Northrop. *Fools of Time: Studies in Shakespearean Tragedy*. Toronto: U of Toronto P, 1967.

———. *A Natural Perspective: The Development of Shakespearean Comedy and Romance*. New York: Columbia UP, 1965.

Garner, Shirley Nelson, and Madelon Sprengnether, eds. *Shakespearean Tragedy and Gender*. Bloomington: Indiana UP, 1996.

Hodgdon, Barbara. *The End Crowns All: Closure and Contradiction in Shakespeare's History.* Princeton: Princeton UP, 1991.

Hoy, Cyrus. *The Hyacinth Room: An Investigation into the Nature of Comedy, Tragedy, and Tragicomedy.* New York: Knopf, 1964.

Knight, G. Wilson. *The Imperial Theme: Further Interpretations of Shakespeare's Tragedies Including the Roman Plays.* 3rd ed. London: Methuen, 1951.

―――. *The Wheel of Fire: Interpretation of Shakespeare's Tragedy.* Rev. ed. New York: Barnes and Noble, 1965.

Long, John H. *Shakespeare's Use of Music.* 3 vols. Gainesville: U of Florida P, 1955–71.

McElroy, Bernard. *Shakespeare's Mature Tragedies.* Princeton: Princeton UP, 1973.

Miola, Robert. *Shakespeare's Rome.* Cambridge: Cambridge UP, 1983.

Mowat, Barbara. *The Dramaturgy of Shakespeare's Romances.* Athens: U of Georgia P, 1976.

Noble, Richmond. *Shakespeare's Biblical Knowledge and Use of the Book of Common Prayer.* New York: Macmillan, 1935.

Ornstein, Robert. *A Kingdom for a Stage: The Achievement of Shakespeare's History Plays.* Cambridge, Mass.: Harvard UP, 1972.

Palmer, D. J. *Shakespeare's Later Comedies: An Anthology of Modern Criticism.* Harmondsworth: Penguin, 1971.

Rackin, Phyllis. *Stages of History: Shakespeare's English Chronicles.* Ithaca: Cornell UP, 1990.

Salingar, Leo. *Shakespeare and the Traditions of Comedy.* Cambridge: Cambridge UP, 1974.

Snyder, Susan. *The Comic Matrix of Shakespeare's Tragedies.* Princeton, 1979.

Spencer, T. J. B., ed. *Shakespeare's Plutarch.* Harmondsworth: Penguin, 1968.

Watson, Robert N. *Shakespeare and the Hazards of Ambition.* Cambridge, Mass.: Harvard UP, 1984.

Weimann, Robert. *Shakespeare and the Popular Tradition in the Theater.* Trans. Robert Schwartz. Baltimore: Johns Hopkins UP, 1978.

Wells, Stanley. "Shakespeare and Romance." Rpt. in *Later Shakespeare.* Ed. John Russell Brown and Bernard Harris. Stratford-upon-Avon Studies 8. London: Edward Arnold, 1966.

Wheeler, Richard P. *Shakespeare's Problem Comedies: Turn and Counter Turn.* Berkeley: U of California P, 1981.

Young, David. *The Heart's Forest: A Study of Shakespeare's Pastoral Plays.* New Haven: Yale UP, 1972.

CRITICAL AND THEORETICAL WORKS

Adelman, Janet. *Suffocating Mothers: Fantasies of Maternal Origin from "Hamlet" to "The Tempest."* London: Routledge, 1992.

Barton, Anne. *Essays, Mainly Shakespearian.* Cambridge: Cambridge UP, 1994.

Bishop, T. G. *Shakespeare and the Theatre of Wonder.* Cambridge: Cambridge UP, 1996.

Booth, Stephen. *An Essay on Shakespeare's Sonnets.* New Haven: Yale UP, 1969.

―――. *Precious Nonsense: The Gettysburg Address, Ben Jonson's Epitaphs on His Children, and "Twelfth Night."* Berkeley: U of California P, 1998.

Bradshaw, Graham. *Misrepresentations: Shakespeare and the Materialists.* Ithaca: Cornell UP, 1993.

Burkhardt, Sigurd. *Shakespearean Meanings*. Princeton: Princeton UP, 1968.

Calderwood, James. *Shakespearean Metadrama*. Minneapolis: U of Minnesota P, 1971.

Cavell, Stanley. *Disowning Knowledge in Six Plays of Shakespeare*. Cambridge: Cambridge UP, 1987.

Colie, Rosalie. *Shakespeare's Living Art*. Princeton: Princeton UP, 1974.

Dean, Leonard F. *Shakespeare: Modern Essays in Criticism*. Rev. ed. Oxford: Oxford UP, 1967.

Dollimore, Jonathan. *Radical Tragedy*. Chicago: U of Chicago P, 1984.

Drakakis, John. *Alternative Shakespeares*. London: Methuen, 1985.

Enterline, Lynn. *The Rhetoric of the Body from Ovid to Shakespeare*. Cambridge: Cambridge UP, 2000.

Fineman, Joel. *Shakespeare's Perjured Eye: The Invention of Poetic Subjectivity in the Sonnets*. Berkeley: U of California P, 1986.

Freedman, Barbara. *Staging the Gaze: Postmodernism, Psychoanalysis, and Shakespearean Comedy*. Ithaca: Cornell UP, 1991.

Goddard, Harold C. *The Meaning of Shakespeare*. 2 vols. Chicago: U of Chicago P, 1951.

Goldberg, Jonathan. *James I and the Politics of Literature*. Baltimore: Johns Hopkins UP, 1983.

Howard, Jean E., and Marion F. O'Connor. *Shakespeare Reproduced: The Text in Ideology and History*. London: Methuen, 1987.

Hunt, Maurice. *Shakespeare's Romance of the Word*. Lewisburg: Bucknell UP, 1990.

Jordan, Constance. *Shakespeare's Monarchies: Ruler and Subject in the Romances*. Ithaca: Cornell UP, 1997.

Kott, Jan. *Shakespeare Our Contemporary*. Trans. Boleslaw Taborski. New York: Norton, 1964.

Lenz, C. S., Gayle Greene, and Carol Thomas Neely. *The Woman's Part: Feminist Criticism of Shakespeare*. Urbana: U of Illinois P, 1980.

Levin, Harry. *The Question of Hamlet*. Oxford: Oxford UP, 1965.

Mack, Maynard. *Everybody's Shakespeare*. Lincoln: U of Nebraska P, 1993.

———. *King Lear in Our Time*. Berkeley: U of California P, 1965.

Maus, Katharine E. *Inwardness and Theater in the English Renaissance*. Chicago: U of Chicago P, 1995.

McDonald, Russ. *Shakespeare and Jonson/Jonson and Shakespeare*. Lincoln: U of Nebraska P, 1988.

Parker, Patricia, and Geoffrey Hartman, eds. *Shakespeare and the Question of Theory*. London: Methuen, 1985.

Patterson, Annabel. *Shakespeare and the Popular Voice*. Oxford: Blackwell, 1989.

Pechter, Edward. *What Was Shakespeare?: Renaissance Plays and Changing Critical Practice*. Ithaca: Cornell UP, 1995.

Rabkin, Norman. *Shakespeare and the Common Understanding*. New York: Free, 1967.

Roberts, Jeanne Addison. *The Shakespearean Wild: Geography, Genus, and Gender*. Lincoln: U of Nebraska P, 1991.

Rose, Mark. *Shakespearean Design*. Cambridge, Mass.: Harvard UP, 1972.

Rossiter, A. P. *Angel with Horns and Other Shakespearean Lectures*. Ed. Graham Storey. London: Longmans Green, 1961.

Schwartz, Murray M., and Coppélia Kahn. *Representing Shakespeare: New Psychoanalytic Essays*. Baltimore: Johns Hopkins UP, 1980.

Sousa, Geraldo U. de. *Shakespeare's Cross-Cultural Encounters*. New York: St. Martin's, 1999.

Summers, Joseph. *Dreams of Love and Power: On Shakespeare's Plays.* Oxford: Oxford UP, 1984.

Taylor, Gary. *Reinventing Shakespeare: A Cultural History, from the Restoration to the Present.* London: Weidenfield and Nicolson, 1989.

Traub, Valerie. *Desire and Anxiety: Circulations of Sexuality in Shakespearean Drama.* London: Routledge, 1992.

Traversi, Derek. *An Approach to Shakespeare.* Rev. ed. 2 vols. New York: Anchor, 1969.

Turner, Robert Y. *Shakespeare's Apprenticeship.* Chicago: U of Chicago P, 1974.

Vendler, Helen Hennessy. *The Art of Shakespeare's Sonnets.* Cambridge, Mass.: Harvard UP, 1997.

APPENDIX

Shakespeare Resources on the Web

✂

The following sites will provide you with a wealth of material about Shakespeare. (These sites are included in the "Links" section of the Bedford Shakespeare Series site at www.bedfordstmartins.com/litreprints.)

STARTING POINTS FOR SHAKESPEARE INTERNET SEARCHES

Mr. William Shakespeare and the Internet
http://daphne.palomar.edu/shakespeare/
Terry Gray at Palomar College created this annotated guide to Shakespeare resources available on the Internet. This enormous site provides Shakespeare biographies, information about Elizabethan theaters, and excellent guides to finding secondary sources on Shakespeare on the Web. Among the many links worth investigating are the "Shakespeare Timeline" and the "Shakespeare Genealogy." Gray also lists links to sites and study guides on specific plays and to scholarly articles available online.

Shakespeare Resource Center
http://www.bardweb.net
This site, designed by J. M. Pressley, provides a brief biography of Shakespeare, a short essay on Shakespeare's works, synopses of the major plays, the text of Shakespeare's will, a summary of the Elizabethan era, a commentary on Shakespeare's language, a reading list, and links to related sites.

Surfing with the Bard
http://www.ulen.com/shakespeare
Amy Ulen's "Shakespeare Classroom on the Internet" includes lesson plans for teaching Shakespeare, "Shakespeare 101" (an introduction to studying Shakespeare's plays), a study guide for *A Midsummer Night's Dream,* a photo album of BBC costumes, links to other resources, and even a page on Shakespearean references in *Star Trek.*

The Furness Shakespeare Library at the University of Pennsylvania
http://www.library.upenn.edu/etext/furness
Selected resources from the Furness Library's extensive collection of primary and secondary sources have been scanned and mounted on the Web site. Browse through digital facsimiles of texts and images and try out the interesting split-screen feature that allows you to view two documents at once for comparison.

The Folger Shakespeare Library, Washington, D.C.
http://www.folger.edu/welcome.htm
The Folger holds the world's largest collection of Shakespeare's printed works and is a major center for scholarly research. Find out about the library and its museums, upcoming public events (such as theater productions and poetry readings), and academic resources.

THE LIFE OF SHAKESPEARE

The Shakespeare Birthplace Trust
http://www.shakespeare.org.uk
Take a look at houses associated with Shakespeare and his family and read about their histories. The "About Shakespeare" section covers his life, family history, schooling, and hometown of Stratford.

Shakespeare's School
http://homepages.nationwideisp.net/~gsa/welcome.htm
Learn more about King Edward VI School in Stratford-upon-Avon and the education of boys in Elizabethan England.

Shakespeare's Life and Times
http://www.uvic.ca/shakespeare/Library/SLT/
Michael Best's extensive Web site is a valuable resource for information on Shakespeare's life and on many aspects of the era in which Shakespeare wrote, such as the stage, society, history, politics, ideas, drama, literature, music, and art. There is also interesting coverage of Elizabethan English, including brief sound recordings of passages from *Henry IV, Part 1* and *Julius Caesar* that illustrate Elizabethan pronunciation.

THE AUTHORSHIP DEBATE

The Shakespeare Authorship Page
http://www.clark.net/pub/tross/ws/will.html
"Dedicated to the proposition that Shakespeare wrote Shakespeare," this site
provides scholarly articles and essays contending that William Shakespeare of
Stratford was the author of the plays.

The Shakespeare Oxford Society
http://www.shakespeare-oxford.com/
The articles on this Web site support the theory that Edward de Vere, seventeenth earl of Oxford, was the author of Shakespeare's works.

The Shakespeare Mystery by PBS Online and WGBH/Frontline
http://www.pbs.org/wgbh/pages/frontline/shakespeare/index.html
For a more impartial presentation of the authorship question, take a look at
this site based on a recent *Frontline* program. Find viewer responses to the
show, a reading list, updates from both sides of the argument, and recent
debates.

PERFORMANCES AND THEATERS

Shakespeare's Globe Research Database
http://www.reading.ac.uk/globe/
This database contains photos, drawings, research bulletins, articles, and
reports on Shakespeare in performance. There are extensive sections on the
history and archaeology of the Old Globe and the design and building of the
New Globe as well as a virtual tour of the New Globe with detailed information on the reconstruction.

Shakespeare Examined through Performance
http://www.tamut.edu/english/folgerhp/folgerhp.htm
The "Shakespeare Performance Recipe Book" contains a variety of performance exercises developed by participants in a 1995–96 Folger Institute session
and is a good resource for those interested in teaching and staging Shakespeare.

The Interactive Shakespeare Project, College of the Holy Cross
http://sterling.holycross.edu/departments/theatre/projects/isp/measure/
teachguide/intro.html
This online study guide for *Measure for Measure* offers a glossed, annotated
text of the play, a teacher's guide, essays, performance exercises, photos, video
clips, and a virtual tour of Shakespeare's Globe.

SHAKESPEARE'S TEXTS

MIT Shakespeare Homepage
http://tech-two.mit.edu/Shakespeare/
Billing itself as "the Web's first edition of the Complete Works of William Shakespeare," this site presents the full text of Shakespeare's plays in an easy-to-navigate format.

The Works of the Bard
http://www.gh.cs.su.oz.au/~matty/Shakespeare/Shakespeare.html
This Complete Works site also features a glossary and a great Shakespeare search engine. (You can type in a particular phrase from a poem or play, and the engine will locate the source.)

Internet Shakespeare Editions
http://web.uvic.ca/shakespeare/index.html
ISE's growing site offers annotated, old-spelling transcriptions of the plays.

CULTURAL AND HISTORICAL SITES

Shakespeare Illustrated
http://www.cc.emory.edu/ENGLISH/classes/Shakespeare_Illustrated/Shakespeare.html
Offering a cross disciplinary approach to Shakespeare, this site examines nineteenth-century paintings and performances of Shakespeare's plays and their influence upon each other.

Royalty of England
http://www.peak.org/shrewsbury/SHOH/
This page, part of the Shrewsbury Renaissance Faire site, provides a chronological bloodline of the British monarchy, a map of the British Isles in 1595, a chart of currency values in Elizabethan England, and links to resources on Renaissance England.

A SAMPLE OF COURSE WEB SITES

(See "Best Educational Sites" at *Mr. William Shakespeare and the Internet* for a more complete list.)

New Approaches to Renaissance Studies
http://www.english.upenn.edu/~bushnell/english-330
Rebecca Bushnell's Web site for English 330 contains a gallery of images relevant to the course.

Bardology: Introduction to Shakespeare
http://www.english.wayne.edu/~aune
Designed by Mark Aune, this Web site offers outlines of lectures on selected topics such as "Gender and Family in Early Modern England," tips on reading Shakespeare and on writing about Shakespeare, and a filmography.

Shakespeare by Individual Studies
http://www.engl.uvic.ca/Faculty/MBHomePage/ISShakespeare/Index.html
Michael Best's virtual course relies on multimedia and computer interaction — instead of lectures — to educate students about Shakespeare.

The Shakespeare Classroom
http://www.jetlink.net/~massij/shakes/
J. M. Massi's Web site contains teaching materials, answers to Shakespeare FAQs, a list of film versions of Shakespeare's plays, and links to other Shakespeare resources.

Surfing with the Bard
http://www.ulen.com/shakespeare
See page 423 for more information about this site.

SHAKESPEARE JOURNALS

Early Modern Literary Studies
http://purl.oclc.org/emls/emlshome.html
Available here are full-text articles and reviews from this online scholarly journal of English language and literature of the sixteenth and seventeenth centuries.

Shakespeare Magazine Online
http:http://www.shakespearemag.com/
Only selected articles from this magazine for teachers and Shakespeare enthusiasts are available online, but the "News on the Rialto" section offers current information about Shakespeare events, including performances, films, conferences, and lectures.

Acknowledgments (continued from copyright page)

CHAPTER 1
The House Known as Shakespeare's Birthplace. Reprinted by permission of the Folger Shakespeare
   Library.
Record of Shakespeare's Baptism. Reprinted by permission of Vicar and Churchwardens, Holy Trinity
   Church, Stratford-upon-Avon.
Map of Stratford-upon-Avon. Reprinted by permission of the Shakespeare Birthplace Trust.
A Plague Bill. The Report of All the Burials and Christenings within the City of London. Reprinted
   by permission of the Folger Shakespeare Library.
Detail from the "Agas" Map of London (With Shakespeare's Lodging Indicated). Reprinted with per-
   mission of Guildhall Library, Corporation of London.

CHAPTER 2
Desiderius Erasmus, From the Foreword to the Third Edition of the Latin New Testament. From *The
   Praise of Folly and Other Writings,* trans. and ed. Robert M. Adams. Copyright © 1992 by Robert M.
   Adams. Reprinted by permission of W. W. Norton & Company.
Baldassare Castiglione, From *The Book of the Courtier,* trans. George Bull (Penguin Classics, 1967).
   Copyright © 1967 by George Bull. Reprinted by permission of Penguin UK.
Chart of the Relative Proportions of Poetry and Prose in Shakespeare's Plays. From *The Complete Peli-
   can Shakespeare* by William Shakespeare, ed. Alfred Harbage. Copyright © 1969 by Penguin Books,
   Inc. Used by permission of Viking Penguin, a division of Penguin Books USA Inc.

CHAPTER 3
Aristotle, From *Poetics.* Reprinted from Aristotle's *Poetics,* trans. Ingram Bywater from *The Oxford
   Translation of Aristotle,* ed. W. D. Ross, vol. II (1925) by permission of Oxford University Press.
Title Page of *Richard III* (First Quarto). Reprinted by permission of the Folger Shakespeare Library.
William Lambarde, From His Notes of a Conversation with Queen Elizabeth I about *Richard II.*
   Reprinted by permission of The British Library.

CHAPTER 4
Map Showing the Playhouses in Shakespeare's Time. From *The Living Monument: Shakespeare and the
   Theatre of His Time,* by Muriel C. Bradbrook (© 1976). Reprinted with permission of Cambridge
   University Press.
Henry Peacham, Sketch Accompanying Lines from *Titus Andronicus.* Reproduced by permission of
   the Marquess of Bath, Longleat House, Warminster, Wiltshire, Great Britain.
Inventory of Theatrical Costumes (From Henslowe's Papers). Reprinted by kind permission of the
   Governors of Dulwich College.
Remains of the Rose Playhouse. Reprinted by permission of Andrew Fulgoni Photography.
Two Plans of the Rose Playhouse. From *The Shakespearean Stage* by Andrew Gurr. Reprinted by per-
   mission of Cambridge University Press and John Orrell, University Professor of English at the Uni-
   versity of Alberta.
C. Walter Hodges, Illustration of the Second Globe. Reprinted from *Shakespeare's Second Globe* by
   C. Walter Hodges (1973) by permission of Oxford University Press.
Copy of De Witt's Sketch of the Swan Playhouse. After a drawing by Arnold Buchelius. Reprinted by
   permission of University Library, Utrecht, MS. 842, fol. 132R.
Wenceslas Hollar, Detail from *Long View of London.* Reprinted by permission of Guildhall Library,
   Corporation of London.
Philip Henslowe, Log of Plays from His *Diary.* Reprinted by kind permission of the Governors of
   Dulwich College.
Record of King James's Payment to the King's Men. Reprinted from the Dramatic Records in the
   Declared Accounts of the Treasurer of the Chamber, 1558–1642. Reprinted by permission of Her
   Majesty's Stationery Office.
Edward Alleyn, Letter to His Wife. Reprinted by kind permission of the Governors of Dulwich
   College.

CHAPTER 5
Giovanni Battista Giraldi Cinthio, From *Gli Hecatommithi* (The Principal Source for Othello). From
   Narrative and Dramatic Sources in Shakespeare by Geoffrey Bullough. Copyright © 1957, 1961 by
   Columbia University Press. Reprinted with the permission of the publisher.

From the Geneva Bible, 1560, Title page, RB 55362. This item is reproduced by permission of The Huntington Library, San Marino, California.

From *The Book of Common Prayer* (The Order for the Burial of the Dead). Reprinted by permission of the Folger Shakespeare Library.

Christopher Marlowe, From *Tamburlaine the Great*, 1590, RB 136105. This item is reproduced by permission of The Huntington Library, San Marino, California.

CHAPTER 6

Illustration of the Folding and Printing Process. Reprinted from G. B. Harrison, *Introducing Shakespeare* (Penguin Books, 1939, 1954, 1966) by permission of David Higham Associates Limited.

Title Page of *Titus Andronicus* (First Quarto). Reprinted by permission of the Folger Shakespeare Library.

Title Page and Catalogue of the First Folio. Reprinted by permission of the Folger Shakespeare Library.

Illustration of a Seventeenth-Century Print Shop (Frontispiece to Edmund Rive's *Twelve Rules Introducing to the Art of Latin*). Reprinted by permission of the Folger Shakespeare Library.

Facsimile of the Last Page of King Lear (First Quarto). Reprinted by permission of the Folger Shakespeare Library.

A Comparison of the Work of the Compositors A and B on the 1623 Folio. From Peter Blayney, *The First Folio of Shakespeare.* Reprinted by permission of the Folger Shakespeare Library.

Facsimile of "To be or not to be" from *Hamlet, Prince of Denmark* (First Quarto), 1603, RB 69304. This item is reproduced by permission of The Huntington Library, San Marino, California.

Facsimile of "To be or not to be" from *Hamlet, Prince of Denmark* (1623 Folio). Reprinted by permission of the Folger Shakespeare Library.

CHAPTER 7

Thomas Platter, From *Travels in England* (The Thames River), trans. Clare Williams. Reprinted by permission of the Clare Williams Estate and the publishers, Jonathan Cape, London.

Lupold von Wedel, From *Journey through England and Scotland Made by Lupold Von Wedel in the Years 1584 and 1585,* ed. Gottfried von Bulow, from *Transactions of the Royal Historical Society* ns 9 (1895). Reprinted by permission of the Royal Historical Society, Univeristy College London, Gower Street, London WC1E 6BT.

Gervase Markham, From *The English Husbandman* (Rural Domestic Architecture and Interior Design). Photo courtesy of the Boston Public Library.

CHAPTER 8

Lady Anne Southwell, "Letter on Poetry." From *The Southwell-Sibthorpe Commonplace Book:* Folger MS V.b.198, ed. Jean Klene, C.S.C., MRTS vol. 147 (Tempe, AZ 1997), pp. 4–5. Copyright © Arizona Board of Regents for Arizona State University.

Sir Robert Filmer, From *Patriarcha, or The Natural Power of Kings,* ed. Johann P. Summerville. Copyright © 1991 by Cambridge University Press. Reprinted with permission of Cambridge University Press.

Queen Elizabeth I, List of Royal Proclamations, Royal Proclamation against Vagabonds and Unlawful Assemblies, and Edict Arranging for the Expulsion from England of Negroes and Blackamoors. Reprinted by permission of James F. Larkin and Paul L. Hughes, *Tudor Royal Proclamations* (New Haven: Yale University Press, 1964–69).

CHAPTER 9

The "Ermine Portrait" of Elizabeth I, by unknown artist. Reproduced by permission of the Marquess of Salisbury.

Portrait of James I, by Paul von Somer, c. 1620. Reproduced by permission of the Royal Collection Enterprises.

King James I, Secret Letter to Robert Cecil. Reproduced by permission of the Marquess of Salisbury.

King James I, Letter to George Villiers, Duke of Buckingham. Reprinted by permission of G. P. V. Akrigg, the University of California Press and the Bodleian Library, University of Oxford, MS. Tanner 72, fol. 14v.

Sir John Harington, Letter Describing the Revels at King James's Court. From *Letters and Epigrams of John Harington,* ed. Norman McClure, University of Pennsylvania Press, 1930.

Niccolò Machiavelli, From *The Prince and Selected Discourses* by Niccolò Machiavelli, trans. Daniel Donno. Copyright © 1966 by Bantam, a division of Bantam Doubleday Dell Publishing Group, Inc. Used by permission of Bantam Books, a division of Random House, Inc.

Simon Forman, From His *Diary* (On a Dream about an Encounter with Queen Elizabeth). Reprinted by permission of Bodleian Library, University of Oxford, MS. Ashmole 226, fol. 44r.

CHAPTER 10

Illustration of David Garrick as King Lear (After a Painting by Benjamin Wilson). By permission of the Harvard Theatre Collection.

Photograph of Sarah Siddons as Lady Macbeth. By permission of the Harvard Theatre Collection.

Photograph of Ellen Terry as Lady Macbeth. Courtesy of the Tate Gallery, New York.

Photograph of Judi Dench as Lady Macbeth. © Donald Cooper/Photostage.

Illustration of Ira Aldridge as Othello. By permission of the Victoria and Albert Museum/Art Resource, New York.

Playbill Advertising a Gala Performance of *Julius Caesar* (Featuring the Three Booth Brothers). Reprinted by permission of the Folger Shakespeare Library.

Photograph of Norman Wilkinson's Set for *Twelfth Night*. By permission of the Raymond Mander and Joe Mitchenson Theatre Collection.

Photograph of Robert Edmund Jones's Set for John Barrymore's *Hamlet*. By permission of the Raymond Mander and Joe Mitchenson Theatre Collection.

John Barrymore's Script for *Hamlet* (Directed by Arthur Hopkins). Reprinted by permission of the Folger Shakespeare Library.

Illustration of Charles Kean's Production of *A Midsummer Night's Dream*. By permission of the Victoria and Albert Museum/Art Resource, New York.

Photograph from Peter Brook's Production of *A Midsummer Night's Dream*. © Donald Cooper/Art Resource.

Robert Speaight, Review of Peter Brook's *A Midsummer Night's Dream*. From "Shakespeare in Britain," *Shakespeare Quarterly* N51, vol. 21, no. 4 (Autumn 1970), pp. 448–49. Reprinted by permission of the Folger Shakespeare Library.

Photograph of Laurence Olivier as Henry V. Photofest.

Kenneth Tynan, From *He That Plays the King*. Copyright © 1950. Reprinted by permission of Pearson Custom Publishing.

Photograph from *Titus* (Directed by Julie Taymor). By permission of Clear Blue Sky Productions.

Index

Italic page numbers indicate illustrations and documents reprinted in *The Bedford Companion.*

Absolute monarchy, 304–06
Actaeon myth, 161, 162
Act of Uniformity, 316
Actor-managers, 361–62
Actors, 120. *See also specific companies*
   boys as, 112–13, 122
   as a class, 275
   criticism of, 250
   female roles and, 113–14
   Heywood's apology for, *141–42*
   hypothetical 1595 production and, 109–14
   introduction of actresses, 353, 354–55
   modern productions and, 2, 357–63
   parts written for, 122–23
   play publication and, 198
   presentational style of performance by, 123
   royal support for, 125, *140–41,* 324
   sexual aspects of roles and, 113–14
   Shakespeare's acting work in theatrical
     companies, 14, 17, 18–19, 156
   touring companies and, 365–66
   wages for, 235, 364
   women's roles and, 112–13
Acts and Monuments (Foxe), 5, 154, *174–78,*
   315
Adelman, Janet, 88
Admonition to the Parliament, An (Field and
   Wilcox), *340–43*
Adultery, 271
Advertising, 233–34, *252*
Aeneid (Virgil), 52
Aesop, 148
Africans, in Elizabethan society, 276–77, *302*
"Agas" map of London, 34, *35 (map)*
Agriculture, 225–26, 228–30, *245–47,* 274
Alchemist, The (Jonson), 234, 325
Aldridge, Ira, 365, *388 (illus.)*
Alençon, François, duke of, 313, 320

Alleyn, Edward, 112, 120, 121, 125, 126, 129,
   143–44, 156
All for Love, 356
All's Well That Ends Well, 20, 77, 80, 83, 85,
   153, 380
Almereyda, Michael, 380
Amoretti (Spenser), 157
Amphitruo (Plautus), 149
Amussen, Susan, 260, 261, 275
Amyot, Jacques, 149
Anatomy of Abuses, The (Stubbes), 325, *351–52*
Anderson, Judith, 379
Anglica Historia (Polydore Vergil), 150
Anglican Church. *See* Church of England
Anjou, duke of. *See* Henry III
Anne, queen of England, 125, 126, 155, 184,
   307, 311, 312, 333
Answer to the Catholics' Supplication, An
   (Muriel), 317, 343, *344–45*
Antony and Cleopatra, 19, 85, 197, 254
   female roles in, 113
   language in, 42, 53, 78
   modern performances of, 356
   sources for, 159–60, *186–87*
   staging of, 116, 117
   as tragedy, 87, 88, 98
Apollonius of Tyre, 153
Apology for Actors, An (Heywood), *141–42*
"Apology of Raymond Sebond, An" (Mon-
   taigne), 157
Apprenticeships, 270, 275–76
Apuleius, 151
Arcadia (Sidney), 152
Architecture
   of playhouses, 114–20, 361–62, 371
   privacy and, 270–71
   of rural houses, *243–45*
Aristocracy, 274, 275, 304

Aristotle, 79, 86, 254
  Historia Animalium, 278
  Poetics, 88, 89, *101–05*
Armada, 313, 321
Armin, Robert, 33, 122–23, 158
Arraignment of Lewd, Idle, Froward, and
  Unconstant Women (Swetnam), 258
Art of English Poesy (Puttenham), 43, *68–73,*
  158
Art of Reason, Rightly Termed Witcraft, The
  (Lever), 40, *66–68*
Art of Rhetoric, The (Wilson), *60–62*
Ascham, Roger, 43, *64–66*
Ashcroft, Peggy, 369, 370
Astrophil and Stella (Sidney), 16, 157, *183–84*
As You Like It, 20, 77, 80, 197, 265, 298
  actors and actresses in, 355
  as comedy, 85
  female roles in, 113
  film version of, 377
  language in, 48, 58
  modern productions of, 371
  sources for, 152, 162
Aubrey, John, 14
Audiences, 20, 21
  court performances and, 121, *333–34*
  hypothetical 1595 production and, 109–14
  makeup of, 118–20
  modern productions and, 355, 373
  onstage seating for, 119
  social-class considerations of, 119–20
  space in playhouses for, 118–19
  stage setting and, 110
  types of plays available to, 94

Babington conspiracy, 312
Bacon, Francis, 24, 25, 26, 41, 307
Baconiana (journal), 25
Bad quartos, 201, 202
Bale, John, 90
Ballads, as source material, 154–55, *178–79*
Bandello, Matteo, 151
Bankside district, London, 21, 115, 120, 224,
  225
Barish, Jonas A., 316
Barnet, Sylvan, 208
Barnfield, Richard, 273, *298–99*
Barroll, J. Leeds, 125
Barrymore, John, 367, 377, *391 (illus.), 392*
  (illus.)

Bartholomew Fair (Jonson), 228, 256
Barton, John, 374
Basilikon Doron (James I), 311, *336–39*
Baylis, Lilian, 369
Bearbaiting, 116, 224, *241–42*
Beaumont, Francis, 22, 94, 107
Bedford, countess of. *See* Russell, Lucy
  Harington
Beggars, 274, *301–02*
Bentley, Gerald Eades, 23
Berliner Ensemble, *370*
Betterton, Sir Thomas, *357–58*
Bevington, David, 197, 208, 209
Bible, 43, 146, 154, 256, 319. *See also* Geneva
  Bible
  Adam and Eve story in, 260, 261
  Erasmus on, 40, *59–60*
  King James (Authorized Version), 318,
    366
  marriage customs and, 260–61, *285–90*
  patriarchy and, 259, 260
  power of kings and, *283–85*
Bingo (Bond), 22
Bishop's Bible, 154
Blackfriars district, London, 115
Blackfriars Theatre, 17, 20–21, 116, 118, 119,
  121, 125
Blacks, in Elizabethan society, 276–77, *302*
Blank verse, 47, *51–53*
Blayney, Peter, 218
Bloom, Claire, 378
Blount, Edward, 204
Boaistuau, Pierre, 151
Boccaccio, Giovanni, 152, 153
Bond, Edward, 22
Book of Common Prayer, The, 154, *171–74,* 315
Book of Husbandry, The (Fitzherbert), 230,
  246–47
Book of the Courtier, The (Castiglione), 46,
  73–76, 158
Book Named the Governor, The (Elyot), 323
Book of the play, 198–99
Boose, Lynda, 88
Booth, Edwin, 365, 366, *389 (illus.)*
Booth, John Wilkes, 365, *389 (illus.)*
Booth, Junius Brutus, 364–65, 366, *389 (illus.)*
Booth, Junius Brutus, Jr., 365, *389 (illus.)*
Booth, Stephen, 158, 254
Bowers, Fredson, *203–04*
Boy actors, 112–14, 122. *See also* Actors

Bracegirdle, Anne, 355, 357
Branagh, Kenneth, 371, 378–79, 380, 381
Brecht, Berthold, 370
Brinsley, John, 43
British Broadcasting Company (BBC),
    379–80
Broadsides, as source material, 154–55
Broë, Pierre, *295*
Brook, Peter, 110, 374–75, 395, *397 (illus.)*,
    398–99
Brooke, Arthur, 151–52
Brothels, 224, *242–43*, 256
Buchell, Arend van, 116, 135
Bullough, Geoffrey, 150, 164
Burbage, Cuthbert, 121, 122
Burbage, James, 19, 109, 115, 116, 120, 121, 122
Burbage, Richard, 2, 17, 19, 33, 109, 121, 122,
    123, *140*, 357
Burge, Stuart, 380
Burghley, Baron. *See* Cecil, William
Burton, Richard, 378

Caesar, Julius, 150
Cagney, James, 377
Calvin, John, 315, 317
Calvinism, 166, 315, 318
Cambyses (Preston), 54
Cardenio, 21, 29, 94
Carey, Henry, Lord Hunsdon, 17, 109, 257
Carr, Robert, earl of Somerset, 307
Cary, Elizabeth, viscountess of Falkland,
    79, *100–01*, 256–57
Castiglione, Baldassare, 46, *73–76*, 158
Casting off copy, 200–201
Catesby, Robert, 317
Catharsis, 88, 90
Catherine of Aragon, 271
Catholicism, 171, 174, 306
    ballads about, 155
    dissolution of the abbeys and, 225, 264
    Elizabethan politics and, 307, 308, 315–16
    James I and, 317, *343–47*
    meatless days and, 222, 227
    Shakespeare's early years and sympathies
        for, 13, 14
Catholics' Supplication, The, 317, *343–44*
Caxton, William, 39
Cecil, Robert, 155, 306, 307, 314, 317, 331
Cecil, William, Baron Burghley, 26, 306,
    307, 313

Chapman, George, 32, 125, 158
Charing Cross district, London, 220, 221
Charles I, king of England, 261, 321, 325
Charles II, king of England, 112, 354, 355
Chaucer, Geoffrey, 40, 43, 52, 153, 224
Cheek by Jowl, 371
Chekhov, Anton, 98
Cherry Orchard, The (Chekhov), 98
Children. *See also* Family
    apprenticeship and training of, 270,
        275–76
    education of, 270
    illegitimate, 257, 263, 271
    inheritance and, 263–65
    Jonson on loss of, *295*
    negotiated marriages and, 266–67, *292–93*
Chimes at Midnight (film), 379
Cholmley, John, 120
Christian, king of Denmark, 333
Christianity. *See* Catholicism; Church of
    England; Protestantism; Religious
    doctrine
Christ's Tears over Jerusalem (Nashe), 225,
    242–43, 256
Chronicles of England, Scotland, and Ireland
    (Holinshed), 146, 150, 158–59, 162,
    185–86, 237, 370
Chrysostom, St. John, 258
Church of England
    Catholics' supplication against, 317,
        343–45
    Elizabeth and, 303
    Elizabethan Settlement in, 315–17
    enemies of, 317–18
    episcopacy and, 318
    homily on marriage and, *285–90*
    homily on obedience and, *345–49*
    Hooker's defense of, 317, 323, *349–51*
    ideology of order and, 318–21
    Puritans and, *340–43*
    religious literature and, 154, *166–74*
    Shakespeare's early years and, 13, 14
Cibber, Colley, 357, 358
Cicero, 43, 148
Cinthio, Giovanni Battista Giraldi, 6
    Gli Hecatommithi, 152, *169–70*
Citizens, 274
City of London, 221, 222–23, 225
Civil Wars, 261, 304, 354
Civil Wars, The (Daniel), 150

Class
    clothing and, 232–33
    eating habits and, *248*
    groups in, 274–75
    marriage and, 266, 271
    patriarchy and, 275
    social structure and, 273–77
Classics, 256
    comedy and, 82, 91
    Shakespeare's familiarity with, 14, 18, 32,
        146
    as a source for Shakespeare, 147–49, 153,
        161–62, *186–87, 190–93*
    tragedy and, 85
Cleese, John, 380
Clinton, Elizabeth, countess of Lincoln,
        269, *293–94*
Closet drama, 187, 257
Clothing, 4, 231–33, 235, 250–52, 275
Clown role, 122
Cockpit theater, 224
Coins, 234
Coke, Sir Edward, 22, 272, *296–98*
Coleman, D. C., 229, 230
Color, in costumes, 112
Comedy, 79, 81–85, 98
    customs of society and, 83–84
    paradox in, 82–83
    Sidney on, *99*
    use of term, 81, 82
Comedy of Errors, The, 28, 32, 80, 86, 109
    as comedy, 83, 85
    language in, 42, 47, 77
    printing of, 205
    sources for, 149, 153, 164
Commercial life, 233–36
    apprenticeship and, 270, 275–76
    daily routine in, 231
    enclosure and, 230
    guilds and, 222
    in London, 221–24, 233
    markets and, 228
    money in, 234–35
    property laws and, 265
    tradesmen and, 222, *239–40*
    women and, 256
Companies. *See* Theatrical companies *and
        specific companies*
Complementarity, 162
Compositors, 203, *218*

Condell, Henry, 24, 33, 204
Conduct books, *295–96*
Confessio Amantis (Gower), 153
Contracts, marriage, 271–72
Cook, Ann Jennalie, 265
Cook, George Frederick, 360
Copyists, 198–99
Coriolanus, 19, 78, 121, 212, 258, 277, 305
    enclosure and, 230
    female roles in, 113
    modern productions of, 370, 371
    sources for, 159
    as tragedy, 87, 88
Cosmetics, 232
Costumes
    color of, 112
    in 1595 production of *Romeo and Juliet,*
        111–12
    inventory list for the Lord Admiral's
        Men, 112, *129–31*
    modern productions and, 361, 368
    richness of, 111–12
    sexual aspects of roles and, 113–14
    sketch for *Titus Andronicus* showing, *127*
        (illus.)
Countess of Lincoln's Nursery, The (Clinton),
        269, *293–94*
Countess of Montgomery's Urania, The
        (Wroth), 256
Country life, 225–28, 235, *243–45*
Court life, 258
    Elizabeth and, 314
    James and, 311, *333–34*
    masques in, 125–26, 312
    revels in, 333–34
Courts. *See* Judicial system
Cowley, Richard, 33
Craftsmen, 256, 275–76
Craig, Edward Gordon, 367, 368, 391
Crane, Ralph, 198, 205
Crewe, Jonathan, 277
Crime and criminals, 224, *301–02,* 320–21,
        351
Cromwell, Oliver, 276, 325
Crosse, Henry, 235
Cryptographic schemes, in Shakespeare's
        plays, 26
Cukor, George, 377
Cultural materialism, 88, 324
Cultural poetics, 2, 93

Culture. *See also* Society in early modern England
    literary criticism and forces in, 2
Cumming, Alan, 381, *405 (illus.)*
Currency, value of, 8, 234–35
Curtain Theatre, 115, 116, 223
Cutpurse, Moll, 256
Cymbeline, 21, 78, 212
    as a romance, 94, 95
    sources for, 152, 158, 185
Czinner, Paul, 377

Dancing, 98, 125–26
Daniel, Samuel, *62–63*, 150, 157
Dante, 81–85
Dark comedies, 80
Dark Lady mystery, and Shakespeare's sonnets, 16, 257, 277
Davenant, Sir William, 354, 356, 358
Davies, Godfrey, 317
Davies, Thomas, 359, 369
Davison, William, 313
Defense of Poesy, The (Sidney), *51*, *82*, 99–100, 158
Dekker, Thomas, 221, 256
Delightful Daily Exercise for Ladies and Gentlewomen, A (Murrell), 234, *252*
Dench, Judi, 357, 371, 380, *387 (illus.)*
Denmark, 306
De Republica Anglorum: The Manner of Government or Policy of the Realm of England (Sir Thomas Smith), *292*, 304, *326–27*
Description of England (Harrison), 4, 220, 222, 231, 232, *237–38*, *248*, *250–52*
de Vere, Edward, earl of Oxford, 24, 25, 26
Devereux, Robert, earl of Essex, 94, 107, 124–25, 140, 296, 313, 314
de Witt, Johannes, 6, 116, 117, *135 (illus.)*
Dexter, John, 371, 400
Diana Enamorada (Montemayor), 152
Diana myth, 161, 162, *190–93*
Diaries. *See* Forman, Simon; Henslowe, Philip; Ward, John
Dickens, Charles, 361
Directions for Speech and Style (Hoskyns), 43
Discovery space, 117
Divers Voyages Touching the Discovery of America (Hakluyt), 156
Divine Comedy, The (Dante), 81

Divorce, 262
Doctor Faustus (Marlowe), 116, 120
Dogg's Hamlet (Stoppard), 98
Dolan, Frances, 270
Dollimore, Jonathan, 324
Domestic service, 270
Donizetti, Gaetano, 314
Donne, John, 43, 157
Donnellan, Declan, 371
Double meanings, in wordplay, 45–46
Dower, 266
Dowry, 266–67
Drake, Sir Francis, 321
Dramatists, fees for, 235
Drayton, Michael, 22, 32, 34, 157
Dress, 4, 231–33, 235, 250–52, 275
Dryden, John, 356
Dudley, Robert, earl of Leicester, 306, 313
Duncan-Jones, Katherine, 17

Early modern (as term), 7
Eastward Ho! (Jonson, Marston, and Chapman), 125
Eating habits, 222, 226–27, 231, *248*, *252*
Economy of England, 219–36
    commercial life of London and, 221–24
    enclosure and, 230, *245–46*
    farming and, 228–30
    fashion and, 231–32
    marriage and, 266–67
    merchants and tradesmen in, 222, *239–40*
    opportunities for economic advancement and, 275–76
    trade and, 233–34
    wages in, 227, 232, 234–35
    women and, 256
Education, 270
    Ascham on, 43, *64–66*
    changes in language and, 39
    of women, 256, 258
Edward II (Marlowe), 273
Edward VI, king of England, 150, 306, 315
Elderton, William, *179*
Eliot, T. S., 366
Elizabeth I, queen of England, 55, 64, 124, 253, 257, 303, *339*
    absolute monarchy and, 304–06
    Arbella Stuart and, 258
    ballads about, 155

Church of England and, 303, 315–17
councillors to, 306–07
court life of, 307–08
fashion and, 231–32
international affairs and, 306, 313, 321
London and, 222
marriage question and, 262, 306, 313–14
A Midsummer Night's Dream and, 27–28
portrait of, *309 (illus.)*
proclamations of, 276–77, *299–302*
productions of Shakespeare's plays and,
    17, 25, 26, 27, 28, 94, *107*, 125, 312, 324
royal symbolism and, 308
sense of performance used by, 313, *328*
state and, 259, 271
succession issues and, 265, 314, *331–32*
Elizabethan Settlement, 315–17
Elyot, Sir Thomas, 323
Enchanted Island, The, 356–57
Enclosure, 230, 236, *245–46*
England's Helicon (miscellany), 158
English Husbandman, The (Markham), 228,
    243–45
English Revolution, 305, 318
Erasmus, Desiderius, 40, *59* 60
Essays (Montaigne), 156–57
Essex, earl of. *See* Devereux, Robert
Evans, Edith, 369
Evans, G. Blakemore, 207
Evans, Maurice, 379
Every Man in his Humour (Jonson), 19, 156,
    223
Executions, 321
Eyre, Richard, 371, 381

Faerie Queene, The (Spenser), 95, 157
Fairbanks, Douglas, 376, 378
Fair copy, 198–99
Faithful Shepherdess, The (Fletcher), *107*
Falkland, viscountess of. *See* Cary, Elizabeth
Falstaff, Sir John (character), 45, 46–47,
    49–50, 77, 91–93, 161, 219, 221, 226, 264,
    312, 380
Family, 269–73
    daily routines and, 231
    housekeeping chores and, 230, *246–47*
    inheritance and, 263–65
    nursing of infants in, 269–70, *293–94*
    patriarchy and, 256–57
    privacy in, 270–71

property ownership and, 253
social class and, 274
Famous Victories of Henry V, The (anony-
    mous play), 150
Farmer, Richard, 147
Farming, 225–26, 228–30, *245–47,* 274
Fashion, 4, 231–33, 236, *250–52,* 275
Fasti (Ovid), 148
Fawkes, Guy, 317
Felperin, Howard, 94
Feminist criticism, 2, 84, 88
Festivals, 227–28
Feudal system, 228, 236, 259, 264, 276
Field, John, *340–43*
Fielding, Henry, 81
Fiennes, Ralph, 2, 371, 374
Filmer, Sir Robert, 6, 259, *283–85*
Film versions of plays, 110, 314, 374, 376–82,
    400 (illus.), 405 (illus.)
First Folio (1623), 1, 28, 197, 203, 208
    catalogue of, 212, *213*
    contents of, 80, 205
    Jonson's verses introducing, 147, 148
    King Lear as printed in, 202–03
    printing of, 24, 199, 204–05
    sources of works printed in, 205
    title page of, 4, *212*
    Titus Andronicus as printed in, 206–07, *211*
    work of different compositors in, 203, *218*
Firth, C. H., 154–55
Fishing industry, 222, 227
Fitzherbert, Sir Anthony, 230, *246–47*
Fitzroy, Henry, 271
Fleming, Abraham, 159
Fletcher, John, 80, 93, 94, *107,* 121, 356
    plays written with Shakespeare, 21–22,
    80, 94, 205
Fletcher, Lawrence, 33
Florio, John, 63, 157
Flower of Friendship, The (Tilney), 260,
    261–62
Folger Shakespeare Library, 203, 207, 211, 372
Folios. *See also* First Folio
    printing process and, 199–201, *200 (illus.)*
Food, 222, 226–27, 231, *248, 252*
Food riots, 275
Ford, John, 121
Forman, Simon, 257, 313, *339*
Forrest, Edwin, 365
Fortescue, Sir John, 320, 323

Fortune Playhouse, 116, 118, 121
Foucault, Michel, 27, 324
Foul papers, 198
Foxe, John, 5, 154, *174–78, 315*
France, 276, 308
Francis II, king of France, 312
French language
    English-language borrowings from, 40
    Shakespeare's knowledge of, 147–48, 157
Fringe, 371–72
Frith, Mary, 256
Frye, Northrop, 85

Gade, Svend, 376
Gainsborough, Thomas, 359
Galen, 254
Gallery, of playhouse, 117, *133 (illus.), 134
    (illus.)*
Games, 231, *248–50*
Garnet, Father Robert, 317, 318
Garnier, Robert, 160, *187–89*, 257
Garrick, David, 357, 358–59, 368, 376, *383
    (illus.)*
Gatherers, 109, 122
Gender. *See also* Men; Women
    sexual aspects of roles and, 113–14
Geneva Bible, 4, 154, *164–69*, 261
Gentry, 274
Gielgud, John, 357, 369, 379
Gli Hecatommithi (Cinthio), 152, *169–70*
Globe Playhouse, 2, 18, 115, 116, 118, 119n2,
    120, 225
    architectural remains of, 114–15
    conjectural drawing of, 115, *134 (illus.)*
    erection of, 19
    in Hollar's *Long View of London, 136
    (illus.),* 137
    re-creation of, 115, 372–73, 377
    Shakespeare as a shareholder in, 19, 122
    size of, 119
    the Theatre and, 116
Golden Ass, The (Apuleius), 151
Golding, Arthur, 148, 190. *See also* Ovid
Goodman, Henry, 371
Gorboduc (Sackville and Norton), 90
Gorgeous Gallery of Gallant Inventions, A
    (miscellany), 158
Gosson, Stephen, 158, 325, 363
Gouge, William, 5, 261, *290–91*
Gower, John, 153

Granville Barker, Harley, 353, 367–68, 369,
    374, 390
Great Chain of Being, 319–20, 324
Greek literature
    as source for Shakespeare, 147–49, 151
    tragedy and, 85, 88–90
Greenblatt, Stephen, 27, 93, 324
Greene, Richard, *22*
Greene, Robert, 15, 152
Greene, Thomas, 22
Greenwich Palace, 18
Greg, W. W., 203
Gregory XIII, Pope, 316
Gresham, Sir Thomas, 221, 306
Griffith, D. W., 376
Guarini, Giovanni Battista, 107
Guilds, 222
Guinness, Alec, 372
Gunpowder Plot, 20, 26, 87, 296, 317–18
Gurr, Andrew, 115, 117, 118, 122, 123
Guthrie, Tyrone, 369, 372, 373
Guy, John, 316
Gwynne, Nell, 355

Hakluyt, Richard, 156
Hall, Edward, 4, 6, 150–51, 153–54, *163–64*
Hall, John, 23, 34
Hall, Peter, 369–70, 371
Hall, Susanna. *See* Shakespeare, Susanna
Hall (indoor) theaters, 115, 355
Halliday, F. E., 13, 147
Halliwell, Stephen, 89
Hamartia, 88, 90,
Hamlet, Prince of Denmark, 19, 80, 98, 123,
    232, 320, 325
    differences in quarto versions of, 201–02,
    204, 206, 208, 210, *216, 217*
    film versions of, 378, 379
    Ghost in, 41, 116
    language in, 41, 42, 44, 45, 49, 53, 78
    modern productions of, 2, 358, 361, 364,
    367, 368, 371, 374, 380, 381, *391 (illus.),
    392 (illus.),* 400
    sources for, 158, 162
    staging of, 112–13, 116, 117
    textual differences in modern editions of,
    194
    as tragedy, 85, 87, 88
Hampton Court Conference, 318
Handfasts, 272

Hands, Terry, 370
Harbage, Alfred, 77, 208
Harington, Sir John, 308, 311, 313, *333–34*
Harrison, William, 4, 220, 222, 231, 232, *237–38*, 248, *250–52*
Hathaway, Anne. *See* Shakespeare, Anne
Hazlitt, William, 360, *393–95*
Heavens, 116, 117, *134 (illus.)*
Hell, 116, 117, *134 (illus.)*
Heminges, John, 24, 33, 122, *140–41*, 204
Henley Street, Stratford-upon-Avon (Shakespeare's birthplace), 11, 13, 22, *29 (illus.)*, *31 (map)*, 265, 382
Henry III, king of France, 313
Henry IV, king of England, *185–86*
Henry IV, Part 1, 91, 150, 196, 219, 220, 223, 312, *312*, 370
    Falstaff in, 46–47, 91–93
    inn scene in, 219–20
    language in, 46, 49, 78
    sources for, 150, 151, 159, 185
Henry IV, Part 2, 78, 196, 226, 312, 319, 370
    sources for, 151
    tragic elements in, 91, 92–93
Henry V, 39, 196, 370
    language in, 45, 78
    film versions of, 377, 378, *400 (illus.)*
    sources for, 151, 162
    staging of, 110
    tragic elements in, 91, 92
Henry V (film), 110, *400 (illus.)*
Henry VI, Part 1, 77, 150, 196
Henry VI, Part 2, 77, 150, 196, 375
Henry VI, Part 3, 15, 77, 150, 196, *218*, 334
Henry VII, king of England, 55, 91, 150, 303
Henry VIII, king of England, 13, 124, 163, 259, 307, 321
    break with Rome by, 174, 225, 315
    power of state under, 271, 303
Henry VIII, 21, 78, 80, 115, 134, 205, 212
Henslowe, Philip, 5, 120–21, 126, 235
    Diary of, 116, 121, *137–39*
    inventory of theatrical costumes owned by, 112, *129–31*
    Rose Playhouse and, 133
Heptameron of Civil Discourses, An (Whetstone), 267, *292–93*
Herbert, Mary Sidney, countess of Pembroke, 160, *187–89*, 257
Heywood, Thomas, 112, *141–42*

Hinman, Charlton, 203
Hirst, Derek, 275
Historia Animalium (Aristotle), *278*
Historicity of texts, 93
History plays, 80, 90–94
Histriomastix (Prynne), 112, 363
Hoby, Sir Thomas, 158, 73
Hodges, C. Walter, 115, *134 (illus.)*
Holbein, Hans, 308
Holinshed, Raphael, 4, 6, 146, 149–50, 152, 154, 158–59, 162, *185–86*, 237, 370
Hollar, Wenceslas, 116, *136–39*
Holm, Ian, 371
Holy Trinity Church, Stratford-upon-Avon, 13, 24, 29
Homer, 158
Homily against Disobedience and Willful Rebellion, An, 319, *345–49*
Homily of the State of Matrimony, An, 260, *285–90*
Homonyms, 45
Homosexuality
    Dark Lady mystery in Shakespeare's sonnets and, 16, 273, 277
    Elizabethan society and, 272–73, *298–99*
    James and, 268, 307
    laws and, 272–73, *296–98*
Hooker, Richard, 317, 323, *349–51*
Hopkins, Anthony, 371, 381
Hopkins, Arthur, 392
Horace, 32, 148
Hoskyns, John, 43
Housekeepers of theaters, 122
House of Commons, 304, 305
House of Lords, 304
Housewives, 230, *246–47*
Housing, 223, *243–45*, 270–71
Howard, Alan, 376
Howard, Leslie, 377
Humanism, 62, 63, 248, 254, 256, 262
Humours, 254–55, *279*
Hundred Merry Tales, A (miscellany), 158
Hunsdon, Lord. *See* Carey, Henry
Hunt, Leigh, 360
Hussey, Olivia, 377
Hut, 117, *134 (illus.)*
Hytner, Nicholas, 375

Iambic pentameter, 47, 51–53
Illegitimate children, 257, 263, 271

Importance of Being Earnest, The (Wilde),
    151
Ingram, William, 234, 235
Inheritance, 263–65, 266, *292*
Inns, *219–20*, *237–38*, *271*, *295–96*
Inns of Court, London, 118, 221, 223, 354
Institutes (Coke), 272, *296–98*
Irving, Henry, 357, 360, 363, 364, 367, 369,
    374, 387, 393
Italian language, Shakespeare's knowledge
    of, 147–48, 164
Italy, 311, 334

Jackson, Barry, 368, 369
Jacobi, Derek, 380
Jacobs, Sally, 375
Jaggard, Isaac, 204
James I, king of England, 221, 258, 305,
    332–33
    ballads about, 155
    Basilikon Doron, 311, *336–39*
    Catholics and, 317, *343–47*
    councillors to, 307
    court life of, 307, 308, 311, *333–34*
    Elizabeth's succession and, 314, *331–32*
    Gunpowder Plot and, 317–18
    homosexuality of, 272, 307, *332–33*
    judicial system and, 308, 321
    license for the King's Men from, 17, *33*, 311
    Macbeth and background of, 20, 87
    as a monarch, 308, 311–12
    politics and, 303, 304, 306
    portrait of, *310 (illus.)*
    Puritans and, 318
    support for productions by, 20, 125,
        140–41, 311–12, 324
    regulation of playhouses and, 124
    on the role of monarchy, 5, 304, *328–31*,
        336–39
James, Henry, 361
Jardine, Lisa, 114*n*1
Jerome, St., 258
Jew of Malta, The (Marlowe), 137
Jews, 277
John, king of England, 304
Johnson, Samuel, 45, 357, 358
Jointure, 266
Jones, Ernest, 378
Jones, Inigo, 125, 312, 356

Jones, Robert Edmond, 367, *391 (illus.)*
Jonson, Ben, 22, 26, 34, 43, 121, 123, 145, 146,
    184, 221, 356
    The Alchemist, 234, 325
    Bartholomew Fair, 228, 256
    Eastward Ho!, 125
    Every Man in his Humour, 19, 156, 223
    First Folio verses of, 24, 147, 148
    masques and, 125, 312, 356
    "On My First Son," 270, *295*
    on Shakespeare's knowledge of Latin
        and Greek, 147–48
    Sejanus, 19, 156
    Workes (1616 Folio), 24
Journey through England and Scotland
    (Wedel), 224, *241–42*
Judge, Ian, 114
Judicial system
    complaints seen in, 275
    crime and criminals in, 320–21
    Elizabeth and, 307
    James and, 308
    marriage regulations and, 272
Julius Caesar, 19, 87, 123, 197, 382
    film versions of, 376
    language in, 48, 52–53, 78
    modern productions of, 353, 362, 365, *389
        (illus.)*
    sources for, 150, 159, 164

Kahn, Michael, 372
Kean, Charles, 360, 362, 364, 365, 366, 395,
    396 (illus.)
Kean, Edmund, 357, 360, 361, 364, 365, 374,
    388
Keats, John, 162, 360
Kemble, Charles, 360
Kemble, Fanny, 360
Kemble, John Philip, 359, 360
Kemp, Will, 122
Kenyon, J. P., 305, 311
Kestleman, Sara, 375
King and No King, A (Beaumont and
    Fletcher), 94
King Johan (Bale), 90
King John, 78, 362, 375, 376
King Lear, 20, 80, 96, 275, 277, 315
    film version of, 379
    language in, 39, 78

primogeniture theme in, 263
printing of, 201, *215*
modern productions of, 359, 371, 374, *383
    (illus.)*, *384–85*
sources for, 152, 158, 161, 162, 185
textual alterations of, 357
textual differences in editions of, 28, 197,
    202–03, 210
as tragedy, 86–87
King Leir (chronicle play), 152
King's Men, 17, 21, 87, 98, 121, 354. *See also*
    Lord Chamberlain's Men
  plays owned by, 196, 197, 202, 204
  Shakespeare as a shareholder with, 156
  Shakespeare's writing of plays for, 17, 18,
    20, 21–22, 23, 26, 107
  support from James for, 17, *33, 140–41,*
    311
  theaters used by, 116, 118
King's New School, Stratford-upon-Avon,
    42, 148
Kittredge, George Lyman, 208, 209
Komisarjevsky, Theodore, 369
Kott, Jan, 374
Kozintsev, Grigori, 377, 379
Kurosawa, Akira, 379
Kyd, Thomas, 79, 123, 137, 156

Laborers, 227, 274
"L'Allegro" (Milton), 145
Lambarde, William, 94, *107*
Land ownership
  enclosure and, 230, *245–46*
  families and, 253
  inheritance and, 263–64
  marriage and, 265–66, 272
  rural life and, 228–30
Lange, Jessica, 381, *405 (illus.)*
Language, 36–78
  blank verse and, 51–53
  foundations of, 40
  homonym in, 45
  homosexuality and, 272, 273
  imaginative associations of, 37
  impetus for changes in, 39
  Lever on, *66–68*
  older forms of words in, 38–42
  proportion of poetry and prose in Shake-
    speare's plays, *77–78*

prose and, 47–49
Puttenham on, *68–73*
rhetoric and, 42–44, *60–62*
rhyme and, 50–53
Shakespeare's vocabulary and, 40
as theme, 55–57
wordplay in, 44–47, *73–76*
Lanyer, Aemilia, 257, *281–83*
la Salle, Jean Baptiste de, *295–96*
Laslett, Peter, 268
Latimer, Hugh, 174, *175–78,* 315
Latin language
  English language borrowings from, 40
  Shakespeare's knowledge of, 14, 26, 41,
    43, 146, 147, 148
  teaching of, *64–66*
Laws and legislation, 222
  class and, 275
  clothing regulation with, 233
  Great Chain of Being doctrine and,
    324
  homosexuality and, 272–73, *296–98*
  inheritance and, 263–65, *292*
  marriage contracts and, 271–72
  meatless days enforced by, 222, 227
  performances during the Civil Wars and,
    354
  religious issues and, 316
Leary, Penn, 26
Lee, Sydney, 155
Leicester, earl of. *See* Dudley, Robert
Leigh, Vivien, 374
Lemnius, Levinus, 254–55
Lennox, Charlotte, 145
Lesbians, 273
Lever, Ralph, 40, *66–68*
Lewalski, Barbara, 258
Lewis, C. S., 44, 46
"Liberties" districts, London, 115, 124, 224,
    324
Lincoln, countess of. *See* Clinton, Eliza-
    beth
Literary criticism
  concepts of authorship and, 26–28, 206
  cultural factors and, 2
  feminist, 2, 84, 88
  as influence on Shakespeare, 158
  on political conflicts in the plays, 324
  Shakespeare's works and, 2–3

Lives of the Noble Grecians and Romans (Plutarch), 146, 148–49, 149, 158, 159–60, 162, *186–87*
Livy, 148
Lodge, Thomas, 152
Loncraine, Richard, 381
London, 26, 221–24, 275
  "Agas" map of, 34, *35 (map)*
  bearbaiting in, 224, *241–42*
  brothels in, 224, *242–43*
  clothing fashions in, 4
  commercial life, 221–24, 233, 256
  daily life in, 231
  description of, 221–24, *240–41*
  Hollar's engraving of, 116, *136 (illus.)*, 137
  inns in, 219–20
  Jews in, 277
  location of playhouses in, 115–16, 127, *128 (map)*
  merchants and tradesmen in, 222, *239–40*
  plague in, 15, 21, *33*, 123–24, 126, 143
  Shakespeare's first decade in, 15–19
  Shakespeare's mature years in, 19–22
  Shakespeare's residences in, 18, 19, 34, *35 (map)*
  streets of, *222, 223, 240–41*
  suburbs of, 224–25
  supervision of theaters in, 115
  theatrical companies in, 120–24
  travel within and beyond, 221–22, 224, *241*
London Bridge, 222, 224, 241
Long View of London (Hollar), 116, *136 (illus.)*, 137
Lope de Vega (Felix Lope de Vega Carpio), 202
Lord Admiral's Men, 120, 123, 196, 235
  inventory of theatrical costumes of, 7, 112, *129–31*
  log of plays performed by, 121, *137–39*
  tours to the provinces by, *143–44*
Lord Chamberlain's Men, 19, 33, 121, 122, 361. *See also* King's Men
  performance of *Richard II* by, 94, 124–25, *140*
  royal support for, 33, 125
  Shakespeare as a shareholder with, 109
  Shakespeare's plays performed by, 312, 314
  theaters used by, 109, 116

Lord Pembroke's Men, 120
Lords' rooms, 117, 118, *134 (illus.)*
Lord Strange's Men, 17, 120
Lord Worcester's Men, 112, 120
Love, 265, 267–68
"Lover's Complaint, A," 16–17
Love's Labor's Lost, 109, 325
  authorship disputed, 25
  as a comedy, 83
  film version of, 378, 379
  language in, 44, 55, 77
  modern productions of, 374
  printing of, 18, 196
Love's Labor's Won, 32n1
Lucy, Sir Thomas, 12
Luhrmann, Baz, 381
Lyly, John, 148, 156
Lyly, William, 148

McArdell, Jo, *383 (illus.)*
Macaulay, Thomas Babington, 108
Macbeth, 19, 80, 96, 197, 205, 318
  authorship of, 26
  background of James and, 20
  female roles in, 113, *386–87 (illus.)*
  film versions of, *376*, *379*
  language in, 37, 46–47, 58, 78
  modern productions of, 356, 359–60, 361, 365, 374, 381, *386–87 (illus.)*
  sources for, 158, 185
  television versions of, 379, 380
  as tragedy, 85–86, 87–88, 89
McCarthy, Cormac, 97
McCarthy, Lillah, 367, 368, *390 (illus.)*
Machiavelli, Niccolò, 311, *334–36*
McKellen, Ian, 380, 381
McKeon, Richard, 101
McKerrow, R. B., 203
Macready, William Charles, 357, 360, 364, 365
Magna Carta, 304
Mahood, M. M., 46
Malone, Edmond, 121
Malory, Sir Thomas, 95
"Manner of Her Will, and What She Left to London, The" (Whitney), 222, *240–41*
Markets, 227, 228
Markham, Gervase, 228, *243–45*

Marlowe, Christopher, 24, 26, 32, 90, 143, 146, 156, 273, 307
  Doctor Faustus, 116, 120
  Edward II, 273
  The Jew of Malta, 137
  Tamburlaine the Great, 120, *182–83*
Marriage, 265–68
  age of partners in, 268
  betrothal and arrangement of, 266–67, 271, *292–93*
  children outside, 271, 272
  conjugal oneness in, 260–61
  contracts in, 271–72
  Gouge's treatise on, *290–91*
  homily on, *285–90*
  inheritance of property and, 265–66, 272
  principle of mutuality (companionate marriage) in, 262
  romantic love in, 265, 267–68
  social order and, 260–61
Marston, John, 125
Marxist criticism, 324
Mary (Mary Stuart), Queen of Scots, 306, 307, 308, 312–13, 319, 321, 343
Mary I (Mary Tudor), queen of England, 174, 303, 307, 308, 311, 315, 316
Masque of Blackness, The (Jonson), 125
Masque of Queens, The (Jonson), 125, 312
Masques, 125–26, 184, 312, 356
Massinger, Philip, 121
Master of the Revels, 124
Mather, Increase, 363
Maugham, Somerset, 79
Measure for Measure, 20, 77, 80, 272, 320
  as comedy, 85
  critics on, 324
  modern productions of, 361, 367, 380
  sources for, 152
  textual problems in, 208–09
Men
  clothing for, 232
  homosexuality and, 272–73, *298–99*
  inheritance and, 263–65
  opportunities for economic advancement of, 275–76
  patriarchy and, 259–63
  social class and, 274
  women and superiority of, 254–55
Menaechmi (Plautus), 149

Mendes, Sam, 375
Merchant of Venice, The, 77, 97, 277
  as comedy, 85
  female roles in, 113
  modern productions of, 361, 369, 371, 374, 380, 400
  printing of, 196
Merchants, 222–23, 231, 264
Meres, Francis, 16, 18, *32–33*
Merry Wives of Windsor, The, 77, 125, 158, 161, 202, 292
Metamorphoses (Ovid), 32, 146, 149, 158, 160–62, *190–93*
Michaelmas Term (Middleton), 234
Middle Ages, 221, 255, 258, 263, 319
Middle class, 236, 257, 267
Middleton, Thomas, 80, 121, 221, 234, 256, 264–65
Midsummer Night's Dream, A, 26, 80, 86, 226, 267, 292, 325
  as comedy, 81, 83–84
  film versions of, 377
  historical and social background for, 27–28
  language in, 38, 48, 51, 52, 53–54, 77
  modern productions of, 355, 362, 368, 374, *375, 393–95, 396–97 (illus.), 398–99*
  printing of, 196, 205
  Queen Elizabeth and, 27–28
  roles in, 113, 122
  sources for, 160
  textual differences in editions of, 196, 196, 207
  theatrical companies and productions of, 17
Miles gloriosus, 91
Miller, Jonathan, 371, 380, 400
Milton, John, 19, 145, 262
Mirror for Magistrates, A, 150
Miscellanies, as source material, 157–58
Mitchell, Katie, 375–76
Modern dress productions, 368–69
Modjeska, Helena, 364
Moiseiwitsch, Tanya, 373
Monarchy, 304–06
  homily on obedience to, *345–49*
  James I on, 5, 304, *328–31, 336–39*
  Smith on authority of, *326–27*
Money, 8, 234–35

Montaigne, Michel de, *63–64*, 156–57, 160, 273
Montemayor, Jorge de, 152
Montrose, Louis Adrian, 27, 308
Moore, John, 230, *245–46*
More, Sir Thomas, 150, 154, 308
Morte d'Arthur (Malory), 95
Mountjoy, Christopher, house of, 18, 34, *223*
Much Ado about Nothing, 20, 80, 86, 97, 196, 263, 266, 268, 270
  as comedy, 82, 85
  film version of, 378
  language in, 44–45, 57–58, 77
  modern productions of, 364, 367
  roles in, 113, 122
Mulcaster, Richard, 231, *248–50*
Mullaney, Steven, 225
Muriel, Christopher, 343, *344–45*
Murrell, John, 234, *252*
Musophilus (Daniel), *62–63*
Mystery cycles, as source material, 156
Mythology, as source material, 160–62, *190–93*

Nashe, Thomas, 15, 225, *242–43*, 256
National Theatre, London, 370–71, 375, 380, 381, 401
Natural and Artificial Directions for Health (Vaughan), 255, *279*
Natural law, 349
Neale, Sir John, 308, 313, 320–21, 328
Negroes, in Elizabethan society, 276, 277, *302*
Nelson, Adelaide, 364
Nest of Ninnies (Armin), 158
Netherlands, 306, 308, 321
New criticism, 2
New historicism, 93, 324
New Place residence, Stratford-upon-Avon, 18, 19, 22, 23, *31 (map)*, 235
New Testament, 154
  Erasmus's foreword to, *59–60*
New York Shakespeare Festival, 372
Noble, Adrian, 370, 378
Norman Conquest, 276
North, Sir Thomas, 149, 158, 159, 160. *See also* Plutarch
Northern Rebellion, 319, 320, 345
Norton, Thomas, 90

Nunn, Trevor, 370, 371, 373, 375, 380, 387
Nursing, of infants, 269–70, *293–94*

Odyssey (Homer), 95–96
Of Domestical Duties: Eight Treatises (Gouge), 5, *290–91*
Of Good Manners and Proper Behavior (Broë), *295*
"Of the Cannibals" (Montaigne), 157
Of the Laws of Ecclesiastical Polity (Hooker), 317, 323, *349–51*
"Of the Vanity of Words" (Montaigne), *63–64*
Old Testament, 154, 319
Olivier, Laurence, 110, 357, 369, 370–71, 374, 376, 377–78, *400 (illus.)*, 401
"On Friendship" (Montaigne), 273
Onions, C. T., 155
"On My First Son" (Jonson), 270, *295*
Order for the Burial of the Dead, The (*The Book of Common Prayer*), *171–74*
Orrell, John, 133
Orwell, George, 41
Othello, the Moor of Venice, 20, 80, 96, 117, 277, 292
  critical response to, 97–98, *108*
  film versions of, 378, 379, 400
  language in, 49, 57, 58, 78
  modern productions of, 364, 365, 371, 380, *388 (illus.)*
  sources for, 152, 161, 164, 169
  as tragedy, 85, 88
Ovid, 32, 43, 148
  Golding's translation of, 148, *190–93*
  Metamorphoses, 32, 146, 149, 158, 160–62, *190–93*
Oxford, 174, 315
Oxford, earl of. *See* deVere, Edward

Palladis Tamia: Wit's Treasury (Meres), 16, 18, *32–33*
Pamphilia to Amphilanthus (Wroth), 157, *184–85*
Pamphlets, as source material, 154, 158
Pandosto, or The Triumph of Time (Greene), *152–53*
Papp, Joseph, 372
Paradox
  comedy and, 82–83
  tragedy and, 86, 88

Parliament, 223, 305
  closing of theaters by, 17
  Elizabeth and, 303, 312, 315
  James and, 5, 304, 311
  role of, 305
  Smith on authority of, *326–27*
  sumptuary laws and, 233, 275
Parma, duke of, 313
Paster, Gail Kern, 269
Pastor Fido, Il (Guarini), 107
Patriarcha, or The Natural Power of Kings
      (Filmer), 6, 259, *283–85*
Patriarchy, 259–63
  class and, 275
  family and, 259–61
  marriage and, 261
Paul, St., 255, 260, 261
Paul's Boys, 113
Pavier, Thomas, 204
Peacham, Henry, 112, *128 (illus.)*
Peele, George, 156
Pembroke's Men, 17
Pentateuch, 259
Performance
  actors' shaping of roles in, 357–63
  American productions and, 363–66
  festivals and, 359, 360, 371
  film version of plays and, 110, 314, 374,
      376–82
  later alteration of texts for, 355–56, 362–63
  major changes in practice of, 354–57
  modern dress, 368–69
  movement indoors, 355
  role of director in, 373–75
  scenery used in, 355
  suspension of, for Civil Wars, 354
  television productions of plays, 379–80
  touring companies and, 365–66
  twentieth-century technical innovations
      and, 366–76
Pericles
  brothel scenes in, 256
  omission from Folio, 205, 212
  as romance, 94
Petrarch, 16
Phelps, Samuel, 360
Philaster (Beaumont and Fletcher), 94
Philip II, king of Spain, 306, 315
Phillips, Augustine, 33, 122, 125, *140*
Philosophy, 157, 256

Pickford, Mary, 376, 378
Pit, in theater, 119
Pius V, Pope, 316
Plague, outbreaks of, 15, 21, *33 (illus.)*,
      123–24, 126, 143
Plato, 89
Platter, Thomas, 221, 224, *241*
Plautus, 18, 32, 83, 148, 149
Players. *See* Actors *and specific companies*
Playhouses, 114–20. *See also specific theaters*
  admission charges to, 109, 235
  architectural remains of, 114–15
  audience makeup in, 118–20
  audience space in, 118–19
  conventions and performance practices
      common to, 110–11
  criticism of attendance at, 235, 250, 325,
      351–52
  discovery space in, 117
  gallery in, 117
  gatherers at, 109, 122
  heavens in, 116
  hut in, 117
  indoor or hall, 115–19
  location of, 115–16, *127 (map)*, 128, 225, 324
  lords' rooms in, 118
  modern productions and, 361–62
  outdoor or amphitheater, 114–20
  pit in, 119
  plague and closing of, 15, 16, 21, 123–24,
      126, 143
  regulation of, 17, 120, 123, 124, 125, 324–25
  stage in, 110, 116–17, 361–62
  tarras in, 117
  tiring-house in, 109
Plays
  actors in, 112–14
  audiences for, 118–20
  conventions and performance practices
      common to, 110–11
  costumes used in, 111–12, *129–31,* 361
  criticism of attending, 235
  female roles in, 113
  hypothetical 1595 production of, 109–14
  meaning of "publication" for, 196
  passage of time marked in, 111
  politics and production of, 124–25
  presentational style of performance in,
      123
  printing process for, 198–201

Plays *(cont'd)*
  scene in, 110
  sexual aspects of roles in, 113–14
  women as authors of, *100–01*, 257
Plays Confuted in Five Actions (Gosson),
    158, 325, 363
Plutarch, 146, 147, 148–49, 158, 159–60, 162,
    186–87, 277
Poel, William, 366–67, 368
Poetics (Aristotle), 88, 89, *101–05*
Poetry, 47–55, *77–78. See also* Blank verse
  lyric, 17, 157
  women as authors of, 157, *184–85*, 256, 257,
    279–83
Politics
  Great Chain of Being doctrine and,
    319–20, 324
  homily on obedience and, *345–49*
  Machiavelli's *The Prince* and, 311, *334–36*
  Stuart lineage in *Macbeth* and, 20, 87
  productions of theatrical companies and,
    55, 94, 107, 124, 140
Polydore Vergil, 150
Poor Laws, 304
Pope, Alexander, 197
Portion (dowry), 266
Positions . . . for the Training Up of Children
    (Mulcaster), 231, *248–50*
Potter, Lois, 202
Preston, Thomas, 54
Primogeniture, 263–65, 266, *292*
Prince, The (Machiavelli), 311, *334–36*
Principal Navigations, Voyages, and Discoveries of the English Nation (Hakluyt),
    156
Printing, 196, 198–201
  bad quartos and, 201, 202
  casting off copy in, 200–201
  copyists in, 198–99
  setting type for, 199–200
  sheets in, 199
  work of different compositors in, 203,
    218
Printing press, 39, 200, *214*
Prisons, 224
Privacy, and family life, 270–71
Privy Council
  Elizabeth and, 307
  regulation of theatrical companies by,
    120, 123, 124, 125

Problem plays, 80
Property. *See* Land ownership
Prose, 47–49, *77–78*
Protestantism, 264, 306, 317, 343
  companionate marriage principle and,
    262
  education and, 256
  Elizabethan Settlement and, 315–17
  opposition to plays by, 325
  subordination of women in, 255
Prothero, R. E., 229
Prynne, William, 112, 363
Puns. *See* Wordplay
Purchas, Samuel, 156
Puritans, 316–17, 319, 343
  Church of England and, 313, *340–43*, 349
  Elizabeth and, 314
  fashion and, 232
  homosexuality and, 273
  James and, 318
  marriage and, 262
  opposition to playhouses by, 124, 325,
    351–52
  use of term, 316
Puttenham, George, 43, *68–73*, 158

Quarto texts, 28, 197, 204
  bad quartos and, 201, 202
  Hamlet and, 201–02, 204, 208, *216*
  King Lear and, 202–03, *215*
  sheets in the printing process for,
    199–200
  Titus Andronicus and, 206–07
Quayle, Anthony, 380
Queen's Men, 17
Quin, James, 358
Quiney, Judith. *See* Shakespeare, Judith
Quiney, Thomas, 23
Quintilian, 43

Rabkin, Norman, 92
Racism, 277
Ran (film), 379
Rape of Lucrece, The, 15, 148, 149, 160, 196,
    212
Recreation, 231, *248–50*
Red Bull Playhouse, 116, 118
Red Lion Playhouse, 115, 121
Reformation, 318
Register of the Stationers' Company, 155

Rehan, Ada, 364
Reinhardt, Max, 368, 374, 377
Religious doctrine. *See also* Catholicism;
    Church of England; Protestantism
    criticism of the theatergoing and, 235
    education of women and, 256, 258
    Great Chain of Being doctrine and,
        319–20, 324
    homosexuality and, 273, *296–98*
    ideology of order and, 318–21
    marriage regulations and, 271–72
    meatless days in, 222, 227
    patriarchy and, 259–60
    subordination of women in, 255
Religious documents as source material,
    154, 158
Renaissance (as term), 7
Renaissance Theatre Company, 372
Revels, *333–34*
Revels Office, 124
Reynolds, Frederic, 393
Reynolds, Sir Joshua, 358, 360
Rhetoric, 42–44, *60–62*
Rhetorica ad Herennium (anonymous), 45
Rhyme, 50–53
Rhythm, 51–53
Ribner, Irving, 208
Richard I, king of England, 13
Richard II, 78, 85, 91, 156, 196, 305, 312, 321, 362
    authorship disputed, 25
    modern productions of, 371, 375, 380
    politics and production of, 94, *107,* 124–25
    sources for, 150, 151
    testimony about a performance of, *140*
    theatrical companies and productions of,
        17
Richard III, king of England, 150, 153, 163,
    303
Richard III, 28, 121, 156, 202, *218*
    authorship disputed, 25
    film versions of, 376, 378
    language in, 39, 46, 49, 53, 55–57, 77
    modern productions of, 358, 363, 366, 370,
        372, 374, 381
    political factors in production of, 55
    sources for, 150, 153
    title page of, 105, *106 (illus.)*
    as tragedy, 91
Richardson, Ralph, 369, 378, 401
Ridley, Nicholas, *174–78,* 315

Righter, Anne (Anne Barton), 96
Rive, Edmund, 214
Roaring Girl, The (Middleton and Dekker),
    256
Roberts, Jeanne Addison, 2
Rollo, Duke of Kent, 354
Roman Catholic Church. *See* Catholicism
Romance, 80, 94–97
    use of term, 80, 94–95
Roman literature
    comedy and, 82, 91
    Shakespeare's familiarity with, 14, 18, 32,
        146
    as source for Shakespeare, 147–49, 149,
        153, 160–62, *190–93*
    tragedy and, 85
Romantic love, 265, 267–68
Romeo and Juliet, 80, 267, 268, 269
    film versions of, 377, 378, 381
    hypothetical 1595 production of, 109–14,
        126
    language in, 39, 46, 78
    modern productions of, 369, 381
    printing of, 18, 196, 198
    roles in, 122
    sources for, 151–52
    staging of, 110, 117
    theatrical companies and productions of,
        17
    as tragedy, 84, 85
Rooney, Mickey, 377
Rosalynde (Lodge), 152
Rose Playhouse, 115, 116, 120, 225
    architectural remains of, 114, *132 (illus.)*
    conjectural drawing of, 114, *133 (illus.)*
    foundations of, 4
    size of, 114, 118
Rowe, Nicholas, 197
Royal Shakespeare Company (RSC),
    369–70, 371, 372, 375, 378
Rules of Decency and Christian Manners, The
    (la Salle), *295–96*
Rural life, 228–30
Russell, Lucy Harington, countess of Bed-
    ford, 257
Rylance, Mark, 373
Rymer, Thomas, 98, *108*

Sackville, Thomas, 90
St. Paul's Cathedral, London, 221–22

Salve Deus Rex Judaeorum (Lanyer), 257, 281–83
Sargent, John Singer, *387 (illus.)*
Scene, 110
Schiller, Leon, 368
Schoenbaum, Samuel, 3, 23, 112
Schoolmaster, The (Ascham), *64–66*
Scofield, Paul, 374
Sejanus (Jonson), 19, 156
Senden, Casper van, 276–77, 302
Seneca, 18, 32, 148, 149
Servants, 231, 233, 253, 271, 274
Sexual behavior
 brothels and, 224, *242–43*
 education of women and, 258
 marriage and, 271–72
Shadwell, Thomas, 356, 357
Shakespeare (*formerly* Hathaway), Anne (wife), 14, 18, 22, 23, 272
Shakespeare, Edmund (brother), 13, 265
Shakespeare, Gilbert (brother), 13, 22
Shakespeare, Hamnet (son), 14, 18, 20
Shakespeare, Joan (aunt), 265
Shakespeare, Joan (sister), 13, 22
Shakespeare, John (father), 11, 12–13, 14, 18, 20, 22, 29
Shakespeare (*later* Quiney), Judith (daughter), 14, 23, 34, 268
Shakespeare, Mary (mother), 12–13, 22, 29
Shakespeare, Richard (brother), 13, 22
Shakespeare (*later* Hall), Susanna (daughter), 23, 34, 268
Shakespeare, William: LIFE
 as an actor, 12, 15, 17, 18–19, 156
 baptismal record, 13, 29, *30*
 birth, 11, 12–13
 business activities, 18, 19, 21, 22, 234–35
 childhood house, 11, 13, *29 (illus.), 31 (map)*
 children, 14
 death, 13, 22, 23
 early years in Stratford-upon-Avon, 12–15
 education, 14, 24–26, 41, 42–43, 147, 148
 family coat of arms, 13, 18
 first decade in London, 15–19
 French and Italian languages known by, 147–48, 157, 164
 knowledge of Greek and Roman authors, 14, 18
 as landowner, 11, 18, 19, 22

London residences, 18, 19, 34, *35 (map)*
"Lost Years," 14
marriage, 14, 268, 272
mixture of fact and legend concerning, 11–12
poaching deer story, 12, 14
religious background, 13, 14
sexual proclivities, 16, 272, 273
as shareholder in companies, 19, 109, 122, 156
siblings, 13
social and economic advancement, 276
Stratford residences, 18, 22, 23, *31 (map)*, 235, 264, 265
tomb and stone inscription, 23
Ward's anecdote about death of, 22–23, *34*
will, 23
Shakespeare, William: PLAYS
adaptation of sources for plots of, 153
American productions of, 363–66
audiences, 20–21
authorship disputes, 24–26
contemporary popularity of, 381–82
cryptographic schemes, 26
Elizabeth and productions of, 17, 25, 26, 27, 28, 94, *107*, 125, 312, 324
female roles, 113
festivals of, 359, 369, 372
film versions of plays, 110, 314, 374, 376–82, *400 (illus.), 405 (illus.)*
later alterations of texts of, 355–57
later years, 21–22
literary criticism and, 2
modern productions, 2, 112, 114, 357–63
plays-within-plays, 325
plays written with Fletcher, 21, 22, 80, 94, 205
political authority portrayed in, 322–24
printing of, 18, 24, 196–97
productions by Elizabethan theatrical companies, 17–18
proportion of poetry and prose in plays, *77–78*
Puritans and, 325
representatives of Otherness in, 276–77
shift of direction to tragedies, 20
social order portrayed in, 276–77
sources for, 145–93
success of plays, 18, 20, 109, 381–82
television productions of plays, 379–80

textual authority issues affecting, 195–98
theatrical companies and, 33, 120
touring companies and, 365–66
writing of plays for Lord Chamberlain's–
King's Men, 17, 18, 19–22, 23, 26, 107
Shakespeare, William: SONNETS
Dark Lady mystery, 16, 257, 273, 277, 298
dating, 16–17
printing of, 15, 16–17, 196
reference in Meres to, 16, 18, 32–33
sources for, 183
style, 16
Shakespeare Memorial Theatre, Stratford-
upon-Avon, 369, 370, 373
Shakespeare-Oxford Society, 25
Shareholders in theatrical companies, 19,
109, 121–22
Shaw, Fiona, 375
Shaw, George Bernard, 361, 366, 371
Shearer, Norma, 377
Sheep and sheepshearing, 227, 230
Sheet, in printing, 199
Sher, Anthony, 374
Sheriden, Richard Brinsley, 358
Shirley, James, 121
Shoreditch district, London, 109, 223
Short View of Tragedy, A (Rymer), 98, 108
Shutter-and-wing system, 355
Siddons, Sarah (Mrs. Siddons), 354, 357,
359–60, 368, 386 (illus.)
Sidney, Sir Philip, 32, 43, 156, 157, 187, 256,
277, 308, 321
Arcadia, 152
Astrophil and Stella, 16, 157, 183–84
Defense of Poesy, 51, 82, 99–100, 158
Sinfield, Alan, 88
Sir Thomas More, 195
Skura, Meredith, 28
Slaves, 302
Sly, William, 33
Smith, Bruce, 272, 273
Smith, Maggie, 371, 380
Smith, Sir Thomas, 263, 292, 304, 326–27
Social life. See Society in early modern
England
Social order. See also Class; Patriarchy; State
Society in early modern England
Africans in, 276–77, 302
authorship disputes concerning Shake-
speare's plays and factors in, 24–26

bearbaiting in, 224, 241–42
brothels in, 224, 242–43, 256
class and social structure in, 273–77
clothing and fashion in, 4, 231–33, 236,
250–52
comedy and customs in, 83–84
country life in, 225–28, 235, 243–45
criticism and factors in, 2
daily routine in, 231
education of women in, 256–58
family life in, 269–73
festivals in, 227–28
food and eating habits in, 222, 227, 231,
248, 252
homosexuality in, 272–73, 298
isolation of England and, 276
London life in, 221–24
marriage and social order in, 260–61,
265–68, 285–90, 292–93
masques in, 125–26, 312
meatless days and, 222, 227
merchants and tradesmen in, 222–23,
239–40
opportunities for economic advancement
in, 275–76
patriarchy in, 259–63
primogeniture in, 263–65, 292
privacy in, 270–71
Shakespeare's representation of social
order in, 276–77
suburban life in, 224–25
superiority of men in, 255–56
travel in, 219–21, 237–38, 271, 295–96
value of currency used in, 8
Somerset, earl of. See Carr, Robert
Somerset House, London, 223
Songs and Sonnets (miscellany), 158
Sources for Shakespeare's plays, 145–93
accounts of the New World as, 155–56
ballads as, 154–55, 178–79
contemporary fictions as, 151–53
definition of source, 146
Greek and Roman classics as, 147–49
historians as, 149–51
major, 149–54
miscellanies as, 157–58
Montaigne's Essays as, 156–57
poetry as, 157
Southampton, third earl of. See Wriothesley, Henry

Southwark borough, London, 224, 225, 241–42, 256, 372
Southwell, Lady Anne, 257, 279–81
Spain, 276, 306, 312, 314, 315, 316, 321
Spanish Armada, 313, 321
Spanish Tragedy, The (Kyd), 79, 123, 137, 156
Speaight, Robert, 360, 375, 398–99
Spenser, Edmund, 32, 43, 95, 158
Sports, 231, 248–50
Spousal agreements, 271–72
Stage, of playhouse
    description of typical, 116–17
    discovery space in, 117
    as "Empty Space," 110
    modern changes to, 373–74
    in Rose Playhouse, 133 (illus.)
    spectators on, 119
    unit set and, 369
Stallybrass, Peter, 113n1
Stanislavsky, Konstantin, 98, 367
State
    absolute monarchy and, 304–06
    Elizabeth and, 303
    ideology of order and, 318–21
    James I on role of monarchy and, 5, 304, 328–31
    patriarchy and, 259–60
    Shakespeare's treatment of authority in, 322–24
Stationers' Register, 155
Stone, Lawrence, 264, 265–66, 270, 272, 274
Stoppard, Tom, 98
Stow, John, 15, 222, 224, 239–40
Strachey, Sir William, 6, 156, 180–82
Stratford, Ontario, Shakespeare festival, 372, 373
Stratford-upon-Avon
    Holy Trinity Church at, 13, 23–24, 29
    land owned by Shakespeare at, 11, 18, 19, 22
    layout of, 13, 31 (map)
    markets at, 228
    modern productions at, 114, 369, 370, 373, 375
    Shakespeare's birthplace at, 11, 13, 29 (illus.), 31 (map), 382
    Shakespeare's early years at, 12–15, 29
    Shakespeare's residences in, 18, 21, 23, 31 (map), 235, 264, 265
    Shakespeare's retirement to, 22–23

Street, Peter, 120–21
Stuart, Arbella, 258
Stubbes, Philip, 325, 351–52
Stubbs, John, 320–21
Suburbs, 224–25, 242–43
Suetonius, 148
Sumptuary laws, 233, 275
Survey of London (Stow), 222, 224, 239–40
Swan Playhouse, 4, 115, 116, 118
    de Witt's sketch of, 6, 116, 117, 135 (illus.)
    stage in, 117
Sweet Nosegay, A (Whitney), 239, 257
Swetnam, Joseph, 258

Tamburlaine the Great (Marlowe), 120, 182–83
Taming of the Shrew, The, 84, 266
    film versions of, 376, 378
    language in, 39, 44, 77
    modern performances of, 356
    sources for, 161
Target for Tillage, A (Moore), 230, 245–46
Tarras, 117
Tate, Nahum, 357, 383–85
Taxation, 304, 305
Taylor, Elizabeth, 378
Taylor, Gary, 80, 208, 209
Taylor, John, 259
Taylor, Sam, 376
Taymor, Julie, 381, 405
Tears of an Affectionate Shepherd Sick for Love, The (Barnfield), 273, 298–99
Television productions of plays, 379–80
Tempest, The, 21, 78, 80, 126, 212, 235, 276, 312
    authorship of, 26
    modern productions of, 363, 381
    printing of, 197, 205
    as romance, 94, 95, 97
    sources for, 156, 158, 180
    staging of, 117
    textual alterations of, 356–57
Terence, 148
Terry, Ellen, 357, 360, 361, 362, 367, 369, 374, 387 (illus.)
Testimony Against Several Prophane and Superstitious Customs Now Practised by Some in New-England (Mather), 363
Textual scholarship
    concepts of authorship and, 27–28, 206
    idea of textual instability in, 206–09

lack of ideal original, 204
meaning of "publication" and, 195–96
printing process and, 198–201
reprinting plays and problems in, 203–04
textual authority issues affecting, 195–98
Textuality of history, 93
Thalberg, Irving, 377
Thames River, 221, 224, *241*
Theater buildings. *See* Playhouses *and specific theaters*
Theatre, the (playhouse), 115, 116, 120, 121, 223
  Globe Playhouse and, 116
  hypothetical 1595 production at, 109–14
Theatrical companies, 120–23. *See also specific companies*
  average size of, 122
  collaborative nature of playwriting for, 28
  conventions and performance practices common to, 110–11
  costumes used by, 111–12
  court performances and, 20, 121, 333
  fees paid to playwrights by, 121
  inventory of costumes used by, 7
  log of plays performed by, 121, *137–39*
  playwrights and ownership of plays by, 18
  politics and, 124–25
  printing of Shakespeare's plays by, 18, 197
  Privy Council regulation of, 120, 123, 124, 125
  repertory system and, 123
  royal support for, 125
  Shakespeare's work as actor in, 15–16, 17, 18–19
  Shakespeare's writing of plays for, 17, 18, 19–22, 23, 26, 107
  shareholders (housekeepers) in, 19, 109, 121–22, 156
  tours to the provinces by, 126, *143–44*
Theobald, Lewis, 208, 209
Third Part of the Institutes of the Laws of England, The (Coke), 272, *296–98*
Thirty-nine Articles, 317
Throne of Blood (film), 379
Thyestes (Seneca), 149
Tilbury speech (Elizabeth I), 313, *328*
Tillyard, E. M. W., 93, 320, 323–24
Tilney, Edmund, 260, 261–62
Timon of Athens, 78, 80, 87, 159, 356

Tiring-house, 109, 117, *134 (illus.)*
Titus (film), 381, *405 (illus.)*
Titus Andronicus, 78, 80, 277
  film version of, 381, *405 (illus.)*
  modern productions of, 365, 374, 375
  publication of, 18, 196
  sketch for production of, 112, *128 (illus.)*
  sources for, 149
  textual instability in, 206–09
  title page of, *211*
Tottel's Miscellany, 158
Tower of London, 221, 313
Trade, 228, 230, 233–34
Tradesmen, 222, *238–39*, 270
Tragedy, 80, 85–90, 98
  Aristotle's theory of, 86, *101–05*
  audiences and, 90
  catharsis and, 88, 90
  paradox and, 86, 88
  Shakespeare's familiarity with, 149
  Sidney on, *99–100*
  tragic flaw and, 88
  use of term, 85, 87
Tragedy of Antonie (Garnier), 160, *187–89*, 257
Tragedy of Mariam, Fair Queen of Jewry, The (Cary), 79, *100–01*, 257
Tragical History of Romeus and Juliet, The (Brooke), 151–52
Tragic flaw, 88
Tragicomedy, 80
Trapdoor, 116, 117, *134 (illus.)*
Traub, Valerie, 273
Travel
  inns and, 219–20, *237–38*, 271, *295–96*
  perils involved in, 220
  on the Thames, 221, 224, *241*
  within and beyond London, 221–22, 224
Travels in England (Platter), *241*
Tree, Sir Herbert Beerbohm, 360, 361, 362, 363, 364, 369, 376
Troilus and Cressida, 20, 78, 80, 204–05, 212, 322–23, 325
Trojan War, 322–23
Troublesome Reign of John, King of England, The, 156
"True Form and Shape of a Monstrous Child, The" (ballad), *178–79*

True Reportory of the Wreck and Redemption of Sir Thomas Gates . . . , A (Strachey), 156, *180–82*
Twelfth Night, 97, 98, 255, 270, 273, 325
  actors and actresses in, 355
  as comedy, 83
  film versions of, 376
  language in, 47, 48, 53, 58
  modern productions of, 353, 367, 374, 380, 390 *(illus.)*
  printing of, 197, 205
  sexual aspects of roles in, 114
  sources for, 149, 155, 164
  staging of, 117
Two Gentlemen of Verona, The, 77, 205, 152
Two Noble Kinsmen, The, 21, 205, 212, 94
Tynan, Kenneth, 369, *401–04*
Tyrell, James, *163–64*

Ulysses, 322–23, 325
Underhill, William, 235
Union of the Two Noble and Illustre Families of Lancaster and York, The (Hall), 150–51, *163–64*
Unit set, 369
Urkowitz, Steven, 202

Vagabonds and vagrants, 274, *301–02*
van Senden, Casper, 276–77, 302
Vaughan, William, 255, *279*
Venus and Adonis, 15, 160, 196, 212
Vertues Commonwealth: or The High-way to Honour (Crosse), 235
Victoria, queen of England, 273
Villages, 228, 229, 230
Villiers, George, duke of Buckingham, 307, *332–33*
Virgil, 52, 148

Wages, 227, 232, 234–35
Walsingham, Francis, 306–07, 312
Wanamaker, Sam, 372
Ward, John, 23–24, *34*
Warner, Deborah, 374
War of the Roses, The, 370
Wars of the Roses, 150
Washington, George, 364
Water taxis, 221, 241
Weather, 226, 231

Webster, John, 121
Wedel, Lupold von, 224, *241–42*
Welles, Orson, 374, 377, 379
Wells, Stanley, 80, 208, 209, 358, 359
Werstine, Paul, 198
Westminster, 220, 223
Wet nurses, 269
Whetstone, George, 267, *292–93*
White, E. B., 41
Whitgift, John, 317
Whitney, Isabella, 222, 257, *240–41*
Wilcox, Thomas, *340–43*
Wilde, Oscar, 151
Wilkinson, Norman, 368, *390 (illus.)*
Williams, Clifford, 371
Williams, Raymond, 324
William the Conqueror, 40
Wilson, Thomas, 41, *60–62*
Winter, Samuel, 31
Winter's Tale, The, 21, 78, 80, 126, 197, 212, 258
  audience reaction to, 119
  modern productions of, 353, 367–68
  as romance, 94, 95, 96
  sheepshearing festival in, 227
  sources for, 152–53, 154, 155, 161, 162, *178–79*
Woman Killed with Kindness, A (Heywood), 112
Women
  as actors in plays, 112
  clothing for, 232
  country life and, 230, *246–47*
  education of, 256–58
  friendship among, 273
  as gatherers, 122
  inheritance and, 263–65
  nursing by, 269–70, *293–94*
  opportunities for advancement of, 276
  patriarchy and, 259–63
  as playgoers, 118
  plays and poetry written by, *100–01,* 157, *184–85, 256–257, 279–83*
  resistance of, to social roles, 256
  social class and, 274
  society and situation of, 253–59
  superiority of men to, 254–56
  work of, 230, *246–47,* 253–54
Woodstock (anonymous play), 150
Wool trade, 227, 230, 234

Wordplay, 44–47, *73–76*
Workers, 227, 230
Workes (Jonson), 24
Wotton, Sir Henry, 134, 321
Wright, James, 118
Wriothesley, Henry, third earl of
    Southampton, 15–16, 146

Wroth, Lady Mary, 157, *184–85,* 256, 257

Yeomen, 274
Your Five Gallants (Middleton), 264–65

Zeffirelli, Franco, 377, 378
Zimmerman, Susan, 113*n*1